2

# Wandermore in Kansas

### Your ultimate guide to the Sunflower State!

## Written by Seth Varner
### Published by Wandermore Publishing LLC

Library of Congress Control Number: 2023921417

ISBN: 978-1-7361368-5-0

Printed by DiggyPOD, Inc., in the United States of America. Distributed from Omaha, Nebraska

Seventh printing edition, April 2024.

Publisher may be reached at
sethvarner@wandermorepublishing.com
https://www.wandermorepublishing.com

# Table of Contents

5

VISIT627Kansas

# Content Disclaimer

Note that communities are dynamic entities and that town attractions, breweries, campgrounds, distilleries, festivals, golf courses, lodging locations, National Register of Historic Places locations, restaurants, Scenic Byways, wineries, and other similar places of business are subject to change. **Please do your homework prior to traveling!**

An attempt has been made to provide as accurate travel information as possible, but there is the assured possibility that some addresses, business names, etc. will change over time. Additionally, please note that not every business entity (brewery, golf course, National Register of Historic Places locations, etc.) is included in this guide. If you would like to suggest a new or existing place of interest to be added, please contact the publisher.

Wandermore's QR Code photo albums are subject to the longevity of Google Photos, a photo sharing and storage service developed by Alphabet Inc. Should the photo albums become defunct in the future, please contact the publisher.

We try to update our Wandermore guides at least once per calendar year. You may see when your guide was published at the bottom of page 4 on the copyright page.

All photographs in this guide are the property of Wandermore Publishing LLC and may not be reproduced or distributed without the express written consent of Wandermore Publishing LLC. We ask that readers take the time to enjoy the printed photos and the QR code photo albums, but to not use them for their own works and projects without first receiving permission from the publisher.

Publisher may be reached at
sethvarner@wandermorepublishing.com
https://www.wandermorepublishing.com
(Updated April 2024)

# Road Trip Games

**Wandermore's My Cows:** The objective of this game is to "collect" as many herds as possible before reading your destination. To play, whenever you see a group of cows (or even a single cow roaming the countryside by its lonesome), say "My Cows" to claim the herd as your own. If two players say "My Cows" simultaneously, they must play rock-paper-scissors to determine the rightful herd owner.

If your caravan comes across a cemetery, the first player to shout, "Dead Cows!" effectively "kills" the herds of all the other players, and their scores are reset to zero. If another player mistakes a group of animals (pigs, sheep, horses, etc.) for a herd of cows, they lose one herd (one point). The game revolves around spotting cattle and cemeteries before any of the other players in the car.

**Wandermore's A-Z Game:** Players must agree on a category and then proceed to name a noun that fits within it while alternating letters of the alphabet. The game continues until (a) there are no longer nouns that fit the corresponding letter and category, (b) a player repeats a noun that another player has already said. For situation (a), if no players can think of a noun, the letter is skipped and the next letter is used to continue the game with all players.

Example Category: Kansas towns
Player 1: "Abbyville." Player 2: "Basehor." Player 3: "Coolidge." Player 1: "Denton." Player 2: "Ellsworth." and so forth.

**Wandermore's Music Game:** One individual is designated as the "DJ" and will connect to the vehicle AUX. The DJ will play a song from their music library, and all other players in the vehicle must try to guess (1) the name of the song, and (2) the name of the main artist. Players who successfully name either (or both) options earn one point per correct guess. If two players simultaneously say the artist's name or the song name, the DJ determines who the rightful owner of the point is, or the players play rock-paper-scissors.

**Wandermore's License Plate Game:** Ideal for cross-state travelers, players compete to "collect' as many out-of-state license plates as possible before reaching their destination. Plates are claimed by saying "License Plate Claimed" followed by the state listed on the other vehicle's plate. Once a state or province is claimed, another player cannot again claim it as their own.

**Wandermore's Road Kill Bingo: Kansas Edition:** Everybody gets bored on the road sometimes! Pass time by using coins, stickers, or a pencil to play Wandermore's "Road Kill Bingo: Kansas Edition!" The first individual to match four spaces in a row wins.

| Water Fowl | Deer | Rabbit | Squirrel |
|---|---|---|---|
| Opossum | Toad | Tire | Deer |
| FREE SPACE | Raccoon | Coyote | Pheasant |
| Skunk | Bird | Pheasant | Raccoon |

| Coyote | Skunk | FREE SPACE | Deer |
|---|---|---|---|
| Opossum | Pheasant | Tire | Squirrel |
| Bird | Rabbit | Water Fowl | Raccoon |
| Toad | Deer | Raccoon | Pheasant |

| Squirrel | Rabbit | Pheasant | Coyote |
|---|---|---|---|
| Opossum | Bird | Raccoon | Pheasant |
| Deer | Raccoon | FREE SPACE | Toad |
| Tire | Deer | Skunk | Water Fowl |

9

# Road Trip Travel Tips

(1) The most common public restrooms can be found at gas stations, although if you're in a pinch, check local bars/restaurants, or public parks, baseball fields, and recreation areas for outhouses.

(2) There are several ways you can earn cashback on the gas you buy. Consider checking out an app such as Upside (use referral code 2UR6XH for a bonus) to earn up to 25-cents back per gallon. Many credit cards, some grocery chains, and gas-station rewards programs also offer cashback on gas.

(3) Always buy your drinks in bulk. Summer temperatures in the Midwest can be extreme at times, so always stock up on water by buying a 24-pack at a gas station (they typically range from $3.00-$6.00). Even better, bring along a reusable bottle and ask to refill it with water at local gas stations or restaurants.

(4) If you plan to visit several state parks or recreation areas within the same year, be sure to purchase an annual Park Entrance License rather than paying for the daily park licenses (https://ksoutdoors.com/State-Parks/Parks-Passport).

(5) When visiting small town bars or restaurants, it is necessary to carry cash. Many establishments outside of cities do not accept credit or debit cards and withdrawing cash from a local ATM will often cost you a hefty fee. Also, *always* call ahead to see if they're open.

(6) Typically, the "sketchier" the exterior of the bar or restaurant, the tastier the food will be.

(7) When using a smartphone or GPS to route from town to town (a general area), use Apple Maps. When routing to a particular place such as a museum (an address), use Google Maps.

(8) Your roadside emergency kit should include a spare tire (if possible), extra water, snacks, a sleeping bag, blankets, first aid kit, jumper cables, a phone charger, a flashlight, a towel, an extra quart of oil, windshield washer fluid, a jack and lug wrench, a portable compressor, a small shovel, hand warmers, tow strap, and a bag of cat litter (for extra grip for your tires).

# Prologue

Who doesn't love a good road trip? While in broader terms we may think of them as a half-country haul to the Grand Canyon or a car ride to the sandy white beaches of Florida, in reality, we take our own miniature "road trips" every day. Whether it's a morning cross-city commute, picking up a prescription from the local pharmacy, or driving down to grandma and grandpa's house for the weekend, we're constantly hitting the road to visit somewhere.

I'm a bit of a roadtripper myself, but I like to take things to the extreme. Over the years, I've had the privilege of traveling to every incorporated town in Nebraska, Iowa, South Dakota and Kansas. By my count, that's 2,407+ communities I've had the pleasure of exploring, despite the constantly changing number of new incorporations and disincorporation of old railroad and mining towns. Whenever an opportunity arises to hit the road with friends or family, I hit the road and seek out what makes whatever region of the country I'm in stand out in its own way. In 2023 alone, prior to the publication of this book, I wiped my schedule clean for friends trips to Denver, CO, Washington D.C., Memphis, TN, Oxford, MS, and Branson, MO, dates with my girlfriend to Des Moines, IA, Newton and Pella, IA, Waco, TX and Oklahoma City, OK, sporting events in Minneapolis, MN and Kansas City, MO, and a mega-family road trip to Grand Canyon National Park, Zion National Park, Great Sand Dunes National Park, Canyonlands National Park, Horseshoe Bend, and Durango and Georgetown, CO. In between all those excursions, I took on my fourth Wandermore project in visiting every one of Kansas's 625+ incorporated towns.

It's evident that I've got a constant travel bug. No matter the occasion, I'm constantly on the lookout for another adventure. It's a blast traveling from city to city to take in historical sites like the monuments of D.C. and the National Civil Rights Museum, or marveling at the beautiful National Parks of the western portion of the country, but sometimes, I like to put my tourist hat and sunglasses away and travel for a different reason. Something deeper and more meaningful. After sixty odd days of traveling to every nook and cranny of Kansas, I was able to document every municipality through nearly 50,000 photographs, from the sprawling cityscapes of the Kansas City metro to the towns with a population in the single digits. I made an effort to explore the history, architecture, cuisine, and all the other quirky attractions that made every town stand out in its own way.

A lot of people are baffled by how I came up with the idea to visit every town in a state. You'd think it's not exactly the kind of idea that somebody comes up with without some sort of backstory or long-winded explanation. And to that, my friend, you think correctly! It all started with the COVID-19 pandemic in March of 2020. We all know how that went. Life was good and normal, and within a week's period the world came crashing down. Workplaces ushered employees out the doors, as did schools and universities, and everyone was sent home as the world struggled to learn how to deal with a modern-day pandemic. At that time, I was a 19-year-old freshman in college at the University of Nebraska at Omaha. I worked for the Omaha Athletics department taking stats for the basketball, hockey, and soccer teams, and I was attending in-person classes and living on campus. One day I was sitting in class learning about volcanoes, and watching the NBA on television, and the next, I was told I was being required to move back in with my parents in my hometown of Wahoo, Nebraska.

For a month or so, I worked at the local Dairy Queen and attended my classes on Zoom. I played basketball and video games with my high school buddy Austin, who had also been sent home from Concordia University in Seward because of pandemic mandates. We were fine for a while, playing games and cruising main, but quarantine began to take its toll on us. Boredom started creeping in as we realized there wasn't much to do in a world where businesses were closed, and public gatherings of any degree weren't allowed. In a time where travel was limited, everything was closed, and making connections with next to impossible, I had the urge to make a something-out-of-nothing summer and do something that (to my knowledge then) nobody had done before: "Hey Austin, want to visit every town in Nebraska this summer?"

The idea spurred from some core memories I had as a child. Circa 2009, when I was about nine years old, my father Dave began to work on a family tree project. In addition to your typical family tree information like birthdays, names, and the like, he wanted to expand his project to include photographs of the headstones of deceased relatives, the churches they had attended, and the homes they lived in. He recruited little ole' me and his mother to accompany him on a series of road trips throughout Butler and Seward County, Nebraska so he took take some up-to-date photos of the sites. While he photographed points of family interest, I had an agenda of my own. Equipped with my disposable Wal-Mart camera, I took photos of the things that interested me: primarily population signs, and sites like the Baloney Shop of Malmo or the green Wal-Mart in York. Things that captured the attention of a third-grader, you know, the important stuff! Around the same time, my mother Leigh instilled a love for traveling in me by taking my brother and I on a trip to the Caribbean, where I first began to understand that there was an entire world to explore outside of the little bubble of Wahoo. As my dad finished up the family tree project, we stopped our road trips. I remember pouring over a map of Nebraska on our way home from one trip and asking dad, "can we visit every town in Nebraska?" To which I likely got a chuckle and a "maybe someday, Seth" response.

The thought of visiting all of Nebraska's communities must've stuck in the back of my mind, but my obsession with traveling, geography, and writing was more profound. In third grade, I started writing books about "Fluffy the Kitten," the adventures of my favorite farm cat who went on adventures and loved spending time with his friends. One such rendition of the fifteen-book series was "Fluffy the Kitten Travels the World," in which Fluffy flew his plane to all corners of the world to take in world's most famous points of interest. My classmates Eli and Marcela (now the owner of the small business Kookaburra Cookies in the Omaha area, and an English teacher at my alma mater high school, respectively) drew the pictures for my books and helped my present them to my classmates at the time. As I continued to see the world through our family vacations, I became more enthralled with geography and travel, and in the fifth grade I launched my then-second website, "SVGeography." I compiled articles, photos, and videos from around the web, and my teacher Mrs. Simons would incorporate them in her lesson plans when applicable. By the time I was fifteen, I was in charge of planning our first true family road trip to Oklahoma City and Kansas City, a responsibility that I have maintained throughout the years as we've made our way to places like the Great Smoky Mountains of Tennessee, the Wisconsin Dells, and the aforementioned adventure to the Grand Canyon and the American West. All things considered, I think it's easy to see how my interests as a child have influenced my career choice of being a traveler and a writer, and how a few little trips around my dad's stomping grounds turned into the ambition to start the pioneer Wandermore project around Nebraska.

On April 22, 2020, Austin and I began our two-and-half month trek across the Cornhusker State. We didn't travel continuously though. We'd go out for a day and visit a handful of towns but return to Wahoo to work at Dairy Queen for a few more. It became a weekly thing where every four to eight days or so we'd hit the road for the day but come back home to sleep in our own beds. Honestly, for the first few weeks of traveling, the project wasn't very serious. We'd visit the towns and take our selfie with something that said the town name on it—typically the welcome sign—and continue to the next community. Sometimes we'd stop for fast food or wander the town a little bit, but we weren't taking pictures, meeting with people (as we didn't yet then know much about COVID), or touring businesses, restaurants, or museums. The point of the trips then was solely for our own enjoyment of getting out of the house and to have a little fun at the welcome signs by making a funny pose with our Energizer bunny, a little pink plush rabbit that Austin's mom thought we should have tag along as our "mascot." At the end of our trip, we planned to hand over the photos to our mothers so they could make a scrapbook of our travels, and that would be that.

I didn't tell my parents about the first few trips. I had a feeling they wouldn't be too pleased with my idea to visit every town in the state amid an ongoing pandemic. But as Austin and I kept disappearing with our friends for entire days at a time, I eventually broke the news to them about fifty towns into the project. It took a little convincing, but after I insisted that we were playing things safe and mostly keeping to ourselves, they ended up being okay with it. It was my mom who came up with the idea that I should begin sharing my photos on Facebook. I had started an Instagram page for our friends, but she thought that we'd reach more people if we shared our travels on the larger platform.

She couldn't have been more correct! Within a couple of weeks of starting the Facebook page, we began receiving interview requests from television and radio stations, and every small-town newspaper out there. We couldn't believe it. Within the first month we had already gained well over ten-thousand followers, and the comments, likes, and messages came pouring in. It was in that moment that I recognized that the project could be a lot more than just a scrapbook adventure, and so I embraced the attention and started to incorporate the suggestions of followers into trips and start meeting people.

As the months progressed and we continued to hear stories from locals of their favorite memories of town and what seeing our few photos (at this time we only took a few since Instagram only allowed us to share ten in a single post) meant to them, a theme came to light. No matter how big or small the community, its residents of past and present were eager to show their hometown pride and make it known to the world what their community was known for. Austin and I saw this theme unfold as we continued our trek around Nebraska: that

14

there's something to do in every town, but you've got to go out and find it. A great example that brings this principle to light is our visit to Monowi, population one. It's the smallest incorporated town in the United States, with Elsie being the sole resident, mayor, bartender, and librarian. Even in this community of one, we were able to keep ourselves busy. We ate at the bar and talked with Elsie about her life and her memories of the town that once was. She showed us Rudy's Library, a collection of thousands of books of her late husband, and an old church in which she was one of the last people in attendance. What many would hardly consider to be a dot on the map was in reality a several-hour adventure that took us through the life cycle of a small farming town. Even if a town had a population of 50 people, 500 people, or 5,000 people, we discovered the truth that there was always something to learn, something to do, or something to explore.

We amassed a following of 21,000 individuals by the conclusion of our trip around Nebraska and finished off our journey in our hometown on July 17, 2020, with a small parade and a celebration. In attendance was *Nebraska Stories*, a public television series that showcased clips and photos from our adventure around Nebraska, two other news stations, and a couple hundred people from the community. It was a wonderful sendoff for an incredible accomplishment. As I read through the Facebook comments on our final town post, I saw that several people were calling for our adventure to be documented in a coffee table book, so people could relive the journey over again and again. I gave it some thought and decided that I would give it a go. I worked day and night throughout the fall of my sophomore year of college to compile a book that featured photos and some brief information about every incorporated town in Nebraska. I went into detail about the things my friends and I saw, heard, and tasted throughout our two-and-a-half-month escapade, shared historical facts and tidbits, and created a living photo album feature by using QR codes. I knew the feature would come in handy down the road, because as I traveled Nebraska, I would be able add more photos of community buildings, or inside looks at museums and restaurants as I continued my travels. Since then, thousands of photos have been added to the living albums, and those who purchased the books in 2020 are able to see where else I've been to in Nebraska in 2021, 2022, and 2023 since the conclusion of the Visit531Nebraska project. The book, a complete afterthought of a project that was supposed to be a way to avoid boredom during a global pandemic, has evolved in the subsequent years to hold information on restaurants, lodging, festivals, recreation parks and areas, museums, and more.

The book "Visit531Nebrasla: Our Journey to Every Incorporated Town in the State," was an incredible success. I'll never forget the feeling of having to take loans from my family members and pouring my life savings into buying the inventory, or the joy I felt when I held a copy of my published work for the very first time that November. After hundreds of hours of planning, writing, and traveling, I had managed to self-publish a book and completed the project of a lifetime. As most reading this already know, the adventure didn't end there either. It was only just the beginning.

In March of 2021, I decided to conduct a similar project called "Visit939Iowa" across the Mighty Mo' and visit every one of Iowa's incorporated communities. Austin joined me on these escapades as well, but this time, I made it known to Iowans that it was my intention to create a book on Iowa at the conclusion of my travels. Much to my surprise, the people of Iowa rallied around the project, and we were met with an equal amount of hospitality and support. I took more photos, met more people, ate at more local eateries, and checked out more sites. Towards the end of the journey, I had taken on somewhat of a documentation mindset when I realized that people wanted to see *everything* that was left in a town. Instead of focusing solely on notable sites like restaurants, historical markers, and downtown areas, by the end of the project in September I was trying to capture older buildings or even sites like repair shops and city parks. In September, our travels concluded, and I had the book ready to go by November. After another successful trip, the idea cemented in my mind that these projects could become a full-time career.

As I got deeper into my business classes in the Fall of 2021, it dawned on me that if I needed to make the business look more professional if I were going to pursue it as a full-time endeavor. The company was then just called "Visit531Nebraska," but people were confused why a business with that name had visited every town in Iowa and written a book about both states. I needed to change the name. I loved the term wanderlust but found it overused, and I kept thinking on a play on words that could showcase what I was trying to do. I wondered. And my thoughts wandered. And they wandered some more. And, thirty minutes into my first brainstorming session in the shower, it came to me: Wandermore Publishing, a book-publishing company whose guides combine travel with history to encourage people to go out and explore their home states throughout the Midwest. I revamped the website, set up the company, printed the business cards, and thus Wandermore Publishing was born.

The "Wandermore's Visit310SouthDakota" project was put into action in February of 2022, and this time, I would be accompanied to every community by my college friend Jack. This was the first trip in which I embraced the documentation mindset and began to spend extra time on the road to capture more photos per town than I had in even in Nebraska or Iowa. In the smaller towns I made sure to take several laps to ensure that I didn't miss churches or other buildings on the outskirts, and in the larger communities, I focused on capturing as many of the "big ticket" buildings and attractions as I could. The project lasted about four months, and it was then that I had come up with the idea to start the Wandermore Travel Fund to allow people to contribute funds in exchange for having the names of their friends, family, loved ones, pets and businesses placed in the back of a book. Still being in college at the time, the extra funds allowed Jack and I to spend more time on the road as I put together the photos and information for my third book. It was released in August of 2022.

Looking back, it's funny to see how a person's career can develop out of their childhood interests in hobbies. For a kid who was writing books about his cat, loved traveling and taking photos at a young age, and who always took an interest in geography and history, it seems like Wandermore Publishing would've come to fruition at one point or another. Maybe it's easy to say that now that COVID is largely a thing of the past, but without that pandemic, who knows if I would have ever had the intention to "wander more" and learn more about Nebraska, Iowa, South Dakota and all the other little farm towns of the Midwest.

The "Wandermore in Kansas" book you hold now in your names is a culmination of my efforts for what was the most thorough and compressive Wandermore project of the four. After finishing Nebraska and traveling east to Iowa and north to South Dakota, it only made sense to look south and take on the Sunflower State. After 17,000+ miles on the road and over eight months of traveling, writing, and research, I successfully visited every one of Kansas's incorporated communities and snapped 50,000+ photos—more pictures than I've taken in any other state by a landslide. This was the first state that I was able to focus nearly one-hundred-percent of my attention, because until then, I had always had to work another job and be in school. I remained proactive in my studies in February through May of 2023, when I graduated with my degree in Business Administration, Marketing, and Management, and from thereon I was able to devote the entirety of my attention to this project. The extra time and freedom allowed me to meet with hundreds of people from all trades: convention and visitors bureaus, chambers of commerce, restaurant owners, attorneys, doctors, blue-collar and white-collar workers alike. I ate at nearly one-hundred local establishments around Kansas and toured over sixty museums. Had it not been for the support I received for the previous three states, and that of all those who followed along with the Kansas project and left their tips, history, anecdotes, memories, and kind words, the project would not have been able to reach the level of thoroughness that it did. I cannot thank all 125,000+ people that follow the four Facebook pages enough for all they've done to help me promote and expand small-town tourism and generate interest in their storied histories.

Reader, I challenge you to follow in my footsteps and experience Kansas for yourself. Make a day trip to tour that museum you've been meaning to check out. Drive two hours to a small-town burger joint for lunch and make a road trip out of it. Treat yourself to a luxurious night in Marion's Elgin Hotel or spook yourself out with a ghost tour in Shawnee or the haunted Wolf Hotel of Ellinwood. Drive Route 66 by Baxter Springs and Galena or explore the mysterious Garden of Eden in Lucas! Support local businesses like your flower shops and breweries, utilize your local libraries, and stop and chat with the locals and learn what makes their town unique from all the others. If you take nothing else away from this project, I ask you to remember this: EVERY community has something to do, you've just gotta go out and find it. Every one of them. Continue to wander more and explore as much as Kansas as you possibly can, because sometimes, the best road trip of your life is waiting for you closer than you realize.

This book serves as a testament to all the communities and the history that makes Kansas so unique, and as a guide to exploring all aspects of tourism in each town, no matter how big or small. I hope you find this guide useful in discovering all that the Sunflower State has to offer. Thank you for helping me in my journey to preserve Midwest history and promote small town tourism across the country.

*Seth Varner*

Be sure to keep up with all my travels and book updates by following the Wandermore network of Facebook pages (updated 4-2024):
Wandermore in Nebraska
Wandermore in Iowa
Wandermore in South Dakota
Wandermore in Kansas
Wandermore in North Dakota

# Kansas County Map

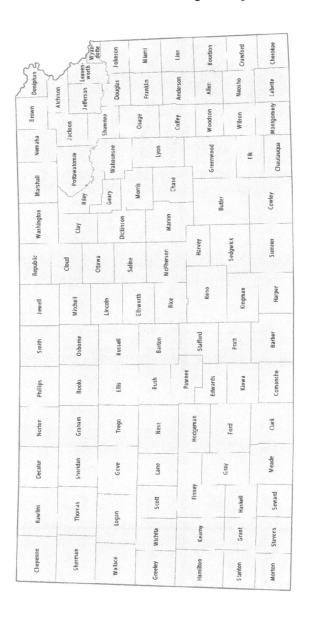

Source: GISGeography.com

# Kansas Highway Map

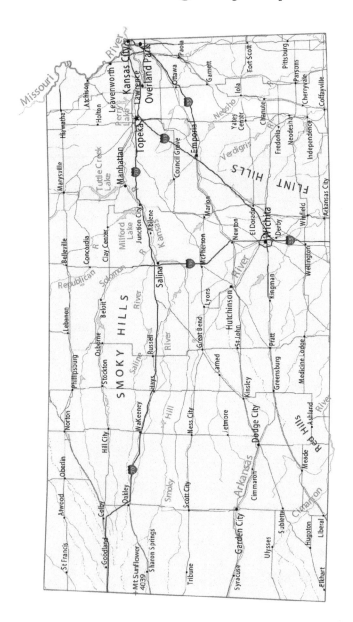

Source: GISGeography.com

# ALLEN COUNTY
## EST. 1855 - POPULATION: 12,526

Allen County was named in honor of the 31st Governor of Ohio and a promoter of Manifest Destiny, William Allen.

# BASSETT, KS
### POPULATION: 20 – TOWN 318 OF 627 (6-28-23)
Bassett, now a hamlet of only 20 residents in Allen County, was founded and incorporated in 1903. It is located south of Iola and was once connected to the county seat via an electric railroad streetcar line. Its highest population on record was 415 residents as of the 1910 Census, around the same time the first concrete road in Kansas was constructed there in 1914.

# ELSMORE, KS
### POPULATION: 50 – TOWN 326 OF 627 (6-29-23)
Elsinore was formed by N. L. Ard, J. A. Nicholson, O. P. Mattson, J. L. Roberts, and W. D. and H. W. Cox in 1888 because of the anticipated arrival of the Missouri, Kansas & Texas Railroad. Its nomenclature is a nod to the Danish castle of Shakespeare's play Hamlet, although the name would later be changed to Elsmore (likely because of a transcription error). By 1909, Elsmore was incorporated, and several small manufacturers and businesses were located there by its citizens. Its population is now just 50 as of the 2020 Census, although it was 237 persons in 1920.

# GAS, KS
### POPULATION: 475 – TOWN 320 OF 627 (6-29-23)
Gas City, Kansas, had a late start in 1898, as it wasn't founded until large volumes of natural gas were discovered in Elm Township of Allen County. Local farmer E. K. Taylor sold off 60 acres of his land so that companies could start extracting the resource, and the rest of the lots were turned into housing for the workers and early settlers. They naturally gave the newly founded community the name Gas, and the resource sparked a flurry of industrial activity that led to

manufacturing plants, an opera house, a bank and post office, and other lines of business. The Missouri, Kansas & Texas Railroad and the Missouri Pacific Railroad were allowed to exploit the economy by building their railroad lines through Gas. It incorporated in 1901.

# HUMBOLDT, KS

## POPULATION: 1,847 – TOWN 357 OF 627 (7-17-23)

The land that would become Humboldt was located by B. M. Blanton circa 1857, who told J. A. Coffey of Lawrence of the site. Coffey platted the town that year and recruited a group of German migrants from Hartford, Connecticut, to settle there. He would go on to construct the town's first frame building, and in consecutive years, a gristmill and church founded by the United Brethren Church were raised. Its name was drawn from the surname of Alexander von Humboldt of Germany, a scientist whose most extraordinary feats laid the foundations for geomagnetic and meteorological monitoring and biogeography. Twice, the town was raided during the American Civil War as Confederate forces looked to recapture formerly enslaved people, and it was throughout this time that Humboldt operated as the Allen County Seat from 1858 to 1865. Humboldt lost the title to Iola in an 1865 election despite maintaining it through two prior elections in 1858 and 1860. Its incorporation came in 1866, and in 1870, the Missouri, Kansas & Texas Railroad and Atchison, Topeka & Santa Fe Railroad were extended to that point. The town's population has wavered between lows of 1,202 persons according to the 1870 Census and highs of 2,558 people as of the 1930 Census. Oil refineries, cement and brick plants, flour mills, and plentiful oil and gas deposits spurred the early economy of Humboldt. Walter Johnson, one of the great MLB pitchers of all-time and the holder of the MLB shutout record with 110 was born here on November 6, 1887. He still holds numerous records and is a member of the National Baseball Hall of Fame. George Sweatt was another notable area player who is recognized as being the only regular position player to have appeared in the first four World Series of the Negro League. The Humboldt Historical Museum tells the stories of the city.

 **Restaurant Recommendation:**
**HoneyBee Bruncherie**
**822 Bridge St**
**Humboldt, KS 66748**

# IOLA, KS ★☆

After the city of Humboldt was located in the southwestern part of Allen County, area residents expressed their dissatisfaction and called for a meeting at the Deer Creek schoolhouse near the home of settler J. C. Clark. They began the formation of a new, centrally located town to become the county seat. John W. Scott, John Hamilton, and J. M. Perkins headed the town company, and the city was named in honor of Iola Colborn, the wife of the first man to build a frame house on the land. A nearby town called Cofachique, the first town and judicial seat of Allen County, was annexed into Iola, and its buildings moved to the present townsite. Iola won the support of the majority of the county to become the county seat when a vote was held on May 19, 1865, to move it to Iola formally. Like several other area communities, Iola benefited substantially from the discovery of natural gas, and its population boomed as high as 9,032 in the 1910s. At that time, the city was widely developed and had five public grade schools, churches of all the leading denominations, nine zinc smelters that were then said to produce a third of the world's total supply, and numerous lines of enterprise from rug, broom and ice factories to planing and flour mills, and bottle, iron, and brick and tile works. The Missouri Pacific Railroad, Atchison, Topeka & Santa Fe Railroad, and the Missouri, Kansas & Texas Railroad were all instrumental in its development. Allen Community College was founded here in 1923 as the Iola Junior College. The Allen County Museum and the Old Jail Museum sit in the city's downtown square, claimed by locals as the "Largest Courthouse Square" in the country as it is two blocks wide by two blocks wide with no roads dividing it. The Major General Frederick Funston Home is a Victorian mansion available for tours via the Allen County Historical Society. Eight miles west of Iola in the unincorporated town of Piqua is a small museum dedicated to the life of Buster Keaton, one of the greatest Hollywood actors of all time (noted for his silent film work). Other local persons of fame have included Dean Hargrove (television producer and 1974 Primetime Emmy Award winner for *Columbo*), actresses Randy Stuart and Lila Leeds, John H. Adams (jockey and United States Racing Hall of Fame member who won 3,270 races), and the 52nd (incumbent) Lieutenant Governor of Kansas, David Toland.

# LA HARPE, KS

**POPULATION: 480 – TOWN 321 OF 627 (6-29-23)**

Platted in 1881 by the Fort Scott, Wichita & Western Railroad Company, La Harpe took its name from the city of La Harpe, Illinois, which honors the French explorer, Bernard de la Harpe. The population skyrocketed to 2,080 citizens, according to the 1920 Census, after natural gas was discovered in the area and a booming economy came to fruition. It was once home to some of the largest zinc smelters on the planet, which were partially brought about by the arrival of the Missouri, Kansas & Texas Railroad to the city. By the 1920 Census, the population had dropped back to 1,001 persons. Today, it sits around 480 people. MLB pitcher Ad Brennan, who played between 1910 and 1918, was born here.

# MORAN, KS

**POPULATION: 466 – TOWN 322 OF 627 (6-29-23)**

This Allen County community went by the name "Morantown" after its first post office (which was named for Daniel C. Moran), although its full name was Moran City until 1900 when the "City" was dropped. It was founded when it was certain circa 1881 that the Saint Louis, Fort Scott & Wichita Railroad would be extended to that point. That line would later be annexed by the Missouri Pacific Railroad. The Missouri, Kansas & Texas Railroad was built through town at a later date and helped bring multiple general merchandise stores, a bank, and other infrastructure to Moran. Miss America 1968, Debra Dene Barnes, heeds from Moran, having been born there in 1947.

# SAVONBURG, KS

**POPULATION: 74 – TOWN 327 OF 627 (6-29-23)**

The etymology of Savonburg is still being determined, although the town is known to have been founded in 1879 when the Missouri, Kansas & Texas Railway built a line through the area. The Savonburg Improvement Company was instrumental in helping the early Swedish settlers build up the town's schools and businesses until the city was finally incorporated in 1902. The U.S. Postal Service established an office in Savonburg the year it was founded, and John Keen was its first postmaster.

**Adjacent Counties:** Anderson (N), Linn (NE), Bourbon (E), Neosho (S), Wilson (SW), Woodson (W), Coffey (NW)

**Unincorporated/Ghost Towns:** Bayard, Carlyle, Cofachiqui, Geneva, Leanna, Mildred, Octagon City, Petrolia

**National Register of Historic Places:**
**Humboldt:** City Square Park Bandstand, Lander's Wagon and Carriage Shop
**Iola:** Allen County Jail, Iola Theatre, Kress Building, Northrup House

**Breweries/Wineries/Distilleries:**
Union Works Brewing Company (Humboldt, KS)

**Golf Courses:**
Allen County Country Club Golf Course, Private (Iola, KS)
Cedarbrook Golf Course, Public (Iola, KS)
Sunny Meadows Golf Course, Semi-Private (Moran, KS)

**Town Celebrations:**
Biblesta, Humboldt, KS (1st Saturday in October)
Elsmore Day, Elsmore, KS (2nd Saturday in September)
Farm City Days, Iola, KS (3rd Weekend of October)
Moran Days, Moran, KS (3rd Saturday in September)
Water Wars, Humboldt, KS (Middle Saturday of August)

# ANDERSON COUNTY
## EST. 1855 - POPULATION: 7,836

A former member of the Kansas Territorial Legislator and border ruffian Joseph C. Anderson is this county's namesake.

# COLONY, KS
## POPULATION: 381 – TOWN 303 OF 627 (6-27-23)

Colony, formulated in 1870, was once known by the name Divide until its present name was given two years later when it was formally platted in August of 1872 with the railroad's arrival. Emigrants from Ohio and Indiana colonies were amongst the first to settle in the area, and so the name Colony seemed appropriate. The town established itself as a shipping point for stock and hay along the Missouri Pacific and the Atchison, Topeka & Santa Fe Railroads early on, leading to the construction of all of the typical early town structures like schools, churches, and general stores, as well as an opera house and a hotel.

Dean Brooks, a noted psychiatrist and the superintendent of the Oregon State Hospital from 1955 to 1982, was born here in July 1916.

# GARNETT, KS ★☆

**POPULATION: 3,242 – TOWN 300 OF 627 (6-27-23)**

The county seat of Anderson County, Garnett, was founded circa 1857 when Dr. George W. Cooper of Louisville, Kentucky, selected a parcel of land to establish a town. His town company was made up of W. A. Garnett, later the namesake of the city, R. B. Hall, Theodore Harris, George A. Dunn, and himself. After an early mill was constructed, the county seat was moved from Shannon to Garnett (1859), and later, cigar factories, furniture factories, a creamery, multiple newspapers, banks, schools, and even eleven churches by 1910 would be built by the settlers. Incorporation came in 1861, which attracted the attention of both the Missouri Pacific and the Chicago, Rock Island & Pacific Railroads to utilize the town and its facilities as a shipping point. Archaeologists adore Garnett for its rich and easy-to-access deposits of Lagerstätte, which are 300-million-year-old deposits of sediment that contain a variety of fossils from early reptiles from the Carboniferous period. The Anderson County Museum and the 1888 Harris House are some local points of interest for history buffs. Two former Governors of Kansas, Arthur Capper (the 20th and first governor born in Kansas) and Sam Brownback (the 46th), heed from Garnett, as did Edgar Lee Masters, the author of *Spoon River Anthology* and dozens of other works.

 **Restaurant Recommendation:
Dutch Country Cafe
309 N Maple St
Garnett, KS 66032**

# GREELEY, KS

**POPULATION: 273 – TOWN 346 OF 627 (6-30-23)**

The first European settlers, Valentine Gerth and Francis Myer, came to Greeley in 1854, during which the Myer cabin temporarily served as the judicial seat of Anderson County until a town called Shannon overtook the designation in April 1856. The townsite wouldn't be formally platted until circa 1856 when the Greeley Town Company (made up of three Ashkenazi Jews, Jacob Benjamin, Theodore Wiener, and abolitionist August Bondi) laid out the town. The town was named for Horace Greeley, the founder of the New-York Tribune, but for some time, the post office was called Walker, and then Mount Gilead because the postal service didn't want an office to be named for such a prominent anti-slavery newspaper owner. The Missouri Pacific Railroad would reach Greeley in 1879, and two years later, it was incorporated as a city of the third class, with Clark Decker being its first mayor. Several of Greeley's streets–Brown, Bondi, Kaiser, and Mitchell–are named in honor of early abolitionists. James G. Blunt, noted for his anti-slavery views and work on the Wyandotte constitutional convention that laid out the Constitution still in use by Kansas today, was another crucial area figure. The first MLB player from the University of Kansas, Dale Gear, was born here in 1872.

# KINCAID, KS
## POPULATION: 103 – TOWN 302 OF 627 (6-27-23)
Kincaid was organized in 1885 and named for Robert Kincaid of Mound City. It was once served by both the Missouri Pacific and the Missouri, Kansas & Texas Railroads. It was home to a post office, numerous stores, schools, and an impressive five churches of different denominations circa 1910. Its 2020 population of 103 people is the lowest in the city's history, whereas the highest was 443 as of the 1920 Census.

# LONE ELM, KS
## POPULATION: 27 – TOWN 301 OF 627 (6-27-23)
The founding of Lone Elm came in the 1870s when the postal service established an office in the area. It would not be incorporated until 1924, following the extension of the Missouri Pacific Railroad through Anderson County. Its population has shrunk to only 27 residents as of 2020, a steady decline from its peak in the 1930s. One of the co-creators of the capital asset pricing model, used to make decisions about expanding portfolios, was born here: John Virgil Lintner Jr.

# WESTPHALIA, KS
## POPULATION: 128 – TOWN 304 OF 627 (6-27-23)
Cornell was established in 1880 once it was inevitable that the Missouri Pacific Railroad would be extended to the area. It was named in honor of S. P. Cornell for a short time before the local post office and railroad changed it to Westphalia after Westphalia, Germany, the motherland of many early settlers. The postal service founded the local post office on June 12, 1880, and subsequently, establishments like churches, schools, and other lines of enterprise

came about. Incorporation was awarded in 1920 when the city was incorporated in the third class. A. A. Adams is credited with snapping the first photograph of a tornado in history when he captured the beginnings of one descending over Westphalia on April 26, 1884.

**Adjacent Counties:** Franklin (N), Miami (NE), Linn (E), Bourbon (SE), Allen (S), Woodson (SW), Coffey (W)

**Unincorporated/Ghost Towns:** Amiot, Bush City, Central City, Glenlock, Harris, Hyattville, Mont Ida, Northcott, Scipio, Selma, Welda

**National Register of Historic Places:**
**Garnett:** Anderson County Courthouse, Sennett and Bertha Kirk House, Shelley-Tipton House
**Greeley:** Spencer's Crossing Bridge
**Harris:** Samuel J. Tipton House

**Golf Courses:**
Garnett Country Club, Public (Garnett, KS)

**Town Celebrations:**
Greeley Days Smoke Off, Greeley, KS (Friday & Saturday after Labor Day)
Kincaid World's Fair, Kincaid, KS (Last Full Weekend in September)

# ATCHISON COUNTY
## EST. 1855 - POPULATION: 16,348

Atchison County's name seeks to honor the legacy of David Rice Atchison, who served as a Senator from Missouri and as President pro tempore of the Senate from late 1852 to 1854.

# ATCHISON, KS ★
## POPULATION: 10,885 – TOWN 60 OF 627 (3-14-23)
Atchison was founded in 1854 and served as the eastern terminus of the Atchison, Topeka, and Santa Fe Railroad. Its name was taken from David Rice Atchison, a former United States Senator from Missouri and the President pro tempore of the United States Senate from December 1852 to December 1854. He wanted to begin a city, but Dr. John H. Stringfellow, Leonidas Oldham, James B. Martin, Ira

Norris, and Neal Owens didn't like his chosen site, so they founded their own near the river with rich soil. It didn't take long for the town's first post office to arrive on April 10, 1855, and for the city to be formally incorporated on August 30, 1855. The town boomed following the completion of its railroad lines to St. Joseph, Missouri, although it had initially hoped to become a massive railroad center (it lost out to Kansas City and Omaha due to those towns' connections to Texas and Chicago, respectively). Resident Harry Muchnic invented a diesel locomotive piston ring in 1914, and in 1924, the John Seaton Foundry created an electric arc melting furnace. The two inventions would lead to the nationwide switch from steam to diesel locomotives. Atchison is home to Northeast Kansas Technical College and Highland Community College Technical Center, as well as Benedictine College, a private Benedictine liberal arts college established in 1971 (after the merger of St. Benedict's College and St. Scholastica College). Several notable people have ties to Atchison, including George Glick, John Alexander Martin, and Willis J. Bailey (the 9th, 10th and 16th Governors of Kansas), Jesse Stone (the creator of the basic rock 'n' roll sound), Laura M. Cobb of the United States Navy Nurse Corps, Ernie Jennings (NFL wide receiver), Oscar "Heavy" Johnson (early baseball player), James M. Stanton (sixth Catholic bishop of the Episcopal Diocese of Dallas), Rory Feek (country music singer and songwriter), Paul Christoph Mangelsdorf (known for his work on the origins and hybridization of maize), and perhaps most notably, aviator Amelia Earhart, the first female aviator to fly solo across the Atlantic Ocean and an early promoter of commercial air travel. Earhart's birthplace is operated today as a museum, and in the southwest corner of town at Warnock Lake, there is the earthwork face of the famed pilot. In April of 2023, the Amelia Earhart Hangar Museum, a state-of-the-art STEM & history museum focused on Amelia's Muriel—the world's last remaining Lockheed Electra 10-E (the same plane that she flew on her final worldwide flight)—will begin to welcome the general public to enjoy its major piece of aviation history and any of its 14 interactive exhibits. One last noteworthy individual is "Deafy" Boular, a child who lost his hearing at four years old and both legs at the age of twelve to a train that he couldn't hear coming. He never wore his prosthetic legs, instead opting for specially made boots, and as it would turn out, his height was perfect for laying the brick streets and sidewalks of Atchison. It is said that he once laid 46,000 bricks in a single day, according to *Ripley's Believe It or Not!* Other community points of interest are the Atchison County Courthouse (as it is the county seat), the Santa Fe Depot Rail Museum (that doubles as the Atchison County Historical Museum), the International Forest of Friendship, the Evah C. Cray Historical Museum, and the Sallie House. The house is said to be haunted by a young girl who died while undergoing appendicitis surgery; it has been featured on the television shows *Sightings* and *Ghost Adventures*.

**Restaurant Recommendation:
Willie's Sports Pub
701 Commercial St
Atchison, KS 66002**

# EFFINGHAM, KS ☆
**POPULATION: 495 – TOWN 57 OF 627 (3-13-23)**
The Missouri Pacific and Central Branch Railroads gave life to Effingham in its early days. The town was founded on a section of the McGilvery farm and eventually consisted of several churches, stores, and even a school by 1882. Its name seeks to honor Effingham Nichols of Boston, Massachusetts, a railroad promoter of the Central Branch of the Union Pacific Railroad.

# HURON, KS
**POPULATION: 74 – TOWN 59 OF 627 (3-13-23)**
Colonel D. R. Anthony of Leavenworth, Kansas, was this town's original townsite owner. He donated twenty acres of land to the Missouri Pacific Railroad to construct the Omaha Branch of their line through his land. The town was named and platted in 1882, although its etymology is unknown.

# LANCASTER, KS
**POPULATION: 246 – TOWN 58 OF 627 (3-13-23)**
Lancaster, population 246, was once almost named the county seat of Atchison County. It was platted in 1857 by J. W. Smith, the president of the townsite company, who also served as the community's first postmaster. It served as a station on the Missouri Pacific Railroad and was named after the city of Lancaster, Pennsylvania.

# MUSCOTAH, KS

**POPULATION: 155 – TOWN 56 OF 627 (3-13-23)**

The westernmost town in Atchison County, Muscotah, was first platted in 1857. It is thought that it was named by Paschal Pensoneau, a Kickapoo trader and interpreter. Its name is of Kickapoo Native American origin and is said to mean "beautiful prairie." The town moved a couple of miles south near the Delaware River shortly after its founding to be situated on the Central Branch of the Union Pacific Railroad. The city is proud of former resident Joe Tinker of baseball fame. He won two World Series championships, became a member of the National Baseball Hall of Fame in 1946, and was a part of the famous "Tinker-to-Evers-to-Chance" play. The World's Largest Baseball was created here in 2013 from the remnants of the old water tower; it measures 20 feet wide.

**Adjacent Counties:** Doniphan (N), Leavenworth (SE), Jefferson (S), Jackson (W), Brown (NE)

**Unincorporated/Ghost Towns:** Arrington, Cummings, Curlew, Eden, Farmington, Good Intent, Hawthorn, Kennekuk, Larkinburg, Monrovia, Mount Pleasant, Oak Mills, Pardee, Parnell, Port Williams, Potter, St. Pats, Shannon, Sumner

**National Register of Historic Places:**
**Atchison:** Atchison & Santa Fe Freight Depot, Atchison County Courthouse, Atchison County Memorial Hall, Atchison Post Office, Atchison YMCA, Francis and Harriet Baker House, Benedictine College North Campus Historic Complex, George T. and Minnie Searles Bolman House, Henry Braun House, J. P. Brown House, Burnes Rental Houses Historic District, Campbell Chapel AME Church, Central School, Chicago, Burlington & Quincy Railroad Freight Depot, John Drimmel Sr. Farm, Amelia Earhart Birthplace, Amelia Earhart Historic District, Ebenezer Baptist Church, James M. Edmiston House, Glancy/Pennell House, Glick-Orr House, A. J. Harwi Hardware Company Building, A. J. Harwi House, Hausner House, W. W. Hetherington House, Michael J. and Mattie Horan House, Frank Howard House, Edgar W. Howe House, Jansen House, Julius Kuhn Block, Lanphear-Mitchell House, Lincoln School, John A. Martin Grade School, McInteer Villa, Mount St. Scholastica Convent, H. E. Muchnic House, Robert L. Pease House, Price Villa, Ronald and Dorcas Ramsay House, St. Patrick's Catholic Church, Schmitt House, Frederick W. Stein House, Trinity Episcopal Church, B. P.

Waggener House, Baile P. Waggener House, Wherrett-Mize Drug Company Building
**Farmington:** Stranger Creek Warren Truss Bridge

**Breweries/Wineries/Distilleries:**
High Plains Distillery (Atchison, KS)
Subiaco Wine Bar (Atchison, KS)
The Whiskey Depot (Atchison, KS)

**Golf Courses:**
Bellevue Country Club, Semi-Private (Atchison, KS)
Pineview Country Club, Semi-Private (Atchison, KS)

**Town Celebrations:**
Amelia Earhart Festival, Atchison, KS (3rd Weekend of July)

# BARBER COUNTY
## EST. 1867 - POPULATION: 4,228

Free-Stater Thomas W. Barber, who perished in the Wakarusa War that began the state's "Bleeding Kansas" period of history, is the namesake of Barber County.

# HARDTNER, KS ☆
## POPULATION: 167 – TOWN 499 OF 627 (9-21-23)

Dr. John Hardtner of Springfield, Oregon, an early area landowner, is the namesake of Hardtner, Kansas (population 167). The townsite was platted in 1887 by Jacob Achenbach, the same year a post office was established that summer. Some two decades later, the townspeople decided that the Atchison, Topeka & Santa Fe Railroad was insufficient to support their interests, and they formed a company with the help of Mr. Achenbach to land their town on the Missouri Pacific line. The superintendent of the A, T & SF was not particularly pleased with the idea of splitting business with another railroad, so he took measures into his own hands by parking his car at the spot where the two railroads were to cross. His idea temporarily worked until 45 cowboys banded together and threatened to "riddle his car with bullets" if he didn't move it. He obliged, and the line was completed, thus connecting Hardtner to the outside world and leading to its incorporation in 1911. Approximately twenty retail stores had been founded by 1912, only years after the introduction of the

Missouri Pacific. An extremely slow-moving tornado whizzed by Hardtner on June 2, 1929, and a photographer captured some of the highest-quality images of a tornado ever taken at that point in time. Although likely unrelated to this event, the former Hardtner High School mascot had been the Tornadoes.

# HAZELTON, KS
## POPULATION: 82 – TOWN 501 OF 627 (9-21-23)
Incorporated in 1887 but founded four years earlier in 1883, this railroad town (once host to two railroad lines, the Atchison, Topeka & Santa Fe, and the Missouri Pacific) got its name from Reverend J. H. Hazelton, one of its first settlers. A post office opened its doors there for the first time on October 18, 1883, and it was once home to three churches and two banks.

# ISABEL, KS
## POPULATION: 68 – TOWN 513 OF 627 (9-22-23)
The townsite of Isabel was formed in 1887, and as was the case with many early towns of that time, its primary purpose was to act as a shipping point and station on the Atchison, Topeka & Santa Fe Railroad. Its etymology is disputed, although the standard story is that it was named for the daughter of an area surveyor. Some of its first structures were the town post office, a bank and a newspaper, and all of the necessary businesses needed for a Midwestern town at the turn of the century.

# KIOWA, KS
## POPULATION: 902 – TOWN 500 OF 627 (9-21-23)
The original Kiowa townsite began in 1872, but its buildings were later moved to be in closer proximity to the railroad by a new town company in the 1880s. Its name honors the Kiowa people, one of the many tribes that roamed the Great Plains before the arrival of Europeans. The Missouri Pacific and the Denver, Enid, and Gulf Railroad (later sold to the A, T & SF) were the two railways of note, bringing with them all the necessary things to start over one hundred different businesses. On June 7, 1900, radical temperance movement activist Carrie Nation destroyed her first saloon in Kiowa following a "heaven-sent vision." As many as 1,674 Kansans called Kiowa home in the 1960s, but four Kiowans stand out as being the most famous in the town's history: Marcellus Boss (Governor of Guam from 1959 to 1960), James Wilson (a Colorado Congressman

from 2013 to 2021), Charles E. Brown Jr. (Chief of Chaplains of the U.S. Army from 1962 to 1967), and Bill Tidwell (the athletic director of Emporia State University from 1971 to 1979 and a member of the NAIA Hall of Fame).

# MEDICINE LODGE, KS ★
## POPULATION: 1,781 – TOWN 509 OF 627 (9-22-23)

In the summer of 1866, the Kiowa tribe of Native Americans built a medicine lodge of tree trunks, branches, and other greens that would serve as a sacred place where they could celebrate their sun dance. The location was in a valley of the nearby Medicine Lodge River, although the tribe's name for the tributary was *A-ya-dalda P'a*. By October 1867, the Medicine Lodge Treaty, actually a set of three treaties signed between the United States government and the Kiowa, Comanche, Southern Cheyenne, Southern Arapaho, and the Plains Apache, were signed near here after the Indian Peace Commission determined that the United States was mistreating the tribes. Sadly, the treaties were skewed in favor of the government, further diminishing tribal land. In the mid-1900s, several tribes sought reparations through settlements of tens of millions of dollars. In February of 1873, John Hutchinson and a group of men decided to build a townsite of 400 acres at the confluence of Elm Creek and Medicine Lodge River and name it after the body of water. D. Updegraff built a hotel, the first of many buildings constructed over the following year, alongside two general merchandising stores, a physician's and lawyer's office, a drug store, and a post office with S. A. Winston as the first postmaster. A stockade was built in 1874 to help protect the town against Native American raiders, and in 1879, it was incorporated as a city of the third class. The Atchison, Topeka & Santa Fe Railroad would arrive later and lead the townspeople to erect five churches, two banks, a library, schools, and a gypsum cement mill. Carrie Nation, a famous temperance movement activist known for wielding a hatchet and attacking saloons, taverns, and other places that served alcohol, lived in Medicine Lodge from 1899 to 1902. It was here that she had her "vision from the heavens" that told her to wreck three saloons in nearby Kiowa. Her home, located adjacent to the Stockade House Museum, was listed on the National Register of Historic Places in 1971 and, at present, displays her infamous hatchet. Edward Hunkeler, the Roman Catholic Bishop of the Diocese of Grand Island, Nebraska from 1945 to 1951 and Kansas City, Kansas from 1951 to 1969, B. H. Born, the 1953 NCAA Final Four most outstanding player and a FIBA World champion in 1954, famous violin instructor Dorothy DeLay, and political activist and journalist Carleton Beals are other noted individuals with ties to Medicine Lodge.

## Lodging Recommendation:
## Swin Housing (Any)
## 206 W Washington Ave
## Medicine Lodge, KS 67104

# SHARON, KS
**POPULATION: 147 – TOWN 508 OF 627 (9-21-23)**
Sharon is the hometown of Martina McBride, a 14-time Grammy Award-nominated country music singer who has also won the CMA Award for Female Vocalist of the Year and the Academy of Country Music's "Top Female Vocalist" award three times each. She is by far the most noted figure in the history of the small Barber County town, which was founded in 1883 as a station on the Atchison, Topeka & Santa Fe Railway system. The original industries of the city pertained to flour mills and grain elevators, and there were once several stores alongside the post office. Orville Brown, a thirteen-time world champion in professional wrestling, was also born in Sharon on March 10, 1908.

# SUN CITY, KS
**POPULATION: 37 – TOWN 510 OF 627 (9-22-23)**
As many as 404 people called this bright spot of Barber County home in the 1930s, but the town has dissipated with time due to the Dust Bowl and the Great Depression, and other issues regarding its location and opportunities for growth. The small city was founded in 1872, and one year later, in August, the Sun City post office went into service. The office closed in May of 1894, but three weeks later, another one was opened under the name "Sun." This office would return the "City" to its name in May 1909. Sun City took on incorporation status in 1919 and has retained the title, even with its dropping population figures. One creepy-crawly anecdote of southern Kansas is that in late August to early October each year, thousands of male tarantulas "migrate" across the prairie in search of a mate.

**Restaurant Recommendation:**
**Buster's Saloon**
**104 W Main St**
**Sun City, KS 67143**

**Adjacent Counties:** Pratt (N), Kingman (NE), Harper (E), Comanche (W), Kiowa (NW)

**Unincorporated/Ghost Towns:** Aetna, Deerhead, Eldred, Elm Mills, Forest City, Gerlane, Lake City, Lasswell, Mingona, Pixley, Stubbs

**National Register of Historic Places:**
**Medicine Lodge:** Carry A. Nation House, Medicine Lodge Peace Treaty Site

**Golf Courses:**
Medicine Lodge Golf Club, Semi-Private (Medicine Lodge, KS)

# BARTON COUNTY
## EST. 1867 - POPULATION: 25,493

Barton County's name differs from many others in Kansas in that it was named after a woman, specifically Clara Barton, the founder of the American Red Cross.

# ALBERT, KS
### POPULATION: 132 – TOWN 416 OF 627 (8-14-23)
The City of Albert, one of the many less-densely populated municipalities of Barton County, comprises the homes and businesses of 132 inhabitants according to the 2020 Census. Its primary reason for coming into existence was to be a station on the Great Bend and Scott line of the Atchison, Topeka, and Santa Fe Railroad, which rolled through the vicinity in the early 1880s. It was named for the community's earliest store owner, Albert Kriesinger. Albert elected to incorporate in 1929.

# CLAFLIN, KS
Once it was certain that the Missouri Pacific Railroad would be laying its tracks through the area, the plans to plat a townsite were underway. The land north of the railroad station was owned by J. H. Williamson, who had purchased the land from George Platt in 1875. Land south of the station was under the ownership of William Albro Giles, and it was this parcel of 40 acres that the railroad wished to buy to build its facilities upon. Giles declined and, in doing so, forced the railroad to change the station's name from Giles City to Claflin after they purchased Williamson's land instead. It was surveyed by Judge Oliver P. Hamilton, who elected to name it Claflin after the maiden name of his wife, Adelia Maria Claflin. Once the townsite was formally established, a grain elevator and a flour mill, a lumber yard, a machine shop, a creamery, a cafe, a bank, a blacksmith, and a newspaper became some of the first businesses to be opened. Jackie Stiles, a 2001 WNBA All-Star and the WNBA Rookie of the Year attended Claflin High School, and Walter Hickel, the 2nd Governor of Alaska and the 38th United States Secretary of the Interior grew up on a farm outside of the community. The Claflin Museum contains a plethora of artifacts that pertain to the town's history.

# ELLINWOOD, KS
Ellinwood's history begins in 1871 when William Misner built a small frame house and became the first settler of the newly platted townsite. As it began to steadily grow in its first couple of years of its existence, a nearby town called Zarah elected to move its citizens and buildings to Ellinwood, and soon there was a hotel, a general store, and several homes by the time that the Atchison, Topeka & Santa Fe Railroad completed its construction of the line through town circa 1872. The townspeople elected to name the city in honor of Colonel R. Ellinwood, a railroad engineer. A small group of Germans arrived at the site, bringing their customs and the idea to establish a brewery in 1875, the first of its kind in the western portion of Kansas. Many of Ellinwood's early streets were given German names. Ellinwood holds a certain level of fame with Kansans because of the historic tunnels–essentially once an underground shopping district– built beneath several downtown businesses. They had been home to saloons and storefronts, and throughout the years, they also served as a refuge from tornadoes, a passageway for locals to avoid trudging through the muddy streets, a sanctuary for Germans during World

War I, and a haven for those engaging in prohibited activities (namely the consumption of alcohol) during the Prohibition era of Kansas. Tens of thousands of tourists have admired the tunnels that remain beneath the Wolf Hotel, the Dick Building, and the 1883. Amongst the other notable buildings of early Ellinwood were sets of creameries, banks, flour mills, three-grain elevators, hotels, and a post office. The rock band Kansas borrowed the town's Opera House in 1973 in a bid to impress Wally Gold, who would later become the band's producer after there was an impressive showing of locals at the show (primarily because of the free beer that was handed out to those in attendance). For years, Ellinwood also played host to the Kansas State Wristwrestling Championship. Born here in 1919 was Walter Joseph Hickel, who served as the 2nd Governor of Alaska from December 1966 to January 1969 and from December 1990 to December 1994.

## Lodging Recommendation:
## The Historic Wolf Hotel
## 1 N Main St
## Ellinwood, KS 67526

# GALATIA, KS
**POPULATION: 45 – TOWN 408 OF 627 (8-13-23)**
For nearly thirty-five years, Galatia was without rail service until the Atchison, Topeka, and Santa Fe Railroad opted to extend a rail line to the community. Before the railroad's arrival, settlers had relied on the Missouri Pacific Railroad line in nearby Olmitz for transportation or the transmission of goods. The site had once been known as Four Corners when it was laid out by David C. Barrows in 1885, but the name was ultimately changed by Henry G. Weber for his stomping grounds in Galatia, Illinois. The United States Postal Service operated an office in the area from 1889 to 1966. At the town's peak, it boasted multiple grain elevators and general merchandise outlets, a bank, and a lumberyard.

# GREAT BEND, KS ★☆
**POPULATION: 14,733 – TOWN 421 OF 627 (8-15-23)**
Named for its geographic location on the "great bend" of the Arkansas River, this active central Kansas city was located by the Great Town Company in 1871 under C. R. S. Curtis, J. L. Curtis, J. T. Morton, M. F. Bassett, A. R. McIntyre, and James Israel. The men opted first to build a hotel to begin the first instance of a long line of economic

activity in the townsite because they foresaw the arrival of the Atchison, Topeka & Santa Fe Railroad to that part of Kansas. Early settlers and those looking to begin a new life on the western frontier saw great promise in the newly founded community. After voting to incorporate the town and designating it as the Barton County seat in 1872, its growth became inevitable. The cattle trade headquartered itself in the community, making Great Bend a rowdy cowtown for its first half-decade until the Kansas Legislature passed a bill extending the "deadline" that would restrict Texas cattle from being present 30 miles west of Barton County. Following the departure of the trade, its industries flourished. By 1912, there were broom and mattress factories, a creamery, mills, elevators, three banks and newspapers, an opera house, an ice plant, eight churches, a public library, and an institution of higher learning. There is still a college in Great Bend today known as Barton Community College, which was established in 1965 by a measure proposed by residents of Barton County. Two specific early events of community importance occurred in 1882 when a smallpox epidemic required a multi-week quarantine of the city, and in 1943, when the U.S. Army Air Forces formed Great Bend Army Airfield to train pilots in the usage of B-29 bombers during the Second World War. The base has since been converted into Great Bend Municipal Airport, which for a time had the only runway long enough to land the President's Air Force One. It was here that the NHRA held its first national drag event called "The Nationals" in 1955, making the city a pioneer location for motorsport. The Argonne Rebels Drum and Bugle Corps furthered Great Bend's notoriety when it won the American Legion national championships from 1971 to 1973 and became one of the thirteen charter members of Drum Corps International. Modern points of interest are the Great Bend Zoo and Raptor Center within Britt Spraugh Park, known for its five-dozen species of animals, the Shafer Art Gallery, the Kansas Oil and Gas Hall of Fame & Museum, and the Barton County Historical Society Museum. Amongst its most notable historic residents are Jack Kilby, the co-inventor of the integrated circuit, thermal printer, and handheld calculator, filmmaker Nicholas Barton, Oscar Micheaux, widely known as the "most successful African-American filmmaker for the first part of the 20th century," NFL punter Monte Robbins, John Keller, a member of the 1952 Olympic men's basketball gold medalist team, five-time Grammy-award nominated pianist and singer Karrin Allyson, Steve Kufeld, the inventor of the reflector sight for telescopes, Joseph W. Henkle Sr., the 33rd Lieutenant Governor of Kansas from 1957 to 1961, baseball scout John R. Keenan, and 2007 NFL Special Teams Coach of the Year Steve Crosby. Kilby is honored with a statue in front of the Barton County Courthouse.

# HOISINGTON, KS

**POPULATION: 2,699 – TOWN 418 OF 627 (8-14-23)**

The second-largest town in Barton County, Hoisington, was founded by the Central Kansas Town Company in 1886 to attract the attention of the Kansas and Colorado Railroad (a line of the Missouri Pacific) and divert the construction of the railroad line through that section of the county. The plan succeeded, and the name Hoisington was assigned to the community in honor of A. J. Hoisington, a member of the townsite company and a capitalist from Great Bend, Kansas. Former names for the area were Monon, as assigned by the railroad, and Buena Vista, given to the area post office in April 1887. The railroad heavily influenced the town's industry and population growth. It was instrumental in bringing forth the town's first four churches, an automobile livery, hotels, banks, grain mills and elevators, a public library, and a roundhouse and shops for their personal business use. South Hoisington (now unincorporated) truly began its growth in the 1920s and 1930s and was the location of South Haven, more popularly known as "The Big House," which provided county residents with their fix for gambling, alcohol, and prostitution. The business is widely remembered by residents of Hoisington today for its unseemly offerings and its notoriety as an outlier amongst other businesses of that era. A peak population of 4,248 residents called Hoisington home in the 1960s thanks to the gas and oil industries, although, with time, those numbers have fallen to 2,699 people as of the last Census. After an F4 tornado made its way through Hoisington on April 21, 2001, the Weather Channel featured Hoisington in an episode of *Storm Stories* because the high school prom had been going on at that time, and most in attendance had no idea that there had been a tornado. More tales on the city's extensive past can be read at the Hoisington Historical Museum. Also worth noting are Phil Webb's tiny folk-art cement creations throughout the Hoisington City Cemetery that add character and charm to the graveyard. Kathryn Eames, an actress whose career spanned five decades, former NFL lineman Doug Dumler, L. Worth Seagondollar, a Manhattan Project scientist, and voice actress Kari Wahlgren, known for her work in *Teenage Mutant Ninja Turtles, Ben 10, Kung Fu Panda: Legends of*

*Awesomeness, Rick and Morty, The Fairly OddParents*, and several other projects, all have affiliations with Hoisington.

# OLMITZ, KS
## POPULATION: 90 – TOWN 417 OF 627 (8-14-23)

Formally platted in 1885 but not incorporated as a municipality until 120, Olmitz was brought up by Austrian settlers who sought to name it after Olomouc, now a city of 102,000 residents in the Czech Republic. It has always remained a small, agricultural community and never recorded a population of more than 166 inhabitants (1930 Census). The Missouri Pacific Railway was the principal driver of the town's economy, as early infrastructure included a post office, a bank, and several lines of general mercantile.

# PAWNEE ROCK, KS
## POPULATION: 193 – TOWN 419 OF 627 (8-14-23)

Pawnee Rock was named after the nearby landmark of the same name that served as a marker for the approximate halfway point on the Historic Santa Fe Trail. The landmark stood 150 feet tall until much of it was destroyed by the railroad for roadbed material and by settlers to assist in building early homes. It is now a protected site under the authority of the Kansas Historical Society and has been named the Pawnee Rock State Historic Site. The townsite, established in 1874 by the Arkansas Valley Town Company, was located on the Atchison, Topeka & Santa Fe Railway and was once home to over twenty businesses. It was incorporated in 1887.

# SUSANK, KS
## POPULATION: 31 – TOWN 407 OF 627 (8-13-23)

Susank was founded in the 1920s when the postal service established a post office there on June 24, 1921. It would later close on August 1, 1991. The town's name seeks to honor Ed Susank, an official of Barton County. Incorporation status given by the legislature in 1940.

**Adjacent Counties:** Ellis (NW), Russell (N), Ellsworth (NE), Rice (SE), Stafford (S), Pawnee (SW), Rush (W)

**Unincorporated/Ghost Towns:** Beaver, Boyd, Dartmouth, Dent Spur, Dubuque, Dundee, Farhman, Heizer, Hitschmann, Millard, Odin, Redwing, South Hoisington, Stickney, Zarah

## National Register of Historic Places:
**Beaver:** Beaver Creek Native Stone Bridge, Bridge No. 218-Off System Bridge, Bridge No. 222-Off System Bridge, Bridge No. 640-Federal Aid Highway System Bridge
**Ellinwood:** Wolf Hotel, Wolf Park Band Shell
**Great Bend:** Abel House, A.S. Allen Buildings, Crest Theater, Great Bend Army Air Field Hangar, Great Bend Central Business District, High Rise Apartments, Nagel House, Norden Bombsight Storage Vaults
**Great Bend (township):** Walnut Creek Crossing
**Heizer:** Walnut Creek Bridge
**Hoisington:** Hoisington High School, Manweiler-Maupin Chevrolet, US Post Office-Hoisington
**Pawnee Rock:** Pawnee Rock

## Breweries/Wineries/Distilleries:
Dry Lake Brewing (Great Bend, KS)
Rosewood Ranch & Winery (Pawnee Rock, KS)
Rosewood Wine Cellar (Great Bend, KS)

## Golf Courses:
Claflin Golf Club, Public (Claflin, KS)
Golden Belt Country Club, Semi-Private (Great Bend, KS)
Grove Park Golf Club, Private (Ellinwood, KS)
Lake Barton Golf Course, Semi-Private (Great Bend, KS)

## Town Celebrations:
After Harvest Festival, Ellinwood, KS (3rd Weekend of July)
K-96 June Jaunt Festival, Great Bend, KS (Early June)
Labor Day Celebration, Hoisington, KS (Labor Day Weekend)
Party in the Park, Great Bend, KS (2nd Saturday in August)

Allen County Photos: Bassett, Elsmore, Gas, Humboldt, Humboldt, Iola, Iola, Savonburg

43

Anderson County Photos: Garnett, Garnett, Garnett, Garnett, Garnett, Greeley, Kincaid, Westphalia

Atchison County Photos: Atchison, Atchison, Atchison, Atchison, Atchison, Atchison, Effingham, Muscotah

45

Barber County Photos: Hardtner, Isabel, Kiowa, Kiowa, Kiowa, Medicine Loge, Medicine Lodge, Sun City

Barton County Photos: Claflin, Ellinwood, Ellinwood, Great Bend, Great Bend, Hoisington, Olmitz, Pawnee Rock

# BOURBON COUNTY
## EST. 1855 - POPULATION: 14,360

Because several of its earliest settlers emigrated from Bourbon County, Kentucky, they opted to transfer the name to their new western home in Kansas.

# BRONSON, KS
### POPULATION: 304 – TOWN 323 OF 627 (6-29-23)

Once called Wilsonville, this Bourbon County community was later named for Ira D. Bronson, an attorney from Fort Scott. The community was founded in the 1880s at one site but later moved to be integrated into the Missouri Pacific Railroad line. It was formally incorporated in 1881, the same year that G. H. Requa and Mr. Martin opened the first store, and the postal service established an office there. Because of its location at the midpoint between the bustling cities of Fort Scott and Iola, its industries multiplied. In 1910, residents came up with the idea to hold a horseshoe pitch tournament, the first of its kind in history. Jonathan Davis, the 22nd Governor of Kansas, spent his entire life in and around Bronson. Perry's Pork Rinds & General Store (est. 2017) is a popular area store that sells fudge, groceries, other goods, and, of course, pork rinds.

# FORT SCOTT, KS ★☆
### POPULATION: 7,552 – TOWN 335 OF 627 (6-30-23)

Fort Scott began in 1842 as a military outpost for the United States Army to help maintain peace between the local Native American tribes and pioneers traveling westward. Now a U.S. National Historic Site, it remained in operation until 1853, when the buildings were decommissioned and soon sold to W. H. Wilson (also the town's first postmaster), A. Hornbeck, J. Mitchell, and Edward Greenwood, who turned the buildings into homes and hotels. In 1857, the Fort Scott Town company was organized with George A. Crawford at its helm, and the board would donate land to erect a courthouse and jail, multiple churches, and even Fort Scott National Cemetery. It was incorporated in 1860 after building up several homes and businesses. When the Civil War broke out, the Union army would return to defend the Midwest from a Confederacy invasion. The Battle of Dry Wood Creek would be fought just across the border in what is now Vernon County, Missouri, culminating in a victory for the Confederacy (although they opted not to seize the fort). The fort is noted for putting together the 1st Kansas Colored Infantry, the first platoon of African-American soldiers in the country who banded together to help emancipate all other enslaved people at that time. The men went into service on January 13, 1863, and would later be reorganized as the 79th United States Colored Troops. Following the war, Fort Scott grew substantially from about 262 permanent residents to over 4,000 by 1870. The sudden increase in population attracted the attention of the Missouri River, Fort Scott & Gulf Railroad (later the Missouri, Kansas & Texas), Missouri Pacific Railroad, and the St. Louis & San Francisco Railroad line. It narrowly lost to Kansas City in a battle to become the largest railroad center west of the Mississippi River. However, the three lines helped bring over 36 manufacturing firms to the city by 1909, ranging from brickworks (a company so large that its bricks were used in the construction of the Panama Canal and of which 14 miles of them would be laid throughout the city) to mineral paint, as well as a historic brewery, planing, woolen, and flour mills, coal mines, and a foundry. Today, Gunn Park (the largest municipal park in Kansas), the Fort Scott National Historic Site, Fort Scott Community College (the oldest community college in Kansas, founded in 1919), the Museum of Creativity, and the Lowell Milken Center for Unsung Heroes (a one-of-a-kind center that focuses on the unsung heroes of past and present America) are amongst its most notable attractions for visitors. In 2008, community members banded together to raise enough funds to renovate Ellis Park, but with a twist: the donations were made in pennies. Three million four hundred six thousand two hundred thirty-four pennies were donated and laid out at the Fort Scott Middle Scott parking lot, a 40.32-mile chain that set the Guinness World Record for the "most pennies laid down." Many notable persons have ties to Bourbon County's judicial seat: Medal of Honor recipient William D. Hawkins, musician Mark Hart (known for touring with the bands Supertramp and Crowded House), Clark Clifford, the 9th United States Secretary of Defense, William C. McDonald, the 1st Governor of New Mexico, notable 1940s to 1970s photojournalist Gordon Parks (known for his photos depicting the struggles of African Americans), drummer Richard Christy, and former MLB players Andy LaRoche, Adam LaRoche, and Louis Ury.

 **Restaurant Recommendation:**
**Crooner's Lounge**
**117 S Main St #1414**
**Fort Scott, KS 66701**

# FULTON, KS

**POPULATION: 165 – TOWN 337 OF 627 (6-30-23)**

Now home to only 165 people, this town was called Osaga until 1878, but the postal service changed the name because of its similarity in spelling to Osage (a city in nearby Osage County). Its new name, Fulton, is an eponym for Fulton, Illinois. The St. Louis & San Francisco Railway once ran through Fulton, helping the local grain elevators, mills, hotels, and fraternity organizations like I.O.O.F. and the Masonic Lodge to flourish. Its founding date was set in 1869, and in 1884, it was incorporated.

# MAPLETON, KS

**POPULATION: 96 – TOWN 338 OF 627 (6-30-23)**

This town of 96 people started under the name Eldora in May of 1857 when a group of New Englanders worked to locate it. The Eldora Town Company waited before seeking to plat the townsite. When the decision was made, they renamed their company and Mapleton site after the local post office. The latter name was taken from an early settler's suggestion that the town be named after the plentiful groves of maple trees. Fred Burke, born Thomas A. Camp in Mapleton, was a prominent Prohibition-era gangster thought to have taken part in the Saint Valentine's Day Massacre of 1929 in Chicago.

# REDFIELD, KS

**POPULATION: 90 – TOWN 325 OF 627 (6-29-23)**

The town of Redfield came about in 1866 to fulfill its purpose of being a supply and shipping point on the Missouri Pacific Railroad. It was named in honor of one of its pioneer settlers, Dr. Redfield. The postal service positioned an office here on May 22, 1872, and in 1905, Redfield was incorporated as a city of the third class. Despite its small size, the town was the birthplace of Elmer McCollum, the biochemist who co-discovered Vitamin A and was known for using rats in nutrition research. Drummer Richard Christy, former drummer for the heavy metal band Death, grew up on a farm outside of town.

# UNIONTOWN, KS
## POPULATION: 293 – TOWN 324 OF 627 (6-29-23)

The name Uniontown was given to this Bourbon County community because of the undying loyalty of the early settlers to the Union during the American Civil War. Although a post office has remained in operation in the area since 1856, it wasn't until 1865 that a town company was formed, and buildings like general stores, a wagon shop and lumber yard, a mill, and a Methodist church were constructed. The Missouri Pacific Railroad was crucial to the town's development and led to it being incorporated in 1895. The "Life in a Jar: The Irena Sendler Project" began at the local high school when students Megan Stewart, Elizabeth Cambers, and Sabrina Coons uncovered the incredible story of Sendler and how she rescued over 2500 Jewish children from the Warsaw Ghetto as the events of World War II unfolded.

**Adjacent Counties:** Linn (N), Crawford (S), Neosho (SW), Allen (W), Anderson (NW)

**Unincorporated/Ghost Towns:** Barnesville, Berlin, Devon, Garland, Godfrey, Hammond, Harding, Hiattville, Hidden Valley, Hollister, Marmaton, Pawnee Station, Ronald, Xenia, Xerox

**National Register of Historic Places:**
**Fort Scott:** Claude and Alberta Brant House, First Congregational Church, First Presbyterian Church, Fort Scott Downtown Historic District, Fort Scott National Cemetery, Fort Scott National Historic Site, Fort Scott Public Carnegie Library, Thomas L. and Anna B. Herbert House, Marmaton Bridge, Moody Building, Union Block, Eugene Ware Elementary School
**Fulton:** Fulton High School and Grade School, Long Shoals Bridge

**Golf Courses:**
Fort Scott Country Club, Semi-Private (Fort Scott, KS)

**Town Celebrations:**
Good Ol' Days, Fort Scott, KS (1st Weekend of June)
Independence Day Bash, Uniontown, KS (Around the 4th of July)
Old Settler's Picnic, Uniontown, KS (Labor Day Weekend)

# BROWN COUNTY
## EST. 1855 - POPULATION: 9,508

Albert G. Brown, the 14th Governor of Mississippi and a significant supporter of admitting Kansas into the Union is remembered by the name of this county in northeast Kansas.

# EVEREST, KS
## POPULATION: 265 – TOWN 42 OF 627 (3-1-23)
Everest came about because of the building of a railroad, specifically the Missouri Pacific Railroad, through the area circa 1882. A station was constructed there that would ultimately lead to a small boom in population. The town's name honors Colonel Aaron S. Everest of Atchison, Kansas. He worked with the railroad and served as the attorney for Atchison County in the Kansas Senate.

# FAIRVIEW, KS
## POPULATION: 240 – TOWN 33 OF 627 (2-28-23)
This community of 240 individuals in Brown County was founded in October of 1886 and named by Mrs. O. Fountain. The town's founding date has been set at 1872, and its prominent railroad was once the Rock Island Railroad. David Floyd Lambertson, known primarily for his role as the United States Ambassador to Thailand in the early 1990s, and Bernard W. Rogers, the Supreme Allied Commander of NATO in Europe, both have ties to Fairview.

# HAMLIN, KS
## POPULATION: 25 – TOWN 39 OF 627 (3-1-23)
Although its population has dwindled to only twenty-five residents, Hamlin was once home to 258 individuals (according to the 1900 Census). It was laid out in 1870 as a station on the St Joseph & Grand Island and the Missouri Pacific Railroads and named for Hannibal Hamlin, the 15th Vice President of the United States (under Abraham Lincoln). The poet behind "Walls of Corn", "Beautiful Things", and "The Trail of Forty-Nine", Ellen Palmer Allerton, is buried in the Hamlin Cemetery.

# HIAWATHA, KS ★

Hiawatha, one of the oldest towns in Kansas, was both founded and incorporated in the same year, 1857. It only took a year for the town to be named the county seat of Brown County, and it wasn't much longer until the Missouri Pacific and St. Joseph & Grand Island Railroads had tracks laid through town. Its name was taken from the character in Henry Wadsworth Longfellow's famous poem, "The Song of Hiawatha." Hiawatha was also a real person and leader who helped to create the Iroquois Native American Confederacy. Its main street is named "Oregon Street" in reference to the Oregon Trail. All roads north of Main Street are named for Native American tribes that once roamed north of the trail, and subsequently, all streets to the south are named for tribes that once called the lands south of the trail their home. Hiawatha is known for hosting the oldest continuous Halloween parade in the United States, the Hiawatha Halloween Frolic, which started in 1914. Mrs. John Krebs started the event for the city's children so they could dress up and decorate their toys, and the event enlarged from there. Notable area attractions include the Brown County Historical Museum, the Brown County Ag Museum and Windmill Lane, and the Davis Memorial. The Davis Memorial at Mount Hope Cemetery is an interesting Italian marble monument that was constructed by John Milburn Davis for $200,000 to honor the life of his wife. It was built between 1930 and 1934, amid the Great Depression. John L. Goldwater, the co-founder of MLJ (later Archie) Comics, is said to have derived his inspiration for the famous comic strip character Archie Andrews from his memories of working as a reporter at the Hiawatha Daily World. Famous Hiawathans include pinup artist Al Buell, the 1953 Pulitzer Prize for Photography winner William M. Gallagher, and Joe Wilhoit, the record holder for the longest hitting streak in baseball history at 69 games (as a member of the Wichita Jobbers of the Western League). Joe's hit record stretched from June 14 to August 19, 1919. John McLendon (member of the Basketball Hall of Fame), Bion Barnett (co-founder of the former largest bank in Florida before its 1997 acquisition, Barnett Bank), Bill Martin Jr. (author of famous children's books such as *Chicka Chicka Boom Boom* and *Brown Bear, Brown Bear, What Do You See?*), and Tod D. Wolters (NATO's Supreme Allied Commander in Europe from May 2019 to July 2022) are other notable town figures.

 **Restaurant Recommendation:**
**The Hiawatha Creamery**
**725 Oregon St**
**Hiawatha, KS 66434**

**Lodging Recommendation:**
**The Country Cabin**
**2534 Kestrel Rd**
**Hiawatha, KS 66434**

# HORTON, KS ☆
**POPULATION: 1,523 – TOWN 55 OF 627 (3-13-23)**

Once located on the Chicago, Rock Island & Pacific Railway, the city of Horton was established in September of 1886 and named in honor of Albert H. Horton. It was the host city for the railroad's most extensive line of shops in the western part of the country, which was completed in 1887. It was in that same year that Horton was incorporated as a city of the second class. Historical Census data states that the population was as high as 4,049 individuals in 1930, but the population has since shrunk to 1,523 as of the 2020 Census. In January 2013, Marcus Lemonis of the CNBC television program *The Profit* visited Horton, intending to revitalize the community. As a result of his visit, residents started a "Reinvent Horton" campaign in which they installed curbs, sidewalks, and light poles and worked to clean up the town. The longest-serving cabinet secretary in Kansas history, Robert Harder, and Kenneth "Boots" Adams, long-time president of the Phillips Petroleum Company (perhaps more commonly known as Phillips 66), heed from Horton. Danny J. Petersen (Medal of Honor recipient) is from here as well.

# MORRILL, KS
**POPULATION: 218 – TOWN 38 OF 627 (3-1-23)**

Morrill was named in honor of Edmund Needham Morrill, the 13th Governor of Kansas. It was started following the construction of the St. Joseph & Western Railroad. The layout for the town was produced on February 27, 1878, and it was to be built on the land of T. J. Elliott.

# POWHATTAN, KS
**POPULATION: 69 – TOWN 32 OF 627 (2-28-23)**
Powhattan was once a stagecoach station named Locknane, but it was later renamed in honor of the father of Pocahontas (of historic Jamestown, Virginia fame). The town was established in 1877, and its prominent railroad was the Rock Island Railway.

# RESERVE, KS
**POPULATION: 67 – TOWN 40 OF 627 (3-1-23)**
Reserve, Kansas (population 67) sits a short 1.5 miles south of the Nebraska-Kansas border. For one hundred and one years, a post office remained in operation until it shut down in 1983. The town was founded on the location of a former Native American Reservation and was once a part of the Missouri Pacific Railroad line.

# ROBINSON, KS
**POPULATION: 183 – TOWN 46 OF 627 (3-1-23)**
Robinson once had an atypical etymology, as it was formerly called Lickskillet. The unique name was derived from the story that an old area trapper would give his dirty dishes to his dog to lick clean. By the time the area began to resemble the early beginnings of the townsite in 1871, the St. Joseph & Grand Island Railroad had arrived, and a new name was given: Robinson, in honor of the 1st Governor of Kansas, Charles Lawrence Robinson. He was once the owner of the townsite, and despite the recognition, he was ironically the first state governor to be impeached by its legislature (although he was found to be not guilty). The 6th Governor of Oklahoma, Martin E. Trapp, was born in Robinson on April 18, 1877. Brown State Fishing Lake and Wildlife Area is a hotspot for area anglers.

# WILLIS, KS
**POPULATION: 24 – TOWN 41 OF 627 (3-1-23)**
Willis had its start as a station on the Missouri Pacific Railroad. The First Presbyterian Church of Willis and the Willis Wesleyan Methodist Church were two crucial early community gathering places for this town with a modern population of 24. The town's post office operated from June 14, 1882, to January 31, 1960. A giant fishing pole and fish at the base of the town's water tower welcome visitors to the city.

Sabetha is only partially located in Brown County (see Nemaha County).

**Adjacent Counties:** Doniphan (W), Atchison (SE), Jackson (SW), Nemaha (W)

**Unincorporated/Ghost Towns:** Baker, Fidelity, Kickapoo Site 1, Kickapoo Site 2, Kickapoo Site 5, Kickapoo Site 6, Kickapoo Site 7, Kickapoo Tribal Center, Mercier, Padonia

**National Register of Historic Places:**
**Fairview:** Delaware River Warren Truss Bridge
**Hamlin:** Bethany Brethren Church
**Hiawatha:** Samuel Bierer House, Davis Memorial, A. J. Eicholtz House, Seward Graham House, Hiawatha Courthouse Square Historic District, Hiawatha Memorial Auditorium, Hiawatha National Guard Armory
**Horton:** Fete Apartments, Horton Civic Center, U.S. Post Office-Horton
**Iowa Township:** Site No. RH00-062
**White Cloud:** Iowa Tribe Community Building

**Golf Courses:**
Hiawatha Country Club, Semi-Private (Hiawatha, KS)
Horton Lakeview Country Club, Semi-Private (Horton, KS)

**Town Celebrations:**
Everest Fun Day, Everest, KS (1st Saturday in August)
Hiawatha Halloween Frolic, Hiawatha, KS (October 31st)
Hiawatha Maple Leaf Festival, Hiawatha, KS (3rd Weekend in September)

# BUTLER COUNTY
## EST. 1855 - POPULATION: 67,380

Butler County was named for Andrew Butler, a United States Senator from South Carolina and a co-author of the Kansas-Nebraska Act of 1854.

# ANDOVER, KS

While this suburb of Wichita is presently named after Andover, Massachusetts, earlier names for the area were Minneha (alternatively spelled Minnehaha) and Cloud City. The "Minneha" name was used on four separate occasions by the post office between 1887 and 1900 to name post offices in Butler and neighboring Sedgwick County, but the one of note about Andover was founded on November 28, 1877, moved to Cloud City on March 8, 1880, and then renamed Andover on June 7, 1880. Andover was settled in the 1870s by Vincent Smith, G. M. Pattison, and Mr and Mrs. Ephraim Waggoner, amongst many others; eventually, enough bond money was raised to bring the St. Louis & San Francisco Railroad to town. Before the advent of the Frisco, Andover had a population of 130 people in 1910, but fifty years later, it still had only 186 citizens calling it home. On February 4, 1957, the townspeople decided to incorporate formally, and manufacturers began to move into their factories. The population of Andover steadily grew, and as of 2020, it is the home of 14,892 people. Aside from an 1898 train robbery, the single most notable day in Andover's tenure as a city came on April 26, 1991, when an F5 tornado destroyed hundreds of structures and took the homes of over a third of the residents. A flag-and-plague memorial marks where the trailer park, the area most affected by the tornado, stood. Kevin Schmidt, most famous for his role as Henry Baker in the 2003 film *Cheaper by the Dozen*, was born in Andover in 1988. Roe Messner, the founder of Messner Construction and known for having over 1,700 churches constructed, started his business here.

**Restaurant Recommendation:**
**Bob & Luigi's Andover**
**325 W Central Ave**
**Andover, KS 67002**

# AUGUSTA, KS

Located at the confluence of the Walnut and Whitewater Rivers lies Augusta, a town of 9,256 inhabitants in western Butler County. Attempts were made as early as 1857 to formulate a city under names like "Fontanella" and "Orizonia." Still, it wouldn't be until the establishment of the trading post of Shamleffer and C. N. James in

1868 that the Osage tribe tolerated any European settlement. James was the town's first postmaster, taking over the duties in October of that year, and as the man in charge, he elected to call the office and town Augusta after his wife. The city's growth was spurred by the arrival of the St. Louis & San Francisco Railroad in 1880, the Atchison, Topeka & Santa Fe Railway, and the Missouri Pacific Railroad. These lines connected Augusta to other central area communities like El Dorado and Arkansas City, which aided in bringing the means and the men to build up a substantial town. The discovery of oil and the establishment of the White Eagle Oil Company, the Walnut Refining Company, and Lakeside Refinery led to an enormous boom in population between 1910 and 1920 (1,235 residents to 4,219, a growth of 241.6%), and from thereon Augusta's growth could not be slowed. Amongst the most notable points of interest today are the Augusta Historical Museum and Henry's Sculpture Hill. The Kansas Museum of Military History showcased military history from 1990 to 2022 before it closed, and the collection was moved to Enid, Oklahoma. The grandmother of former President Barack Obama, Madelyn Dunham, attended Augusta High School.

# BENTON, KS
## POPULATION: 943 – TOWN 593 OF 627 (10-10-23)
Benton has been steadily growing since its inception in 1884 when it began as a stopping point on the Missouri Pacific Railroad. The name seeks to honor former Kansas legislator Thomas Benton Murdock. At its incorporation in 1909, Benton residents had already built up three churches—Christian, Methodist, and Presbyterian—and a handful of businesses and schools for their youth. The community was the focal plot location of the 1969 drama film *The Gypsy Moths*. Stearman Airfield Bar & Grill is famous because of its location at an airport, where its patrons can watch small aircraft take off and land as they enjoy a meal.

**Restaurant Recommendation:**
**Stearman Field Bar & Grill**
**14789 SW 30th St**
**Benton, KS 67017**

# CASSODAY, KS
## POPULATION: 113 – TOWN 221 OF 627 (5-3-23)
The "Prairie Chicken Capital of Kansas" in northeastern Butler County, Cassoday, was named in honor of John B. Cassoday, the 9th Chief Justice of the Wisconsin Supreme Court from 1895 to 1907. It was founded over twelve miles away from the closest railroad station in De Graff, and while it still developed multiple lines of business as well as schools, a bank, and a post office (established July 9, 1906), its population never crossed a threshold of more than 130 individuals (2000 Census). The townspeople elected to incorporate the town in 1960. Local history can be studied and enjoyed at the Cassoday Historical Museum.

# DOUGLASS, KS
## POPULATION: 1,555 – TOWN 567 OF 627 (10-7-23)
Joseph W. Douglass is responsible for bringing about the City of Douglass circa 1869. He was an early store owner, and one of the leading products he supplied for town residents was chicken. In 1873, Douglass captured a man suspected of stealing his fowl and went around town questioning other store owners as to whether or not the man had bought a chicken from their store. After everyone denied him having made a purchase and the prisoner was sure that he would be held accountable for his actions, he shot Douglass, who died only a couple of days later. The town's development marched onward despite losing its founder, and soon, there was a hotel and an opera house, more unique businesses like a jewelry store and a sugar mill (a failed investment at the time), banks, general stores, a newspaper, and more. A line of the Atchison, Topeka & Santa Fe Railroad developed by the Florence, El Dorado, and Walnut Valley Railroad Company was the principal railroad of Douglass. The community retains a strong sense of pride today, and its early history is on display at the Douglass Historical Museum. Four particularly famous people have called the city home: William Couch (leader of the Boomer Movement to Oklahoma and the first mayor of Oklahoma City), Phyllis Haver (silent film era actress), George Hill (silent film era director), and Monty Beisel (an NFL linebacker from 2001 to 2010). The Nutsch family of Douglass was featured on season 3 of Extreme Makeover: Home Edition in January 2006, after their Rose Hill home exploded because of a gas leak.

# ELBING, KS

**POPULATION: 226 – TOWN 597 OF 627 (10-10-23)**

When the Chicago, Kansas, and Nebraska Railway was laying their tracks through Butler County, they appreciated the land of Jacob W. Reiger so much that they wished to build a depot there and formulate a town. It was to be named in honor of the Reiger family, but Mr. Reiger respectfully declined and insisted that it be named after one of three Prussian cities: Danzig, Elbing, or Marienburg. The name was appropriate since there were several other families of the same descent living in the vicinity. The name "Elbing" was selected, and on November 2, 1887 (about six months after the town was founded), the Worth post office was moved here to provide mail services to the residents. In 1919, Elbing was incorporated and experienced a minor boom when oil was discovered. At that point, it had everything from a hotel and a doctor's office to a blacksmith shop and a grain elevator.

# EL DORADO, KS ★☆

**POPULATION: 12,870 – TOWN 555 OF 627 (10-5-23)**

The El Dorado (meaning "golden land" in Spanish) of the present day is primarily remembered for its substantial oil fields, but the city had a considerable amount of success before the 1915 discovery that catapulted its economy and population. It is said that William Hildebrand, one of several horse thieves of the 1850s that plagued the early settlers, was the first semi-permanent resident until he was run out of town at the end of the decade. In 1868, the Eldorado Town Company was formed by B. F. Gordy, Samuel Langdon, Byron O. Carr, and Henry Martin, who began to promote the town. The California Trail ran right through the townsite, and the ideal conditions prompted many pioneers to forgo the rest of their journey and instead settle in Eldorado. They worked diligently to build a flour mill, sawmill, and stores. Within the decade, the Florence, El Dorado, and Walnut Valley Branch Company connected it with other area towns via the Atchison, Topeka & Santa Fe Railroad system. The Kansas City, Mexico, and Orient Railway Company were constructed through the area in the same time frame, and it, too, was later merged into the Santa Fe network. The Missouri Pacific ensured they got in on the town's impressive trade and economy. Great fortune came to El Dorado in 1915, when the first oil field ever discovered using geologic mapping was found there. The "oil field that won World War I" became the most significant single-field producer in the country within three years, accounting for 9.0% of all oil production on the planet at that point in time. Such an incredible discovery dramatically increased the population threefold from 3,129 residents in 1910 to 10,995 in 1920, and it never again receded to a four-digit count. The El Dorado Refinery, once owned by the Skelly Oil Company, is now the largest in Kansas and operated by HF Sinclair. Butler Community College came about in 1927 under the El Dorado Junior College namesake and has since produced many professional athletes (2003 NBA champion Stephen Jackson, 2004 NFL Pro-Bowler Rudi Johnson, the 2007 Israeli Basketball Premier League MVP, Lee Nailon, and 3x NBA All-Defensive First Team member Tony Allen, amongst nearly forty others). Other notable points of interest include the Erman B. White Gallery at the college, El Dorado State Park (the largest state park in Kansas at 4,500 acres), the Butler County Courthouse (as El Dorado is the Butler County seat), the World War II History Center, Coutts Memorial Museum of Art, and the Kansas Oil Museum. The old El Dorado theater was featured on a July 2010 episode of the History Channel's *American Pickers* when it was the Hot Rod Cafe. Aside from specifically Butler Community College athletic alums, several other famous people have called El Dorado home at one point or another: Almon Brown Strowger (the inventor of the Strowger switch, the first successful electromechanical stepping switch telephone exchange), Mort Walker (creator of the *Beetle Bailey* comic strip), Alex Graves (film and television director), Stanley A. Dunham (the grandfather of President Barack Obama), Bobby Douglass (predominantly 1970s NFL quarterback), Steve Brodie (actor born as John Stephens), Ralph Graham (a former coach who supported the integration of African Americans into mainstream sports), Maude Fulton (actress and screenwriter), Marion Koogler McNay (founder of the McNay Art Museum in San Antonio, Texas), Beals Becker (MLB outfielder), and Alfred W. Ellet (a Union Army brigadier general).

 **Restaurant Recommendation:
True Lies Ranch Hand Cafe
607 Oil Hill Rd
El Dorado, KS 67042**

# LATHAM, KS
## POPULATION: 96 – TOWN 556 OF 627 (10-6-23)
This town of 96 on the Frisco Railway (a common nickname for the St. Louis and San Francisco Railway) has a name that likely honors Latham Young, a former railroad official. Latham as a townsite sprung up in 1885, but a post office named Bodock had been established

here on August 21, 1883, before it was moved to Latham in October 1885. It was incorporated by an act of the legislature in 1902.

# LEON, KS

Noble was the original name of this community until it was discovered that there was already another town of that name in Kansas. The town company renamed it Leon, after Leon, Iowa, which in turn commemorated Ponce de Leon. It was laid out in 1879 by M. A. Palmer, J. M. Watson, C. Tabing, J. King, and C. R. Noe, and by March 15, 1882, it was incorporated as a city of the third class. The first building was a blacksmith shop, and later, there were schools, churches, and homes of all designs erected with the advent of the St. Louis & San Francisco Railroad. The post office was established in 1880 with G. A. Kenoyer as the first postmaster.

**Lodging Recommendation:**
**Beaumont Motel & RV Park**
**11651 SE Main St**
**Beaumont, KS 67012**

# POTWIN, KS

Charles W. Potwin was the principal owner of the land that would later host the Missouri Pacific Railroad, so when the town was established in the early 1880s, it was named in his honor. Before that, the postal service had called their office there "Ayr" up until September 22, 1885. William I. Joseph is credited with being the town's founder because he was determined to attract a railroad to Mr. Potwin's earth. In its heyday, it had a flour mill, an alfalfa mill, and several institutions of learning and religion. Some buildings were moved from Plum Grove to Potwin after the ghost town failed to attract a railroad. Two particularly notable (but entirely different) town events occurred first in 1920 when the Vickers Oil Refinery (later sold to oil companies Mobil Oil and Total Petroleum) was started here after oil was discovered in the region, and later in the 2010s, when MaxMind accidentally set the default geolocation of 600 million IP addresses to the farmstead of James and Theresa Arnold at (38.0000, -97.0000). The mistake resulted in the Arnolds being visited by the FBI and the local sheriff's department and hundreds of accusations of fraud, theft, scamming, and just about every other crime imaginable, despite them being completely innocent. The mistake happened because as law enforcement was trying to locate actual criminals, they were often provided with this "default" location, which was interpreted as being the whereabouts of the offender when, in actuality, it was a dead end. Since then, the data company has changed the default IP address locations to bodies of water near the continental center of the contiguous 48 states (throughout Kansas).

# ROSE HILL, KS
**POPULATION: 4,185 – TOWN 570 OF 627 (10-7-23)**

After being founded in 1892, Rose Hill served as a small rural community along the Atchison, Topeka & Santa Fe Railroad for some years before real population growth occurred. For a long while, it was not much more than a handful of stores and homes, limited infrastructure, and a branch of the post office that initially arrived on June 23, 1874. Early settlers are thought to have given the name as a descriptive representation of the townsite when they came, a land full of wild roses. Its most famous resident is Kendall Gammon, the first long snapper selected for the Pro Bowl (in 2004). Resident Phil Brinkley has dedicated years to his Jurassic Art project, a collection of welded scrap metal sculptures in his yard that range from dinosaurs and dragons to animals and other exciting characters.

# TOWANDA, KS
**POPULATION: 1,447 – TOWN 594 OF 627 (10-10-23)**

"Towanda" is an Osage Native American term meaning "big village," which is what its first settlers hoped it would become. With a present population of 1,447 residents, it can be said that they were successful, as early businesses and industries ranging from stone quarrying and livestock to a plethora of retail stores helped make the town into what it is today. Like other Midwestern communities, Towanda's history largely begins with the construction of a railroad line (the Missouri Pacific) through the plains. The townsite was first settled by Europeans around 1870, and in 1905, it filed for incorporation. In 1917, it became the wealthiest town in the world for a short period after oil was discovered on the land of a couple of trap-loving men. The oil boom brought thousands of workers, new residents, and tourists to the area who hoped to glimpse the literal pounds of oil. The Towanda Area Historical Museum showcases exhibits on this and other early town events, buildings, and people. Paradise Doll Hospital & Museum is located nearby. Jordan Phillips, a defensive tackle for the Buffalo Bills of the NFL as of the 2023 season, attended Circle High School in Towanda.

# WHITEWATER, KS
**POPULATION: 661 – TOWN 596 OF 627 (10-10-23)**
The original townsite was established several miles eastward of its present location, and it was there that a post office was designated under the name "White Water" in 1871. For several years, only the post office and minimal structures were in place until it was decided that a town should be started there in 1878. In July 1882, its name was temporarily changed to Ovo, but after many of the buildings were relocated to the Missouri Pacific that had just been constructed through this section of the county, the town resumed the White Water namesake on May 15, 1888. Around the same time that the Missouri Pacific rolled into town, so did the Chicago, Kansas, and Nebraska Railway. The presence of two rail systems was instrumental in the town's success, as they provided the means to erect alfalfa and flour mills, grain elevators, and all varieties of stores. Hattie Horner Louthan, known predominantly for her work on The *Great Southwest: A Monthly Journal of Horticulture*, was a long-time resident of Whitewater.

**Adjacent Counties:** Chase (NE), Greenwood (E), Elk (SE), Cowley (S), Sumner (SW), Harvey (W), Sedgwick (W), Marion (NW)

**Unincorporated/Ghost Towns:** Aikman, Alki, Amador, Beaumont, Bois d'Arc, Brainerd, Browntown, Chelsea, De Graff, Durachen, Frazier, Gordon, Haverhill, Keighley, Lorena, Magna City, Midian, Oil Hill, Oil Valley, Ophir, Plum Grove, Pontiac, Providence, Ramsey, Rosalia, Salter, Vanora, Wingate

**National Register of Historic Places:**
**Augusta:** Augusta Theater, C. N. James Cabin, Loomis-Parry Residence, John Moyle Building, US Post Office-Augusta, Viets Block
**Beaumont:** Beaumont Hotel, Beaumont, St. Louis & San Francisco Railroad Retention Pond, Beaumont, St. Louis & San Francisco Railroad Water Tank
**Bois D'Arc:** Little Walnut River Pratt Truss Bridge
**De Graff:** First Presbyterian Church of De Graff
**Douglass:** Creed-Mills House, Douglass Township Community Building, Muddy Creek Bridge, Polecat Creek Bridge

**El Dorado:** Butler County Courthouse, El Dorado Carnegie Library, El Dorado Historic District, El Dorado Missouri Pacific Depot, Amos H. Gish Building, James T. Oldham House, Ray L. Smith House, Walnut River Crossing of the Cherokee/Fayetteville Oregon-California Trail, Yingling Brothers Auto Company
**Towanda:** Towanda Masonic Lodge No. 30 A.F. and A.M., Whitewater Falls Stock Farm
**Whitewater:** Oak Lawn Farm Dairy Barn

### Breweries/Wineries/Distilleries:
Grace Hill Winery & Vineyards (Whitewater, KS)
Walnut River Brewing Company (El Dorado, KS)

### Golf Courses:
American Legion Golf Course, Public (El Dorado, KS)
Augusta Country Club, Semi-Private (Augusta, KS)
Cedar Pines of Andover, Public (Andover, KS)
Flint Hills National Golf Club, Private (Andover, KS)
Prairie Trails Golf And Country Club, Public (El Dorado, KS)
Terradyne Country Club, Private (Andover, KS)

### Town Celebrations:
Old People's Day, Potwin, KS (4th Saturday in September)
Potwin Watermelon Festival, Potwin, KS (Late August)
Prairie Rose Western Days, Benton, KS (May)
Rose Hill Fall Festival, Rose Hill, KS (2nd Full Weekend of October)

# CHASE COUNTY
## EST. 1859 - POPULATION: 2,572

A politician named Samuel P. Chase is the namesake of Chase County. Chase was a Governor of Ohio and the U.S. Secretary of the Treasury and Chief Justice at different points.

# CEDAR POINT, KS
## POPULATION: 22 – TOWN 234 OF 627 (5-4-23)
This humble town of 22 people once boasted a population of nearly tenfold in the 1920s (190 as of the 1920 Census). Its founding came in 1862, as did the post office in June of that year. Cedar Point Mill was the earliest establishment in the town in 1867, and in 1870, it was changed to the Drinkwater & Schriver Mill. The mill remains

today and was placed on the National Register of Historic Places in 2006. The Atchison, Topeka, and Santa Fe Railroad laid tracks through Cedar Point in 1871, although they called their station Cedar Grove and located it just north of the townsite.

# COTTONWOOD FALLS, KS ★☆
**POPULATION: 851 – TOWN 223 OF 627 (5-3-23)**
Cottonwood Falls welcomed its first settlers in 1854 when trader Seth Hayes established himself on the Cottonwood River. Other immigrants would make their way to the townsite over the next several years, and on September 16, 1858, a post office was established. Area residents voted to designate the city as the county seat in 1862; in 1872, it was incorporated as a city of the third class (with W. S. Smith being its first mayor), and in 1873, the Atchison, Topeka, and Santa Fe Railway built the first of its two lines through the community. An essential historical moment in town history occurred on March 31, 1931, when a Transcontinental & Western Air flight crashed ten miles south of Cottonwood Falls, killing University of Notre Dame head coach Knute Rockne and seven others. Its central point of interest is the Chase County Courthouse, a gorgeous structure built in 1873 in the French Renaissance Revival architectural style that remains the oldest operating courthouse in Kansas. The Chase County Historical Society Museum and the Roniger Memorial Museum are also here. Politicians William Morgan (the 21st Lieutenant Governor of Kansas), Samuel Wood, Harley Martin, and Dudley Doolittle are all affiliated with the community, as is the 1985 Disney film *Return to Oz*, the 2005 war drama film *Jarhead*, and an episode (Season 8, Episode 13) of NBC's crime drama series *The Blacklist*.

**Lodging Recommendation:**
**Spring Street Retreat**
**371 Spring St**
**Cottonwood Falls, KS 66845**

# ELMDALE, KS
**POPULATION: 40 – TOWN 235 OF 627 (5-4-23)**
Elmdale began when the Atchison, Topeka, and Santa Fe Railway built a line in 1871. With the railroad came several storefronts, a bank and newspaper, telegraph and express offices, and a post office that had once been known as Middle Creek (a ghost town) opened its

doors on January 1, 1873. Incorporation as a city of the third class came in 1904, and by 1916, Camp Wood YMCA was founded by local farmers, teachers, and other townspeople as the state's first YMCA residence camp. The town's present population of 40 individuals is the lowest of any Census, and its highest population was 253 as of the 1910 Census.

**Lodging Recommendation:**
**Clover Cliff Ranch B&B**
**826A US-50**
**Elmdale, KS 66850**

# MATFIELD GREEN, KS
**POPULATION: 49 – TOWN 222 OF 627 (5-3-23)**
This small, progressive Kansas town incorporated in 1924 was founded on the banks of the southern fork of the Cottonwood River, nine miles south of the nearest railroad station in Bazaar. Early settlers named it after Matfield, England. It was once home to a school, bank, livery and blacksmith, flour mill, hardware and grocery stores, lumberyard, and a post office that remained in operation from January 1867 to September 1995. A local site of interest is the Pioneer Bluffs ranch headquarters and projects created by local artists. The population has decreased steadily with time since its high point of 324 citizens as of the 1880 Census.

# STRONG CITY, KS
**POPULATION: 386 – TOWN 224 OF 627 (5-3-23)**
William Barstow Strong, the vice-president and general manager of the Atchison, Topeka, and Santa Fe Railroad at the time this town was founded, is its namesake. Strong City is unique in that it was founded by the Cottonwood Town Company in 1872 as a depot on the railroad under the name Cottonwood Station, and it was located only a couple of miles north of Cottonwood Falls, which was incorporated that same year. Citizens in 1881 changed the town's name to Strong, partially to avoid confusion between the two cities as an interurban streetcar system connected them. Early establishments included the largest limestone quarry in the state at the time, two banks and hotels, a six-stall engine roundhouse, a theater, a substantial livestock market, and merchant stores. The word "City" wasn't added to the end of the town's name until 1945. The Tallgrass Prairie National Preserve is one of the final patches of the once-

prominent tallgrass prairie biome and ecosystem that had covered much of the Great Plains prior to the arrival of European settlers.

**Adjacent Counties:** Morris (N), Lyon (E), Greenwood (SE), Butler (SW), Marion (W)

**Unincorporated/Ghost Towns:** Bazaar, Birley, Clements, Clover Cliff, Elk, Ellinor, Gladstone, Homestead, Hymer, Morgan, Neva, Rockland, Rural, Saffordville, Thurman, Toledo, Wonsevu

**National Register of Historic Places:**
**Cedar Point:** Cedar Point Mill, Cottonwood River Pratt Truss Bridge
**Clements:** Clements Stone Arch Bridge, William C. & Jane Shaft House
**Cottonwood Falls:** Carter Building, Chase County Courthouse, Chase County National Bank, Cottonwood Falls Grade School, Cottonwood River Bridge, Wood House
**Elmdale:** Clover Cliff Ranch House, McNee Barns
**Hymer:** Whitney Ranch Historic District
**Matfield Green:** Crocker Ranch, Pioneer Bluffs Ranch Historic District
**Strong City:** Fox Creek Stone Arch Bridge, Lower Fox Creek School, Spring Hill Farm and Stock Ranch House, Strong City Atchison, Topeka & Santa Fe Railroad Depot

**National Register of Historic Places:**
Symphony in the Flint Hills, Cottonwood Falls, KS (Early June)

# CHAUTAUQUA COUNTY
## EST. 1875 - POPULATION: 3,379

Many early settlers of this area of Kansas came from Chautauqua County in New York, so the county was named as such.

# CEDAR VALE, KS
## POPULATION: 476 – TOWN 561 OF 627 (10-6-23)
Situated at the junction of the two major area railways at the beginning of the 20th century, the Atchison, Topeka & Santa Fe Railroad and the Missouri Pacific, Cedar Vale was given a descriptive name for its location in the valley. A town company laid out the townsite in 1870 on the land of E. W. Davis, who attempted to back

out of his deal with them to allow the plans to commence. The company, not playing around with Davis's antics, threatened to hang him if he did not keep up his end of the bargain. To no surprise, he obliged, and from thereon, a grist mill, general stores, hotels, blacksmiths, and a post office with J. R. Marsh as postmaster came into existence. The city's success stopped the expansion of another community a few miles down the Big Cheney River called Osrow. In 1884, it was incorporated by an act of the Kansas legislature. A crowd of nearly 1,000 people flocked to Cedar Vale in its primary year of existence to enjoy Fourth of July festivities, but the town's population did not reflect the same number of inhabitants for the first time until 1920 when 1,044 called it their home. The Cedar Vale Museum serves as the local history center. George Beuoy is one notable town figure credited with inventing the caponizing tool, used to geld male chickens and make them capons with more tender meat.

# CHAUTAUQUA, KS
## POPULATION: 108 – TOWN 390 OF 627 (7-20-23)
The former full name for this settlement was Chautauqua Springs, named after the water source in another part of the county. Like many early springs at the time, they were advertised as being able to cure ailments and illnesses, which town promoters used to help attract new settlers to the townsite. Doctors G. W. Woolsey and T. J. Dunn are credited as founders of the town since they were the first to donate land for the site in 1881. As the Atchison, Topeka & Santa Fe Railroad brought with it the materials and people to construct a grist mill, livery stables, a hotel, blacksmiths, and a line of hardware, drug, and grocery establishments, the town grew to a peak of 401 citizens before dropping off after the 1920s.

# ELGIN, KS
## POPULATION: 60 – TOWN 391 OF 627 (7-20-23)
L. P. Getman founded the town of Elgin in 1869 after building his first store. The town's primary line of business was the cattle trade throughout its earliest days, and it served as a shipping point on the Atchison, Topeka & Santa Fe Railroad. A sawmill was founded in 1870, and soon, banks, churches, and schools followed. Elgin's incorporation date was set in 1919. The present-day population is just 60 residents as of the 2020 Census; it had as many as 600 people in the 1920s. Many of Elgin's streets are still made entirely of brick, a highly unusual feature for a town of this size.

# NIOTAZE, KS

Niotaze was lucky to be located at the junction of two historic railroad lines, the Missouri Pacific and the Atchison, Topeka & Santa Fe. The unusual nomenclature of its name is disputed, although it is speculated that it was derived from either Niota, Tennessee, or Niota, Illinois. The North Caney River proved to be a popular stopping point for early pioneers to settle around, and so a townsite was made that would ultimately have the typical lines of churches, schools, and stores. It is one of several Chautauqua County towns with a present-day population in the double digits.

# PERU, KS

Belleville was an early consideration for the name of this town until it was discovered that there was already a settlement of that name on the opposite side of the state in Republic County. Its founding came in 1870, with the principal member of the town company being E. R. Cutler. He opted to name the newly platted town Peru after his hometown of Peru, Illinois. Although today's population would suggest otherwise, Peru was once a booming town with upwards of 628 citizens (1930s) and boasted numerous hotels, general stores, hardware stores, and saloons. It was a proper town of the west, as it has been said that seven of the first nine townspeople to have been buried in the cemetery died in shootouts and similar affairs. As the town settled down, the Atchison, Topeka & Santa Fe, and the Missouri Pacific Railroads would be extended to that part of the state. The town's claim to fame is that it was the birthplace of Madelyn Dunham in 1922, the maternal grandmother of President Obama.

# SEDAN, KS ★☆

The growth of Sedan can be directly attributed to the designation of the city as the county seat of Chautauqua County because of its positioning near the geographical center of the county. When it was selected as the judicial seat, there were only a couple of homes, a single store and blacksmith shop, a post office, and most surprisingly, a school. The earliest establishments of the first post office and store in Sedan in the early 1870s were futile, as both closed due to a lack of support. The townsite was saved by its location within the county and its designation as the county seat and from the generosity and will of Mr. Kelly, who operated the fundraising efforts to erect a courthouse building. The town was incorporated in 1876 and was likely named commemorative for the Battle of Sedan between the French and the Prussians in September of 1870. It is a sister city to Sedan, France, and the two towns maintain a special economic relationship. Of Sedan's most notable historical figures, three worth mentioning are Charlie Weatherbie, a college football head coach on and off between 1981 and 2009, Emmett Kelly, the mind behind "Weary Willie," a "hobo-clown" type of character, and Elmer S. Riggs, a noted paleontologist. The Emmett Kelly Museum honors the life of the circus clown but is also home to the world's most extensive collection (1,500+) of commemorative Jim Beam bottles. Other popular tourist photo-ops are the Yellow Brick Road) throughout downtown Sedan, "The Hollow," and the mannequin-vehicle remnants of an old Safari Mark's Bar & Bistro advertising campaign.

 **Restaurant Recommendation: Buck's BBQ & Steakhouse 1898 US Highway 166B Sedan, KS 67361**

**Adjacent Counties:** Elk (N), Montgomery (E), Cowley (W)

**Unincorporated/Ghost Towns:** Boston, Cloverdale, Grafton, Hale, Hewins, Jonesburg, Layton, Leeds, Lowe, Matanzas, Monett, Moore, Osro, Rogers, Wauneta

**National Register of Historic Places:**
**Cedar Vale:** L.C. Adam Mercantile Building, Hewins Park Pavilion, Otter Creek Bridge
**Elgin:** Cedar Creek Bridge
**Niotaze:** Niotaze Methodist Episcopal Church
**Sedan:** Bradford Hotel

**Breweries/Wineries/Distilleries:**
Gunnar's Bourbon Company (Sedan, KS)

**Golf Courses:**
Sedan Country Club, Semi-Private (Sedan, KS)

## Town Celebrations:

Chautauqua Hills Blues Festival, Sedan, KS (Memorial Day Weekend)
Labor Day Celebration, Cedar Vale, KS (Labor Day Weekend)

Bourbon County Photos: Bronson, Bronson, Fort Scott, Fort Scott, Fort Scott, Fort Scott, Fulton, Redfield

Brown County Photos: Everest, Hiawatha, Hiawatha, Hiawatha, Hiawatha, Horton, Horton, Willis

Butler County Photos: Andover, Augusta, Benton, Douglass, El Dorado, Latham, Leon, Rose Hill

Chase County Photos: Cedar Point, Cedar Point, Cottonwood Falls, Cottonwood Falls, Cottonwood Falls, Matfield Green, Strong City, Strong City

Chautauqua County Photos: Cedar Vale, Chautauqua, Elgin, Niotaze, Peru, Sedan, Sedan, Sedan

# CHEROKEE COUNTY
## EST. 1855 - POPULATION: 19,362

The southeasternmost county in Kansas was named for the Cherokee tribe of Native Americans.

# BAXTER SPRINGS, KS
## POPULATION: 3,888 – TOWN 379 OF 627 (7-19-23)

Although founded in 1858, the earliest history of the Baxter Springs townsite is entirely preceded by the Osage Nation and skirmishes relating to the American Civil War. The Union established crude military outposts at the site of Baxter Springs surrounding a former area trading post; they consisted of Fort Baxter, Camp Hunter, and Camp Ben Butler. The fort was abandoned and destroyed after 400 of Quantrill's raiders killed nearly one hundred Union men who were caught meandering in the nearby prairie. After the war, the townsite began to take shape, and two men, Armstrong and Davis, built a home. They continued to call their address "Baxter Springs" in honor of A. Baxter on the town site's mineral springs. The area seemed promising to Captain M. Mann and J. J. Barnes, who laid out a town site in 1866 and began welcoming settlers and men associated with the Texas cattle trade. The demand for beef was rising throughout the rest of the United States, so Baxter Springs naturally became a point between Kansas City and Texas used by ranchers and cowboys. It was the first true Kansas cowtown and the "toughest town on earth," according to notable Kansas historian Eugene F. Ware. The Stockyards and Drovers Association would be the responsible party for instrumenting the purchase and sale of cattle and supplying housing, food, water, and other necessities for the animals and the respective businessmen (cowboys). It would serve as the county seat of Cherokee County from November 1867 until February 1869, when a majority of the county's residents voted to move the seat to Columbus following a dispute regarding the land rights of early settlers. As the cattle drive moved westward, growth quickly subsided until lead deposits were discovered some years later and revived the town's prosperity. The Missouri, Oklahoma & Gulf, and the San Francisco & St. Louis Railroads would aid immensely in growing the town's economy. Today, Baxter Springs is one of only two incorporated communities (the other being Galena) in Kansas to be located on Historic Route 66, which drives many potential patrons to local businesses. Several murals and local sites pay homage to the town's location on the ultimate road trip road. Amongst the most noted Baxter Springs residents are Lee Scott (CEO of Wal-Mart from 2000 to 2009), Joe Don Rooney (lead guitarist in the country band Rascal Flatts), Hale Irwin (professional golfer and three-time U.S. Open champion in 1974, 1979, and 1990), Charles F. Parham (founder of American Pentecostalism), actor Byron Stewart, composer Gladys Robinson Youse, and Max McCoy, the author of four *Indiana Jones* novels, the most notable being *Indiana Jones and the Philosopher's Stone*, 1995. The Baxter Springs Heritage Center & Museum is a local resource for those interested in learning more about the Cherokee County community.

 **Restaurant Recommendation: Bricks & Brews Woodfire Grill 1531 Military Ave Baxter Springs, KS 66713**

# COLUMBUS, KS ★☆
**POPULATION: 2,929 – TOWN 377 OF 627 (7-18-23)**
The county seat of Cherokee County, Columbus, was formerly located at the junction of multiple divisions of the Missouri, Kansas & Texas Railroad and the St. Louis & San Francisco line. John Appleby, the first settler who had arrived in February 1868, alongside William Little, John Hanson, and Dr. Bailey, founded a town company. Later, Appleby would form a separate town company with H. A. Scovell, H. Scovell, and F. Fry, who each donated twenty-five acres to start the townsite. Mr. Fry, a native of Columbus, Ohio, is responsible for the town's name. Incorporation as a city was awarded in 1871, and once coal was discovered, the town's growth took off and led to a powder mill, bottle works, cigar (once the largest in Kansas) and canning factories, brick and tile works, marble works, machine shops, carriage and wagon works, and the Long-Bell Lumber Company, ultimately one of the largest vertically integrated companies in the United States. The International Paper Company, the largest pulp and paper company in the world, bought out founder Robert A. Long and Victor Bell's company in 1956. The population of Columbus has varied only slightly over the last century, its smallest population being 2,929 residents as of the latest Census and the highest being 3,490 people in the 1950 Census. Some noteworthy past residents have been Merle Evans, the circus band conductor of the Ringling Bros. and Barnum & Bailey Circus for half a century, actresses Norma Terris and Doro Merande, author and activist Elizabeth W. Crandall, the 5th Civilian Governor of Guam, Marcellus Boss, and the formerly noted

Robert A. Long, a pioneer of the lumber industry, reforestation, and the founder of the communities of Longville, Louisiana and Longview, Washington. Those looking for more information on town and family history utilize the Columbus Museum as the prominent area resource.

# GALENA, KS
## POPULATION: 2,761 – TOWN 378 OF 627 (7-19-23)

Cornwall, Short Creek, and Bonanza were all early variations of the settlement that would later be called Galena after the lead ore was discovered in the area in 1877. The Missouri, Kansas & Texas Railroad had been extended through this part of Kansas in 1871, the same year that Galena was incorporated as a city. It was the discovery that led to a massive influx in population and growth for the community at large. The plat was filed by the Galena Mining and Smelting Company, who purchased 120 acres of land and sold the lots to hopeful prospectors. It only took two months for the population to top two thousand residents, but because of this rapid growth, much of the town's early infrastructure was saloons filled with rough and rowdy gamblers and drunks. By 1900, the population had risen to an all-time peak of 10,155 people. As things settled, Galena would become home to stamping and smelting works, foundries and machine shops, a broom factory, elevators, and an opera house. The St. Louis & San Francisco Railroad would also be extended to this point, and in 1907, Galena would annex the growing town of Empire City into its limits. Jayhawk Ordnance Works, the largest worldwide producer of ammonium nitrate fertilizer for some time, is located just outside town and is now called the Jayhawk Fine Chemicals Corporation. George Grantham, a 1925 MLB World Series champion baseman, heeds from Galena, as does former California Congressman James C. Corman (a member of the House of Representatives from 1961 to 1981). Route 66 briefly passes through Galena, and the city ensures its presence on the route is well-known to passersby. A Kan-O-Tex Service Station was restored to serve as a diner and souvenir shop for tourists. The station is home to an International Harvester L-170 truck that was the inspiration behind "Mater" of Disney's *Cars* franchise. Lightning McQueen, Sheriff, and several other characters are located throughout the town's main street as part of a project that is referred to as "Cars on the Route." Other notable city attractions are the Bonnie and Clyde Shotgun at Galena Liberty Pawn and the Galena Mining and Historical Museum, which naturally pays tribute to the area's extensive mining history. A few miles west of Galena in unincorporated Riverton stands a beautiful 1923 Marsh Arch bridge over Brush Creek, an original part of Route 66.

# ROSELAND, KS
**POPULATION: 76 – TOWN 375 OF 627 (7-18-23)**
As the name suggests, this town of 76 people in Cherokee County was likely named by early settlers for the wild roses found in the area or after an early settler's hometown. It was incorporated in 1906 and once had a post office. The peak population was 482 people according to the 1920 Census, around the time that the coal mining industry in southeast Kansas was at its best. West of Roseland in the unincorporated town of Carona is the Caron Depot Complex, home to two depots, locomotives, and other railroad memorabilia.

# SCAMMON, KS
**POPULATION: 376 – TOWN 374 OF 627 (7-18-23)**
A couple of early name variations for this town were Stilson and Scammonville until the '-ville' of the latter title was dropped. The name comes from the Scammon brothers, the first men to operate a coal mine in an area that would ultimately become one of the largest shipping points for coal in Kansas (along the St. Louis & San Francisco Railroad) by the 1910s. David Mackie was one of the town's founders circa 1884, and he worked extensively to build up the infrastructure. He was also the first President of the Scammon State Bank. The post office predated the townsite, having been placed in 1879. Like other Cherokee County towns, the population peaked during the heyday of the coal mining industries at 2,233 persons in 1910. Three sporting figures–the 1900 and 1901 World Welterweight Champion boxer Rube Ferns, 1917 World Series champion Fred McMullin (and member of the Black Sox Scandal in which the White Sox allegedly threw the 1919 World Series title away in exchange for money), and tenured MLB umpire George Barr (2,757 major league games in 19 years)–all called Scammon home at some point.

# WEIR, KS
**POPULATION: 569 – TOWN 373 OF 627 (7-18-23)**
Named for T. M. Weir, this Cherokee County town started in 1872 after Mr. Weir donated forty acres to found a city. Its population skyrocketed to 2,977 by the late 1890s as men flooded the area looking to work in the coal mines. It was amongst the first towns in Kansas to commercially mine coal, which helped to bring the St. Louis

& San Francisco Railroad there. At its peak population, its most notable constructions and businesses were an opera house, a public library, and a feed mill. The Weir post office was established in 1875, the same year the legislature approved the request to incorporate. Weir's scoutmaster and school principal in 1905, Frank Rose, was so perturbed by flies and their diseases that he nailed together screen wires and wooden yardsticks to create the first "fly bat," more commonly known today as the flyswatter.

# WEST MINERAL, KS
## POPULATION: 154 – TOWN 376 OF 627 (7-18-23)

This small Kansas coal town is well-known across the state for Big Brutus, the second largest electric coal shovel (Bucyrus Erie Model 1850-B) that was once used in coal strip mining operations by the Pittsburg & Midway Coal Mining Company to dig anywhere from 20 to 69 feet below the earth's surface. It was built in the early 1960s at the cost of 6.5 million dollars; its height was 160 feet, the width was 58 feet, and the length was 79.5 feet. It weighs an impressive 9,300,000 pounds (4,650 tons) and can move at 0.22 miles per hour. It is now the centerpiece of West Mineral's mining museum, which opened its doors in 1985. The town's history is fascinating, as it was first started under the name Cherry and then changed to Mineral in 1895. West Mineral was founded as an extension of the original townsite (and actually as a separate town) and incorporated in 1907. As of the 1910 Census, it was home to 1,770 people involved in the coal mining industry. The Missouri, Kansas & Texas Railway served both communities, but eventually, the town of Mineral became no more. Orval Grove, a pitcher for the Chicago White Sox and a 1944 MLB All-Star, was born here on August 29, 1919.

**Adjacent Counties:** Crawford (N), Labette (W)

**Unincorporated/Ghost Towns:** Carona, Cokedale, Crestline, Daisy Hill, Empire City, Faulkner, Hallowell, Keelville, Kniveton, Lawton, Lowell, Mackie, Melrose, Neutral, Quaker, Riverton, Sherman, Sherwin, Skidmore, Stippville, Treece, Turck

**National Register of Historic Places:**
**Baxter Springs:** Baxter Springs High School, Baxter Springs Independent Oil and Gas Service Station, Brush Creek Bridge, Johnston Library, Kansas Route 66 Historic District-North Baxter Springs, Rial A. Niles House

**Columbus:** Columbus Public Carnegie Library
**Galena:** Kansas Route 66 Historic District-East Galena, Edgar Backus Schermerhorn House
**Riverton:** Williams' Store
**West Mineral:** Big Brutus, Soffietti-Boccia Grocery Store

**Golf Courses:**
Baxter Springs Golf & Country Club, Public (Baxter Springs, KS)
Columbus Country Club, Semi-Private (Columbus, KS)

**Town Celebrations:**
Columbus Day Festival Hot Air Balloon Regatta, Columbus, KS (Saturday before Columbus Day)
Columbus Saddle Club Rodeo, Columbus, KS (Last Weekend in June)
Freedom Fest, Columbus, KS (Saturday after Independence Day)

# CHEYENNE COUNTY
## EST. 1873 - POPULATION: 2,616

Cheyenne County was named for the Cheyenne Native American tribe that once called this part of Kansas home.

# BIRD CITY, KS
### POPULATION: 437 – TOWN 169 OF 627 (4-12-23)
Bird City got its name from cattleman Benjamin Bird, the president of the Northwestern Land Cattle Company. Although Bird himself was not affiliated with the town, many of the earliest pioneers and families in this part of Kansas were heavily involved in raising livestock. The city was founded in 1885, and it served as a shipping point and station on the Chicago, Burlington & Quincy Railroad. One of the barnstorming stops for famous aviator Charles Lindbergh was Bird City, where he stayed at a local boarding house and was said to have entertained the town by landing his plane on the football field.

 **Restaurant Recommendation: Big Ed's**
**104 W Bressler**
**Bird City, KS 67731**

# ST. FRANCIS, KS ★☆

The county seat of Cheyenne County, St. Francis, was platted in 1887 with the arrival of the Chicago, Burlington, and Quincy Railroad to the area. It was started by residents of Wano, Kansas, a small community located two miles southwest who wanted to relocate their townsite to be closer to the railroad. After many of the buildings and citizens were moved, in February of 1889, St. Francis was given the title of county seat, and by April 1903, it was incorporated as a city of the third class. Its etymology is disputed, although it was likely named for the wife of founder A. L. Emerson. The St. Francis Motorcycle Museum is home to 145 vintage motorcycles, one of the finest collections of early bikes in this region of the country, and the Cheyenne County Museum is responsible for telling the story of local history. Ray Stafford, a participant in the 1968 Summer Olympics in trapshooting, and Ronald Evans, one of only 24 astronauts to have flown to the Moon (Apollo 17 mission), were born here.

**Adjacent Counties:** Rawlins (E), Sherman (S)

**Unincorporated/Ghost Towns:** Calhoun, Hourglass, Jaqua, Lawnridge, Marney, Orlando, Wano, Wheeler

**National Register of Historic Places:**
**Bird City:** Henry Hickert Building
**St. Francis:** Cheyenne County Courthouse, St. Francis City Park

**Golf Courses:**
Bird City Golf Course, Public (Bird City, KS)
Riverside Recreation Association, Semi-Private (St. Francis, KS)

**Town Celebrations:**
Horse and Mule Show, Bird City, KS (1st Saturday in October)
Military Show, Bird City, KS (End of April)
Thresher Show, Bird City, KS (Last Weekend of July)

# CLARK COUNTY
## EST. 1885 - POPULATION: 1,991

Captain Charles F. Clarke of the 6th Regiment Kansas Volunteer Calvary was given the honor of having this county named for him for his service in the American Civil War.

# ASHLAND, KS ★☆
## POPULATION: 783 – TOWN 495 OF 627 (9-21-23)

Cement works, drug and jewelry stores, flour mills, confectionaries, and beautiful schools and churches of all the leading Christian denominations were all early establishments of the progressive community known today as Ashland, now the county seat of Clark County. Although not platted until 1884, Ashland was in line with the Fort Dodge and Fort Supply military road that connected western Kansas to Indian Territory. The Bear Creek Redoubt and the Cimarron Redoubt, both fortifications designed from earth and stone that were meant to protect area settlers and military personnel, were constructed near Ashland and this former pathway. "Ashland" was selected as an eponym for the city of Ashland, Kentucky. Big Basin Prairie Preserve is an 1,818-acre nature preserve known for a water-filled sinkhole called Jacob's Well and its herds of buffalo. History buffs of the area assist in the running of the Pioneer-Krier Museum and its early exhibits on toys, kitchen items, a country store, a school, a bank, and more. The poet Ronald Johnson and David "Wes" Santee, a runner noted for his silver medal in the 1500m relay at the 1955 Pan American Games in Mexico City, heed from Ashland.

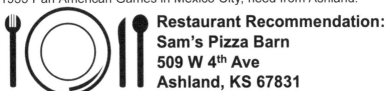 **Restaurant Recommendation:
Sam's Pizza Barn
509 W 4th Ave
Ashland, KS 67831**

# ENGLEWOOD, KS
## POPULATION: 58 – TOWN 494 OF 627 (9-20-23)

In 1884, a town company was formed after an idea was hatched to begin a new townsite in southwestern Clark County. Its members were N. E. Osborn, M. L. Mun, Grant Hatfield, and B. B. Bush, who worked to establish a stage line to Dodge City and attract the attention of the Atchison, Topeka & Santa Fe Railroad. The railroad agreed to extend their line to that point, and thus, the future of Englewood, named for Englewood, Illinois, was secured. The post office came to town in 1885, and eventually, there was a hotel, grain elevators, flour mills, and at least seven attempts at starting a community newspaper before 1911. Its population as of the 2020 Census is only 58 people, but it was once called home by 518 residents in the 1910s.

# MINNEOLA, KS

## POPULATION: 738 – TOWN 493 OF 627 (9-20-23)

"Minneola" is a name derived from the surnames of two wives of some of the community's earliest settlers, Mrs. Minnie Davis and Mrs. Ola Watson. The town's origins can be traced to 1887, and the Chicago, Rock Island & Pacific Railroad is the railway of note that brought life to it. The Appleton post office, then located in what is now a defunct town, moved to Minneola on April 23, 1888, where it has serviced the area ever since. Grain elevators and mills, hardware, general and drug stores, and a hotel were some of the first businesses, as was the Minneola Record newspaper, which has remained Minneola's longest-operating business since its inception in 1906. Eric F. Melgren, the present Chief Judge of the United States District Court for the District of Kansas as of 2023, was born here.

**Adjacent Counties:** Ford (N), Kiowa (NE), Comanche (E), Meade (W)

**Unincorporated/Ghost Towns:** Acres, Cash City, Englewood, Letitia, Lexington, Minneola, Sitka, Vanham

**National Register of Historic Places:**
**Ashland:** Ashland Grade School, Girl Scout Little House, Hodson Hotel, Stein House, Stockgrowers State Bank
**Center Township:** Bear Creek Redoubt, Cimarron Redoubt
**Golf Courses:**
Ashland Country Club, Semi-Private (Ashland, KS)

**Town Celebrations:**
4th of July Celebration, Ashland, KS (Independence Weekend)

# CLAY COUNTY
## EST. 1857 - POPULATION: 8,117

Clay County is one of several counties around the country named after Henry Clay, a three-time presidential candidate and the 9th United States Secretary of State.

# CLAY CENTER, KS ★☆
## POPULATION: 4,199 – TOWN 80 OF 627 (3-15-23)

Clay Center was first settled in May of 1862 by Orville Huntress and John and Alonzo F. Dexter. It was named for its geographical position near the center of the county. When word came around that the town was the choice spot for the county seat circa 1900, Dexter donated the land for a courthouse to be constructed. Clay Center would grow rapidly because of its railroad prominence as a junction for two lines of the Union Pacific Railroad and the Chicago, Rock Island & Pacific Railroad. In June of 1875, it was incorporated as a city of the third class, and by 1880, it had moved up to the second class. In 2020, Clay Center started "A Mural Movement," a collection of over twenty colorful murals hand-painted by artists from all over the country. The murals invite visitors to explore the city and celebrate local heritage, as does the Clay County Museum. Some of Clay Center's most notable individuals are Warren Henry Cole (the pioneer behind using X-rays in medicine), Steve Doocy (television host and anchor of *Fox & Friends* on the Fox News Channel), Nicole Ohlde (WNBA player and champion), Otto D. Unruh (football player and coach credited with inventing the T-Wing offensive football formation), George Docking (the 35th Governor of Kansas), Tracy Claeys (former head coach and defensive coordinator for Minnesota football), Tenney Frank (ancient Rome historian), Herb Bradley (MLB pitcher), and Lady Greyhound (1950s marketing mascot for the Greyhound Lines bus company).

**Restaurant Recommendation:**
**Tasty Pastry Bakery & Coffee**
**511 Court St**
**Clay Center, KS 67432**

# CLIFTON, KS
**POPULATION: 454 – TOWN 12 OF 627 (2-19-23)**
Clifton is situated in both Clay and Washington County along the Republican River. It once served as an essential railroad junction where the lines of the Missouri Pacific, Union Pacific, and Rock Island & Pacific Railroads met. The town was originally platted in 1859, and its name seeks to honor the surveyor. 1870 is the town's official inaugural year of existence. Fort Clifton was a 19th-century fort built in 1862 so settlers could protect themselves from Native Americans. The founder of the publishing house Contact Editions (that published the works of Ernest Hemingway and other notable era authors), Robert McAlmon, was born in Clifton. William P. Henderson, noted particularly for his work in Santa Fe, New Mexico, lived here briefly with his family in the late 1880s. Clifton's primary historical point of interest is the Clifton Community Historical Society Museum.

# GREEN, KS
**POPULATION: 95 – TOWN 78 OF 627 (3-15-23)**
The fourth Governor of Kansas and former Methodist minister Nehemiah Green offered to donate a church bell to the town if he were awarded the town's naming rights. His offer was accepted, so the city was named in his honor. Green would later become a shipping point on the Union Pacific Railroad, and in 1908, it was incorporated. Its first post office served Powellsburgh, now a ghost town, until 1881, when it was moved to the community.

# LONGFORD, KS
**POPULATION: 73 – TOWN 82 OF 627 (3-15-23)**
Once located on a branch line of the Atchison, Topeka, and Santa Fe Railway, Longford had its beginnings in 1870. The town was once called Chapman. Its first post office was established in 1875. The city prides itself on its annual PRCA-sanctioned rodeo that has been running since 1955, and "The Smithalo," a 60-ton monument dedicated to the American buffalo built by Ray Omar Smith, welcomes visitors to the town from atop a hill. Bob Cain, an MLB pitcher from 1949 to 1954, was from Longford and is best known for pitching to Eddie C. Gaedel (the shortest person to ever appear in a major league game at 3 feet, 7 inches tall) on his sole career at bat.

**Restaurant Recommendation:
Coachlight Restaurant
114 Weda St
Longford, KS 67458**

# MORGANVILLE, KS
**POPULATION: 180 – TOWN 79 OF 627 (3-15-23)**

Established in 1870, Morganville was named after its founder, Ebenezer Morgan. It was on the Union Pacific and Chicago, Rock Island & Pacific Railways. Former names for the town included Morgan City and Della (the original name for the post office established in 1871).

# OAK HILL, KS
**POPULATION: 24 – TOWN 81 OF 627 (3-15-23)**

Oak Hill (historically spelled Oakhill for a short time) was awarded its first post office in 1871, and a year later, the town was founded. In 1887 the Atchison, Topeka, and Santa Fe Railroad was constructed through the area.

# WAKEFIELD, KS
**POPULATION: 858 – TOWN 187 OF 627 (4-30-23)**

Established in 1869 by the Kansas Land and Emigration Company, Wakefield was once located on the Union Pacific Railroad. It was named in honor of one of its founders, Reverend Richard Wake. The railroad arrived circa 1873 and brought many businesses, including a flour mill, grain elevators, and other commerce institutions. The town's first postmaster was A. Maitland. Some of Wakefield's most notable points of interest are Milford Lake, the Wakefield Museum, and the Kansas Landscape Arboretum. This 193-acre arboretum sprouted its roots in 1972 and is now home to over one thousand native and exotic plants. The 37th Governor of Kansas, William H. Avery, was born outside of Wakefield in 1911.

Vining is only partially located in Clay County (see Washington County).

**Adjacent Counties:** Washington (N), Riley (E), Geary (SE), Dickinson (S), Ottawa (SW), Cloud (W)

**Unincorporated/Ghost Towns:** Broughton, Browndale, Idana, Industry, Ladysmith

**National Register of Historic Places:**
**Blaine Township:** Mugler Lodge Site
**Clay Center:** Clay Center Carnegie Library, Clay Center Downtown Historic District, Clay County Courthouse
**Republican Township:** Auld Stone Barn

**Breweries/Wineries/Distilleries:**
15-24 Brew House (Clay Center, KS)

**Golf Courses:**
Clay Center Country Club, Private (Clay Center, KS)

**Town Celebrations:**
Piotique Celebration, Clay Center, KS (Last Saturday in September)

# CLOUD COUNTY
## EST. 1866 - POPULATION: 9,032

Union general William F. Cloud, known primarily for leading battles in Kansas and Missouri throughout the American Civil War, is the namesake of Cloud County, Kansas.

# AURORA, KS
## POPULATION: 56 – TOWN 84 OF 627 (3-15-23)

The name of this town is an eponym for Aurora, Illinois, the hometown of many of its pioneer settlers. The post office was briefly called St. Peter from 1886 to 1888 before the name was changed to its present one. It was in the middle of that stint that the Atchison, Topeka, and Santa Fe Railroad was extended through the village.

# CLYDE, KS
## POPULATION: 694 – TOWN 14 OF 627 (2-19-23)

The oldest town in Cloud County, Clyde, was founded in 1867 and named after either the River Clyde in Scotland or Clyde, Ohio. The typical story is that the town was named after the river by B. V. Honey, who had seen the name in a newspaper and liked it so much that he suggested it to the dismay of Charles Davis (whose proposition was to name the town Elkhart). The majority of the townspeople at the meeting agreed to call it Clyde. Clyde experienced its most significant growth in population after 1877 when the Central Branch Railroad was constructed through the vicinity. Reverend Louis Mollier, a Roman Catholic priest, lived in the area and performed services in several towns as they established their parishes. George Dockins, who appeared briefly in the MLB in the 1940s and pitched a shutout on August 8, 1845, was from Clyde. The Clyde Community Museum, located in the old Presbyterian church, is particularly proud of its 1903 Votteler-Hettche pipe organ.

# CONCORDIA, KS ★☆
## POPULATION: 5,111 – TOWN 88 OF 627 (3-27-23)

The history of Concordia is unusual in that the town was declared to be the county seat of Cloud County (defeating the now nonexistent town of Sibley in a 165 to 129 vote) when the only two structures in town were a couple of small ones owned by G. W. Andrews and J. M. Hagaman. Concordia won the vote because Hagaman had constructed a complete town layout and plan that included a courthouse, organized streets and blocks, parks, and more. Early town promoters decided to name it Concordia for their former hometown of Concordia, Missouri, and to pay tribute to the early settlers' German heritage. The town was founded in 1870, platted in 1871, and incorporated in August 1872. In 1887, the Atchison, Topeka, and Santa Fe Railroad rolled into town. Buffalo Bill Cody, Wild Bill Hickok, and the Ringling Brothers frequently stopped in Concordia to entertain the townspeople throughout the late 1800s. Between 1908 and 1910, Carrie Nation of the temperance movement visited the town, intending to shut down its saloons for their sale of alcohol. Cloud County Community College was founded in 1965 and reported an enrollment of about 3,500 undergraduates throughout the mid-2000s. There are multiple points of interest throughout the community such as the national Orphan Train complex (dedicated to preserving the stories and artifacts of the 1854 to 1929 Orphan Train Movement), the Cloud County Historical Museum, Camp Concordia (a prisoner of war camp during World War II), the Nazareth Convent and Academy (the Motherhouse for the Sisters of St. Joseph of Concordia), and the Brown Grand Theatre, a historic performing arts and community center that was built in 1905. One oddity is the "World's Longest Sculpted Brick Mural," a 6,400-piece installation depicting a train that measures 15 feet high and 140 feet long. It also dubs itself as "The Stained Glass Capital of Kansas" for the large number of stained-glass pieces found in the town's private homes and churches. Garth Brooks's song "Friends in Low Places," which spent four weeks at number one on the Hot Country Songs list in 1990, calls out a former bar in Concordia called "The Oasis." Dozens of noted individuals have ties to Concordia, a handful of which are Frank Carlson (the 30th Governor of Kansas), Boston Corbett (the man who shot and killed John Wilkes Booth, who later went mad and lived in a hole in the ground not far from town), Pop Hollinger (a pioneer in comic book collecting), Robert E. Pearson (movie director), Kay Vaughan (1956 and 1957 CFL Outstanding Lineman award winner), Helen Talbot (actress and pin-up girl), Jim Garver (guitarist for Garth Brooks), Ernest C. Quigley (basketball referee and member of the National Basketball Hall of Fame), Marilyn Schreffler (voice actor in Hanna-Barbera Productions like *Scooby-Doo*, *The Yogi Bear Show*, and multiple other shows), Shanele Stires (WNBA player and women's basketball coach), former NFL players Larry Hartshorn, Keith Christensen, and Billy Dewell, MLB player Greg Brummett, and Charles J. Chaput (ninth Catholic Archbishop of Philadelphia, Pennsylvania from 2011 to 2020 and former Bishop of Denver, Colorado and Rapid City, South Dakota).

 **Restaurant Recommendation:
Easy G Sports Grill
107 W 6th St
Concordia, KS 66901**

# GLASCO, KS
**POPULATION: 441 – TOWN 86 OF 627 (3-15-23)**
Dell Ray was the original name for this town until the Kansas legislature changed it in 1878. The city was founded in 1870 by H. H. and A. H. Spaulding, J. M. Copeland, and Captains H. C. Snyder and J. A. Potts. The Solomon Branch Railway adopted the name Glasco (after Glasgow, Scotland) following the naming reassignment, and later, the Union Pacific Railroad would arrive in 1878. In 1886, the town was incorporated as a city of the third class. Glasco had such a prominent football team in the late 1890s that they were invited to compete against Kansas University in October 1897, although they would lose the game 23-0. The Glasco club would go on to beat or tie other university schools like Ottawa University and Washburn University in the years to follow. In 1902, they were considered the best team in the state. Elmer Stricklett, an early pioneer of the spitball (now an illegal baseball pitch), is from Glasco.

# JAMESTOWN, KS
## POPULATION: 237 – TOWN 89 OF 627 (3-27-23)

The small agricultural community of Jamestown, Kansas, was founded in 1878 by C. I. Gould and later incorporated in 1883. The town was located on a couple of branches of the Missouri Pacific Railroad and named for either Senator James Pomeroy or James P. Pomeroy of the railroad. In 1912, the community was reported as having as many as fifty businesses, although major fires in 1911 and 2000 led to the town being rebuilt twice. Born outside of town in June of 1916 was Martha Peterson, the former president of Barnard College (1967-1975) and Beloit College (1975-1981).

# MILTONVALE, KS
## POPULATION: 440 – TOWN 83 OF 627 (3-15-23)

Milton Tootle of St. Joseph, Missouri, was the original townsite owner and founder of the town. Proposed names for the newly founded village (December 1, 1881) included Tootletown and Tootleville, but the townspeople thought that Miltonvale sounded the best. The Kansas Central narrow-gauge railroad once ran through town until it was annexed by the Union Pacific Railroad, and later, the Atchison, Topeka, and Santa Fe Railway would be built through the vicinity. One of the best baseball teams in Central Kansas once called Miltonvale home; they were known as the "Miltonvale Light Weights" and later the "Miltonvale Heavy Weights" as they continued to defeat team after team. Miltonvale Wesleyan College was the area's institution of higher learning from 1909 to 1972 until it merged with Bartlesville Wesleyan College (now a part of Oklahoma Wesleyan University). Three very notable persons heed from Miltonvale: Nellie Tayloe Ross, the 14th Governor of Wyoming and the first woman governor in United States history, Patrice Wymore of vaudeville performing fame (and the third wife of Errol Flynn), and Jim Garlow, the author of *Cracking DaVinci's Code* and an evangelical pastor.

Simpson is only partially located in Cloud County (see Mitchell County).

**Adjacent Counties:** Republic (N), Washington (NE), Clay (E), Ottawa (S), Mitchell (W), Jewell (NW)

**Unincorporated/Ghost Towns:** Ames, Hollis, Huscher, Macyville, Minersville, Rice, Sibley, St. Joseph, Yuma

**National Register of Historic Places:**
**Clyde:** Clyde School, Charles W. Van De Mark House
**Concordia:** Bankers Loan and Trust Company Building, Brown Grand Opera House, Nazareth Convent and Academy, Republican River Pegram Truss, Union Pacific Railroad Depot
**Glasco:** Glasco Downtown Historic District, Pott's Ford Bridge
**Hollis:** County Line Bowstring

**Golf Courses:**
Concordia Country Club, Private (Concordia, KS)

**Town Celebrations:**
Clyde Watermelon Festival, Clyde, KS (1st Weekend of September)
Fall Fest, Concordia, KS (September)
National Orphan Train Complex Annual Celebration, Concordia, KS (1st Weekend of June)
Tootlefest, Miltonvale, KS (4th Weekend of August)

Cherokee County Photos: Baxter Springs, Galena, Galena, Galena, Galena, Riverton, Weir, West Mineral

Cheyenne County Photos: Bird City, Bird City, Bird City, St. Francis, St. Francis, St. Francis, St. Francis, St. Francis

Clark County Photos: Ashland, Ashland, Ashland, Ashland, Englewood, Englewood, Englewood, Minneola

Clay County Photos: Clay Center, Clay Center, Clay Center, Clay Center, Clay Center, Green, Morganville, Wakefield

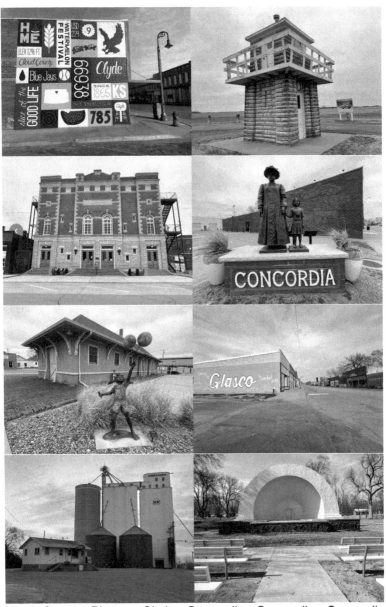

Cloud County Photos: Clyde, Concordia, Concordia, Concordia, Concordia, Glasco, Jamestown, Miltonvale

# COFFEY COUNTY
## EST. 1855 - POPULATION: 8,360

Coffey County was one of the counties named after a former territorial legislator, in this case, A. M. Coffey.

# BURLINGTON, KS ★☆
## POPULATION: 2,634 – TOWN 306 OF 627 (6-28-23)

The county seat of Coffey County, Burlington, was founded in 1857 and named after Burlington, Vermont, the former residence of O. E. Learnard. Learnard was the town's promoter and member of the Burlington Town Company alongside Charles Morse, C. W. Southway, T. T. Parsons, and J. A. D. Clark. There was one nearby smaller town by the name of Hampden, from which the first Burlington post office, store, and wagon shop took residence in its relocated buildings. As the city grew and the Atchison, Topeka & Santa, and the Missouri, Kansas & Texas Railroads laid down their lines and met there at a junction, it would eventually take the judicial seat from Le Roy. Numerous industries unfolded throughout Burlington as entrepreneurs founded a carding and woolen mill, three cigar factories, a creamery, a tile factory, a carriage and wagon factory, and other lines of enterprise. It was incorporated in 1870 once several of the town's men returned home from the American Civil War. The population grew considerably between the 1970 Census (2,099 residents) and the 1980 Census (2,901 residents) as hundreds of workers moved to Burlington to work at Wolf Creek Generating Station, a nuclear power plant. The town's two most famous residents were Tyrel Reed, the winningest player in the history of the University of Kansas men's basketball team with a record of 132-17, and Christian Braun, a member of the Denver Nuggets and recent 2023 NBA champion. A sizable collection of antique dolls is one of the many highlights of the Coffey County Historical Society Museum in Burlington. Since 1880, the Coffey County Fair has operated without a hitch, making it the longest consecutively held fair in Kansas.

# GRIDLEY, KS
## POPULATION: 313 – TOWN 315 OF 627 (6-28-23)

Gridley, named for its early promoter Walter Gridley, was once located at the junction of the Atchison, Topeka & Santa Fe, and the Missouri Pacific Railroads. Established in 1886, it played a small role in the area's trade throughout its early days with its bank and post office (founded in June 1886). Its maximum historical population was 434 individuals circa the 1930s.

# LEBO, KS
**POPULATION: 885 – TOWN 309 OF 627 (6-28-23)**
Located as an early community on Atchison, Topeka & Santa Fe Railroad in 1883, Lebo's name was taken from Captain Joe Lebo (a Civil War merchant), whose name was also given to the nearby Lebo Creek. The postal service was established there in June of the same year. By 1910, it had been incorporated for 24 years, and it had considerable businesses, including two banks and all the other typical infrastructure. The population grew to a peak of 966 residents in the years leading up to the 1980 Census.

# LE ROY, KS
**POPULATION: 451 – TOWN 316 OF 627 (6-28-23)**
Once the county seat of Coffey County, Le Roy once served as the junction point for the Missouri Pacific and the Missouri, Kansas & Texas Railroads. It was founded by General John B. Scott in 1855 and named after Le Roy, Illinois. He was the town's first judge and postmaster when the office arrived in the subsequent year. LeRoy's post was formed on September 12, 1861, and operated until May of 1864 to protect the town from potential attacks by the Confederacy. Early lines of business included a vitrified brick plant, a wagon factory, and a flour mill.

# NEW STRAWN, KS
**POPULATION: 414 – TOWN 305 OF 627 (6-28-23)**
Old Strawn was located on the Missouri, Kansas & Texas Railroad in 1871 and was once the site of many businesses and places of worship and learning. After the Great Flood of 1951 and several decades of floods in the Neosho River valley, the U.S. Army Corps of Engineers claimed the townsite and required that it be moved 6 miles eastward on higher ground so that the John Redmond Reservoir could be built. When water levels are low, Old Strawn's Main Street can be thoroughly explored by visitors. New Strawn was incorporated in 1970 and had 414 citizens living there as of the 2020 Census.

# WAVERLY, KS
## POPULATION: 574 – TOWN 307 OF 627 (6-28-23)

Waverly is one of several communities nationwide named in honor of the main character in Sir Walter Scott's 1814 novel, "Waverley." An early settler suggested the name after his hometown of Waverly, Indiana. The post office, placed on June 10, 1878, predates the platting of the townsite by Isaac Pierson and the formation of the town company in 1880. A. N. Sylvester and Thomas Donnell were the first men to open mercantile stores, and later, both the Missouri Pacific and the Atchison, Topeka & Santa Fe Railroads would lay tracks through Waverly. The town's lowest population came in 1960 when it shrunk to 381 residents, and its highest was 751 people as of the 1910 Census. The most famous former resident of Waverly is Olive Ann Beech, "The First Lady of Aviation" and the co-founder of the Beech Aircraft Corporation.

**Adjacent Counties:** Osage (N), Franklin (NE), Anderson (E), Allen (SE), Woodson (S), Greenwood (SW), Lyon (NW)

**Unincorporated/Ghost Towns:** Agricola, Aliceville, Halls Summit, Jacobs Creek Landing, Ottumwa, Sharpe

**National Register of Historic Places:**
**Burlington:** Burlington Carnegie Free Library, Plaza Theater, U.S. Post Office-Burlington
**Hartford:** Neosho River Bridge
**Lebo:** Cleo F. Miller House

**Golf Courses:**
Indian Plains Golf Course, Semi-Private (New Strawn, KS)
Rock Creek Country Club, Private (Burlington, KS)

**Town Celebrations:**
Christmas Craft Fair, Burlington, KS (Saturday before Thanksgiving)
Independence Day Celebration, Burlington, KS (4th of July)
Independence Day Celebration, Gridley, KS (Weekend closest to 4th of July)
LeRoy Homecoming, LeRoy, KS (Last Weekend in August)
Strawnfest, New Strawn, KS (Last Saturday in June)
Waverly Ohio Days, Waverly, KS (2nd Weekend of July)

102

# COMANCHE COUNTY
## EST. 1867 - POPULATION: 1,689

Comanche County is one of a handful of jurisdictions in Kansas that was named for a Native American tribe, the Comanche, who once lived throughout the region.

# COLDWATER, KS ★☆
## POPULATION: 687 – TOWN 497 OF 627 (9-21-23)

The county seat of Comanche County began as a station on the Wichita & Englewood line of the Atchison, Topeka & Santa Fe Railroad. For a short period, the site had been referred to as Smallwood, but when G. W. Vickers, Timothy Shields, C. D. Bickford, C. M. Cade, J. P. Grove, and Samuel Sisson decided to formulate a townsite here in 1884, they opted to name it Coldwater after Coldwater, Michigan. The men successfully brought a post office to town in October of that same year, and by February 1885, they had organized Coldwater into an incorporated city. The railroad arrived in 1887 and brought more traffic and residents to Coldwater. But when the lands that once belonged to the Cheyenne were opened up for settlement in northern Oklahoma in 1889, most of those inhabitants headed southward to make their claims. The population rebounded in the coming decades to a pinnacle of 1,296 people in the 1930s, but over the last century, many residents have moved away, and the population now sits at 687. Harold S. Herd, the minority leader of the Kansas Senate from 1969 to 1973, was born in Comanche County in 1918, as was Chick Brandom, who had a brief career as an MLB pitcher in the early decades of the 20th century. The history of the Comanche Cattle Pool, the largest cattle pool in Kansas (84,000+ cattle) up until its dissolution in 1885, is the highlighted exhibit of the Comanche County Historical Museum.

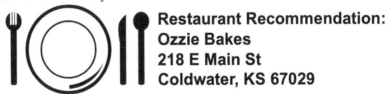 **Restaurant Recommendation:
Ozzie Bakes
218 E Main St
Coldwater, KS 67029**

# PROTECTION, KS
Protection was established in 1884, the same year there was widespread support for a protective tariff in the 1884 presidential election. Protective tariffs are intended to cause the sales of domestically produced goods to rise and support local industry, which is why the name "Protection" was chosen for the town. August 27, 1884, was the first date the post office went into operation. Protection's earliest industries ranged from mills and grain elevators to a newspaper, a bank, and other typical small-town businesses. The National Polio Foundation selected Protection as its center for distributing free Salk vaccine shots in 1957, making it the first city in the United States to be 100% protected against the terrible disease. Later, Protection would also become the first U.S. City to claim that it was fully protected against the proposed disk failures and dilemmas of Y2K. The farming community's highest historical population was 1,109 residents, according to the 1920 Census. Olympic athlete and high jumper Nathan Leeper, and Stan Herd, an artist connected to the Prairie Renaissance Movement, heed from the Comanche County community.

# WILMORE, KS
This small Atchison, Topeka & Santa Fe Railroad town had its start in 1887. It was named for the first town merchant, Thomas Wilmore, who kicked off some of the first recorded trade in the community. Amongst the proudest businesses were a mill, a grain elevator, and a volcanic ash mine. A post office was introduced to Wilmore on June 7, 1887, and the Kansas legislature approved its application to become incorporated in 1920. Visitors to Wilmore can't miss the bright red-and-yellow carousel in the backyard of a local couple, who will allow anybody who "honks" to ride it if they are home.

**Adjacent Counties:** Kiowa (N), Barber (E), Clark (W)

**Unincorporated/Ghost Towns:** Buttermilk, Smallwood

**National Register of Historic Places:**
**Coldwater:** Chief Theater, Comanche County Courthouse
**Protection:** Protection High School

# COWLEY COUNTY
## EST. 1867 - POPULATION: 34,549

Cowley County, established in 1867 off a section of Butler County, was named for Matthew R. Cowley of the Union Army.

# ARKANSAS CITY, KS
## POPULATION: 11,974 – TOWN 563 OF 627 (10-6-23)

Before the founding of Arkansas City circa 1870, there was once a great city called Etzanoa. It had a population of over 20,000 members of the Wichita tribe, and from 1450 to 1700, it was one of the greatest Native American settlements of the Great Plains. Because of its location between the Arkansas and Walnut Rivers, early variants of the newly proposed town included Adelphia, Walnut City, and Cresswell before settlers finally adopted the name Arkansas City, given initially to the post office on May 16, 1870. G. H. Norton was the first postmaster and one of the first business owners in town. In 1872 came incorporation, and by the end of the decade, the Atchison, Topeka & Santa Fe Railroad was extended to this point. The St. Louis & San Francisco, the Missouri Pacific, the Kansas Southwestern, and the Midland Valley Railroad would follow suit, and Arkansas City would establish itself as one of the premier cities of Kansas. The existence of so many railroads spurred manufacturing interests, and soon, there were factories established to make brooms, paint, overalls, cement, ice, alfalfa meal, and a range of other products. Creameries, mills, a meat packing plant, The Kirkwood Wind Engine Company (a windmill manufacturer), and Kanotex Refining Company (then a popular oil refining business) were amongst the other businesses, and by 1912, there was an impressive opera house, a fire department, churches and schools and the area-famous Paris Lake swimming area. From 1880 to 1890, the population rose by 724.8% to 8,347 people because of the Cherokee Strip Land Run that was set to take place in Oklahoma in the 1890s. A quarter of the population was lost following the land run, but the city bounced back after many of the industries mentioned above came into existence at the turn of the century. Cowley College was established in September 1922 as the Arkansas City Junior College and helps to serve the higher education needs of southern Kansas to this day. The Cherokee Land Run Museum covers the famous 1893 event and contains several exhibits on Arkansas City history. Jim Sheets (once an executive director of Kiwanis International), Billy Mize (a country music singer), Dick Metz (former PGA Tour golfer), Robert Docking

105

(the 38th Governor of Kansas), Les Miller (former NFL defensive end), Darren Daulton (3x MLB All-Star catcher), Jim Sherwood (Mothers of Invention band member), Robert J. Eaton (former CEO of Chrysler Corporation), Nila Mack (the creator of the 1934 to 1954 CBS radio series *Let's Pretend*), Lionel Hollins (member of the 1978 NBA All-Star team), Michael Bradford (former director of the Connecticut Repertory Theatre), Richard E. Killblane (the author of several military novels), and Helen Parsons (biochemist known for her discoveries on biotin, avidin, thiamine, and vitamin B) are amongst Arkansas City's most beloved past residents.

**Restaurant Recommendation:
Burger Junkie
611 W Madison Ave
Arkansas City, KS 67005**

# ATLANTA, KS
## POPULATION: 168 – TOWN 557 OF 627 (10-6-23)
Glenn Cunningham, largely considered one of the greatest middle-distance runners in the history of the United States because of the multiple records he broke in the 1930s, was born in the sleepy town of Atlanta, Kansas, on August 4, 1909. Atlanta was a St. Louis & San Francisco Railroad town, having once been home to several businesses before experiencing several drops in population. It was founded in 1885, the same year the postal service established an office there, and incorporated in 1903. The Atlanta Cafe has long served as the town's hub for history, conversation, and good eats.

# BURDEN, KS
## POPULATION: 512 – TOWN 558 OF 627 (10-6-23)
Robert F. Burden, the namesake of Burden and an original member of the town company was one of the primary men responsible for bringing this town on the Kansas City, Lawrence, and Southern Railroad into existence. The town was laid out in 1879, the same year the post office came to town with the name "Burdenville." The suffix was dropped on May 19, 1884, leaving behind the present nomenclature. Baptist, Christian, and Methodist churches provided religious services to community members early on, and inhabitants had many businesses and resources to help grow the town. Since 1900, the fewest number of people to call Burden home in any

Census year was in 1910 (424), and the highest in 1960 (580 people).

**Restaurant Recommendation:**
**Ma's Cafe**
**421 W 5th St**
**Burden, KS 67019**

# CAMBRIDGE, KS
### POPULATION: 92 – TOWN 559 OF 627 (10-6-23)
One of Kansas's many small agricultural-based communities, Cambridge, was platted in May 1880 by Benjamin H. Clover after the construction of the Kansas City, Lawrence & Southern Railroad (later incorporated into the A, T & SF Railroad) through Cowley County. The name Cambridge is a nod to England's prestigious Cambridge University. The post office predates the town, established on January 30, 1880. Other institutions of the early days included a hotel, churches, a bank, and mercantile of all varieties. Cambridge has an interesting tie to Cold War history, as it was selected as one of only two communities (the other being Ault, Colorado) in the 1970s to be the site of a distribution control station that would start the warning broadcast system in the case of a nuclear attack of the United States.

# DEXTER, KS
### POPULATION: 224 – TOWN 560 OF 627 (10-6-23)
A trotting horse from New York that was the property of Robert Bonner is to thank for the name of this Cowley County community. The first permanent European activity in the area came about on July 14, 1870, when a post office was founded to serve the needs of the settlers. That same year, citizens from Emporia decided to start the Dexter Town Company with the hopes of locating a new townsite, but they only laid out their town in October of 1875. The Missouri Pacific Railroad brought the means to build and keep a flour mill, banks, stores, a hotel, and a newspaper in operation through at least the 1910s. Researchers from the University of Kansas, in conjunction with the United States government, discovered the presence of gas in one of Dexter's wells that was nonflammable. The "Dexter Gas" prompted the discovery that helium could be produced from the extensive gas fields found throughout Kansas, Oklahoma, and other neighboring states. Travelers to Dexter are interested in visiting the Cowley Lake Waterfall, Cowley State Fishing Lake, and the Henry's Candies factory that sells a sweet similar to the "Oh Henry!" caramel,

fudge, and peanut bar invented in 1920. In downtown Dexter, the Lighthouse Library has a 25-foot-tall functional lighthouse and an impressive saltwater aquarium.

# PARKERFIELD, KS
**POPULATION: 406 – TOWN 562 OF 627 (10-6-23)**
Seeking to avoid annexation by the much larger Arkansas City, residents of this 0.91 square mile area of Cowley County sought refuge by petitioning the county government for incorporation status in 2004. Their reasoning for resisting annexation was that they were against the tax laws and city codes of Arkansas City. The County Commissioners reviewed their case and granted incorporation status to the "City of Parkerfield" on March 16, 2004, and two weeks later, they had elected local government officials. Its population as of the 2020 Census was 406 people, down 4.7% from the 2010 Census.

# UDALL, KS
**POPULATION: 661 – TOWN 579 OF 627 (10-9-23)**
Town founders J. M. Napier and P. W. Smith established Udall in 1881, two years after they had purchased the land for the townsite and the postal service had placed an office in the vicinity. They chose Udall to commemorate the noted English writer Cornelius Udall. D. C. Green was the first to construct his home and build a store, and soon others followed with their drug stores, farm and implement businesses, mills, and other enterprises. The Atchison, Topeka & Santa Fe Railroad was the principal mode of commerce and transportation from one town to the next. Hardships have long plagued the community, as in January 1883, resident Charles Cobb shot and killed the Cowley County Sheriff Shenneman. On May 25, 1955, the deadliest tornado to ever strike Kansas blew apart every single structure in Udall, from the high school to the water tower and three churches. It killed 77 residents. Its residents stayed strong, and the population increased in subsequent years from 410 people in 1950 to as many as 891 persons in 1980.

# WINFIELD, KS ★☆
**POPULATION: 11,777 – TOWN 566 OF 627 (10-6-23)**
One of the most prosperous cities of southern Kansas, Winfield, was founded in 1870 and named for Reverend Winfield Scott, who promised the town company that he would build a church if they named their new community in his honor. Colonel Edwin C. Manning

served as the president of the town company and as the postmaster when the postal service located a branch here on May 5, 1870. He was the main driver in making his town the county seat of Cowley County as opposed to the nearby Arkansas City, which has a similar yet slightly larger population today. Haste was made to ensure that Winfield had all the necessary infrastructure to make it a formidable town. Structures from homes and hotels to banks, stores, and schools were built, and Winfield earned incorporation status as a city of the third class by 1872. Lines of St. Louis & San Francisco, the Missouri Pacific, and the Atchison, Topeka & Santa Fe Railroads all passed through town, and an interurban rail system was put in place to connect Winfield to their neighbors in the south in Arkansas City. Winfield's proudest early industries were marble works, an ice and cold storage plant, a carriage and wagon factory, stone quarries, and a foundry and machine shop. The "State Asylum for Idiotic and Imbecile Youth," sometimes referred to as a "state mental hospital for feeble-minded juveniles," served as one of three state mental hospitals from 1887 to its closure by the 2000s. St. John's College sent over nine thousand students through its programs between 1893 and 1986; John Peter Baden had initially funded it. Southwestern College, founded in 1885 as a private Methodist school, is now the lone college-level place of learning in Winfield. It was the founding site of the "oldest interdisciplinary social science honor society," Pi Gamma Mu. Despite the thought that Winfield and Arkansas City should be competitors in all regards, they share Strother Field, once a World War II army air base used to train cadets in flying Vultee BT-13 Valiant airplanes. GE Aerospace (then General Electric Aviation) remains a major Winfield employer in the 2020s. The Cessna Aircraft Company and the old Crayola plant (what used to be the only one to make paint) were other significant employers until their closures by the end of the twentieth century. From a cultural perspective, Winfield is well-known throughout this region of the United States because of the Walnut Valley Festival, one of the oldest and largest bluegrass and acoustic music festivals every September. It was briefly mentioned in an episode of the teen sitcom *iCarly* and the CBS sitcom *Gilligan's Island*. Guy McAfee, responsible for creating many of Las Vegas's casinos and the Las Vegas Strip, Bob Kenney, a 1952 Olympic gold medalist in basketball, Dean C. Strother, a four-star general of the United States Air Force, Darren E. Burrows, an actor known for his role in the CBA comedy-drama *Northern Exposure*, Robert A. Alberty, the author of several physical chemistry textbooks, Steve Sidwell, a 38-year-long tenured football coach, Eugene Pallette, a silent film era actor for 33 years, Bob Brannum, a former NBA center, Broadway actor Ruth Maycliffe, and artists Gilbert

Bundy, Richard Mawdsley, Karen Wheeler, and Caroline Thorington highlight the town's noted residents. The Cowley County Historical Society Museum chronicles the stories, people, and events that made Winfield into the prominent settlement it is today.

Geuda Springs is only partially in Cowley County (see Sumner County).

**Adjacent Counties:** Butler (N), Elk (NE), Chautauqua (E), Sumner (W), Sedgwick (NW)

**Unincorporated/Ghost Towns:** Akron, Etzanoa, Floral, Grand Summit, Hackney, Hooser, Kellogg, Maple City, New Salem, Rock, Silverdale, Tisdale, Vinton, Wilmot

## National Register of Historic Places:
**Arkansas City:** Arkansas City Commercial Historic District, Old Arkansas City High School, Pilgrim Congregational Church, Spring Creek Stone Arch Bridge
**Burden:** Weigle Barn
**Creswell Township:** Arkansas City Country Club Site
**Dexter:** Esch's Spur Bridge
**Rock:** Bucher Bridge
**Winfield:** Bryant School, W. H. Coffin House, Cowley County National Bank Building, East Badger Creek Culvert, Grace Methodist Episcopal Church, W. P. Hackney House, Magnolia Ranch, Pettit Cleaners Building, St. John's Lutheran College-Baden Hall, St. John's Lutheran College Girls Dormitory, St. John's Lutheran College West Dormitory, Silver Creek Bridge, Strother Field Tetrahedron Wind Indicator, Wilmer House, Winfield Fox Theatre, Winfield National Bank Building, Winfield Public Carnegie Library

## Breweries/Wineries/Distilleries:
Ladybird Brewing (Winfield, KS)

## Golf Courses:
Arkansas City Country Club, Private (Arkansas City, KS)
Quail Ridge Golf Course, Public (Winfield, KS)
Spring Hill Municipal Golf Course, Public (Arkansas City, KS)
Winfield Country Club, Private (Winfield, KS)

## Town Celebrations:
Arkalalah Festival, Arkansas City, KS (Last Weekend of October)

K & O Tractor Show, Winfield, KS (3rd Weekend in August)
Last Run Car Show, Arkansas City, KS (Last Weekend of September)
Walnut Valley Festival, Winfield, KS (3rd Weekend of September)

# CRAWFORD COUNTY
## EST. 1867 - POPULATION: 38,972

Crawford County's name was derived from the surname of the third Governor of Kansas, Samuel J. Crawford.

# ARCADIA, KS
## POPULATION: 254 – TOWN 334 OF 627 (6-29-23)
In 1862, Arcadia was founded under its present name (after Arcadia of ancient Greece) and then temporarily changed to Findlay City for George W. Findlay. The post office had been established in January 1866 under the name Coxe's Creek until it was moved to serve the Arcadia townsite in April 1867. It is unknown why the name suddenly changed from Arcadia to Findlay City and back to Arcadia. The early townspeople built a hotel, a brick and tile plant, planning and grist mills, and an extensive array of different denominations of churches to serve their needs following the construction of the St. Louis & San Francisco Railway in the area. Like many other area towns, Arcadia's population spiked from 694 residents to 1,175 from the 1910s to the 1920s before dropping again.

# ARMA, KS
## POPULATION: 1,407 – TOWN 332 OF 627 (6-29-23)
Arma's post office came before the platting of the townsite, as it was founded on May 13, 1891. It was in 1894 that Arma was formally established and named in honor of W. F. Armacost. The Missouri Pacific Railway brought enterprise to the community, the most notable of which were an early flour mill and lumber yard. Its highest single decade of population growth came between 1910 and 1920 when it grew 566.7% from 327 citizens to 2,180. The annual Arma V-J Homecoming celebration is the oldest continuously running World War II celebration in the United States; it began in 1946, only a year after the conclusion of World War II. Miners Hall Museum in the nearby unincorporated town of Franklin was built on the site of Union Hall, where the Army Amazon marches first started in 1921.

111

# CHEROKEE, KS

Cherokee was located at the junction of the Missouri Pacific, the Kansas City, Fort Scott & Gulf, and the Memphis, Kansas & Colorado Railroads. The intersecting of the lines led to the formal founding of a town in 1870 when William Sharp built the first store, and the Kansas City, Fort Scott & Gulf Railroad began to sell lots to settlers. The town was named Cherokee because it was thought to be located within the boundaries of Cherokee County, but it is located in south Crawford County on the county line. The local post office arrived in the year the town was founded, and with time, there were coal mines, a broom factory and an ice plant, hotels, schools, banks, and the other typical lines of enterprise found in Kansas at that time. Cherokee was incorporated as a city in 1874. Three noted figures have called Cherokee home at one time or another, them being Patricia Miles Martin, a 1972 Newbery Honor recipient for her children's book *Annie and the Old One*, Medal of Honor recipient Samuel Triplett, and Page Cavanaugh, a noted pianist and musician.

# FRONTENAC, KS

Frontenac grew alongside its neighbor in Pittsburg and took equal advantage of the railroad and the coal-mining industries of that area. The Atchison, Topeka & Santa Fe, and the Kansas City Southern Railroads serviced it. Named after the French explorer Louis de Buade de Frontenac, the founding date was set in 1886, when it began as a coal mining town. A disaster struck only a couple of years later, on November 9, 1888, when the worst mining accident in state history occurred when an explosion of coal dust took the lives of 44 mine workers. A post office was established in 1887 and succeeded by the construction of all the other typical lines of enterprise. The annual Festa Italiana, A Taste of Nations event, invites residents and locals to taste family recipes from any one of the city's rich Italian, Slavic, Sicilian, or Austro-Hungarian lines of heritage. Chicken Mary's (est. 1941) and Chicken Annie's (est. 1934), two local fried chicken competitors across the street from one another, rose to national fame when Pittsburg journalist and the former NBC Nightly News anchor (amongst other titles) from 1993 to 2021 Brian Williams covered the story for the Travel Channel. Author Clare Vanderpool wrote a book in 2010 called *Moon Over Manifest*, which was based on Frontenac and won the Newbery Medal and the Spur Award. Biophysics scientist Douglas Youvan, American football coach Andy Pilney, and

1936 Summer Olympic Archie San Romani, who placed 4th in the 1500 meters, are affiliated with the city. Noted Chicago mobster Joey Aiuppa earned his nickname "Joey Doves" after FBI agents searched his vehicle outside Frontenac and Girard and found that he was carrying 563 frozen doves (well over the 24-doves-a-person limit).

# GIRARD, KS ★☆
## POPULATION: 2,496 – TOWN 331 OF 627 (6-29-23)
C. H. Strong, the first town resident, postmaster, and secretary of the town company, decided to name this community after his hometown of Girard, Pennsylvania. It was platted in 1868 along the future site of the Kansas City, Fort Scott, and Gulf Railroad to make it a rival of nearby Crawfordsville. Development of the town continued throughout 1868 as the first stores, post office, and courthouse building were raised by the conclusion of the year. The Atchison, Topeka & Santa Fe Railroad was built through town at a later date, and in March of 1871, Girard became incorporated as a city of the third class (it is now a second-class city). Many industries overtook Girard around the turn of the century, including factories for canning, fences, stoves, coffee, blacksmith, milk, and vinegar, as well as flour mills, an ice plant, and coal mines. Percy Daniels, Eugene V. Debs, and Emanuel Julius were three early town figures who worked to spread socialist ideas through their writings, most notably Julius's "Little Blue Books" of the Haldeman-Julius Company. The Museum of Crawford County in the late 1880s Episcopal Church holds some of the earliest artifacts of the surrounding area. Crawford State Park, located at the far edge of the Ozarks, is renowned for its fishing, boating, and scuba diving opportunities. Jane Grant (the co-founder of *The New Yorker* newspaper), 2x NFL champion and 1962 Pro Bowl football star Ron Kramer, jazz pianist Edythe Baker, gardening book author Ruth Stout, Dennis Hayden, the actor who played Eddie in the 1988 movie *Die Hard*, and former college football NAIA Division I Coach of the Year Dennis Franchione all have connections to Girard.

# HEPLER, KS
## POPULATION: 90 – TOWN 330 OF 627 (6-29-23)
Hepler, now home to only 90 residents, was founded in January of 1871 by B. F. Hepler and T. H. Annable. Hepler's surname was given to the town because he was the president of the town company when it was established. In June 1871, the post office arrived, and after the Missouri, Kansas, and Texas Railroad laid down its tracks through

Hepler, the schools, hotels, businesses, and churches were formed to serve the needs of the townspeople.

# MCCUNE, KS
**POPULATION: 370 – TOWN 369 OF 627 (7-18-23)**
Isaac McCune was an early settler and founder of the town of McCune. He was designated the first postmaster when the postal service elected to start an office there on August 12, 1878. The area office had originally been established at a site known as "Time" in January 1875. McCune platted his town in 1879 and built a store of which J. D. Rodgers would be the owner. He remained in a position of authority for several years and became the first mayor when McCune was incorporated in 1881. Its railroad of note was the St. Louis & San Francisco Railroad, on which the largest grain elevator along the line was constructed and still stands to this day in 2023.

 **Restaurant Recommendation:**
**McCune Farm to Market**
**604 Hickory St**
**McCune, KS 66753**

# MULBERRY, KS
**POPULATION: 409 – TOWN 333 OF 627 (6-29-23)**
First called Mulberry Grove after a nearby grove of mulberry trees, this small Crawford community was founded to provide housing and materials for early coal mine workers circa 1875. The post office and town followed that name until May 21, 1892, when the suffix was dropped. Workers from all around piled into the newly founded community, and the Kansas City Southern and St. Louis & San Francisco Railroad helped launch the town towards incorporation status (in 1902) by transporting coal from Mulberry to neighboring areas. Its population dwindled almost as quickly as it had swelled, going from 997 residents in 1910 to 2,697 in 1920 and down to 779 people by 1950.

# PITTSBURG, KS
**POPULATION: 20,646 – TOWN 371 OF 627 (7-18-23)**
Pittsburg has established itself as the hub of economic activity and population for southeastern Kansas. As of the 2020 Census, it has more residents than ever in its recorded history, thanks to the

continuous arrival of new industries, housing development, and progressive ideas. Named after Pittsburgh, Pennsylvania, "New Pittsburgh" was founded by George Hobson and Franklin Playter circa 1876 at the base of a coal mining camp. Colonel E. H. Brown is credited with laying out a formal plan for the townsite, an idea that sprouted because of the meeting of four railroads around that point: the Missouri Pacific, the Atchison, Topeka & Santa Fe, St. Louis & San Francisco, and the Kansas City Southern Railroads. It was the hub for the Kansas City Southern, the largest employer in the earliest days of the town. The name of the city and the post office were changed to "Pittsburgh" in 1881 and later to "Pittsburg" in 1894, when the United States Board on Geographic Names declared a standardization measure across the country that would drop the letter 'h' from most cities ending in the suffix '-burgh." Although Pittsburg never asserted itself to capture the Crawford County seat, what they lacked in a title was disregarded as the railroad and the coal industries (there were 55 coal companies as of 1904, employing nearly 12,000 men, according to a 1912 source) spurred the growth of the town. One such coal company was Pittsburg & Midway Coal Company, one of the oldest continuous coal companies in the United States and is now owned by Chevron. There were at one point four newspapers and banks, foundries, boilers, cornices, sewer pipe works, zinc smelters, and factories manufacturing everything from gloves and clothes to cigars and tents. The Auxiliary Manual Training Normal School, later the Kansas State Teachers College of Pittsburg and Kansas State College of Pittsburg and now Pittsburg State University, has been serving the area's need for an institution of higher learning since its inception on March 6, 1903. The "gorillas" are well-known throughout the region, and statues of the Gus the Gorilla mascot can be found throughout the city. Satellite campuses of Labette Community College and Fort Scott Community College are also located here, as are tourist sites such as the Veteran's Memorial, Crawford County Historical Museum (noted for its two-headed half), Green Elm School, Kansas Crossing Casino, and The Bicknell Family Center for the Arts. Chicken Mary's (est. 1941) and Chicken Annie's (est. 1934), two local fried chicken competitors across the street from one another, rose to national fame when local journalist and the former NBC Nightly News anchor (amongst other titles) from 1993 to 2021 Brian Williams covered the story for the Travel Channel. Other persons of note are Paul White, a broadcasting pioneer whose name is used to this day for the lifetime achievement award given out by the Radio Television Digital News Association, railroad executive William N. Deramus III, 3x MLB All-Star, and 2x World Series champion Bill Russell, actor Roy Glenn, Harold Bell Wright, thought to be the first writer to sell one million copies of their book, the founder of the world's largest ammonium nitrate producer, Kenneth A. Spencer, 1944 MLB All-Star Ray Mueller, Russell Myers, and his *Broom-Hilda* comic strip, Dale Hall, the 1945 Sporting News Men's College Basketball Player of the Year, and Waylande Gregory, an innovative sculptor.

**Restaurant Recommendation: Chicken Annie's Original**
**1143 E 600th Ave**
**Pittsburg, KS 66762**

**Restaurant Recommendation: Chicken Mary's**
**1133 600th Ave**
**Pittsburg, KS 66762**

**Restaurant Recommendation: Toast**
**401 N Broadway St Ste D**
**Pittsburg, KS 66762**

# WALNUT, KS
## POPULATION: 187 – TOWN 329 OF 627 (6-29-23)
Walnut's name is a descriptive one for the walnut groves that once dotted the area surrounding Walnut Creek. Its founding came in 1871 under the name Glenwood, until it was changed to Walnut in 1874 to match the name of the local post office. The postal service first called their office Walnut Creek when it was established in 1866, but would later change the suffix to Station in 1873 before dropping it altogether in 1877. The Missouri, Kansas & Texas, and the Atchison, Topeka & Santa Fe Railroads would help the town rapidly develop and erect a flour mill, feed mill, and sawmill, a screen door and a washing machine factory, two hotels, an opera house, and other business practices and stores.

# Restaurant Recommendation:
## His & Hers Bar & Grill
## 203 S Main St
## Walnut, KS 66780

**Adjacent Counties:** Bourbon (N), Cherokee (S), Labette (SW), Neosho (W)

**Unincorporated/Ghost Towns:** Beulah, Brazilton, Camp 50, Capaldo, Cato, Chicopee, Coalvale, Cornell, Croweburg, Curranville, Dry Wood, Dunkirk, Englevale, Farlington, Fleming, Foxtown, Franklin, Fuller, Greenbrush, Gross, Kirkwood, Klondike, Kniveton, Litchfield, Lone Oak, Midway, Monmouth, Opolis, Radley, Red Onion, Ringo, South Radley, Yale

## National Register of Historic Places:
**Cato:** Cato District No. 4 School
**Franklin:** Franklin Sidewalk
**Girard:** Crawford County Courthouse, First Presbyterian Church, Girard Carnegie Library, Hudgeon Bridge, J. T. and Anna Leonard House, J. E. Raymond House, S-W Supply Company, St. John's Episcopal Church, State Bank of Girard, Julius A. Wayland House
**Pittsburg:** Besse Hotel, Colonial Fox Theatre, Fourth and Broadway Historic District, Frisco Freight Depot, Hotel Stilwell, Pittsburg Foundry & Machine Company, Pittsburg Public Library, Washington Grade School, Whitesitt-Shirk Historic District
**Walnut:** Little Walnut Creek Bowstring

## Breweries/Wineries/Distilleries:
Drop the H Brewing Company (Pittsburg, KS)
Jolly Fox Brewery (Pittsburg, KS)

## Golf Courses:
Countryside Golf Course, Public (Pittsburg, KS)
Crestwood Country Club, Private (Pittsburg, KS)
Four Oaks Golf Course, Public (Pittsburg, KS)
Girard Municipal Golf Course, Public (Girard, KS)

## Town Celebrations:
Festa Italiana, Frontenac, KS (September or October)
Hepler Rodeo, Hepler, KS (Independence Day)

Little Balkans Festival, Pittsburg, KS (Labor Day Weekend)
McCune Fall Festival, McCune, KS (4<sup>th</sup> Full Weekend of September)
Walnut Days, Walnut, KS (Labor Day Weekend)

# DECATUR COUNTY
## EST. 1873 – POPULATION: 2,764

Commodore Stephen Decatur of Sinepuxent, Maryland, a prominent naval man and a hero in the War of 1812, is the man responsible for the etymology of Decatur County.

# DRESDEN, KS
**POPULATION: 43 – TOWN 177 OF 627 (4-13-23)**
Dresden, population 43, once served the Chicago, Rock Island, and Pacific Railway as a shipping point. It was built by German settlers (starting in 1888, the same year the town got its post office) and named after the city of Dresden, Germany. It was incorporated in 1920. The town's population has steadily decreased from its peak of 231 in the 1930s, although it grew by 4.9% between 2010 and 2020.

# JENNINGS, KS
**POPULATION: 81 – TOWN 176 OF 627 (4-13-23)**
Jennings was an early station on the Chicago, Rock Island, and Pacific Railroad founded circa 1888. Its name honors an early settler and landowner, Warren Jennings. The town's post office was called Slab City from October 1874 to October 1879 until the Postal Service changed it to Jennings.

# NORCATUR, KS
**POPULATION: 159 – TOWN 174 OF 627 (4-13-23)**
Norcatur's name was given because of its location at the eastern border of Decatur County and the western border of Norton County. Its first post office arrived in October 1885, the same year the town was founded. It was located on the Chicago, Burlington & Quincy Railway. A couple of Major League Baseball players, Dewey Adkins and Elden Auker were born here in 1918 and 1910, respectively. Auker was a 1935 World Series champion and was well-known for his submarine style of throwing pitches. Norcatur's highest population came during the 1930 Census: 524 citizens.

# OBERLIN, KS ★☆

**POPULATION: 1,644 – TOWN 173 OF 627 (4-13-23)**

Oberlin was named after Oberlin, Ohio, and founded in 1878, the same year the United States Postal Service established an office there. The town was incorporated in 1885 following rapid growth from its distinction as a terminus of the Chicago, Burlington & Quincy Railroad and the founding of numerous industries and businesses, including a foundry, creamery, grain elevator, three newspapers, two banks, flour mill, an opera house, and much more. The Decatur County Museum contains a room dedicated to the "Last Indian Raid in Kansas" event, which occurred on September 30, 1878, when a band of Northern Cheyenne Native Americans attacked early area homesteaders. Nearby, Sappa Park was once a state park with a WPA shelter house, disc golf course, and other recreational opportunities for residents and visitors. Famous people from Oberlin include Brun Campbell, a renowned pianist; Cora E. Simpson, the founder of the Florence Nightingale School of Nursing in Fuzhou, China; and NFL running backs Elmer Hackney and Sam Francis (the #1 pick in the 1937 NFL Draft).

## Lodging Recommendation:
## The Landmark Inn
## 189 S Penn Ave
## Oberlin, KS 67749

Clayton is only partially located in Decatur County (see Norton County).

**Adjacent Counties:** Norton (E), Sheridan (S), Thomas (SW), Rawlins (W)

**Unincorporated/Ghost Towns:** Allison, Bassetville, Cedar Bluffs, Decatur, Hawkeye, Hooker, Jackson, Kanona, Leoville, Lund, Lyle, Sheffield, Shibboleth, Stephen, Traer, Vallonia

**National Register of Historic Places:**
**Norcatur:** Norcatur City Hall
**Oberlin:** Bank of Oberlin

**Breweries/Wineries/Distilleries:**
Wahlmeier Farms Vineyard (Jennings, KS)

Coffey County Photos: Burlington, Burlington, Burlington, Burlington, Lebo, Le Roy, New Strawn, Waverly

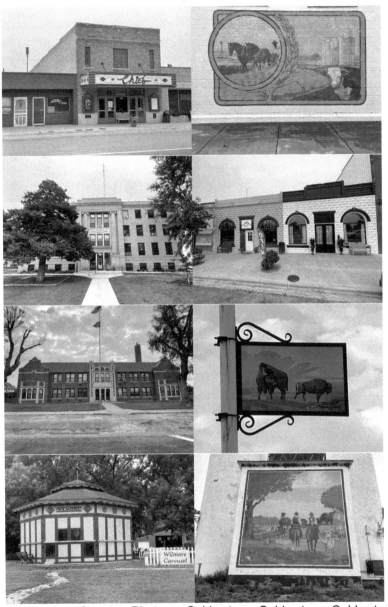

Comanche County Photos: Coldwater, Coldwater, Coldwater, Coldwater, Protection, Protection, Wilmore, Wilmore

Cowley County Photos: Arkansas City, Arkansas City, Arkansas City, Arkansas City, Atlanta, Burden, Dexter, Winfield

Crawford County Photos: Arma, Frontenac, Girard, McCune, Mulberry, Pittsburg, Pittsburg, Pittsburg

Decatur County Photos: Dresden, Jennings, Jennings, Norcatur, Norcatur, Oberlin, Oberlin, Oberlin

# DICKINSON COUNTY
## EST. 1857 - POPULATION: 18,402

After this county was established in 1857, its creators deemed it appropriate to name it in honor of Daniel S. Dickinson, a noted U.S. Senator from New York.

# ABILENE, KS ★☆
## POPULATION: 6,460 – TOWN 193 OF 627 (5-1-23)

Historic Abilene, Kansas, began as a station on a stagecoach line circa 1858. Its name was derived from a word in the Bible (referenced explicitly in Luke 3:1) that means "grassy plains." By 1860, the town was selected to be the county seat of Dickinson County. It wouldn't be until 1867 that the Kansas Pacific Railroad was completed, and Joseph G. McCoy decided it would be a suitable cattle shipping point. It didn't take long for Abilene to reach notoriety as the west's first authentic "cow town" as cattlemen herded hundreds of thousands of cattle through the area. With the cattle came unruly men who did not believe in law and order, who took command of Abilene until Thomas "Bear River" Smith was elected as town marshal and reestablished a level of peace. Following his death, famous folk hero Wild Bill Hickok took over his duties for a brief period. As the town progressed, the Atchison, Topeka & Santa Fe Railroad and the Chicago, Rock Island & Pacific Railroads would establish railroad lines in the area and bring with them ice, carriage, cigar & organ factories, flour mills, and creameries, banks, an opera house, and a Carnegie library. Today, Abilene is most famous for being the birthplace of Sprint Corporation, a telecommunications company founded in 1899 by Cleyson L. Brown under the name Brown Telephone Company, and the boyhood home and burial place of Dwight D. Eisenhower, the 34th President of the United States. The Eisenhower Presidential Center and Presidential Library and Museum are now local points of interest for the town, as are the Greyhound Hall of Fame, the Abilene and Smoky Valley Railroad (a tourist railroad that takes passengers between Abilene and Enterprise), Old Abilene Town, the A. B. Seelye Mansion and Museum, Museum of Independent Telephony, and the Heritage Museum of Dickinson County. Local welder Jason Lahr recently constructed the World's Largest Belt Buckle, a 20-foot-wide and 14-foot-high creation that now stands proudly by the grandstands. The buckle is one of two local "World's Largest" objects, the other being a 28-foot-high spur outside Rittel's Western Wear. It was introduced in 2002 by artist Larry Houston. In the world of pop culture, Abilene has made appearances in video games (*Call of Juarez: Gunslinger*), films (*Abilene Town*, 1946), and songs "Abilene" (George Hamilton IV, 1963) and "Buffalo Ballet" (John Cale, 1975). Other persons of note with ties to Abilene are Harry Beaumont (film director nominated for an Oscar), Charles Olin Ball (food scientist and inventor who created the thermal death time formula), Mike Racy (former vice president of the NCAA and current president of the MIAA), Marlin Fitzwater (White House Press Secretary for Ronald Reagan and George H. W. Bush), Hy Vandenberg (MLB pitcher), Cody Whitehair (NFL guard and 2018 Pro-Bowler), and Everett W. Stewart (flying ace of World War II).

**Restaurant Recommendation:**
**M & R Grill**
**1720 N Buckeye Ave**
**Abilene, KS 67410**

**Lodging Recommendation:**
**Abilene's Victorian Inn B&B**
**820 NW 3rd St**
**Abilene, KS 67410**

# CARLTON, KS
**POPULATION: 40 – TOWN 211 OF 627 (5-2-23)**
Carlton began as a station and shipping point on the Missouri Pacific Railroad and was once home to telegraph and express offices, a handful of general stores, and a post office that remained in operation from February 1872 to July 1995. Its population peaked at 138 people per the 1930 Census, although it is today home to 40 residents.

# CHAPMAN, KS
**POPULATION: 1,377 – TOWN 191 OF 627 (4-30-23)**
Chapman's name is derived from the nearby Chapman Creek, the tributary on which Jackman's mill had been established. The town's first settlers arrived in 1868, and in 1871, the townsite was laid out by James Streeter and S. M. Strickler. The area's post office was in operation before the town existed, having been founded on July 30, 1866, under the name "Chapman's Creek," but it was shortened on May 16, 1872, to its present name. After a devastating tornado obliterated most of the town on June 11, 2008, ABC's *Extreme Makeover: Home Edition* assisted the Tutweiler family and other

nearby neighbors in rebuilding their homes and providing furniture. As a part of the episode and project, the town was given its first community center, complete with a tornado safety shelter. Four other notable residents from Chapman's past are Joseph Henry Engle (former NASA and original Space Shuttle astronaut), Harvey T. Hollinger (one of the first well-known collectors of comic books), Franke Burke (actor known for his role in the 1938 crime drama *Angels with Dirty Faces*), and Henry Varnum Poor (architect and grandnephew of the ultimate founder to Standard & Poor's). The Kansas Auto Racing Museum of Chapman seeks to preserve the history of Kansas motorsports and the state's impact on the sport on a global scale.

# ENTERPRISE, KS
## POPULATION: 708 – TOWN 192 OF 627 (4-30-23)
Enterprise got its name for the "enterprising qualities of its first settlers" and because of its progressive movements to become a center of industry for the region throughout the 1870s. At the time it was laid out in 1872, and the town company was formed in 1875 with V. P. Wilson and John Johntz at the helm, the townspeople had erected one of the largest flour mills in Kansas, a flour mill machinery manufacturer, multiple hotels and banks, a creamery, schools, and more. A lot of the town's industry came about because of its location at the junction of the Union Pacific Railroad, Chicago, Rock Island & Pacific Railroad, and the Atchison, Topeka & Santa Fe Railroad. The first post office was established in January 1873, and another anecdote of town history is that it was the victim of one of Carrie Nation's Temperance Movement strikes in January 1901. Its population peaked at 1,015 citizens according to the 1960 Census.

# HERINGTON, KS
## POPULATION: 2,109 – TOWN 241 OF 627 (4-30-23)
Monroe Davis Herington established the city of Herington in January of 1884 and had the town named in his honor. Places of industry and commerce came quickly after its founding, as within its first year, the amount of money that had circulated local businesses equated to $485,300 (equal to $15,190,000 in January 2024 dollars). Early lines of business ranged from a creamery and an ice and cold storage plant to hotels, railroad shops, and mercantile stores. The post office was opened on February 21, 1884. M. D. Herington convinced the Chicago, Kansas, and Nebraska Railroad to extend their line through his community in 1887, and later, the Missouri Pacific Railroad would

follow suit. Herington Army Airfield served as a World War II staging base from 1942 to 1947 until it was later converted into the Herington Regional Airport. The Herington Historical Museum welcomes visitors to explore its exhibits on early area history. Some famous people from the Herington area are painter Alan Shields, WNBC radio show host Brad Crandall, race car driver Louis Durant, the 1950 Democratic nominee for Governor of Idaho, Calvin E. Wright, army chaplain and the writer of the "Airman's Prayer," John H. Eastwood, Medal of Honor recipient and Catholic "Servant of God" Emil Kapaun, and Bruce P. Blake, a former United Methodist Church bishop of Oklahoma and Dallas, Texas. The bomb that was used in the 1995 Oklahoma City bombing of the Alfred P. Murrah Federal Building was built and tested by the proprietors at a lake outside of town.

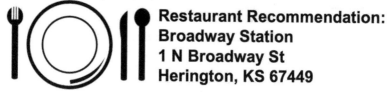 **Restaurant Recommendation:**
**Broadway Station**
**1 N Broadway St**
**Herington, KS 67449**

# HOPE, KS
**POPULATION: 317 – TOWN 239 OF 627 (5-4-23)**
This unique town name was named for the son of Newell Thurstin, who was a leader of a colony of settlers that sought to create a town site in the area that is now Dickinson County. He and the other colonists platted the site in 1871, the same year the post office was established. The Missouri Pacific Railroad laid its tracks through the townsite when Hope was incorporated in 1886. The Atchison, Topeka, and Santa Fe Railroad followed suit the following year. With the activity of the bustling railroad came multiple telephone companies and banks, flour mills, a hospital, gypsum plaster works, and other lines of business. The father of Dwight D. Eisenhower (the 34th President of the United States), David Jacob Eisenhower, lived on a ranch not far from Hope and helped operate a local general store. Edgar N. Eisenhower, Dwight's brother, was born in Hope in January 1889, as was Don Ihde, the first individual to create a work on the philosophy of technology.

# MANCHESTER, KS
**POPULATION: 47 – TOWN 195 OF 627 (5-1-23)**
Once called Keystone, the name Manchester was later given to this small Dickinson County community between 1888 and 1890. When

the town was founded in 1887, the Atchison, Topeka, and Santa Fe Railway was completed through the area, and a year later, the Chicago, Kansas, and Western Railroad was established. The Manchester post office operated from October 28, 1889, to November 13, 1993.

# SOLOMON, KS
**POPULATION: 993 – TOWN 194 OF 627 (5-1-23)**
Solomon was founded circa 1866 at the confluence of the Solomon and Smoky Hill Rivers, of which it took its name from the primary mentioned. The town was based on the land of H. Whitney, a member of the town company. The first merchant opened their doors in 1867, a hotel came in 1868, and the following year, the Union Pacific Railroad was extended to that point. The Chicago, Rock Island & Pacific Railroad and Atchison, Topeka & Santa Fe Railroads would later build or annex area railroad lines. The town's population has remained relatively constant from 1890 to the present day, having reached a low of 817 citizens (1900 Census) and a high of 1,095 residents (2010 Census). Of that population, four individuals are particularly of note: Alberta, Canada politician Kenneth McLeod, the first president of Antioch College Algo Henderson, former head coach of Ottawa University and Oklahoma Baptist University Archie W. Butcher, and 1920 vice-presidential candidate Seymour Stedman.

# WOODBINE, KS
**POPULATION: 157 – TOWN 240 OF 627 (5-4-23)**
James Allen Gillett Sr. gave life to Lyons in 1871 and named it after an area stream. The name wouldn't be changed until 1887 when the Chicago, Rock Island, and Pacific Railroad was extended to that point, and he instead changed it to honor his hometown of Woodbine, Illinois. While its post office, which opened on January 31, 1872, is still in operation, other early town services and facilities such as stockyards, a grist mill, a depot, and other merchants have since gone out of business. Two Methodist Churches (one English and the other German), Baptist, and Lutheran churches also once called Woodbine home.
**Adjacent Counties:** Clay (N), Geary (E), Morris (SE), Marion (S), McPherson (SW), Saline (W), Ottawa (NW)

**Unincorporated/Ghost Towns:** Acme, Bonaccord, Buckeye, Dayton, Detroit, Dillon, Donegal, Elmo, Holland, Industry, Lyona,

Manchester, Moonlight, Navarre, Pearl, Rhinehardt, Shady Brook, Stitt, Stoney, Sutphen, Talmage, Upland

## National Register of Historic Places:
**Abilene:** Abilene City Park Historic District, Abilene Downtown Historic District, Abilene Historic No. 1, Abilene Union Pacific Railroad Freight Depot, Abilene Union Pacific Passenger Depot, ATSF Steam Locomotive No. 3415, Berger House, John W. Birchmore House, Emerson Coulson House, Eisenhower Home, Elms Hotel, Jacob S. Engle House, Garfield Elementary School, David R. Gordon House, Hotel Sunflower, John Johntz House, Gustave A. Kubach House, Lander Park Carousel, C. H. Lebold House, Litts-Dieter House, Mead-Rogers House, Naroma Court Historic District, Perring Building, Rock Island Depot, St. John's Episcopal Church, A. B. Seelye House, D G. Smith Building, Trinity Evangelical Lutheran Church, Union Electric Warehouse, United Building, Versteeg-Swisher House, Vine Street Historic District
**Chapman:** Chapman Creek Pratt Truss Bridge, Freeman-Zumbrunn House, J. S. Hollinger Farmstead, Prospect Park Farm, Smoky Hill Trail and Butterfield Overland Despatch Segment, Wheatland Farm Historic District, Wilson Pratt Truss Bridge
**Enterprise:** Hoffman and Lamb Buildings
**Herington:** Herington Carnegie Public Library, William and Minnie Liggett House, U.S. Post Office-Herington
**Holland Township:** Eliason Barn
**Junction City:** Staatz House
**Solomon:** Brewer Scout Cabin

## Breweries/Wineries/Distilleries:
Kanza Cattle, Vineyards, Honey & Flora (Chapman, KS)

## Golf Courses:
Abilene Country Club, Private (Abilene, KS)
Chisholm Trail, Public (Abilene, KS)
Herington Country Club, Semi-Private (Herington, KS)
Indian Hills Golf Course, Public (Chapman, KS)

## Town Celebrations:
Herington Air Base Showdown, Herington, KS (May and September)
Hope Heritage Festival, Hope, KS (Saturday after Labor Day)
Woodbine Fall Festival, Woodbine, KS (2nd Saturday of October)

# DONIPHAN COUNTY
## EST. 1855 - POPULATION: 7,510

Doniphan County's name honors the memory of Alexander W. Doniphan, an attorney and politician who held a prominent position in the Mexican-American War.

# DENTON, KS
## POPULATION: 130 – TOWN 43 OF 627 (3-1-23)

This town was once called Darwin (1882 to 1888) and later Dentonville until February of 1905, when the post office finally settled on Denton. The Chicago, Rock Island & Pacific Railroad came to town in its early days, and the city was laid out by D. C. Kyle, Moses William, and John Denton in 1886. Its name honors the latter founder.

# ELWOOD, KS
## POPULATION: 1,125 – TOWN 51 OF 627 (3-2-23)

Once called Roseport, Henry Thompson founded a trading post in 1852 that would ultimately begin the town of Elwood. It is said that in its early days, it rivaled the prosperity of St. Joseph, Missouri, now a bustling city of 72,473 residents just across the Missouri River. Nature, however, was not kind to Elwood as the Missouri River would wash away several acres of ideal property and discourage the town's growth. The city was named for pioneer settler John B. Elwood and incorporated in 1860.

# HIGHLAND, KS
## POPULATION: 903 – TOWN 48 OF 627 (3-2-23)

"The Snowflake City of Kansas," Highland, had its beginnings as the Iowa and Sac & Fox Mission. The mission was started by Reverend Samuel and Eliza Irvin and Reverend William and Julia Hamilton under the sponsorship of the Presbyterians. Some pieces of the original mission still stand a few miles east of Highland as a Kansas State Historic Site. The first structure of what is now Highland Community College (home to the Scotties), Irvin Hall, was built in 1858 and is still in use today. The entire community was essentially built around the idea that it would eventually become an educational town. Two other notable points of interest are the Yost Art Gallery at the college and the oldest Masonic Lodge in Kansas, Smithton Lodge No. 1 A.F. & A.M., organized in 1854 and chartered in 1856. John

Misse, who played briefly in Major League Baseball, was born in Highland on May 30, 1885.

# LEONA, KS
**POPULATION: 41 – TOWN 45 OF 627 (3-1-23)**
The first child born in the newly founded community, Leona Shock, is the namesake of this now-town of 41. Mrs. Lenora Hauser named the town. Laid out in 1873, it was once a stop along the Missouri Pacific Railroad, and its post office was in operation from 1873 to 1986.

# SEVERANCE, KS
**POPULATION: 76 – TOWN 44 OF 627 (3-1-23)**
John Severance, one of the town's founders, is the namesake of Severance. He established it in 1869 with the help of C. C. Clonch and Dr. Robert Gunn, and five years later, in 1874, the St. Joseph & Grand Island Railway arrived. The town was seldom meant to be, as after promoters gifted $500 to the railroad to build a platform, they came under litigation from Joel Ryan of Ryan's Station, whom they had made an agreement with to "not build a station within three miles of his town." It wasn't long before the community was incorporated as a third-class city in 1877. Harry E. Chapman, a catcher in Major League Baseball from 1912 to 1916, heeds from Severance.

# TROY, KS ★☆
**POPULATION: 964 – TOWN 49 OF 627 (3-2-23)**
Troy is the county seat of Kansas's northeasternmost county, Doniphan. It was named after the ancient city of Troy (in Greece) upon its establishment in 1855. It would later serve as an important stop and junction for the Chicago, Rock Island & Pacific, Burlington & Missouri River, and the St. Joseph & Grand Island railways. Its post office has been in operation since 1857, and in 1860, it was incorporated by an act of the state legislature. Its first courthouse was burned to the ground in 1867 due to a skirmish between towns to claim the county seat title. Peter Toth, the famous artist who carved over 70 giant Native American heads across North America (and at least one in each state), decided to place his Kansas statue here. Novelist Chloe Gartner, former Associate Justice of the United States Supreme Court (1957 to 1962) Charles Evans Whittaker, and Charles "Buffalo" Jones, the co-founder of Garden City and the first game warden of Yellowstone National Park, have ties to the community.

132

# WATHENA, KS
## POPULATION: 1,246 – TOWN 50 OF 627 (3-2-23)
Wathena was named in honor of Chief Wathena, the former chief of the Kickapoo tribe of Native Americans. He and his tribe were once residents of the area. For four years, between 1855 and 1859, the town's post office was known as Bryan before the name was changed. The city was founded in 1856 and would later welcome the Chicago, Rock Island & Pacific, and the St. Joseph & Grand Island Railroads. It was incorporated in 1873.

# WHITE CLOUD, KS
## POPULATION: 115 – TOWN 52 OF 627 (3-2-23)
White Cloud was named for Francis White Cloud, son of Chief White Cloud of the Iowa tribe of Native Americans. The city serves as the seat of government for the Iowa Tribe of Kansas and Nebraska. In July of 1855, the first post office was started, and in 1857, land promoters John Utt and Enoch Spaulding spurred the town's growth by purchasing the townsite and convincing steamboat traffic from the Missouri River to settle there. Three significant points of interest in the city are the "Four State Lookout," which allows visitors to enjoy a view of Kansas, Missouri, Iowa, and Nebraska at a glimpse, a 40th parallel marker that was the initial surveying point for Nebraska, Kansas, and large parts of South Dakota, Wyoming, and Colorado, and a monument to the pig, "Pete," that inspired the creation of the piggy bank. Pete was sold for $25 in 1910 by a ten-year-old Wilbur Chapman as a fundraiser for a leper colony.

**Adjacent Counties:** Atchison (SW), Brown (W)

**Unincorporated/Ghost Towns:** Bendena, Blair, Brenner, Doniphan, Eagle Springs, Fanning, Geary City, Iowa Point, Moray, Palermo, Purcell, Sparks
**National Register of Historic Places:**
**Bendena:** Albert Albers Barn, St. Benedict's Church, J. A. Symns Barn, T. L. White Barn, M. D. L. Williams Barn
**Denton:** Mathew Eylar Barn No. 1 & No. 2
**Doniphan:** Brenner Vineyards Historic District
**Elwood:** Lincoln School, District 2
**Highland:** First National Bank Building, John R. Hale Barn, Highland Christian Church, Highland Presbyterian Church, Iowa, Sac and Fox Presbyterian Mission, Irvin Hall, Highland Community Junior College,

Abram M. Minier House, St. Martha's AME Church and Parsonage, A. L. Wynkoop House
**Iowa Township:** Site No. RH00-062
**Leona:** George Hanson Barn, John Streib Barn
**Purcell:** St. Mary's Catholic Church
**Sparks:** Godfrey Nuzum Barn
**Troy:** Nicholas Bohr Barn, Doniphan County Courthouse, Doniphan County Courthouse Square Historic District, Doniphan County Waddell Truss Bridge, George Kinkhead Barn
**Wathena:** Herman Chrystal Barn, Fred W. Kienhoff Barn, John Silvers Barn, Wathena Fruit Growers' Association Building
**White Cloud:** Poulet House, White Cloud Historic District, White Cloud School

# DOUGLAS COUNTY
## EST. 1855 - POPULATION: 118,785

Stephen A. Douglas had this county appropriately named in his honor because of the Senator's efforts to decide the state's stance on slavery by popular sovereignty.

# BALDWIN CITY, KS
## POPULATION: 4,826 – TOWN 279 OF 627 (6-11-23)

Robert and Richard Pierson were the first settlers to claim the land that would later become the town of Palmyra. In the summer of that year, 1854, the Palmyra Town company was established by James Blood at its helm and ten other men who sought to begin a trail stop along the Santa Fe Trail. The company went to work at once, furnishing the town with dwellings, stores, a hotel, doctor's offices, and even a post office on June 29, 1857, with N. Blood as the first postmaster. During this time, the Battle of Jack Black took place on June 2, 1856, when Free-Stater forces led by John Brown attacked and captured Henry C. Pate and his men. It was one of the major contributing incidents that led to the beginning of the American Civil War. John Baldwin of Berea, Ohio, was instrumental in donating funds (particularly to the establishment of a saw and grist mill) to aid in the town's growth, and so it was later renamed in his honor. All of the buildings of Palmyra would be moved to the area where his mill was built. After a successful start, the town company purchased a tract of land in 1858 and donated it to the Kansas Educational Association of the Methodist Episcopal church on the condition that a university be built there. Baker University, named after the Methodist

Episcopal bishop Osman Cleander Baker, remains in operation today as the oldest four-year university in Kansas. They pride themselves on being the champions of the intercollegiate football game to be played in Kansas, in which they defeated the Jayhawks of the University of Kansas by a score of 22-9 in 1890. Famous alums include persons such as Andrew Cherng (the founder of Panda Express), George LaFrance (one of the greatest Arena Football League players of all-time, a 2x MVP, 5x champion, and 3x Arena Bowl MVP), Patrick Tubach (visual effects artists noted for his work on the 2013 film *Star Trek Into Darkness* and *Star Wars: The Force Awakens* (2015)), Candice Millard (former editor of *National Geographic* magazine), and Ernest Eugene Sykes (noted freemason), among others. The campus serves as the site of the Quayle Bible Collection at the Collins Library, the Holt-Russell Gallery [of Art], the Osbourne Chapel, and the Old Castle Museum. President Abraham Lincoln donated one hundred dollars towards building Parmenter Hall, and several years later, President William Howard Taft visited campus to give a speech. In 1870, the town was incorporated, and it was around then that the Leavenworth, Lawrence, and Galveston (later the Atchison Topeka & Santa Fe) Railroad arrived in Baldwin City. The railroad was bought out in 1987 by the Midland Railway, which has recently operated as a 16-mile heritage railroad. Since 1957, Baldwin City has been the site of the Maple Leaf Festival, a celebration that attracts nearly 30,000 people each year to enjoy shows, tours, and other entertainment options.

# EUDORA, KS
## POPULATION: 6,408 – TOWN 550 OF 627 (9-30-23)
Deutsche-Neusiedlungsverein, a German Company based out of Chicago, Illinois, sent a party to the Kansas and Missouri area to prospect for a location to lay out a townsite. They decided that a parcel on the southern bank of the Kansas River would serve their needs well, and so they negotiated with then-landowner and Chief Paschal Fish of the Shawnee Nation a deal to acquire the land and begin to settle it. As a part of the deal, he was to own every other lot according to the plat map, and the community would be named in honor of his daughter, Eudora. Foreseeing the impending economic opportunities, Chief Fish built a cabin-hotel called the "Fish House" to help serve the needs of the earliest settlers. P. Hartig and his party arrived on April 18, 1857, and by September 1 of the same year, they had attracted a post office and built a sawmill, offices, and buildings for all of the leading professions. The Atchison, Topeka & Santa Fe Railroad further drove up the town's population and industry as time

passed. Because of its location directly between Lawrence and the Missouri border, William Quantrill and his raiders marched through Eudora on their way to sack Lawrence during the American Civil War. Residents of Eudora attempted without success to warn Lawrence of the intruders, but they helped to rebuild the city as they were strong supporters of the Union. The Eudora Community Museum is supported and run by the members of the Eudora Area Historical Society. Noteworthy Eudorians include Charles Parham, one of the principal founders of American Pentecostalism, actor Hugh Beaumont of *Leave It to Beaver*, former NASCAR driver Chase Austin, Vic Edelbrock, the founder of Edelbrock Corporation and a presiding figure in the hot rod movement, and Mitch Ballock, a professional basketball player in Germany.

# LAWRENCE, KS ★☆
**POPULATION: 94,934 – TOWN 280 OF 627 (6-12-23)**
The history of Lawrence runs deep as it was heavily influential in the state during the time of "Bleeding Kansas" and the events that led to the outbreak of the American Civil War in 1861. It was in June of 1854 that the New England Emigrant Aid Society sent Dr. Charles Robinson and Charles H. Branscomb to select an area fit for an abolitionist-based settlement to prevent the spread of slavery into Kansas from neighboring Missouri. The first settlers arrived in July of that year, and subsequent parties made their way to the newly founded town site throughout the following months. By the end of the year, nearly 750 emigrants had descended on the townsite. The name Lawrence was selected as a nod to Amos A. Lawrence, an important benefactor and supporter of the newly founded settlement. For several years, the settlers would undergo consistent threats from proslavery rivals throughout the area, including the Wakarusa War and Quantrill's Raid in 1863, in which the entire city was burned. Its men were massacred, and even an earlier threat from John Baldwin (namesake of the nearby Baldwin City) to "expel the free-state men with the aid of 3,000 Missourians." The townspeople's drive to continuously rebuild and protect their city despite being constantly attacked led them to be called "Jayhawkers," a name given to those who supported the free-state movement throughout the American Civil War. They would soon be called the "antislavery capital of Kansas" because the antislavery legislature met there and, therefore, made it a de facto capital of Kansas Territory between 1858 and 1861. In November of 1861, Lawrence lost the vote to Topeka (7,966 votes to 5,291) for the formal title of the state capital, although it had acquired the judicial seat of Douglas County from Lecompton only a

few years prior in January 1858. Following the war, per a stipulation in the Kansas Constitution for a state university to be founded, Lawrence was selected as the site for the University of Kansas to be established. They won the legislature's approval by a single vote, beating out the City of Emporia for the honor. As of Fall of 2022, its enrollment was over 27,500 students, and its most prominent buildings are the University of Kansas Natural History Museum, the Spencer Museum of Art, Wilcox Classical Museum, David Booth Kansas Memorial Stadium (the eighth oldest college football stadium in the country), and Allen Fieldhouse, the noted basketball arena that broke the Guinness World Record for the "loudest roar in an indoor arena" at 130.4dB in a 2017 matchup. The Kansas men's basketball team has made 16 Final Four appearances since 1940 and won four national championships. They are first in all-time wins with 2,385 and in regular-season conference championships with 64. (as of June 2023). Lawrence is also home to the Haskell Indian Nations University (formerly known as the United States Indian Industrial Training School, the Haskell Institute, and the Haskell Indian Junior College), the nation's oldest continuously operated federal school for Native Americans. Its campus is the site of the American Indian Athletic Hall of Fame, the Haskell Cultural Center and Museum, the oldest student-run newspaper in the United States, the Indian Leader, and it was the site of the first touch-typing class in the state. The university was the alma mater of the famous 1912 Olympic decathlon and pentathlon gold medalist Jim Thorpe. Tourist sites aside from those on the two university campuses include the Watkins Museum of History, the Lawrence Arts Center, Liberty Hall, Oak Hill Cemetery, Freedom's Frontier National Heritage Area, Museum of the Odd, The Eldridge Hotel, the Lied Center of Kansas, and Clinton State Park for recreationists. More offbeat attractions are the Wishing Bench, the Haunted Bathroom of Wonder Fair, and the "mermaid experience" at Sandbar. The community has been featured numerous times in pop culture throughout the decades, in television series such as *The Immortal*, *Jericho*, and *Supernatural* (it is the hometown of main characters Sam and Dean Winchester), and the 1983 film *The Day After*, in which hundreds of locals appeared as extras. Google Earth engineer Brian McClendon paid homage to his hometown by setting his childhood apartments (Meadowbrook) as the default starting point upon the program's opening. Numerous persons of note have called Lawrence their home throughout its existence: John Hadl (2x NFL Pro-Bowl quarterback and the 1971 league leader in passing yards and touchdowns), Alan Mulally (former CEO of Ford Motor Company and Boeing Commercial Airplanes), Charles L. Robinson (1st Governor of Kansas), William A. Starrett (the architect who oversaw the construction of the Empire State Building in New York City), Patty Jenkins (director of *Monster* (2003), *Wonder Woman* (2017), and *Wonder Woman 1984* (2020)), Elmer "Dr. Vitamin" McCollum (scientist known for using rat colonies to research diet and health in humans), Langston Hughes (poet and leader of the Harlem Renaissance), Bart D. Ehrman (six-time *New York Times* bestselling author), David G. Booth (co-founder of Dimensional Fund Advisors), Leo Beuerman (Academy Award-nominated short film director), Ralph Houk (six-time MLB World Series champion), and hundreds of notable University of Kansas alumni.

**Restaurant Recommendation:
Burger Stand at The Cabash
803 Massachusetts St
Lawrence, KS 66044**

**Lodging Recommendation:
The Oread Hotel
1200 Oread Ave
Lawrence, KS 66044**

# LECOMPTON, KS
**POPULATION: 588 – TOWN 289 OF 627 (6-12-23)**

Upon being settled in 1854 by A. W. and A. G. Glenn, this part of Kansas was named "Bald Eagle" after one of the predatory birds was spotted nesting on a nearby bluff of the Kansas River. Its name would later be changed to honor Samuel Dexter Lecompte, the Chief Justice of the Supreme Court of the Kansas Territory from 1854 to 1859 and the president of the town company. Less than a year after its founding, the city was incorporated by an act of President Franklin Pierce and the territorial legislature, and it was designated as the county seat of Douglas County and the capital of Kansas Territory. The land to construct a capitol building was surveyed by D. H. Harting, and although the building never came to fruition, its cost would have been estimated at $500,000 at that time ($18.5 million in 2024). It held the position of capital city until Topeka won a January 1861 vote to the claim. Throughout its earliest years, Lecompton was a prominent advocate for the slave trade, and it was here in 1857 that the Lecompton Constitution, a document that would have inducted Kansas into the Union as a slave state, was drafted at Constitution Hall. The constitution never came to fruition as abolitionists took control of the legislature, and the downfall of the city's infrastructure began. A university was raised in 1865 by the United Brethren Church and is located in the historic Rowena Hotel (the former site of the territorial legislature). In 1882, a building was constructed to host Lane University. The institution remained in Lecompton until 1902, when it became a part of Campbell College and later Kansas City University (both now defunct). The university building is now the Territorial Capital Museum and the adjacent Constitution Hall State Historic Site also serves as a museum. Two of Lecompton's notable historical figures were Robert S. Stevens, U.S. Congressman for New York from 1883 to 1885, and Chuck Wright, the mayor of Topeka when the destructive F5 tornado leveled the city in 1966. Locals insist that Stull Cemetery, a short ten-minute drive from town, is haunted and a portal to one of the "seven Gates of Hell" in the United States.

**Adjacent Counties:** Jefferson (N), Leavenworth (NE), Johnson (E), Miami (SE), Franklin (S), Osage (SW), Shawnee (NW)

**Unincorporated/Ghost Towns:** Belvoir, Big Springs, Black Jack, Clearfield, Clinton, Franklin, Globe, Grover, Hesper, Kanwaka, Lake View, Lapeer, Lone Star, Louisiana, Media, Midland, Pleasant Grove, Prairie City, Sibleyville, Stull, Twin Mound, Vinland, Weaver, Worden

## National Register of Historic Places:
**Baldwin City:** School and Auditorium-Gymnasium, Barnes Apple Barn, Black Jack Battlefield, Case Library, Clearfield School-District 58, Elmwood Stock Farm Barn, Kansas Homestead of Thomas McQuillan, Marion Springs School, Old Castle Hall, Parmenter Memorial Hall, William A. Quayle House, Santa Fe Depot, Santa Fe Trail-Douglas County Trail Segments, Star Cash Grocery Store and Residence, Stoebener Barn, Stony Point Evangelical Lutheran Church, Trail Park and Trail Park DAR Marker, Willow Springs Santa Fe Trail Segment and DAR Marker
**Eudora:** Beni Israel Cemetery, Cohn-Gardner-Hill & Company Store, Holy Family Catholic Church, Charles Pilla House
**Lawrence:** Ralph and Cloyd Achning House, Bailey Hall, George Malcom Beal House, George and Annie Bell House, Benedict House, Col. James Blood House, Breezedale Historic District, Chewning House, Clinton School District 25, Double Hyperbolic Paraboloid House, Douglas County Courthouse, Charles Duncan House, Dyche Hall, University of Kansas, East Lawrence Industrial Historic District, Eldridge House Hotel, English Lutheran Church, Fernand-Strong House, First Methodist Episcopal Church, First Presbyterian Church,

Charles & Elizabeth Haskell French House, Eugene F. Goodrich House, Green Hall, University of Kansas, Michael D. Greenlee House, Andrew Jackson and Marry Carrol Griffin House, Hancock (12th Street) Historic District, Haskell Institute, Edward House House, Johnson Block Historic District, Kibbee Farmstead, Klock's Grocery & Independent Laundry, Lawrence's Downtown Historic District, Lone Star Lake Civilian Conservations Corps (CCC) Camp, Lone Star Lake Dam, Ludington House, George K. Mackie House, Handel T. Martin House, Witter S. McCurdy House, Robert H. Miller House, Dr. Frederic D. Morse House, Mugan-Olmstead House, North Rhode Island Street Historic Residential District, Oak Hill Cemetery, Old Lawrence City Hall, Old Lawrence City Library, Old West Lawrence Historic District, Oread Historic District, Oregon-California Trail Segments, Pinckney I Historic District, Pinckney II Historic District, Plymouth Congregational Church, Priestly House, Reuter Organ Company Buildings, Samuel A. Riggs House, Roberts-Luther-Mitchell House, John N. Roberts House, St. Luke African Methodist Episcopal Church, Santa Fe Depot, Snow House, South Rhode Island and New Hampshire Street Historic Residential District, Spooner Hall, University of Kansas, Judge Nelson T. Stephens House, Strong Hall, Lucy Hobbs Taylor Building, Trinity Lutheran Historic District, United Presbyterian Center, University of Kansas East Historic District, University of Kansas Historic District, Upper Wakarusa River Crossing, John Palmer Usher House, U.S. Post Office-Lawrence, Vermilyra-Boener House, Henry Waters House, Zimmerman Steel Company, S. T. Zimmerman House
**Lecompton:** Constitution Hall, William Henry House, Lane University, Winter School No. 70
**Lone Star:** Chicken Creek Bridge
**Overbrook:** John and Anna O'Sullivan Farmstead, Somers-Crawford Farms Historic District
**Vinland:** Knud Anderson Farmstead, Barnes-Hoskinson Farmstead, Coal Creek Library, Vinland Fair Association Fairgrounds, Vinland Fair Association Fairgrounds Exhibit Building, Vinland Grange Hall, Vinland Presbyterian Church


# Breweries/Wineries/Distilleries:
23rd Street Brewery (Lawrence, KS)
Black Stag Brewery (Lawrence, KS)
BlueJacket Crossing Vineyard & Winery (Eudora, KS)
Crescent Moon Winery (Lawrence, KS)
Crescent Moon Winery Tasting Room (Lawrence, KS)
Davenport Orchards, Vineyards & Winery (Eudora, KS)
Empty Nester's Winery (Lecompton, KS)

Fields & Ivy Brewery (Lawrence, KS)
Free State Brewing Company (Lawrence, KS)
Irvine's Just Beyond Paradise (Lawrence, KS)
Lawrence Beer Company (Lawrence, KS)
Lawrence Beer Company West (Lawrence, KS)
Pane e Vino Wine Bar & Academy (Lawrence, KS)
Rappaho Vineyard on Coal Creek (Baldwin City, KS)
The Vines Vineyard & Farm (Baldwin City, KS)
Trivedi Wine (Lawrence, KS)
Z&M Twisted Vines Vineyard (Lawrence, KS)

**Golf Courses:**
Alvamar Country Club, Private (Lawrence, KS)
Alvamar Golf Club, Public (Lawrence, KS)
Alvamar Orchards, Public (Lawrence, KS)
Baldwin Golf Association, Semi-Private (Baldwin City, KS)
Eagle Bend Golf Course, Public (Lawrence, KS)
Eudora Riverview Golf, Public (Eudora, KS)
Haven Pointe Winery (Baldwin City, KS)
Lawrence Country Club, Private (Lawrence, KS)

**Town Celebrations:**
Lawrence Busker Festival, Lawrence, KS (4th Weekend of May)
Maple Leaf Festival, Baldwin City, KS (3rd Full Weekend of October)
Territorial Days, Lecompton, KS (Varies between June to September)
Vinland Fair, Vinland, KS (1st Week of August)

# EDWARDS COUNTY
## EST. 1874 - POPULATION: 2,907

State senator John H. Edwards was a leading voice for the creation of Edwards County from Kiowa County in 1874, so it was named for him when the measure passed.

# BELPRE, KS
## POPULATION: 97 – TOWN 452 OF 627 (8-18-23)
The Belpre post office began circulating mail in the area on July 7, 1879, and a townsite was established that same year. Although the population has since dipped to 97 residents as of the last Census, upwards of 488 people called it home in the 1920s because of considerable shipping capabilities along the Atchison, Topeka &

Santa Fe Railroad. In 1906, Belpre was formally incorporated as a city of the third class.

# KINSLEY, KS ★☆

**POPULATION: 1,456 – TOWN 450 OF 627 (8-18-23)**

"Midway USA," located equidistant (approximately 1,561 miles) between the metropolises of San Francisco, California, and New York City, was laid out in 1873 and is the county seat of Edwards County. Former names for the community were Petersburg and Peter's City until the name Kinsley was settled upon to honor E. W. Kinsley. He was a Boston businessman who funded the construction of Kinsley's first church. The post office went by the name "Peters" from April 1873 to January 1874 and was located in Kiowa County before being moved to Edwards County to serve the needs of the newly founded town. The development of Kinsley was quite impressive because of its lonely location in western Kansas. With the assistance of the Atchison, Topeka & Santa Fe Railroad, its citizens erected a cement and brick factory, flour mills and grain elevators, churches, schools, and as many as one hundred unique business establishments by 1912. Its two large draws for tourists are the Carnival Heritage Center & Museum (focusing on farmer Charles Brodbeck's idea to build one of the largest family carnivals in the country) and the Edwards County Historical Sod House and Museum. The population has dropped substantially since the 1950s, when Kinsley was then home to 2,479 people, although many former citizens have left their mark on American history through their achievements: Earl Winfield Spencer Jr. (the first commanding officer of the Naval Air Station in San Diego), Freddy Johnston (a famous songwriter), Kyle Burkhart (briefly under contract with the NFL's Seattle Seahawks and New York Jets), Madge Blake (actress who played Margaret Mondello in *Leave it to Beaver* and Aunt Harriet Cooper in ABC's *Batman* series in 96 of the series 120 episodes), and Peter Mehringer (1932 Olympic gold medalist in light heavyweight men's freestyle wrestling).

# LEWIS, KS

**POPULATION: 400 – TOWN 451 OF 627 (8-18-23)**

Founded in 1885 and incorporated in 1906, the City of Lewis was named in honor of James M. Lewis, who was influential in getting the railroad to extend its line to this section of Edwards County and his Hollingsworth Ranch. Its original purpose for being platted was to assist with the needs of the Atchison, Topeka & Santa Fe Railroad as a station and shipping point. When it was established, it was a relatively new Kansas settlement, and its economy prospered. Two banks, a cement plant, a flour mill and grain elevators, a newspaper, and even a soda pop factory were amongst the earliest businesses. The post office arrived in November 1886.

# OFFERLE, KS
## POPULATION: 179 – TOWN 449 OF 627 (8-17-23)
Town founder Lawrence Offerle is the namesake of this community that was once a part of the Atchison, Topeka & Santa Fe Railroad line. A mill and elevators were amongst the first agricultural industries in town, although there were once several general merchandise stores and a creamery. The postal service elected to place a post office in Offerle the same year the city was founded, 1876. It was incorporated in 1917.

**Adjacent Counties:** Pawnee (N), Stafford (E), Pratt (SE), Kiowa (S), Ford (SW), Hodgeman (NW)

**Unincorporated/Ghost Towns:** Centerview, Fellsburg, Nettleton, Trousdale

**National Register of Historic Places:**
**Kinsley:** Gano Grain Elevator and Scale House, Kinsley Civil War Monument, Palace Theater

**Golf Courses:**
Kinsley Country Club, Semi-Private (Kinsley, KS)

**Town Celebrations:**
Lewis Days, Lewis, KS (Early July leading up to Independence Day)

# ELK COUNTY
## EST. 1875 - POPULATION: 2,483

Elk County got its name from the Elk River, a tributary of the Verdigris River that flows through the county.

# ELK FALLS, KS
## POPULATION: 113 – TOWN 395 OF 627 (7-20-23)
The first permanent European settler of Elk Falls was R. H. Nichols,

who built himself a home and an office for his loan and real estate company in 1870. The name of the settlement was given by early settlers for a nearby waterfall of the Elk River, which meanders through the townsite. Incorporation as a city of the third class was awarded in 1887 by the legislature shortly after the arrival of the Atchison, Topeka & Santa Fe Railroad, and the highest recorded Census population of 513 residents came in the year 1880. One such early settler was Prudence Crandall, the founder of the Canterbury Female Boarding School, the first African-American girl-only school in the country.

# GRENOLA, KS
**POPULATION: 151 – TOWN 396 OF 627 (7-20-23)**
"Grenola" is an amalgamation of the former names of two townsites, Greenfield and Canola. Both towns were passed over by the Atchison, Topeka & Santa Fe Railroad when it was built through the vicinity in 1879 (halfway between both communities). So, they united with one another to formulate a new settlement. The population grew to encompass coal, gas, and building stone industries, as well as an opera house, banks, saloons, schools, churches, and a post office to accommodate the needs of the railroad workers and early settlers. The first child born in Grenola took the town's name as given by her parents, and they were rewarded with a pristine town lot. After the Grenola grain elevator ceased operations in 1989 after eighty years of milling, the local historical society converted it into a museum and relocated two country schools to the grounds. Trixie Friganza, a vaudeville and theater performer from 1889 to 1940, and Jake L. Hamon Sr., a millionaire by the railroad and oil industries who was instrumental in acquiring Warren G. Harding the 1920 Republican presidential nomination, were born in Grenola in the early 1870s.

# HOWARD, KS ★
**POPULATION: 570 – TOWN 398 OF 627 (7-20-23)**
Howard City was founded on an overlook of the Elk River and its tributaries in 1870 and named for Oliver O. Howard of American Civil War and Howard University fame. Amongst its founders were Samuel McFarland and T. A. Dodd, then the president and the secretary of the town company. A post office was started in the area on February 14, 1870, when Elk County had formerly been a part of Howard County. In 1875, Howard County was split into a northern (now Elk County) and southern (Chautauqua) portion because settlers could not agree on a singular county seat, so Howard became the seat of

the newly founded Elk County. Early notable businesses were the opera house, a printing office, a saloon, and the Howard House. A. B. Steinberger was named the first mayor of Howard upon the settlement's incorporation as a municipality in October of 1877. The Atchison, Topeka & Santa Fe Railroad serviced the town and its people throughout the turn of the century, leading to a population as high as 1,207 people circa 1900. The six buildings of the Benson Historical Museum include the Union Center District #2 Schoolhouse and the Gragg Agricultural Building. Hubble's Rubble is a fun, can't-miss roadside attraction on Highway 99 full of the sculptures of artist Jerry Hubble.

 **Restaurant Recommendation: Toots Drive-In 1251 K-99 Howard, KS 67349**

# LONGTON, KS ☆
**POPULATION: 288 – TOWN 394 OF 627 (7-20-23)**
Longton, England, is the city in Europe after which early pioneers decided to name this settlement. It was originally called Elk Rapids by founders J. W. Kerr, J. Hoffman, J. C. Pinney, and others until the post office decided that the name was too similar to the nearby towns of Elk Falls and Elk City. Both the postal service and the townsite were established in the year 1870. For years, Longton was considered for the county seat title, but after the local government failed for a short time (no mayor or city council were elected at one point) and the town risked disincorporation, those aspirations went by the wayside. Like other towns throughout the area, the Atchison, Topeka & Santa Fe Railroad was the significant area rail line.

# MOLINE, KS
**POPULATION: 345 – TOWN 397 OF 627 (7-20-23)**
On July 21, 1879, Major J. H. Chapman chartered the land in the name of the Moline Town Company to establish a townsite that would benefit from the arrival of the Atchison, Topeka & Santa Fe Railroad's westward expansion. Chapman was from Moline, Illinois, home of the Moline Plow Company, a prominent tool used by area farmers in Kansas history. The name stuck for good when the postal service placed an office there in September. Many of its earliest settlers and buildings were annexed from the nearby town of Boston, and the

earliest industries were carriage works, cement and brick plants, lime kilns, and mills. Moline has maintained a number of exciting attractions and traditions, such as the Shaffer House Museum and Art Center and Moline Crazy Days, known around the area for its superb ham and beans "bean feed." Kansas's Oldest Swinging Bridge, built in 1904, swings today over a local creek on which little waterfalls can sometimes be seen. Leon Johnson, a Medal of Honor recipient for his strikes on the Ploesti oil fields during Operation Tidal Wave in World War II, attended the local high school.

**Adjacent Counties:** Greenwood (N), Wilson (E), Montgomery (SE), Chautauqua (S), Cowley (SW), Butler (NW)

**Unincorporated/Ghost Towns:** Busby, Cave Springs, Fiat, Oak Valley, Upola

**National Register of Historic Places:**
**Elk Falls:** Elk Falls High School Gymnasium, Elk Falls Pratt Truss Bridge
**Grenola:** Grenola Mill and Elevator
**Howard:** Elk County Courthouse, Howard National Bank

Dickinson County Photos: Abilene, Abilene, Abilene, Enterprise, Herington, Herington, Hope, Woodbine

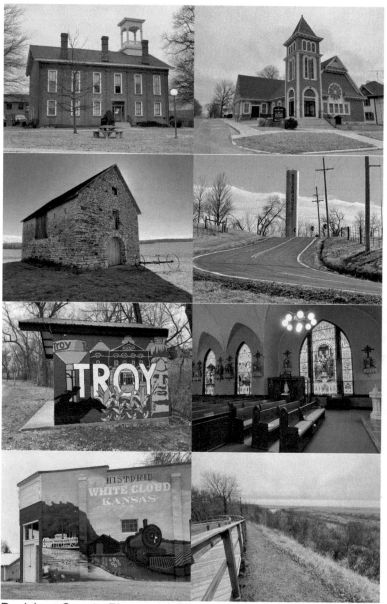

Doniphan County Photos: Highland, Highland, Leona, Severance, Troy, Wathena, White Cloud, White Cloud

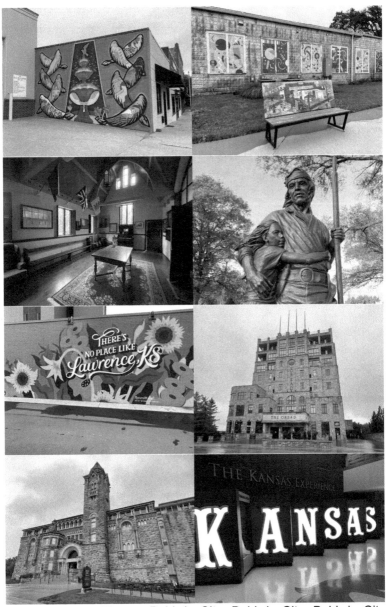

Douglas County Photos: Baldwin City, Baldwin City, Baldwin City, Eudora, Lawrence, Lawrence, Lawrence, Lawrence

Edwards County Photos: Belpre, Kinsley, Kinsley, Kinsley, Kinsley, Kinsley, Lewis, Offerle

Elk County Photos: Elk Falls, Elk Falls, Elk Falls, Grenola, Grenola, Howard, Howard, Howard

151

# ELLIS COUNTY
## EST. 1867 - POPULATION: 28,934

Ellis County is one of several in Kansas that honors the legacy of former American Civil War heroes from the Union; it was named for Lieutenant George Ellis.

## ELLIS, KS
### POPULATION: 1,958 – TOWN 152 OF 627 (4-11-23)

Ellis first served as a water station on the Kansas Pacific Railroad in 1867. It was around 1873 that the townsite was formally established, and it quickly became a cow town (a common shipping point for cattle drives heading from the south to the north). Early settlers came from predominantly Louisville, Kentucky, and Syracuse, New York, to assist with the construction of the railroad line. Incorporation came about in January of 1888, and in 1896, the town made history when an all-woman council and mayor won the local elections. Former residents of the community created a couple of early inventions, the first being the electric streetcar (developed by John Henry in 1882, an early train dispatcher in Ellis), and the other being the Cross Process for converting oil, natural gas, and similar resources into gasoline (invented by residents Walter and Roy Cross). Walter P. Chrysler, the founder of the Chrysler Corporation, which employs over 90,000 individuals, grew up here and spent his early days working for the railroad and a local machinist. His former home is now the Walter P. Chrysler Boyhood Home and Museum. It is one of four museums in town, the other three being the Railroad Museum, the Ellis High School Alumni Association Museum, and the Bukovina Society Headquarters and Museum. The Bukovina Society of the Americas operates the latter institution at the former First Congregational Church. Famous jeweler and businesswoman Martha L. Addis is another person of note from Ellis.

## HAYS, KS ★☆
### POPULATION: 21,116 – TOWN 151 OF 627 (4-11-23)

The old American west town of Hays today serves as the largest center of industry and culture in northwest Kansas, as well as the county seat of Ellis County. The United States Army was the first organization to colonize the future townsite when they built Fort Fletcher in 1865 along the Smoky Hill Trail to assist and protect pioneers working their way westwards. One year later, the fort was renamed Fort Hays after Brigadier General Alexander Hays, who had recently been killed in the Battle of the Wilderness in the American Civil War. When the Kansas Pacific Railway expanded its line through the area, William Webb and other early colonists began to work on platting a townsite. Fort Hays would later move several miles northwest to accommodate the railroad, and Buffalo Bill Cody would work with a railroad contractor to establish a new town, Rome, next to it. However, Webb's town, which he called Hays City, would survive because of how the railroad was constructed through the area. The wild west history of Hays was extensive as several notable figures such as Buffalo Bill Cody, Elizabeth Bacon Custer, George Armstrong Custer, Wild Bill Hickok, and Calamity Jane all lived there at different points. The nation's first "Boot Hill Cemetery," a term given to graveyards where people who "died with their boots on" in violent gunfights, was established in Hays and is today a tourist attraction. A brief timeline places Hays's designation as the county seat in 1870, its incorporation in 1885, and its renaming to simply "Hays" in 1895. The old Fort Hays became the Fort Hays Historic Site in 1967 after the Kansas Historical Society acquired it, and some of the fort's land was repurposed into Fort Hays State University. As of Fall of 2022, the university boasted an enrollment of nearly 13,000 students and was the first school to be considered an agriculturally based institution. It was formed in 1902 and was formerly known as the Western Branch of the Kansas Normal School (1902-1914), Fort Hays Kansas State Normal School (1914-1923), Kansas State Teacher College of Hays (1923-1931), and Fort Hays State College (1931-1977). The university operates the Sternberg of Natural History. It boasts an impressive collection of fossilized creatures and specimens, of which one such exhibit is the famous Gillicus in Xiphactinus (the fish within a fish) fossil. The Moss-Thorns Gallery of Art and the Ellis County Historical County Historical Society Museum are the two other museums in town. Hays has a handful of appearances in popular culture, mainly in the movies *The Plainsman* (1936), *Paper Moon* (1973), and *Wild Bill* (1995). It has two sister cities in Xinzheng, Henan, China, and Santa Maria, Paraguay, and ties with dozens of notable individuals such as actress Rebecca Staab, businessman Philip Anschutz, former NBA guard Ron Baker, feminist legal pioneer Frances Tilton Weaver, actor Robert Bogue, the "blue light lady" Elizabeth Polly, sportscasters Dave Armstrong and Bob Davis, writer Elizabeth Bacon Custer, Jeff Colyer, the 47th Governor of Kansas, and MLB players Willard Schmidt, Otto Denning and Elon Hogsett.

# SCHOENCHEN, KS

**POPULATION: 170 – TOWN 412 OF 627 (8-13-23)**

Russian Germans, more accurately referred to as Volga Germans, were the founders of Schoenchen in the spring of 1877 after they sought to resolve a dispute to relocate the townsite of Liebenthal. The disagreement was concerning where Liebenthal should be appropriately located so settlers would have easier access to water. Many families had already constructed their homes and did not wish to move, whereas others opted to do so shortly after John Schaefer donated four acres for a church to be completed at Liebenthal. Liebenthal officially built up around Section 21, Township 16, Range 18 West in Rush County, whereas Schoenchen was founded at Section 28, Township 15 South, Range 18 West in Ellis County. Schoenchen's settlers named it after a town from their motherland of the same name (although San Antonio was an alternate proposed option) and went straight to work to construct St. Anthony Catholic Church and area homes. In 1902, the post office opened its doors, and the townsite grew thereon.

# VICTORIA, KS

**POPULATION: 1,129 – TOWN 150 OF 627 (4-11-23)**

George Grant and a group of British colonists were the first to settle in the area that would eventually become Victoria on land sold to Grant by the Kansas Pacific Railroad circa 1873. They decided it would be fitting to name the town after Queen Victoria, the Queen of the United Kingdom. Many of the colonists of this early settlement left throughout the late 1870s because of their lack of interest in raising livestock, which opened the door for a group of Volga Germans to annex their community into Herzog, which was located only half a mile northward. Herzog and Victoria would combine their settlements and adopt Victoria's name in 1913. Herzog's settlements were predominantly Roman Catholic and were responsible for constructing the Basilica of St. Fidelis, otherwise known as The Cathedral of the Plains. The church was built between 1908 and 1911 from limestone and includes two massive towers, each 141 feet tall. Walker Army

Airfield would be constructed a few miles northeast of Victoria in the 1940s as an airfield designed to train soldiers for World War II, some of whom were members of the 58th Bombardment Wing who were amongst the first to bombard the Japanese mainland in the spring of 1944. Other unusual points of interest include the lone grave and monument to the man (George Grant) who imported the first Angus beef cattle to the United States in 1873, and at the local cemetery, a memorial to six men working on the railroad who were ambushed by the Cheyenne in 1867. Former NFL linebackers Monty Beisel and Nate Dreiling are from Victoria, as are actor Lucy Isabella Buckstone and rancher James "Scotty" Phillip, known for his role in preventing the extinction of the American Bison.

 **Restaurant Recommendation: Library Grill & Bar 1102 3rd St Victoria, KS 67671**

**Adjacent Counties:** Rooks (N), Osborne (NE), Russell (E), Rush (S), Ness (SW), Trego (W)

**Unincorporated/Ghost Towns:** Antonino, Catharine, Chetola, Easdale, Emmeram, Hog Back, Martin, Mendota, Munjor, Palatine, Pfeifer, Rome, Smoky Hill City, Stockrange, Toulon, Turkville, Walker, Yocemento

**National Register of Historic Places:**
**Ellis:** Walter P. Chrysler House, Ellis Congregational Church, Memorial City Hall, Merchants Bank of Ellis, Papes Barn
**Hays:** Justus Bissing Jr. Historic District, Chestnut Street Historic District, Drees House, First Presbyterian Church, Fort Hays, Gallagher House, J. A. Mermis House, Pawnee Tipi Ring Site and Golden Spring Beach, Phillip Hardware Store, St. Joseph's Church and Parochial School, Washington Grade School
**Victoria:** Brungardt-Dreiling Farmstead, George Grant Villa, St. Fidelis Catholic Church
**Walker:** Fort Fletcher Stone Arch Bridge

**Breweries/Wineries/Distilleries:**
Defiance Brewing Co. Downtown (Hays)
Defiance Brewing Co. Taproom (Hays)
Gella's Diner & Lb. Brewing Company (Hays)

Resurrection Vineyard (Hays)

**Golf Courses:**
Ellis Country Club, Semi-Private (Ellis, KS)
Fort Hays Municipal Golf Course, Public (Hays, KS)
Smoky Hill Country Club, Private (Hays, KS)

**Town Celebrations:**
Ellis High School Alumni Celebration, Ellis, KS (Memorial Day Weekend)
Herzogfest, Victoria, KS (2nd Weekend off August)
Oktoberfest, Hays, KS (1st Weekend of October)
Riverfest, Ellis, KS (3rd Weekend of June)

# ELLSWORTH COUNTY
## EST. 1867 - POPULATION: 6,376

Ellsworth County was named for Fort Ellsworth of Alexandria, Virginia, a structure that assisted the Union Army in its defense against the Confederacy from 1861 to 1865.

# ELLSWORTH, KS ★☆
## POPULATION: 3,066 – TOWN 201 OF 627 (5-2-23)

Ellsworth was surveyed in the spring of 1867 by a townsite company headed by H. J. Latshaw. It took its name from the nearby Fort Ellsworth. "The Stockade," a hotel and store establishment, was the first building to be constructed by E. W. Kingsbury. The population grew rapidly to over two thousand individuals with the anticipation that the construction of the Kansas Pacific Railroad would soon be completed in the area and bring new people and industries. However, in June 1867, the town was hit with a series of catastrophes ranging from flooding by the Smoky Hill River to Native American raids and an outbreak of cholera. The population dwindled to less than 50 individuals but soon rebounded thanks to the 1,500+ soldiers stationed near Fort Harker. The town was incorporated in 1867 and soon obtained a large share of the cattle industry. It made a name for itself as "The Wickedest Cattletown in Kansas" for all the saloons, brothels, gambling halls, and shootouts that took over the town. By the late 1870s, the stockyard closed, and with it went the cattle drives and cowboys to other Kansan cities such as Dodge City and Abilene. Today, Ellsworth serves as the county seat of Ellsworth County, and one of its major draws is Mushroom Rock State Park, the smallest state park in Kansas that is home to mushroom-shaped rocks from the Cretaceous Period that are 66 to 144 million years old. Old western figures that once roamed the town's streets include Wyatt Earp, Ben, Billy and Libby Thompson, John Morco, and Wild Bill Hickok. The Anglican Bishop of Damaraland, South Africa, from 1960 to 1968, Robert Herbert Mize Jr., and the Episcopal Bishop of the Anglican Diocese of Quincy, Keith Ackerman, have ties to Ellsworth too, as does Kelvin Droegemeier, the 10th Director of the Office of Science and Technology Policy.

 **Restaurant Recommendation:**
**A El De Oros**
**1408 Foster Rd**
**Ellsworth, KS 67439**

# HOLYROOD, KS
## POPULATION: 403 – TOWN 463 OF 627 (9-17-23)

Holyrood, the former home of the Cardinals, was an essential early town of Ellsworth County and a part of the Atchison, Topeka & Santa Fe Railroad system. The etymology of Holyrood differs from most cities in that it was named for Holyrood Abbey, now the Abbey and Palace of Holyroodhouse in Edinburgh, Scotland. Interestingly enough, the first settlers of the community were not Scottish but of German, Czech, and Irish descent. A post office was established in 1874 under the name "Hollyrood," although it would be changed in 1898 to match the spelling used by local newspapers and the railroad. Because of the differing origins of the pioneer settlers, three churches were erected slightly before the turn of the century: St. Mary's Catholic Church, St. Paul's Evangelical Church, and St. Peter's Lutheran Church. Other enterprises of note at that time were a hotel, mercantile stores, a bank, and a cigar factory. Author James Fugaté and former MLB pitcher Fay Thomas have ties to Holyrood.

# KANOPOLIS, KS
## POPULATION: 443 – TOWN 200 OF 627 (5-1-23)

Kanopolis was once a town that had vied to capture the title of the state capital of Kansas. The townsite began as a military installation, Fort Harker, that began construction under the orders of General Winfield S. Hancock in November 1866. It was designed to be a replacement for the nearby Fort Ellsworth, which was located approximately one mile to the southwest. When the fort closed in 1872, it temporarily became the Fort Harker Military Reservation until its 10,240 acres of land were sold to Colonel Henry Johnson in August 1881 for $4,117.50. Seventeen members of a group from Ohio led by Ross Mitchell, F. M. Bookwalter, and John H. Thomas purchased 4,740 acres of this land in 1885 for $71,000 and started to print advertisements with pictures of skyscrapers and major commerce for what they thought would become the "great metropolis" and ultimately the state capital of Kansas. The advertisements went as far as to claim that the area surrounding the townsite was the authentic Garden of Eden from the Bible and that the produce grew so large that cabbage leaves were used as circus tents and pea pods as ferry boats on the Arkansas River. Another claim was that jackrabbits in the area grew to be "as large as horses." The Kanopolis Land Company laid out a townsite to accommodate 150,000 people, but alas, the population never even reached 1,000 individuals, peaking at 868 as of the 1940 Census. Its status as a "paper town" was solidified in history when it lost the vote to become the county seat of Ellsworth County and when a January 1887 issue of the *Leavenworth Times* exposed the advertisements as fraud and led to a significant drop in advertising abilities and land sales. In 1893, there was another vote to attempt to move the state capital to Kanopolis from Topeka. Kanopolis is home to the state's first state park, Kanopolis State Park, the site of sandstone canyons, Kanopolis Lake, a prairie dog town, and ample opportunities for hunting, hiking, and fishing. Fort Harker can be toured with the help of the Ellsworth County Historical Society.

# LORRAINE, KS
**POPULATION: 137 – TOWN 202 OF 627 (5-2-23)**
Lorraine was founded in 1888, and it didn't take long for both the Atchison, Topeka & Santa Fe Railroad and the St. Louis & San Francisco Railroad to extend their lines to that point. Notable early establishments included a flour mill, two grain elevators, a bank, several merchants, and a post office starting in February 1888.

# WILSON, KS
**POPULATION: 859 – TOWN 148 OF 627 (4-11-23)**
"The Czech Capital of Kansas" is unique in that it is rich in Czech history. Many of its earliest settlers were immigrants from Bohemia who moved to America to help construct the railroad. The town's history, like many others in this area of Kansas, began with the

construction of a stagecoach station by the Butterfield Overland Despatch to carry out their mail service. The Kansas Pacific Railroad built stations in the same areas as the Despatch, and it was in 1868 that they established Wilson Station (a name taken from the station's location in Wilson Township of Ellsworth County). A short-lived name for the area was Bosland, given by the National Land Company, but the post office went by the name Wilson. The historic Midland Railroad Hotel was constructed in 1899 by Wilke Power and, for a long time, was considered to be one of the best lodging accommodations in the Midwest. It was frequently shown in the 1973 film, *Paper Moon*. As a tribute to its Czech heritage, residents painted the "World's Largest Hand-Painted Czech Egg," a 22-foot-long creation that was painted in 2015 and put on display the following year. Several smaller eggs dot the streets of the Wilson, and Czech artifacts are on display at the Wilson Czech Opera House & Museum. Three noted Wilsonians were Dennis D. Farney (1993 Pulitzer Prize writer for *The Wall Street Journal*), Neva Egan (the 1st First Lady of Alaska), and John Kuck (gold-medalist in the shot put at the 1928 Summer Olympics).

# Lodging Recommendation: Midland Railroad Hotel
## 414 26th St
## Wilson, KS 67490

# Lodging Recommendation: Atlas Ad Astra Adventure Resort
## 354 4th Rd
## Wilson, KS 67490

**Adjacent Counties:** Lincoln (N), Saline (E), McPherson (SE), Rice (S), Barton (SW), Russell (NW)

**Unincorporated/Ghost Towns:** Arcola, Black Wolf, Carneiro, Delight, Elkhorn, Frantz, Langley, Midway, Terra Cotta, Venango, Yankee Run

**National Register of Historic Places:**
**Ellsworth:** Ellsworth Downtown Historic District, Perry Hodgden House, Insurance Building, Arthur Larkin House, Ira E Lloyd Stock Farm
**Holyrood:** Holyrood Santa Fe Depot

**Kanopolis:** Fort Harker Guardhouse, Fort Harker Officers' Quarters
**Marquette:** Indian Hill Site
**Wilson:** Midland Hotel, Weinhold House, Wilson Downtown Historic District #1-Main St., Wilson Downtown Historic District #3-Southside

**Golf Courses:**
Ellsworth Golf Municipal Course, Public (Ellsworth, KS)

**Town Celebrations:**
After Harvest Czech Festival, Wilson, KS (Last Weekend of July)
Fort Harker Days, Kanopolis, KS (2nd Weekend in July)

# FINNEY COUNTY
## EST. 1883 - POPULATION: 38,470

Kansas's 10th Lieutenant Governor, David W. Finney, is the namesake of this county established in 1883 from Arapahoe, Grant, Kearney, and Sequoyah Counties.

# GARDEN CITY, KS ★☆
## POPULATION: 28,151 – TOWN 444 OF 627 (8-17-23)

This sister city of Oristano, Sardinia, Italy, and Ciudad Quesada, Costa Rica, has its roots in the sugar beet industry and its construction of an irrigation system that helped begin a series of bountiful agricultural harvests throughout southwestern Kansas. It was founded in 1878 when the Fulton family settled here, and Charles Van Trump surveyed the land for a townsite. A few homes were built, but the real population boom didn't occur until town promoter Charles Jesse "Buffalo" Jones enticed the Atchison, Topeka & Santa Fe Railroad to run their tracks through the area. The General Land Office, now a part of the Bureau of Land Management, located their office in Garden City as well to make it a junction point for those wanting to make land claims throughout the region. The community's growth was immaculate, as the earliest settlers rallied to make Garden City amongst the best early establishments of the entire western portion of the state. At one point, there were thirteen drug stores, nine lumber yards, three lines of newspapers and banks, a broom factory, bottling works, mills, and elevators of all varieties, and an impressive sugar beet plant that brought in 1,000 tons of beets every daily and produced 200,000 pounds of sugar every day in 1912. The factory cost $1,000,000 to construct but churned out far more value than it was built for. The Garden City, Gulf & Northern Railroad would soon make the town's railroad line to get in on the local trade scene. Following the construction of a meat packing plant in the 1970s and the arrival of Vietnamese refugees due to the Fall of Saigon in 1975, several different ethnic groups began to incorporate themselves into the community. Garden City is now the most ethnically diverse community in the entire state. The city's first and only secondary education institution, Garden City Community College, was established in 1919 and is home to the "Broncbusters." Noted points of interest include the Finney County Historical Museum (home of the World's Largest Hairball and crime exhibits on the Clutter Family and the Fleagle Gang), the Windsor Hotel, Lee Richardson Zoo, the Finney County Courthouse (because of its designation as the Finney County seat), and "The Big Dipper," a massive 2.2 million gallon pool that once advertised itself as the "World's Largest, Free, Outdoor, Municipal, Concrete Swimming Pool." It has multiple water slides, accommodations for water skiing, a bathhouse, and seven 50-meter Olympic swimming lanes. Noted Garden City residents include Thurman McGraw (College Football Hall of Fame inductee), Jeremy Hubbard (former ABC News correspondent in New York), Sanora Babb (novelist), Charles "Buffalo" Jones (co-founder of Garden City and a noted conservationist), Hal Patterson (one of the Top 50 players in Canadian Football League history), Todd Tichenor (MLB umpire), Frank Mantooth (pianist), Victor Ortiz (boxer), Brandon Ríos (boxer), Roy Romer (the 39th Governor of Colorado), and Joe Exotic, "The Tiger King," known from the Netflix series of the same name and for operating the Greater Wynnewood Exotic Animal Park.

 **Restaurant Recommendation:**
**El Paisa Restaurant & Bar**
**3101 W Jones Frontage Rd**
**Garden City, KS 67846**

**Lodging Recommendation:**
**Sunnyland B&B**
**501 N 5th St**
**Garden City, KS 67846**

# HOLCOMB, KS

**POPULATION: 2,245 – TOWN 443 OF 627 (8-16-23)**

Holcomb is a relatively new Kansas community, having only been founded in the early 1900s, around the same time (December 3, 1909) that the postal service took an interest in the area to start a post office. Its name honors Mr. Holcomb, an early area hog farmer. The small village served as a simple shipping point for the Atchison, Topeka & Santa Fe Railroad for many years and only had 272 residents as of the 1970 Census. Incorporation had occurred in 1961, which began to fuel its growth. As the nearby Garden City continued to build up its status as a regional trading center, Holcomb also benefited and became a sort of bedroom community. In November of 1959, Holcomb rose to international fame as a result of the Clutter murders, when four members of a family were found dead at their River Valley Farm home. The murders spawned the inspiration for Truman Capote's 1966 novel, *In Cold Blood*, who, with the help of noted author Harper Lee, interviewed locals and crime scene investigators to write the book. Several adaptations of the book were turned into films, and the house still stands today on private property. Beat Generation poet Charles Plymell was born in a chicken coop on a farm outside of the city in 1935.

**Adjacent Counties:** Scott (N), Lane (N), Ness (NE), Hodgeman (E), Haskell (S), Gray (S), Grant (SW), Kearny (W)

**Unincorporated/Ghost Towns:** Eminence, Friend, Ganoo, Kalvesta, Lowe, Mansfield, Peterson, Pierceville, Plymell, Quinby, Ravanna, Ritchal, Rodkey, Tennis, Terry, Wolf

**National Register of Historic Places:**
**Garden City:** 900 Block North Seventh Street Historic District, Buffalo Hotel, Bungalow Historic District, Cedar Cliff, Hope House, Little Finnup House, Sabine Hall, Sen. William H. Thompson House, Windsor Hotel
**Pierceville:** Finney County Point of Rocks

**Breweries/Wineries/Distilleries:**
Flat Mountain Brewhouse (Garden City, KS)
Hidden Trail Brewing (Garden City, KS)

**Golf Courses:**
Buffalo Dunes Golf Course, Public (Garden City, KS)

Golden Locket Golf Course, Public (Garden City, KS)
Southwind Country Club, Private (Garden City, KS)

**Town Celebrations:**
Beef Empire Days, Garden City, KS (Late May to Early June)

# FORD COUNTY
## EST. 1867 - POPULATION: 34,287

James H. Ford served as a brevet brigadier general in the American Civil War near Kansas and Missouri, so this county was named to commemorate him.

# BUCKLIN, KS
## POPULATION: 727 – TOWN 473 OF 627 (9-18-23)
Once as Corbitt upon the platting of the townsite in 1885, this town would later take on the name Bucklin in honor of the Township in Ford County where it had been established. Because of its location at the junction of two divisions of the Chicago, Rock Island & Pacific Railroad, Bucklin enjoyed fruitful beginnings and was once home to a grain elevator, post office, a flour mill, hotels, churches, schools, and banks. Its proximity to Dodge City has enabled it to maintain a relatively stable population since its incorporation as a municipality in 1909, as the population has ranged from 696 persons (1910 Census) to 917 people (1930 Census) over the past 110-plus years. Its most famous past resident is Eddie Sutton, a college basketball coach who, between 1966 and 2008, was the head coach of the College of Southern Idaho, Creighton, Arkansas, Kentucky, Oklahoma State, and San Francisco men's basketball programs. He is a member of the Basketball Hall of Fame.

# DODGE CITY, KS ★☆
## POPULATION: 27,788 – TOWN 447 OF 627 (8-17-23)
Dodge City's reputation precedes itself because of its distinction of being the rowdiest cowtown of the West in its heyday. "The Wickedest Little City in America" started as a series of forts constructed by locals or the government that were established to protect travelers along the Santa Fe Trail: Fort Mann 1847 to 1848, Fort Atkinson 1850 to 1853, and Fort Dodge 1865 to 1882. The townsite, the origins of which can be traced to the settlement of rancher Henry J. Sitler and his sod house near the Arkansas River, was established in 1872 and took its

name from the fort that was still in operation at that time. Because of its location along the Santa Fe Trail and the forthcoming of the Atchison, Topeka & Santa Fe Railroad, the idea came about to plat a townsite whose commerce would focus primarily on the buffalo trade and whatever industries the railroad brought with it. Thousands of buffalo hides were shipped out, forming the foundation for a strong economy. Then a spur of luck hit Dodge City when it was suddenly thrust into being the "King of Cowtowns" after the Kansas State Legislature forced the Texas cattle trade westward of a quarantine line and ended the cattle trade in Baxter Springs, Abilene, Newton, Ellsworth, and Wichita. Throughout the first fifteen-odd years of its existence, the city grew rapidly, but so did its reputation for being home to outlaws, gamblers, and those with little regard for human life or the law. On May 13, 1874, an ordinance was established that abolished the presence of any illicit firearms, knives, drunkards, or rebels with the promise that they would be fined up to $100 or imprisoned for up to three months for bad behavior. The ordinance did little to curb the town's rowdy atmosphere. As gunfighters, Mexican bullfighters, and saloons and brothels continued to operate undeterred, everything culminated in the "Dodge City War" of 1883 in which mayor Lawrence E. Deger banished Luke Short, then owner of the Long Branch Saloon, from continuing his operations in the city. On June 4, 1883, Deger issued an ordinance that effectively banned gambling within city limits, and after that, the rowdiest residents moved westward. Substantial peace unlike any Dodge City had experienced before overcame the townspeople, and they went to work to build up or improve city infrastructure. An alfalfa mill, an ice plant, machine shops, flour mills, elevators, an opera house, a public library and school, three banks, and a fire department were among the most notable early accomplishments. The modern-day "Cowboy Capital of the World" has capitalized on its historic past, with some of its most famous points of interest being The Boot Hill Museum and the city's original Boot Hill Cemetery, the Long Branch Saloon and its corresponding old-west show, the Kansas Cowboy Hall of Fame, Boot Hill Casino & Resort (the first state-owned casino in the United States), Dodge City Raceway Park, United Wireless Arena, the Kansas Teachers Hall of Fame and the Gunfighters Wax Museum, Dodge City Zoo, Dodge City Public Library, the Ford County Courthouse (as the city is the Ford County judicial seat), the Mueller-Schmidt House Museum, La Salsa Muffler Man, and ruts from the original Santa Fe Trail. At nearby Fort Dodge, the Kansas Soldiers' Home operates the nursing facility and two cemeteries and allows for tours of the 19th-century fort buildings. In 1935, Dodge City Community College was founded as the city's public school of higher learning, and from 1952 to 1993, it was also the site of St. Mary of the Plains College, a private four-year Catholic university. The famous Western drama series *Gunsmoke*, which first ran as a radio broadcast throughout the 1950s and was later adapted into a 20-season, 635-episode run from 1955 to 1975, is based in Dodge City. It is the source of the famous quotation, "Get the heck out of Dodge." As with any city of this size and stature, Dodge City has been home to a number of famous residents throughout its history. Amongst those people are Old West legends Doc Holliday, Big Nose Kate, Clay Allison, Nat Love, Wyatt Earp, and Bat Masterson, professional wrestler Sputnik Monroe, the 33rd Governor of Kansas Fred Hall, actor and director Dennis Hopper, the present Catholic Bishop of Green Bay, Wisconsin David L. Ricken, comedian Eddie Foy, 1932 Olympic gold-medalist in pole vault Bill Miller, and former NFL running back Robert Delpino.

**Restaurant Recommendation:**
**Casey's Cowtown Club**
**503 E Trail St**
**Dodge City, KS 67801**

**Restaurant Recommendation:**
**Bella Italia Ristorante**
**312 W Wyatt Earp Blvd**
**Dodge City, KS 67801**

# FORD, KS
**POPULATION: 203 – TOWN 474 OF 627 (9-18-23)**
The namesake of Ford comes from its location within Ford County, which was, in turn, named in honor of Colonel James Hobart Ford. He served in the Union Army as a colonel and a brevet brigadier general during the Civil War. The history of the community can be traced back to February of 1885 when the United States Postal Service established an office in the area. A townsite would soon follow, as would the Chicago, Rock Island & Pacific Railroad.

# SPEARVILLE, KS
**POPULATION: 791 – TOWN 448 OF 627 (8-17-23)**
Alden H. Speare of Boston, Massachusetts, was honored with having this newly founded community named on his behalf, as he was then

the director of the Atchison, Topeka & Santa Fe Railroad and the president of the Arkansas Valley Town Company. It was in 1873 that the town got its start on a section of the Santa Fe Trail, and the first resident was railroad foreman Jonas Stafford and his family. The postal service started servicing Spearville in June 1877. When George Hall, M. Wear, and a colony of settlers from Cincinnati, Ohio, arrived, the city's development was in full swing. Sheep farmers, flour mills, and grain elevators provided their products for shipment along the railroad, and banks, hotels, and all the typical lines of business and general merchandising stores were created to serve the needs of the settlers. After the Dalton Gang was foiled in Coffeyville, Kansas, a new group known as the "Bill Doolin Gang" took their place and plotted their second robbery around the Ford County Bank in Spearville. They made off with $1,697, equal to about $57,203 in 2024 dollars. Willie Cauley-Stein, an NBA player from 2015 to 2022, was born and raised in Spearville. Former NFL defensive end Rick Dvorak and Ignatius Jerome Strecker, the archbishop of the Archdiocese of Kansas City, Kansas, from 1969 to 1993, heed from here as well.

**Adjacent Counties:** Hodgeman (N), Edwards (NE), Kiowa (E), Clark (S), Meade (SW), Gray (W)

**Unincorporated/Ghost Towns:** Bellefont, Bloom, Fort Dodge, Howell, Kingsdown, South Dodge, Wilroads Gardens, Windhorst, Wright

## National Register of Historic Places:
**Dodge City:** Atchison, Topeka & Santa Fe Railway Depot, Burr House, Dodge City Downtown Historic District, Dodge City Municipal Building, Dodge City Public Library, Hennessy Hall, Saint Mary of the Plains Campus, Lora Locke Hotel, Mueller-Schmidt House, Sacred Heart Cathedral, Santa Fe Trail Ruts
**Ford:** Santa Fe Trail-Ford County Segment 2
**Windthorst:** Immaculate Heart of Mary Catholic Church

## Breweries/Wineries/Distilleries:
Boot Hill Distillery (Dodge City, KS)
Dodge City Brewing Company (Dodge City, KS)
The Doctors Office Bar (Dodge City, KS)

## Golf Courses:
Dodge City Country Club, Private (Dodge City, KS)

Mariah Hills, Public (Dodge City, KS)

**Town Celebrations:**
City of Windmills Festival, Spearville, KS (2nd Saturday in July)
Dodge City Days, Dodge City, KS (Late July to Early August)

# FRANKLIN COUNTY
## EST. 1855 - POPULATION: 25,996

One of the original 36 counties of Kansas, Franklin County was named for Founding Father Benjamin Franklin, one of the most influential and accomplished Americans of his time.

# LANE, KS
### POPULATION: 241 – TOWN 347 OF 627 (6-30-23)
This town of 241 residents in southeast Franklin County welcomed its first permanent settlers, the Sherman brothers (William, Peter, and Dutch), in the 1840s. Early pioneers used Dutch Henry's Crossing to pass over Pottawatomie Creek, so the postal service took notice and established an office there on March 21, 1855, under the name Shermanville. In 1863, the name was changed to Lane for James H. Lane, an early abolitionist and Kansas state Senator. The Missouri Pacific Railway would put down tracks through the area in 1879, and a small settlement called Avondale would be established. It later merged with Lane so that the two towns would no longer be in contest with one another. The character William Sherman would later be a victim of the Pottawatomie massacre (a violent event in the "Bleeding Kansas" period in which abolitionist John Brown and others would kill several proslavery individuals after the ransacking of Lawrence) because he and his brother had militant ties to proslavery forces.

# OTTAWA, KS ★☆
### POPULATION: 12,625 – TOWN 297 OF 627 (6-27-23)
The first settlers to Ottawa, Jotham Meeker and his wife, arrived in 1837 to live amongst the Ottawa Nation on the banks of the Marais des Cygnes River. It wouldn't be until nearly three decades later that the actions needed to formulate a townsite would be taken by C. C. Hutchinson, I. S. Kalloch, and James Wind, the chief of the Ottawa tribe, amongst others. Its name roughly translates in English to "men of the bulrushes." The first permanent home was constructed on March 31, 1864, by J. C. Richmond, and it was then that the town

truly began to expand as more settlers moved into the area and a sawmill, hotel, and post office were erected. By the end of the year, the newly founded city had been awarded the title of the county seat of Franklin County, and in 1867 it was incorporated. The Leavenworth, Lawrence & Galveston Railroad (later the Atchison, Topeka & Santa Fe) and the Missouri Pacific Railroad were instrumental in the early days of Ottawa's economy; they brought with them the workers and supplies needed to build grain elevators, flour mills, brick, tile, broom, condensed milk, soap and furniture factories, a creamery, and machine works. Significant locations of note around the city are the Plaza 1907 theater, the "oldest purpose-built cinema in operation in the world," Neosho County Community College, and Ottawa University, a private Baptist university established in 1865, not long after the founding of the city. The college was established by four Native Americans and two members of the local Baptist congregation, who had agreed to set aside 20,000 acres of land to build an institution of higher learning. Of historical note are the Old Depot Museum and its well-put-together exhibits on Ottawa history and the Dietrich Cabin in Ottawa City Park. Amongst Ottawa's famous residents of note from years past are Don Harrison (one of the first CNN anchors), Gary Hart (1984 and 1988 Presidential candidate), John G. Thompson (mathematician noted for his work on finite groups), Stanley Sheldon (guitar player known for work with Peter Frampton), Semi Ojeleye (professional basketball player and 2022 Italian Supercup MVP), and Steve Grogan (former NFL quarterback and the passing touchdowns leader in 1979).

 **Restaurant Recommendation:**
**Smoked Creations BBQ**
**222 E Logan St**
**Ottawa, KS 66067**

# POMONA, KS
**POPULATION: 884 – TOWN 278 OF 627 (6-11-23)**
Pomona, one of the medium-sized communities of Franklin County, was founded in 1869 on 320 acres of land in the Marais des Cygnes River valley. Its first permanent resident was A. Jones, and Reverend L. Rickseeker's general and drug store served as the first area post office when the service came to the area on May 5, 1870. It shares its distinctive name with the Roman goddess of fruit trees, gardens, and orchards. The Atchison, Topeka & Santa Railroad and Missouri Pacific Railroad aided the town's early businesses–ranging from the

Pomona House hotel to a lumber yard, furniture and extract factories, flour and feed mills, and hardware store–in having prosperous business and the distinction as an essential early area shipping and supply community. The nearby Pomona State Park was established in 1963 and has ample recreational opportunities.

# PRINCETON, KS
**POPULATION: 248 – TOWN 298 OF 627 (6-27-23)**

Princeton's name is an eponym for Princeton, Illinois, the town after which this one was named. It began in 1869 when the Leavenworth, Lawrence & Galveston Railroad was laying its tracks through Franklin County. The townsite was located not far from an older community called Ohio. A blacksmith and a wagon shop, hardware and general stores, and a post office would come about due to the railroad. The original tracks, initially the first north-south rail line in Kansas, have since been converted into the Prairie Spirit Trail State Park. Princeton is just one of several towns between Ottawa and Iola on the trail.

# RANTOUL, KS
**POPULATION: 165 – TOWN 348 OF 627 (6-30-23)**

Rantoul was incorporated in 1913, although the town's roots can be traced back to 1862 when a post office was established in September. For six years, between June 26, 1866, and March 20, 1872, the office was closed, although it has remained in operation since then. It was named for Robert Rantoul Jr., a Massachusetts Congressman. The Missouri Pacific Railroad would be the town's primary railroad and source of enterprise, bringing with it the people who built the first hardware store, lumber yard, general merchandise stores, schools, and churches. Visitors to this small town may be surprised to find Dodson International Parts, an aircraft salvage company responsible for dismantling several thousands of planes.

# RICHMOND, KS
**POPULATION: 459 – TOWN 299 OF 627 (6-27-23)**

John C. Richmond, an early pioneer farmer who donated 40 acres of his land for the Atchison, Topeka & Santa Fe Railroad to be built through the townsite, had this community named in honor of his generosity. The town was founded in 1870, with some of its earliest establishments being a broom factory, a blacksmith, lumber yards, a hotel, general stores, and churches and schools. The postal service established a branch of its office there on April 12, 1870. Richmond locals have banded together to formulate the Richmond Community Museum to hold onto notable community keepsakes.

# WELLSVILLE, KS
**POPULATION: 1,953 – TOWN 296 OF 627 (6-27-23)**

The city of 1,953 citizens was platted in 1870 and named in honor of D. L. Wells, an engineer of the Atchison, Topeka & Santa Fe Railroad. It was laid out by J. Emerson, P. P. Elder, and J. J. B. Shute, and it soon attracted stores, a hotel, and the attention of the postal service, who, in October of 1870, elected to build a post office there. W. Brockway was its first postmaster. Its earliest industry of note was the gas and oil distinct, which enabled it to maintain steady growth in both people and enterprise. A horrid train accident recalls when early MLB star Charlie Bennett slipped from a train platform as he was reboarding a passenger train, crushing his legs and immediately ending his baseball career. He was the MLB record holder for games at catcher, double plays, putouts, and fielding percentage for several years. Country music star Chely Wright, artist Elizabeth Layton, and the endeared Kansas City Chiefs broadcaster from 1963 to 2009, Bill Grigsby, each once called Wellsville their home. T.J. Bivins received national acclaim in 2005 for creating the "Slowest Moving Mechanical Object," an ultimate gear reduction machine that can complete only one turn every 3.8 billion years.

# WILLIAMSBURG, KS
**POPULATION: 390 – TOWN 308 OF 627 (6-28-23)**

What began as a part of a 30,000-acre piece of land bought from the Sac and Fox Native American tribe by W. B. McKenna would later be turned over to the Kansas Pacific Railroad Company. A townsite was platted in June 1868 when William H. Schofield, A. C. Henderson, Roger Hickok, and Albert Supernau were amongst the first to settle there and take advantage of the coal seams for an extended period. Several unique lines of business emerged with the arrival of the Atchison, Topeka & Santa Fe Railroad, ranging from cement and culvert pipe mold works, clayworks, silkworms, and stoneworks to a blacksmith and wagon shop and stores of all varieties. The post office went by Williamsburgh until the "h" was dropped in March 1894. Two former professional MLB players, James Willard Ramsdell and Lou McEvoy, heed from Williamsburg. Guy & Mae's Tavern is a local favorite and was named one of the "8 Wonders of Kansas" by the Kansas Sampler Foundation.

**Restaurant Recommendation:**
**Guy & Mae's Tavern**
**119 W William St**
**Williamsburg, KS 66095**

**Adjacent Counties:** Douglas (N), Johnson (NE), Miami (E), Linn (SE), Anderson (S), Coffey (SW), Osage (W)

**Unincorporated/Ghost Towns:** Centropolis, Homewood, Imes, LeLoup, Minneola, Norwood, Peoria, Ransomville, Richter, Silkville

**National Register of Historic Places:**
**Lane:** Judge James Hanway House
**Ottawa:** Dietrich Cabin, Downtown Ottawa Historic District, Eight Mile Creek Warren Truss Bridge, Franklin County Courthouse, Historic Ottawa Central Business District, Tauy Jones Hall, Tauy Jones House, Old Santa Fe Railroad Depot, Ottawa High School and Junior High School, Ottawa Library, James H. Ransom House, Lyman Reid House, Tauy Creek Bridge
**Overbrook:** Appanoose Church of the Brethren and Cemetery
**Princeton:** Middle Creek Tributary Bridge
**Wellsville:** Pleasant Valley School District #2, Walnut Creek Bridge, Wellsville Bank Building
**Williamsburg:** Silkville

**Breweries/Wineries/Distilleries:**
Not Lost Brewing Company (Ottawa, KS)
Pome on the Range Orchard & Winery (Williamsburg, KS)

**Golf Courses:**
Ottawa Country Club, Private (Ottawa, KS)
Silver Lake Golf Course, Public (Ottawa, KS)

**Town Celebrations:**
Ol' Marais River Run Car Show, Ottawa, KS (3rd Weekend of September)
Power of the Past Show, Ottawa, KS (2nd Weekend of September)
Wellsville Days, Wellsville, KS (Late September)

Ellis County Photos: Ellis, Ellis, Hays, Hays, Hays, Hays, Schoenchen, Victoria

172

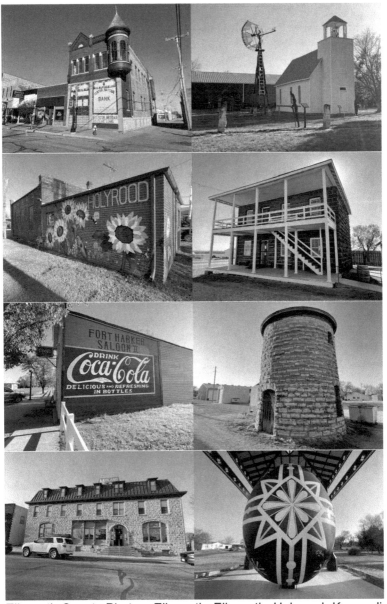

Ellsworth County Photos: Ellsworth, Ellsworth, Holyrood, Kanopolis, Kanopolis, Wilson, Wilson, Wilson

173

Finney County Photos: Garden City (all)

174

Ford County Photos: Bucklin, Dodge City, Dodge City, Dodge City, Dodge City, Dodge City, Dodge City, Dodge City

Franklin County Photos: Lane, Ottawa, Ottawa, Ottawa, Ottawa, Rantoul, Richmond, Wellsville

# GEARY COUNTY
## EST. 1855 - POPULATION: 36,739

Known for his roles as the 16th Governor of Pennsylvania, the 1st Mayor of San Francisco, and the 3rd Territorial Governor of Kansas, John W. Geary is the Geary County namesake.

# GRANDVIEW PLAZA, KS
## POPULATION: 1,697 – TOWN 190 OF 627 (4-30-23)

Grandview Plaza is a relatively new incorporated community, having only been founded in 1963. One of the town's earliest buildings was its school, a two-room school built in the area in 1956 that would eventually become the City of Grandview Plaza. New classrooms would later be added, two being Army barracks from Camp Phillips in Salina. The town's population has risen steadily, from 734 residents as of the 1970 Census to 1,697 persons as of 2020. An Atomic Cannon at nearby Freedom Park overlooks Grandview Plaza, Fort Riley, and the surrounding area.

# JUNCTION CITY, KS ★☆
## POPULATION: 22,932 – TOWN 189 OF 627 (4-30-23)

This large Kansas city owes its inception to Andrew J. Mead, a member of the Cincinnati-Manhattan Company. It was affiliated with the Free-Staters, the name given to pioneers during the "Bleeding Kansas" historical period that opposed the expansion of slavery throughout the United States. Mead and the Free Staters were looking to begin a community in the area and call it Manhattan (or New Cincinnati), but their plans took a turn when the first settlers could not reach the planned townsite due to low water levels. They would instead found the present-day community of Manhattan twenty miles east of this townsite, which would, in turn, go on to be called Millard City in honor of Captain Millard of the steamship Hartford, who had intended to bring the first settlers to the area. The name would change twice more to Humboldt in 1857 and then to Junction City because of the town's geographical location at the "junction" of the Republican River and the Smoky Hill River, which combined to make the Kansas River. Junction City would earn incorporation status in 1859, and it would ultimately be named the county seat of Geary County. The city is featured in author Sidney Sheldon's 1987 novel *Windmills of the Gods*, the 2001 musical film *Hedwig and the Angry Inch*, and film director Kevin Willmott's 1999 drama film *Ninth Street*.

Willmott was born here in 1959. Other individuals of note from Junction City are inventor Amanda Jones (noted for her vacuum canning method), the "Father of the Armored Force," Adna R. Chaffee Jr. (known for his role in developing the tank forces of the United States Army), playwright Velina Hasu Houston, and two-time WWE Champion Bobby Lashley. The Geary County Historical Society operates the local museum and also works to educate the community and preserve modern-day facets of Geary County's story. For recreational adventures, Geary State Fishing Lake and Wildlife Area is the area's go-to lake.

# MILFORD, KS
## POPULATION: 408 – TOWN 188 OF 627 (4-30-23)

The original name for this town, founded in 1855, was Bachelder. The postal service established an office here in 1861 and appointed Major Barry as its first postmaster. A lumber mill was the town's first significant business until the Union Pacific Railroad was extended to the townsite. The nearby Milford Lake and Milford State Park share the town's name and welcome numerous hunters throughout the year searching for mammals, fish, and fowl. The lake is the largest artificial lake in the state, at 33,000 acres. Henry D. Linscott of Milford served in both World Wars and is now buried in Arlington Cemetery. Another interesting person in the town's history was John R. Brinkley, a quack doctor famous for his "goat-gland" procedure as a means of curing human male impotence. Brinkley also began one of Kansas's first radio stations in 1923, KFKB, to promote his practice.

**Lodging Recommendation:**
**Acorns Resort**
**3710 Farnum Creek Rd**
**Milford, KS 66514**

**Adjacent Counties:** Riley (N), Wabaunsee (E), Morris (S), Dickinson (W), Clay (NW)

**Unincorporated/Ghost Towns:** Alida, Army City, Fort Riley, Pawnee, Wreford

**National Register of Historic Places:**
**Fort Riley:** First Territorial Capitol, Main Post Area, Fort Riley

**Junction City:** Bartell House, George T. Brown House, Conroe Bridge, Elliott Village Site, First Presbyterian Church of Junction City, Grand Army of the Republic (GAR) Memorial Arch, Jackson-McConnell House, Junction City Downtown Historic District, Leithoff-Powers Ranch Historic District, Old Junction City High School, Christian Wetzel Cabin
**Milford:** James Dixon House
**Wreford:** Lyon Creek Rainbow Arch, Old Katy Bridge

**Golf Courses:**
Custer Hill Golf Course, Military (Fort Riley, KS)
Junction City Country Club, Private (Junction City, KS)
Rolling Meadows Golf Course, Public (Junction City, KS)

**Town Celebrations:**
Freedom Fest, Junction City, KS (Independence Day Weekend)
Riley Fall Festival, Riley, KS (Early October)

# GOVE COUNTY
## EST. 1868 - POPULATION: 2,718

Gove County (est. 1868) was named for Grenville L. Gove, a Captain of the 11th Regiment Kansas Volunteer Calvary in the Civil War.

# GOVE CITY, KS ★
### POPULATION: 80 – TOWN 158 OF 627 (4-11-23)
Gove City, the tiny county seat of Gove County with only 80 residents as of the 2020 Census, began in 1885 and was given the title of county seat a year later because of its geographical location in the middle of the county. The town was unique in that the closest railroad station was located eleven miles north in Grainfield, which stunted its growth and only ever allowed it to attain a high population of 284 people (1940 Census). Grenville Gove of the 11th Kansas Cavalry Regiment, a regiment of soldiers who fought for the Union in the American Civil War, is the community's namesake.

# GRAINFIELD, KS ☆
### POPULATION: 322 – TOWN 157 OF 627 (4-11-23)
Grainfield, a community that reached a high population of 389 residents in the 1960s, was founded when the Union Pacific Railroad

was extended to that point. Mr. Beal of Abilene, Kansas, established Grainfield in 1879 after railroad officials sent him to erect a town in the area. Its name is a testament to the amber waves of grain (wheat) that surrounded the townsite. Grainfield was fortunate enough to have its first post office arrive in May of the year it was founded. Skip Yowell, the co-founder of JanSport and a pioneer of the backpack industry, is from Grainfield.

# GRINNELL, KS
**POPULATION: 260 – TOWN 159 OF 627 (4-11-23)**
Grinnell was named for Grinnell Township of Gove County, which was, in turn, named for Moses Hicks Grinnell, an early Kansas businessman. It began with the arrival of the Union Pacific Railroad to this region of the state in the late 1870s and early 1880s. The town's population reached a height of 449 individuals in the 1970s.

# PARK, KS
**POPULATION: 112 – TOWN 156 OF 627 (4-11-23)**
This small (and first) community of Gove County was founded in the late 1870s as Buffalo Park. It was named for the large number of American bison that used to roam the Great Plains, and the latter part of the name is a reference to British Medieval "park keepers." The Union Pacific Railroad utilized the name Buffalo Park until the postal service elected to shorten it to simply "Park" in 1898.

# QUINTER, KS
**POPULATION: 929 – TOWN 155 OF 627 (4-11-23)**
Quinter, Gove County's largest town by population, was started by the Familton Town Company in 1885 when they built a hotel and platted the townsite under that name. The railroad operated a switching site in the Melota area for a time, but the name was never widely considered for the townsite. The post office decided that the newly-founded community would be called Quinter, for the local Baptist minister Reverend James Quinter, to avoid confusion with other towns in the state with names similar to Familton. Castle Rock, a 70-foot-tall pillar of chalk located several miles south of Quinter, once served as an essential landmark on the Overland Trail. Waldo was the hometown of centenarian Waldo McBurney, famous for being the oldest worker (as a beekeeper) in the United States at 104 years old in 2006. Other notable town figures throughout history include Brent Barrett (musical actor), Robert Maxwell (Medal of Honor

recipient), Scott Huffman (one of the fastest pole vaulters in history and creator of "The Huffman Roll"), and Tracey Mann (the 50th lieutenant governor of Kansas).

Oakley is only partially located in Gove County (see Logan County).

**Adjacent Counties:** Sheridan (N), Graham (NE), Trego (E), Ness (SE), Lane (S), Scott (SW), Logan (W), Thomas (NW)

**Unincorporated/Ghost Towns:** Alanthus, Campus, Hackberry, Jerome, Monument Station, Orion

**National Register of Historic Places:**
**Gove:** Benson Culvert, Jenkins Culvert
**Grainfield:** Grainfield Opera House
**Oakley:** Beamer Barn
**Quinter:** Oxley Barn

**Breweries/Wineries/Distilleries:**
Center Pivot Restaurant and Brewery (Quinter, KS)

**Golf Courses:**
Grinnell Cow Paddy Golf Club, Semi-Private (Grinnell, KS)

**Town Celebrations:**
After Harvest Festival, Grinnell, KS (3rd Weekend of July)
Cruise, Shoes & BBQ's, Grainfield, KS (Memorial Day Weekend)
Old Settlers' Day, Gove, KS (2nd Weekend of August)

# GRAHAM COUNTY
## EST. 1867 - POPULATION: 2,415

Graham County commemorates the late John Graham, a Union captain who perished in the Battle of Chickamauga.

# BOGUE, KS
## POPULATION: 155 – TOWN 107 OF 627 (3-28-23)
Bogue was platted in 1888 by the Lincoln & Colorado Railroad Company and named in honor of its founder and the original owner of the townsite, Virgil Gay Bogue. An early variation of the town's name was Wild Horse, and another was Fagan, the original name for

the post office that was moved to town in September 1888. Located about five miles northeast of Bogue is the now unincorporated community of Nicodemus, home to the Nicodemus National Historic Site that commemorates the only remaining western town that a group of African Americans established during the Reconstruction Period that followed the aftermath of the American Civil War. The site has two churches and a schoolhouse, the St. Francis Hotel, and a Township Hall.

# HILL CITY, KS ★☆
## POPULATION: 1,403 – TOWN 108 OF 627 (3-28-23)
The oldest town in Graham County and its county seat, Hill City, welcomed its first settlers in 1876. W. R. Hill was amongst those early pioneers and was the town's founder, and so it was named in his honor. The Union Pacific Railroad was extended through the community at one point, which helped it to welcome its post office in 1878 and garner the title of county seat by 1880. Hill City made national headlines in the summer of 2012 when it recorded the hottest temperatures in the nation for four consecutive days (114°F, 111°F, 115°F, and 115°F between June 24 and June 27). The city's most notable historical resident was Charles V. Park, a noted librarian born in 1885. Keith Riley, an Industrial Arts teacher for the local high school, holds the Kansas state record for the most wins (764 as of March 2023) by an active coach in boys basketball. He has been the head coach for 54 years. The Graham County Museum, Oil Museum, and Auto & Art Museum are three visit-worthy places for history, car, and art enthusiasts.

# MORLAND, KS
## POPULATION: 115 – TOWN 184 OF 627 (4-13-23)
Morland was called Fremont (in honor of the military officer and politician John C. Fremont) from 1884 to 1888 when it was recognized that there was already another town in Kansas of the same name. The name Kalula was briefly adopted from 1888 to 1892 before it changed one final time to Morland in honor of a railroad employee. The city was incorporated in 1906. Cottonwood Ranch State Historic Site is a focal point of interest located a few short miles across the county line in Sheridan County.

**Adjacent Counties:** Norton (N), Phillips NE), Rooks (E), Ellis (SE), Trego (S), Gove (SW), Sheridan (W), Decatur (NW)

**Unincorporated/Ghost Towns:** Fargo, Happy, Houston, Kebar, Millbrook, Nicodemus, Olean, Penokee, Roscoe, St. Peter, Togo, Turnerville, Whitfield, Wild Horse

**National Register of Historic Places:**
**Morland:** Antelope Lake Park
**Nicodemus:** Nicodemus Historic District, Nicodemus National Historic Site
**Penokee:** Harry Keith Barn

**Golf Courses:**
Graham County Grass Greens, Public (Hill City, KS)

# GRANT COUNTY
## EST. 1888 - POPULATION: 7,352

Formed from lands that formerly made up Finney and Hamilton County, Grant County was named in honor of Ulysses S. Grant, the 18th President of the United States.

# ULYSSES, KS ★☆
### POPULATION: 5,788 – TOWN 481 OF 627 (9-19-23)

"Old Ulysses" was founded in June 1885 in the rough area where famous explorer and mountain man Jedediah Smith was killed by a band of Comanche Native Americans in 1831. It was named in honor of Ulysses S. Grant, the former U.S. President, and American Civil War hero. The town company did an excellent job in promoting the new townsite and attracting settlers, as its inhabitants were prompt to found a couple of newspapers, build the prominent Hotel Edwards and three others, as well as nearly a dozen restaurants and saloons as well as a bank, church, school, and an opera house. It was also named the county seat of Grant County by a direct order of the Kansas Supreme Court, despite a challenge from the nearby towns of Cincinnati and Appotomax (now defunct). As the railroads continued to sweep across the western portion of Kansas at the end of the 19th century, Ulysses fell behind as it did not have its own railway, and settlers left in droves to avoid economic hardships. The troubling times were primarily brought about because the Ulysses city council had bonded $36,000 to county citizens to buy an alleged 388 votes to ensure the victory of the judicial seat title. It wouldn't be until February of 1909 that all of the residents opted to move the town closer to the railroad because of the enormous debts. At the direction of the New Ulysses Town Company, they moved the buildings on sets of skids three miles to the new site. The decision to relocate along the Atchison, Topeka & Santa Fe Railroad saved the town from fading into nothingness, and it has grown substantially ever since (from 103 persons as of the 1920 Census, a year before it was incorporated, to 5,788 citizens today). Although it was never formally proposed to the legislature, Ulysses was briefly chosen as the capital of "West Kansas," resulting from a secessionist movement in 1992 that would have had nine counties secede from Kansas because of a school finance law that disadvantaged several area schools. The attendees of the convention, held on September 11, 1992, went as far as to select a state flower (the yucca) and a state bird (the pheasant). The Grant County Adobe Museum was built in 1938 to serve as a county shop, but forty years later, it was turned into a home for artifacts of the Santa Fe Trail, Native Americans, and other Ulysses history. Some noteworthy Ulysses residents have included Sheri L. Dew (CEO of the Deseret Book Company), Eugene C. Pulliam (founder of Central Newspapers, Inc. and a newspaper publisher), Sarah Noriega (Olympic volleyball player), Karen Dillon (filmmaker and the Executive Director of the Chandler Center for the Arts), and Gary Bender (sportscaster known for being the voice of the NBA's Phoenix Suns from 1993 to 2011).

 **Restaurant Recommendation:
Alejandro's
816 W Oklahoma Ave
Ulysses, KS 67880**

**Adjacent Counties:** Kearny (N), Finney (NE), Haskell (E), Stevens (S), Stanton (W), Hamilton (NW)

**Unincorporated/Ghost Towns:** Appotomax, Cincinnati, Hickok, Ryus, Stano, Sullivans Tracks, (Old) Ulysses

**National Register of Historic Places:**
**Ulysses:** Grant County Courthouse District, Lower Cimarron Spring, Santa Fe Trail-Grant County Segment 1

**Golf Courses:**
Bentwood Golf Course, Public (Ulysses, KS)

**Town Celebrations:**
Grant County Home Products Dinner, Ulysses, KS (3rd Tuesday of September)

# GRAY COUNTY
## EST. 1887 - POPULATION: 5,653

Alfred Gray, once the Kansas Secretary of Agriculture, was honored by having Gray County named for him upon its inception in 1887.

# CIMARRON, KS ★☆
## POPULATION: 1,981 – TOWN 446 OF 627 (8-17-23)

For many years, Cimarron was the only incorporated town of Gray County, as its inhabitants worked tirelessly to grow the city and ensure that it would retain the judicial seat from the nearby competing community of Ingalls. It was platted in April of 1878 as a station of the Atchison, Topeka & Santa Fe Railroad, although it wouldn't be until 1893 that it was awarded the permanent county seat title following a dispute involving Ben Daniels, Bat Masterson, Bill Tilghman, and other Old West figures (that were also associated with the nearby cowtown of Dodge City). Its name comes from its location on a fork of the Chisholm Trail along the Cimarron River. The primary economic purpose of Cimarron was to serve as a shipping point between Garden City to the west and Dodge City to the east. To fulfill that purpose, the townspeople erected banks, a grain elevator, a post office, a newspaper, churches of the leading Protestant denominations, and perhaps most notably, the now-historic three-story Second Empire-style Cimarron Hotel. It was built by Nicholas B. Klaine, newspaper editor of the *New West Echo* and the *Dodge City Times*, at a cost of $15,000. Bill Doolin and the "Wild Bunch" gang robbed a train here on June 10, 1893.

# COPELAND, KS
## POPULATION: 251 – TOWN 477 OF 627 (9-18-23)

In the grand scheme of towns in Kansas, Copeland is one of the relatively newer ones, having only been founded in 1912. Named for railroad official E. L. Copeland, its primary purpose was to act as a water station for the Atchison, Topeka & Santa Fe Railroad as it was being built through Gray County. The Copeland post office started on October 26, 1912, and in 1927, it had finally garnered enough residents to qualify for incorporation status. The population as of the

2020 Census was 251 residents, although it historically had as many as 423 persons living there at one point (1930 Census).

# ENSIGN, KS
## POPULATION: 166 – TOWN 475 OF 627 (9-18-23)
Lone Lake was the original name of this townsite when it was platted in 1886, although it would be renamed to Ensign two years later for its founder, G. L. Ensign. The town's development came late, as it took some time for the Atchison, Topeka & Santa Fe Railroad to extend their line to that point of Gray County, and it was not granted incorporation status until 1929. For many years, Ensign served the area as a post office, and the nearest railroad station was 12 miles north in Wettick (now a ghost town). Gray County Wind Farm was the largest wind farm in the state until 2023 when the Flat Ridge 2 farm in Harper, Barber, Kingman, and Sumner counties went into operation. The 35th Lieutenant Governor of Kansas, John Crutcher, heeds from Ensign.

# INGALLS, KS
## POPULATION: 252 – TOWN 445 OF 627 (8-17-23)
Once very briefly the Gray County Seat, Ingalls has always remained a small center of trade and commerce for the area. The population has ranged from a low of 173 inhabitants in 1950 to a high of 328 persons in 2000, and its official year of incorporation came in 1929. A post office under the name Soule operated here from May 1887 to May 1888 to serve the Atchison, Topeka & Santa Fe Railroad and the early settlers until the name was changed to Ingalls for John James Ingalls. He was a former United States Senator from Kansas and the President pro tempore from February 1887 to March 1891. The Santa Fe Trail Museum tells the tales of those who dared to traverse the historic cross-country trail.

# MONTEZUMA, KS
## POPULATION: 975 – TOWN 476 OF 627 (9-18-23)
The original townsite of Montezuma was established in 1879 near a natural water spring that, like many others of that era in the Midwest, was touted as having curative qualities. It was named after Moctezuma II, the ninth Emperor of the Aztec Empire. Throughout its first thirty-odd years of existence, Montezuma had the aspirations of becoming the judicial seat of Gray County, but without a railroad, it had no opportunity for growth. By 1910, the population had shrunk to

just 11 people, at which point talks came about to relocate the town a mile and a half away to the Atchison, Topeka & Santa Fe Railroad. The decision to move effectively saved Montezuma from becoming a ghost town. Since then, it has enjoyed consistent growth throughout the decades (except for a -19.8% growth rate between 1930 and 1940 due to the Great Depression). Montezuma's incorporation as a city of the third class came in 1917. The local grain elevator made national headlines when it experienced a severe explosion in 1989. The Stauth Memorial Museum has a notable focus on arts and crafts from around the planet.

 **Restaurant Recommendation:
Brianna's Cafe
203 N Aztec St
Montezuma, KS 67867**

**Adjacent Counties:** Finney (N), Hodgeman (N), Ford (E), Meade (S), Haskell (W)

**Unincorporated/Ghost Towns:** Charleston, Haggard, Wettick

**National Register of Historic Places:**
**Cimarron:** Cimarron City Jail, Cimarron Hotel, Old Gray County Courthouse
**Ingalls:** Welborn 'Doc' Barton House, Soule Canal-Gray County Segment 1, Soule Canal-Gray County Segment 2

Geary County Photos: Grandview Plaza, Junction City, Junction City, Junction City, Junction City, Junction City, Milford, Milford

Gove County Photos: Gove City, Grainfield, Grainfield, Grainfield, Grinnell, Grinnell, Park, Quinter

189

Graham County Photos: Bogue, Hill City, Hill City, Hill City, Hill City, Hill City, Hill City, Morland

Grant County Photos: Ulysses (all)

Gray County Photos: Cimarron, Cimarron, Copeland, Ensign, Ensign, Ingalls, Ingalls, Montezuma

# GREELEY COUNTY
## EST. 1873 - POPULATION: 1,284

The well-respected abolitionist and founder of the *New York Tribune*, Horace Greeley, is to thank for the name of the least populous county in Kansas.

# HORACE, KS
## POPULATION: 102 – TOWN 437 OF 627 (8-16-23)
Horace, the only section of Greeley County not considered a part of the city-county of this part of Kansas (see Tribune), was founded in 1886 by a town company affiliated with the Missouri Pacific Railroad. Like its neighbor to the east, its name also honors the legacy of Horace Greeley, the founder and editor of the *New York Tribune*. Its post office only remained in operation from February 10, 1886, to December 30, 1965, although it retained several lines of mercantile enterprise for several years. It was incorporated in 1887 and vied for many years to win the county seat.

# TRIBUNE, KS ★☆
## POPULATION: 772 – TOWN 438 OF 627 (8-16-23)
Tribune is unique in that it is the fifth-largest United States city by area (778.2 square miles) and the largest in the continental United States. This strange case came about on January 1, 2009, when the City of Tribune formally became a unified government with Greeley County. Therefore, by definition, the city-county is technically the "City of Tribune" as well as the whole of Greeley County (with the small 0.24 square mile exception of the City of Horace, which opposed the decision). Its history begins in 1886 with the arrival of the Missouri Pacific Railroad to the area, which brought with it the men and supplies to start a townsite and a railroad depot. The name was chosen by settlers inspired by Horace Greeley, the founder and editor of the *New York Tribune*, to "Go West, young man." Its status as the Greeley County seat would be stalled for a number of years by court cases, but it would eventually pull through and win the title. When the original Greeley County Courthouse was put out of commission in 1975 after nearly eighty-five years of service, it was refashioned into the Horace Greeley Museum.

**Adjacent Counties:** Wallace (N), Wichita (E), Hamilton (S)

193

**Unincorporated/Ghost Towns:** Astor, Colokan, Hector, Walkinghood, Whitelaw

**National Register of Historic Places:**
**Tribune:** Greeley County Courthouse

# GREENWOOD COUNTY
## EST. 1855 - POPULATION: 6,016

Greenwood County was named for Alfred B. Greenwood, one of several congressmen who fought for Kansas statehood.

# CLIMAX, KS
## POPULATION: 45 – TOWN 552 OF 627 (10-5-23)
This compact community covers just 0.12 square miles and was reported as only being home to 45 persons as of the 2020 Census. It was founded in 1884 and incorporated in 1923, with its principal businesses coming about as a result of the extension of a line of the Atchison, Topeka & Santa Fe Railroad to this point. The likely story of its etymology is that an early settler named it after Climax College in Kalamazoo, Michigan, although it could have also been named for its lofty elevation.

# EUREKA, KS ★☆
## POPULATION: 2,332 – TOWN 553 OF 627 (10-5-23)
"Eureka" literally translates to "I have found it" in Greek, which reflected the positive sentiment of the city's first settlers, who felt as if they had found a prairie paradise in 1857. The original townsite owners were David Tucker and Levi N. Prather, and later just Tucker, who sold off the entire townsite to a town company in 1867 for fifty dollars (the equivalent of a little over one thousand dollars in 2024). Edwin Tucker served as the town's primary postmaster once the postal service elected to establish an office here in 1858 and also as the first teacher and the second storekeeper. The area served little purpose until the conclusion of the American Civil War (although it did have Fort Montgomery to protect from Confederate advances and attacks), and soon, there were men of all the leading professions opting to establish their businesses there. It was incorporated in the 1870s, with Ira P. Nye winning the mayoral election and George H. Lillie being the first city clerk. It took over as the Greenwood County seat in the 1860s. It continued to grow into a thriving community with

the assistance of the Missouri Pacific and the Atchison, Topeka & Santa Fe Railroads. By 1912, it had multiple banks and hotels, a wagon and a broom factory, and flour mills and elevators. It was even the site of a horse racing track, Eureka Downs, that raced quarter horses from 1903 to 2011. An attempt at retaining a successful college institution was made by the community from 1946 to 1970 when Utopia College was in operation and granted certificates (somewhat equal to associate degrees) to students. A couple of tornadoes struck Eureka in July 2016 and June 2018, damaging 143 structures and another 175. The Greenwood County Historical Society Museum has managed to preserve many of the early stories and artifacts of Eureka despite the disasters. Eureka's most famous past residents are Donald L. Hollowell (an attorney famous for freeing Martin Luther King Jr. from prison), Jim Brothers (noted sculptor), Lamon V. Harkness (primary shareholder of Standard Oil until its breakup in 1911), Tyrel Reed (the winningest player in the history of the Kansas Jayhawks men's basketball program), John Woods (an executioner at the Nuremberg trials), John Erickson (the 8th Governor of Montana), Kathy Patrick (the founder of Pulpwood Queens Book Club), and Charles Errickson (a former head coach at Ottawa and Washburn Universities in football and basketball).

# FALL RIVER, KS
## POPULATION: 131 – TOWN 400 OF 627 (7-20-23)
Fall River is very purposefully named after its location on the river of the same name. Now home to about 131 people, it was first laid out in 1879 by the Fall River Town company. The members worked to construct the Fall River House, a home for Mr. J. M. Edminston, and the Romig Brothers general store before acquiring several other buildings from a nearby settlement called Charleston. The town would be incorporated in the same year it was established. Fall River State Park offers several trails for hiking enthusiasts, as well as opportunities for swimming, boating, water skiing, and camping. Johnny Butler, a Fall River native, played in the MLB in the 1920s.

# HAMILTON, KS
## POPULATION: 182 – TOWN 406 OF 627 (7-20-23)
Hamilton, Kansas, is one of many towns around the country bearing this name that looks to honor the first Secretary of the Treasury, Alexander Hamilton. It was founded in 1879 and served as a stop on the Atchison, Topeka & Santa Fe Railroad. The railroad was instrumental in bringing about the town's cement block machinery

factory, its largest industry of note in the town's pioneer days. Hamilton was incorporated in 1903.

# MADISON, KS
**POPULATION: 689 – TOWN 314 OF 627 (6-28-23)**

1872 was set as Madison's official founding year, as it was the start of the area's economy when five men by the names of Smith, Strails, Green, Oglesby, and Crinkle began to do business from their log cabins. When the Atchison, Topeka & Santa Fe Railroad was built in 1879, the townsite was moved to accommodate it. The new site was laid out by L. J. Cunkle, S. J. Wells, and W. Martindale. Eventually, the Missouri Pacific Railroad would join the A., T. & S.F. in taking advantage of the town's ice manufacturing plant, coal mines, and oil wells. The etymology of Madison is different in that it was named after Madison Township of Madison County. This now-defunct county existed only from 1855 to 1861 and was replaced by Greenwood and Breckenridge (now Lyon) Counties. Madison County was named in honor of James Madison, the 4th President of the United States.

# SEVERY, KS
**POPULATION: 205 – TOWN 399 OF 627 (7-20-23)**

Once known as Gould, this southernmost town in Greenwood County was platted with the anticipation of the arrival of the Atchison, Topeka & Santa Fe Railroad being built through the area in 1879. There had been a town called Severy founded by the Arkansas Valley Town company a few years before then to the south of the new site. A blacksmith, general store, livery stables, a hotel, and post office were amongst the first buildings to be erected before they were said to have been moved once or twice before finally ending up at the present-day townsite along the railroad. Luther Severy of Emporia, a railroad employee for the A, T & S.F., was the town's namesake, and the St. Louis & San Francisco Railroad was the other primary line that brought life to the community. An antique store near Severy attracts the attention of passersby with its enormous silo and needle protruding from a haystack at its top. Stanley Vestal, an author most known for his works *Sitting Bull, Champion of the Sioux*, and *Dodge City, Queen of the Cowtowns*, was born near Severy.

# VIRGIL, KS
## POPULATION: 48 – TOWN 405 OF 627 (7-20-23)

Virgil had a boom in population leading up to its record high number of residents in the 1930s (598 residents according to the Census) shortly following its incorporation as a city of the third class in 1922. The area post office was established on February 9, 1863, and named for the town of Virgil, New York (named for the Greek poet). Like many pioneer Kansas towns, Virgil once had schools and several churches of differing denominations, though the population has since shrunk considerably to only 48 people. The Greenwood Review and *The Virgil Leader* shared the town's news from 1887 to 1892 and 1894 to 1907, respectively.

**Adjacent Counties:** Lyon (N), Coffey (NE), Woodson (E), Wilson (SE), Elk (S), Butler (W), Chase (NW)

**Unincorporated/Ghost Towns:** Ivanpah, Lamont, Lapland, Piedmont, Quincy, Reece, Teterville, Thrall, Tonovay, Utopia

**National Register of Historic Places:**
**Eureka:** Eureka Atchison, Topeka & Santa Fe Railroad Depot, Eureka Carnegie Library, Eureka Downtown Historic District, Greenwood Cemetery and Mausoleum, Greenwood Hotel, Paul Jones Building, Robertson House, U.S. Post Office-Eureka, Westside Service Station and Riverside Motel
**Madison:** Madison Atchison, Topeka & Santa Fe Railroad Depot, Verdigris River Bridge
**Piedmont:** North Branch Otter Creek Bridge

**Golf Courses:**
Eureka Country Club, Private (Eureka, KS)
Madison Golf Course, Public (Madison, KS)

**Town Celebrations:**
Fall River BBQ, Fall River, KS (3rd Saturday in September)
Madison Days, Madison, KS (2nd Weekend of June)

# HAMILTON COUNTY
## EST. 1873 - POPULATION: 2,518

The man on the ten-dollar bill and the 1st United States Secretary of the Treasury, Alexander Hamilton, had this county named after him in 1873.

# COOLIDGE, KS
### POPULATION: 80 – TOWN 439 OF 627 (8-16-23)
Coolidge is a proud Hamilton County municipality, largely thanks to its small population of 80 residents and tightly-knit community. It was once a station on the Atchison, Topeka & Santa Fe Railroad, and its name honors its former president, Thomas Jefferson Coolidge. A hotel, newspaper, school building, and churches and stores once dotted its streets, and the postal service moved their office there in July 1881 from Sargent. Coolidge holds a small portion of pop culture fame in that it is mentioned by name in the 1983 road trip comedy movie *National Lampoon's Vacation*. The more widely acclaimed holiday movie, *Christmas Vacation*, is a sequel to the original film.

 **Restaurant Recommendation: Gracie's Cafe 204 Coolidge Ave Coolidge, KS 67836**

# SYRACUSE, KS ★☆
### POPULATION: 1,826 – TOWN 440 OF 627 (8-16-23)
Founded in 1873 and incorporated in 1887, Syracuse began as a railroad town on the Atchison, Topeka, and Santa Fe Railroad. Before 1873, it was known as Holliday in honor of Cyrus K. Holliday, the railroad's first president. Alternate names were also Holidayburg and Hollidaysburg. A name change was agreed upon when a party of settlers from Syracuse, New York, arrived on the scene and opted to name it after their former home. It was awarded the title of county seat in 1886 over the nearby community of Kendall (now defunct), and from there, it progressed rapidly and soon became host to a plethora of early lines of businesses: machine shops, four churches, banks, and flour mills, and even a Fred Harvey hotel (constructed for $75,000). On April 5, 1887, the town held a historic election in which it became the first and only town in the country to elect an all-woman

city council. Mrs. N. E. Wheeler was voted in as mayor, and the council members were Caroline Johnson Barber, Mrs. Charles Coe, Mrs. S. P. Nott, Mrs. G. C. Riggles, and Mrs. W. A. Swartwood. The Hamilton County Museum is responsible for telling the storied history of Syracuse.

**Adjacent Counties:** Greeley (N), Wichita (NE), Kearny (E), Stanton (S)

**Unincorporated/Ghost Towns:** Kendall, Trail City

**National Register of Historic Places:**
**Kendall:** Menno Community Hall
**Syracuse:** Fort Aubrey Site, Northrup Theater

**Golf Courses:**
Tamarisk Golf Course, Public (Syracuse, KS)

# HARPER COUNTY
## EST. 1867 - POPULATION: 5,485

The etymology of Harper County can be traced to Marion Harper, a man who served as a sergeant in the Union Army during the American Civil War.

# ANTHONY, KS ★
### POPULATION: 2,108 – TOWN 503 OF 627 (9-21-23)
Anthony was destined for greatness early on in its history, as it was located at the junction of several railroad lines in its heyday. The St. Louis-San Francisco and the Missouri Pacific Railroads had been completed through town in the 1890s, and two decades later came the Kansas City, Mexico, and Orient and the Kansas Southwestern Railroads (both later a part of the Atchison, Topeka & Santa Fe system), and the Chicago, Rock Island, and Pacific Railroad (formerly known as the Choctaw Northern Railroad). The townsite was platted before the arrival of any railroads in 1878 and named in honor of George T. Anthony, the 7th Governor of Kansas. He had the power to select the county seat, but the case of the Harper County seat was a strange one. In 1873, there had been a fraudulent organization of Harper County in which Bluff City claimed the judicial seat, but the matter was resolved in 1879 following the proper organization of

199

Harper County the prior year. Anthony won the title over Harper City, but the election was fraudulent as nearly 3,000 ballots had been cast in a county with only 800 citizens of legal voting status. Anthony retains its position as the Harper County seat to this day despite the outcries of the Harper residents at that time. The town would establish numerous businesses and industries, such as a glove factory, bottling works, and a salt plant that sent out 50,000 barrels of goods every year by the 1910s. When the Oklahoma land runs took place in the latter part of the 19th century, Anthony was amongst the other Kansas towns of the area that suffered huge lapses in population growth, as nearly half of its settlers emigrated south in search of free land and new opportunity. The Historical Museum of Anthony is located in the town's old Santa Fe Railroad depot that was built in 1928. Neal Patterson, the former CEO of Cerner Corporation (now a part of Oracle Corporation) and the owner of the Sporting Kansas City soccer franchise, grew up near Anthony.

 **Restaurant Recommendation: Irwin-Potter Drug 202 W Main St Anthony, KS 67003**

# ATTICA, KS
**POPULATION: 516 – TOWN 507 OF 627 (9-21-23)**
The name "Attica" refers to the historic region of Greece on the Attic Peninsula that is home to Athens. It was founded in the early 1880s as the eastern terminus of a line of the Atchison, Topeka & Santa Fe Railroad, a major player in the Kansas railroad industry at that time. Its designation as a terminus led to its quick incorporation as a city under Kansas law in 1885, as the population was thought to have been about 1,500 people. Much of the area that the town of Attica would be built upon was once a part of the Osage Land Trust, a swath of land held by the U.S. government that was sold on "behalf of the tribe" for $1.25 an acre. When the most significant land run in United States history began to take place in the Cherokee Strip (now part of present-day Oklahoma), hundreds of settlers headed south to take advantage of the opportunity for as much free soil as they could get their hands on.

# BLUFF CITY, KS
**POPULATION: 45 – TOWN 585 OF 627 (10-9-23)**
Bluff City (first platted under the name Bluff Creek) was the most crucial shipping point between Caldwell and Anthony for many years on the Kansas Southwestern Railway. Although only 45 people inhabit the townsite today, during its heyday in the 1910s, it boasted churches and schools, general stores carrying all the merchandise the townspeople could ever need, and a bank, newspaper office, and post office. It was founded in 1879 and incorporated in 1887.

# DANVILLE, KS
**POPULATION: 29 – TOWN 505 OF 627 (9-21-23)**
This small city has gone through some name changes throughout the years. The area was first called Odell, until Mrs. J. E. Cole laid out a townsite in 1880 and renamed it Coleville after herself. She was the first postmistress. As more settlers came to reside there, T. O. Moffet became the president of the town company, and they purchased the site from Mrs. Cole and changed the name to Danville for Danville, Ohio. The Atchison, Topeka & Santa Fe Railroad helped the town maintain a level of prosperity for many years, and the citizens built up a Presbyterian church founded a newspaper and established a mill, bank, and other lines of enterprise. After its incorporation in 1926 as a city of the third class, the population began to decline, and now only 29 people call Danville home (per the 2020 Census).

# HARPER, KS ☆
**POPULATION: 1,313 – TOWN 506 OF 627 (9-21-23)**
A colony of Iowans arrived in the area in April of 1877 and started a town they named in honor of Sergeant Marion Harper of the 2nd Kansas Cavalry, the same namesake of the county. J. B. Glenn was then the president of the town company and the first man to erect a building on the land. Cora City was the name of the post office for a very brief three-and-a-half-week period from May to June of 1877 before it was changed to Harper. The home of the Bearcats has always been a bustling city, with a high population of 1,899 residents in the 1960s. In its early days, it was a station on the Kansas City, Mexico & Orient, and the Atchison, Topeka & Santa Fe Railroads. It possessed everything from an opera house and seven churches to a flour mill, foundry, machine shops, a creamery, and an impressive economy of agricultural and animal products. The first mayor was Sam S. Sisson, when incorporation status was reached in September

1880. Harper was the subject of an episode of the NBC sitcom *Veronica's Closet*, in which one of the characters returned home for a town celebration.

# WALDRON, KS
## POPULATION: 9 – TOWN 502 OF 627 (9-21-23)

This itty-bitty community on the Kansas-Oklahoma border was home to only nine people as of the 2020 Census. Founded in 1900, Waldron was once a bustling railroad town complete with its one weekly newspaper, bank, and post office, and it was even located at a junction of the Choctaw Northern Railroad and the Kansas, Mexico, and Orient Railroad. When the lines were abandoned, residents began to leave the town in droves, and by 1970, the population had already dropped to 24 people. Roe Messner was born in Waldron on August 1, 1935, and later founded Messner Construction. He is responsible for constructing over 1,800 churches across all 50 states. He eventually married 1980s Hollywood celebrity Tammy Faye Bakker, who was buried at the local cemetery.

**Adjacent Counties:** Kingman (N), Sumner (E), Barber (W)

**Unincorporated/Ghost Towns:** Albion, Corwin, Crisfield, Crystal Springs, Duquoin, Freeport, Midway, Ruella, Runnymede, Shook, Yankton

**National Register of Historic Places:**
**Anthony:** Anthony Public Carnegie Library, Anthony Theater, First Congregational Church, Harper County Courthouse, U.S. Post Office-Anthony
**Harper:** I. P. Campbell Building, Harper Standpipe, Old Runnymede Church

**Golf Courses:**
Anthony Golf Course, Public (Anthony, KS)

**Town Celebrations:**
Attica Saddle Club Rodeo, Attica, KS (Late July or Early August)
Sunflower Balloon Fest, Anthony, KS (May)

# HARVEY COUNTY
## EST. 1872 - POPULATION: 34,024

When Harvey County was formed in 1872 from McPherson, Sedgwick, and Reno Counties, it was decided that its name would honor James M. Harvey, the fifth governor of Kansas.

# BURRTON, KS
**POPULATION: 861 – TOWN 604 OF 627 (10-11-23)**

Not so named because there were a "ton" of burr oak trees at the townsite, but rather for railroad official Isaac T. Burr, Burrton's beginnings as a community date to September 6, 1873. Mr. Burr was then one of the vice presidents of the Atchison, Topeka & Santa Fe Railroad, which laid out the town for its use for transporting goods across Kansas. The St. Louis & San Francisco Railroad joined in on the action later on, which capitulated the city into becoming a regional shipping center for agricultural products. Despite its population never crossing the one-thousand-person threshold, early residents were impressive in bringing about an opera house, well-stocked stores, numerous churches, banks, and newspapers, alongside other feats. Actor Hugh Milburn Stone, perhaps better known as "Doc" from the classic old Western drama *Gunsmoke*, was born here in July 1904.

# HALSTEAD, KS
**POPULATION: 2,179 – TOWN 603 OF 627 (10-11-23)**

Halstead is rooted in German history, as it was they who settled the area in 1872 and brought about the establishment of the townsite under the supervision of John Sebastian of the Atchison, Topeka & Santa Fe Railroad and town company president H. D. Alrbright. Halstead's name was selected to honor Murat Halstead, a well-known Civil War correspondent from Ohio. As the post office moved into the area circa 1873, so did a school, a newspaper, and all the other necessary institutions needed to warrant a bid for incorporation. They succeeded in doing so in 1877, and H. H. McAdams presided as the first mayor of Halstead. Industries only continued to expand with time as larger companies moved in, and eventually, Doctor Arthur Emanuel Hertzler founded the Halstead Hospital. Hertzler was known as the "horse and buggy doctor" for his excellent lectures and teaching ability. The Halstead Heritage Museum and Depot chronicles area history and contains artifacts from two movies filmed in the community: *Picnic* (1955) and *The Parade* (1984). Another site

203

of interest, the Kansas Learning Center or Health, has state-of-the-art displays on the human body for tourists to admire. Valeda III, the "talking transparent woman," is the most famous exhibit of the Center because of the sheer accuracy and inside look at the human body she gives. The winner of the first-ever NASCAR stock car race in 1949, Jim Roper, was from Halstead, as was Adolph Rupp, a 5x NCAA National Coach of the Year recipient and 4x Division 1 men's basketball champion.

# HESSTON, KS
## POPULATION: 3,505 – TOWN 601 OF 627 (10-10-23)
The Elivon post office began in February 1873 in McPherson County, but by April 1878, it had been moved to the neighboring Harvey County. For nearly a decade, it retained that name until it was changed to Hesston (in December 1887) to match the name the railroad gave to the newly established townsite. The site had been platted in 1886 by the Missouri Pacific Railway on the land of the Hess brothers, thus the origin of the name. While churches, schools, and businesses were constructed as expected, Hesston College was founded in 1909 by the Mennonites to serve the higher education needs of the area. It is known for its thirteen-acre botanical garden, Dyck Arboretum of the Plains, and its six-hundred-plus species of native plants. Not long after the college was founded, Lyle Yost was born in 1913. He would go on to invent the unloading auger and found Hesston Manufacturing, now a part of AGCO Corporation (an agricultural machinery manufacturer). Katie Sowers, the first openly LGBTQ+ coach in NFL history, grew up in Hesston.

# NEWTON, KS ★☆
## POPULATION: 18,602 – TOWN 600 OF 627 (10-10-23)
Newton held an important role in Kansas history from the get-go, as it was established as the western terminal for the Atchison, Topeka & Santa Fe Railroad, the most influential railroad in Kansas, and located at the railhead of the Chisholm Trail. The city's first building was moved here in the spring of 1870, but its prosperity didn't begin until the competition of the A, T & S. F. to that point. Several wealthy men who had grown up in Newton, Massachusetts, found it appropriate to name the town after their old stomping grounds, and the post office opted to adopt the name as well. W. A. Russell was the first postmaster. Residents of early Newton experienced all of the effects of the cattle trade, both positive and negative, through 1875. While the town was incredibly wealthy and growing at a fast pace, it

became known as the "wickedest city in the west" for a short while following the Gunfight at Hide Park, where eight men died on August 19, 1871. As the cattle trade moved westward towards Dodge City, so too did the violence, and at last, Newton could grow in peace. It was incorporated as a city of the third class in 1872, and within a few decades, it had attracted the Missouri Pacific Railroad and several manufacturing businesses. Factories made wagons, brooms, grain drills, threshing machines, cornices, and carriages, and other industries such as poultry packing plants, a creamery, an ice plant, a nursery, an alfalfa mill, and three individual grain elevators and flour mills were developed. By 1912, there were seventeen church congregations, a hospital and a library, enormous school systems, a courthouse (to fulfill its duties as the Harvey County seat), and two colleges: Bethel College (now in North Newton) and the Evangelical Lutheran College. While neither of these institutions operates in Newton any longer, there has been a satellite campus of Hutchinson Community College for many years. Noteworthy area attractions include the Harvey County Historical Society Library and Museum, Carriage Factory Art Gallery, the Warkentin House, Sand Creek Station Golf Course, and the World's Tallest Mennonite at Athletic Park. The sculpture was a WPA project completed in 1941 to honor local Mennonite heritage. Newton has raised some famous individuals throughout its time: Harold E. Foster (former head coach and member of the Naismith Basketball Hall of Fame, Class of 1964), Jacob A. Schowalter (the founder of the Schowalter Foundation), Jesse M. Unruh (the 26th Treasurer of California), Reed Crandall (famous comic book illustrator known for the 1940s Quality Comics' *Blackhawk* issues), Donna Atwood (figure skater), Elizabeth P. Hoisington (one of the first women to become a brigadier general in the U.S. Armed Forces), Tony Clark (the Executive Director of the Major League Baseball Players Association), Dallas Wiebe (author), Tom Adair (screenwriter), Miles Johns (UFC fighter), John M. Janzen (anthropologist known for his work in Africa), and Errett Bishop (mathematician who proved several real analysis theorems).

 **Restaurant Recommendation:**
**Genova Italian Restaurant**
**1021 Washington Rd**
**Newton, KS 67114**

# NORTH NEWTON, KS

**POPULATION: 1,814 – TOWN 599 OF 627 (10-10-23)**

The community of North Newton primarily revolves around the presence of Bethel College, the oldest Mennonite college in the United States. It was founded in 1887 after a group of men from Newton and another from the Kansas Conference of Mennonites agreed that it would be mutually beneficial to establish a college to help attract prospective students to the area. The local office of the postal service went by the Bethel College namesake from December 19, 1934, to December 1, 1938, until it was changed to North Newton because of the community's location directly north of its Harvey County seat counterpart. The Luyken Fine Arts Center is renowned for its Robert W. Regier Gallery, focusing on the art of alums and artists from the international sphere. Kate E. Brubacher, the official United States attorney for the District of Kansas since March 2023, and Rachel deBenedet, known for her theater performances in *Catch Me If You Can*, are North Newton's two most notable residents.

# SEDGWICK, KS

**POPULATION: 1,603 – TOWN 615 OF 627 (10-12-23)**

Contrary to what many would expect, the City of Sedgwick is predominantly located in Harvey County, even though a small portion of the town extends southward into Sedgwick County. It was initially laid out in June 1870 under the direction of T. S. Floyd and Sedgwick County on an 80-acre parcel of land and named in honor of John Sedgwick, a major general for the Union Army during the American Civil War. Floyd assumed the duties of postmaster when the post office arrived, and William H. Owen was credited with placing the first store into business. It continued to grow with its banks, newspaper office, drug, implement, and general stores, amongst other commercial lines, until it was incorporated in 1872. Keeping pace with his title as a man of authority, Floyd won the first mayoral election. The surgeon responsible for creating the Department of Neurological Surgery at Northwestern University School of Medicine was born in 1874. Sports figures Briar Moorman, a 2x NFL Pro Bowl punter and a member of the NFL 2000s All-Decade Team, and Harold Manning, the American record holder for the 3,000-meter steeplechase from 1934 to 1952, both attended Sedgwick High School at different points in its history.

**Restaurant Recommendation:**
**Cy's Hoof and Horn**
**425 N Commercial Ave**
**Sedgwick, KS 67135**

# WALTON, KS

## POPULATION: 219 – TOWN 598 OF 627 (10-10-23)

This town of 219 citizens in northeastern Harvey County began with the Atchison, Topeka & Santa Fe Railroad in 1871. The railroad arrived in July, but it wouldn't be until December that William Mathews settled there and laid out a townsite. He and the Santa Fe named it in honor of a railroad shareholder. Not many people moved there until 1876 when J. F. Watson took over the lands, and from thereon, the town grew to encompass stores (the first of which was managed by B. C. Johnson), a schoolhouse, and a post office. The postal service arrived in December 1871, before the rest of Walton's development.

**Adjacent Counties:** Marion (NE), Butler (E), Sedgwick (S), Reno (W), McPherson (NW)

**Unincorporated/Ghost Towns:** Annelly, McLain, Patterson, Putnam, Van Arsdale, Zimmerdale

**National Register of Historic Places:**
**Halstead:** Bergtholdt House, Halstead Santa Fe Depot, U.S. Post Office-Halstead, Bernhard Warkentin Homestead
**Newton:** Samuel A. Brown House, Carnegie Library, Coleman House, E. H. Hoag House, J. J. Krehbiel and Company Carriage Factory, Lincoln School, McKinley Residential Historic District, Mennonite Settler Statue, Jairus Nel House, Newton Main Street Historic District I, Newton Main Street Historic District II, Newton Stadium, Old Railroad Savings and Loan Building, Santa Fe Depot, Warkentin House, Warkentin Mill
**North Newton:** David Goerz House, Wirkler-Krehbiel House
**Sedgwick:** Sedgwick Downtown Historic District

**Breweries/Wineries/Distilleries:**
Equus Beds at McGinn Farms (Sedgwick, KS)

207

## Golf Courses:
Fox Ridge, Semi-Private (Newton, KS)
Hesston Municipal Golf Park, Public (Hesston, KS)
Newton Public Golf Course & Driving Range, Public (Newton, KS)
Sand Creek Station Golf Club, Public (Newton, KS)
Wedgewood Golf Course, Public (Halstead, KS)

## Town Celebrations:
Old Settlers Festival, Halstead, KS (2nd Saturday in August)
Taste of Newton, Newton, KS (Late September or Early October)

Greeley County Photos: Horace, Horace, Tribune, Tribune, Tribune, Tribune, Tribune, Tribune

209

Greenwood County Photos: Climax, Eureka, Eureka, Eureka, Eureka, Eureka, Hamilton, Severy

Hamilton County Photos: Coolidge, Coolidge, Coolidge, Coolidge, Syracuse, Syracuse, Syracuse, Syracuse

Harper County Photos: Anthony, Anthony, Anthony, Anthony, Anthony, Danville, Harper

Harvey County Photos: Halstead, Hesston, Newton, Newton, Newton, Newton, Newton, Walton

213

# HASKELL COUNTY
## EST. 1887 - POPULATION: 3,780

Haskell County's name comes from Dudley C. Haskell, the same Congressman who helped establish Haskell Indian Nations University in Lawrence, Kansas.

## SATANTA, KS
### POPULATION: 1,092 – TOWN 479 OF 627 (9-19-23)

Satanta, Kansas, was founded along the line of the Atchison, Topeka & Santa Fe Railroad in 1912 with the purpose of being a refueling and water station. On October 11th of that same year, the United States Postal Service started an office there and thus began the foundations for a new Kansas community. The unique name "Satanta" was selected by early townspeople to honor a Kiowa Native American chief, one of the most remarkable men in the tribe's history because of his fierce fighting abilities and eloquence. An annual celebration called "Satanta Day" is held every year to commemorate the heritage of the local tribes. Incorporation came in 1929, and from thereon, the city continued to grow and serve as a minor trading hub of southwest Kansas. Gary Spani, a former linebacker for the Kansas City Chiefs and the 1983 NFL Man of the Year, was born here in 1956.

 **Restaurant Recommendation:**
**Triple J's**
**111 Sequoyah St**
**Satanta, KS 67870**

## SUBLETTE, KS ★☆
### POPULATION: 1,413 – TOWN 478 OF 627 (9-19-23)

Sublette is home to 1,413 people and presently serves as the county seat of Haskell County. The town was founded with the arrival of the Atchison, Topeka & Santa Fe Railroad circa 1912 and named for William Lewis Sublette, a "mountain man" affiliated with the Rocky Mountain Fur Company. The locals called him "Cut Face" because of a profound scratch on his face, presumably from one of his encounters with area wildlife. By January 1913, a post office was established, and the earliest settlers went to work on the construction of a grain elevator, general and drug stores, and other necessary structures for the well-being of the town. Sublette would be incorporated in 1923. A century later, the Haskell County Museum is still working to uncover artifacts and tales from the bygone days of the county. Four notable individuals from the town's history are Jack Christiansen, a 3x NFL champion, 5x Pro-Bowler, and a member of the Pro Football Hall of Fame, Otto Schnellbacher, a 2x Pro-Bowler with the New York Giants in the 1950s, and one of the first-ever NBA players (then the BAA in 1948-49), Shalee Lehning, a former WNBA player, and Ted Trimpa, the founder of the Trimpa Group, a consulting firm noted for working on strategy for the Democratic party.

 **Restaurant Recommendation:**
**Cattleman's Cafe**
**110 S Inman St**
**Sublette, KS 67877**

**Adjacent Counties:** Finney (N), Gray (E), Meade (SE), Seward (S), Stevens (SW), Grant (W), Kearny (NW)

**Unincorporated/Ghost Towns:** Santa Fe, Tice

**Golf Courses:**
Cimarron Valley Golf Club, Public (Satanta, KS)

**Town Celebrations:**
Satanta Day, Satanta, KS (2nd Saturday in May)

# HODGEMAN COUNTY
## EST. 1867 - POPULATION: 1,723

Hodgeman County, Kansas, embraced the name of Amos Hodgman, who served in the 7th Regiment Kansas Volunteer Calvary for the Union forces.

# HANSTON, KS
## POPULATION: 259 – TOWN 425 OF 627 (8-15-23)
From 1878 to 1902, this community was known as "Marena" until it took its present name in honor of the Hann family. It served as a station of the Atchison, Topeka & Santa Fe Railroad, which referred to it as Olney for some time. Two churches of the Catholic and Methodist denominations, public schools, a post office, and a bank

and stores once lined the streets of Hanston circa 1912. The population has varied only slightly since it was incorporated in 1929, from a low of 206 residents per the 2010 Census to a peak of 326 citizens in the 1990 Census.

# JETMORE, KS ★☆
**POPULATION: 770 – TOWN 426 OF 627 (8-15-23)**
During its first year of existence in 1879, the town of Buckner began to build its population and industries and was awarded the title of the judicial seat of Hodgeman County. In the spring of the following year, the name was changed to Jetmore for Colonel A. B. Jetmore, a lawyer from Topeka who was instrumental in bringing county seat status and the Atchison, Topeka & Santa Fe Railroad to the community. Following the railroad's arrival and a formal vote to incorporate as a municipality in 1887, Jetmore grew to encompass schools, businesses of all varieties, and three denominations of churches around the turn of the 20th century. Despite its relative isolation from most communities, Jetmore cracked the 1,000-citizen threshold briefly in the 1960s. Judy's Cafe is a world-famous food joint that attracts thousands of visitors every year, and the Haun Museum welcomes history lovers to explore Jetmore's history.

 **Restaurant Recommendation:
Judy's Cafe
303 Main St
Jetmore, KS 67854**

**Lodging Recommendation:
Yurts at HorseThief Reservoir
19005 SW KS-156
Jetmore, KS 67854**

**Adjacent Counties:** Ness (N), Pawnee (E), Edwards (SE), Ford (S), Gray (SW), Finney (W)

**Unincorporated/Ghost Towns:** Beersheba

**National Register of Historic Places:**
**Jetmore:** Hackberry Creek Bridge, T. S. Haun House, Hodgeman County Courthouse

216

**Kinsley:** St. Mary's Catholic Church

**Golf Courses:**
Cheyenne Hills Municipal Golf Course, Private (Jetmore, KS)

# JACKSON COUNTY
## EST. 1855 - POPULATION: 13,232

Jackson County is one of a handful of Kansas counties to honor the name of a former U.S. President, in their case, the 7th President of the United States, Andrew Jackson.

# CIRCLEVILLE, KS
## POPULATION: 153 – TOWN 68 OF 627 (3-14-23)
There are a couple of accounts as to how Circleville received its name. The first is that during its early settlement days, it "circled around the prairie." The other is that it took its name from Circleville, Ohio. The town was founded in 1863 by Major Thomas J. Anderson and was located on the Missouri Pacific and the Union Pacific Railroads.

# DELIA, KS
## POPULATION: 151 – TOWN 250 OF 627 (6-8-23)
Named for Mrs. Delia Cunningham, this community began as a siding for the Union Pacific Railroad in 1905. The name was given by the town's founder, David Cunningham, to honor his mother. The postal service established the Delia post office on January 12, 1906, and by 1918, it was formally incorporated. One notable town figure in recent memory was David Bawden, a sedevacantist claimant to the papacy opposed to Popes John Paul I, Benedict XVI, and Francis. He was elected pope by his parents and three other laypeople in July 1990.

# DENISON, KS
## POPULATION: 146 – TOWN 65 OF 627 (3-14-23)
The town of Denison was started by the Kansas City, Wyandotte, and Northwestern Railroad as a connection point between Valley Falls and Holton, Kansas. It was founded by A. D. and Hollis Tucker and named for Tucker's hometown of Denison, Ohio. A village called Tippinville was once located in the area as well, but Denison would ultimately annex all of its homes and churches. William F. "Buffalo

Bill" Cody's sister, Eliza Cody Myers, lived here and was frequently visited by the showman. Multiple Civil War veterans are buried in the Denison Cemetery.

# HOLTON, KS ★☆

**POPULATION: 3,401 – TOWN 67 OF 627 (3-14-23)**

The county seat of Jackson County, Holton, was founded by a wagon train of settlers from Milwaukee, Wisconsin, who had been sent out by the Kansas Society of Milwaukee and abolitionist Edward Dwight Holton. The town was formed in 1856 at the confluence of Elk Creek and Banner Creek and was named in his honor. The Battle of the Spurs took place north of Holton on January 31, 1859, when U.S. marshals stopped abolitionist leader John Brown while leading a group of 11 escaped enslaved people from Missouri to Iowa. Brown, undeterred by their presence, proceeded forward and caused the posse to run in panic because they feared him. No shots were fired, but the confrontation is today labeled as such as a reference to the flight of the proslavery posse. There was once a university in town called Campbell University (later Campbell College after its merger with Lane University, and later still as Kansas City University) that opened in 1880, but it shut its doors in 1933. Some of Holton's famous residents have included Kendall McComas (child actor), Lynn Jenkins (Vice Chair of the House Republican Conference from 2013 to 2017), and Robin Utterback (contemporary artist). Of particular historic note are the Roebke Memorial Museum, an 1876 era-correct house, and the Jackson County Historical Society Museum.

**Restaurant Recommendation:
Trails Cafe
601 Arizona Ave
Holton, KS 66436**

**Lodging Recommendation:
Hotel Josephine
501 Ohio Ave
Holton, KS 66436**

# HOYT, KS
## POPULATION: 593 – TOWN 293 OF 627 (6-12-23)
George Henry Hoyt, the 6th Attorney General of Kansas and the attorney of abolitionist leader John Brown is the namesake of this town of 593 residents. It was founded in 1886 by a town company consisting of I. T. Price, A. D. Walker, and other men from Holton along the Chicago, Rock Island & Pacific Railroad, and for years it served as a notable area stock and hay market. Joseph Burns opened the first general store.

# MAYETTA, KS
## POPULATION: 348 – TOWN 66 OF 627 (3-14-23)
The etymology of Mayetta honors Mary Henrietta Lunger, a young daughter of the town's founder who passed away at an early age. The community was platted in 1886 by Mrs. E. E. Lunger, who donated land to the Rock Island Railroad to build their line through the area on the condition that she be allowed to name the town. The leader of the Potawatomi Nation, who successfully stopped the termination of her tribe, Minnie Evans, was born in Mayetta. Noted baseball historian Bill James, known for his two-dozen-plus books on baseball history and statistics, also has ties to the community. Mayetta was featured on a 2011 episode of *The Late Show with David Letterman* in which Biff Henderson interviewed town locals as a skit.

# NETAWAKA, KS
## POPULATION: 139 – TOWN 53 OF 627 (3-13-23)
"Netawaka" was derived from a Pottawatami Native American word meaning "grand view." This town was founded in 1866 and was once a part of the Missouri Pacific Railroad. Its first post office was established on January 20, 1868.

# SOLDIER, KS
## POPULATION: 102 – TOWN 69 OF 627 (3-14-23)
The first settlers of Soldier arrived in 1877, the same year that the town was laid out by then President of the Kansas Central Town Company and Paul Havens. In 1896, the city was incorporated. Its name was taken from the nearby creek of the same nomenclature.

**Lodging Recommendation:**
**The Red Rock Guest Ranch**
**4340 270th Rd**
**Soldier, KS 66540**

# WHITING, KS

**POPULATION: 191 – TOWN 54 OF 627 (3-13-23)**
This community, founded in 1866, was named in honor of Martha S. Whiting, the second wife of Samuel C. Pomeroy. Pomeroy served as a United States Senator from Kansas from April 1861 to March 1873. It was located on the Missouri Pacific and Rock Island Railroads. Anna Estelle Arnold, the author of the textbook *A History of Kansas* (published in 1914), was born here in 1879.

**Adjacent Counties:** Brown (NE), Atchison (E), Jefferson (SE), Shawnee (S), Pottawatomie (W), Nemaha (NW)

**Unincorporated/Ghost Towns:** Birmingham, Larkinburg

**National Register of Historic Places:**
**Delia:** Delia State Bank
**Holton:** Holton Bath House, McFadden House, State Bank of Holton

**Golf Courses:**
Firekeeper Golf Course, Resort (Mayetta, KS)
Holton Country Club, Semi-Private (Holton, KS)

**Town Celebrations:**
Delia Days, Delia, KS (2nd Weekend of September)
Glory Days Festival and Car Show, Holton, KS (4th Weekend of May)
Holton Fall Fest, Holton, KS (2nd Saturday of October)
Pioneer Days, Mayetta, KS (Mid-September or October)
Pride of Hoyt Days, Hoyt, KS (3rd Weekend of August)

# JEFFERSON COUNTY
## EST. 1855 - POPULATION: 18,368

Formulated in 1855 as one of the original counties in Kansas, this state division has a name that seeks to honor Thomas Jefferson, the third President of the United States.

# MCLOUTH, KS
### POPULATION: 859 – TOWN 287 OF 627 (6-12-23)

McLouth was named after its founder and the original owner of the townsite, Amos McLouth. It was established and incorporated in the 1880s, during which a post office was formed (May 26, 1882), as were flour mills, banks, creameries, grain elevators, and a grange store. The Leavenworth & Topeka branch of the Atchison, Topeka & Santa Fe Railroad, and the Missouri Pacific Railroad served the early residents of the community. The Threshing Bee and Fall Festival has entertained people since 1957 when Slim Watson had the idea to engage people with farm equipment and machinery. Local road construction crews could not remove a large piece of granite deposited in the ground by glaciers long ago at the intersection of South Granite Street and East Lucy Street, so it sits unmoved in the middle of an active street.

# MERIDEN, KS
### POPULATION: 744 – TOWN 292 OF 627 (6-12-23)

Platted in 1872 on the land of Albert Owens, this westernmost town in Jefferson County was named by Newell Colby for his former hometown of Meriden, New Hampshire. It was located on two branches of the Atchison, Topeka & Santa Fe Railroad, one of which was the Leavenworth & Topeka Railway. The post office was established in the year the town was formed, and in 1891, it was incorporated as a city of the third class. In its early days, it was home to a church, library, newspaper office, banks, and a high school. Meriden is near Perry State Park, established in 1968, and offers camping, hiking, boating, and angling amenities.

# NORTONVILLE, KS
### POPULATION: 601 – TOWN 63 OF 627 (3-14-23)

Nortonville's chief railroad back in the day was the Atchison, Topeka & Santa Fe Railroad. It was platted circa 1873 by the Arkansas Valley

Town Company and named for L. Norton Jr., an early roadmaster (manager of track quality) for the Santa Fe Railroad. The first post office in town was established in May 1873.

# OSKALOOSA, KS ★
**POPULATION: 1,110 – TOWN 288 OF 627 (6-12-23)**
The first settler of Oskaloosa was Dr. James Noble, who arrived in February of 1855. The following year, Jesse Newell and Joseph Fitzsimons platted a townsite, the two of which served as the first sawmill and store owners. The newly founded settlement was named after Oskaloosa, Iowa, and laid out in the same design. On November 25, 1856, the post office was established, and in October 1858, county residents elected to make Oskaloosa the judicial seat of Jefferson County. Two railroads, the Missouri Pacific and the Atchison, Topeka & Santa Fe line, would be constructed in the following decades. The town has made some progressive strides in the past. It was the hometown of Samuel Peppard, who in 1860 created a "sailing wagon" that could travel up to 15 mph. They began to make their way to Pike's Peak near Denver, Colorado until strong winds destroyed the wagon. In 1888, an all-woman city council and mayor Mary D. Lowman were elected as the town's officials, the first instance of its kind in the Sunflower State. Notable past figures of Osky's past have been McKinley Burnett (President of the Topeka NAACP during the Brown v. Board of Education court case), Luther "Dummy" Taylor (deaf MLB pitcher who led the National League in games pitched in 1901), James Reynolds (actor known for his role as Abe Carver on the soap opera *Days of Our Lives*), Roger Barker (founder of environmental psychology), and Charles W. Roberts (briefly the Chairman of the Republican National Committee for a couple of months in 1953).

# OZAWKIE, KS
**POPULATION: 638 – TOWN 291 OF 627 (6-12-23)**
Once historically spelled Osawkie and *Osawkee* (a word derived from the Sauk Nation), Ozawkie was the first town established in Jefferson County. It was the county seat until October of 1858. Its first settlers, the Dyer brothers, arrived in 1854 and founded a trading post on the heavily traveled military road. It served as an important early settlement, having a prosperous hotel, sawmill, and many prosperous lines of enterprise until Oskaloosa gradually took over as the area's trade center. The town remained unincorporated throughout its early existence because of its dwindling population. Because of that, the

original townsite was razed to make way for the Perry Dam Project of 1964-1969 to control the flooding of the Delaware River and create today's Perry Lake. Citizens rallied to move the town to higher ground prior to the first flood, and so in 1967, the present-day Ozawkie was incorporated.

# PERRY, KS
**POPULATION: 852 – TOWN 290 OF 627 (6-12-23)**

Perry was founded in 1865 as a station on the Kansas Pacific Railway, a standard gauge line that remained in operation from 1863 to 1880 until it merged with the Union Pacific. Its former full name, Perryville, was given to pay tribute to the president of the Union Pacific Railroad, John D. Perry. G. B. Carson & Brothers worked to form the first general store of the newly-founded town, and in February of 1866, a post office would be established. Former names for the office were Rising Sun and Medina. N. J. Stark was named as the town's first mayor upon its official incorporation as a city on March 3, 1871.

# VALLEY FALLS, KS ☆
**POPULATION: 1,092 – TOWN 64 OF 627 (3-14-23)**

An early variation of this town's name was Grasshopper Falls, named for the falls of the Grasshopper (later renamed Delaware) River. The name was again briefly changed to Sautrelle Falls by the legislature before its present name was decided upon in 1875. The town was located at a convergence point for the Atchison, Topeka & Santa Fe, Missouri Pacific, and Union Pacific Railroads and welcomed its first settlers circa 1854. The town's streets are named in honor of women pioneer settlers. Noted individuals include George M. Stafford (former Chairman of the Interstate Commerce Commission), Fred Marsh (Major League Baseball infielder), Puella Dornblaser (temperance activist and newspaper editor), and King O'Malley (former member of the Australian Parliament). The Valley Falls Historical Society Museum is the community's center for history and heritage; it contains artifacts from the making of the 1988 crime drama *Kansas* that was primarily filmed in town.

**Lodging Recommendation:**
**The Barn B&B Inn**
**14910 Blue Mound Rd**
**Valley Falls, KS 66088**

# WINCHESTER, KS

Winchester began in June 1854 with William H. Gardiner, who made a claim in the area and eventually built a cabin there. A townsite was laid out in 1857 after Gardiner and another man's cabins being used as hotels had led to a significant growth in population. The town's name is an eponym for Winchester, Virginia. Al Reynolds, who played in the first-ever Super Bowl for the Kansas City Chiefs, and Jerry Robertson, a former MLB pitcher, were born in Winchester.

**Adjacent Counties:** Atchison (N), Leavenworth (E), Douglas (S), Shawnee (SW), Jackson (NW)

**Unincorporated/Ghost Towns:** Boyle, Buck Creek, Dunavant, Grantville, Half Mound, Hickory Point, Indian Ridge, Lake Shore, Lakeside Village, Medina, Mooney Creek, Newman, Rising Sun, Rock Creek, Thompsonville, West Shore, Williamstown

**National Register of Historic Places:**
**Grantville:** Maplecroft Farmstead
**Oskaloosa:** Jefferson Old Town Bowstring Truss, Newell-Johnson-Searle House, Union Block
**Perry:** Buck Creek School, Delaware River Parker Truss Bridge, Morris Harris Farmstead
**Sarcoxie Township:** Sunnyside School
**Valley Falls:** Delaware River Composite Truss Bridge

**Breweries/Wineries/Distilleries:**
Crooked Post Winery (Ozawkie, KS)
Jefferson Hill Vineyards & Guest House (McLouth, KS)

**Golf Courses:**
Village Greens Golf Course, Public (Ozawkie, KS)

**Town Celebrations:**
Heartland Pagan Festival, McLouth, KS (Memorial Day Weekend)
McLouth Threshing Bee, McLouth, KS (3rd Weekend of September)
Meriden Fall Fest, Meriden, KS (1st Weekend of October)
Meriden Threshing Show, Meriden, KS (3rd Weekend of July)
Oskaloosa Old Settlers Reunion, Oskaloosa, KS (4th Weekend of June)

# JEWELL COUNTY
## EST. 1867 - POPULATION: 2,932

The namesake of Jewell County comes from Lewis Jewell, a Lieutenant Colonel of the 6th Regiment Kansas Volunteer Calvary of the Union Army.

## BURR OAK, KS
### POPULATION: 140 – TOWN 125 OF 627 (3-29-23)
Burr Oak was named after the nearby creek of the same name. It was an important shipping point (with grain and livestock being its main products) on the Missouri Pacific Railroad. It once boasted an impressive population of close to 1,132 persons, according to some sources (although the U.S. Census argues that the population was at its peak in 1910 at 746 persons). Burr Oak was laid out in 1871, the same year that its post office was established, and incorporation soon followed in 1880.

 **Restaurant Recommendation:**
**Grate Expectations**
**115 S Main St**
**Burr Oak, KS 66936**

## ESBON, KS
### POPULATION: 69 – TOWN 124 OF 627 (3-29-23)
The westernmost community in Jewell County, Esbon, was laid out in 1873 and served as a shipping point between Mankato and Smith Center on the Chicago, Rock Island & Pacific Railroad. It reached a population high in 1920 of 375 persons, and its year of incorporation was 1904. The town's original post office (founded in January 1874) was also spelled "Ezbon."

## FORMOSO, KS
### POPULATION: 94 – TOWN 128 OF 627 (3-29-23)
Formoso was established in 1889 and located on the Rock Island Railway. The town's first post office arrived only a few years earlier, on December 17, 1887. The town's highest recorded population was 453 in 1910.

# JEWELL, KS
**POPULATION: 370 – TOWN 127 OF 627 (3-29-23)**

Jewell was incorporated in 1880 as a city of the third class, although its beginnings can be traced to an 1870 settlement called "Fort Jewell," a large sod enclosure. It was named in honor of Lieutenant-Colonel Lewis R. Jewell, a member of the Sixth Kansas Cavalry. The town's growth came about due to the Missouri Pacific Railroad. Jewell County State Park is a popular spot amongst fishermen, although there are also limited hunting and camping opportunities.

# MANKATO, KS ★☆
**POPULATION: 836 – TOWN 126 OF 627 (3-29-23)**

Once called Jewell Center for its geographical location at the center of Jewell County, this county seat was later renamed Mankato after the city in Minnesota. The name was changed because individuals began to confuse Jewell Center for the nearby town of Jewell City, from which Jewell Center, now Mankato, had taken the county seat away a few years earlier in a special election. Alta was also considered until it was discovered that there was already another town in the state of that name. It was laid out in 1872 and located at the junction of the Missouri Pacific and the Chicago, Rock Island & Pacific Railroad, although its earliest settler was the blacksmith David Blank, who had arrived a few years before then. Incorporation status was gained in 1880. The Chief Agricultural Negotiator from March of 2018 to January of 2021, Gregg Doud, Kansas Congressman Wint Smith, and 1932 Summer Olympic participant Ernest Tippin (in the 25 m rapid fire pistol) were born in Mankato. The adventurist YouTube channel Yes Theory visited Mankato in 2019 and published a video titled "Throwing a Party in the Most Boring Town in America," where they helped rally residents to throw the largest party the town had ever seen. The video has over 8.5 million views as of January 2024. Jewell County Historical Society Museum hosts a treasure trove of artifacts from days bygone.

# RANDALL, KS
**POPULATION: 79 – TOWN 90 OF 627 (3-27-23)**

The original name for this town was Vicksburg, under which the city was platted in 1870. It was renamed Randall in 1882 in honor of Edward Randall, the original townsite owner, and was located on the Missouri Pacific Railroad.

# WEBBER, KS
## POPULATION: 30 – TOWN 129 OF 627 (3-29-23)

Webber, a town of thirty people in northeast Jewell County, got its first post office in November of 1889. Its name honors Dan Webber, an early settler and landowner. The Atchison, Topeka, and Santa Fe Railroad passed through the area in 1887. Although Webber is a relatively secluded municipality, it does enjoy the proximity of Lovewell State Park and its amenities for camping and swimming.

**Adjacent Counties:** Republic (E), Cloud (SE), Mitchell (S), Osborne (SW), Smith (W)

**Unincorporated/Ghost Towns:** Dentonia, Dispatch, Ionia, Lovewell, Montrose, North Branch, Otego, Wesley Center

**National Register of Historic Places:**
**Burr Oak:** Burr Oak School, Burr Oak United Methodist Church, O. W. Francis House
**Mankato:** First National Bank, Jewell County Courthouse, Jewell County Jail

Haskell County Photos: Satanta, Satanta, Sublette, Sublette, Sublette, Sublette, Sublette, Sublette

Hodgeman County Photos: Hanston, Hanston, Hanston, Jetmore, Jetmore, Jetmore, Jetmore, Jetmore

229

Jackson County Photos: Delia, Holton, Holton, Holton, Holton, Mayetta, Netawaka, Whiting

Jefferson County Photos: McLouth, Meriden, Nortonville, Oskaloosa, Oskaloosa, Perry, Perry, Valley Falls

Jewell County Photos: Burr Oak, Burr Oak, Burr Oak, Jewell, Jewell, Mankato, Mankato, Webber

# JOHNSON COUNTY
## EST. 1855 – POPULATION: 609,863

Johnson County was named after one of the first settlers of Kansas, Methodist missionary Thomas Jackson, who founded the area's famous Shawnee Methodist Mission.

# DE SOTO, KS
## POPULATION: 6,118 – TOWN 548 OF 627 (9-29-23)

Laid out in 1857 by the De Soto Town Company, this community derived its namesake from the famous Spanish explorer Hernando De Soto, likely the first European to have crossed the Mississippi River. The Shawnee tribe of Native Americans had been in the area for several decades following their forced relocation from Cape Girardeau, Missouri. They were the principal landowners when Europeans began to explore the possibility of settling northeast Kansas. John and Hattie Possum are recorded as selling land to settlers as early as 1858, and three years later, the Town Company bought up another 80 acres to get to work erecting buildings and living quarters. The De Soto hotel, the Methodist church, a sawmill, and other businesses were soon opened, and a post office was established in 1860. Its first postmaster was James Smith. The arrival of the Atchison, Topeka & Santa Fe Railroad expanded the economic opportunities of the town. In the 1940s, it received another when the Sunflower Army Ammunition Plant, the largest ammunition plant in the world during its World War II operating days, was built by the U.S. government. It also has the notoriety of having been the world's largest smokeless powder plant. A town called Prairie Center was once located on the site but was destroyed to make room for the facility. It remained in operation until 1993, and as of the 2020s, the site has been undergoing cleanup efforts to transform it into a series of parks, homes, and businesses, one of which will be Panasonic's $4 billion electric vehicle battery factory, the largest in the world. Three noted corporations, Goodcents Deli Fresh Subs, Great American Bank, and Custom Foods, Inc., are headquartered here. In the popular culture stratosphere, De Soto was heavily featured in the 1983 film *The Day After* and the 2018 drama *All Creatures Here Below*. The multi-award-winning 2018 sci-fi novel *The Calculating Stars* by Mary Robinette Kowal features the Ammunition Plant as part of the new United States capital. De Soto has maintained constant growth between the 1860 and the 2020 Census and increased in population every decade with the exception of the 1940 Census, in which it lost one resident overall (384 in 1930 to 383 in 1940). Some of the more famous residents have been Mandy Chick (stock car driver and racer), John H. Outland (the namesake of the Outland Trophy in college football), Howard K. Gloyd (herpetologist noted for his discovery of several new reptile species), and Stanley T. Adams (Medal of Honor recipient).

# EDGERTON, KS
POPULATION: 1,748 – TOWN 295 OF 627 (6-27-23)

Edgerton was named in honor of Mr. Edgerton, the chief engineer of the Atchison, Topeka & Santa Fe Railroad, the town's early prominent railway. It was founded with the railroad extension to that point in 1870. Enterprise arose as the railroad began to ship goods across the state on its line, and Edgerton was soon home to a hardware and implement store, lumber yard, hotel, schools, and a post office. Logistics Park Kansas City Intermodal Facility, an impressive 3,000-acre BNSF Railway shipping facility and hub, is the town's most notable industrial site. The Lanesfield School Historic Site focuses on the history of rural education, particularly in Johnson County. John Henry Balch, a Medal of Honor recipient, was born in Edgerton on January 2, 1896.

# FAIRWAY, KS
POPULATION: 4,170 – TOWN 539 OF 627 (9-27-23)

"The City of Trees" began, like many of the other communities throughout the Kansas City metropolitan area, as a subdivision. Because of its location on a golf course, the town's developers named it Fairway after the numerous driving ranges. Founded in the 1930s, it was formally incorporated by an act of the Legislature in 1949, and it garnered a peak population of 5,398 residents in the 1960s. While the cities of Shawnee and Mission have connections to the Shawnee Methodist Mission established in the area in the 1830s, Fairway is now its home at the Shawnee Indian Mission State Historic Site. The Mission was moved here in 1839 from its original location and, in 1968, was designated as a National Historic Landmark. A few notable past residents include Greg Orman, who ran for Kansas Governor in 2018, and Frank L. Hagaman, the 31st Governor of Kansas.

# GARDNER, KS ☆

The nomenclature of this quickly-growing Johnson County town is still being determined. One story suggests that it was named in honor of Henry Gardner, the 23rd Governor of Massachusetts, when the Kansas town was founded in 1857. The other is that the name honors O. G. Gardner, who laid out the townsite alongside Benjamin B. Francis, A. B. Bartlett, and others. The men selected the area because it was at the division point of the Santa Fe and the Oregon & California Trails, so multitudes of settlers passed through daily. Original businesses include a blacksmith shop, a hotel, a doctor's office, and later, a post office that opened on March 18, 1858. In 1887, it elected to incorporate, not long after the arrival of the Atchison, Topeka & Santa Fe Railroad. The town's population has grown exponentially since 1990 thanks to its proximity to the Kansas City metropolitan area when it was home to just 3,191 residents. A couple of former MLB players, outfielder Bubba Starling and 2019 All-Star pitcher John Means, come from Gardner. Means is one of only 318 pitchers in MLB history to have thrown a no-hitter, an accomplishment he garnered on May 5, 2021. Ray McIntire, the inventor of Styrofoam, was born in Gardner in 1918. The Gardner Historical Museum focuses primarily on local history but also features an in-depth exhibit on the history of reverse mortgages.

**Restaurant Recommendation:
Blazers Restaurant
131 N Center
Gardner, KS 66030**

# LAKE QUIVIRA, KS

A city named after the artificial lake in the same area, Lake Quivira, was founded in the 1920s by Charles E. Gault, a land developer responsible for creating a housing subdivision surrounding the body of water. He did just that, and Lake Quivira met the requirements to become an incorporated city in 1971. "Quivira" was a name for the city of gold and fortune that the great Spanish conquistador Francisco Vásquez de Coronado was in search of as he journeyed through southwestern and middle America. Quivira was also an ancient province of the Wichita tribe somewhere between Lyons and Salina. The town's population is 1,014 people today, although it had as many as 1,087 inhabitants per the 1980 Census. It is a private gated community, and only residents are allowed to enter.

# LENEXA, KS

**POPULATION: 57,434 – TOWN 547 OF 627 (9-29-23)**

One of the first settlers of the land that would one day become Lenexa, the "Spinach Capital of the World," was none other than the notorious James Butler Hickok, perhaps better known by his folk hero title, "Wild Bill" Hickok. He claimed 160 acres of land in 1857, with much of it being located on the heavily traversed Santa Fe Trail. After the United States passed the Pacific Railroad Acts of 1862, encouraging the creation of a transcontinental railroad, a group of businessmen formed the Kansas and Neosho Valley Railroad (later annexed by the St. Louis & San Francisco Railroad). They laid out a townsite in 1869 on land formerly owned by C. A. Bradshaw and wished to name it in his honor. He refused, so they named it in recognition of Nax-Nex-Se, the wife of then Shawnee Chief Thomas Blackhoof. He was the Chief responsible for signing away over 1.6 million acres of Shawnee land to the United States. Lee Freeman and Dr. Bower erected Lenexa's first stores, and soon a post office, the Fountain Head mill, a hotel, Methodist and Catholic churches, and lines of general, hardware, and drug stores were constructed to take advantage of the local trade scene. Its most prominent business venture is Garmin, a GPS and wearable technology company founded in 1989 by Gary Burrell and Min H. Kao. Regarding sites of interest, the National Archives and Records Administration operates "The Caves" Record Center, its most notorious artifacts being from the Parkland Memorial Hospital trauma room of Dallas, Texas, from the day that President John F. Kennedy was assassinated. The Legler Barn Museum focuses on the historic Legler stone barn, early area transportation, and local history. Historical residents of the city include Jason Wiles (actor in the NBC drama series *Third Watch*), Madison Desch (World Champion gymnast), Baron Corbin (WWE wrestler and former NFL offensive lineman), Paul Rudd (actor), Grace VanderWaal (champion singer of season 11 of *America's Got Talent*), William Shaw (the founder of Great Plains Laboratory), Cam F. Awesome (three-time super heavyweight Golden Glove champion), and Lucas Rodríguez (former soccer midfielder and present coach).

# LEAWOOD, KS

An original attempt was made at settling this part of the state prior to the American Civil War, when Oxford, Kansas, was placed into existence. It failed to last through the war's end, and the townsite was abandoned until landowner Oscar G. Lee took a shot in the 1920s at forming a new town named after himself: Leawood. Lee Boulevard was built up for use by the public, and future housing developments led to Leawood's incorporation as a city of the third class in November of 1948. The Johnson County city has fared well since its designation as a municipality, as it has expanded every decade since then. The Johnson County city's largest jump in population (539.8%) came between 1950 and 1960, when it grew to 7,466 inhabitants from 1,167. AMC Entertainment Holdings, Inc., the largest movie theater chain on the planet, relocated its headquarters from Kansas City, Missouri, to Leawood in the early 2010s for tax incentive reasons. It has also since become a Sister City to the Gezer Regional Council in Israel and Yilan City of Taiwan Province in the Republic of China. Julie Garwood (romance novelist best known for her work *A Girl Named Summer*), Trent Green (2x Pro-Bowl NFL quarterback), J. C. Hall (the entrepreneur behind Hallmark Cards), Min Kao (the co-founder of Garmin), Alex Gordon (3x All-Star MLB left fielder), Dan Quisenberry (3x All-Star MLB relief pitcher and 5x AL saves leader), Nancy Opel (a 2002 Tony Award nominee), Phil Keaggy (seven-time Gospel Music Association Dove Award winner), and Jon Kempin (former goalkeeper soccer for multiple professional teams), and Holley Fain (noted actress for her role in ABC's medical drama *Grey's Anatomy*) are all individuals intertwined in the city's history.

**Restaurant Recommendation:**
**Joe's Kansas City Bar-B-Que**
**11723 Roe Ave**
**Leawood, KS 66211**

# MERRIAM, KS

A former secretary of the Kansas City, Fort Scott, and Gulf Railroad (later taken over by the St. Louis & San Francisco Railway), Charles Merriam, had this town named in his honor as he was instrumental in bringing the railroad to the area. At the turn of the century, it was home to a post office and other business lines, one of which was the town's first attempt at a newspaper: the Merriam Herald-Chieftain (only in print from March 21 to April 25, 1913). Incorporation was awarded to Merriam on October 28, 1950, and since then, the population has remained between 10,794 people (1980 Census) and 11,821 (1990 Census) over the last half-century. Until 2019, it held the honor of being the headquarters of the Lee brand of denim jeans (originally founded in Salina in the 1880s), but Seaboard Corporation (an agribusiness and transportation conglomerate) has been based out of Merriam since 1980.

# MISSION, KS
**POPULATION: 9,954 – TOWN 532 OF 627 (9-26-23)**
The etymology of Mission was taken from the Methodist church mission established in the area in 1829 by Reverend Thomas Johnson. A town was formulated by early Santa Fe Trail settlers who elected to stay there to take advantage of clear natural water springs, a precious resource for those looking to settle in the west. The subdivision was called Mission Hill Acres when lots went up for sale in the early portion of the twentieth century, and entrepreneurs soon brought about a grocery store, drug, hardware, and general merchandising stores, and a restaurant and a barbershop. It was incorporated in 1951 and has been home to noted figures Michael Sull, formerly the calligrapher for President Ronald Reagan, Bart Evans, a member of the Museum of Polo and Hall of Fame, sports journalist Grant Wahl, once affiliated with *Sports Illustrated*, CBS Sports, and Fox Sports, and Earl Eugene O' Connor, former Senior Judge of the United States District Court for the District of Kansas.

 **Restaurant Recommendation:**
**The Snack Shack**
**6018 Johnson Dr**
**Mission, KS 66202**

# MISSION HILLS, KS
**POPULATION: 3,594 – TOWN 537 OF 627 (9-27-23)**
The two men who had a major influence in several of the smaller Johnson County municipalities, Reverend Thomas Johnson and J. C. Nichols, the land developer, played a role in the naming and establishing the affluent City of Mission Hills. The name "Mission Hills" is a nod to Johnson's 1829 Shawnee Indian Mission, and J. C. Nichols went to work laying out the townsite about a century later.

Nichols's intentions for the area differed from his other nearby divisions, as he wanted to create an upscale community for wealthy individuals outside of Mission Hills Country Club. He also founded the Club on June 30, 1914, as a strategy to convince the rich to build their homes and settle in the Kansas portion of Kansas City. Indian Hills Country Club and the Kansas City Country Club (then the Community Country Club) were also formulated to provide alternative golfing options. Prior to the establishment of Mission Hills, he was having a difficult time attracting such a class of elitists to his Kansas properties. Fearing annexation like many other communities at the time, Mission Hills elected to incorporate in 1949, then having only about 1,275 residents (per the 1950 Census). Noted writer Ernest Hemingway stayed in the area in 1928 and, during his stay, wrote his famous 1929 war novel *A Farewell to Arms*. In other media, they hosted the ABC drama series *Switched at Birth*, a five-season, 103-episode show that followed two teenagers who lived drastically different lives. Professional golfers Tom Watson (eight-time major championships victor) and Matt Gogel, 13x MLB All-Star third baseman George Brett, the founder of the National Association of Independent Truckers, Cheryl Womack, Henry W., and Richard A. Block, the co-founders of H&R Block, Ewing Kauffman, the creator of Kansas City Royals in 1969 and a pharmaceutical entrepreneur, NFL and NBA sportscaster Kevin Harlan, writer James Ellroy, Donald J. Hall Sr., a majority shareholder of Hallmark Cards, Marcelo Claure, the CEO of Shein in Latin America and the former CEO of Sprint telecommunications, the co-founder of The *Baffler magazine*, Thomas Frank, and David Dreier, the chair of the Fallen Journalists Memorial Foundation and the former chair of the Tribune Publishing Company, all have communal ties.

# MISSION WOODS, KS
## POPULATION: 203 – TOWN 536 OF 627 (9-27-23)

Land developer J. C. Nichols, credited for founding many subdivisions of housing in the Kansas City metro in the 1920s and 1930s, started constructing this future community in 1930. Like the City of Mission, it was named after Reverend Thomas Johnson's 1829 Shawnee Mission and additionally for the area's richness in trees. It, too, was incorporated in 1949 to keep it distinguished from all the other surrounding communities and for tax purposes.

# OLATHE, KS ★

The Johnson County seat was founded by Dr. John T. Barton and his party in 1857 when they surveyed a location in the center of the county to establish a townsite. One of the party members was of the Shawnee Nation, and when the claim was made, he was recorded as saying *olathe*, meaning "beautiful" in his language, and the name stuck with the Europeans. Incorporation was granted that same year from the false Legislature (those wanting to make Kansas a slave state), and it was awarded the title of judicial seat without contention from the other cities of Johnson County. Some of the very first settlers had the surnames of Blake, Boggs, Campbell, Hill, Mayo, Millikin, Osgood, and Whittier. The presence of the Oregon Trail, Santa Fe Trail, and the California Trail enabled early residents of Olathe to establish some homes and businesses to help pioneers continue their trek westward, but the American Civil War drastically impeded the city's growth. Like other abolitionist towns in the area, Olathe built up a military post to defend itself from incoming Confederates from Missouri. The town would be ambushed and razed by Quantrill's Raiders in September of 1862, and it was again raided by him in August 1863 and by Major General Sterling Price in 1864 as he was retreating from "Price's Missouri Expedition." As tensions subsided following the war's end, Olathe finally had the chance to grow without fear of significant setbacks caused by enemy forces. It was re-incorporated in 1868 to ensure its designation as a municipality was legitimate. The push for a transcontinental railroad transpired in the introduction of the Kansas City, Clinton & Springfield, Topeka, Atchison & Santa Fe, and the St. Louis & San Francisco Railroads to Olathe. Within the same time frame, churches of all the leading congregations were established, as were prominent schools, newspaper offices, flour mills by C. M. Ott, pearl mills, general, hardware and implement, and drug stores of all varieties, and Olathe College in 1873. Although the college has since closed, the Kansas School for the Deaf has remained in operation since 1861, when Phillip A. Emery founded it. Its campus is home to the Museum of Deaf History, Arts, and Culture, one of three noted Olathe museums, the other being the Mahaffie Stagecoach Stop and Farm Historic Site and Ensor Park and Museum. A private Nazarene university called the MidAmerica Nazarene University, formulated in 1966 and once called the Mid-America Nazarene College (until 1996), is the other institution of higher learning in Olathe. Once the Eisenhower Interstate System was put into motion in the 1950s, Olathe soon found itself with direct ties to the Kansas City metropolitan area, and the legislation resulted in a staggering boom in population. With a 2020 population of 141,290 residents, it has claimed fourth place in Kansas's list of the most populated cities. Donald J. Tyson (the CEO of Tyson Foods from 1967 to 1991), Darren Sproles (3x NFL-Prowler and the NFL record holder for the most all-purpose yards in a season with 2,696 yards in 2011), Jennifer Bertrand (host of HGTV's *Paint-Over!*), Danielle McCray (former professional women's basketball player), John St. John (the 8th Governor of Kansas), George H. Hodges (the 19th Governor of Kansas), John Anderson Jr. (the 36th Governor of Kansas), Mark Parkinson (the 45th Governor of Kansas), Budd Rogers ("America's Boyfriend," an actor known for his role in the 1927 Academy Award-winning film *Wings*), Johnny Dare (host of Rockfest, the largest one-day concert event in the United States on an annual basis), Charles H. Zimmerman (aeronautical engineer), Earl Browder (leader of the Communist Party USA from 1934 to 1945), Willie Aames (actor in the comedy series *Eight Is Enough*), Herbert S. Hadley (the 32nd Governor of Missouri), Manute Bol (one of the tallest players in NBA history), and Michael McMillian (an actor in *What I Like About You* and HBO's *True Blood*), are just some of Olathe's proudest past residents.

 **Restaurant Recommendation:
54th Street Scratch Bar & Grill
14750 S Harrison St
Olathe, KS 66061**

# OVERLAND PARK, KS
**POPULATION: 197,238 – TOWN 544 OF 627 (9-28-23)**
Even Kansas's second-most populous city, Overland Park (197,238 residents as of the 2020 Decennial Census), came from humble beginnings despite its incredible growth over the past half-century. Railroader William. B. Strang Jr. is credited with starting the city in 1905 when he purchased 600 acres with the intention of creating a "park-like community." He was additionally responsible for creating the Missouri and Kansas Interurban Railway between Olathe and Kansas City, which helped to interconnect the cities of the metropolitan area and further the rapid growth of Overland Park and the surrounding communities. Since its incorporation in May 1960 as a city of the first class, city officials have worked aggressively to grow Overland Park by annexing land and other former municipalities, and new sites of interest appear with each decade. Amongst these sites are the Deanna Rose Children's Farmstead (offering a petting zoo,

241

pony and wagon rides, a 1900s one-room schoolhouse, and more), Overland Park Arboretum and Botanical Gardens, the Museum at Prairiefire, the Overland Park Convention Center, the Overland Park Historical Society, Johnson County Museum and the Strang Carriage House, The Nerman Museum of Contemporary Art, Oak Park Mall, the Epsten Gallery, and the Scheels Overland Park Soccer Complex. Eight institutions of higher learning are based out of or have satellite campuses in the city: Johnson County Community College (est. 1969), Kansas Christian College (a private, four-year Christian college founded in 1938), Rasmussen University (a private university founded in 1900), Cleveland University-Kansas City (private institution created in 1922), and satellites of Baker University, Emporia State University, Ottawa University, and the University of Kansas Edwards Campus. As a result of ample opportunities for education, recreation, and employment, it has made several national lists as being one of the best places to raise kids, a prime suburb for retirees, and one of the top 10 places to live in the United States on several occasions. The population has climbed by double-digits percentage-wise over the past four U.S. Censuses, with the highest single-decade jump having occurred between 1960 and 1970 when the population rose 263.0% from 21,110 people to 76,623. The growth has attracted the corporate headquarters of Compass Minerals and Netsmart Technologies, and it was once one to Applebee's (1993 to 2007) and Sprint Corporation before its 2020 merger with T-Mobile. Worthy notable person mentions include Paul Rudd (actor noted for his roles in movies like *Ant-Man* in the Marvel Cinematic Universe, *Anchorman: The Legend of Ron Burgundy*, and *The 40-Year-Old Virgin*), Jeff Colyer (the 47th Governor of Kansas), Sarah Lancaster (actress in multiple television series), Michael Almereyda (the director of *Hamlet* (2000) and *Twister* (1989), Mike Boddicker (the MLB's 1983 ALCS MVP and 1984 World Series champion), James D. Conley (the bishop of the Roman Catholic Diocese of Lincoln since 2012), 2x World-Series MLB relief pitcher Jason Grimsley, Darren Bousman (the director of four *Saw* movies), comedic actors Rob Riggle and Jason Sudeikis, Anna Glennon (world champion jet ski racer), Tom Kane (voice actor in several *Call of Duty* video games, as well as the television series *Kim Possible*, *The Powerpuff Girls*, *Foster's Home for Imaginary Friends*, and more), Will Shields (former NFL offensive guard and member of the Pro Football Hall of Fame), David Dastmalchian (actor known for roles in *The Dark Knight*, *The Flash*, and *The Suicide Squad*), Johnathan Wendel (a member of the International Video Game Hall of Fame), Ryne Stanek (2022 World Series champion MLB pitcher), and Semi Ojeleye, an NBA player from 2017 to 2022, amongst others.

**Restaurant Recommendation:
Cinzetti's Italian Market
7201 W 91st St
Overland Park, KS 66212**

# PRAIRIE VILLAGE, KS
**POPULATION: 22,957 – TOWN 538 OF 627 (9-27-23)**

Platted in 1941 and incorporated in 1951, Prairie Village is another successful development of J. C. Nichols, the noted Kansas City real estate developer. His goal for this project was to provide sustainable homes for World War II veterans. Its name pays tribute to the original Prairie School built on the land in 1882; its second incarnation, built in 1912, stood until 1990. The National Association of Home Builders, a trade association that largely represents the housing industry, recognized the city in 1949 for being the "best-planned community in the United States." With nearly 23,000 inhabitants, Prairie Village is large enough to have two sister cities: Schaerbeek, Belgium, and Dolyna, Ukraine. Chuck Norris (an actor known for his roles in mixed martial arts films), Robert Bennett (the 39th Governor of Kansas), Joyce DiDonato (3-time Grammy award-winning opera singer), Donald Fehr (the 3rd Executive Director of the MLB from 1983 to 2009 and the 5th Executive Director of the NHL Players' Association from 2012 to 2023), Sandahl Bergman (actress noted for playing Valeria in *Conan the Barbarian*), Dan Connolly (one of the creators of the World Wide Web), Ramesh Ponnuru (political pundit and journalist), David Wittig (former CEO of Westar Energy), Ben and Horace Jones (thoroughbred horse trainers), Robert S. Kaplan (co-creator of the Balanced Scorecard utilized in business), Hank Bauer (3x MLB All-Star), and Eric Darnell (co-director and writer for the DreamWorks comedy film franchise *Madagascar*), are some the city's most famous residents of past and present. Locked behind the gates of a housing development that was once a farm is the grave of Larwin, the only horse from Kansas to win the Kentucky Derby (1938).

**Restaurant Recommendation:
BRGR Kitchen + Bar
4038 W 83rd St
Prairie Village, KS 66208**

# ROELAND PARK, KS

**POPULATION: 6,871 – TOWN 533 OF 627 (9-27-23)**

Incorporated in 1951, Roeland Park was selected to honor John Roe, an Irish immigrant who first settled in the area in 1883. Developers added the other portions of the name to make it more appealing to potential future residents. Its population has fluctuated throughout the decades, but 6,871 inhabitants called it home as of the 2020 Census. Catherine Fox, two-time gold-medal winner in swimming at the 1996 Olympics, John Carmack, a co-founder of iD Software and a programmer for popular video games such as *Doom*, *Commander Keen*, and *Quake*, former professional soccer defender Nia Williams, and Mike Gardner, the head football coach at Tabor College as of 2023, have all claimed Roeland Park as home.

# SHAWNEE, KS

**POPULATION: 67,311 – TOWN 530 OF 627 (9-26-23)**

This American Civil War town has grown extensively over the decades, as its population has gone from 845 inhabitants to 67,311 since the 1950s. Its history begins with the arrival of Reverend Thomas Johnson, who, in 1831, built the original Shawnee Indian Mission to convert the local tribes to Christianity. His Mission took on the name Shawnee after the local tribe. It would be here on February 24, 1835, that Reverend Jotham Meeker would bring his printing press and publish the first newspaper to ever go into circulation in Kansas, the Shawnee Sun. Later, the same building would be utilized by pro-slavery advocates of the false Legislature for their first session, and Governor Reeder would declare the "Shawnee Mission Legislature" to be illegal. In response, they helped to persuade then-United States President Franklin Pierce to dismiss Reeder's role as the first governor of the Territory of Kansas because of his unwillingness to assist in making Kansas a slave state. Shawnee's early history was plagued from the inception of the townsite in 1857 through the end of the war, as it was burned and pillaged on two occasions in 1862 and 1864 by Quantrill raiders and fellow Confederates. The townspeople never wavered, and by the early 1910s, they had for themselves a small, fruitful community complete with businesses like a hotel, harness shop, grocery, drug, and general stores, and a blacksmith and wagon shop. Its modern growth was determined by its proximity to the Kansas City, Missouri, metropolitan area and the location of several large employers in the area. Some of its most prominent attractions are the Wonderscope Children's Museum, the Buster Keaton Museum, the Johnson County

Museum of History, a 1954 All-Electric House, and the Shawnee Town 1929 Museum. Johnny Carver (sports author), Linda Cook (former CEO of Shell Gas & Power), Gary Woodland (PGA golfer and winner of the 2019 U.S. Open), Danni Boatwright (the champion of *Survivor: Guatemala* in 2005), 1957 MLB all-star pitcher Bob Grim, comedian Chris Porter, former NFL running back Ryan Torain, Jason Kander (the 39th Secretary of State of Missouri), professional bowler Bryan Goebel, and Dave Doeren, the head coach of North Carolina State football since 2013, all have connections to Shawnee.

 **Restaurant Recommendation:**
**Pegah's Family Restaurant**
**5354 Roberts St**
**Shawnee, KS 66226**

# SPRING HILL, KS
### POPULATION: 7,952 – TOWN 541 OF 627 (9-28-23)
Spring Hill was surveyed in May of 1857 and first settled by James B. Hovey. He served as the first president of the town company alongside secretary A. B. Simmons. He decided to name the newly founded town after a community of the same name outside of Mobile, Alabama. He went on to construct the town's first building, the Spring Hill Hotel, and become the town's first postmaster. It would be incorporated later that same year. When the St. Louis & San Francisco Railroad was being built, it bypassed the city because of the lack of a smooth grade, and so the tracks were laid half a mile eastward. A station would ultimately be built so that residents did not have to travel to Ocheltree for deliveries, and Spring Hill would grow to encompass multiple stores, a lumber yard, and other facilities. Early notable townspeople included Gary Burrell, the co-founder of Garmin, MLB pitcher Curly Brown, Celia Ann Dayton, the first woman doctor in Kansas, and Navy Cross recipient Stephen J. Chamberlin.

# WESTWOOD, KS
### POPULATION: 1,750 – TOWN 534 OF 627 (9-27-23)
Westwood was selected as the name for this community because of the existence of Westwood, Missouri, located just across the border to the east. At that time, Westwood View Elementary School had already been established on the town site. The community's origins can be traced to Captain Joseph Parks, a former Chief of the Shawnee tribe of Native Americans. He had been moved from Ohio

to a nearly 1,300-acre parcel of land in Kansas as a part of a deal with the U.S. government, although he passed away before being able to make plans for the land's usage. Ultimately, it was given to his granddaughter Catherine Swatzell, who, with her husband John, elected to build their home here. As nearby Kansas City was developed, residents of the Westwood areas wished to remain as an independent entity, and so they incorporated as a city in 1949.

# WESTWOOD HILLS, KS
## POPULATION: 400 – TOWN 535 OF 627 (9-27-23)
This tiny 0.06 square mile city in the middle of the Kansas City metropolitan area first began in 1922, when J. C. Nichols created the subdivision. Like its neighbor to the west, Westwood Hills took its name from the prior existence of Westwood, Missouri, and several other subdivisions with similar names. To keep themselves from being annexed into a larger surrounding community, Westwood Hills was incorporated in 1949. Since then, they have had a peak population of 495 persons (per the 1960 Census).

Bonner Springs is only partially located in Johnson County (see Wyandotte County)

**Adjacent Counties:** Wyandotte (N), Miami (S), Franklin (SW), Douglas (W), Leavenworth (NW)

**Unincorporated/Ghost Towns:** Bonita, Clare, Clearview City, Ocheltree, Stanley, Stilwell, Wilder

**National Register of Historic Places:**
**De Soto:** Sunflower Village Historic District
**Edgerton:** Lanesfield School, John McCarthy House
**Fairway:** Shawnee Methodist Mission
**Gardner:** Downtown Gardner Historic District, Herman B. Foster House, Louis & Rachel Hammer Barn, Mt. Pleasant Four Corners Burying Grounds, William Thomas Turner Barn, WPA Beach House at Gardner Lake
**Leawood:** Herman J. and Ella B. Voigts House
**Merriam:** R. W. Hocker Subdivision, Lot K Spec House, Loomis Historic District
**Mission Hills:** Horn-Vincent-Russell Estate, Wolcott House
**Olathe:** Ensor Farm, Franklin R. Lanter House, Lone Elm Campground Swale, J. B. Mahaffie House, Olathe Cemetery, Albert

Ott House, Martin Van Buren Parker House, I. O. Pickering House
**Overland Park:** Broadmoor Ranch House Historic District, Campbell Dome House, Overland Theater
**Prairie Village:** Harmon Park Swale
**Shawnee:** William and Julia LeCluyse House, Shawnee Indian Cemetery, Virginia School District No. 33
**Spring Hill:** George L. Morrow Barn
**Stilwell:** Blackfeather Farm, Redel Historic District
**Westwood Hills:** Westwood Hills Historic District

## Breweries/Wineries/Distilleries:
Aubrey Vineyards (Overland Park, KS)
Brew Lab Brewery & Kitchen (Overland Park, KS)
Bull Creek Distillery (Spring Hill, KS)
Discourse Brewing (Overland Park, KS)
ExBEERiment Brewing (Gardner, KS)
KC Pumpkin Patch (Olathe, KS)
KC Wine Company (Olathe, KS)
Limitless Brewing (Lenexa, KS)
Lost Evenings Brewing Company (Lenexa, KS)
Louie's Wine Dive (Overland Park, KS)
Martin City Brewing Company Pizza & Tapr. (Overland Park, KS)
Pathlight Brewing (Shawnee, KS)
Red Crow Brewing Company (Olathe, KS)
Rockcreek Brewing Company (Mission, KS)
Sandhills Brewing – Mission (Mission, KS)
Serendipity Farm & Vine (Stilwell, KS)
Servaes Brewing Company (Shawnee, KS)
Stone Pillar Vineyard & Winery (Olathe, KS)
Tall Trellis Brew Company (Olathe, KS)
Transport Brewery (Shawnee, KS)
Transport Brewery – Gardner (Gardner, KS)
Union Horse Distilling Company (Lenexa, KS)
Wandering Vine at the Castle (Shawnee, KS)
White Tail Run Winery (Edgerton, KS)
Wine Bunker (Overland Park, KS)

## Golf Courses:
Brookridge Country Club, Private (Overland Park, KS)
Deer Creek Golf Course, Public (Overland Park, KS)
Falcon Ridge Golf Course, Public (Lenexa, KS)
Falcon Valley Golf Course, Public (Lenexa, KS)
Gardner Golf Course, Public (Gardner, KS)
Hallbrook Country Club, Private (Leawood, KS)

Indian Hills Country Club, Private (Mission Hills, KS)
Ironhorse Golf Club, Public (Leawood, KS)
Kansas City Country Club, Private (Mission Hills, KS)
Lakeside Hills Golf Course, Public (Olathe, KS)
Leawood South Country Club, Private (Leawood, KS)
Meadowbrook Golf & Country Club, Private (Prairie Village, KS)
Milburn Country Club, Private (Overland Park, KS)
Mission Hills Country Club, Private (Mission Hills, KS)
Nicklaus Golf Club, Private (Overland Park, KS)
Oak Country Club, Public (De Soto, KS)
Overland Park Golf Club, Public (Overland Park, KS)
Prairie Highlands Golf Course, Public (Olathe, KS)
Quivira Lake & County Club, Private (Lake Quivira, KS)
Shadow Glen Golf Club, Private (Olathe, KS)
Shawnee Golf & Country Club, Public (Shawnee Mission, KS)
Smileys Executive Golf Club, Public (Lenexa, KS)
St. Andrews Golf Club, Public (Overland Park, KS)
Sycamore Ridge Golf Course, Public (Spring Hill, KS)
Tomahawk Hills Golf Course, Public (Shawnee, KS)
Wolf Creek Golf Club, Private (Olathe, KS)

**Town Celebrations:**
De Soto Days, De Soto, KS (Labor Day Weekend)
Edgerton Frontier Days, Edgerton, KS (3rd Weekend of June)
Lenexa BBQ Challenge, Lenexa, KS (4th Saturday of June)
Lenexa Chili Challenge, Lenexa, KS (3rd Weekend of October)
Lenexa Spinach Festival, Lenexa, KS (2nd Weekend of September)
Old Settlers Day, Olathe, KS (Weekend after Labor Day)
Old Shawnee Days, Shawnee, KS (1st Full Weekend of June)
Fall Festival, Overland Park, KS (Last Full Weekend of September)
Patriotic Days, Lenexa, KS (Independence Day)

# KEARNY COUNTY
## EST. 1887 - POPULATION: 3,983

War hero Philip Kearny, a noted leader in the Civil War and Mexican-American War, is remembered by the name of this county.

# DEERFIELD, KS
## POPULATION: 711 – TOWN 442 OF 627 (8-16-23)
The first settlers to Deerfield arrived in 1878 to form a townsite along the Arkansas River and the newly-built Atchison, Topeka & Santa Fe

Railroad line. The railroad's presence enabled the townspeople to build several Protestant churches and businesses ranging from banks to mills and elevators. A post office was included among the original establishments. Deerfield would be formally incorporated as a municipality in 1907.

# LAKIN, KS ★☆

## POPULATION: 2,205 – TOWN 441 OF 627 (8-16-23)

Lakin's population growth is interesting in that for several decades, between 1890 and 1940, it grew from only 258 inhabitants to 709 before the population spiked by 128.2% in the 1950 Census, and 1,618 people called it home. That number has since climbed to 2,205 people as of the 2020 count. The townsite began in 1872 with the arrival of the Atchison, Topeka & Santa Fe Railroad to western Kansas, and it was named after David Long Lakin. He was a former treasurer for the railroad. A post office was formed on March 6, 1874, and for a short time, was a part of Finney County until the present-day Kearny County was organized in the late 1880s. In 1888, Lakin was first named the Kearny County seat before Hartland took over the honor in 1890. It was only a few years until the county records were returned to Lakin, where they have remained ever since. Country singer and songwriter Frank Luther was born outside town on August 4, 1899. A schoolhouse and a former railroad depot are two major highlights of the Keary County Historical Museum.

 **Restaurant Recommendation: Flashback Diner 210 W Santa Fe Trail Blvd Lakin, KS 67860**

**Adjacent Counties:** Wichita (N), Scott (NE), Finney (E), Grant (S), Stanton (SW), Hamilton (W)

**Unincorporated/Ghost Towns:** Chantilly, Hartland

**National Register of Historic Places:**
**Deerfield:** Deerfield State Bank, Deerfield Texaco Service Station, Santa Fe Trail-Kearny County Segment 1
**Lakin:** Indian Mound

**Golf Courses:**
Lakin Country Club, Public (Lakin, KS)

# KINGMAN COUNTY
## EST. 1872 - POPULATION: 7,470

Kingman County came about in 1872 and was named for Samuel A. Kingman, once the Chief Justice of the Kansas Supreme Court.

# CUNNINGHAM, KS
## POPULATION: 444 – TOWN 521 OF 627 (9-22-23)

Cunningham, named in honor of early settler J. D. Cunningham, was once a prosperous little community and a station on the Atchison, Topeka & Santa Fe Railroad. However, it was not the first town to be founded in the area. There was once another named Ninnescah (named after the nearby river) located a few miles east of present-day Cunningham, but it was surpassed by the railroad. Its residents decided that it would be in their best interest to move their structures to Cunningham as there was more economic opportunity to be had there. A handful of locals opposed the move, but following a March 24, 1888 tornado that wiped out what little remained of Ninnescah, Cunningham took the lead as the most prominent town of Dresden and Rural townships. A hotel, lumber yard, hardware, and general stores, and a post office were amongst the earliest notable structures. The Santa Fe depot remains today and operates as the Cunningham Depot Museum.

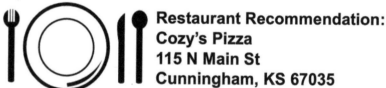 **Restaurant Recommendation:**
**Cozy's Pizza**
**115 N Main St**
**Cunningham, KS 67035**

# KINGMAN, KS ★☆
## POPULATION: 3,105 – TOWN 518 OF 627 (9-22-23)

The founders of Kingman were brothers J. K. and F. S. Fical, who made land claims next to one another in 1873 along the Ninnescah River. The following year Jesse McCarty surveyed the land, and the newly-formed townsite was named in honor of Judge Samuel A. Kingman. He was then the chief justice of the Kansas Supreme Court. The Atchison, Topeka & Santa Fe, and the Missouri Pacific Railroads brought with them the human resources and the aids needed to transform Kingman into a thriving city of the region. By 1912, Kingman had four churches, three hotels and banks, two grain elevators, flour mills, an ice plant, a cereal mill, an opera house, a carpet factory, a salt mine, a creamery, and an ice cream factory that churned out upwards of 400 gallons of ice cream every day. The Kingman County Courthouse was erected between 1907 and 1908 and designed in the Late Victorian style by George P. Washburn, the architect of thirteen courthouses across Kansas. Former MLB players Don Lock and George Aiton, noted orthodontist Martin Dewey, Clyde Cessna, the founder of the Cessna Aircraft Corporation, and The Most Reverend Eugene John Gerber, the Roman Catholic bishop of the Diocese of Wichita from 1982 to 2001, all have ties to Kingman. The Kingman County Historical Museum plays host to a plethora of early community artifacts and anecdotes.

 **Restaurant Recommendation:**
**Smitty's Carry Out**
**233 E D Avenue**
**Kingman, KS 67068**

# NASHVILLE, KS
**POPULATION: 54 – TOWN 514 OF 627 (9-22-23)**
Nashville was named after Nashville, Tennessee, and established as a station on the Atchison, Topeka & Santa Fe Railroad circa 1888. The post office predates the town, starting on August 30, 1887. A mill, grain elevators, churches, and schools were all once essential locations in the little farming community, but as the population decreased with time, so did the need for infrastructure. At present, Nashville is home to 54 people, but its peak population was 234 inhabitants in 1930. Ernest Schmidt, enshrined in the Naismith Memorial Basketball Hall of Fame in 1974, is the most noted resident.

# NORWICH, KS
**POPULATION: 444 – TOWN 517 OF 627 (9-22-23)**
The name of this southeastern Kingman County community is an eponym for Norwich, Connecticut. It began in 1885 and was quick to welcome the arrivals of the Atchison, Topeka & Santa Fe, and the Missouri Pacific Railroad to their little prairie town. Many retail businesses called it home at the turn of the century, as did churches of the leading denominations and a flour mill to process the grain of

251

the local farmers. Norwich's all-time peak population was 551 people per the 2000 Census.

# PENALOSA, KS
**POPULATION: 18 – TOWN 520 OF 627 (9-22-23)**
The Spanish explorer Don Diego Dionisio Penalosa is said to be the namesake of this Kingman County hamlet, which is currently home to only 18 people. It was originally known as Lotta when it was founded in 1885, but the name was changed to Penalosa in 1887 when the Missouri Pacific Railroad rolled into town. Since 1929, the city has remained incorporated despite never recording a U.S. Census population of more than 128 individuals (1930 Census).

# SPIVEY, KS
**POPULATION: 61 – TOWN 516 OF 627 (9-22-23)**
Spivey was founded on the banks of the Chikaskia River in the 1880s and incorporated as a city of the third class in 1887. Its name pays tribute to Colonel E. M. Spivey, one of the original members of the townsite company. Its early structures were a church, bank, several small businesses, including a newspaper, and a post office founded on December 6, 1886, that is still in operation today.

# ZENDA, KS
**POPULATION: 72 – TOWN 515 OF 627 (9-22-23)**
Anthony Hope's 1894 adventure novel "The Prisoner of Zenda" is the source of this town's unique name. It began as a railroad town on the Atchison, Topeka & Santa Fe line in 1887 and would be formally incorporated in 1913. Zenda's economy has always revolved around agricultural products, as its principal shipments in its early days were livestock and grain.

**Adjacent Counties:** Reno (N), Sedgwick (E), Sumner (SE), Harper (S), Barber (SW), Pratt (W)

**Unincorporated/Ghost Towns:** Belmont, Calista, Cleveland, Midway, Mount Vernon, Murdock, Rago, Skellyville, St. Leo, Varner, Waterloo, Willowdale

**National Register of Historic Places:**
**Kingman:** Kingman Carnegie Library, Kingman City Building, Kingman County Courthouse, Kingman National Guard Armory, Kingman Santa Fe Depot, Charles M. Prather Barn, U.S. Post Office-Kingman
**Pretty Prairie:** Louis Werner Barn

**Golf Courses:**
Kingman Country Club, Private (Kingman, KS)

**Town Celebrations:**
All-American Family Fest, Kingman, KS (4th of July)
Christmas Parade Day, Kingman, KS (1st Saturday of December)
Kingman Fall Festival, Kingman, KS (3rd Saturday of September)

# KIOWA COUNTY
## EST. 1886 - POPULATION: 2,460

Kiowa County was created from portions of Comanche and Edwards counties in 1886 and named in honor of the Kiowa Native American tribe.

# GREENSBURG, KS ★☆
## POPULATION: 740 – TOWN 471 OF 627 (9-18-23)

The "greenest town in America," Greensburg, gets its nickname not as a play on words on its name but because of its notoriety around the nation for building its hospital, city hall, school, and all other city buildings to the highest possible certification level issued by LEED (Leadership in Energy in Environmental Design). Ten 1.25 MW wind turbines provide the town's power, and visitors can find bikes and electric vehicle charging stations throughout the municipality. The decision to "go green" came after the events of May 4, 2007, when an EF5 tornado with 205 mile-per-hour winds decimated 95 percent of the city and took the lives of eleven residents. The 250 million dollars in damage was so extensive that President W. Bush and Governor Kathleen Sebelius declared the town a disaster area, and the town's population dropped by 50.6% after that (from 1,574 citizens in the 2000 Census to just 777 in the 2010 Census). There were never more than 2,000 recorded people who called Greensburg home at any point in its history, but early newspaper publishers Hollis & Welles attempted to push that fact in a March 1887 advertisement

253

(two years after the first settlers arrived in the area in 1885) where they claimed that their two-year-old town was a "substantial, thriving, and bustling city, with a population of 2,000 earnest, energetic, educated people." Ironically, at that time, Greensburg was nothing more than a small number of homes and a few businesses, and it was 28 miles from the nearest railroad line. Soon enough, the Chicago, Rock Island & Pacific Railroad was extended to that point, and genuine improvements to the town came with the construction of several churches, schools, hotels, banks, grain elevators and livery stables, and even an opera house. It would be named for Colonel D. R. "Cannonball" Green, an early town promoter who owned the town's first stagecoach company. The acclaimed largest hand-dug well in the world underwent construction in 1888, and after serving as the city's water source for four-and-a-half decades and then sitting empty for another four decades, it is now the Big Well Museum. The well, at 109 feet deep, is only the biggest in the Western Hemisphere, as the Well of Joseph in the Cairo Citadel at 280 feet deep, and the St. Patrick's Well in Orvieto, Italy, at 200 feet deep, are larger. The museum displays history on the well, the city of Greensburg and the tornado, and a half-town pallasite meteorite from a nearby site. Other points of interest are the town's Kiowa County Historical Museum and Soda Fountain, the 5.4.7 Arts Center, and the Kiowa County Courthouse because of its designation as the Kiowa County seat. The town is of a certain level of national fame, as it has been featured in the 2009 ABC documentary *Earth 2100* and a 2008 to 2010 television series featuring the town's name that followed its sustainable measures and rebuilding practices following the tornado. The show was created by noted actor Leonardo DiCaprio and Craig Piligian (also the creator of *Dirty Jobs*, *American Chopper*, and *The Ultimate Fighter*). Several books were also published following the event. A couple of notable Greensburg locals are Manvel H. Davis, who lost to future U.S. President Harry S. Truman in the 1940 U.S. senatorial campaign in Missouri, and Sandra Seacat, an actress noted for her work as an acting coach.

 **Restaurant Recommendation:
Kiowa County Soda Fountain
320 S Main St
Greensburg, KS 67054**

# HAVILAND, KS
## POPULATION: 678 – TOWN 470 OF 627 (9-18-23)
The City of Haviland was founded by Quakers from Indiana in the 1880s, who elected to name it after Laura Smith Haviland. She was herself a Quaker and a noted figure of the Underground Railroad. The town's development was accelerated when the Chicago, Rock Island & Pacific Railroad arrived, which led to the establishment of hotels, a feed mill, and a series of mercantile. A post office was founded in June 1886, and the town's incorporation came in 1906. In 1917, Scott T. Clark founded the Kansas Central Bible Training School, which was later changed to Friends Bible College in 1930 after college courses were added to the curriculum. At present, the institution of higher learning is known as Barclay College, a name given in honor of the first Quaker theologian, Robert Barclay. Locals joke that although they can get a bachelor's or a master's degree from Barclay, they can't get a high school diploma because the only other school in town serves kindergarten through eighth grade. The Haviland Crater is a noted local meteorite crater, one of the smallest impact craters on Earth at a diameter of only 50 feet.

# MULLINVILLE, KS
## POPULATION: 197 – TOWN 472 OF 627 (9-18-23)
The establishment of an area post office precedes the founding of Mullinville, as the office went into service on September 12, 1884, but the townsite was not started until 1886. Located on the Chicago, Rock Island & Pacific Railroad, it has always served the area as a center of agricultural activity with its mills and elevators. It was named after Alfred A. Million, the town's first storekeeper. Some of the most well-known folk art in the state is situated along U.S. Route 400 in Mullinville, a collection of welded metal and farm equipment political sculptures put together by the late M. T. Liggett. One particularly unique Mullinville site is the Fromme-Birney Round Barn, a sixteen-sided structure focusing on agricultural exhibits.

**Adjacent Counties:** Edwards (N), Pratt (E), Barber (SE), Comanche (S), Clark (SW), Ford (W)

**Unincorporated/Ghost Towns:** Belvidere, Brenham, Joy, Wellsford

**National Register of Historic Places:**
**Greensburg:** Greensburg Well, S. D. Robinett Building

# LABETTE COUNTY
## EST. 1867 - POPULATION: 20,184

Labette County took its name from Labette Creek, named for the French fur trapper Pierre LaBette.

# ALTAMONT, KS
**POPULATION: 1,061 – TOWN 365 OF 627 (7-17-23)**
Altamont, a town of 1,061 people in the center of Labette County, Kansas, was initially called Elston upon the establishment of the area post office in 1870. The name would be changed in 1879 after Altamont, Illinois, when the townsite of Altamont arose because of the arrival of the St. Louis & San Francisco Railroad. One of the town's earliest stories lies with the Hutson family, an early family of settlers that used to refer to their home as being "a mile east of the lone tree." Citizens of nearby Oswego and other towns were familiar with the tree because, at that time, there were a tiny handful of trees in this part of Kansas. Incorporation was granted by the legislature in 1884; H. C. Blanchard was the first mayor. The population of Altamont first crossed 1,000 residents in the 1980s, and it has not dipped under the four-figure mark since.

# BARTLETT, KS
**POPULATION: 69 – TOWN 381 OF 627 (7-19-23)**
Bartlett's history dates back to 1886 when it was platted and named in honor of its founder, Robert A. Bartlett. He widely promoted the town to attract residents, and he brought in as many as 249 residents by the time the 1910 Census was conducted. The Missouri Pacific Railroad served the needs of the small community, as did once a bank and a post office established on September 15, 1886.

# CHETOPA, KS
**POPULATION: 929 – TOWN 380 OF 627 (7-19-23)**
The first European to locate here was Larkin McGhee, who, in 1847, formed a trading post to trade with the Osage tribe of Native Americans. A handful of other Europeans joined in throughout the years, and a small settlement began to take shape. Dr. George Lisle of a Powhattan, Ohio colony located Chetopa a decade later, and he

helped to further the settlement's expansion until the American Civil War broke out. On September 18, 1861, the 6th Kansas Calvary and pro-slavery raiders clashed at the site. In 1863, United States troops destroyed the town so that it wouldn't be overtaken by Confederate forces and used as a tactical fort or vantage point. As the war subsided, Lisle tried again to forge a townsite, and this time he would be successful. The Chetopa Town Company was formed in 1868, and in 1870, the Missouri, Kansas & Texas Railroad was built here, intending to locate their rail offices, railyard, and foundry. Unfortunately, the proposal fell through, and the M, K & T withdrew their support. However, that didn't stop Chetopa from keeping their post office (founded April 1867), banks and general stores, a library, creamery, brick plant, flour mill, a public school, and The National Hotel. The Missouri Pacific (then the Nevada and Minden Railway) laid their tracks down later. Regarding the history of the name, Chetopa was derived from the combination of the Osage Nation words *che* and *topah*, meaning four houses. It had been spelled as 'Chepotah' until town postmaster J. M. Cavaness asked to remove the '-h' in 1880. The highest number of residents in the city at any one time was in the 1890s when 2,265 people called Chetopa home. The Chetopa Museum features a wealth of information on the small Labette County community.

# EDNA, KS
### POPULATION: 388 – TOWN 382 OF 627 (7-19-23)
Alexander Patterson and Mr. Booth opened a small general store in the area in 1876 to accommodate the needs of early travelers, and in April 1878, a post office was founded nearby. Because of the lack of infrastructure, growth was nonexistent until the Missouri Pacific Railroad elected to lay its tracks through the area in 1886. This led to the platting of the townsite, and the townspeople thought to name the town after a young child, Edna Gragory. After erecting elevators and flour mills and outputting some economic activity, Edna was incorporated in 1892, and the Edna Historical Museum is responsible for maintaining the historical artifacts and documents of the city.

# LABETTE, KS
### POPULATION: 50 – TOWN 367 OF 627 (7-18-23)
Present-day Labette is the third usage of this name for a town in the county, this one being founded in 1870 in Liberty Township. The former cities were located in Richland township in 1866 by Gilbert Martin and in another part of Richland township in 1868 by an early

group of town promoters. Naming their site Soresco, the men had intended for the Missouri, Kansas & Texas Railroad to pass through that part of the county. The present town was founded by Dempsey Elliott, J. S. Waters, and others looking to make it the judicial seat. They combined with the nearby village of Neola one and a half miles southward, took the post office and whatever other buildings there were, and changed the name to Labette. The name is derived from the surname of Pierre Labette, an early area settler. As of the 2020 Census, Labette has the smallest recorded population in its history, with only 50 residents now calling it home.

# MOUND VALLEY, KS
**POPULATION: 348 – TOWN 364 OF 627 (7-17-23)**
1869 was the year in which Mound Valley got its start when a town company with William M. Rodgers at the helm went to work on founding the townsite. A general, grocery, and drug store were the first three buildings erected, and from there, hotels began to surface. A post office was established in 1870, and for many years, the town was largely disconnected from its neighbors until a stage line was built from Oswego in 1876, and the St. Louis & San Francisco and the Missouri, Kansas & Texas Railroad were constructed. Like other area towns, Mound Valley benefited from the copious amounts of natural gas, oil, and coal throughout much of southeastern Kansas. At one point, Mound Valley's population topped 956 individuals around the height of the Kansas natural gas boom. Country music artist James Wesley was born in Mound Valley on March 9, 1970, as was George Pedderdine, the founder of Pepperdine University in Los Angeles County, California, on June 20, 1886. The Mound Valley Historical Museum assists in preserving area history and stories.

# OSWEGO, KS ★☆
**POPULATION: 1,668 – TOWN 366 OF 627 (7-17-23)**
Oswego, the county seat of Labette County, was named after Oswego, New York, and was initially located on the lines of the Missouri, Kansas & Texas, and the St. Louis & San Francisco Railways. The first true settlement there was a village of the name *No tse Wa spe*, meaning "Quiet Heart," home to part of the Osage tribe of Native Americans. The European name given by Jesuits from nearby Osage Mission to the village was "Little Town Above" because of its distinction of being located on a hill overlooking the Neosho River and the fact the Native Americans of the town were of the Osage tribe's "Little Osage" division. Another early place name was

"White Hair's Village," in honor of Chief Iron Hawk. In 1867, the Oswego town company was formed with Dr. John F. Newlon as President and D. W. Clover as secretary. Town promoters suggested that lots be given away to any individual who would agree to construct buildings on the land, which caused rapid growth and the construction of homes and stores, an opera house and ice plant, a hotel and blacksmith shop, a creamery and flour mills, and a post office. Citizens even raised enough money in 1883 for two colleges to be formed, one of which was Oswego College for women, housed in an impressive three-story building complete with classrooms, dorms, and a library, kitchen, dining room, chapel, and recreation rooms. The legislature awarded Oswego incorporation as a city of the third class in February of 1870, and in 1880, it was upgraded to a municipality of second-class status. Of note for those who enjoy history is the Oswego Historical Museum and Genealogy Center. William Gladstone Steel, the man responsible for convincing Congress to designate Crater Lake as a National Park, Carson Robison, the late country music singer, Playboy model Candy Loving, and Arthur Grant Evans, former president of the Universities of Tulsa and Oklahoma, have ties to Oswego.

# PARSONS, KS
## POPULATION: 9,600 – TOWN 368 OF 627 (7-18-23)
The largest city in Labette County, Parsons, has always played a significant role in the prosperity and economics of Southeastern Kansas. At one point, it had a population of 16,028 per the 1920 Census. Its roots can be tied back to the Missouri, Kansas & Texas Railroad, as its primary purpose for being founded was to serve the needs of the newly established railway. It was here that two lines of the railroad extended from Sedalia, Missouri, and Junction City, Kansas, would meet at the confluence between two creeks, and so extensive facilities consisting of a rail yard, locomotive shop, foundry, etc. were constructed. This facility would be the third-largest of its kind west of the Mississippi River for several years, third to only those in Los Angeles, California, and Kansas City. R. S. Stevens led the town company that would locate the townsite in 1870; the men elected to name it for Levi Parsons, then-president of the railroad. Within ten years of being established as a city, the population is said to have boomed to over 6,500 people, and over one hundred lines of business had been started by the townspeople. Amongst the most notable of these were perhaps the skirt, broom, cornice, corset, mattress, cigar factories, a foundry and creamery, a cider mill, and the Kansas State Hospital for Epileptics (founded in 1903), now called

the Parsons State Hospital & Training Center. The Kansas Army Ammunition Plant is another semi-recent structure of note constructed in 1942 to produce ammunition and bombs for use by the military during World War II. Dwayne's Photo rose to fame circa 2010 when it became the last facility in the world with the capabilities to process Kodak's Kodachrome film, and it was given the last chemicals needed to develop it. Other institutions and points of interest today are Labette Community College (est. 1923 as Parsons Junior College), Lake Parsons, the Parsons Arboretum, the Iron Horse Museum, and the Parsons Historical Society Museum. As it was aforementioned that Parsons had a booming population due to the railroad industry, there are several persons of note with city ties worth mentioning. Some of them are Walter Davison Sr. (co-founder of Harley-Davison), Payne Ratner (the 28th Governor of Kansas), Jeff Kready (Broadway actor known for his role as Jean Valjean in *Les Misérables*), Shaun Hill (NFL Europe passing yards leader in 2003 and the record-holder for the most completions thrown in a single season with 220), Nell Donnelly Reed (fashion designer of the Nelly Don brand of house dresses), actresses ZaSu Pitts and Jamie Anne Allman, William Coffin Coleman (founder of the Coleman Company), college basketball coach Bill Guthridge, Clyde M. Reed, the 24th Governor of Kansas, T. Claude Ryan, the founder of many aeronautical corporations and airlines, Medal of Honor recipient William W. Cranston, *New York Times* best-selling author Pintip Dunn, and Levi Watkins, the first surgeon to implant an automatic defibrillator in a patient.

**Adjacent Counties:** Neosho (N), Crawford (NE), Cherokee (E), Montgomery (W)

**Unincorporated/Ghost Towns:** Angola, Dennis, Montana, Mortimer, Strauss, Valeda, Wilsonton

### National Register of Historic Places:
**Edna:** First State Bank
**Mound Valley:** Pumpkin Creek Tributary Bridge
**Oswego:** Oswego Public Carnegie Library, Riverside Park, U.S. Post Office-Oswego
**Parsons:** Carnegie Library, Labette Creek Tributary Bridge, The Parsonian Hotel, Parsons Filled Arch Bridge, Parsons Katy Hospital

### Breweries/Wineries/Distilleries:
TJ's Brew Distillery & Winery (Parsons, KS)

**Golf Courses:**
Oswego Golf Association, Public (Oswego, KS)
Parsons Country Club, Private (Parsons, KS)
Parsons-Katy Golf Club, Semi-Private (Parsons, KS)

**Town Celebrations:**
Edna Smoke N Motor Show, Edna, KS (1st Saturday in June)
Flagpole Festival, Mound Valley, KS (Last Weekend of June)
Katy Days, Parsons, KS (Memorial Day Weekend)

Johnson County Photos: Fairway, Lenexa, Merriam, Olathe, Olathe, Overland Park, Overland Park, Shawnee

Kearny County Photos: Deerfield, Deerfield, Lakin, Lakin, Lakin, Lakin, Lakin, Lakin

Kingman County Photos: Cunningham, Cunningham, Kingman, Kingman, Kingman, Kingman, Kingman, Penalosa

Kiowa County Photos: Greensburg, Greensburg, Greensburg, Greensburg, Haviland, Haviland, Haviland, Mullinville

Labette County Photos: Chetopa, Chetopa, Chetopa, Mound Valley, Oswego, Oswego, Parsons, Parsons

# LANE COUNTY
## EST. 1873 - POPULATION: 1,574

The abolitionist James H. Lane, a general officer in the Union Army and a Kansas U.S. Senator, is the namesake of Lane County, Kansas.

# DIGHTON, KS ★☆
## POPULATION: 960 – TOWN 434 OF 627 (8-15-23)

Dighton is the sole incorporated community within Lane County, therefore making it the county seat. It was named after Dick Dighton, the surveyor responsible for dividing the townsite into lots for the first settlers to make their claims. The arrival of W. A. Watson in 1879 preceded the presence of other European settlers in the area, and he made a claim through The Homestead Act of 1862 and became the town's first postmaster. The arrival of the Atchison, Topeka & Santa Fe Railroad guaranteed the city a future, and so it was named the Lane County seat. It grew to include churches of the leading denominations, schools and newspapers, elevators and mills, and many lines of general merchandising mercantile. In Frank Baker's popular folk song, "Lane County Bachelor," he sings about living in the area because of its unfavorable weather patterns and the hardships of living in such a wide-open part of Kansas. Following a burglary of the First National Bank of Lamar, Colorado, by the Fleagle Gang, surviving members fled to Dighton and kidnapped and killed local doctor W. W. Wineinger after they forced him to tend to their injuries. This story and others are featured exhibits of the Lane County Historical Museum.

 **Restaurant Recommendation:**
**Frigid Creme**
**433 E Long St**
**Dighton, KS 67839**

**Adjacent Counties:** Gove (N), Ness (E), Finney (S), Scott (W)

**Unincorporated/Ghost Towns:** Alamota, Amy, Farnsworth, Healy, Pendennis, Shields

267

**National Register of Historic Places:**
**Dighton:** Lane County Community High School, Alexander & Anna Schwartz Farm

**Golf Courses:**
Lane County Country Club, Public (Dighton, KS)

# LEAVENWORTH COUNTY
## EST. 1855 - POPULATION: 81,881

Henry Leavenworth founded Fort Leavenworth, the oldest permanent settlement in Kansas. The respective county and city are both named in his honor.

# BASEHOR, KS
## POPULATION: 6,896 – TOWN 285 OF 627 (6-12-23)
Basehor, one of the fastest growing towns in Kansas, would have its start after the Leavenworth, Pawnee, and Western Railroad purchased land from the Delaware Diminished Reserve in January of 1886, and Reuben and Ephraim Basehor would plat a townsite in 1889. The town was to be named Basehor for their surname. The brothers would be the benefactors of the town's first library and school. The Missouri Pacific Railroad served the community as a shipping point, and it remained unincorporated until 1965. Basehor Historical Museum is of local interest to history enthusiasts.

# EASTON, KS
## POPULATION: 213 – TOWN 61 OF 627 (3-14-23)
Once formally called Eastin, this community was established by its founder and namesake, General Eastin J. Trader, in 1854. He was the former editor of the Kansas Herald. The spelling of the name was later changed to "Easton" at the request of Andrew Horatio Reder, the first governor of the Territory of Kansas, for his hometown of Easton, Pennsylvania. The city was located on the Union Pacific Railroad, and its first post office was established in December 1855.

# LANSING, KS
## POPULATION: 11,239 – TOWN 283 OF 627 (6-12-23)
The growth and founding of Lansing came with the construction of the Lansing Correctional Facility (then the Kansas State Penitentiary)

throughout the 1860s. It began housing prisoners in July of 1868, about ten years before the town was platted under the supervision of James Lansing. Lansing had served in the 7th Kansas Cavalry Regiment in the American Civil War as a hospital steward. After leaving his job at the prison, he sought to open a store that served as the foundation of what would become the townsite. Because of the three railroads (the Union Pacific, Missouri Pacific, and the Atchison, Topeka & Santa Fe) that served the town, a coal mine was opened at the penitentiary, and frequent shipments led the city to develop banks, schools, churches, and other business lines. In February 1902, Lansing was the site of the "Lansing Man" archaeological discovery, in which the remains of a man from roughly 3579 B.C. were uncovered. The city was not incorporated until 1959. The Lansing Historical Museum was founded to explain the community's origins and ties to the railroad and the jail. The graves of the *In Cold Blood* killers, Richard Hickock and Perry Smith, are located at Lansing's Mount Muncie Cemetery.

# LEAVENWORTH, KS ★
## POPULATION: 37,351 – TOWN 284 OF 627 (6-12-23)
Leavenworth was the first city incorporated in Kansas in 1854, although its history predates its incorporation. Fort Leavenworth was constructed in 1827 as a military installation for several thousands of settlers, soldiers, and other persons to pass through as they made their way westward into unfamiliar territory. It is the oldest permanent settlement in the state and the second oldest active United States Army post west of the nation's capital in Washington D.C.. After the Kansas-Nebraska Act was enacted in 1854, George W. Gist and his town company went to work to establish a townsite immediately south of the Fort. Lots went up for sale in October 1854, and in the subsequent years, a sawmill, hotel, post office, and all of the other typical lines of business began to form. Much of its rapid growth can be attributed to the Majors, Russell & Company, a large transportation company that required many people and resources to maintain. The military road and Oregon and California Trails would also lead large numbers of pioneers through the city limits, and many elected to stay in the quickly growing town. Factories of various manufacturing capabilities were established, making everything from wagons, shoes, and steam engines to stoves, soap, musical instruments, and bridges. The Atchison, Topeka & Santa Fe, Union Pacific, and Missouri Pacific Railroads would all opt to extend their respective lines through the city to take advantage of its thriving economy. In 1858, a variant of the potential Kansas State

Constitution, the "Leavenworth Constitution," was adopted here (but never officially approved by the federal government) that would have recognized freed African Americans as citizens. The city served as a haven for formerly enslaved persons and was home to a large portion of the state's African-American population by the end of the Civil War. Some of its main tourist destinations are the C. W. Parker Carousel Museum, the Edward Carroll Mansion, the National Fred Harvey Museum, the First City Museum, the Richard Allen Cultural Center and Museum, the Leavenworth County Courthouse (as it is the county seat), and the nearby Fort Leavenworth, home to the Frontier Army Museum. The University of Saint Mary (known as Saint Mary College throughout its first eighty years of existence) has operated since 1923 as a private Catholic university with an enrollment of about 800 students. Because of its age, many persons of notoriety and fame have been affiliated with the city over its lifetime: Brock Pemberton (founder of the Tony Awards and co-founder of the American Theatre Wing), William B. Waddell (co-founder of the Pony Express), Donn B. Murphy (theatrical advisor to the Kennedy Administration and President and Executive Director of the National Theatre from 1974 to 2010), Fred Harvey (creator of the first restaurant chain in the United States, the Harvey House), Jack Beckley (first baseman and member of the National Baseball Hall of Fame), David J. Brewer (Justice of the Supreme Court from 1890 to 1910), Melissa Etheridge (Grammy Award-winning guitarist and singer), Elizabeth Vargas (anchor for A&E Networks and NewsNation), the 2nd and 7th Governors of Kansas, Thomas Carney and George T. Anthony, and William Larimer Jr., the founder of Denver, Colorado, amongst others.

 **Restaurant Recommendation:**
**Pullman Place Restaurant**
**230 Cherokee St**
**Leavenworth, KS 66048**

**Lodging Recommendation:**
**Leavenworth Local Hotel**
**600 Shawnee St**
**Leavenworth, KS 66048**

# LINWOOD, KS
## POPULATION: 415 – TOWN 281 OF 627 (6-12-23)

In the 1860s, Journeycake was founded at the confluence of the Stranger and Kansas Rivers and named in honor of Charles Journeycake, the final chief of the Lenape Delaware people. After the government signed a treaty with Chief Sarcoxie of the Delaware tribe in 1860, the land was sold to the Union Pacific Railroad so they could begin construction on a railroad line from Kansas City to Denver, Colorado. The town was platted in 1867, and the name changed to Stanger until the postal service forced it to be changed once more to Linwood because of another community by the name "Stranger" in that area. The present name was decided upon because of the abundant linden trees that grew throughout the townsite and Stranger Creek. A school, places of worship, and several stores were constructed throughout the early days of the town, and in 1895, it became an incorporated city. Linwood's population has varied only slightly over the decades, having dropped as low as 261 persons (1950 Census) and as high as 415 residents (2020 Census). The town's most famous person was William Alexander Harris, a wealthy politician affiliated with the stock trade, the Union Pacific Railroad, and the Kansas legislature.

# TONGANOXIE, KS ☆
## POPULATION: 5,573 – TOWN 286 OF 627 (6-12-23)

Tonganoxie has grown considerably since its inception in 1866 because of its proximity to the Kansas City metropolitan area. Between the 2000 Census and the 2020 Census alone, the population grew from 2,728 residents to 5,573, an increase of 104.29%. It was laid out by Mrs. Magdalena Bury, who, with other early residents, opted to name it in honor of the Delaware Native American chief Tonganoxie, who operated a tavern in the area for pioneer settlers. Tonganoxie was incorporated in 1871, and its earliest banks, lumber yards, churches, drug, shoe, millinery, general stores, and other lines of enterprise thrived with the introduction of the Union Pacific and the Missouri Pacific Railroads. Artifacts line the walls of the Tonganoxie Community Historical Society and Museum, which consists of the Reno Methodist Church, the Honey Valley Schoolhouse, a dairy barn, a milk parlor, and a firehouse. NFL players Doug McEnulty (1943 NFL champion) and Roy Zimmerman (1942 NFL All-Star and champion and the creator of the rise ball and drop ball in fast-pitch softball), Danni Boatwright (the winner of *Survivor: Guatemala* in 2005), and film historian Terry Ramsaye.

Bonner Springs and Kansas City are only partially located in Leavenworth County (see Wyandotte County), and De Soto is only partially located in Leavenworth County (see Johnson County).

**Adjacent Counties:** Wyandotte (E), Johnson (SE), Douglas (SW), Jefferson (W), Atchison (NW)

**Unincorporated/Ghost Towns:** Bonner-Loring, Coldspur, Delaware City, Fairmount, Fall Leaf, Hoge, Jarbalo, Kickapoo, Lowemont, Maltby, Millwood, Reno, Springdale, Wadsworth

## National Register of Historic Places:
**Fort Leavenworth:** Fort Leavenworth National Cemetery
**Leavenworth:** Abernathy Furniture Company Factory, A. J. Angell House, Arch Street Historic District, Atchison, Topeka & Santa Fe Railroad Passenger Depot, AXA Building, David J. Brewer House, Nathaniel H. Burt House, Edward Carroll House, First Presbyterian Church, Leavenworth, Fort Leavenworth, Greenwood Cemetery, Fred Harvey House, Helmers Manufacturing Company Building, Hollywood Theater, Alice and Edwin Holman Farmstead, Hund School, Merritt Insley House and Outbuildings, Horace and Rosemond Lamborn Farmstead, Leavenworth County Courthouse, Leavenworth Downtown Historic District, Leavenworth Historic Industrial District, Leavenworth Public Library, Leavenworth Terminal Railway & Bridge Company Freight Depot, Little Stranger Church and Cemetery, North Broadway Historic District, North Broadway School, North Esplanade Historic District, Old Union Depot, David W. Powers House, Quarry Creek Archeological Site, William Small Memorial Home for Aged Women, South Esplanade Historic District, Sumner Elementary School, Third Avenue Historic District, Union Park Historic District, Western Branch, National Home for Disabled Volunteer Soldiers, Zacharias Site
**Linwood:** Delaware Cemetery, Senator William A. Harris House
**Millwood:** Begley Bridge
**Tonganoxie:** Stonehaven Farm

## Breweries/Wineries/Distilleries:
11Worth Station BrewHouse (Leavenworth, KS)
Holy-Field Vineyard & Winery (Basehor, KS)
Willcott Brewing Company – Leavenworth (Leavenworth, KS)
Z&M Twisted Vines Wines and Winery (Leavenworth, KS)

**Golf Courses:**
Falcon Lakes Golf Course, Public (Basehor, KS)
Leavenworth Country Club, Private (Lansing, KS)
The Oaks Golf Club, Public (Leavenworth, KS)
Trails West Golf Course, Military (Fort Leavenworth, KS)

**Town Celebrations:**
Basehor Dairy Days, Basehor, KS (1st Saturday of June)

# LINCOLN COUNTY
## EST. 1867 - POPULATION: 2,939

Founded in 1867, Lincoln County's name seeks to honor Abraham Lincoln, the 16th President of the United States.

# BARNARD, KS
### POPULATION: 64 – TOWN 137 OF 627 (4-10-23)
The small city of Barnard owes its existence to the construction of the Chicago, Kansas & Western Railroad Company that built the line through the area circa 1888. The town's name seeks to honor J. F. Barnard, a railroad employee. Not long after the town's founding, the Atchison, Topeka, and Santa Fe Railroad took control of the line in 1901, and in 1904, Barnard was officially incorporated. Although the population has since dwindled from its peak of 425 residents in 1910, Barnard was once the site of multiple banks, churches, and businesses. "The Cookbook House" is a local point of interest run by present city clerk Barb Rathbun that may potentially hold the "World's Largest Collection of Cookbooks."

# BEVERLY, KS
### POPULATION: 135 – TOWN 136 OF 627 (4-10-23)
Beverly is an eponym for Beverly, West Virginia, the home of one of its earliest homesteaders, Volany Ball. It was established in 1886 as a station on the Salina & Plainville line of the Union Pacific Railroad and, in 1904, was incorporated as a city of the third class. The first serviceman to receive a Medal of Honor for his service in World War II, Donald Kirby Ross, was born here on December 8, 1910. As travelers approach Beverly from the east on Highway 18, they will notice a collection of a dozen pieces of art made from old farm equipment, including a 60-foot-long dragon.

# LINCOLN CENTER, KS ★

**POPULATION: 1,171 – TOWN 138 OF 627 (4-10-23)**

The "Post Rock Capital of Kansas," Lincoln, had its beginnings in 1870 with the arrival of early settler George Green. He elected to name the newly founded community "Lincoln Center" for its geographical location at the center of Lincoln County. Although it today serves as the county seat, for a short period between November 1870 and February 1872, the nearby town of Abram took over the responsibilities until citizens later reversed the decision. Incorporation came about in 1879 under the name "Lincoln Center," although the latter part of the name has been dropped in most usages. One oddity in town is the suitcase-shaped tombstone of traveling salesman J. S. Jacobs in the Lincoln Cemetery. The community is more touted for its three museums, the Post Rock Scout Museum, Crispin's Drug Store Museum, and the Lincoln County, Kansas, Historical Museum. The first two museums focus primarily on scouting and pharmaceuticals, and the general history museum includes a school, newspaper office, funeral home, general store, and the historic Kyne House. Noted Lincoln residents of the past include James H. Knight (the pilot who delivered the first overnight transcontinental parcel), Martin Johnson (worldwide adventurer and filmmaker), Jessa Crispin (critic and author), Don Wendell Holter (former bishop of the United Methodist Church), Daniel Ray Hull (landscape architect famous for his work on many of national parks), Uncas A. Whitaker (founder of AMP incorporated, the world's largest manufacturer of electrical devices and connectors), and Bessie Anderson Stanley (author of the well-known 1904 poem, "Success"). Her poem is the origin of the popular saying, "Live, laugh, love."

# SYLVAN GROVE, KS ☆

**POPULATION: 291 – TOWN 139 OF 627 (4-10-23)**

Sylvan Grove was named for a duo of sylvan groves that were located on the original townsite at the time of its founding in 1877. The town was established on the land of William Bender and H. S. Merriam, and its earliest settlers were Louis and Hutchinson Farley, participants in the Battle of Beecher's Island. The Union Pacific Railroad was responsible for the town's growth spurt in its early days, as the city grew from 25 persons in the 1880 Census to a peak population of 540 in 1940. Fly Boy Brewery & Eats is a noted local establishment that has given Sylvan Grove the distinction of being the smallest town in Kansas with a brewery. The Yesterday House Museum showcases items and memorabilia from Sylvan Grove's pioneer days, and Wilson State Park is a noted recreation area that allows swimming, boating, camping, and hiking.

 **Restaurant Recommendation:
Fly Boy Brewery & Eats
105 N Main St
Sylvan Grove, KS 67481**

**Adjacent Counties:** Mitchell (N), Ottawa (E), Saline (SE), Ellsworth (S), Russell (W), Osborne (NW)

**Unincorporated/Ghost Towns:** Ash Grove, Bacon, Bayne, Cedron, Denmark, Herman, Lone Walnut, Milo, Monroe, Orbitello, Orworth, Paris, Pinon, Pleasant Valley, Pottersburg, Rosette, Topsy, Towerspring, Union Valley, Vesper, Woodey, Yorktown

**National Register of Historic Places:**
**Barnard:** Salt Creek Truss Leg Bedstead Bridge
**Grant Township:** Danske Evangelist Lutheran Kirke
**Lincoln:** Cummins Block Building, Lincoln Carnegie Library, Lincoln City Park, Lincoln County Courthouse, Lincoln Downtown Historic District, Lincoln High School, Marshall-Yohe House, Spring Creek Tributary Bridge
**Sylvan Grove:** Behrhorst Brothers Hardware, Evangelical Lutheran School, Nielsen Farm, Sylvan Grove Union Pacific Depot
**Vesper:** Bullfoot Creek Bridge

**Breweries/Wineries/Distilleries:**
Fly Boy Brewery and Eats (Sylvan Grove, KS)

**Town Celebrations:**
Lovegrass Music Festival, Sylvan Grove, KS (2nd Weekend in August)
Post Rock Festival, Lincoln, KS (Labor Day Weekend)

# LINN COUNTY
## EST. 1855 - POPULATION: 9,591

A United States Senator from Missouri, Lewis F. Linn, would go down in the history books forever when this county was named after him in 1855.

# BLUE MOUND, KS
**POPULATION: 219 – TOWN 339 OF 627 (6-30-23)**

John Quincy Adams (not to be confused with the United States President of the same name) named Blue Mound after a local geographical feature that radiated a hue of blue. The local post office was established in 1854, long before the town was platted in 1882 by the Blue Mound Town Company. Some of its earliest lines of business included a harness shop, drug, furniture, general stores, a lumber yard, and a hardware store, all of which were supported by the extension of two lines of the Missouri Pacific Railroad.

# LA CYGNE, KS
**POPULATION: 1,050 – TOWN 343 OF 627 (6-30-23)**

The founding of La Cygne came immediately before the extension of the St. Louis & San Francisco Railroad to that point of Kansas. In 1869, the town was platted on 140 acres of land, and the following January, it was incorporated. F. A. Foote was elected as the first mayor. Henceforth, the town began to grow as residents introduced a flour mill, organ factory, and coal mine as its noteworthy places of early business lines. The community got its name from the Marais des Cygnes River, which comes from an Osage-French term meaning "marsh of the swans." Its local center for history is the La Cygne Historical Society Museum.

 **Restaurant Recommendation: Re-Ohz!**
**115 N Broadway St**
**La Cygne, KS 66040**

# LINN VALLEY, KS
**POPULATION: 956 – TOWN 342 OF 627 (6-30-23)**

Linn Valley is a relatively new city, having only been incorporated since November 1998. Until then, it had been an unincorporated community developing around Linn Valley Lakes (named for the geographical feature of the county in which they are located). The population then was about 375 individuals, 74% of whom voted to incorporate Linn Valley as a city of the third class. In August of 2001, a recall vote was held to determine whether or not the town should remain incorporated, which it did by a vote of 216 to 170. The town's reason for incorporating was so that the covenants of the Property

Owners Association could be better enforced since the county government was insufficient in doing so in a timely manner.

# MOUND CITY, KS ★☆
**POPULATION: 647 – TOWN 340 OF 627 (6-30-23)**
The history of Mound City began in 1855 when it was founded by D. W. Cannon and Ebenezer Barnes and named after the nearby Sugar Mound, a large hill decorated with hundreds of sugar maple trees. Settlers were prompt in building a town hall, post office, and living quarters. As Confederate forces were retreating from the Battle of Westport, they twice attacked the city, which by that time had built a military outpost to defend from attackers. Its designation as the Linn County seat has been a long and tedious matter, as the judicial seat began there in 1859 when it defeated the town of Paris in a vote but then lost the seat in 1865 to Linnville. It regained the honor in 1866, lost it a second time to La Cygne in 1871, and then regained it after the title was moved thrice to Farmers City, La Cygne, and Pleasanton before it returned to Mound City in 1874. At the turn of the century, Mound City became a bustling hub for economic activity, having a blacksmith, glass factory, coal mines, wagon shops, a creamery, stone quarries, and a flour mill. Its current population is 647 citizens, although its highest on record was 888 persons in 1890. Many early buildings are displayed at the open-air Mound City Historical Park, including a school, windmill, log cabin, and railroad depot.

# PARKER, KS
**POPULATION: 241 – TOWN 345 OF 627 (6-30-23)**
Parker was platted in 1889 and named for the original townsite owner, J. W. Parker. The post office predates the town, established on December 22, 1888. After the construction of the Missouri, Kansas & Texas Railroad, the community raised schools and churches, a line of general stores, and a lumber yard and bank. Its highest historical population came in 1920 when the Census reported that 436 persons lived in Parker. One of the most recent governors of Kansas (the 46th), Sam Brownback, grew up on a farm near the community. The Parker Museum focuses its exhibits on the early settlers and stories of the town.

# PLEASANTON, KS

**POPULATION: 1,208 – TOWN 341 OF 627 (6-30-23)**

General Alfred Pleasonton is the namesake of this community. He is best known for leading Union forces to a victory over the Confederates in the Battle of Mine Creek on October 25, 1864, which took place not far from the present-day townsite. The town was founded a short half-decade after the battle when it was sure that the Kansas City, Fort Scott & Gulf Railroad (later bought out by the St. Louis & San Francisco Railroad) would be built through the area. A post office arrived in 1869, and the townspeople erected a hotel, general, hardware and drug store, flour mills, quarries, coal mines, and a hay press factory to further Pleasanton's growth and attract a second railroad line, the Missouri Pacific. Pleasanton is the proud site of the Linn County Museum, Antique Car Museum, Trading Post Museum, Carpenter's Ol' Iron Motorcycle Museum, and the Mine Creek Battlefield State Historic Site. The battle site commemorates the Battle of Mine Creek, in which an army of 2,800 Union soldiers defeated 8,000 Confederates on October 25, 1864. Born here in 1899 was Julius C. Holmes, who served as the Assistant Secretary of State in the latter portion of World War II.

**Lodging Recommendation:**
**Cedar Crest Lodge**
**25939 E 1000th Rd**
**Pleasanton, KS 66075**

# PRESCOTT, KS

**POPULATION: 207 – TOWN 336 OF 627 (6-30-23)**

Prescott (pop. 207) was founded and incorporated in 1870 and named for C. H. Prescott, the auditor and treasurer of the Missouri River, Fort Scott & Gulf Railroad. That railroad line would later become a part of the St. Louis & San Francisco Railroad. Its earliest establishments were a post office, a general store, a drug store, and a blacksmith shop. Its present population is the lowest it has been since shortly after the town's incorporation (1880, 151 citizens).

**Adjacent Counties:** Miami (N), Bourbon (S), Allen (SW), Anderson (W), Franklin (NW)

**Unincorporated/Ghost Towns:** Cadmus, Centerville, Critzer, Farlinville, Hail Ridge, Mantey, Trading Post

**National Register of Historic Places:**
**Goodrich:** Landers Creek Bridge
**Mound City:** Linn County Courthouse, Mine Creek Bridge, Old Linn County Jail
**Pleasanton:** Battle of Mine Creek Site
**Prescott:** Prescott School, Prescott Rural High School
**Trading Post:** Marais des Cygnes Massacre Site

**Breweries/Wineries/Distilleries:**
Blue Dog Wine Company (La Cygne, KS)
Isinglass Vineyard & Winery (La Cygne, KS)

**Golf Courses:**
Deer Trace Golf Links, Private (La Cygne, KS)
Sugar Valley Lakes Homes Association, Private (Mound City, KS)

**Town Celebrations:**
Dancefestopia Music Festival, La Cygne, KS (Early September)
General Pleasonton Days, Pleasanton, KS (1st Weekend of October)
Parker Days, Parker, KS (3rd Weekend in September)
Sugar Mound Arts & Crafts Festival, Mound City, KS (2nd Weekend in October)

# LOGAN COUNTY
## EST. 1888 - POPULATION: 2,762

Logan County got its name from John A. Logan, a United States Senator from Illinois who is widely remembered for his role in recognizing Memorial Day as a federal holiday.

# OAKLEY, KS ★☆
**POPULATION: 2,046 – TOWN 160 OF 627 (4-12-23)**
Former names for the bustling city of Oakley included Carlyle and Cleveland before its name was selected in 1885 to honor Elizabeth Oakley Gardner Hoag, the mother of David D. Hoag. David Hoag and Judge Fredman had founded the community a year prior, although its very first settlers were pioneers following the Smoky Hill Trail toward

Denver, Colorado, in the 1870s and 1880s. Parts of the town extend into Gove and Thomas Counties, although it is the county seat of Logan County. Fick Fossil and History Museum is a large draw for tourists that boasts exhibits of dinosaur fossils, folk art, and other relics, and the Buffalo Bill Kill Statue, a heavily detailed statue of Buffalo Bill Cody hunting his nickname's namesake, is another point of interest. The Monument Rocks and Chalk Pyramids, a National Natural Landmark located twenty-five miles south of Oakley, and the nearby Little Jerusalem Badlands State Park offer some of the best views of Kansas's natural landforms that were created over 80 million years ago during the Cretaceous Period. The Keystone Gallery is near the area and is located in an old country church; it exhibits art and fossils. The 2006 television series *Jericho* is based on a fictional town that largely resembles the geographical location and other similarities to Oakley.

# RUSSELL SPRINGS, KS
## POPULATION: 26 – TOWN 161 OF 627 (4-12-23)

"Russell's Springs" served as a place for weary travelers on the Overland Trail to stop for a fresh drink of water from a natural spring. In 1865, some travelers decided to begin a settlement there, and in the following decades, the Kansas Pacific Railroad was extended to that point. The name of the springs pay homage to Avra P. Russell of the 2nd Regiment Kansas Volunteer Cavalry, a cavalry who fought for the Union in the American Civil War. Although its present population wouldn't reflect it, Russell Springs was the county seat of Logan County until Oakley took the title in 1963. The old courthouse is presently the site of the Butterfield Trail Museum, a building that discusses the history of the Overland Despatch stage line. The population of Russell Springs never broke the 200-person mark. However, hundreds of individuals flock to the town every September to partake in the "Cow Chip Capital of Kansas's" cow-chip throwing contest at the annual Old Settler's Day Celebration. Logan State Fishing Lake fills and disappears depending on weather patterns.

# WINONA, KS
## POPULATION: 193 – TOWN 162 OF 627 (4-12-23)

The name Winona is in reference to a character in Henry Wadsworth Longfellow's 1855 poem, "The Song of Hiawatha." Wenonah is the mother of the main character, Hiawatha. The town of Winona was established in 1884 as Gopher, but the name was changed only three years later. The Union Pacific Railroad brought the first settlers and industries to the area.

**Adjacent Counties:** Thomas (N), Gove (E), Scott (SE), Wichita (S), Wallace (W), Sherman (NW)

**Unincorporated/Ghost Towns:** Henshaw Station, McAllaster, Monument, Page City, Sheridan
**National Register of Historic Places:**
**Oakley:** Oakley High School Stadium
**Russell Springs:** Old Logan County Courthouse
**Winona:** Winona Consolidated School

**Golf Courses:**
Oakley Country Club, Semi-Private (Oakley, KS)

**Town Celebrations:**
Old Settlers' Days, Russell Springs, KS (Labor Day)

Lane County Photos: Dighton (all)

Leavenworth County Photos: Easton, Leavenworth, Leavenworth, Leavenworth, Leavenworth, Leavenworth, Linwood, Tonganoxie

283

Lincoln County Photos: Barnard, Beverly, Lincoln, Lincoln, Lincoln, Lincoln, Sylvan Grove, Sylvan Grove

Linn County Photos: Blue Mound, La Cygne, La Cygne, Mound City, Mound City, Mound City, Pleasanton, Pleasanton

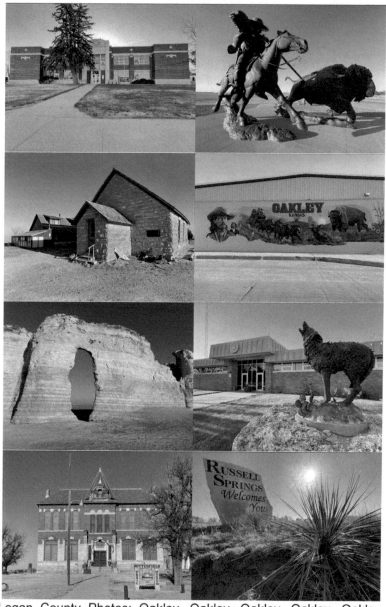

Logan County Photos: Oakley, Oakley, Oakley, Oakley, Oakley, Oakley, Russell Springs, Russell Springs

# LYON COUNTY
## EST. 1855 - POPULATION: 32,179

The name "Lyon" was derived from the surname of Nathaniel Lyon, the first Union general to be killed because of the conflicts of the American Civil War.

# ADMIRE, KS
### POPULATION: 130 – TOWN 228 OF 627 (5-3-23)
This community in northeast Lyon County was named in honor of Jacob Admire, one of its founders. It was built on land originally owned by B. H. G. Wilbur and founded in the year 1886. On November 15, 1886, the post office arrived, and on July 6, 1896, Admire was incorporated as a city of the third class with George W. McDaniel as its mayor. The Missouri Pacific Railroad brought about some of the town's first establishments, such as churches, mercantile stores, a feed mill, and more. A former test pilot for Bell Aircraft and the Boeing Company, Alvin M. Johnston, heeds from Admire.

# ALLEN, KS
### POPULATION: 160 – TOWN 227 OF 627 (5-3-23)
The Missouri Pacific Railroad station was founded in 1854 and incorporated circa 1910. The highest population it ever reached was 343 citizens as of the 1930 Census. It once had numerous churches and mercantile establishments, as well as a school and post office.

# AMERICUS, KS
### POPULATION: 776 – TOWN 225 OF 627 (5-3-23)
The name Americus was derived from Amerigo Vespucci, the famous Italian explorer responsible for proving that the "New World" discovered by Christopher Columbus was an entirely "new" continent. It was founded in 1857 along the Neosho River and located on the Missouri, Kansas & Texas Railroad. The town's population skyrocketed from 441 residents as of the 1970 Census to 915 in 1980, an increase of 107.5%, although it has since dropped slightly to its president-day number of 776 individuals. Born here in February of 1919 was Grant F. Timmerman, a Medal of Honor recipient for his actions during World War II, and Ross Grimsley, an MLB pitcher for the Chicago White Sox.

# BUSHONG, KS
**POPULATION: 27 – TOWN 226 OF 627 (5-3-23)**

Bushong was incorporated in 1926, although its history dates back to the 1880s when the Missouri Pacific Railroad extended its line through the townsite. Its etymology is unique as it is one of only a handful of incorporated towns in the United States named in honor of an athlete, specifically Albert J. "Doc" Bushong, a catcher for the 1886 World Series champion St. Louis Browns. Several team members had Missouri Pacific Railroad depots named in their honor, although Bushong is the only such community remaining today. Bushong once had a post office, bank, school, hotel, and general stores, although industry (and the population, now only 27) has since shrunk.

# EMPORIA, KS ★☆
**POPULATION: 24,139 – TOWN 312 OF 627 (6-28-23)**

Emporia, the county seat of Lyon County, was founded by Preston B. Plumb in 1857. He was the town's first promoter, and he worked with George W. Deitzler, Lyman Allen, G. W. Brown, and Columbus Hornsby to develop the townsite and its first stores, hotels, and homes. They and the other early townspeople settled on the name Emporia, derived from the Latin word "emporium," meaning "a place of trade or commerce." It lived up to its designations as a market town as several lines of business (marble and iron works, a planing mill, factories creating brooms and corrugated culverts, foundries, a brick and tile plant, an ice plant, etc.) thrived there. The city became a railroad hub with the arrival of the Missouri, Kansas & Texas, and three lines of the Atchison, Topeka & Santa Fe Railways. Emporia would be incorporated in 1865 and once more in 1870 as a city of the second class, and for many years, it was known as an educational hub of Kansas because of its superior public school facilities and its distinction of being the home of two large institutions of higher learning, Emporia State University and the College of Emporia. The latter school operated from 1882 to 1974 under the jurisdiction of the Presbyterian church. Emporia State University was established in 1863 and is the third-oldest public university in the state. The University of Kansas was almost located in Emporia by an act of the Kansas Legislature, but it lost the honor to Lawrence by only a single vote. Flint Hills Technical College is the most recent college established in Emporia in 1963; it is the city's only community college. Other sites of interest are the National Teachers Hall of Fame, Schmidt Museum of Natural History, the Johnston Geology Museum, the Norman R. Eppink and Gilson Memorial Galleries, and the

National Memorial to Fallen Educators on the campus of ESU and the historic Granada Theatre and the William Allen White House State Historic Site. Emporia has always been progressive in its ideas for town events, as it was the first town in the United States to observe Veterans Day in 1953, which would be designated a federal holiday by President Dwight D. Eisenhower the following year. It is frequently called the "Disc Golf Capital of the World" because of its large number of disc golf courses and its annual Dynamic Discs Open tournament. "Unbound Gravel" has been referred to as one of the top gravel bike races in the world because it takes riders through a 25-to-350-mile loop throughout Kansas's Flint Hills region. *Murder Ordained*, a 1987 CBS television film, was based on actual events in Emporia and filmed on location. Its higher population relative to the rest of the state has resulted in numerous figures of historical importance or fame: Dean Smith (formerly the NCAA Division I men's basketball leader in wins by a coach with 879 wins between 1961 and 1997), David Green (the founder of Hobby Lobby), Samuel J. Crawford (the 3rd Governor of Kansas), William Allen White (famed writer and leader of the Progressive movement), Cady Groves (pop and country artist), Clint Bowyer (NASCAR driver and 2008 Nationwide Series champion). Lee Ermey (known for his role as Gunnery Sergeant Hartman in the 1987 war drama movie *Full Metal Jacket*), Jim Everett (1990 NFL Pro-Bowler and 2x NFL passing touchdowns leader in 1988 and 1989), Rose Conway (Personal Secretary to President Harry S. Truman), and Arthur Samuel (pioneer of computer games and artificial intelligence).

**Restaurant Recommendation:**
**Casa Ramos**
**707 Commercial St**
**Emporia, KS 66801**

**Restaurant Recommendation:**
**Do-B's**
**704 E 12th Ave**
**Emporia, KS 66801**

**Lodging Recommendation:**
**Guffler Mansion**
**612 W 12th Ave**
**Emporia, KS 66801**

# HARTFORD, KS
**POPULATION: 355 – TOWN 311 OF 627 (6-28-23)**
Hartford is an eponym for Hartford, Connecticut, the hometown of two of its early founders, H. D. Rie and A. K. Hawkes. It was laid out in 1858 by the two men alongside W. H. Martin, E. Quiett, and others. Within the first year, the first lines of business were established, and in 1859, the post office formed with Hawkes at its helm. The Methodist Episcopal Conference decided to establish a branch of Baker University in the newly-founded town circa 1860, so a 32 by 46 structure was built and utilized for many years until the local high school took over the building. Hartford's incorporation came in March 1884; within the same timeframe, the Missouri, Kansas & Texas Railroad rolled into town. Flint Hills National Wildlife Refuge was created in 1966 to protect the habitats of several species of animals. Wildlife viewing is the primary activity for tourists, although fishing, hiking, boating, and a museum are among the other opportunities.

# NEOSHO RAPIDS, KS
**POPULATION: 229 – TOWN 310 OF 627 (6-28-23)**
The whitewater rapids of the Neosho River gave light to the idea of naming this townsite Neosho Rapids. However, the town's first name was Italia when it was laid out in 1855. Florence was another early name, but town promoters F. R. Page, G. J. Tallman, and H. S. Sleeper elected to change it one last time and then work to construct a hotel building. The city's incorporation date was 1923, although there are records of the population as early as 1880 when the town was home to only 80 people. The Atchison, Topeka & Santa Fe Railroad was the early railroad of note, similar to many other area communities. On December 24, 1945, Neosho Rapids and its people were featured in a 5-page feature in *LIFE* magazine that showcased WWII service members returning home for their first post-war Christmas with their families.

# OLPE, KS

Bitlertown was named in honor of its original townsite owner, Gilbert Bitler, upon its founding in 1879 with the knowledge that the Atchison, Topeka & Santa Fe railroad would soon be built through the area. Settlers would later change the name to pay tribute to their homeland of Olpe, Germany. Before the names Bitlertown and Olpe, the site had been formerly called Eagle Creek Station. Throughout the early 20th century, Olpe would continue to grow, and more businesses would be developed, including the Olpe Chicken House in 1958. The restaurant's beginnings date back to 1934, and its visitors have included prominent political figures like Kansas governors and state representatives throughout the years. The city was incorporated in 1905 and is today recognized as being the only community named "Olpe" in the country.

 **Restaurant Recommendation:**
**Chicken House**
**8 KS-99**
**Olpe, KS 66865**

# READING, KS

Reading (pop. 181) was named after Reading, Pennsylvania, because the land that the townsite was founded upon was owned by a firm from that city, McMann & Company. James Fagan, M. S. Sargent, and T. J. Peter worked with one another to survey the land and establish the Atchison, Topeka & Santa Fe Railroad through it. The postal service followed suit by placing an office in town that same year on August 24, 1870. It was incorporated in September 1890 as a city of the third class. The population decreased steadily throughout the 20th century, but following a May 2011 tornado that wiped out over 50% of the town's homes and 67% of its businesses, the population dropped by a quarter between the 2010 and 2020 Census. Bob Price, a Congressman for Texas from 1967 to 1975, and Jim Barnett, a former candidate for Kansas state governor in 2006 and 2018, are from this small city.

**Adjacent Counties:** Wabaunsee (N), Osage (NE), Coffey (SE), Greenwood (S), Chase (W), Morris (NW)
**Unincorporated/Ghost Towns:** Miller, Plymouth

**National Register of Historic Places:**
**Americus:** Harris Bridge
**Emporia:** Anderson Carnegie Memorial Library, Col. H. C. and Susan Cross House, Emporia Downtown Historic District, Warren Wesley Finney House, Granada Theater, Harris-Borman House, Richard Howe House, Keebler-Stone House, Kress Building, Walt Mason House, Snowden S. Mouse Service Station and Tourist Home, Old Emporia Public Library, Mrs. Preston B. Plumb House, Rocky Ford Bridge, Soden's Grove Bridge, Hallie B. Soden House, William Allen White House
**Hartford:** Hartford Collegiate Institute

**Breweries/Wineries/Distilleries:**
Bobwhite Vines (Hartford, KS)
Broken Spoke Vineyard (Emporia, KS)
Radius Brewing Company (Emporia, KS)
Trolley House Distillery (Emporia, KS)

**Golf Courses:**
Emporia Country Club, Private (Emporia, KS)
Emporia Golf Course, Public (Emporia, KS)

**Town Celebrations:**
Great American Market, Emporia, KS (2nd Saturday in September)

# MARION COUNTY
## EST. 1860 - POPULATION: 12,660

When Marion County was organized in 1860, it was decided that it would be named for the American Revolution war hero Francis "Swamp Fox" Marion.

# BURNS, KS
## POPULATION: 234 – TOWN 220 OF 627 (5-3-23)

The Florence, El Dorado, and Walnut Valley Railroad Company founded Burns in 1877 as a station on their line. The station was located north of the present-day townsite. In 1880, a city named St. Francis had its beginnings, but town officials then realized that a town of the same name already existed in the state in Cheyenne County. They decided that the name of the community and the station should match, so it was selected to be Burns in honor of an official of the railroad company. It was in November of the same year that the town was founded that the postal service began to service the area. The Burns Community Museum is in the old Burns Union School, which closed in 1965. Some of the scenes of the 1996 comedy sci-fi film *Mars Attacks!* were filmed in and around the city.

# DURHAM, KS
## POPULATION: 89 – TOWN 213 OF 627 (5-2-23)
Durham's name pays tribute to the Durham cattle, known as the "Shorthorn" breed. The name was given because of its early distinction of being a rich cattle land and home to the thoroughbred stock maintained by early German farmers. The postal service established an office nearby in June 1874 under the name Durham Park, and in the Fall of 1887, they moved it to the newly founded community. That same year, the Chicago, Kansas, and Nebraska Railroad rolled through town, and in 1906, Durham was incorporated as a city of the third class by an act of the legislature. An early variation of the town name was Funk. A short half-mile from Durham is the Donahue Corporation, a large manufacturer of farm implement carriers that has built and distributed 50,000 carriers internationally since the company's founding in 1962 by James C. Donahue.

# FLORENCE, KS
## POPULATION: 394 – TOWN 233 OF 627 (5-4-23)
Florence was named in honor of the daughter (Miss Florence Crawford) of the third Governor of Kansas, Samuel J. Crawford. An original name for the area was Doyle, in honor of Patrick Doyle, who had first settled the area in 1859. The post office shared the nomenclature from November 1866 to March 1871. The men behind Florence Town Company (of which Samuel J. Crawford was its president) knew that the construction of the Atchison, Topeka, and Santa Fe Railway was imminent, so they platted the town in 1870 to ensure that the railroad would be routed through that area along the Cottonwood River. The Florence, El Dorado, and Walnut Valley Railroad Company, as well as the Marion and McPherson Railway Company, both began lines that went through Florence in the 1870s, both of which were leased and operated by the A, T & SF Railroad. Having multiple railroad lines helped Florence to quickly grow to 1,517 residents as of the 1920 Census, although the population has since significantly declined. The second Harvey House Restaurant to ever exist was founded by Fred Harvey in the old Clifton Hotel in 1878; it is now the Harvey House Museum. The 1977 biological film

*Mary White* and the 2006 episode (season 1, episode 3) "High Plains Feaster" of *Feasting on Asphalt* had scenes from them filmed throughout Florence. The 27th President of the United States, William Howard Taft, gave a speech in the area from his train car circa 1908. And, to top off an extended list of anecdotes for the small community, Florence is famous for its exceptionally pure (99.96%) spring water, as is advertised by the town's water tower and a small pump at Moses Shane Memorial Park.

# GOESSEL, KS
### POPULATION: 556 – TOWN 218 OF 627 (5-3-23)
Goessel was named in honor of Captain Kurt von Goessel, who perished with his ship Elbe in 1895 when it sank in the English Channel. The first settlers were a group of Russian Mennonites seeking asylum from Russia to preserve their heritage. As a third of all Russian Mennonites began to flee the country in the 1870s, many of them elected to settle in Kansas, specifically in Buhler, Inman, and what would become Goessel. The Alexanderwohl group founded Gnadenfeld, the original town on which Goessel would be built, and in the early 1890s, the city began to see its first public structures and businesses flourish. The post office accepted the name Goessel in 1895, a formal townsite was platted in 1910, and incorporation came in 1952. The Mennonite Heritage Museum is an impressive complex of eight buildings that contain the Bethesda Mennonite Hospital and early Mennonite artifacts, and another point of interest is the Alexanderwohl Mennonite Church, a mile north of town. One of the museum's prized artifacts is its Liberty Bell Made of Wheat that hung in the Smithsonian during the 1976 U.S. Bicentennial celebration. Eight-time Primetime Emmy Award nominee, Golden Globe award winner, and Tony Award winner Shirley Knight was born in Goessel on July 5, 1936. Former collegiate head coach Wes Buller and the present CEO of the National Naval Aviation Museum Foundation heed from the city as well.

# HILLSBORO, KS ☆
### POPULATION: 2,732 – TOWN 214 OF 627 (5-2-23)
John Gillespie Hill, an early area homesteader who built his home here in 1871, is the town's namesake. The town was laid out in 1879 under the name Hill City and later Hillsboro after discovering that there was already another town of the prior name in Graham County, Kansas. The post office was called Risley from April 1873 to August 1879. The Atchison, Topeka & Santa Fe Railroad elected to build a

line through the area in the late 1870s and early 1880s, which helped to bring multiple lines of business, banks, and even Tabor College to Hillsboro. The private Mennonite college began in 1908 under the direction of the Mennonite Brethren and Krimmer Mennonite Brethren churches. History buffs may take interest in the 1876 P. P. Loewen House, the last remaining Russian clay brick house of its kind left in North America, the Jacob Friesen Flouring Windmill, and the Mennonite Settlement Museums, and the William F. Schaeffler House Museum. T. R. Schellenberg, an archival theorist known for setting the foundations for much of archival theory and practice throughout the United States, attended Hillsboro Middle School and High School, Tabor Academy, and Tabor College.

# LEHIGH, KS
## POPULATION: 161 – TOWN 215 OF 627 (5-2-23)
Lehigh, population 161, was founded in 1881 by Alden Speare of Boston, Massachusetts. Its etymology appears disputed, although it was likely named for its geographical location "high above the plains" or potential early settlers from Lehigh County, Pennsylvania. The first pioneer travelers of the area traversed the nearby Santa Fe and Chisholm Trails, both of which passed by the site that would eventually become Lehigh. The Atchison, Topeka, and Santa Fe Railroad reached the area shortly before Speare founded the community. It was also around then that the post office was established on April 23, 1880, and Boston L. Monniger was named as the first postmaster. It was incorporated as a city in 1901.

# LINCOLNVILLE, KS
## POPULATION: 168 – TOWN 236 OF 627 (5-4-23)
Lincolnville was named in honor of the 16th President of the United States, Abraham Lincoln. The town's first settler was Heman Deal in 1860, although it wasn't until the final day (December 31) of 1868 that an area post office was established. Robert C. McAllister sought to begin the townsite in 1872, although it was not approved until 1878. It was built on Clear Creek, later attracting the Chicago, Rock Island & Pacific Railroad (then known as the Chicago, Kansas, and Nebraska Railroad) to lay tracks through the townsite. Lincolnville was incorporated in 1910. Father Emil Kapaun, a faithful priest nearing canonization as a saint in the Catholic Church, grew up outside the nearby unincorporated community of Pilsen. It is still the site of St. John Nepomucene Catholic Church and the Chaplain Kapaun Museum.

# LOST SPRINGS, KS
## POPULATION: 55 – TOWN 237 OF 627 (5-4-23)
The community of Lost Springs began near an area that was once a landmark stop on the Santa Fe Trail (between 1821 and 1866) because of the plentiful water that could be enjoyed there by the pioneers. The springs were first mentioned in 1845 in Josiah Gregg's "Commerce of the Prairies," although there is written history that J. H. Costello and Joshua Smith operated a trading post there in 1859. The primary part of the name comes from the periodicity of the springs, as they would dry up at different intervals throughout the year. Lost Springs Station began in 1859, and there was very briefly a post office there from 1861 to 1864 before it closed and then returned on July 9, 1879. The town was incorporated in 1904, a couple of decades after the Atchison, Topeka, and Santa Fe Railway and the Chicago, Kansas, and Nebraska Railway came through town. The Metzler paradox and Metzler matrices, functions of economics and mathematics, were both named after Lloyd Metzler, who was born in Lost Springs in 1913.

# MARION, KS ★
## POPULATION: 1,922 – TOWN 232 OF 627 (5-4-23)
Marion Centre was founded in 1860 with the intention of making it the county seat of Marion County. Its name seeks to honor Francis Marion, the "Swamp Fox" of the American Revolutionary War known for his guerrilla warfare tactics. The town was formally laid out in 1866, shortly after its first store opened in 1861, and the postal service established an office there in September 1862. By 1878, the Atchison, Topeka, and Santa Fe Railway had arrived and helped to spur rapid growth of the county seat. An early account of the town states that it had a hotel, creamery, flour mills, a fire department, three banks, schools, a library, and numerous storefronts. The Chicago, Kansas, and Nebraska Railway, eventually called the Chicago, Rock Island & Pacific Railroad, and later the Union Pacific Railroad, built a line through Marion in 1887. There was a brief third railroad line called the Marion Belt and Chingawassa Springs Railroad, which remained in operation from 1889 to 1893. The Historic Elgin Hotel, now a boutique hotel serving the Flint Hills Region of Kansas, was completed in September 1886 by local real estate firm Case and Billings and several local artisans. The Marion City Museum plays a vital role in telling the early history of the city. Like many early towns of its size, Marion too has been the home of several notable people, such as Pulitzer Prize nominee Eric Meyer, the 1904 Olympic bronze-

medalist in the 60 meters event, Fay Moulton, Samuel Peters, a Union Army Captain and the composer of "Great Is Thy Faithfulness," MLB players Tex Jones and Charlie Faust, the 17th Governor of Kansas Edward Hoch, and opera singer Beverly Hoch. Marion County was recognized by the Guinness Book of World Records in 2012 when 1,272 people were credited with participating in the "Most People Roasting Marshmallows (concurrently)" record attempt at Marion County Park and Lake.

## Lodging Recommendation:
### Historic Elgin Hotel
### 115 N 3rd St
### Marion, KS 66861

# PEABODY, KS
## POPULATION: 937 – TOWN 219 OF 627 (5-3-23)

The early etymology and history of the city are complex as it underwent numerous name changes and legal troubles. The first settler, W. C. Coble, began his ranch in the area in 1864, and six years later, another colony of settlers arrived. The townsite company named it Coneburg for their president, John Cone. When some immigrants left during the winter to gather more supplies back home in the east, those who had remained behind became restless, and claim jumping became rampant throughout the site. In the same year, T. M. Potter and five men founded the Peabody Town Company (named for the former president of the A, T & SF Railroad, F. H. Peabody) in the southern portion of the land section, which attracted the attention of the settlers of Coneburg, as well as the post office (which moved its office from Coneburg to Peabody in October 1871). As legal disputes continued, Coneburg would be renamed North Peabody, but with time, Peabody and North Peabody agreed to merge in 1879. With this settlement, the town grew substantially, becoming a significant shipping point for hogs and cattle around Kansas. Many of its earliest lines of business and infrastructure, ranging from a windmill factory and creamery to banks, an opera house, and a public library, came after the Atchison, Topeka, and Santa Fe Railway came to town in 1871, and the Chicago, Kansas, and Nebraska Railway built their line through town in 1887. The Kansas State Fair was once held in town from September 1-4, 1885, with its greatest attraction being a 40-foot-tall obelisk built from forty bushels of ears of corn and dubbed "the First Monument to General Grant," who had recently passed away. Another interesting anecdote is that several championed racehorses in the late 1890s were raised here: Joe "Iron Horse" Young, Joe Patchen, and Dan Patch. Modern attractions include the Peabody Historical Complex and Library Museum, the Peabody Printing Museum, Peabody City Park, the W. H. Morgan House, and the 1880s Peabody Downtown Historic District. Some of Peabody's most famous individuals are Oscar Stauffer (founder of Stauffer Communications), Warren Bechtel (founder of Bechtel Corporation), C. M. Arbuthnot (founder of Arbuthnot Drug Company), Nick Hague (NASA astronaut), Frederic Remington (American Old West artist), William Weidlein, Lamar Hoover, and Dennis Franchione (all former college head football coaches), and Rebecca Ediger (Distinguished United States Secret Service agent).

# RAMONA, KS
## POPULATION: 78 – TOWN 238 OF 627 (5-4-23)
One of several small communities that dot the beautiful Flint Hills, Ramona is another community that once played an essential role as a shipping and receiving point for the Chicago, Rock Island & Pacific Railroad in its early days. It was platted in 1887 and incorporated in 1909, and the post office arrived on August 9, 1887. Trade was fruitful at the turn of the century, leading Ramona to grow to a population of 303 persons by 1920. The name is of Spanish origin, a nod to when Manuel De Lisa of Spain petitioned the Spanish government for a land grant in the area in 1799.

# TAMPA, KS
## POPULATION: 105 – TOWN 212 OF 627 (5-2-23)
This small Marion County community was platted in 1887 by the Golden Belt Town Company and incorporated in 1908. An early engineer of the Chicago, Kansas, and Nebraska Railway gave its namesake. The Chicago, Rock Island, and Pacific Railroad would eventually take over the line, which, like many other railroad lines in the area, would undergo a series of mergers and become a part of the modern Union Pacific Railroad system. The post office was founded shortly after the town began in April 1888. Prior to the existence of the town between the 1820s and 1860s, early pioneers wandered the Santa Fe Trail in the area that would eventually become the townsite.

**Adjacent Counties:** Dickinson (N), Morris (NE), Chase €, Butler (SE), Harvey (SW), McPherson (W), Saline (NW)

**Unincorporated/Ghost Towns:** Alexanderfeld, Antelope, Aulne, Blumenfeld, Blumenort, Canada, Creswell, Eastshore, Ebenfeld, Emmathal, Elk, Fred, Friedenstal, Gnadenau, Gnadenfeld, Gnadenthal, Gruenfeld, Hampson, Hochfeld, Hoffnungsthal, Horners, Jacobs, Kuhnbrook, Marion County Lake, Morning Star, Oursler, Pilsen, Quarry, Schoenthal, Springfield, Steinbach, Strassburg, Wagner, Waldeck, Watchorn, Youngtown

## National Register of Historic Places:
**Antelope:** Amelia Park Bridge
**Burns:** Burns Union School, Keystone Ranch
**Durham:** Donahue's Santa Fe Trail Segment, Santa Fe Trail – Marion County Trail Segments
**Florence:** Bichet School, District 34, Doyle Place, Florence Opera House, Florence Water Tower, Harvey House
**Hillsboro:** 1927 Hillsboro Water Tower, Pioneer Adobe House, William F. and Ida G. Schaeffler House
**Lehigh:** French Frank's Santa Fe Trail Segment
**Lincolnville:** Bethel School, Island Field Ranch House
**Lost Springs:** Lost Spring
**Marion:** Bown-Corby School, Donaldson and Hosmer Building, Elgin Hotel, Hill Grade School, Marion Archeological District, Marion County Courthouse, Marion County Park and Lake
**Peabody:** W. H. Morgan House, Old Peabody Library, Peabody City Park, Peabody Downtown Historic District, Peabody Township Carnegie Library, J. S. Schroeder Building
**Tampa:** P. H. Meehan House

## Golf Courses:
Hillsboro Municipal Golf, Public (Hillsboro, KS)
Marion Country Club, Semi-Private (Marion, KS)

## Town Celebrations:
Art in the Park, Marion, KS (3rd Weekend of September)
Chingawassa Days, Marion, KS (1st Weekend of June)
Father Kapaun Day and Pilgrimage, Pilsen, KS (Early June)
Hillsboro Arts & Crafts Fair, Hillsboro, KS (3rd Saturday in September)
Old Settler's Day, Marion, KS (Last Saturday in September)
Peabody 4th Fest & Annual Fireworks, Peabody, KS (Independence Day)
Tampa Trailfest, Tampa, KS (Last Saturday in August)
Threshing Days, Goessel, KS (1st Weekend of August)

# MARSHALL COUNTY
## EST. 1855 – POPULATION: 10,038

Marshall County honors the legacy of Frank J. Marshall with its name, as he was the first settler to operate a ferry across the Big Blue River.

# AXTELL, KS
## POPULATION: 399 – TOWN 3 OF 627 (2-19-23)
Axtell's first settlers arrived circa the 1860s, and by December of 1871, a post office had arrived in town. The railroad rolled into town not long after the post office was established, and in 1872, the depot was named Axtell in honor of railroad official Jesse Axtell. Two railroads once went through town: the St. Joseph & Grand Island and the Wyandotte & Northwestern Railroads.

# BEATTIE, KS
## POPULATION: 197 – TOWN 4 OF 627 (2-19-23)
The "Milo Capital of the World," Beattie, was laid out in June of 1870 by the Northern Kansas Land Company (out of St. Joseph. Missouri) and was named in honor of Armstrong Beattie. He served as the eighth Mayor of St. Joseph. Its claim to fame came about at the town's 1970 centennial celebration because, at that time, Marshall County, Kansas, was the largest producer of milo in the state (and, therefore, the world per the townspeople). Governor Robert Docking formally declared the title.

# BLUE RAPIDS, KS ☆
## POPULATION: 928 – TOWN 6 OF 627 (2-19-23)
The Blue Rapids Town Company worked in the late 1860s to survey a potential townsite and found a new colony, and in 1870, the town's first colonists moved to the area from Genesee County, New York. By 1872, the city was officially incorporated due to its booming population and the construction of a dam and stone flour mill. The town's public library was built in 1875 and still operates as the oldest library west of the Mississippi River in continuous operation in the same building. The city has other claims to fame as well, such as its distinction as the smallest town in the country to have ever hosted a National League baseball game, a world tour exhibition game played between the Chicago White Sox and New York Giants on October 24, 1913. The pancreatic cancer drug Streptozotocin was discovered

from a soil sample taken from Blue Rapids in the late 1950s. To further its notoriety, the town dedicated "The Monument to the Ice Age" in its town square in May of 2012 to pay tribute to the abundant natural resources brought by glaciers during the Pleistocene era (as recent as 11,700 years ago).

# FRANKFORT, KS
**POPULATION: 730 – TOWN 5 OF 627 (2-19-23)**
Frankfort was organized in 1867 after the Central Branch Union Pacific Railroad constructed a depot there. Two miles southeast of the townsite, there had been a post office established called "Nottingham," but it was later moved to town and renamed Frankfort for town company member Frank Schmidt. It is noted for its significant loss of life during World War II. Frankfort lost 32 men during the war, more persons per capita than any other community in the country.

# MARYSVILLE, KS ★
**POPULATION: 3,447 – TOWN 25 OF 627 (2-20-23)**
Marysville was founded circa 1855 by Francis J. Marshall with the intention of making it the county seat. The territorial legislature elevated the town to incorporated status in 1861. For years, it was an important stop on notable routes of American History, such as the Oregon Trail, the Overland Stage, and the Pony Express, amongst others. The Pony Express Home Station No. 1 was established in a stone barn constructed by settler Joseph Cottrell in 1859. For eighteen months, it was used by riders carrying letters between St. Joseph, Missouri, and Sacramento, California. The station is still standing to this day in downtown Marysville as the "Pony Express Home Station & Museum." Historic Trails Park commemorates the community's rich historical trail history and even includes a replica of an old rope-powered ferry. Other points of interest include the Koester House Museum, the Marysville Doll Museum, and the Marshall County Courthouse Museum. The town prides itself on its large population of black squirrels, even going so far as to hold an annual Black Squirrel Celebration and designate the "Black Squirrel Song" as the city's national anthem: "Lives in the city park, runs all over town…The coal black squirrel will be our pride and joy…Many more years to come!" The population began in the 1920s after a group of squirrels escaped from a traveling circus and has today come to include several large decorative black squirrel statues. Notable people with ties to Marysville include poet and playwright Michael McClure, Ralph Elliott, an accountant known for developing

the Wave Principle regarding trends and reversals about financial markets, Major League Baseball pitcher Brian Duensing, the 9th United States Deputy Secretary of the Treasury, Kenneth W. Dam, WNBA player Kendra Wecker, and Louis "Moondog' Hardin known for his music compositions and work as a music theoretician.

**Restaurant Recommendation:
Wagon Wheel
703 Broadway St
Marysville, KS 66508**

# OKETO, KS
## POPULATION: 64 – TOWN 26 OF 627 (2-28-23)
Oketo's name seeks to honor that of "Ar-Ka-Ke-teh," once the head chief of the Otoe tribe of Native Americans. The community, incorporated in 1870, served as a stopping point on the overland stage line and was a part of the Blue Valley branch of the Union Pacific Railroad. The Oketo Cutoff was a popular cutoff established by Ben Holladay for $50,000 for his mail and passenger coaches to bypass Marysville. However, its use was limited to only a few months due to the nearby Military Road. Before the establishment of a post office here on May 7, 1873, there was an enormous swath of land without mail service. Thomas Olmsted, born in 1947, served as the bishop of the Diocese of Wichita from 2001 to 2003 and the Diocese of Phoenix, Arizona from 2003 to 2022.

# SUMMERFIELD, KS
## POPULATION: 125 – TOWN 2 OF 627 (2-19-23)
Elias Summerfield, the superintendent of the Kansas City & Northwestern Railroad branch at the time of the community's founding, is its namesake. Its first post office was established in February of 1889, and by 1890, the town had reached incorporation status. Despite now having a population of 125, this small community once boasted over five miles of sidewalks in 1916.

# VERMILLION, KS
## POPULATION: 76 – TOWN 27 OF 627 (2-28-23)
Vermillion is a small Marshall County village that was once a stop on the Missouri Pacific Railroad. Founded in 1869, it takes its name from

the stream on which the town was established, the Black Vermillion River. The town's first post office arrived on May 2, 1870.

# WATERVILLE, KS
## POPULATION: 658 – TOWN 7 OF 627 (2-19-23)
Waterville's etymology can be traced to the hometown of Mr. R. Osborne, the superintendent of the Central Union Pacific Railroad at that time. He was initially from Waterville, Maine. It was incorporated as a village in 1870 and then as a city of the third class a year later. Josephine Thorndike Berry, a noted home economist within the university system, was born here on February 25, 1871.

**Lodging Recommendation:**
**Weaver Hotel**
**126 Kansas Ave**
**Waterville, KS 66548**

**Adjacent Counties:** Nemaha (E), Pottawatomie (S), Riley (SW), Washington (W)

**Unincorporated/Ghost Towns:** Alcove Springs, Bigelow, Bremen, Herkimer, Home, Irving, Lillis, Marietta, Vliets

**National Register of Historic Places:**
**Blue Springs:** Alcove Springs, Blue Rapids Library
**Bremen:** Oregon and California Trails-Pacha Ruts
**Frankfort:** Barrett Schoolhouse, Frankfort School, Old Frankfort City Jail, Robidoux Creek Pratt Truss Bridge
**Marysville:** Perry Hutchison House, Koester Block Historic District, Charles Koester House, Marshall County Courthouse, Marysville High School-Junior High School Complex, Marysville Pony Express Barn, Marysville Union Pacific Depot, Pusch-Randell House
**Oketo:** Z. H. Moore Store
**St. Bridget Township:** St. Bridget Church
**Summerfield:** Transue Brothers Blacksmith & Wagon Shop
**Waterville:** Samuel Powell House, Waterville Opera House, Weaver Hotel

**Golf Courses:**
Marysville Country Club, Private (Marysville, KS)

**Town Celebrations:**
Beattie Milo Fest, Beattie, KS (3$^{rd}$ Weekend in August)
Big Blue River Days, Marysville, KS (1$^{st}$ Saturday in June)
Frankfort Summerfest, Frankfort, KS (Last Saturday in June)

# MCPHERSON COUNTY
## EST. 1867 - POPULATION: 30,223

McPherson County took its name from James B. McPherson, the second-highest-ranking Union Army official to perish during a battle.

# CANTON, KS ☆
## POPULATION: 685 – TOWN 216 OF 627 (5-2-23)

Canton was platted in 1879 with the construction of the Atchison, Topeka, and Santa Fe Railroad through that portion of Kansas. It was incorporated the following year and named by one of the early settlers after the town of the same name in Ohio. As the city grew and developed a flour mill, creamery, two grain elevators, and other lines of business, the Chicago, Kansas, and Nebraska Railway (later the Chicago, Rock Island, and Pacific Railway) built a line of their own through Canton. An early tourism marketing idea by Mrs. M. D. Fisher led the community to paint the words "HOT" and "COLD" on the town's two water towers despite the water inside being the same temperature. The town drew national attention in 2008 when Stephen Colbert made questionable remarks about the community on The Colbert Report, which led then-Kansas governor Kathleen Sebelius to invite Colbert to spend a night at the city's historic jail. The Maxwell Wildlife Refuge northwest of Canton is home to rolling hills, natural prairie, and a couple hundred head of bison and several dozen elk.

# GALVA, KS
## POPULATION: 834 – TOWN 217 OF 627 (5-2-23)

The first white settlement in McPherson County came in 1855 when Charles O. Fuller established a ranch (a couple of miles outside of Galva's present townsite) to accommodate early pioneers on the Santa Fe Trail. Like many other area towns, Galva was platted in 1879 as a depot station on a branch of the Atchison, Topeka, and Santa Fe Railroad. It was organized by the Marion & McPherson Railroad Company on the Florence & Ellinwood branch. In 1887, the Chicago, Kansas, and Nebraska Railway built a line through Galva as well. The town's name is an eponym for Galva, Illinois, the hometown of early settler Mrs. J. E. Doyle. It was incorporated as a city of the third class in 1887 and reached its highest population of 870 citizens at the 2010 Census. The Galva Museum looks to preserve local history.

# INMAN, KS
**POPULATION: 1,341 – TOWN 606 OF 627 (10-11-23)**

Major Henry Inman, the noted frontiersman who boasted ties with Buffalo Bill Cody and General George A. Custer, had the City of Inman and the nearby Lake Inman named in his honor. It owes its existence to the construction of the Chicago, Kansas, and Nebraska Railway through Kansas in 1887, which enabled the residents to build a newspaper, bank, post office, and all sorts of homes, religious institutions, and businesses. The railroad first called it Aiken but changed its name in 1889. The Inman Historical Museum is an extensive complex covering the town's inception to several of its earliest businesses and people. Dean Wade of the NBA's Cleveland Cavaliers spent his earliest days in Inman. One of the strongest advocates for rural tourism in the United States, the Kansas Sampler Foundation, is headquartered here on the farm of Marci Penner, who, in 1990, began work with her father (Mil) to compile a list of things to see and do around Kansas. What started as a family endeavor has developed into a state-wide campaign to showcase that every town in Kansas, no matter how big or small, has something to offer to everyone. The organization hosts the Big Kansas Road Trip every year, which puts three counties in the spotlight every year and drives hundreds of people to tour those regions of the state.

 **Restaurant Recommendation:**
**Inman Harvest Cafe**
**112 S Main St**
**Inman, KS 67546**

# LINDSBORG, KS
**POPULATION: 3,776 – TOWN 207 OF 627 (5-2-23)**

"Little Sweden" prides itself on its rich Swedish history and its large population of residents of Swedish, Nordic, and Scandinavian descent. The town was platted in 1868 by the Chicago Swedish Company, and the following year, a charter of settlers came from Värmland, Sweden, to settle the area. The Salina & McPherson branch of Union Pacific Railroad would be built through the site in

1879, the same year Lindsborg was incorporated as a city, and in 1887, the Missouri Pacific Railroad was extended to that point. The name Lindsborg is a Swedish term meaning "Linden Castle" in English, although the community takes its name from the first part of the surname of four important members (N. P. Linde, S. A. Lindell, J. O. Lindh, and S. P. Lindgren) of the First Swedish Agricultural Company that was instrumental in bringing settlement to the area. There are numerous sites of interest throughout the community related to the city's Swedish heritage, including several gift stores (such as Hemslöjd, Inc.), the Lindsborg Old Mill & Swedish Heritage Museum (also home to the 1904 World Fair's Swedish Pavilion), the International Chess Institute of the Midwest, Broadway RFD (longest-running outdoor theater in Kansas, established 1959), the Birger Sandzén Memorial Gallery, the Clara Hatton Center, Red Barn Studio Museum, Smoky Valley Arts and Folk Life Center, and Coronado Heights, where it is said that Francisco Vásquez de Coronado ceased his expedition to find the seven cities of gold. Bethany College, home of the Swedes, was established here in 1881 as a private Christian college. There are nearly a dozen events held in Lindsborg throughout the calendar year, the most notable of which is the Svensk Hyllningsfest. This biennial event celebrates Swedish heritage through dance, food, and art. Ted Kessinger, one of the winningest coaches in college football history and a member of the College Football Hall of Fame, evangelical Christian music songwriter and member of the Gospel Hall of Fame John W. Peterson, Ebba Sundstrom Nylander, a violinist, and perhaps the first American-born woman to conduct a full symphony orchestra (Women's Symphony Orchestra of Chicago in the 1930s), and artist Birger Sandzén all have ties to the community.

 **Restaurant Recommendation:**
**Happy Swede Restaurant**
**435 E McPherson St**
**Lindsborg, KS 67456**

**Lodging Recommendation:**
**Dröm Sött Inn B&B**
**112 W Lincoln St**
**Lindsborg, KS 67456**

# MARQUETTE, KS

**POPULATION: 599 – TOWN 206 OF 627 (5-2-23)**

Marquette's history begins with the establishment of H. S. Bacon's flour mill in the area in 1873. In February of the following year, S. J. Darrah, president of the Town Company, sought to start a town on land surveyed by J. D. Chamberlain. The town healthily supported incoming traffic from the Missouri Pacific Railroad, as well as a blacksmith shop, a hotel, seven stores, two banks and newspapers, churches, schools, and a post office, of which J. A. Foster was the primary postmaster. Early Swedish immigrant settlers opted to name it Marquette after Marquette, Michigan. Notable points of historical interest include the Range School Museum, the Hans-Hanson 1888 Victorian home, Smoky Valley Distillery, and the Kansas Motorcycle Museum founded in 2004 by "Stan the Man" Engdahl.

# MCPHERSON, KS ★

**POPULATION: 14,082 – TOWN 627 OF 627 (10-13-23)**

L. G. Skancke led the efforts in 1872 to have a town established in an area that was then referred to as McPherson Flats. The name was derived from General James B. McPherson of the Union Army, the second-highest-ranked Union officer to perish in the American Civil War. He and eleven other individuals formed the McPherson Town Company upon hearing that a colony from Kentucky was set on moving to the area. In June of that year, they located the townsite and made some improvements (by simply turning over the sod) to ensure that the settlers would stick around. H. Bowker was amongst the first of the arrivals and the first store owner, and as other general merchandising stores and structures were erected, word of the new settlement reached the United States Postal Service. On January 21, 1873, they opened an office there to serve the mail needs of the locals. That same year, McPherson was named the county seat of the newly established McPherson County because of its central location. In 1874, it was incorporated with Sol Stephens as its first mayor. Because of its relatively central location in Kansas and the presence of four major railroad lines, the Union Pacific, Missouri Pacific, Atchison, Topeka & Santa Fe, and the Chicago, Kansas and Nebraska Railway (later the Rock Island line), officials of the city vied with the legislature to make McPherson the state capital, but to no avail. The presence of so many railroads did, however, result in the arrival of several large businesses by the 1910s: factories for stove drums, carriages, brooms, and sorghum, an oil refinery, four grain elevators, five banks, and some of the largest flour mills in the state at that point in time. Higher education has always been of great importance to the residents of McPherson, as in 1884, Central Christian College of Kansas was established by the Free Methodist Church, and in 1887, the Church of the Brethren founded McPherson College. The latter institution has always retained the same name, but the former was formally called Orleans Seminary (1884 to 1914), Central Academy and College (1914 to 1940), Central College (1940 to the 1950s), and the Central College of the Free Methodist Church (from the 1950s to 1999). The Swedish Evangelical Church also attempted to start Walden College in 1908 but sold the buildings to Orleans Seminary. McPherson put itself on the map in the 1930s when members of their AAU McPherson Globe Refiners basketball team, "The Tallest Team in the World," helped lead the 1936 Olympic men's basketball team to a gold medal. Seven famous McPhersonites worth mentioning are Sue Raney (noted jazz singer since 1957), Harry Stine (the founder of Stine Seed, the world's largest private seed company), Jonathan Coachman (a WWE announcer), George Magerkurth (an umpire in over 2,800 MLB games), Brad Underwood (the present head coach of the Illinois men's basketball team), V. John Krehbiel (the United States Ambassador to Finland in the mid-1970s), and Harvey H. Nininger (the "father of modern meteoritics"). McPherson Museum exhibits items from all aspects of the town's history, from Native American history and geology to paleontology. Dr. J. Willard Hershey, a noted chemist, fabricated the first synthetic diamond in the world in 1926 at McPherson College using Moissan's technique.

 **Restaurant Recommendation:**
**Neighbors Café**
**204 S Main St**
**McPherson, KS 67460**

# MOUNDRIDGE, KS
**POPULATION: 1,974 – TOWN 602 OF 627 (10-10-23)**
Despite its mid-sized population of only about two thousand residents, Moundridge boasts two extensive manufacturing facilities for Bradbury Group (the largest manufacturer of roll-forming equipment on the planet) and The Grasshopper Company (a ground care and lawnmower company). Manufacturing has always been a strong suit for the local economy, as in the 1910s, Moundridge was the site of three impressive grain elevators, a plethora of merchantiles, and a vast roller mill. Predominantly, Germans and

Mennonites had brought up the sites as they arrived in droves in the 1870s and settled at the townsite once known as Christian. By 1887, it had been renamed Moundridge because of its lofty elevation, and the Missouri Pacific Railroad was introduced. Two museums are located here: The Moundridge Depot Museum and the Cole House Museum, with its neighboring buildings on heritage and agriculture. The most famous of all Moundridge residents was Laurie Koehn, a former professional women's basketball player and now the assistant head coach at Washington State's women's basketball program.

 **Restaurant Recommendation:**
**The Hub Brick Oven**
**100 S Christian Ave**
**Moundridge, KS 67107**

# WINDOM, KS
**POPULATION: 85 – TOWN 626 OF 627 (10-13-23)**
Windom, formerly the home of the Tigers, has a couple of possibilities as to how it got its name. It could have been named in honor of William Windom, a United States Senator from Minnesota and later the 33rd and 39th United States Secretary of the Treasury, or for Windham County, Connecticut, the former home of an early settler. Windom served as a station on the Atchison, Topeka & Santa Fe Railroad and once boasted a bank and several general stores.

**Adjacent Counties:** Saline (N), Dickinson (NE), Marion (E), Harvey (SE), Reno (SW), Rice (W), Ellsworth (NW)

**Unincorporated/Ghost Towns:** Alta Mills, Battle Hill, Christian, Conway, Doles Park, Elivon, Elyria, Groveland, Johnstown, King City, New Gottland, Roxbury, Sveadal

**National Register of Historic Places:**
**Canton:** Canton Township Carnegie Library, Heinrich H. Schroeder Barn
**Inman:** Inman I.O.O.F. Hall
**Lindsborg:** Berquist & Nelson Drugstore Building, Bethany Lutheran Church and Parsonage, Farmers State Bank, Hjerpe Grocery, Holmberg and Johnson Blacksmith Shop, Johnson House, P. J. Lindquist Building, Paint Creek Archeological Site, Anton Pearson House and Studio, Rosberg-Holmgren-Clareen Block, Sharps Creek

Archeological Site, Smoky Valley Roller Mill, Swedish Pavilion, Teichgraeber-Runbeck House, U.S. Post Office-Lindsborg
**Marquette:** Hans Hanson House
**McPherson:** Kuns-Collier House, McPherson Community Building, McPherson County Courthouse, McPherson Opera House, Power Plant No. 1, John R. Wright House
**Roxbury:** North Gypsum Creek Truss Leg Bedstead Bridge

## Breweries/Wineries/Distilleries:
Smoky Valley Distillery (Marquette, KS)
The Hub Brick Oven & Brewery (Moundridge, KS)
Three Rings Brewery (McPherson, KS)
Under the Cork (Lindsborg, KS)

## Golf Courses:
Lindsborg Golf Course, Semi-Private (Lindsborg, KS)
McPherson Country Club, Private (McPherson, KS)
Midway Golf Course, Public (Inman, KS)
Rolling Acres Golf Course, Semi-Private (McPherson, KS)
Turkey Creek Golf Course, Public (McPherson, KS)

## Town Celebrations:
Black Kettle Festival, Moundridge, KS (1st Saturday in June)
Canton Flea & Craft Markets, Canton, KS (Last Saturday of September)
Canton Heritage Days, Canton, KS (Last Weekend of September)
Heritage Christmas, Lindsborg, KS (2nd Saturday in December)
Lindsborg in Bloom, Lindsborg, KS (Last Saturday in April)
Lindsborg Våffeldagen, Lindsborg, KS (March 25)
McPherson County All Schools Day, McPherson, KS (2nd Friday in May)
Messiah Festival of the Arts, Lindsborg, KS (Begins one month before Easter)
Midsummer's Festival, Lindsborg, KS (3rd Weekend of June)
Millfest, Lindsborg, KS (1st Saturday in May)
Smoky Valley Classic Car Show, Lindsborg, KS (1st Saturday of August)
Smoky Valley Saddle Club Rodeo, Marquette, KS (1st Weekend of August)
Svensk Hyllningsfest, Lindsborg, KS (2nd Weekend of October, Biannually on Odd Years)
Thunder on the Smoky, Marquette, KS (3rd Saturday of September)

# MEADE COUNTY
## EST. 1885 - POPULATION: 4,055

Meade County was named for George Meade, the Union general who emerged victorious at the Battle of Gettysburg.

# FOWLER, KS
### POPULATION: 534 – TOWN 492 OF 627 (9-20-23)

Formerly known as Gilbert, the name "Fowler" was assigned in 1886 in honor of the original townsite owner, George Fowler. The Chicago, Rock Island & Pacific Railroad's arrival enabled the community to make significant strides in building several churches, hotels, and schools, and even alfalfa mills, grain elevators, and a lumber yard. The goods were shipped along the railroad to other towns in the immediate area and beyond. Incorporated as a city of the third class in 1908, the historical population of Fowler has remained steady over the last half-century and ranged from 534 residents as of 2020 to as many as 592 in the eighties. Kansas's Representative from its 1st District from 2011 to 2017, Tim Huelskamp, was raised on a farm outside of Fowler.

 **Restaurant Recommendation: Medrano's Restaurant 406 Main St Fowler, KS 67844**

# MEADE, KS ★☆
### POPULATION: 1,505 – TOWN 491 OF 627 (9-20-23)

1885 was a significant year for Meade, as it was founded, incorporated, and named the judicial seat of Meade County in rapid succession over six months. A couple of former names for the community were Skidmore and Meade Center, but on February 26, 1889, it was permanently shortened to Meade to honor General George Meade. He was the commander of the Army of the Potomac during the American Civil War. The town's population nearly doubled (from 838 people to 1,552) between the 1920 and 1930 Census on account of the Chicago, Rock Island & Pacific Railroad being extended throughout the region. Many of the town's original buildings, including its first courthouse, a bank, and other structures on Main Street, were constructed of native stone. The jewel of the community is the Dalton Gang Hideout and Museum, one of only two locations in the county to be listed on the National Register of Historic Places. The small Victorian home, owned by John N. Whipple, the husband of Eva Dalton (whose siblings comprised the notorious Dalton Gang), has a small hidden tunnel underneath it that leads to a barn. This secret area is said to have been used as the gang's hideout. The Meade County Historical Museum focuses on the local history of Meade and its past residents. Naturalists looking for an excellent outdoor spot to fish, hike, and boat enjoy the amenities of nearby Meade State Park. David A. R. White was born and raised in Meade and is known for his role in the 2014 Christian film *God's Not Dead.*

# PLAINS, KS
## POPULATION: 1,037 – TOWN 490 OF 627 (9-20-23)
Platted as West Plains in 1885, the "West" portion of the name would later be dropped, and this town would become known as plain old "Plains." The Chicago, Rock Island & Pacific Railroad was extended to Plains later, and the city elected to incorporate in 1908. The town's claim to fame is that it has the widest main street in the United States and a width of 155 feet and 5 inches from storefront to storefront. Onawa, Iowa, makes a similar claim, as in the 1980s, a local high school student measured their main street at 157 feet from curb to curb. The width of both streets likely depends on how an individual measures a "street," whether measured between curbs, sidewalks, or storefronts.

**Adjacent Counties:** Gray (N), Ford (NE), Clark (E), Seward (W), Haskell (NW)

**Unincorporated/Ghost Towns:** Missler

**National Register of Historic Places:**
**Fowler:** Fowler Swimming Pool and Bathhouse
**Meade:** Dalton Gang Hideout and Museum

**Golf Courses:**
Joyce L. Hamm Country Club, Public (Plains, KS)

Lyon County Photos: Allen, Bushong, Emporia, Emporia, Emporia, Emporia, Hartford, Olpe

313

Marion County Photos: Burns, Florence, Florence, Florence, Goessel, Hillsboro, Marion, Marion

Marshall County Photos: Axtell, Beattie, Frankfort, Marysville, Marysville, Marysville, Vermillion, Waterville

315

McPherson County Photos: Inman, Inman, Lindsborg, Lindsborg, Marquette, Marquette, McPherson, Moundridge

316

Meade County Photos: Fowler, Fowler, Meade, Meade, Meade, Meade, Plains, Plains

317

# MIAMI COUNTY
## EST. 1855 - POPULATION: 34,191

Once called Lykins County, it was later decided that this county be named for the Miami Native American tribe.

# FONTANA, KS
### POPULATION: 210 – TOWN 344 OF 627 (6-30-23)

The name Fontana is derived from the French word *fontaine*, meaning "fountain" or "spring." Early settlers of the area adopted the title after the nearby springs. Old Fontana existed for a year before the townsite was moved to be closer to the St. Louis & San Francisco Railroad. By 1910, the new settlement grew to encompass all of the typical lines of business and even a mill and lumber yard. Fontana was incorporated in 1889. Miami County State Park began as a duck marsh but now serves the area as a fishing lake.

## Lodging Recommendation:
## Netherfield Natural Farm B&B
## 24126 KS-7
## Fontana, KS 66026

# LOUISBURG, KS
### POPULATION: 4,969 – TOWN 542 OF 627 (9-28-23)

Once known as "New St. Louis," the name of this fast-growing Miami county city was eventually changed to Louisburg by the Missouri, Kansas, and Texas Railroad to avoid confusion with St. Louis, Missouri. It was laid out in 1868, and the town soon comprised general stores, livery stables, a drug store, a school, significant nurseries, and many churches. The post office predates the establishment of Louisburg by a year. On November 3, 1882, Louisburg was incorporated, and since then, the population has grown exponentially. The most significant decade-long resident increase occurred between 2000 and 2010 when it grew by 67.5%. One such resident, Joe Towne, is the author of the true-crime novel *Tongues on Fire*, which documents the memories of those who were alive when the cold case murder of town postmaster George McElheny occurred in 1912. Notable points of interest in Louisburg are the Cedar Cove Feline Conservatory & Sanctuary, a home for big cats, the Powell Observatory, the Louisburg Cider Mill, and the Little

Round House at Louisburg City Lake that once served as World War II housing, an inspection station for truckers, and originally, part of an old Victorian-style home in Paola.

 **Restaurant Recommendation:**
**Louisburg Cider Mill**
**14730 K-68 Highway**
**Louisburg, KS 66053**

# OSAWATOMIE, KS
## POPULATION: 4,255 – TOWN 546 OF 627 (10-29-23)

The proud city of Osawatomie, whose name is an amalgamation of the words "Osage' and "Pottawatomie" taken from the names of the nearby bodies of water (although the Osage River is now the Marais des Cygnes River), has its earliest roots in Bleeding Kansas and American Civil War history. The townsite was selected in February of 1855 by the Emigrant Aid Society, who hoped to bring more abolitionists to Kansas to have it enter into the Union as a free state. The town company comprised Orville C. Brown, S. C. Pomeroy, and Mr. Ward, the three of whom went to work to build residences, a sawmill, a blacksmith, a drug store, and a general merchandise store. The post office would open its doors on December 21, 1855. It was also here that noted anti-slavery leader John Brown would establish his base at the cabin of his half-sister, Florella, and her husband, Reverend Samuel Adair. The log cabin is now a part of the John Brown Museum State Historic Site, which hosts Civil War artifacts and displays on John Brown and other abolitionists. The Osawatomie and the Missouri Pacific Railroad Depot Museum aid in telling the story of Brown and more about the townsite's past. The Battle of Osawatomie, which took place on August 30, 1856, was a devastating blow to the community after a party of 250 pro-slavery activists plundered the town and rained down destruction on all but three of the buildings. The battle, however, only strengthened Jayhawker activity throughout the area, and in 1859, they would host the Kansas Republican Party convention. The Osawatomie State Hospital, once known as the "Kansas Insane Asylum," was established in 1863 by an act of the legislature, and it quickly became one of the largest institutions in Kansas. The asylum campus is still intact, with its historic bridge, buildings, and graveyard. The Missouri Pacific would later aid the growth of local industry and business until the town's incorporation in 1883. Because of the major events that unfolded as precursors of the Civil War, it has since been visited by

President Theodore Roosevelt in 1910 when he gave his New Nationalism speech, and President Barack Obama, who gave a similar speech in 2011. Three former NFL players, Derrick Jensen (noted for his punt-block returned for a touchdown in Super Bowl XVIII as a member of the Raiders), Lynn Dickey (the NFL passing touchdowns and passing yards leader in 1983), and Lafayette Russell (known for his roles in Old Western films) were raised in Osawatomie.

# PAOLA, KS ★☆
## POPULATION: 5,768 – TOWN 545 OF 627 (9-29-23)

Baptiste Peoria, a former Indian agent and Chief of the Peoria tribe, gifted the 1,240 acres of land that would ultimately become the bustling, proud community of Paola. For nearly two decades, the area was known as Peoria Village until the Paola Town Company platted a townsite in 1855 and authorized Peoria, A. M. Coffey, Isaac Jacobs, David Lykins, and a handful of other men to begin the development of a town. Father Paul D. Ponziglione renamed the town for a small coastal Italian city. After the passage of the American Civil War and an extended pause in its growth, Paola soon welcomed the Missouri Pacific, Missouri, Kansas & Texas, and the St. Louis & San Francisco Railroads. The introduction of three lines into the area aided in the establishment of a radiator factory, brick plant, and a creamery, and following the discovery of natural gas in 1882, it became the first town west of the Mississippi River to light its streets with natural gas lanterns and use the resource in a commercial manner. Paola has grown steadily throughout the years because of its distinction as the Miami County seat, with the population now sitting at 5,768 persons as of the 2020 Census. Famous Paolans with city ties include Ed, Gus, and Zeke Justice, the founders of the Justice Brothers line of car care products, noted immunologist Barney S. Graham, Steve Pepoon (writer of the second *The Simpsons* episode to win a Primetime Emmy Award for Outstanding Animated Program), the "First Lady of Aviation" Olive Ann Beech, film critic and historian John C. Tibbetts, one of the greatest drummers of all time, Danny Carey, and former NFL quarterback Lynn Dickey. Three historic 19th-century buildings house the artifacts of the Miami County Historical Museum, and Hillsdale State Park offers locals and tourists the chance to enjoy the scenic outdoors.

**Restaurant Recommendation:**
**We B' Smokin BBQ**
**32580 Airport Rd**
**Paola, KS 66071**

**Lodging Recommendation:**
**Casa Somerset B&B**
**16315 W 287th St**
**Paola, KS 66071**

Spring Hill is only partially located in Miami County (see Johnson County).

**Adjacent Counties:** Johnson (N), Linn (S), Anderson (SW), Franklin (W), Douglas (NW)

**Unincorporated/Ghost Towns:** Antioch, Bucyrus, Drexel Corner, Hillsdale, Jingo, Lento, New Lancaster, Ringer, Somerset, Stanton, Wagstaff, Wea

**National Register of Historic Places:**
**Louisburg:** Jake's Branch of Middle Creek Bridge
**New Lancaster:** New Lancaster General Store, New Lancaster Grange Hall, No. 223
**Osawatomie:** Asylum Bridge, John Brown Cabin, Carey's Ford Bridge, Congregational Church, Creamery Bridge, William Mills House, Pottawatomie Creek Bridge, Soldiers' Monument
**Paola:** Jackson Hotel, Martin Farm, Miami County Courthouse, Miami County Mercantile Company

**Breweries/Wineries/Distilleries:**
5A Vineyard (Osawatomie, KS)
Bourgmont Winery (Bucyrus, KS)
Casa Somerset Bed & Breakfast (Paola, KS)
Fossil Springs Winery (Paola, KS)
Nighthawk Winery & Vineyard (Paola, KS)

**Golf Courses:**
Osawatomie Golf Course, Public (Osawatomie, KS)

Paola Country Club, Private (Paola, KS)
The Club Of The Country, Private (Louisburg, KS)

**Town Celebrations:**
Blocktoberfest, Paola, KS (3rd Saturday in September)
Freedom Festival, Osawatomie, KS (3rd Saturday in September)
John Brown Jamboree, Osawatomie, KS (3rd Weekend of June)
Labor Day Parade, Louisburg, KS (Labor Day)
Lights on the Lake, Osawatomie, KS (Saturday before 4th of July)
Paola Roots Festival, Paola, KS (Last Full Weekend of August)
Third Saturday, Osawatomie, KS (3rd Saturday April through October)

# MITCHELL COUNTY
## EST. 1867 - POPULATION: 5,796

Mitchell County, founded in 1867, got its name from the Union captain William D. Mitchell.

# BELOIT, KS ★☆
**POPULATION: 3,404 – TOWN 92 OF 627 (3-27-23)**
Early area settler A. A. Bell arrived in 1868 to take advantage of the power of the Solomon River by building a mill. He called his settlement Willow Springs, but a year later, T. F. Hersey purchased the site and put up a sawmill and a grist mill. A small town began to form, and by 1870, Beloit was declared the county seat of Mitchell County. The city was platted and first incorporated in 1872 (in March and July, respectively). A. A. Bell would become the first postmaster, and he and Hersey worked together as town promoters. Contrary to what some may believe, the name Beloit is not derived from that of Bell's surname but rather from the hometown of another early settler: Beloit, Wisconsin. The Union Pacific and Missouri Pacific Railroads would eventually arrive and further the town's industry. The Kansas Industrial School for Girls, once one of the longest-operating reformatories for juvenile girls, operated here from February 1888 to August 2009. Notable Beloit figures include Rodger Ward (two-time winner of the Indianapolis 500), Gene Keady (head coach of Purdue University's men's basketball team from 1980 to 2005), former MLB catcher Dean Sturgis, former NFL punter Scott Fulhage, 1976 Summer Olympics participant and javelin thrower Sam Colson, dance instructor and creator of the first ever dance university major, Margaret H'Doubler, Nancy Moritz (Judge of the United States Court of Appeals for the Tenth Circuit), and Waldo McBurney, one of the

oldest workers in the world upon his death in July of 2009. He worked as a beekeeper and was featured on the CBS television program *Assignment America*. The Mitchell County Museum is located in Beloit and welcomes visitors to explore local history.

 **Restaurant Recommendation:
Kettle
100 S Mill St
Beloit, KS 67420**

# CAWKER CITY, KS
**POPULATION: 457 – TOWN 94 OF 627 (3-27-23)**
Founded circa 1870 and incorporated in 1874, the right to name the town was won by Colonel E. H. Cawker (one of its founders) after he defeated the other three founders (J. P. Rice, R. G. F. Kshinka, and John J. Huckle) in a game of poker. Its first post office was established in 1870, and it was about a decade later that the Missouri Pacific Railway made its way through the area. The town is a popular stop for road trip enthusiasts as it is the site of the "World's Largest Ball of Twine," or more specifically, the "largest ball of sisal twine built by a community." It had its beginnings in 1953 after local farmer Frank Stoeber began to roll the excess twine from the floor of his barn into a ball, and today, visitors are still welcome to add their own twine to the ball with the help of the locals. The ball in August of 2014 had a circumference of 41.42 feet, a diameter of 8.06 feet, and a height of 10.83 feet, and contained over 1,600 miles of twine. Its estimated weight at the time was 28,000 pounds. Eyegore's Curiosities and Monster Museum is another local attraction that features absurd oddities such as a Feejee Mermaid, the one and only Vampire Chicken, and even a "baby alien" from Roswell, New Mexico. Social reformer Martha L. Davis Berry is buried in the local Prairie Grove Cemetery, and silent film actress Claire Windsor has connections to the town.

# GLEN ELDER, KS
**POPULATION: 362 – TOWN 93 OF 627 (3-27-23)**
Once called West Hampton, this community was first laid out in 1871 following the construction of Jon Neve and Albert Spencer's gristmill. Residents quickly changed its nomenclature to Glen Elder after a post office was moved to the area under that name. Within that same decade, the Missouri Pacific Railroad was completed through town.

The name is a tribute to the large groves of box elder trees that grow across Kansas's valleys. Waconda Lake and Glen Elder State Park is home to the living Waconda Heritage Village Museum and a marina, amphitheater, visitor's center, and amenities for hikers, campers, swimmers, and boaters. The "Best Little Town by a Dam Site" has a tiny chapel in the City Park not far from one of the Boy Scouts' twenty-five miniature Statue of Liberty replicas that can be found throughout Kansas.

## HUNTER, KS
**POPULATION: 51 – TOWN 96 OF 627 (3-27-23)**
Hunter is a relatively newer community in the area, having only been established in 1915 (although a post office for the site was created on May 14, 1895). It was named for Al Hunter, a resident of Jewell County since September of 1879.

## SCOTTSVILLE, KS
**POPULATION: 26 – TOWN 91 OF 627 (3-27-23)**
Scottsville came about in October of 1878 following the extension of the Missouri Pacific Railroad to that point. It was named for one of its earliest settlers, Tom Scott. The Scottsville post office existed from November 12, 1878, to May 5, 1967; it was once called "Lulu." The highest recorded population of the town was 248 individuals in 1910, although there are now just twenty-six residents in town as of the 2020 Census.

## SIMPSON, KS
**POPULATION: 82 – TOWN 87 OF 627 (3-15-23)**
Known originally as Brittsville, this town of 82 straddling the borders of Cloud & Mitchell Counties, was established in 1871 with the construction of a mill on the Solomon River. Later, in 1879, when the Union Pacific Railroad reached the area, Alfred Simpson donated land for the new town to be moved, and so the city was named in his honor (in 1882).

 **Restaurant Recommendation: Trapper Joe's 304 S Elkhorn St Simpson, KS 67478**

# TIPTON, KS
## POPULATION: 193 – TOWN 95 OF 627 (3-27-23)

Tipton was initially founded under the name Pittsburg in 1872 by Fred Sackoff, J. F. Steinberg, and W. A. Pitt and named in honor of the latter individual. It was soon discovered that another Pittsburg was already located in southeast Kansas, so the name was changed to Tipton after Tipton, Iowa, the hometown of early settler Chris Reinking. The Meades Ranch Triangulation Station, listed on the National Register of Historic Places in 1973 as the Geodetic Center of the United States, was used as a reference location for establishing geodetic datum. A geodetic datum is used for navigation, surveying, and other purposes by measuring a location across the Earth's surface in latitude or longitude.

**Adjacent Counties:** Jewell (N), Cloud (E), Ottawa (SE), Lincoln (S), Osborne (W)

**Unincorporated/Ghost Towns:** Asherville, Blue Hill, Buel, Coursens Grove, Elmira, Saltville, Solomon Rapids, Victor, Waconda, Walnut Grove, West Asher

### National Register of Historic Places:
**Beloit:** Cather Farm, Abram Click Farmstead, F. H. Hart House, Mitchell County Courthouse, C. A. Perdue House, Porter Hotel, St. John the Baptist Catholic Church
**Cawker City:** Old Cawker City Library, Wisconsin Street Historic District
**Glen Elder:** Brown's Creek Tributary Masonry Arch Bridge, E. W. Norris Service Station
**Hunter:** North Rock Creek Masonry Arch Bridge
**Tipton:** Antelope Creek Masonry Arch Bridge

### Golf Courses:
Beloit Country Club, Private (Beloit, KS)
Lakeside Golf Course, Public (Cawker City, KS)

### Town Celebrations:
Cruz'n Mill Street, Beloit, KS (Memorial Day Weekend)
Tipton Picnic, Tipton, KS (1st Weekend of August)
Twine-A-Thon, Cawker City, KS (3rd Weekend of August)
Wakonda Indian Festival, Glen Elder, KS (1st Saturday in October)

# MONTGOMERY COUNTY
## EST. 1867 - POPULATION: 31,486

Carved out of Wilson County in 1867, Montgomery County was named for Richard Montgomery, a major general of the Continental Army during the American Revolution.

# CANEY, KS
## POPULATION: 1,788 – TOWN 386 OF 627 (7-19-23)

Caney, located on the Oklahoma border and now home to 1,788 citizens as of the 2020 Census, was named after the Caney River that flows into the larger Verdigris River. Dr. J. W. Bell was the first settler to open his doors for business in 1869, and soon after, the postal service elected to establish a post office in the area on May 16, 1870. This was when the town was indeed established, although it didn't reach incorporation status until the year 1887. Most of the town's early growth can be directly attributed to the discovery of gas in the area, as in 1912, the city was outputting an impressive 175,000,000 cubic feet of the resource per day. It was home to the largest farm of oil tanks in all of Kansas, which covered 800 acres. Catastrophe struck the industry in 1906 and made national headlines when a gas well fire (shooting 150 feet into the sky at some points) burned over several months, attracting thousands of tourists from around the country and deafening the countryside for several miles in all directions. One such company that took advantage of the vast supply of fuels was the Kanotex Refining Company, later the Anderson-Prichard Oil Corporation. There were other industries as well, such as glass factories, brick and tile works, a zinc smelter, and all the other typical lines of business for an early Kansas town. The Missouri, Kansas & Texas Railroad and the Missouri Pacific Railroad were the notable exporters of the town's products. A few famous folks have ties to Caney: Glenn Shafer (co-creator of the Dempster-Shafer theory, a mathematical theory regarding evidence and probability), Clancy Hayes (a jazz musician), Rosalie E. Wahl (the first woman to serve as an Associate Justice of the Minnesota Supreme Court), and Kenneth McFarland, the superintendent of the Topeka school system when Brown v. Board of Education was making its way through the justice system. The Caney Valley Historical Society Museum hosts memorabilia commemorating the town's early people and places.

# CHERRYVALE, KS

**POPULATION: 2,192 – TOWN 362 OF 627 (7-17-23)**

The Kansas City, Lawrence & Southern Kansas Railway (later a part of the Atchison, Topeka & Santa Fe) gave life to the community of Cherryvale in 1871 after it purchased the property from Mr. Abe Eaton and built its line through this former area of Osage Native American territory. The name Cherryvale was given because of its location in the Cherry Creek valley. Manufacturing enterprises of all lines became prevalent, ranging from six brick and tile plants and shovel and implement factories to flour and planing mills, a creamery, a foundry, iron works, an oil refinery, a glass plant, and a zinc smelter. By 1912, 31 gas wells were pumping out 160,000,000 cubic feet of gas per day; one such well was likely the largest in the state at a production of 11,000,000 cubic feet daily. Later, the St. Louis & San Francisco Railroad would opt to extend their line through Cherryvale to take advantage of the economy of the boomtown. The South Kansas and Oklahoma Railroad, owned by Watco, is headquartered in Cherryvale and still operates 511 miles of rail lines throughout the immediate area. The town's early history has been plagued by the presence of the Bloody Benders, a family of serial killers who were thought to have killed between twelve and twenty travelers who had stayed at the Bender family inn between 1871 and 1873. Then-governor Thomas A. Osborn put out a bounty of $2,000 (nearly $51,000 in 2024 dollars) for the capture of the family, but they were never found and are thought to have escaped the townspeople after several locals became suspicious of them. Artifacts left behind by the Benders are on display at the Cherryvale Museum, as are other items of note from Cherryvale's history. Amongst the town's other historic famous residents are actress Vivian Vance of the sitcom *I Love Lucy*, Frank Bellamy, one of many potential authors of the "Pledge of Allegiance", Louise Brooks, known for popularizing the bob hairstyle and flapper culture, Sam Avey, a former professional wrestling promoter, and Billy Sandow, the manager of the professional wrestler Ed "Strangler" Lewis.

# COFFEYVILLE, KS ☆

**POPULATION: 8.826 – TOWN 383 OF 627 (7-19-23)**

Colonel James A. Coffey founded the town of Coffeyville in 1869 when he built a trading post to conduct business with Native Americans in what was then Indian Territory and is now the state of Oklahoma, a short mile south of Coffeyville's present-day city limits. He was a member of the original townsite company that consisted of fellow promoters N. B. Blanton, William Wilson, Edward Pagan, and John Clarkson. Their town was absorbed into another of the same name, as were other communities of Parker, Claymore, Verdigris City, and Westralia. Together, all the settlements make up today's bustling cityscape of Coffeyville, Kansas. It was incorporated in 1873 after an unsuccessful attempt in 1872, and following the designation, they became a center for railroad activity as the Atchison, Topeka & Santa Fe, Missouri Pacific, Missouri, Kansas & Texas, and the St. Louis & San Francisco all opted to lay tracks through the townsite. The presence of four railroad lines, coupled with the headquarters of the Missouri Pacific's railroad shops and the natural gas fields, led to an unbelievably prosperous period of growth for Coffeyville through the 1950s and 1960s, when the population peaked at 17,382 residents (1960 Census). These fields produced over a billion cubic feet of gas per day, allowing it to be sold at the low cost of just three cents per 1,000 feet to any enterprise willing to start their enterprise there. In the 1910s, the townspeople were fortunate enough to have nine public school buildings, four theaters, five banks, six brick plants, nine glass factories (it was one of the largest glass manufacturers in the country from the 1890s to the 1930s), four foundries, two of each of ice plants, planing mills and box factories, a hospital, oil refinery, plow, paper, carriage and wagon, wire fence, plaster, egg case and excelsior factories, implement, novelty, roof tile, and pottery works, and zinc smelters, amongst other industries still. As is commemorated every year by the annual town celebration, Coffeyville was the location of a famous shootout and botched robbery attempt by the Dalton Gang, in which four of its members were killed by townspeople who sought to protect the community. They were in the process of looting the First National and the Cordon & Company banks when, in the latter, they were recognized underneath their disguises, and civilians began to ambush them as they tried to escape. They were met by even more townsfolk, who, for twelve minutes, battled the Dalton Gang until all but one (Emmett Dalton, who survived with 23 gunshot wounds) were killed. $31,000 was recovered, and the perpetrators stopped, but at the cost of the lives of local marshal Charles T. Connelly and three civilians. Invented here by Douglas Brown and the Coffeyville Multiscope company was the Norden bombsight, which significantly aided the United States military in their precision daylight bombing missions during World War II. Coffeyville Community College, one of the first of many schools established around the turn of the century in Kansas (1923), is celebrating its centennial this year. As a part of a project in the school's art program, students work to put together their grassroots art that is placed on display in a nearby empty lot. In recent years, the city has been the subject of multiple mediums of pop culture, having been referenced in The Eagles song "Doolin-Dalton" (1973) and the 2002 and 2019 (respectively) films *Reign of Fire* and *The Highwayman*. Earth science plays an essential role in Coffeyville's history, as on September 3, 1970, the "World's Heaviest Hailstone," a 1.67-pound ball of ice, slammed into the earth at 105 miles per hour. It was the largest hailstone on record until 2003 when an Aurora, Nebraska storm dropped a later hailstone. Amongst Coffeyville's most famous residents of the past are Wade Flemons, formerly of the band Earth, Wind and Fire, Mildred Burke, three-time women's world champion wrestler and member of the Professional Wrestling Hall of Fame, Omar Knedlik, inventor of the ICEE machine and drink, Grammy-award winning songwriter Gary S. Paxton (known for his songs "Monster Mash" and "Alley Oop" in the 1960s), a three-time winner of the Indianapolis 500, Johnny Rutherford, the first woman to fly a B-29, Micky Axton, actress Cynthia Yorkin, jazz musician Kenyon Hopkins, Frank "The Red Ant" Wickware, a long-time baseball pitcher in the Negro leagues, World War I flying ace Field Eugene Kindley, and Wendell Willkie, the 1940 Republican nominee for President of the United States. The Coffeyville Aviation Heritage Museum, the Dalton Defenders Museum, and the Brown Mansion work together to tell the rich history of Coffeyville.

 **Restaurant Recommendation: Sunflower Soda Fountain 125 W 8th St Coffeyville, KS 67337**

# DEARING, KS
## POPULATION: 382 – TOWN 384 OF 627 (7-19-23)
Dearing, one of the cities of Montgomery County, was founded around 1888 when the post office arrived that year. Two lines of the Missouri Pacific Railroad met there, helping spur the growth of the ore-mining industry and attracting early settlers looking for work. Dearing was incorporated in 1909, and sixteen years later, it would be involved in the Tri-State tornado outbreak, one of the deadliest outbreaks in history that killed over 750 people and injured thousands more. Dearing was largely spared from the damages, although the same system spurred a tornado that lasted for nearly four hours and traveled over 219 miles across Missouri, Illinois, and Indiana.

# ELK CITY, KS
**POPULATION: 260 – TOWN 393 OF 627 (7-20-23)**

Elk City, the birthplace of the 53rd United States Secretary of War and the 25th Governor of Kansas, Harry Hines Woodring, was the first town to be founded in Montgomery County. The first settler was John Kappel in 1868, who established a trading post there. Within the calendar year, the town was founded, and several lines of enterprise ranging from general and hardware stores to sawmills and brick and tile works began to develop. The duties of postmaster were bestowed on William H. H. Southard when it was established on November 5, 1869. Once the Missouri Pacific and Atchison, Topeka & Santa Fe Railroads rolled into Elk City, the population grew to as many as 896 people per the 1890 Census.

# HAVANA, KS
**POPULATION: 84 – TOWN 387 OF 627 (7-19-23)**

The small farming settlement of Havana sprung to life circa 1869 when Callow & Myers opened their general store there. A bank, post office (established in 1871), and other businesses would follow suit. In 1886, the Atchison, Topeka & Santa Fe Railway paved the way for future growth and the decision to incorporate as a city of the third class in 1909. The town's name was taken from Havana, Illinois, the county seat of Mason County.

# INDEPENDENCE, KS ★
**POPULATION: 8,548 – TOWN 361 OF 627 (7-17-23)**

This patriotic community and county seat of Montgomery County, Independence, takes its name as a commemorative one remembering the signing of the Declaration of Independence. Initially, the townsite was purchased by George A. Brown in September of 1869 from the Osage tribe of Native Americans for fifty dollars. Large-scale settlement did not occur until the government took over the land following the forced migration of Native Americans to Indian Territory. Brown had wanted to name the townsite Colfax for Schuyler Colfax, vice president in the Ulysses S. Grant administration, but he thought the name Independence would be more attractive to potential settlers. A large colony of Indiana families moved to the site in the Fall of 1869, and E. E. Wilson and F. D. Irwin founded a general store to accommodate their needs. The following year, it would be formally incorporated and named the judicial seat, and as the discovery of oil, coal, and natural gas in the area boosted the local economy, more industries developed: cracker, shirt, asphalt, candy, cotton twine, rubber, and multiple glass and ice factories, a paper mill, hospital, cement works, and oil refineries, four banks and newspapers, and an impressive number of paved streets. It was by far the most developed community in what is today referred to as the Kansas gas belt, partially thanks to the arrival of the Atchison, Topeka & Santa Fe, and the Missouri Pacific Railways. The town made further history when, on April 17, 1930, it hosted the first professional night baseball game between the Independence Producers and the House of David from Benton Harbor, Michigan. Baseball history runs deep within the town, as in 1949, one of the most notable baseball players of all time, Mickey Mantle, made his professional debut as a member of the 1949 Independence Yankees team. Another progressive moment for Independence occurred in the late 1950s, when Miss Able, a rhesus monkey born at the city's Ralph Mitchell Zoo, became one of the first two monkeys to fly in space. Independence Community College, founded in 1925 as a part of the Independence public school system, enrolls roughly 800 students and serves the town's needs for a higher learning institution. The Corythosaurus at Riverside Park (a part of the 1964 New York World's Fair), Elk City State Park, the Ralph Mitchell Zoo, the Independence Historical Museum and Art Center, and the childhood home of Laura Ingalls Wilder several miles south of town (the Little House on the Prairie Museum) are amongst the most noted points of interest. Due to the size of the community, several famous people have affiliations with the community: Harry F. Sinclair, the founder of Sinclair Oil, W. W. Hodkinson, "The Man Who Invented Hollywood" and began Paramount Pictures, Donald G. Burt, the Academy Award winner for Best Art Direction in 2009, actors and actresses Benny Bartlett, Gerry Bamman, Vivian Vance, and Mary Howard de Liagre, William Inge, "the Playwright of the Midwest and a Pulitzer Prize and Academy Award winner, Alf Landon, the 26th Governor of Kansas and 1936 Republican Party nominee for President, author Gareth Porter, Taylor Armstrong of the Real Housewives of Beverly Hills, Lyman U. Humphrey, the 7th Governor of Kansas, Sheila Bair, the 19th Chair of the FDIC (Federal Deposit Insurance Corporation), Jim Halsey, a noted music artist manager, and Bill Kurtis, the anchor of The CBS Morning News in New York City for some time, among others.

 **Restaurant Recommendation:
Maria Mexican Restaurant
3064 W Main St
Independence, KS 67301**

# LIBERTY, KS
**POPULATION: 99 – TOWN 363 OF 627 (7-17-23)**

For a brief few months, the original townsite of Liberty was the county seat of Montgomery County. It was located in 1869, approximately six miles south of Independence, but it was relocated the following year to be a part of the Atchison, Topeka & Santa Fe railroad line. The first settlers came from the towns of Verdigris and Montgomery, who wanted to consolidate their communities and grow and prosper as one. While prosperity came thanks to the railroad and a flour mill, businesses, a newspaper and bank, and a post office (in 1870), like many small Kansas towns, its industries have been lost, and the population has contracted back to double digits. Its etymology is similar to that of the nearby city of Independence in that it was named for the American value of liberty.

# TYRO, KS
**POPULATION: 177 – TOWN 385 OF 627 (7-19-23)**

The name "Tyro" means "beginner." It was founded as a railroad town on the Denver, Memphis & Atlantic Railroad, the precursor to the Kansas and Colorado Pacific Railway and eventually the Missouri Pacific line. When its citizens voted to incorporate the town circa 1906, it had established itself as an essential agricultural and gas shipping point. The first Census conducted in Tyro in 1910 placed its initial population at 603.

**Adjacent Counties:** Wilson (N), Neosho (NE), Labette (E), Chautauqua (W), Elk (NW)

**Unincorporated/Ghost Towns:** Avian, Blake, Bolton, Corbin, Jefferson, Le Hunt, Sycamore, Videtta Spur, Wayside

**National Register of Historic Places:**
**Cherryvale:** Cherryvale Carnegie Free Library
**Coffeyville:** Charles M. Ball House, Bethel African Methodist Episcopal Church, W. P. Brown Mansion, Coffeyville Carnegie Public Library Building, Condon National Bank, Hotel Dale, Midland Theater, Onion Creek Bridge, Terminal Building
**Fredonia:** Cedar Manor Farm
**Independence:** Blakeslee Motor Company Building, Booth Hotel, Booth Theater, Brown Barn, Cook's Hotel, Dewlen-Spohnhauer Bridge, Federal Building-U.S. Post Office, First Congregational Church, Independence Bowstring, Independence Downtown Historic

District, Independence Junior High School, Independence Public Carnegie Library, Infinity Archeological Site, William, Inge Boyhood Home, Memorial Hall, Pennsylvania Avenue Rock Creek Bridge, Union Implement and Hardware Building-Masonic Temple, Washington School

**Breweries/Wineries/Distilleries:**
Indy Brew Works (Independence, KS)

**Golf Courses:**
Caney Golf Club, Semi-Private (Caney, KS)
Coffeyville Country Club, Private (Coffeyville, KS)
Hillcrest Golf Course, Public (Coffeyville, KS)
Independence Country Club, Private (Independence, KS)
Lakeview Country Club, Semi-Private (Cherryvale, KS)
Sycamore Valley Golf Course, Public (Independence, KS)

**Town Celebrations:**
Cherry Blossom Festival, Cherryvale, KS (Early May)
Dalton Defenders Days, Coffeyville, KS (1st Full Weekend of October)
End of Summer Bash, Cherryvale, KS (2nd Weekend of September)
Inge Festival, Independence, KS (3rd Week of April)
MayFest, Caney, KS (Memorial Day Weekend)
Pioneer Days, Caney, KS (1st Weekend of June)
Neewollah, Independence, KS (Last Weekend before Halloween)
Old Settlers Day Fair, Elk City, KS (Saturday after Labor Day)

# MORRIS COUNTY
## EST. 1855 - POPULATION: 5,386

Wise County was the first name of this section of Kansas, although it would later take on the name of Thomas Morris, a U.S. Senator from Ohio.

# COUNCIL GROVE, KS ★☆
## POPULATION: 2,140 – TOWN 230 OF 627 (5-3-23)
The county seat of Morris County, Council Grove, was named after the grove of trees where pioneers would band together wagon trains to prepare for their journey westward along the Santa Fe Trail. The "Council" portion of the name refers to a meeting between the pioneers and the Osage Nation tribe of Native Americans, who

allowed the early settlers to move through the area with their convoys. Seth M. Hays, a great-grandson of frontiersman Daniel Boone, was the first to settle in the Council Grove area in 1847 so that he could trade with the Kaw Native Americans. He opened a restaurant in 1857, now known as the Hays House 1857 Restaurant & Tavern, largely believed to be the longest continuously operating restaurant west of the Mississippi River. The post office began on February 26, 1855 (the oldest in the county), and incorporation was awarded by an act of the legislature in 1858. After the Missouri Pacific and the Missouri, Kansas & Texas Railroads completed their lines through the area, Council Grove grew to contain multiple hotels, an opera house, marble and granite works, a library and school, and several churches, stores, and even three newspapers. In addition to having "more historic markers per capita" than any other town in Kansas, Council Grove is home to the Kaw Mission State Historic Site, an early mission for the children of the Kaw tribe of Native Americans, and Trail Days Historic Site, a set of numerous buildings that tell the early story of Council Grove's residents and how they lived. The Stump of the Council Oak, where representatives of the U.S. government and the Osage tribe signed a deal in 1825, is one of the many historic sites in town. Famous persons from Council Grove are John Jacob Rhodes (House Minority Leader from 1973 to 1981), the 31st Vice President of the United States, Charles Curtis, actor Don Harvey, and author Clara H. Hazelrigg.

 **Restaurant Recommendation:
Hays House 1857 Restaurant
112 W Main St
Council Grove, KS 66846**

# DUNLAP, KS
## POPULATION: 27 – TOWN 229 OF 627 (5-3-23)
Although its population is now only 27 as of the 2020 Census, Dunlap once played an important role by serving as a "promised land" for African Americans seeking refuge shortly after the American Civil War. It began circa 1870 and was named after the Indian agent Joseph Gage Dunlap. Benjamin "Pap" Singleton, an abolitionist known for moving thousands of black colonists, "Exodusters," to the plains of Kansas, first visited Dunlap in the spring of 1878 and made it his headquarters where he would help move African Americans from the south to "Singleton's Colony" outside of Topeka, Wyandotte, and the City of Dunlap. Because of the large influx of residents,

several churches popped up throughout town around the turn of the century, as did a hotel, ice cream lounge and dairy factory, flour mill, drug, hardware, general stores, and a blacksmith shop. The Dust Bowl of the 1930s caused many to flee the area for a better life in the big cities, and by 1988, the post office had closed. The Dunlap Colored Cemetery is a historical local cemetery and point of interest that was added to the National Register of Historic Places in 2018.

# DWIGHT, KS
**POPULATION: 217 – TOWN 245 OF 627 (5-4-23)**
The name Dwight pays homage to one of the original owners of the townsite, Dwight Rathbone. It was founded in 1887 with the arrival of the Chicago, Nebraska, and Kansas Railway. Impressively, despite never reporting a population of more than 365 individuals (1990 Census), it was once home to multiple Christian, Presbyterian, Episcopal, and Methodist churches. The post office was established in November 1880 (known as Damorris until March 1887), and incorporation was granted in 1903. It took effect in 1905.

# LATIMER, KS
**POPULATION: 31 – TOWN 242 OF 627 (5-4-23)**
First known as Far West upon its founding in 1883, this town would be renamed Latimer five years after one of its founders. The Chicago, Rock Island & Pacific Railroad was the town's central railway in its early days, although it was the Chicago, Nebraska, and Kansas Railway that was first built there in 1887. Incorporation for the community didn't come until 1929, right around its highest recorded population of 124 individuals in the 1930 Census. The population has remained between twenty to forty residents since the 1950s. Strangely, the town's postal service operations opened and closed on three different occasions: September 1887 to June 1888, February 1889 to April 1895, and November 1895 to January 1961.

# PARKERVILLE, KS
**POPULATION: 46 – TOWN 244 OF 627 (5-4-23)**
Charles G. Parker (the town's namesake), W. M. Thomas, J. A. Rogers, and G. W. Clark worked to incorporate Parkersville in February 1871. When it failed to gain county seat status, and Council Grove took the honor instead, the townspeople worked to make it a center of commerce and trade by starting two cheese factories, two harness shops, a wagon shop, multiple grocery stores, and a

hardware store, dry goods store, and two drug stores. The "s" was dropped from the name when the post office elected to change it on June 23, 1892.

# WHITE CITY, KS
**POPULATION: 447 – TOWN 243 OF 627 (5-4-23)**
The Missouri, Kansas & Texas Railroad preceded the founding of White City when it was constructed through the vicinity in 1868. It wasn't until three years later that a colony of forty families of settlers from Chicago, Illinois, would make their way to the area and start a town. Thomas Eldridge constructed the first home, James Thornley and W. N. Dunbar began the first store, and on January 2, 1872, the postal service established an office there. White City was incorporated as a city of the third class in 1885, and a second railroad line, the Chicago, Kansas, and Nebraska Railway (later annexed by the Chicago, Rock Island & Pacific Railroad), would be extended through the area. Early settlers considered naming the town New Chicago or Swedeland after their former homes, but they decided it would be best to honor F. C. White, a Missouri, Kansas & Texas Railroad superintendent at that time.

# WILSEY, KS
**POPULATION: 139 – TOWN 231 OF 627 (5-3-23)**
Wilsey, incorporated as a city of the third class in 1910, was named after John Wilsey. It was once home to a business district made up of a grain elevator, bank, flour mill, a hotel, and a post office that remained in operation from May 23, 1884 to September 27, 1997. Mildred and Hill Spring were other early names for the post office and the surrounding area. The Missouri Pacific Railroad was the city's railroad line of note.

Herington is only partially located in Morris County (see Dickinson County).

**Adjacent Counties:** Geary (N), Wabaunsee (NE), Lyon (SE), Chase (S), Marion (SW), Dickinson (W)

**Unincorporated/Ghost Towns:** Burdick, Comiskey, Delavan, Diamond Springs, Skiddy

**National Register of Historic Places:**
**Burdick:** Oscar Carlson House, Six Mile Creek Stage Station Historic District
**Council Grove:** Big John Farm Limestone Bank Barn, Cottage House Hotel, Council Grove Carnegie Library, Council Grove Downtown Historic District, Council Grove Historic District, Council Grove Missouri, Kansas & Texas Depot, Council Grove National Bank, Farmers and Drovers Bank, First Baptist Church, Furney Farm, Greenwood Cemetery, Seth Hays House, Hermit's Cave on Belfry Hill, Last Chance Store, Little John Creek Reserve, Madonna of the Trail, Old Kaw Mission, Simcock House, U.S. Post Office-Council Grove
**Dunlap:** Dunlap Colored Cemetery
**Latimer:** Herington Army Airfield Chapel
**White City:** Jenkins Building
**Wilsey:** Diamond Spring, Four Mile Creek Lattice

**Breweries/Wineries/Distilleries:**
Riverbank Brewing (Council Grove, KS)

**Golf Courses:**
Council Grove County Club, Private (Council Grove, KS)

**Town Celebrations:**
4th of July Celebration, Wilsey, KS (Independence Day)
Candlelight Charm, Council Grove, KS (2nd Saturday in November)
Girls Getaway in the Grove, Council Grove, KS (Last Weekend in July)
Labor Day Festival, Burdick, KS (Labor Day)
Second Saturdays, Council Grove, KS (Every 2nd Saturday of the Month, Yearlong)
Spooky Halloween, Council Grove, KS (Saturday before Halloween)
Voices of the Wind People Pageant, Council Grove, KS (Mid-September, biannually)
Washunga Days, Council Grove, KS (3rd Full Weekend of June)

# MORTON COUNTY
## EST. 1886 - POPULATION: 2,701

Formed from Seward County circa 1886, this county in the far southwest corner of Kansas got the name Morton from the 14th Governor of Indiana, Oliver P. Morton.

# ELKHART, KS ★☆

Elkhart is the southwesternmost town in all of Kansas, as it lies only a short eight-and-a-half miles east of the Colorado border and is connected to the Oklahoma border on its southern edge. Like most other communities in this region of Kansas, Elkhart had a late start as it wouldn't be founded until 1913 with the arrival of the Atchison, Topeka & Santa Fe Railroad. The Santa Fe Railway specifically elected to start its Elkhart and Santa Fe Railway from here, ultimately running to its intended destination in New Mexico. The name of the city is an eponym for Elkhart, Indiana. With time, Elkhart would soon boast a cement block factory, churches, schools, a post office, and all the lines of enterprise necessary for a town's survival. Its fruitfulness led to it becoming the county seat of Morton County in 1961 when they took the honor from nearby Richfield (now population 30). Cimarron National Grassland, the largest area of public land in Kansas, comprises over 100,000 acres of shortgrass prairie grassland and a section of the Cimarron River. Those who adventure far enough into its far reaches may find themselves standing on a marker designating the precise point where Kansas, Oklahoma, and Colorado meet. The Morton County Historical Society Museum tells the story of those who passed through the grasslands and what life as a pioneer on the Santa Fe Trail would have been like. Literary editor Sanora Babb has ties to Elkhart, as do many former professional athletes: Robelyn Garcia, a 4x Women's Basketball Association All-Star, Glenn Cunningham, once the world record holder in the one-mile race with a time of 4 minutes and 4.4 seconds, Jerry Simmons, an NFL and college football strength and conditioning coach from 1978 to 2010, Thane Baker, a four-time Olympic medalist in different sprinting events, and Darrin Simmons, the special teams coordinator for the NFL's Cincinnati Bengals since 2003.

 **Restaurant Recommendation:**
**Dairy Kreem**
**350 Morton St**
**Elkhart, KS 67950**

# RICHFIELD, KS

This hamlet of 30 people along the Cimarron River was named for the supposed rich quality of its soil and was once a hub of activity for

Morton County and the surrounding rural area. It was platted in November 1885 by the Aurora Town Company, one year before the Kansas legislature established the county, and it was subsequently named the county seat. The townsite was incredibly prosperous, as within the first year, it had already boasted 600 inhabitants and a series of retail businesses and other structures that had been moved here from another town called Sunset. Jacob Ridleman was the first to construct a building, a general store. It was incorporated in 1887, and V. N. Sayer was named mayor. Just as quickly as the population swelled to an estimated 2,000 individuals, it dropped to 164 people by the 1890 Census because of its isolation from other towns due to the lack of a railroad. Residents continued to leave until the 1920s when the Atchison, Topeka & Santa Fe Railroad finally arrived to "save" the town. However, it was far too late. The population slightly recovered from 62 residents in 1920 to 106 in 1930, but it has since sunk to 30 due to the Dust Bowl and the movement of the county seat from Richfield to Elkhart in 1961.

# ROLLA, KS
## POPULATION: 384 – TOWN 486 OF 627 (9-19-23)
Rollie Ray Williamson is the namesake of this Morton County town of 384 people. He was an early pioneer who came to Kansas in 1907 to live on the land of his father, who had established a homestead in the area. A post office began to service this section of the county on August 31, 1907, and in 1913, a townsite was platted because of the imminent arrival of the Santa Fe Railroad. Before the railroad, the nearest shipping point had been over 35 miles away in Hooker, Oklahoma. Rolla was incorporated as a city of the third class in 1921 and had a top population of 482 people, according to the last Census.

**Adjacent Counties:** Stanton (N), Stevens (E)

**Unincorporated/Ghost Towns:** Wilburton

**National Register of Historic Places:**
**Elkhart:** Point of Rocks – Middle Spring Santa Fe Trail Historic District, Santa Fe Trail – Cimarron National Grassland Segments 1-4
**Richfield:** Morton County WPA Bridge
**Wilburton:** Santa Fe Trail – Cimarron National Grassland Seg. 5

**Golf Courses:**
Point Rock Golf Club, Public (Elkhart, KS)

Miami County Photos: Louisburg, Louisburg, Louisburg, Osawatomie, Osawatomie, Osawatomie, Paola, Paola

Mitchell County Photos: Beloit, Beloit, Beloit, Cawker City, Cawker City, Cawker City, Glen Elder, Tipton

341

Montgomery County Photos: Caney, Cherryvale, Coffeyville, Coffeyville, Coffeyville, Coffeyville, Independence, Independence

Morris County Photos: Council Grove, Council Grove, Council Grove, Council Grove, Dunlap, Dwight, Parkerville, Wilsey

Morton County Photos: Elkhart, Elkhart, Elkhart, Richfield, Richfield, Rolla, Rolla, Rolla

344

# NEMAHA COUNTY
## EST. 1855 – POPULATION: 10,273

Known as Dorn County, when first organized in 1855, this county would later be named for one of its most prominent geographical features: the Nemaha River.

# BERN, KS
## POPULATION: 161 – TOWN 36 OF 627 (3-1-23)
Early Swiss settlers named Bern after the capital of Switzerland of the same name, although it was briefly known as Lehman in honor of Christian Lehman, then Basel, and almost Collins. It was established in 1888 along the Rock Island Railroad. An old record of Bern in a 1916 Nemaha County history book claims that there were approximately 213 cats in town. The Speaker of the House of Representatives for the State of Wyoming throughout a portion of the 1930s, Herman F. Krueger, was born here in 1894.

# CENTRALIA, KS
## POPULATION: 485 – TOWN 28 OF 627 (2-28-23)
The original townsite of Centralia began in 1859, and seven years later, it was moved one mile south to be located along the Missouri Pacific Railway. The town was named for its location in the center of Home Township. A well-known former newspaper editor of the *Topeka Commonwealth* (now a part of *The Topeka Capital-Journal*) and member of the Kansas State Legislature, Floyd Baker, lived here briefly. The Most Valuable Player of Super Bowl XVII and Pro Football Hall of Famer John Riggins attended Centralia High School, where he was a standout athlete in football, basketball, and track. He once held the NFL record for touchdowns in a season with 24 (in 1983).

# CORNING, KS
## POPULATION: 212 – TOWN 29 OF 627 (2-28-23)
This town's name is an eponym for the surname of Erastus Corning, a member of New York's House of Representatives from 1861 to 1863. It was given by Dr. McKay, the town's first postmaster and Corning's partner in medicine. Corning was founded in 1857 and later moved to a new site in 1867 to accommodate the Missouri Pacific Railroad.

# GOFF, KS
Goff, population 106, started in 1880 with the construction of the Missouri Pacific Railroad through the area. Its name honors Edward H. Goff, a former railroad official for the Central Branch of the Union Pacific Railroad. The Central Branch and Missouri Pacific Railroads eventually merged in 1909 before returning to the Union Pacific railway system in 1982. The town's post office and name was officially "Goff's" until it was shortened in 1894.

# ONEIDA, KS
Oneida received its name from the Native American tribe of the same name that once lived predominantly in Wisconsin and New York. Although the town now has a population of just 61, it was as high as 350 in 1910. Its street layout was planned after Chicago, Illinois, so they were named after the main thoroughfare. The town was platted circa 1873 by Colonel Cyrus Shinn.

# SABETHA, KS
The name "Sabetha" is derived from the word "Sabbath," the day in Christianity that is commonly set aside for rest. It is said that the very first settler to the townsite arrived on that day in 1857. It was formally incorporated in 1874 and was founded at the junction of the St. Joseph & Grand Island and the Chicago, Rock Island & Pacific Railroads. Today, the city boasts nearly twice as many jobs as it does residents, and as a result, many of the smaller surrounding towns now play host as "bedroom communities" to Sabetha. Wenger Manufacturing Inc. is one of these employers and the world's largest exporter of extruder food processing systems. A major point of interest for tourists is the Albany Museum, an old schoolhouse in what was formerly the town of Albany. Located on the grounds are a caboose, farmhouse, museum, and several transportation-related artifacts. Famous individuals from Sabetha include Arthur Schabinger (member of the Basketball Hall of Fame and the originator of college football's first forward pass), Wilbur Bestwick (the first Sergeant Major of the United States Marine Corps from 1957 to 1959), and Krishna Shenoy (noted for his contributions to neurotechnology).

 **Restaurant Recommendation:
Downtown Coffee Company
901 Main St
Sabetha, KS 66534**

# SENECA, KS ★☆
**POPULATION: 2,139 – TOWN 34 OF 627 (3-1-23)**
The county seat of Nemaha County, Seneca, was established in 1857 and named after Seneca County in Ohio. A former name for the community was Rock Castle. The town has always served as the county's center of industry thanks to the early arrivals of the St. Joseph & Grand Island and Missouri Pacific Railroads to the town. Pioneers once traversed the lands that would later become the city of Seneca along wagon trails, and in the early 1860s, the town boasted a Pony Express station and what was then the Smith Hotel. The Second Largest Hand Dug Well in Kansas, measuring 65 feet deep and 34 across, was dug in the late 1890s and is available for touring. The town has four other museums focusing on general history: Nemaha County, military history, the local fire department, and the Pony Express. For a brief period, Seneca had a minor league baseball team that played its home games at City Park. NFL fullback John Riggins, of Super Bowl XVII fame, was born here in August of 1949, as was Medal of Honor recipient Edward White (January of 1877). The Bancroft Depot Museum is a seasonal museum outside of Seneca that talks about the history of the now-ghost town and its role on the Kansas City, Wyandotte, and Northwestern Railroad.

 **Restaurant Recommendation:
Sweet Pea Bakery
420 Main St
Seneca, KS 66538**

**Lodging Recommendation:
Altenhofen Inn & Suites
1615 North St
Seneca, KS 66538**

# WETMORE, KS
**POPULATION: 348 – TOWN 31 OF 627 (2-28-23)**

Founded in 1866 and incorporated in 1882, Wetmore was named for W. T. Wetmore, then vice president of the Central Branch Union Pacific Railroad. The town's first post office arrived in 1867, and A. O. McCreary served as its first postmaster. Former California Congressman Lee E. Geyer (in office from January of 1939 to October of 1941) and Zip Zabel, Major League Baseball's record holder for the "most relief innings in a single game" with 18⅓ innings, heed from Wetmore.

**Adjacent Counties:** Brown (E), Jackson (SE), Pottawatomie (SW), Marshall (W)

**Unincorporated/Ghost Towns:** Albany, America City, Baileyville, Bancroft, Berwick, Capioma, Kelly, Neuchatel, St. Benedict, Woodlawn

**National Register of Historic Places:**
**Baileyville:** Clear Creek Camel Truss Bridge, Marion Hall
**Berwick Township:** Old Albany Schoolhouse
**Sabetha:** U.S. Post Office-Sabetha
**Seneca:** Hand-Dug City Water Well, Lake Nemaha Dam Guardrail, Nemaha County Jail and Sheriff's House, Prairie Grove School, Seneca Main Street Historic District, U.S. Post Office-Seneca
**St. Benedict:** St. Mary's Church

**Golf Courses:**
Sabetha Golf & Country Club, Private (Sabetha, KS)
Seneca Golf Club, Public (Seneca, KS)

**Town Celebrations:**
Corning Days, Corning, KS (2nd Weekend of August)

# NEOSHO COUNTY
## EST. 1855 - POPULATION: 15,904

Formerly a part of Dorn County, Neosho County is like Nemaha County in that it, too, renamed itself after a major geographical feature: the Neosho River.

# CHANUTE, KS

Octave Chanute, the father of aviation and a pioneer in American bridges and wood preservation, was honored by area settlers by having this town named for him after he suggested that they be incorporated together as one to attract the railroad's land office to the community. He was then the chief engineer and the superintendent of the LL&G Railroad. The townsite began after the Leavenworth, Lawrence & Galveston Railroad (later the Atchison, Topeka & Santa Fe) line crossed over the Missouri, Kansas & Texas Railroad. This led to the founding of four different towns, New Chicago, Chicago Junction, Tioga, and Alliance, all of which were vying to win over the business of the railroads. New Chicago was incorporated in 1871 and was the biggest of the communities. When the four towns opted to join forces on January 1, 1873, at the request of Chanute, the buildings from the other three sites were moved to it, and the present-day town was born. Chanute's industries would be quite progressive, as within its first decades of existence, it would become home to glass, drilling tool, broom, egg case, and torpedo factories, the headquarters of multiple oil and gas companies, refineries, numerous mills, gas engine and boiler works, and the Ash Grove Cement Company, now the sixth largest cement manufacturer on the North American continent. Neosho County Community College started as the city's first and only institution of higher learning in 1936 under the name Chanute Junior College. The Chanute Historical Museum invites visitors to learn more about the early railroad and town history, the Chanute Art Gallery showcases over 500 unique works, and the Martin and Osa Johnson Safari Museum contains exhibits on the duo's trips to Africa and their filmmaking experiences. Residents of note include Granny-Award nominated singer Jennifer Knapp, Basketball Hall of Fame coach Ralph Miller, George Aberle (better known as Eden Ahbez), a hippie-era songwriter and artist, herpetologist Grace Olive Wiley, 3x World Series champion Paul Lindblad, and Gilbert Baker, the creator of the rainbow flag.

**Restaurant Recommendation:**
**The Grain Bin Restaurant**
**314 E Main St**
**Chanute, KS 66720**

# EARLTON, KS
**POPULATION: 60 – TOWN 355 OF 627 (7-16-23)**
Founded in 1870 and incorporated in 1912, this small community in northwest Neosho County has always maintained a simple history. It was located on the Atchison, Topeka & Santa Fe Railroad, which came through town in about 1876. The founder of the townsite, J. C. Lantz, served as the first postmaster and was the first storekeeper. Its name from its founding until October 1, 1950, was "Earleton," until the second "e" was dropped, and the name was shortened to its present state. The postal service shut the office doors on July 3, 1976, only a day before the bicentennial. The population of Earlton soared as high as 381 people in 1920.

# ERIE, KS ★☆
**POPULATION: 1,047 – TOWN 358 OF 627 (7-17-23)**
Present-day Erie was founded when two rival townsites, one called Crawfordsville and the other "Old Erie" in later years, abandoned their respective towns and elected to unionize at a new location between the two. A combined 160 acres of land was donated by D. W. Bray, Peter Walters, J. F. Hemilwright, and Luther Packet, who effectively became the leaders of the Erie Town Company and helped lay the foundations for what would eventually grow into a bustling early city. They named it for a nearby lake. A. H. Roe was appointed as the town's postmaster in 1866, and after much contention with the town of Osage Mission (later St. Paul), it was awarded the permanent title of the Neosho County seat circa 1874. Because of the arrival of the Atchison, Topeka & Santa Fe Railroad in 1863 and the Missouri, Kansas & Texas Railroad in 1887, the town's industries blossomed and came to include an oil refiner, canning factory, creamery, stone quarries, several mills, and banks. The discovery of oil and gas and the formation of the Erie Gas and Mineral Company contributed to the town's economy and growth in population, and since the 1880s, the town has not seen a dip in population under 1,000 residents. The longest-running Old Soldiers and Sailors Reunion in the United States (since 1873) is known for its Free Erie Bean Feed, which consists of cooking 1,400 pounds of Great Northern navy beans, 125 pounds of bacon, and 50 pounds of onions in 53 cast-iron kettles on the courthouse lawn from 7 am to 6 pm. The Mem-Erie Museum features exhibits about community history under the direction of the Neosho County Historical Society. Paleontology and art lovers marvel at the creations of Robert Dorris at Erie Dinosaur Park, a collection of twenty life-size dinosaurs formed from welded steel.

# GALESBURG, KS
## POPULATION: 149 – TOWN 360 OF 627 (7-17-23)
Land donated by Christopher and Elvina Boje was divided into suitable plats for a townsite by Mr. Tracy, J. W. Crees, and a group of men. The Missouri, Kansas & Texas Railroad rolled into the area in 1871, which led to the construction of the first store owned by J. W. Snyder. A post office had existed in the nearby town of Rose Hill from May 1870 until March 1871, until it was abandoned and the office moved to Galesburg. In 1907, Galesburg was formally incorporated.

# STARK, KS
## POPULATION: 69 – TOWN 328 OF 627 (6-29-23)
The Stark post office predates the townsite itself, as it was established on January 7, 1886, and the townsite didn't come about until 1888 with the arrival of the Missouri, Kansas & Texas Railroad. Its name is an eponym for Stark County, Illinois. Although the population is now only 69 people, Stark was once the site of a bustling train depot, bank, and multiple lines of business. Three attempts were made at founding a town newspaper, none of which lasted longer than a year (the longest being the Stark Enterprise from December 1898 to December 1899).

# ST. PAUL, KS
## POPULATION: 614 – TOWN 359 OF 627 (7-17-23)
Osage Mission started in April of 1847 when Father John Schoenmakers settled in the area to assist pioneers and attempt to convert the Osage Native American tribe to Catholicism. He served as the first postmaster of the newly appointed office when it arrived in 1851. Nearly two decades after his arrival, two stores were built up by L. P. Foster & Company and S. A. Williams, and in 1867, the idea to plat a townsite was formed by George A. Crawford, C. W. Blair, the aforementioned Williams, and others. The nearby settlement of Catholic Mission would be absorbed by Osage Mission, and in 1869, it was incorporated as a city of the third class by the Kansas legislature. It wasn't until the 1880s that the townspeople decided that the settlement needed a change in name because it was no longer solely a Native American mission. So, in April of 1895, the name "St. Paul" was voted upon to honor St. Paul of the Cross, the founder of the Passionists. The Missouri, Kansas & Texas Railroad maintained the town's growth through the turn of the century. Mary Lease, of the

suffrage and temperance movement and Populist Party fame, was an early teacher at the Osage Mission School.

# THAYER, KS
## POPULATION: 432 – TOWN 354 OF 627 (7-16-23)
Thayer, a town of 432 people in Neosho County, was founded in 1870 by J. M. Walker to accommodate the forthcoming arrival of the Atchison, Topeka & Santa Fe Railroad. Walker was then the president of the railroad company. He named it in honor of Nathaniel Thayer Jr., one of his employees and a well-known financier from Boston. Several general stores and hotels were constructed when the community was incorporated in 1871. Nellie Ellen Shepherd, an early artist by trade, was born in Thayer and known for her Impressionistic oil portraits.

**Adjacent Counties:** Allen (N), Bourbon (NE), Crawford (E), Labette (S), Montgomery (SW), Wilson (W), Woodson (NW)

**Unincorporated/Ghost Towns:** Kimball, Ladore, Leanna, Morehead, Odense, Rollin, Shaw, South Mound, Urbana

**National Register of Historic Places:**
**Chanute:** Austin Bridge, Murray High School, Tioga Inn, James and Ella Truitt House
**Erie:** First Christian Church, State Street Bridge
**St. Paul:** Maxwell's Slough Bridge, Oak Grove School, District 20, Osage Mission Infirmary

**Breweries/Wineries/Distilleries:**
On the Edge Vineyard (Erie, KS)

**Golf Courses:**
Chanute Country Club, Private (Chanute, KS)
Osage Hills Golf Course, Private (St. Paul, KS)
Prairie Ridge Golf Club, Public (Erie, KS)
Safari Public Golf Course, Public (Chanute, KS)

**Town Celebrations:**
Artist Alley, Chanute, KS (Last Saturday of September)
Galesburg Days, Galesburg, KS (3rd Saturday of September)
Mission Days, St. Paul, KS (Memorial Day Weekend)
Old Soldiers and Sailors Reunion, Erie, KS (2nd Full Week of July)

# NESS COUNTY
## EST. 1867 - POPULATION: 2,687

The 7th Regiment Kansas Volunteer Calvary, also known as "Jennison's Jayhawkers," has several veterans who had counties named in their honor, such as Noah V. Ness.

# BAZINE, KS
### POPULATION: 282 – TOWN 428 OF 627 (8-15-23)

François Achille Bazine, an officer of the French army under King Louis-Philippe and President Napoleon III, is the namesake of Bazine, Kansas. The city was platted along the Atchison, Topeka, and Santa Fe Railroad, and the area post office arrived in 1874. It was incorporated in 1924, and shortly after that, it achieved its highest number of residents in its history, 465 inhabitants, in 1940. When Bazine High School closed in 2004 due to consolidation, the building was listed on eBay to prevent it from disrepair. It sold for $55,000.

# BROWNELL, KS
### POPULATION: 23 – TOWN 431 OF 627 (8-15-23)

While its population has since fallen to only 23 residents, the hamlet of Brownell was once a bustling community and a station on the Missouri Pacific Railway. Named after a railroad official, as of 1912, Brownell had a post office and a bank, multiple lines of enterprise, and even a Baptist and Methodist church. A former name for the post office had been Vansburgh until it unified with the name given by the railroad. Elon Hogsett, of MLB baseball fame, was a Brownell and Ness County native and a 1935 World Series champion.

# NESS CITY, KS ★☆
### POPULATION: 1,329 – TOWN 427 OF 627 (8-15-23)

Ness City, the county seat of Ness County, was started in 1878 by Richard Dighton, and early capitalist Robert Stephens was responsible for expanding the townsite to ultimately assist in attracting the Atchison, Topeka & Santa Fe Railroad in 1886. The railroad is credited with giving the community its first economic boom, as its arrival spurred growth and the establishment of a creamery, an ice plant, stone quarries, grain elevators and mills, and baking facilities. Over thirty years, from 1886 to 1915, eight different newspapers attempted to headline the local journalism industry, with the last surviving paper by 1915 being the Ness County News. The Skyscraper of the Plains, the Ness County Bank, was built in the late 1880s in the Romanesque Revival style and has been widely dubbed as being the most magnificent building in this part of Kansas. More history on agriculture, oil, and heritage can be enjoyed at the Ness County Historical Museum.

## Lodging Recommendation:
## Grain Bin Inn
## 511 S Court St
## Ness City, KS 67560

# RANSOM, KS
### POPULATION: 260 – TOWN 432 OF 627 (8-15-23)
Ogdensburgh was the name assigned by the postal service for this townsite until the Missouri Pacific Railroad requested that it be simplified and changed to honor Thomas E. G. Ransom. He had been a general of the Union Army, a surveyor, and a land speculator. On March 3, 1905, Ransom was incorporated by an act of the legislature; at this point, it had a hotel and a handful of small businesses. 2x WNBA champion, 2005 WNBA All-Star, and the first woman to ever win the Most Valuable Player award in an NCAA and a WNBA championship, Ruth Riley was born here. She is not the only all-star champion professional athlete to heed from the town, though, as NFL safety Nolan Cromwell won Super Bowl 31 (XXXI) and was selected to four Pro Bowl appearances.

# UTICA, KS
### POPULATION: 99 – TOWN 433 OF 627 (8-15-23)
Established in 1880 as a station on the Missouri Pacific Railroad, the small Ness County community of Utica is thought to have been named by early settler C. W. Bell for his former stomping grounds of Utica, New York. Although the town's economy has shrunk substantially, Utica was once home to many thriving storefronts, as well as a post office. The first office was in operation from July 1879 to early January 1883, and the second from late January 1883 to the present day. A former name for it was Saint Sophia.

**Adjacent Counties:** Trego (N), Ellis (NE), Rush (E), Pawnee (SE), Hodgeman (S), Finney (SW), Lane (W), Gove (NW)

**Unincorporated/Ghost Towns:** Arnold, Beeler, Nonchalanta, Sidney

**National Register of Historic Places:**
**Bazine:** Ness County Bridge FS-450, Pawnee River Tributary Bridge
**Beeler:** George Washington Carver Homestead Site
**Ness City:** Lion Block, Ness County Bank
**Ransom:** Henry Tilley House
**Utica:** Thornburg Barn

**Town Celebrations:**
Ness County's Old Settlers Reunion, Ness City, KS (Early June, Every Five Years)

# NORTON COUNTY
## EST. 1867 - POPULATION: 5,459

Norton County's name comes from Orloff Norton, who served as a Union captain in the Civil War.

# ALMENA, KS
**POPULATION: 363 – TOWN 112 OF 627 (3-28-23)**
Almena was located at the junction of the Chicago, Burlington & Quincy Railroad and the Chicago, Rock Island & Pacific Railroad, which assisted immensely in helping it grow its peak population of 703 residents by 1930. Its name was given by Margaret Coleman, the town's first postmistress, a native of Almena, Wisconsin. Coleman's post office was established in the summer of 1872.

# CLAYTON, KS
**POPULATION: 44 – TOWN 175 OF 627 (4-13-23)**
Clayton is split between Decatur and Norton counties and was named after the abundant amount of clay that could be found at the townsite when it was founded circa 1879. The post office arrived on approximately March 31, 1879. It was incorporated as a city of the third class in 1907 and was located on the Chicago, Rock Island & Pacific Railroad.

# EDMOND, KS
## POPULATION: 28 – TOWN 109 OF 627 (3-28-23)
This small town's population has dwindled from its high of 213 residents in 1920 to just 28 as of the 2020 Census. It is thought to have been founded in the 1870s with the arrival of the post office, which closed in 1996. It was named in honor of Jack Edmond, who offered a supply of flour to the town if he were awarded the naming rights for it.

# LENORA, KS
## POPULATION: 207 – TOWN 185 OF 627 (4-14-23)
Lenora was once located on the Missouri Pacific Railroad and was founded in 1873. Its name pays tribute to early settler Mrs. Lenora Hauser. Early town infrastructure encompassed three churches, two hotels, an opera house, a bank, a post office, and schools. The post office has remained in operation since its inception in 1874.

# NORTON, KS ★☆
## POPULATION: 2,747 – TOWN 186 OF 627 (4-14-23)
Norton County and its county seat were both named for Captain Orloff Norton, an officer of the Kansas Cavalry who died in 1865. The town was started in 1872 and once boasted two major railroad lines: The Chicago, Rock Island & Pacific Railway and the Chicago, Burlington & Quincy Railway. Norton's first hotel was constructed in 1884 by George Griffin, who would later pass it on to the women's clubs of the city. The State Sanitarium for Tuberculosis was placed in Norton in 1913 because of the town's location, pleasant climate, and "exceptionally pure drinking water." Keith Sebelius Lake is a popular area attraction with Prairie Dog State Park on its northern shores and activities for swimmers, boaters, campers, and hikers. The last original adobe house in Kansas is located at the State Park. Visitors may also enjoy exploring Station 15, an old stagecoach stop, the Norton County Historical Museum, or the restored 1930s Conoco and 1940s Sinclair gas stations. Norton's First State Bank showcases a gallery of "Presidential Also-Rans," a collection of portraits and the history of every runner-up in the United States Presidential election. Kathleen Sebelius (the 44th Governor of Kansas and the 21st United States Secretary of Health and Human Services), Keith Gary Sebelius (former Magistrate Judge for the United States District Court for the District of Kansas), and MLB catcher "Roarin'' Nick Allen have ties to the community.

**Restaurant Recommendation:**
**110 Bar & Grill**
**110 S State St**
**Norton, KS 67654**

**Adjacent Counties:** Phillips (E), Graham (S), Sheridan (SW), Decatur (W)

**Unincorporated/Ghost Towns:** Bower, Brett, Cactus, Devizes, Fairhaven, Hanback, Hedgewood, Rayville, Rockwell, Smithton, Wakeman

**National Register of Historic Places:**
**Lenora:** Barbeau House, Sand Creek Truss Leg Bedstead Bridge
**Norton:** North Fork Solomon River Lattice Truss Bridge, Norton Downtown Historic District, West Sappa Creek Lattice

**Golf Courses:**
Prairie Dog Golf Course, Semi-Private (Norton, KS)

# OSAGE COUNTY
## EST. 1855 - POPULATION: 15,766

Although it was known as Weller County when it was organized in 1855, it would later be renamed after the Osage River that flows through it.

# BURLINGAME, KS
### POPULATION: 971 – TOWN 269 OF 627 (6-10-23)

Founded as Council City in 1855, this town was the first to be established in the area that would eventually be organized as Osage County in 1859. It served as an essential stopping point for early travelers along the Santa Fe Trail (second only to the City of Council Grove), and it was quick to accommodate them with well-stocked general stores and even a brick main street wide enough for oxen to pull a pioneer "U-turn." The post office was placed on April 30, 1855. In January of 1858, the town's name was changed to honor Anson Burlingame, an abolitionist, lawyer, and politician who later served as the United States Minister to the Qing Empire under President

Abraham Lincoln. Incorporation by the legislature was awarded in 1860, and for a few years, it served as the county seat of Osage County until Lyndon took over the title in 1875. Its early railroad of note was the Atchison, Topeka & Santa Fe line, which encouraged the construction of fraternity buildings, churches, schools, and the typical lines of business and services found in early towns of the era. During the Civil War, Burlingame's Fort was constructed by the townspeople to protect it from Bloody Bill Anderson, who had threatened to burn the town to the ground after being evicted from a neighboring county and Confederate pro-slavery forces. It would later be torn down, and its stones used to build a Baptist church. Allen Community College has operated a branch of its institution in Burlingame since 1991. The Schuyler Museum of Burlingame is in the old Burlingame Grade School, originally constructed in 1902. Earl Wilbur Sutherland Jr. (the 1971 Nobel Prize winner in Physiology or Medicine), Kenny Starr (country singer), Maurice Mehl (noted paleontologist), Muriel Window (vaudeville performer), Carla Provost (former Chief of the United States Border Patrol), Victor Murdock (the 1916 Progressive party presidential nominee), and Ron Thornburgh (the 29th Secretary of State of Kansas) all heed from Burlingame.

# CARBONDALE, KS
## POPULATION: 1,352 – TOWN 266 OF 627 (6-10-23)
Carbondale's name is a nod to its basis of existence, the large coal seams that attracted the Carbon Coal Company to the area circa 1869 and enabled them to begin the townsite. It was founded by T. J. Peter, L. R. Adams, and C. P. and J. F. Dodds, who worked to build homes for the coal mine workers. The Atchison, Topeka & Santa Railroad fueled the town's economy by transporting coal around the rest of the state, which led to the founding of several businesses, churches, banks, and schools. C. P. Dodds of the town company was named the first postmaster. The townspeople elected to incorporate on October 15, 1872. Barnum Brown, a famous paleontologist noted for discovering the first Tyrannosaurus rex remains, was born in Carbondale a year after its incorporation. David Forbes Jr., the namesake of Forbes Air Force Base (now Topeka Regional Airport), also heeds from this city. Carbondale is home to Osage State Fishing Lake, located near Santa Fe Trail High School.

# LYNDON, KS ★
The Sac and Fox Nation once called these lands their home until the government took complete control of the land in 1869 to open it up for homesteading (a result of the Homestead Act of 1862). M. M. Snow was the community's first store owner and postmaster, and in 1870, the town company was formed, and a push began to make Lyndon the county seat of Osage County. It wasn't until 1878 that Lyndon was formally awarded the title (despite county records being moved as early as 1875), around the same time that the Atchison, Topeka & Santa Fe, and the Missouri Pacific Railroads began to lay tracks through that part of Kansas. Incorporation came in 1871, and since then, the population has hovered between 729 (1950 Census) and 1,132 (1980 Census) residents. The Osage County Museum offers an inside look at a bygone era of Lyndon's history.

# MELVERN, KS
The name Melvern alludes to the Malvern Hills of Worcestershire, England; it was chosen by early town company members S. B. Enderton, Charles Cochran, and eight other men who aspired to start a town in the area in 1870. The future expected arrival of the Atchison, Topeka & Santa Fe Railroad led to the quick construction of a cheese factory, school, church, bank, flour mill, stone quarries, coal mines, and a post office with J. W. Beck as its first postmaster. Nearby Melvern Lake was filled in 1975 by the United States Army Corps of Engineers as a means of controlling the damaging floods of the Marais des Cygnes River (responsible for the Great Flood of 1951). The reservoir attracts boaters, anglers, campers, and hunters.

# OLIVET, KS
Reverend A. J. Bartels, J. R. Elder, and C. P. Loricke gave life to this small Osage County community when they founded it in 1869 after raising $10,000 to start a town. Within its first year, the funds had already helped furnish a wagon and blacksmith shop, H. J. Davis's hotel, a Bartels & Munger's sawmill, and a general store by William Haslam. This rapid growth attracted the attention of the postal service, which established an office there on April 15, 1870, before closing it down on September 16, 1971. For a brief period between August 1885 and October 1888, the post office went by the names of

Penfield and Aurora before resuming the name Olivet. It is the closest municipality to Eisenhower State Park, which has 1,345 acres of prairie. The Melvern Wildlife Area is right next door and is home to several types of fowl and mammals.

# OSAGE CITY, KS
**POPULATION: 2,861 – TOWN 272 OF 627 (6-10-23)**
Onion Creek post office was established circa 1869 by the postal service and named after a tributary of the Marais des Cygnes River. Later that year, town promoters T. J. Peter and John N. Witherell brought the Atchison, Topeka & Santa Fe Railroad to the site, and in 1870, it was renamed Osage City. It shares the exact name of the county in which it is located, both of which were named to honor the Osage Nation tribe of the Great Plains. The Osage Carbon, Coal & Mining Company established itself as the first coal operation that summer, helping spur the town's growth as over 1,200 men worked across a couple dozen mine shafts. The local industry grew to include the output of ochre (a regional naturally occurring clay pigment), flagstone, a canning factory, machine shops, a creamery, and original buildings ranging from churches, schools, and hotels to an opera house and multiple lines of business. 2018 MLB All-Star and 2020 World Series champion Blake Treinen, the co-founder of the Marine Corps Marathon and Navy Cross recipient Michael P. Ryan, and 1937 Pulitzer Prize winner C. D. Batchelor (known for his political cartoons) have ties to the city.

**Restaurant Recommendation:**
**Henry's Coffee House**
**413 Market St**
**Osage City, KS 66523**

# OVERBROOK, KS ☆
**POPULATION: 1,005 – TOWN 267 OF 627 (6-10-23)**
Overbrook began in 1888 as a stop along the Missouri Pacific Railroad line. Its name is an eponym of Overbrook, Pennsylvania, the hometown of one of the railroad's early engineers. Although the town's population has swelled to over 1,005 individuals as of the 2020 Census because of its proximity to Topeka, it had humble beginnings. For many years, it had not much more than a post office, newspaper, bank, and schools and churches.

# QUENEMO, KS
**POPULATION: 288 – TOWN 277 OF 627 (6-11-23)**
The name "Quenemo" comes from the name of a well-known chief of the Sac and Fox Native American tribe that formerly lived in the area. George Logan and William Whistler were amongst the first Europeans to claim settlement in the area and assist the government in forming and manning the Sac and Fox Indian agency. The town was platted circa 1870, although the Atchison, Topeka & Santa Fe Railroad wasn't extended to that point until some fourteen years later. The Missouri Pacific Railroad soon followed with their line. A mill, coal mine, creamery, and several lines of enterprise were amongst the first industries in Quenemo. In the 1970s, upwards of 1,500 bike riders would converge on Quenemo every Friday the 13th to "celebrate" the semi-rare event.

# SCRANTON, KS
**POPULATION: 653 – TOWN 268 OF 627 (6-10-23)**
The first settlers came to this area of Kansas in 1871 when miners Alexander Thomas and O. H. Sheldon discovered coal veins. The discovery led to the creation of the Burlingame and Scranton Coal company and several other public and private interests, and infrastructure for a town soon followed when the Atchison, Topeka & Santa Fe Railroad was extended to that point. Scranton was officially incorporated in August 1880 and named in honor of Scranton, Pennsylvania, formerly another coal town. The following year, the population grew to over 1,700 persons, according to some reports, and the townspeople formed multiple congregations, schools, mercantile establishments, and banks. The post office was the first service established in the area on September 6, 1872.

**Adjacent Counties:** Shawnee (N), Douglas (NE), Franklin (E), Coffey (S), Lyon (SW), Wabaunsee (NW)

**Unincorporated/Ghost Towns:** Barclay, Michigan Valley, Peterton, Vassar

**National Register of Historic Places:**
**Burlingame:** Schuyler Grade School
**Burlingame Township:** Samuel Hunt Grave
**Carbondale:** Karnes Stone Bran
**Lebo:** Arvonia School, Arvonia Township Hall, Calvinistic Methodist Church

**Lyndon:** Lyndon Carnegie Library, Osage County Courthouse
**Melvern:** Atchison, Topeka & Santa Fe Pratt Truss Bridge
**Osage City:** Osage City Santa Fe Depot, Rapp School District No. 50, Star Block
**Reading:** Luther Severy & Son Stock Farm
**Scranton:** Banner Hereford Farm

## Golf Courses:
Hidden Springs Golf Course, Public (Overbrook, KS)
Lamont Hill Resort, Resort (Vassar, KS)
Osage City Country Club, Semi-Private (Osage City, KS)

## Town Celebrations:
Rodeo Days, Burlingame, KS (3rd Weekend of May)
Smoke in the Spring, Osage City, KS (1st Full Weekend of April)

Nemaha County Photos: Bern, Centralia, Goff, Sabetha, Seneca, Seneca, Seneca, Wetmore

363

Neosho County Photos: Chanute, Chanute, Chanute, Erie, Erie, Saint Paul, Saint Paul, Thayer

Ness County Photos: Bazine, Bazine, Brownell, Ness City, Ness City, Ness City, Ransom, Utica

Norton County Photos: Almena, Almena, Edmond, Norton, Norton, Norton, Norton, Norton

Osage County Photos: Burlingame, Burlingame, Lyndon, Lyndon, Lyndon, Osage City, Overbrook, Scranton

367

# OSBORNE COUNTY
## EST. 1867 - POPULATION: 3,500

The etymology of Osborne County comes from the surname of a former soldier of the Union Army, Vincent B. Osborne.

# ALTON, KS
## POPULATION: 100 – TOWN 100 OF 627 (3-28-23)
Alton began in 1870, but at that time, it was known as Bull City, named for the business and politician Hiram C. Bull. Female residents requested that the town's name be changed in 1885, so the townspeople agreed on Alton after Alton, Illinois. The Missouri Pacific Railway brought industry to the city, and in February 1885, the first post office was established. The highest recorded temperature in the history of Kansas was recorded on July 24, 1936, when the temperature reached a sweltering 121 °F. The famous entrepreneur and confectionist Russell Stover was born in Alton in 1888; his company would sell for 1.6 billion dollars in 2014. Two other notable former residents are Bruce Goff (a famous architect admired by even Frank Lloyd Wright) and Len Dugan (an NFL player in the 1930s).

# DOWNS, KS
## POPULATION: 800 – TOWN 97 OF 627 (3-27-23)
The city of Downs was once home to two lines of the Missouri Pacific Railroad, of which the Central Branch Railroad was established first in 1879. John A. Beal and A. Z. Blunt platted the community later that year and named it after railroad official Major William F. Downs of Atchison, Kansas. The former head coach of the University of Tulsa (1919 to 1921), University of Arkansas (1922 to 1928), Texas Christian University (1929 to 1933), Ohio State University (1934 to 1940), and University of Idaho (1941 to 1942) college football programs, Francis Schmidt was born here on December 3, 1885. He doubled as Tulsa, TCU, and Arkansas's head basketball coach for some time as well.

# NATOMA, KS
## POPULATION: 302 – TOWN 144 OF 627 (4-10-23)
Founded in 1888 and incorporated in 1905, Natoma's nomenclature was derived from a Native American of the same name. An employee of the railroad chose the name that roughly translates to "newborn."

The area's first post office came about circa 1878 under the name "Tapley," but by July 1890, the name had been changed to match that of the townsite. The town's high population sat at 775 individuals according to the 1950 and the 1960 Census. In a bizarre coincidence of natural disaster history, a little village called Codell (located eight miles west of Natoma) was hit by a tornado on three consecutive years in 1916, 1917, and 1918. A 15-foot-tall memorial made by Tobias Flores and Danielle Robinson memorializes the events and those affected by the disasters.

# OSBORNE, KS ★☆
## POPULATION: 1,335 – TOWN 99 OF 627 (3-28-23)

The county seat of Osborne County was founded by a group of 38 men, one woman, and two boys from southeastern Pennsylvania in the spring of 1871. The colony leader, Colonel William Bear, suggested that the newly founded community be named in honor of Vincent B. Osborne, a fighter for the Union in the American Civil War. A year and a half later, it was awarded the title of county seat, but it wasn't until 1878 that the town was formally incorporated. The town's full name was Osborne City until the "City" portion was dropped in the mid-1890s. Today, it serves as a terminus of both the Kyle Railroad and the Kansas & Oklahoma Railroad. Its largest points of interest are the Osborne County Historical Museum (Osborne's center of local history), its Shady Bend recreational area (known for its golf course and shooting range), and a roadside park that is home to a replica of the marker for the geodetic center of North America (located 18 miles to the southeast). The NCK Youth Fair is held here annually and is the largest fair of its kind in Kansas. Numerous persons of notoriety heed from Osborne: Elsie Reasoner Ralph, the first female war correspondent in U.S. history, entomologist Edward L. Kessel, former NFL tight end Fred Cornwell, professional wrestler Lee Wykoff, and steel drummer Chris Arpad.

 **Restaurant Recommendation:**
**Yopos Mexican Restaurant**
**119 S 1st St**
**Osborne, KS 67473**

# PORTIS, KS
**POPULATION: 86 – TOWN 98 OF 627 (3-27-23)**

Bethany came into existence when a trading post was established at the soon-to-be townsite in 1871. The Central Branch Railroad rolled through town in 1879 and was later bought out and renamed to the Missouri Pacific Railroad. The railroad changed the name from Bethany to Portis because there was already a Bethany, Missouri, located further east on the line. Its present name honors Thomas J. Portis, then Vice-President of the railroad. Melvin "Tubby" Millar, who worked as an animator for *Looney Tunes* and as an assistant to other show creators, called Portis his hometown and included subtle nods to the community in the cartoon episodes "Porky's Pet" (King, 1936) "Bingo Crosbyana" (Freleng, 1936), and "Porky of the North Woods" (Tashlin, 1936).

**Adjacent Counties:** Smith (N), Jewell (NE), Mitchell (E), Lincoln (SE), Russell (S), Ellis (SW), Rooks (W)

**Unincorporated/Ghost Towns:** Banks, Bloomington, Bristow, Cheyenne, Corinth, Covert, Delhi, Deliverance, Dial, Emley, Forney, Free Will, Handy, Pleasant Plain, Potterville, Roundmound, Twin Creek, Vincent, Yoxall

**National Register of Historic Places:**
**Delhi:** East Fork Wolf Creek Pratt Truss Bridge
**Downs:** Downs Carnegie Library, Downs Missouri Pacific Depot
**Natoma:** Natoma Presbyterian Church
**Osborne:** Geodetic Center of the United States, Osborne County Courthouse, Osborne Public Carnegie Library

**Golf Courses:**
Shady Bend Golf Course, Public (Osborne, KS)

**Town Celebrations:**
4th of July Celebration, Alton, KS (Independence Day)
Alton Jubilee, Alton, KS (4th Saturday in August)
Downs Celebration, Downs, KS (3rd Weekend of June)
Kansas Storytelling Festival, Downs, KS (Last Full Weekend of April)
Labor Day Celebration, Natoma, KS (Labor Day Weekend)

# OTTAWA COUNTY
## EST. 1860 - POPULATION: 5,735

Named in honor of the Ottawa Native American tribe, Ottawa County came into existence in 1860.

# BENNINGTON, KS
## POPULATION: 622 – TOWN 196 OF 627 (5-1-23)
The etymology of Bennington's name is disputed. The most likely story, however, is that George R. Parker, an original town founder and the first town store owner, named it after the City of Bennington, Vermont. It was founded in 1870 along the Solomon River, which later attracted the Kansas Pacific Railroad to build a line there. Early lines of business in Bennington included a flour mill, an opera house, and a couple of grain elevators and banks.

# CULVER, KS
## POPULATION: 114 – TOWN 134 OF 627 (4-9-23)
This community of 114 residents in Southwest Ottawa County welcomed its first post office on April 14, 1873, and it was later, in 1878, that the foundations for the town would be created. Its railroad of notoriety was the Union Pacific, and the town's name is thought to have been taken from George Washington Culver.

# DELPHOS, KS
## POPULATION: 302 – TOWN 85 OF 627 (3-15-23)
Levi and Dan Yockey started the town of Delphos in 1867 alongside several early settlers looking to start anew after the American Civil War. Its name was taken from Delphos, Ohio, the former hometown of the Yockey brothers. Grace Bedell, noted for encouraging Abraham Lincoln to grow his famous beard, is buried in the Delphos Cemetery. A local tale recalls the time that a UFO landed outside of town in 1971 on the farm of a teenager and his family, leaving him with nightmares. The Delphos Museum encapsulates the town's interesting tidbits of history and tales. Archie "Happy" McKain, former MLB pitcher, and L. E. Katterfeld, a founding member of the Communist Labor Party of America and a magazine editor, have connections to Delphos.

# MINNEAPOLIS, KS ★☆

Minneapolis, the county seat of Ottawa County, was founded in 1866 and first called Markley's Mills. Less than half a decade later, the name was changed to match that of Minneapolis, Minnesota. The town's industry of flour and alfalfa mills, an ice plant, several newspapers, three banks, and other businesses came about because of Minneapolis's location at the junction of the Atchison, Topeka & Santa Railroad and the Union Pacific Railroad. Rock City is an unusual park and National Natural Landmark on the outskirts of the community where visitors admire, climb, and play on any one of 200+ spherical boulders. The Ottawa County Historical Museum serves as a small regional center for history and heritage, and Ottawa State Fishing Lake offers opportunities for local recreationists. Famous Minneapolisans throughout history have included Frank "Cannonball" Richards (performer known for taking shots to the belly from objects such as a 104-lb cannonball or boxer's punches), Alyssa George (Miss Kansas 2007), Alexander P. Riddle (11th lieutenant governor of Kansas), Bessie S. McColgin (first woman elected to Oklahoma's House of Representatives in 1920), and George Washington Carver, an agricultural scientist known for his contributions to preventing the depletion of nutrients from soil.

 **Restaurant Recommendation:**
**Papa's Burger Mill**
**121 N Mill St**
**Minneapolis, KS 67467**

# TESCOTT, KS

Established in 1866, this town was once called Churchill until the name was changed to Tescott in honor of T. E. Scott, an early area farmer. The name combines his first and middle initials and his last name. The Union Pacific Railway once rolled through town.

**Adjacent Counties:** Cloud (N), Clay (NE), Dickinson (SE), Saline (S), Lincoln (W), Mitchell (NW)

**Unincorporated/Ghost Towns:** Ada, Lindsey, Niles, Sumnerville, Verdi, Vine Creek, Wells

**National Register of Historic Places:**
**Minneapolis:** Minneapolis Archeological Site

**Breweries/Wineries/Distilleries:**
The FARM & The Odd Fellows (Minneapolis, KS)

**Town Celebrations:**
Art in the Park, Minneapolis, KS (2nd Weekend of October)
Del-Fest, Delphos, KS (2nd Weekend of August)

# PAWNEE COUNTY
## EST. 1867 - POPULATION: 6,253

Pawnee County was named for the indigenous tribe once widely prevalent throughout Kansas.

# BURDETT, KS
## POPULATION: 228 – TOWN 424 OF 627 (8-15-23)

Burdett's reason for existence can be traced directly to the arrival of the Atchison, Topeka & Santa Fe Railroad to this part of Pawnee County. A post office had been started in the area in 1877 under the name Brown's Grove, once a different townsite, until it was moved to the site of Burdett in April 1887. The town's etymology honors Robert Jones Burdette, a comedian noted for his work in *The Hawk Eye* newspaper of Burlington, Iowa, at that time. The city was once home to fundamental lines of business like a hotel, grain elevator, and general stores. Clyde Tombaugh, who discovered Pluto in 1930 at the Lowell Observatory in Flagstaff, Arizona, grew up in Burdett in his teen years.

# GARFIELD, KS
## POPULATION: 151 – TOWN 422 OF 627 (8-15-23)

Garfield (population 151) is one of a handful of places in the country named to honor President James A. Garfield, the 20th President of the United States. Like the other incorporated towns of the area, its industries came forth with the arrival of the Atchison, Topeka & Santa Fe Railroad. The town's infrastructure was impressive in its heyday for its size, as it was home to four grain elevators, three churches, a bank, a flour mill, a public library, a hotel, and a post office, amongst other businesses. The existence of the postal service in the area dates back to May 28, 1873. Incorporation as a municipality came in the year 1910. The Garfield Memorial Wayside Chapel is a peaceful attraction that holds great significance within the community, partially because President Garfield donated its bell as an appreciation gift for naming the town in his honor.

# LARNED, KS ★☆

**POPULATION: 3,769 – TOWN 420 OF 627 (8-14-23)**

Once located on the Missouri Pacific and the Atchison, Topeka & Santa Fe Railroad, Larned took its name from Colonel Benjamin F. Larned, the former Paymaster General of the United States Army. Although he never visited Kansas, a small military outpost (Fort Larned) bore his name during its operating days between 1859 and 1878. The fort, like many others in the American West, was established by the government to provide supplies and protection to settlers traveling westward along the Santa Fe Trail. The area was so dangerous at one point that all merchants and wagon trains in 1865 were required to be guided by an armed escort if traveling west of the fort. Fort Larned Historic Site now welcomes visitors to tour the refurbished barracks, shops, officers' row, and other buildings. The city of Larned began with a post office in 1872, and the townsite came about a year later. Early town industry ranged from a foundry, creamery, and mills to grain elevators and machine shops and upwards of fifty lines of enterprise. An opera house and a hospital were also amongst the early establishments, as Larned was then (and still is today) the county seat of Pawnee County. The Santa Fe Trail Center Museum & Research Library educates visitors on the effect of Westward Expansion throughout the Sunflower State that largely came with the Santa Fe Trail, and the Central States Scout Museum has unique exhibits on the history of the Boy Scouts and the Girl Scouts. Amongst Larned's most notable residents of the past are Gene Keady (member of the Basketball Hall of Fame and 5x National Coach of the Year as head coach of the Purdue Boilermakers), Ralph Terry (2x MLB All-Star and World Series champion, and the 1962 World Series MVP), John Zook (1973 NFL Pro-Bowl defensive end), Belle Benchley (the director of the San Diego Zoo from 1927 to 1953 responsible for the zoo's massive expansion), Hal Patterson (one of Top 50 players in Canadian Football League history as of 2006 and a 3x All-Star and Grey Cup champion), and former MLB outfielder Mitch Webster.

**Restaurant Recommendation:**
**Edwards Street Brew & Bites**
**603 Edwards St**
**Larned, KS 67550**

# ROZEL, KS

**POPULATION: 102 – TOWN 423 OF 627 (8-15-23)**

Only established in the 1890s, this small Pawnee County community was named in honor of Roseila, the daughter of a prominent area businessman when it was founded. The post office was amongst the first of the town's buildings, having been moved to Rozel on June 15, 1893. It had formerly been known as the Ben Wade and the Keysville office. The Atchison, Topeka & Santa Fe Railroad helped to bring a mill, grain elevator, and a bank to Rozel, although the town never reached a population of more than 236 persons (1970 Census). One such resident at that time was Gary Patterson, who would grow up to become the most-winning head coach in Texas Christian University football program history during his 2000 to 2021 tenure.

**Adjacent Counties:** Rush (N), Barton (NE), Stafford (E), Edwards (S), Hodgeman (W), Ness (NW)

**Unincorporated/Ghost Towns:** Ash Valley, Frizell, Sanford, Zook

**National Register of Historic Places:**
**Garfield:** Coon Creek Crossing on the Santa Fe Trail (Wet Route)
**Larned:** Babbitt-Doerr House, Fort Larned National Historic Site, Lewis Site, Ooten House, Patterson House, Pawnee Fork Crossing and Boyd's Ranch Site on the Santa Fe Trail (Dry Route)
**Rozel:** Township Line Bridge

**Golf Courses:**
Larned Country Club, Public (Larned, KS)

**Town Celebrations:**
Santa Fe Trail Days, Larned, KS (4th Weekend of May)

375

# PHILLIPS COUNTY
## EST. 1867 - POPULATION: 4,981

William A. Phillips, a former Kansas Congressman and abolitionist who was widely responsible for the creation of Phillips County, had it named in his honor.

# AGRA, KS
### POPULATION: 208 – TOWN 122 OF 627 (3-29-23)

The name Agra is an eponym for the city in India of the same name. The first settlers came to the area in 1888, and eventually, the Chicago, Rock Island, and Pacific Railroad were constructed through the vicinity. The townspeople elected to formally incorporate the community in 1904.

# GLADE, KS
### POPULATION: 52 – TOWN 115 OF 627 (3-29-23)

Not incorporated as a city until 1948, Glade started as a shipping station on the Atchison & Lenora line of the Missouri Pacific Railroad. Former names for the town included Marvin and Chillicothe. Its post office remained in operation from its founding in 1908 to 1989.

# KIRWIN, KS
### POPULATION: 139 – TOWN 116 OF 627 (3-29-23)

Colonel John Kirwin, the former commander of a stockade in the area when this town was organized in 1869, is to thank for Kirwin's present name. The Missouri Pacific Railroad was the noted railroad that brought industry to the community. The town's original post office was founded in 1871 with H. P. Gandy as the postmaster, and nine years later, the city was incorporated. Kirwin Reservoir was built in March of 1952, and the first national refuge in Kansas was soon organized nearby in 1954 as the Kirwin National Wildlife Refuge to help conserve migratory birds and other species like black-tailed prairie dogs and greater prairie chickens.

# LOGAN, KS
### POPULATION: 460 – TOWN 110 OF 627 (3-28-23)

General John A. Logan of Illinois is this town's namesake. Located on the Missouri Pacific Railroad, Logan was established in the early

1870s and welcomed a post office into town at that time. The railroad wasn't completed until 1880, when the city became incorporated with Charles H. Bridges as its first mayor and W. W. Gray as its clerk. The Hansen Museum, established in 1972, offers a look into town history, the life of entrepreneur Dane Gray Hansen, and rotating exhibits throughout the year. The nearby Logan Area Historical Museum focuses predominantly on area history. The people of Logan are currently working to construct the "Logan Intergenerational Family Education Center," a one-of-a-kind (in North America) marvel of engineering that will contain a school, nursing home, community center, and recreational center all in one.

# LONG ISLAND, KS
**POPULATION: 137 – TOWN 113 OF 627 (3-28-23)**
Located on the Chicago, Burlington & Quincy Railroad, Long Island was established in 1873. Its post office had been founded a year earlier, on May 16, 1872. The town's name was given after it was discovered that after a heavy rainfall, the floodwaters from Elk Creek and Prairie Dog Creek (on the north and south sides of town, respectively) would fill the floodplain and create a "Long Island" on which the community was located.

# PHILLIPSBURG, KS ★☆
**POPULATION: 2,337 – TOWN 114 OF 627 (3-29-23)**
The city of Phillipsburg was established in 1872 and was awarded the title of the county seat of Phillips County before a single resident ever set foot on the townsite. Its name sought to honor Colonel William A. Phillips and was spelled "Phillipsburgh" at the local post office until 1893. In 1880, the town was incorporated as a third-class city thanks to its status as the county's center of industry and commerce and the recent arrival of the Chicago, Rock Island & Pacific Railroad. The town made history in 1939 when the Consumer's Cooperative Association opened the world's first cooperative oil refinery in Phillipsburg, but it was closed in 1992. After being paved in 1926, downtown Phillipsburg was the site of the only traffic light between Kansas City and Denver along U.S. Highway 36. Today, the community promotes itself as playing host to the "biggest rodeo of Kansas" every year during the first week of August. The Fort Bissell Museum comprises several 1880s frontier buildings of the original army fort, and the C & R Railroad Museum at the Huck Boyd Community Center maintains artifacts and memorabilia about the history of the "iron horse" in Phillipsburg. Former NFL linebacker and

Super XLIV Super Bowl champion Mark Simoneau, petroleum geologist Wallace Pratt, and McDill Boyd, a newspaper publisher and two-time candidate for Kansas governor, have ties to the city.

# PRAIRIE VIEW, KS
**POPULATION: 106 – TOWN 111 OF 627 (3-28-23)**
Prairie View's population remained relatively steady between 1910 and 1970 (between 183 and 205 residents) until it began to drop significantly. Today, it is home to 106 people. The town was established circa July of 1879 with the arrival of the post office, and its name is a geographical description of the beautiful view of the prairie enjoyed by the townsite's original settlers.

# SPEED, KS
**POPULATION: 37 – TOWN 248 OF 627 (5-28-23)**
This area was once referred to as "Big Bend" by the Missouri Pacific Railroad, although it was incorporated under the name "Speed" in 1928 in honor of James Speed. He served as the United States Attorney General under President Abraham Lincoln. Speed was once home to numerous retail businesses, a hotel, a bank, a grain elevator, a newspaper, and a post office that remained in service from March 1895 to December 1964. In honor of its 40th Anniversary in 2008, Hot Wheels designated the town as one of six stops on a cross-country road trip because of its unique name and named it the "Birthplace of America's Need for Speed." Over 10,000 people showed up to the community to celebrate the event.

**Adjacent Counties:** Smith (E), Rooks (S), Graham (SW), Norton (W)

**Unincorporated/Ghost Towns:** Crow, Dickeyville, Goode, Gretna, Jimtown, Luctor, Matteson, Myrtle, Pleasant Green, Powell, Stuttgart, Wagnerville, West Cedar, Woodruff

**National Register of Historic Places:**
**Agra:** Agra Consolidated School, Agra Lake and Park
**Kirwin:** Hoff School District No. 42, Kirwin City Hall
**Long Island:** Battle Creek King Post Truss Bridge, Jack Creek Kingpost, Long Island School
**Phillipsburg:** Phillipsburg Community Building, Pleasant Ridge Church

**Golf Courses:**
Logan Country Club, Public (Logan, KS)
Phillipsburg Golf Course, Semi-Private (Phillipsburg, KS)

**Town Celebrations:**
Kansas' Biggest Rodeo, Phillipsburg, KS (1st Weekend of August)
Old Settler's Day, Kirwin, KS (1st Saturday in October)

# POTTAWATOMIE COUNTY
## EST. 1857 - POPULATION: 25,348

Created from former portions of Calhoun and Riley counties, Pottawatomie County got its name from the Native American tribe of the same nomenclature.

# BELVUE, KS
## POPULATION: 177 – TOWN 252 OF 627 (6-8-23)
Malcolm Gregory and A. J. Baker laid out the townsite of Belvue in 1871 and named it after the French term meaning "beautiful view." The Union Pacific Railroad would bring several lines of business, including a post office, in the year the town was platted. Census population figures have remained relatively constant since its incorporation in 1913, never dropping lower than 161 individuals in the 1970s or higher than 228 persons in the 2000s.

# EMMETT, KS
## POPULATION: 170 – TOWN 249 OF 627 (6-8-23)
The town of Emmett, located in eastern Pottawatomie County, filed for incorporation in 1920. It started as a station along the Union Pacific Railroad and once boasted a telephone company, a bank, a handful of merchants, and a post office that began on November 11, 1905. It was named in honor of Robert Emmet, an Irish nationalist who sought to overthrow the British Crown.

# HAVENSVILLE, KS
## POPULATION: 119 – TOWN 70 OF 627 (3-14-23)
Havensville was created by constructing the Leavenworth & Miltonvale branch of the Union Pacific Railroad through the area. It was platted in 1878 by the railroad company (the same year that the post office was established), and for a short while, the station was

called just "Havens" while the post office was referred to as Havensville. It owes its name to Paul F. Havens, a railroad employee.

# LOUISVILLE, KS
**POPULATION: 131 – TOWN 253 OF 627 (6-8-23)**
Louisville was an early incorporated community (1870) of Pottawatomie County that was once connected to the nearby cities of Westmoreland and Wamego via a daily stagecoach line. It had vied to garner the title of county seat in 1861, opposing St. George, and in 1882, opposing Westmoreland, but lost both elections. Robert Wilson preemptively settled the area in 1857 and lived at a log cabin on Rock Creek that acted as a hotel stop for early travelers along the Oregon Trail. He called the area "Rock Post" after the creek. His son Louis and prominent area businessman Louis Vieux are the community's namesakes. Vieux lies at rest today at the Vieux Family Cemetery, not far from an 1849 Oregon Trail cholera cemetery home to about fifty graves, only two of which are still marked.

# OLSBURG, KS
**POPULATION: 218 – TOWN 74 OF 627 (3-15-23)**
Olsburg was built by Swedes beginning in the late 1870s and named for pioneer settler Ole Thrulson. Its name was once spelled as "Olesburgh" until 1887. The Union Pacific railroad rolled through town not long after its founding, and in 1873, its first post office was established. Several little Dala horses dot the time, paying homage to the town's Swedish heritage.

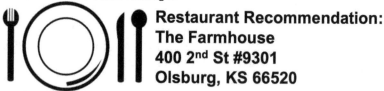

**Restaurant Recommendation:**
**The Farmhouse**
**400 2nd St #9301**
**Olsburg, KS 66520**

# ONAGA, KS ☆
**POPULATION: 679 – TOWN 71 OF 627 (3-14-23)**
This city of 679 residents in Pottawatomie County was platted in 1877 by the Union Pacific Railroad and Paul F. Havens. Its name was derived from the name of a member of the Potawatomi Native American tribe, "Onago." The post office arrived in December of the year the town was established, and by 1881 it was incorporated. The city is home to an incredibly comprehensive museum complex

consisting of two buildings of artifacts, a schoolhouse, a caboose, and a log cabin.

# ST. GEORGE, KS

**POPULATION: 1,054 – TOWN 255 OF 627 (6-8-23)**

St. George was platted in 1857 and named for a group of early settlers with the surname George. When it was discovered that the Union Pacific Railroad would be constructed a mile away in 1879, the entire townsite was moved to be located alongside it. The town's movement fulfilled the goals of the town promoters, who had wanted the settlement to be connected to St. Joseph, Missouri, via a railroad line. It was formerly the county seat of Pottawatomie County until Westmoreland took over that designation in 1882. The town has been growing rapidly the previous two decades, from 434 citizens as of the 2000 Census, to 639 in 2010, and 1,054 in 2020. The growth comes from its newfound distinction as a bedroom community to the City of Manhattan. The country singer Wendell Woods Hall, known as the "Red-haired Music Maker," heeds from St. George.

# ST. MARYS, KS

**POPULATION: 2,759 – TOWN 251 OF 627 (6-8-23)**

Circa 1848, a group of Jesuit missionaries traveling the Oregon Trail established a mission in the area in an attempt to guide the Pottawatomie tribe of Native Americans in the Catholic faith. One of the mission's original buildings from 1855, the Pottawatomie Indian Pay Station, remains to this day. Government agents used it to pay an annuity to the tribe for their agreement to move from the Great Lakes Region to reservation land in Kansas. Following the founding of the townsite in 1866 by town promoter B. H. Bertrand, many industries began to form in the town, including brick, tile and cement works, and multiple banks and grain elevators. The city is unique in that it is home to Saint Mary's Academy and College, a private religious school operated by the Society of St. Pius X that offers a K-12 program and a four-year secondary education program. Most of the town's population is made up of members of SSPX, a group that was formed out of opposition to changes in the Catholic Church brought about by the Second Vatican Council in the 1960s. In May 2023, the Immaculata church, one of the most impressive churches in the state with a seating capacity of 1,500, was dedicated by The Most Reverend Bernard Fellay. Immaculate Conception Catholic Church, closer to the center of the original town, is the oldest parish in the Archdiocese of Kansas City, Kansas, having begun in 1848.

**Restaurant Recommendation:**
**Froggys**
**311 E Bertrand Ave**
**St. Marys, KS 66536**

# WAMEGO, KS
## POPULATION: 4,841 – TOWN 254 OF 627 (6-8-23)

Wamego, known today as Kansas's "Wizard of Oz" city, was platted in 1866 by Hugh S. Walsh and named in honor of Pottawattamie Chief Wamego. It was home to many business lines ranging from barrel and broom factories, grain elevators to flour and alfalfa mills, a cement plant, multiple banks, newspapers, and a post office established in the Fall of 1866. Although there are no longer tornadoes that'll take you to the magical land of Oz today, the Oz Museum seeks to mesmerize visitors with its extensive collection of Oz-related relics. It was founded in 2004 as a tribute to Frank Baum's 1900 children's book *The Wonderful Wizard of Oz* and the famous 1939 film. Nearby businesses allude to the movie with names such as Toto's Tacoz, Oz Winery, Barleycorns, and Lincoln Street Station. An Old Dutch Windmill built in 1879 to grind grain welcomes visitors to the Wamego City Park, and the Wamego Historical Museum and the Columbian Theatre, Museum & Art Center are frequented tourist locations. OZtoberFEST takes place in early October and allows people to take to the sky in hot air balloons, enjoy a beer garden, and bike the Yellow Brick Road. The town was featured in the 2005 thriller *Firecracker*, directed by Steve Balderson. Balderson was raised in Wamego, and other notable figures include Walter Chrysler, founder of Chrysler Corporation, (Playboy model Maggie May, MLB players Wiley Taylor and Travis Metcalf, and painter Benjamin Butler.

**Restaurant Recommendation:**
**Toto's TacOz!**
**515 Lincoln Ave**
**Wamego, KS 66547**

# WESTMORELAND, KS ★
## POPULATION: 740 – TOWN 73 OF 627 (3-14-23)

The name Westmoreland is an eponym for Westmoreland County, Pennsylvania. Westmoreland was established in 1871 by Volney

Baker and is located on the Kansas Southern & Gulf Railroad. Circa 1882, the community became the county seat of Pottawatomie County, and it remains today as one of Kansas's smaller county seats. A primary museum building, a church, and a log cabin make up the bulk of the Rock Creek Valley Historical Society Museum. Three particularly notable individuals once called the city home: Billie Moore (women's college basketball coach in the Basketball Hall of Fame noted for being the first head coach in history to lead different women's programs to national championships), painter Benjamin Butler, and Frank Wiziarde (television personality known for his role as Whizzo the Clown).

# WHEATON, KS
## POPULATION: 98 – TOWN 72 OF 627 (3-14-23)
Wheaton, population 98, was once called Leghorn up until 1883. Its post office was first established in 1870, and it later closed in 1992. Frank Bushey, a pitcher for the Boston Red for a couple of stints in 1927 and 1930, was born here on August 1, 1906. The story of how the town got its name appears to be disputed.

Manhattan is only partially located in Pottawatomie County (see Riley County).

**Adjacent Counties:** Marshall (N), Nemaha (NE), Jackson (E), Shawnee (SE), Wabaunsee (S), Riley (W)

**Unincorporated/Ghost Towns:** Blaine, Duluth, Flush, Fostoria, Juniata, Saint Clere, Swamp Angel

**National Register of Historic Places:**
**Belvue:** Vermillion Creek Crossing, Oregon Trail
**Flush:** Joseph Heptig Barn
**Lincoln Township:** Dennis Quarry
**Olsburg:** Coffey Site
**Onaga:** Pottawatomie County Fair Pavilion, Teske Farmstead, Vermillion Creek Tributary Stone Arch Bridge
**St. Marys:** Pottawatomie Indian Pay Station
**Wamego:** Cassius & Adelia Baker House, Old Dutch Mill, George and Virginia Trout House
**Westmoreland:** German Evangelical Church, John McKimmons Barn, Pottawatomie County Courthouse

**Breweries/Wineries/Distilleries:**
456 Wineries (Wamego, KS)
OZ Winery (Wamego, KS)

**Golf Courses:**
Cool Spring Golf Course, Public (Onaga, KS)
St. Marys Public Golf Course, Public (St. Marys, KS)
Wamego Country Club, Private (Wamego, KS)

**Town Celebrations:**
Boomtown, Wamego, KS (Independence Day)
Flint Hills Shakespeare Festival, St. Marys, KS (Late September to Early October)
Tulip Festival, Wamego, KS (Mid-Late April)
OZtoberFEST, Wamego, KS (1st Saturday in October)

Osborne County Photos: Alton, Downs, Natoma, Natoma, Osborne, Osborne, Osborne, Osborne

Ottawa County Photos: Bennington, Culver, Delphos, Minneapolis, Minneapolis, Minneapolis, Minneapolis, Tescott

Pawnee County Photos: Burdett, Garfield, Garfield, Larned, Larned, Larned, Larned, Rozel

Phillips County Photos: Kirwin, Kirwin, Logan, Phillipsburg, Phillipsburg, Phillipsburg, Phillipsburg, Speed

Pottawattamie County Photos: Olsburg, Olsburg, St. Marys, St. Marys, Wamego, Wamego, Westmoreland, Westmoreland

389

# PRATT COUNTY
## EST. 1867 - POPULATION: 9,157

Caleb Pratt (a Union lieutenant) of Civil War fame is the gentleman whose name is commemorated by this county.

# BYERS, KS
## POPULATION: 38 – TOWN 468 OF 627 (9-18-23)
Byers, a tiny hamlet in rural Pratt County, was established in 1914. It was named after Otto Phillip Byers of Hutchinson and was once located on the Anthony & Northern Railroad. The local post office began on April 12, 1915, the same year the town was incorporated, but has since ceased operations. The present population sits at just 38 people.

# COATS, KS
## POPULATION: 68 – TOWN 511 OF 627 (9-22-23)
The land on which a railroad station for the Wichita & Englewood division of the Atchison, Topeka & Santa Fe Railroad would be built in Grant township of Pratt County was decided upon in 1887 by William A. Coats, the city's namesake. In that same year, a post office was founded, and subsequently, the townspeople founded a cement block factory, hotel, grain elevator, and a bank to serve their needs. Coats was incorporated in 1909 and had its highest number of residents in the 1920s (383 people).

# CULLISON, KS
## POPULATION: 83 – TOWN 469 OF 627 (9-18-23)
Cullison, population 83, began in the 1880s as a shipping point for the Chicago, Rock Island, and Pacific Railroad. It was named after the original owners of the townsite prior to the arrival of the railroad, John B. and Mary M. Cullison. Its earliest establishments were a grain elevator, a bank, a hotel, and a postal office that remained in operation from 1885 to 1967. Several attempts were made at starting a community newspaper (*The Banner* from April 1886 to 1888, *The Tomahawk* from September 1888 to 1890, and *The Times* from March 1913 to 1915), which lasted a couple of years at maximum.

# IUKA, KS
## POPULATION: 151 – TOWN 466 OF 627 (9-18-23)
First settled in 1877, Iuka's name is a commemorative one for the Battle of Iuka of the American Civil War. The battle occurred on September 19, 1862, in Iuka, Mississippi, where the Union stopped the Confederates from advancing. Its post office first opened its doors on December 6, 1877. At the time of incorporation in 1908, Iuka was home to a hotel, a bank, churches, schools, elevators, and general stores. It was even the county seat for a short period until Pratt overtook the honor. Otto P. Myers, seeing an opportunity to bring a railroad to the area mills, hatched a plan to build the line from Iuka to Pratt in 1913. His line was known as the Anthony & Northern Railroad (later the Wichita Northwestern Railroad), and portions remained in operation until 1941. The Missouri Pacific Railroad would ultimately extend its line through Iuka as well.

# PRATT, KS ★☆
## POPULATION: 6,603 – TOWN 467 OF 627 (9-18-23)
Pratt was founded and incorporated in 1884 on the Ninnescah River and was once located on the Chicago, Rock Island & Pacific, and the Atchison, Topeka & Santa Fe Railroad. It was named in honor of Caleb S. Pratt, a young man of the Kansas Infantry who was killed in the Battle of Wilson's Creek at the age of 29 years old. Only a few months before his death, he had administered the oath of office to the first state governor, Charles L. Robinson. Pratt was built up relatively quickly, as it received its first post office on June 17, 1884, and in the subsequent years, its inhabitants founded an opera house, ice plant, three banks and grain elevators, a flour mill, and a steam laundry, amongst other places of note. The historic Hotel Roberts was designed by Samuel S. Voigt and Webster L. Elson in the late 1920s and through 1930 and went by that name until it was purchased in 1959 and renamed by the new owner Monte Parrish himself. It ceased activities as a hotel in the seventies and was added to the National Register of Historic Places in 2015. Other notable sites within the town are the Pratt County Historical Museum, the Pratt County Courthouse, the "Hot and Cold Water Towers" that were playfully labeled in 1956, the state headquarters of the Kansas Department of Wildlife and Parks, and Pratt Army Airfield. This early World War II military base was used to train the bomber crews of the Boeing B-29 Superfortress aircraft. Pratt Community College, home of the Beavers, was established in 1935. For decades, Pratt has hosted the Miss Kansas beauty pageant, in which a representative is

crowned to represent the state in the Miss America pageant. Of historical and national fame are Pearl Farmer Richardson, a member of the woman's club movement and a United Nations promoter, professional baseball players Brad Ziegler and William Marriott, actress Vera Miles, known for her role as Lila Crane in Alfred Hitchcock's 1960 American horror film *Psycho*, and Bill Farmer, the voice of Disney characters Goofy (since 1987), Pluto (since 1990), and Horace Horsecollar (since 1990). Pratt is noted in popular culture several times in the television series *Prison Break* and Stephen King's 1978 novel *The Stand*.

 **Restaurant Recommendation:**
**N'Cahoots Coffee & Shoppe**
**210 S Main St**
**Pratt, KS 67124**

# PRESTON, KS
**POPULATION: 115 – TOWN 522 OF 627 (9-22-23)**
Preston (population 115) was once located on the lines of the Chicago, Rock Island & Pacific and the Missouri Pacific Railroad. Its founding date has been set at 1887, the same year that a post office began to service this portion of Haynesville township. The office would be discontinued in 1990. Other early establishments included a bank, elevators, flour mills, and a weekly newspaper.

# SAWYER, KS
**POPULATION: 89 – TOWN 512 OF 627 (9-22-23)**
Sawyer, once the home of the Eagles, is a hamlet of southern Pratt County with a population of 89 people. It was founded in 1886 on the Atchison, Topeka & Santa Fe Railroad and was home to an impressive number of industries, ranging from a thriving sugar factory and a foundry to a machine shop and brick and stone yards. The town's name honors the legacy of Warren Sawyer, who was then an official of the A, T & SF Railway. Incorporation came about circa 1914.

**Adjacent Counties:** Stafford (N), Reno (NE), Kingman (E), Barber (S), Kiowa (W), Edwards (NW)

**Unincorporated/Ghost Towns:** Cairo, Croft, Hopewell, Natrona

**National Register of Historic Places:**
**Cullison:** J. R. Rice Barn and Granary, J. R. Rice Farmstead
**Isabel:** Thornton Adobe Barn
**Pratt:** Earl H. Ellis VFW Post No. 1362, S. P. Gebhart House, Hotel
Roberts, Norden Bombsight Storage Vaults, Parachute Building
**Sawyer:** Sawyer City Jail

**Golf Courses:**
Green Valley Golf Course, Public (Pratt, KS)
Park Hills Golf & Supper Club, Private (Pratt, KS)

# RAWLINS COUNTY
## EST. 1873 - POPULATION: 2,561

Rawlins County was organized in 1873 and named after the Union
Army general John Aaron Rawlins, who would later serve as the 29th
United States Secretary of War.

# ATWOOD, KS ★☆
**POPULATION: 1,290 – TOWN 171 OF 627 (4-13-23)**
T. A. Andrews and J. M. Matheny founded Attwood in April 1879 and
named it in honor of Matheny's 14-year-old son at the time, Attwood.
The town would become the county seat of Rawlins County in 1881,
with much of its early growth being attributed to its designation as a
shipping point on the Chicago, Burlington & Quincy Railroad between
Orleans, Nebraska and St. Francis, Kansas. The second 't' in its
name was dropped by the post office in 1882 to avoid transcription
errors on parcels. The Rawlins County Museum exhibits local history
ranging from Hopi kachina dolls to clocks and tools, as well as art
created by Rudolph Wendelin, the artist behind Smokey Bear's
appearance. The 41st Governor of Kansas, Mike Hayden, and MLB
outfielder Ted Uhlaender have ties to Atwood.

 **Restaurant Recommendation:**
**Legends**
**202 S 4th St**
**Atwood, KS 67730**

**Restaurant Recommendation:**
**MOJO Espresso & Bistro**
**113 S 4th St**
**Atwood, KS 67730**

**Lodging Recommendation:**
**It'll Do Motel**
**205 Grant St**
**Atwood, KS 66730**

# HERNDON, KS
### POPULATION: 119 – TOWN 172 OF 627 (4-13-23)

The town of Pesth was founded in 1878 and named after Pest, Hungary (now a part of modern-day Budapest), but a year later, it was renamed Herndon for William H. Herndon, a gentleman known for his ties to Abraham Lincoln as a law partner. It was located on the Chicago, Burlington & Quincy Railroad and was incorporated in 1906 thanks to its growth. Facilities throughout the town once included a hotel, flour mill, multiple general stores and churches, and a newspaper, bank, and post office. Herndon was the birthplace of the Smokey Bear artist Rudy Andreas Wendelin in 1910.

# MCDONALD, KS
### POPULATION: 113 – TOWN 170 OF 627 (4-12-23)

Once called Celia, the postal service moved the post office from that now-defunct city to the townsite of McDonald in July 1888. Its name honors Rice McDonald, an early pioneer settler who gave land for the Chicago, Burlington, and Quincy Railroad to be constructed through the town. Former five-time NFL All-Pro offensive tackle and member of the Pro Football Hall of Fame (Class of 1964) William Roy "Link" Lyman attended high school here but ironically did not play football because there weren't enough boys enrolled to form a team.

**Adjacent Counties:** Decatur (E), Thomas (S), Sherman (SW), Cheyenne (W)

**Unincorporated/Ghost Towns:** Achilles, Beardsley, Beaverton, Blakeman, Burntwood, Celia, Chardon, Gladstone, Greshamton, Ludell, Mirage, Rawlins, Rotate

**National Register of Historic Places:**
**Atwood:** Sappa Creek Massacre Site, Shirley Opera House
**McDonald:** Minor Sod House

**Golf Courses:**
Atwood Country Club, Semi-Private (Atwood, KS)

**Town Celebrations:**
Atwood Early Rod Run, Atwood, KS (3rd Weekend in May)
Smokin' on the Beaver, Atwood, KS (4th Weekend in September)

# RENO COUNTY
## EST. 1867 - POPULATION: 61,898

Major General Jesse L. Reno of the Union Army is the namesake of Reno County, Kansas.

# ABBYVILLE, KS
## POPULATION: 83 – TOWN 526 OF 627 (9-22-23)

The original name of this town was Nonpariel before it was changed to Abbyville when the Atchison, Topeka & Santa Fe Railway laid its tracks through western Reno County. The name comes from Abby McLean, the first baby born in the newly founded community. Its founding can be traced to the 1880s, the same year that some railroads were making their way across Kansas, and the decade in which the Abbyville post office was moved to the townsite on June 1, 1886, from Salt Creek (now a ghost town). It was said to have a population of about 300 people in the 1910s before the first Census was conducted there in 1920. At that point, it boasted several Protestant churches and general stores. Abbyville celebrated the Kansas Centennial on July 15, 1961, with a rodeo event, and the event has been continued on an annual basis since the second rodeo was hosted in 1963. The music video for the 2011 single "Good Day at the Races" by the Canadian rock band Hollerado was filmed at the rodeo grounds.

# ARLINGTON, KS
**POPULATION: 435 – TOWN 527 OF 627 (9-22-23)**

Named for the "Heights" of Arlington, Massachusetts, upon the townsite's platting in 1877, Arlington is one of the fifteen incorporated towns of Reno County. The postal service elected to establish service here on February 7, 1878, where it has remained in operation ever since. By the 1920s, it had a population of over 500 residents. It proudly boasted a cornet band, grain elevators, retail establishments, and more because of its location on the Chicago, Rock Island & Pacific Railroad. In April of 1980, the Associated Press ran an unusual story in the Los Angeles Times that "Arlington [Kansas] has not had a murder in its entire history." In the article, the town's first full-time policeman, Ralph Almquist, said, "We don't have any murders here because I don't allow crime." Only four years later, the small town was the victim of the triple homicide of Andy and Jamie Vogelsang and Tammey Mooney.

# BUHLER, KS
**POPULATION: 1,325 – TOWN 605 OF 627 (10-11-23)**

The establishment of Buhler came with the arrival of the Mennonites circa 1888, former natives of Russia who wished to begin a new life in the Midwest. They successfully raised schools, churches, two grain elevators, a creamery, a hotel, and a post office. The office was called Hamburg from January 20 to October 20 until it was changed to Buhler for Bernard Buhler. Other than Mr. Buhler, the town's most prominent past resident was the medical missionary Katharina Schellenberg, one of the first North American women Mennonite doctors. The town's lowest recorded Census population was in 1920 (486 people), seven years after its incorporation. Four threshing stones, used by Mennonites to thresh wheat, are on display at Buhler High School. It is the largest quantity of stones on public display in the United States. Aside from Hutchinson, residents of Buhler are some of the closest individuals to Sand Hills State Park. The park was established in 1974 on land formerly owned by the Kansas State Industrial Reformatory.

# HAVEN, KS
**POPULATION: 324 – TOWN 620 OF 627 (10-12-23)**

The Missouri Pacific Railway town was laid out as a townsite in 1886, but a post office had been in operation long before then, since April 10, 1873. After residents opted to take on the name Haven after New

Haven, Connecticut, they went to work at once at building their flourishing community's creamery, flour mill, elevator, and banks, amongst other structures. Their prosperity continued through the school's high school athletics programs in the 1920s, as in 1927, they defeated county rival Sylvia in a 256-0 football game. Many records were shattered at the state and national levels, many of which will never be broken. Elvin McCoy still holds the Kansas state record for individual touchdowns scored with 13 and most points with 90. Born here only seven years after the town's founding was Flossie Page, who lived a fruitful life to the age of 112.7 years before her passing in 2006. By 2024 standards, she was around for 113 of the town's 138 years of existence (81.88%). One final individual worth mentioning is Andy Dirks, who graduated from Haven High School and went on to play for the Detroit Tigers in the MLB.

 **Restaurant Recommendation:
Carriage Crossing Restaurant
10002 S Yoder Rd
Yoder, KS 67585**

# HUTCHINSON, KS ★☆
**POPULATION: 40,006 – TOWN 609 OF 627 (10-11-23)**
The county seat of Reno County had its beginnings in 1871 when C. C. Hutchinson, a real estate officer, worked with the Atchison, Topeka & Santa Fe Railroad to establish a new town on the banks of the Arkansas River. Because of his work to make the town a reality, the railroad named it in his honor, and by August of 1872, it was incorporated. Amongst the first businesses and proprietors were general store owners W. Bailey, Jordan & Bemis, hotel operator J. S. Fay, hardware and farm implement store owner E. Wilcox, grocer T. F. Leidigh, and C. McMurray, the owner of the first livery stable. Hutchinson himself would go on to start the Reno County Bank in 1873, as well as the first water mill in Kansas in 1878. He was known for his hatred of alcohol, and so for many years, the sale of such substances was banned in "Temperance City," and U.S. marshals would arrest offenders. As the population grew over the next decade, the Chicago, Kansas, and Nebraska Railway (later the Chicago, Rock Island & Pacific Railroad) would extend their line through Hutch in 1887. That same year, the town's fate would be changed forever when oil speculator Ben Blanchard struck a large salt deposit on September 26th. This discovery led to the start of the first salt-processing plants west of the Mississippi River, which by 1912 were

producing nearly 2,500 to 5,000 barrels of salt per day. The vein then measured approximately "400 feet thick" and was 375 feet underground. The Carey Salt Company in 1923 ultimately became the sole salt mine in Hutchinson, today known as the Hutchinson Salt Company. They operate alongside other big-name salt brands like Morton Salt and Cargill. Because of the mine's extensiveness, Underground Vaults & Storage has made a business out of storing irreplaceable movie and television masters (including classics such as *The Wizard of Oz* (1939) and *Star Wars* (1977)), business records, and other data in the abandoned sections of the salt mines. The only salt mine in the country open to tourists, the Strataca salt mine museum, is located in the Hutchinson Salt Company mine and allows tourists to go 650 feet underground to tour the shafts for themselves. The impact of the salt discovery on Hutchinson is truly immeasurable. It affected the local economy so dramatically that hundreds of other entrepreneurs, making everything from blank books, automobiles, furniture, cans, boilers, paint, strawboard, and soda ash to founding creameries, foundries, flour and alfalfa mills, grain elevators, a packing house, and other business ventures, flocked to the area. The soda ash plant was at one point thought to be the largest of its kind in the United States; it made the base of most soda products found at that time. Agriculture would continue to be a big part of Hutchinson's history, too, as in 1961, the world's longest grain elevator was built there, and earlier in the century, in 1913, the city lobbied the Kansas Legislature to become the permanent site of the Kansas State Fair. It is the largest singular event in Kansas and draws in an impressive 350,000 annual visitors to its 280-acre 70-structure complex. Other noteworthy points of interest and activities include Carey Park and the Hutchinson Zoo, the Reno County Museum, the Cosmosphere, a space museum home to over 13,000 artifacts on American and Russian space expeditions, Hutchinson Community College (founded in 1928 as Hutchinson Junior College), and the National Junior College Athletic Association Basketball Tournament. Although the NJCAA offices relocated to Colorado Springs from Hutchinson in 1985, the annual tournament is still held at Hutchinson Sports Arena. The city continues to make history today in unusual ways. On January 17, 2001, an explosion due to a compressed natural gas leak occurred downtown and damaged 28 buildings, and another explosion happened the following day in a trailer park. The events made national headlines and were featured on the History Channel's "Gas Explosion" segment. It holds a tight grip in pop culture because of its designation as Smallville, the home of Superman's fictional hometown. Every year since 2013, the city traditionally changes its name to Smallville for a few days to coincide with the

Smallville Con comic book convention. The city has been featured on other television series such as *Modern Marvels*, *Dirty Jobs*, *How Stuff Works*, and *Rocket Power*, and in the films *Picnic* (1955), *Mysterious Skin* (2004), *Salvation U.S.A.* (2013), and *Wait till the Sun Shines, Nellie* (1952). Naturally, because of the success of the city and its notoriety, it has been home to dozens of noteworthy citizens over the years: screenwriters Kay Alden and Mitch Brian, David Dillon (former CEO of Kroger) and J. S. Dillon (founder of Dillons), the 21st Governor of New Mexico, Jack M. Campbell, 2005 Pulitzer Prize-winning composer Steven Stucky, Leland Barrows, the 1st United States Ambassador to Togo and Cameroon, former NFL or CFL quarterbacks Pat Ryan, Tommy Thompson, and Buck Pierce, Walter A. Huxman, the 27th Governor of Kansas, Hal Prewitt (founder of several technology firms, including Core International, the creators of the world's first disk drives, host adapters, disk controllers, and swappable power supplies), Murry Wilson, the father of Brian, Dennis, and Carl Wilson of the Beach Boys rock band, writers Margaret St. Clair, Scott Heim, and William Mark Simmons, actresses Aneta Corsaut and Lucinda Dickey, Jamie Carey, a former WNBA player, and L. H. Hausam, the founder of the Great Western Business and Normal College, amongst many others.

**Restaurant Recommendation:**
**Anchor Inn Restaurant**
**128 S Main St**
**Hutchinson, KS 67501**

**Restaurant Recommendation:**
**Dutch Kitchen Restaurant**
**6803 KS-61**
**Hutchinson, KS 67501**

**Restaurant Recommendation:**
**R-B Drive In**
**201 E Ave A**
**Hutchinson, KS 67501**

# LANGDON, KS
## POPULATION: 39 – TOWN 524 OF 627 (9-22-23)

Little Langdon once had a population as high as 208 people in the 1940s, but it has since subsided to 39 people as of the last Decennial Census in 2020. It began in 1873 and was formerly known for its private fish hatchery, which has long since gone by the wayside. In its heyday, the Chicago, Rock Island & Pacific Railroad supplied enough trade to the community to warrant the construction of a few businesses, a bank, and a post office (that operated from December 1873 to April 1881 and then from June 1881 to May 11, 1992). The original office was called Leonville for six months in 1873.

# NICKERSON, KS
## POPULATION: 1,058 – TOWN 622 OF 627 (10-13-23)

Thomas Nickerson, the president of the Atchison, Topeka & Santa Fe Railway between 1874 and 1880, is the namesake of this town of 1,058 citizens who owe their town's existence to the railroad company. The depot was constructed in 1872, although it would be a few years before moves were made to build homes and stores. The first of these merchandising establishments was the store of Dr. L. A. Reeves. He would serve as the town's first postmaster when the postal service established an office in Nickerson in 1873, and he moved his store to a new townsite in 1878 that was founded on the land of farmer Sears. It was on this new townsite that Nickerson flourished, as it would be home to a couple of livery stables, banks, and lumber yards, as well as a printing office, mills, elevators, and other stores before its incorporation in June 1879. Because of its proximity to Hutchinson, Nickerson has done well with maintaining its population over the last century, having as few as 1,013 residents in 1950 and as many as 1,292 in 1980. Its highest number of inhabitants ever recorded to have lived in the city at one time was 1,662 people in 1890. Hedrick's Exotic Animal Farm is a unique local point of interest that allows visitors to get up close and personal with camels, zebras, ostriches, and other animals. People can stay and play as it doubles as a bed and breakfast. Curtis, Ernest, and George Baldwin of Nickerson were responsible for the founding of The Gleaner Manufacturing Company in 1923 and inventing an innovative self-propelled combine harvester.

# PARTRIDGE, KS
**POPULATION: 209 – TOWN 528 OF 627 (9-22-23)**
Partridge was named after the land fowl of the same name, a prominent type of bird found throughout the eastern hemisphere. The first townsite was founded in 1874 and named Reno Centre for its geographical location near the middle of Reno County but was later moved three-quarter miles in 1886 to be located on the Atchison, Topeka & Santa Fe, and later the Chicago, Rock Island & Pacific Railroad (then the Chicago, Kansas and Nebraska Railway). The name change came with the move to the railroad. Its most notable early structures were its grain elevator, bank, and post office when it was incorporated in 1906.

# PLEVNA, KS
**POPULATION: 85 – TOWN 525 OF 627 (9-22-23)**
Plevna, founded in the 1870s, was named after Pleven, Bulgaria, which at present is the seventh most populous country of the European nation. The Siege of Plevna took place here in 1877 between the Ottoman Empire, the victorious Russian Empire, and the Kingdom of Romania, which led to an independent Bulgaria. The Plevna post office was established on October 25, 1877, almost two months before the siege ended on December 10. Plevna was a suitable townsite because of its location on the Ninnescah River and later the Atchison, Topeka & Santa Fe Railroad. As of the 2020 Census, it was home to 85 people.

# PRETTY PRAIRIE, KS
**POPULATION: 660 – TOWN 610 OF 627 (10-12-23)**
The Pretty Prairie post office, established in January of 1874, predates the townsite by fifteen years. In 1889, lots were laid out so that settlers could accommodate the needs of the Atchison, Topeka & Santa Fe Railroad, which had recently extended their line to that point. The settlers loved the prairie scenery and thought it was so pretty that their community should be named after it. Incorporation as

a city of the third class came in 1907 following the construction of grain elevators, flour mills, and enough commerce to warrant the action. Noteworthy people from town include Carl Switzer, a child actor known for his role as Alfalfa in the early short film series *Our Gang*, Walter A. Huxman, the 27th Governor of Kansas, and artists Jon Gnagy (a television art instructor) and Jack Unruh (known for his outdoor advertising work).

# SOUTH HUTCHINSON, KS
## POPULATION: 2,521 – TOWN 608 OF 627 (10-11-23)
South Hutchinson is a southern suburb of Hutchinson, thus its name, although it operates as its municipality. It was founded in 1887 by Benjamin Blanchard (the oil prospector who accidentally found salt instead and forever changed the history of the region) of Terre Haute, Indiana, the same year that the post office arrived there. Because of its proximity to Hutch, the South Hutchinson post office was only in operation from August 22, 1887, to July 19, 1898. Although it now primarily serves as a bedroom community for 2,521 residents, South Hutchinson is the site of the salt discovery well, where the first salt deposits of Reno County were discovered on September 27, 1887. Part of the exhibit is a 1,260-pound salt block.

# SYLVIA, KS
## POPULATION: 215 – TOWN 459 OF 627 (8-18-23)
Zenith was the first name for this town of 215 persons in Reno County; it was assigned in 1874 when the city was founded. By 1886, when the Atchison, Topeka & Santa Fe Railroad came to town, the name had been changed to Sylvia after the wife and daughter of a railroad worker. For years, it was an important shipping point for agricultural products in this part of Kansas. It was home to general stores, a post office, a mill, an elevator, and a bank to accommodate the needs of the local farmers and citizens. When incorporation was given by the legislature in 1887, T. J. Ialhott was elected as the first mayor of the community. Sylvia perhaps has a love-hate relationship with the sporting world, as in 1927, they were on the losing side of a 256-0 football game blowout loss against cross-county rival Haven. Sylvia was, however, the birthplace of a highly-noted former NAIA and United States Olympic administrator, Alva Duer, who was inducted into the Basketball Hall of Fame in 1982 for his achievements. He was known as "Mr. NAIA" for his work on improving intercollegiate basketball and promoting sportsmanship.

# THE HIGHLANDS, KS

**POPULATION: 349 – TOWN 607 OF 627 (10-11-23)**

Founded on July 25, 2017, The Highlands is one of the newest incorporated towns in Kansas. The idea to formulate 21 subdivisions surrounding the Crazy Horse Golf Club came about when locals wanted to raise tax dollars to fix poor roads in the area. The town is approximately 1.02 square miles and was home to 349 people, according to the 2020 Census.

# TURON, KS

**POPULATION: 309 – TOWN 523 OF 627 (9-22-23)**

Located at the junction of the Missouri Pacific and the Chicago, Rock Island & Pacific Railroad in 1886, Turon joined the ranks of Kansas's incorporated towns in 1905. In its heyday, it was home to a creamery, grain elevator, flour mill, bottling factory, two banks, a newspaper, and a post office. Historically, its largest population was 631 people in the 1920s, although that number has since subsided to 309 people as of the 2020 Census.

 **Restaurant Recommendation:
Jerry's Bar
508 N Burns St
Turon, KS 67583**

# WILLOWBROOK, KS

**POPULATION: 71 – TOWN 621 OF 627 (10-13-23)**

Willowbrook is a relatively new Kansas municipality, having only been incorporated on July 10, 1952. Located along Cow Creek, it serves primarily as a bedroom community for Hutchinson. The population has varied wildly throughout its existence, having as few as 36 residents in 2000 but as many as 109 persons in the 1980s.

**Adjacent Counties:** Rice (N), McPherson (NE), Harvey (E), Sedgwick (SE), Kingman (S), Pratt (SW), Stafford (W)

**Unincorporated/Ghost Towns:** Castleton, Darlow, Huntsville, Kent, Lerado, Medora, St. Joe, Yaggy, Yoder

**National Register of Historic Places:**
**Buhler:** Wall-Ratzlaff House
**Hutchinson:** Downtown Core North Historic District, Downtown Core South Historic District, Fox Theater, John P. O. Graber House, Hamlin Block, Hoke Building, Houston Whiteside Historic District, Hutchinson Public Carnegie Library, Kelly Mills, G. W. Norris House, Reno County Courthouse, St. Teresa's Catholic Church, Soldiers and Sailors Memorial, Terminal Station, U.S. Post Office-Hutchinson, Frank D. Wolcott House
**Medora:** Ranson Hotel
**Nickerson:** Anna Richardson-Brown House
**Sylvia:** Sylvia Rural High School

**Breweries/Wineries/Distilleries:**
Inland Ocean Vineyards (Hutchinson, KS)
Salt City Brewing Company (Hutchinson, KS)
Sandhills Brewing (Hutchinson, KS)

**Golf Courses:**
Carey Park Golf Course, Public (Hutchinson, KS)
Crazy Horse Sports Club & Golf Club, Private (The Highlands, KS)
Prairie Dunes Country Club, Private (Hutchinson, KS)
The Links At Pretty Prairie, Public (Pretty Prairie, KS)

**Town Celebrations:**
Kansas Largest Night Rodeo, Pretty Prairie, KS (3rd Week of July)
Kansas State Fair, Hutchinson, KS (10 days beginning the Friday after Labor Day)
Klear Nearly Days, Nickerson, KS (Last Full Weekend of July)

# REPUBLIC COUNTY
## EST. 1868 - POPULATION: 4,674

When Republic County was formed out of Washington County in 1868, it was decided that it would be named for its primary water source, the Republican River.

# AGENDA, KS
## POPULATION: 47 – TOWN 15 OF 627 (2-19-23)
The name "Agenda" is a Latin word meaning "what ought to be done." The town began in 1887 along the Chicago, Rock Island & Pacific

Railroad. The city was referred to as Neva for a short while until the post office and the railroad depot were established with the name Agenda, and the latter name stuck.

# BELLEVILLE, KS ★☆

**POPULATION: 2,007 – TOWN 1 OF 627 (2-9-23)**

Belleville was established in 1869 as an essential shipping point for the Chicago, Rock Island & Pacific Railroad, and in 1878, it was formally incorporated as a city. The town that was once considered to be a gateway to the homesteading country now serves as the county seat of Republic County. Its name honors Arabella Tutton, the wife of A. B. Tutton, a member of the town company. Three museums call the town home: the High Banks Hall of Fame & National Midget Auto Racing Museum, the Paul Boyer Museum of Animated Carvings, and the Republic County Historical Society Museum. The High Banks Museum pays tribute to the town's extensive racing history and the Belleville High Banks racetrack, commonly called the "World's Fastest Half Mile." Notable racers like Jeff Gordon, Kasey Kahne, and Tony Stewart have competed here. The museum also features several "midget" cars in honor of the specialized auto racing sport. Although not open, the Paul Boyer Museum of Animated Carvings features 65 hand-carved wooden sculptures built and animated using hand-built motors and mechanisms by the late Paul Boyer. The Republic County Historical Society Museum boasts several outdoor exhibits, including a church, schoolhouse, smokehouse, and several indoor exhibitions. Other points of interest include Rocky Park and the Blair Theatre. Notable individuals with ties to Belleville are Nick Hague, a NASA astronaut and flight engineer on the International Space Station, Larry Cheney, the 1912 National League wins leader in the MLB, and Dean Nesmith, a professional football player for the AFL's New York Yankees.

 **Restaurant Recommendation:
Los Primos
2006 Old US Hwy 81
Belleville, KS 66935**

# COURTLAND, KS

**POPULATION: 294 – TOWN 131 OF 627 (3-29-23)**

The city of Courtland was settled in 1885 and located at the junction of the Atchison, Topeka & Santa Fe, and the Chicago, Rock Island &

Pacific Railroads. It was in 1878 that its first post office (once called Prospect) was established until it was moved to its present site in 1888. Its etymology is disputed, and the town is thought to have taken its name from either Cortland, New York, or Courtland, Minnesota. Incorporation status was granted to Courtland on July 18, 1892.

# CUBA, KS
**POPULATION: 140 – TOWN 16 OF 627 (2-19-23)**
Cuba was formed not long after the American Civil War (in 1868) by Southern migrants. Its name was given by one of the early settlers who had once been a resident of Cuba. In 1884, the entire town moved to be located along the railroad, and it would later sit at the junction of the Chicago, Rock Island & Pacific and Chicago, Burlington & Quincy Railroads. Photographer Jim Richardson shone a light on the town after he helped it to be recognized on the *CBS News Sunday Morning* show in 1983 and 2004, as well as in the May 2004 issue of *National Geographic*.

# MUNDEN, KS
**POPULATION: 96 – TOWN 17 OF 627 (2-19-23)**
Started in September of 1887, Munden was named after the original townsite owner, John Munden. It was situated along the Chicago, Rock Island & Pacific Railroad and, at its peak in 1920, had a population of 339 individuals.

# NARKA, KS
**POPULATION: 81 – TOWN 18 OF 627 (2-20-23)**
Narka was established by M. A. Low and C. J. Gilson, the president and secretary of the town company at the time of its founding (1887). It was incorporated in 1894 as a third-class city and located on the Chicago, Rock Island & Pacific Railroad. It got its name from the daughter of an employee of the railroad.

# REPUBLIC, KS
**POPULATION: 82 – TOWN 130 OF 627 (3-29-23)**
Founded in 1871, Republic got its name from the county in which it is located. In turn, the county is named after the Republican River that flows through it. Republic was one of many small towns on the Missouri Pacific Railroad and prospered because of its arrival. Republic's maximum population reached 450 individuals in 1910. A

fun anecdote claims that it was near here in 1806 that the first American flag was flown in present-day Kansas. The Pawnee Indian Museum Historic Site showcases the remains of a former Pawnee Native American village; it was added to the National Register of Historic Places in 1971.

# SCANDIA, KS
**POPULATION: 344 – TOWN 132 OF 627 (3-29-23)**
After famine swept through Sweden in 1867 and 1868, several Swedes fled their home country in search of a better life in America. They decided to settle in New Scandinavia in Republic County on lots that the Scandinavian Agricultural Society of Chicago had purchased. The name was changed by the post office in 1876 to Scandia, and in 1879, the town was incorporated. It was located on the Rock Island and Missouri Pacific Railroads, which brought with them much of the town's growth and industry in the early 1900s. Film and television actress Greta Granstedt comes from Scandia. Richard B. Wilke (creator of The DISCIPLE Bible Study) and Edwin C. Johnson (the 26th and 34th Governor of Colorado) also have communal ties. The Scandia Museum focuses heavily on the Swedish, Norwegian, and Danish origins of the city's people.

 **Restaurant Recommendation:
Tags Grill & Bar
319 Cloud St
Scandia, KS 66966**

**Adjacent Counties:** Washington (E), Cloud (S), Jewell (W)

**Unincorporated/Ghost Towns:** Harbine, Kackley, Norway, Rydal, Sherdahl, Talmo, Wayne, White Rock

**National Register of Historic Places:**
**Belleville:** Belleville High School, East Riley Creek Bridge, Republic County Courthouse, Riley Creek Bridge, S. T. Stevenson House, U.S. Post Office-Belleville
**Courtland:** Woodland Place Stock Farm
**Cuba:** Cuba Blacksmith Shop
**Mahaska:** Site No. JF00-072
**Munden:** Shimanek Barn
**Narka:** Cossaart Barn

**Republic:** Pawnee Indian Village Site
**Wayne:** County Line Bowstring

**Breweries/Wineries/Distilleries:**
Irrigation Ales (Courtland, KS)

**Golf Courses:**
Republic County Rec. As. Golf Course, Semi-Private (Belleville, KS)

**Town Celebrations:**
Courtland Fun Day, Courtland, KS (Last Saturday of July)
Cuba Harvest Festival (3$^{rd}$ Saturday in July)
Cuba Rock-A-Thon, Cuba, KS (March)
NCK Free Fair, Belleville, KS (1$^{st}$ Weekend of August)
Scandia Riverfest, Scandia, KS (2$^{nd}$ Weekend of July)

# RICE COUNTY
## EST. 1867 - POPULATION: 9,427

Samuel A. Rice is the Union Army general who was bestowed the honor of having this county named after him when it was created in 1867.

# ALDEN, KS
## POPULATION: 122 – TOWN 460 OF 627 (8-18-23)
Alden Speare is the namesake of this town of 122 residents in southwestern Rice County. He was a former employee of the Atchison, Topeka & Santa Fe Railroad, the town's primary railroad of note and the reason for the community's existence. It had its start as a station on the railroad in 1872, and in February of 1882, the postal service elected to establish a post office there. For many years, it was an important shipping point and was home to a bank, several lines of business, and a public school.

# BUSHTON, KS
## POPULATION: 203 – TOWN 203 OF 627 (5-2-23)
The Missouri Pacific Railroad started Bushton as a station in the northwest corner of Rice County in the early 1880s and named it after the large number of wild bushes that grew on the townsite. It was called Sorghum until 1887, and in 1907, the legislature approved its

application for incorporation. The population reached as many as 532 persons in the 1950s thanks to its flour mill, grain elevator, retail stores, and jobs. Bushton prides itself on the Bushton Museum and its working soda fountain, drug store, and bank exhibits.

# CHASE, KS
**POPULATION: 396 – TOWN 462 OF 627 (8-18-23)**
Chase was founded in 1880 when it was confirmed that the Marion and McPherson Railway of the Atchison, Topeka & Santa Fe Railroad would be extended to that point. It was named in honor of a railroad employee called Chase, although the area post office was once referred to as Wildwood. The community's highest recorded population came from the 1950 Census when 961 residents called Chase home.

# FREDERICK, KS
**POPULATION: 8 – TOWN 204 OF 627 (5-2-23)**
Frederick is the smallest incorporated town in Kansas (as of the 2020 Census), with a population of only eight individuals. It was once located at the junction of the St. Louis & San Francisco and the Missouri Pacific Railroads and served as a shipping point for the area. Early facilities included telegraph and telephone offices and multiple banks, churches, and schools. Incorporation came in 1909, but in recent years, its residents have voted to disincorporate the small city. Because of an election error in 2016 when voting ballots were delivered to nearby residents who didn't live in Frederick, it remained incorporated by a 13-7 outcome. It remains unclear if citizens have officially unincorporated the community as of 2023.

# GENESEO, KS
**POPULATION: 236 – TOWN 205 OF 627 (5-2-23)**
This town of 236 residents in Rice County was founded in 1886 and incorporated the following year. It was once situated at the junction of the Atchison, Topeka & Santa Railroad and two lines of the Missouri Pacific Railroad (once running north to south and another east to west). The unique name is an eponym for Geneseo, Illinois. The town's highest population of 660 citizens was recorded in the 1950 Census, and the early 1900s, it boasted three hotels because of its distinction as being a notable regional transfer point for travelers. In 1923, resident John S. Gibson Jr. made history when he became the

youngest mayor in the United States at 21 years old. The town has worked to preserve its history at the Geneseo City History Museum.

# LITTLE RIVER, KS
**POPULATION: 472 – TOWN 625 OF 627 (10-13-23)**
Founded in 1880 and named for its location on the banks of the Little Arkansas River, the history of Little River can be traced to the plans to construct the Atchison, Topeka & Santa Fe Railroad through this section of Rice County. The railroad advanced the town's prosperity in that it brought with it the means and men for the construction of a grain elevator, two banks, a post office, and all the typical lines of business to be established within a short period. Walker & Russ of nearby McPherson built the first of its many stores. A peak population of 749 inhabitants was reached in the 1920s per the decade's Census, but it has since dropped to 472 people.

# LYONS, KS ★☆
**POPULATION: 3,611 – TOWN 624 OF 627 (10-13-23)**
The story of Lyons can only be told by first acknowledging the town of Atlanta, which was an adjoining community. The two townsites were both formed in 1870, but Lyons would later absorb Atlanta in 1876 so that the communities could grow together. The year they combined was when Lyons was awarded its title as the judicial seat of Rice County. An alternate name for the area given by the post office was Brookdale, although it too would be changed to match the present name that honors Truman J. Lyon, the original townsite owner. When the Atchison, Topeka & Santa Fe Railroad rolled through town at the tail end of the decade, industries of all varieties began to sprout across Lyons: salt works, cement building block works, three banks, a wagon and carriage shop, gasoline engine works, two hotels, machine shops, mills and elevators, and all the other typical merchandising establishments found in a town of that era. The salt works were the Western Salt Company, which in 1890 dug its first salt mine shaft and would later become one of the world's largest salt-producing centers. Capitalizing on the success already brought about by the Santa Fe Railroad, the Missouri Pacific and the St. Louis & San Francisco Railroads would also route their lines through Lyons. Because of the townspeople's skill with working underground in the salt mines, the federal government briefly considered making Lyons the burial site of large quantities of nuclear waste in the 1970s. They instead opted to send it to Carlsbad, New Mexico. The Coronado Quivira Museum, situated in the city's former

Carnegie Library, boasts an impressive selection of artifacts from multiple area archaeological sites. Some of the town's most notable past residents include Marcia Rodd (actress known for playing Dorothy in a 1964 production of *The Wizard of Oz*), Jerry Cox Vasconcells (a World War I flying ace), James Fankhauser (a choral music conductor noted for his contributions to the art form in Canada), Orville Harrold (theatre actor), Milton R. Wolf (radiologist and second-cousin once removed of former President Barack Obama), and James Pulliam (Modernist architect noted for his work in California).

 **Restaurant Recommendation:
Scrambled Sam's
802 W Main St
Lyons, KS 67554**

**Lodging Recommendation:
The Slammer
120 E Main St
Lyons, KS 67554**

# RAYMOND, KS
**POPULATION: 85 – TOWN 461 OF 627 (8-18-23)**
Rice County's oldest town, Raymond, welcomed its first settlers in 1871 and was awarded a post office the subsequent year. In its earliest days, Raymond was a typical "wild west" cowtown, serving as a shipping point for cows, grain, and other agricultural products along the Atchison, Topeka & Santa Fe Railroad. It had all of the typical lines of enterprise that small towns had in the early days, like a general store, bank, and even a newspaper (the Raymond Advance) from November 1885 to April 1886. Emmaus Raymond, a railroad official, is credited with being the town's namesake. Raymond was not incorporated until 1954 when it was close to having its highest number of residents (143) in its recorded history.

# STERLING, KS
**POPULATION: 2,248 – TOWN 623 OF 627 (10-13-23)**
A town called "Peace" was established in the area circa 1871, but five years later would have its name changed to Sterling upon its incorporation as a municipality. Judge Samuel Peters ordered the change at the suggestion of two brothers, who wanted the name to

honor their father, Sterling Rosan, an early settler. J. S. Chapin was elected as the first mayor. The Atchison, Topeka & Santa Fe Railroad and the Missouri Pacific Railroads served the town well in enabling it to erect a myriad of factories and other establishments, amongst the earliest being two broom factories, a washing machine factory, a seed cleaner factory, marble works and salt works, machine shops, and an opera house, library, and churches and lodges of all the leading denominations. In 1890, a man named Jonathan S. Dillon began to sell groceries at his Sterling location, and by 1913, he had expanded into the nearby city of Hutchinson with his "J. S. Dillon Cash Store." He pioneered the "cash and carry" concept in which customers would be required to come to the store and pay in cash for their goods rather than have them delivered to their homes or bought on credit. Dillons would ultimately be acquired by The Kroger Company in 1983, and as of 2023, it has 94 locations around the Midwest. This progressive mindset was not atypical for Sterling, as in 1887, the Synod of Kansas of the United Presbyterian Church of North America chose the town as the founding point for Sterling College, then known as Cooper Memorial College, before a 1920 name change. The "Warriors" of Sterling College total about 700 students as of 2023. Some famous Sterling people include Nicolle Galyon, a songwriter whose work has been selected as the CMA's Single of the Year and the ACM's Song of the Year and nine number 1 hits, Doris Fleeson, the first woman in the country to have a nationally syndicated political column, Richard G. Weede, a Marine Corps General, actor Windell Middlebrooks, Lorene Harrison, a choir director and musician, and professional soccer player Osman Mendez.

**Adjacent Counties:** Ellsworth (N), McPherson (E), Reno (S), Stafford (SW), Barton (NW)

**Unincorporated/Ghost Towns:** Beach Valley, Crawford, Galt, Mitchell, Pollard, Saxman, Silica

**National Register of Historic Places:**
**Chase:** Santa Fe Trail-Rice County Trail Segments
**Geneseo:** Tobias-Thompson Complex
**Little River:** Archeological Site Number 14RC10, Santa Fe Trail-Rice County Segment 2
**Lyons:** Malone Archeological Site, Rice County Courthouse, Rice County Jail and Sheriff's Residence
**Saxman:** Saxman Site

**Sterling:** Cooper Hall, Shay Building, Sterling Free Public Carnegie Library
**Windom:** Little Arkansas River Crossing, Santa Fe Trail-Rice County Segment 3, Station Little Arkansas

## Golf Courses:
Geneseo Golf Course, Public (Geneseo, KS)
Lyons Town & Country Club, Semi-Private (Lyons, KS)
Paradise Pastures, Public (Sterling, KS)

## Golf Courses:
Little River Fall Festival, Little River, KS (Late October)

Pratt County Photos: Coats, Iuka, Pratt, Pratt, Pratt, Pratt, Preston, Sawyer

Rawlins County Photos: Atwood, Atwood, Atwood, Atwood, Atwood, Herndon, Herndon, McDonald

415

Reno County Photos: Arlington, Buhler, Haven, Hutchinson, Hutchinson, Hutchinson, Hutchinson, Nickerson

416

Republic County Photos: Belleville, Belleville, Belleville, Courtland, Cuba, Cuba, Republic, Scandia

Rice County Photos: Alden, Geneseo, Little River, Lyons, Lyons, Sterling, Sterling, Sterling

418

# RILEY COUNTY
## EST. 1855 - POPULATION: 71,959

The 7th Military Governor of California, Bennet C. Riley, was also widely regarded as a Mexican-American war hero and had Riley County named for him.

# LEONARDVILLE, KS
## POPULATION: 432 – TOWN 77 OF 627 (3-15-23)

Leonard T. Smith, the former President of the Kansas City Railroad, is the namesake of this town of 432 individuals. The town was known as simply "Leonard" for a while. It was founded in 1881 and located on the Union Pacific Railroad. Leonardville has enjoyed a post office since 1882. Boxer Quentin "Baby" Breese was born here in 1918, as was Albin K. "Birdman" Longren in 1882, an aviation pioneer who established the Longren Aircraft Corporation and successfully flew many of his plane designs.

# MANHATTAN, KS ★☆
## POPULATION: 54,100 – TOWN 256 OF 627 (6-9-23)

"The Little Apple" of Manhattan, Kansas, had humble beginnings in 1854 when it began as two smaller hamlets called Poleska and Canton. The first site was founded by Colonel George S. Park, and the latter by a town company whose members were Samuel D. Houston, Judge J. M. Russell, Dr. A. H. Wilcox, E. M. Thurston, and Judge Saunders W. Johnston. Both parties elected to start their communities in the area because of the confluence of the Big Blue and the Kansas Rivers. A year later, Free-Staters from the New England Emigrant Aid Company, under the direction of Isaac Goodnow, arrived to found an abolitionist community. The men merged Canton and Poleska into one settlement, Boston, after the city in Massachusetts. The name would be changed one final time in June 1855 following the arrival of the paddle steamer Hartford and 75 settlers from the Cincinnati-Manhattan Company. This group had originally intended to settle 20 miles upstream at the present-day location of Junction City, but after becoming stranded, they were incentivized to stay in this area in exchange for half the townsite and naming rights. At this point, the name Manhattan was selected, and in 1857, the legislature acted to incorporate the city. Its growth was quickly spurred thanks to the prominence of Fort Riley, which protected the settlement from the violence often experienced in the area by other free-state communities, the arrival of the Chicago, Rock Island & Pacific, and the Union Pacific Railroads, and its designation as the county seat of Riley County in 1858. Blue Mont Central College, the predecessor to today's Kansas State University, was formed only days after the county seat announcement under the direction of Kansas Governor James W. Denver. The university was transformed into the Kansas State Agricultural College on February 16, 1863, following a series of lobbying efforts led by Isaac Goodnow. It was the first public college in Kansas, as well as the first land-grant institution created from the terms of the Morrill Act of 1862. They intentionally enrolled 26 men and 26 women in its first semester of operation, making them only the second public institution of higher learning to admit women and men equally, and they were one of the first two schools to pioneer a home economics program of study. The university is still known for its high research activity, and as of Fall of 2022, it had an enrollment of nearly 20,000 students. On January 19, 1968, the campus had a very important visitor as that was the day that Martin Luther King Jr., the well-respected leader of the Civil Rights Movement at the time, gave his final speech on a college campus before his assassination only months later in Memphis, Tennessee. Other area institutions include Manhattan Christian College (est. 1927), Manhattan Area Technical College (est. 1965), and the American Institution of Baking International (est. 1919). Major points of interest range from a sprawling nightlife, shopping, and music scene in Aggieville to the Flint Hills Discovery Center, Sunset Zoo, the Harold M. Freund American Museum of Banking, the Marianna Kistler Beach Museum of Art, Kansas State University Gardens, the Insect Zoo at Kansas State University, the Riley County Historical Museum, the Historic Costume and Textile Museum at KSU's Justin Hall, the historic Wolf House, Colbert Hills Golf Course, Goodnow House State Historic Site, Johnny Kaw at City Park, Tuttle Creek State Park, Cedar Ridge State Park, Rocky Ford State Fishing Area, and the First Territorial Capitol State Historic Site at Fort Riley. Because of its sheer size and large number of collegiate graduates, there are hundreds of famous people with ties to Manhattan. Some of them include Eric Stonestreet (known for his role as Cameron Tucker in the sitcom *Modern Family* and appearances in *CSI: Crime Scene Investigation*), Earl Woods (father of PGA golfer Tiger Woods), Albert E. Mead (the 5th Governor of Washington), Luraine Tansey (creator of the Universal Slide Classification System for libraries), Tom Oberheim (inventor of the Oberheim synthesizer and founder of four audio electronics companies), Bob Anderson (founder of *Runner's World* magazine), Alice Stebbins Wells (first American-born female police officer in the United States), Frank B. Morrison (the 34th

420

Governor of Nebraska), Tim Jankovich (collegiate basketball coach), Gary Spani (former NFL linebacker and member of the College Football, Kansas City Chiefs, and Kansas State Hall of Fames), William Buzenberg (former vice-president of news at National Public Radio), Del Close (comedian), and the 4th, 40th, and 42nd Governors of Kansas, Nehemiah Green, John W. Carlin, and Joan Finney.

**Restaurant Recommendation:**
**Nico's Little Italy**
**1101 Moro St Suite 111**
**Manhattan, KS 66502**

**Restaurant Recommendation:**
**So Long Saloon**
**1130 Moro St**
**Manhattan, KS 66502**

**Restaurant Recommendation:**
**Vista Drive In**
**1911 Tuttle Creek Blvd**
**Manhattan, KS 66502**

# OGDEN, KS
## POPULATION: 1,661 – TOWN 247 OF 627 (5-4-23)
The City of Ogden began in 1857 after an act of the legislature established it. It was incorporated as a city of the second class in 1870, and for a short time, it served as the county seat of Riley County. The Union Pacific Railroad was responsible for bringing much of the town's early industries to fruition, as was the placement of the nearby Fort Riley, a U.S. Army Installation first established in January 1853. Major E. A. Ogden from the United States Army Corps of Engineers, who was instrumental in the construction of the fort, is the namesake of the community.

# RANDOLPH, KS
## POPULATION: 159 – TOWN 75 OF 627 (3-15-23)
An original name for this town located on the Union Pacific Railroad was Waterville (until 1876). It was founded in 1856 and named in

honor of early settler Gardner Randolph. The original townsite was located a mile east, but when Tuttle Creek reservoir was filled in 1962, ten towns were affected, and four were submerged underwater (Cleburne, Stockdale, Garrison Cross, and Randolph). Randolph rebuilt, whereas the others did not, but its street names pay tribute to the submerged towns. The ruins of "Old Randolph" are sometimes visible on the north side of Kansas Highway 16 over the lake, which also hosts Randolph State Park and Fancy Creek State Park. The actress and go-go dancer who plays the lead role in *Elvira, Mistress of the Dark*, Cassandra Peterson, has ties to the town.

# RILEY, KS
**POPULATION: 938 – TOWN 76 OF 627 (3-15-23)**
A former name for this community is Union. It was later renamed in the late 1870s to Riley Center after an Irish railroad employee, as the Rock Island Railroad began its construction through town. Riley's official founding date is set as 1871. Jordy Nelson of National Football League fame (Super Bowl XLV champion, 2014 Pro-Bowler, and the 2016 NFL receiving touchdowns leader and Comeback Player of the Year) attended high school at Riley County High School. Fort Riley is a nearby United States Army installation with the U.S. Calvary Museum, the 1st Infantry Division Museum, and the Custer Home.

 **Restaurant Recommendation:
Big Papa's Pizza
119 S Broadway St
Riley, KS 66531**

**Adjacent Counties:** Marshall (NE), Pottawatomie (E), Wabaunsee (SE), Geary (S), Clay (W), Washington (NW)

**Unincorporated/Ghost Towns:** Ashland, Bala, Bodaville, Cleburne, Fort Riley, Garrison Cross, Keats, Lasita, May Day, Pawnee, (Old) Randolph, Rocky Ford, Stockdale, Walsburg, Winkler, Zeandale

**National Register of Historic Places:**
**Manhattan:** Anderson Hall, The Avalon, Bethel A.M.E. Church, Bluemont Youth Cabin, Community House, Dawson's Conoco Service Station, Downtown Manhattan Historic District, Mattie M. Elliot House, First Christian Church, First Congregational Church,

Leslie A. Fitz House, F. B. Forrester House, Goodnow House, Grimes House, Hartford House, Houston and Pierre Streets Residential Historic District, Samuel D. Houston House, Hulse-Daughters House, Jesse Ingraham House, KSAC Radio Towers, Francis Byron (Barney) Kimble House, Landmark Water Tower, Lyda-Jean Apartments, Manhattan Carnegie Library Building, McFarlane-Wareham House, Persons Barn and Granary, Pioneer Log Cabin, Jeremiah Platt House, Riley County Courthouse, Rocky Ford School, Damon Runyon House, Second Baptist Church, Seven Dolors Catholic Church, Strasser House, Robert Ulrich House, Viking Manufacturing Company Building, Daniel and Maude Walters House, E. A. and Ura Wharton House, Wolf House Historic District, Woman's Club House, Yuma Street Historic District

**Breweries/Wineries/Distilleries:**
Little Apple Brewing Company (Manhattan, KS)
Liquid Art Winery & Estate (Manhattan, KS)
Manhattan Brewing Company (Manhattan, KS)
Tallgrass Tap House (Manhattan, KS)

**Golf Courses:**
Colbert Hills Golf Course, Public (Manhattan, KS)
Leonardville Golf Course, Public (Leonardville, KS)
Manhattan Country Club, Private (Manhattan, KS)
Stagg Hill Golf Club, Semi-Private (Manhattan, KS)
Wildcat Creek Sports Center, Public (Manhattan, KS)

**Town Celebrations:**
BayoU GatorCraw Fest, Manhattan, KS (April or May)
Fall Festival, Ogden, KS (Late September or Early October)
Independence Day Celebration, Randolph, KS (Weekend before 4th of July)
Leonardville Hullabaloo, Leonardville, KS (2nd Weekend in August)

# ROOKS COUNTY
## EST. 1867 - POPULATION: 4,919

Rooks County honors the legacy of John Rooks of the 11th Kansas Calvary Regiment, a Private who perished in the Battle of Prairie Grove during the Civil War.

# DAMAR, KS
**POPULATION: 112 – TOWN 106 OF 627 (3-28-23)**

Damar is unique in that it was founded by a group of French Canadians who had emigrated from Canada to the area in the early 1870s. The land was sold to early settler Francis St. Peter by President Grover Cleveland (made available by the Homestead Act) for $4.00. Damar had its start in 1888 along the Union Pacific Railroad and was named for D. M. Marr, the original townsite owner. The town is particularly fond of St. Joseph Catholic Church, a marvel of architecture built in 1912 and placed on the National Register of Historic Places in 2005.

 **Restaurant Recommendation:**
**Dad's Place Damar Cafe**
**210 Main St**
**Damar, KS 67632**

# PALCO, KS
**POPULATION: 208 – TOWN 105 OF 627 (3-28-23)**

The name Palco is an amalgamation of the names "Palmer" and "Cole," a couple of early officials for a line of the Union Pacific Railroad. The town's founding date is set in 1888, although the town's history begins earlier than that. Its first post office came from the now-defunct town of Cresson, whose post office was established in 1879. Residents formed a new community called New Cresson a couple of miles south when they heard rumors that the railroad would be laid through that area. Unfortunately, their suspicions were incorrect, and the track was laid closer to where the original Cresson had once been located. Those early settlers would go on to join the town that we know today as Palco. In 1906, it was incorporated as a city.

# PLAINVILLE, KS
**POPULATION: 1,746 – TOWN 103 OF 627 (3-28-23)**

Plainville's history starts in 1877 with the arrival of Washington Irving Griffin, who settled along a freight trail and sought to found the town's post office. The local Justice of the Peace, Lambert P. Darland, was in charge of reviewing Griffin's application, and he suggested that the establishment be called Plainville as a descriptive name for its location on the Great Plains. About a decade later, in 1888, the Union Pacific Railroad built a railway through Plainville, and the town was incorporated. Carl Weeks, the founder of several pharmaceutical-cosmetic companies such as Weeks & Leo Company, actor Brent Collins, known for his role as Mr. Big in *As the World Turns*, Rob Beckley of the Christian rock band Pillar, and Jack Hartman, the head coach of Southern Illinois (1962-1970) and Kansas State's (1970-1986) men's basketball programs have ties to Plainville. A local memorial pays tribute to Clarence Auburn Gilbert, a pioneer airmail pilot and member of the Air Force Reserves who was born here on April 25, 1898.

# STOCKTON, KS ★☆
**POPULATION: 1,480 – TOWN 102 OF 627 (3-28-23)**
A large number of the area's earliest settlers were cattlemen, and so they came to call the town "Stocktown." The name was later shortened to Stockton with the arrival of the Missouri Pacific Railway in 1885. The town's founding date was in 1872, and in 1879, it was incorporated as a city of the third class. Today, it serves as the county seat of Rooks County. It is the site of the Rooks County Historical Society's Frank Walker Museum, the Waller-Coolbaugh 1905 High Classical Revival home, Rooks County State Park, and Webster State Park. British author Tony Parker wrote a book in 1989 called *Bird, Kansas*, in which he wrote about the stories of residents. Famous locals in Stockton's past have included Lorenzo Fuller (singer and actor), Dale Dodrill (defensive tackle for the NFL's Pittsburgh Steelers for nine years), Mal Stevens (member of the College Football Hall of Fame), Elam Bartholomew (horticulturist), Roy Fisher (former Editor-in-Chief of the *Chicago Daily News*), and Ken Randle, a project leader for NASA that led to the Voyager Mission and Mariner 10.

# WOODSTON, KS
**POPULATION: 94 – TOWN 101 OF 627 (3-28-23)**
Charles C. Woods, a businessman from the nearby town of Stockton who was instrumental in bringing the Missouri Pacific Railroad to that community, had this town named in his honor. Woods also donated $500 towards the founding of the town's first school on the condition that it be named for him. The city was founded in 1885 as a connecting railroad town between Alton and Stockton, and the area post office was known as Rooks Centre before it was changed to coincide with the town's name in February of 1886. In 1905, Woodston was incorporated.

# ZURICH, KS

**POPULATION: 89 – TOWN 104 OF 627 (3-28-23)**

This town of 89 residents in southwest Rooks County was founded in the late 1870s, and in 1880, John and Amanda Webb sought to bring the first post office to town under the name Zurich. Zurich is an eponym for their birthplace of Zurich, Switzerland. The Union Pacific Railway would ultimately extend one of its lines to the town and help spur growth in its population. The town's slogan, "Zurich It's Never Idle," was sold as an emblem to be placed on car radiators throughout the 1920s.

**Adjacent Counties:** Phillips (N), Smith (NE), Osborne (E), Ellis (S), Trego (SW), Graham (W)

**Unincorporated/Ghost Towns:** Adamson, Alcona, Amboy, Chandler, Codell, Cresson, Earnest, Frankton, Gould City, Highhill, Hoskins, Igo, Laton, McHale, Motor, Nyra, Portage, Slate, Sugarloaf, Survey, Rockport, Webster

**National Register of Historic Places:**
**Damar:** St. Joseph Catholic Church
**Stockton:** Rooks County Courthouse

**Golf Courses:**
Cedar Links Country Club, Private (Plainville, KS)

**Town Celebrations:**
Paradise Creek Festival and Rodeo, Plainville, KS (2nd Weekend of June)
Swing Into Summer Festival, Stockton, KS (Father's Day Weekend)
Webster State Park Car Show, Stockton, KS (Mid to Late September)

# RUSH COUNTY
## EST. 1867 - POPULATION: 2,956

Rush County's name follows suit with several others in Kansas in that it was named for a hero of the Civil War, in particular for Union Captain Alexander Rush.

# ALEXANDER, KS
**POPULATION: 54 – TOWN 429 OF 627 (8-15-23)**
This town of 54 inhabitants was the first settlement of Rush County, having been established in 1869 as a trading post on the Hays-Fort Dodge Military Trail (also a part of the Santa Fe Trail). Its name honors Alexander Harvey, the proprietor of the Harvey's Ranch trading post that kicked off the development of a future community. J. C. Young and his family arrived in 1872, and a couple of years later, a post office was founded to serve the needs of early settlers. The Atchison, Topeka & Santa Fe Railroad would ship anything from sheep and cattle to agricultural products, and the trade of the area generated enough interest for there to be the presence of two creameries, a hotel, hospital, lumberyard, grocery stores, churches, and general stores throughout Alexander.

# BISON, KS
**POPULATION: 179 – TOWN 410 OF 627 (8-13-23)**
Bison expectedly got its name from the abundant herds of American bison that once freely roamed the Great Plains, many of which were once found in Rush County. The town came into existence in 1888 when officials of the Missouri Pacific Railroad opted to continue their push to cross Kansas with their line. In May of the same year, a post office was established, and a cement factory, elevator, and mill would soon follow. Attendees of Bison High School once called themselves "the Buffaloes," ironic in the fact that buffalo and bison are two different (yet in the same bovidae family) animals. Buffaloes are native to the African and Asian continents, whereas bison are the creatures that call Europe and the North American Plains their home.

# LA CROSSE, KS ★☆
**POPULATION: 1,266 – TOWN 413 OF 627 (8-15-23)**
"The Barbed Wire Capital of the World" of La Crosse was established in 1876 and located as a station on the Missouri Pacific Railroad. Its name is an eponym for La Crosse, Wisconsin, a city of 52,000 citizens. The town was founded by Denman A. Stubbs, his wife Ellen, and his surveyor brother David, who worked to lay out the townsite shortly after Rush County was reorganized and Denman's land suddenly became the center of the county. In its principal years, it battled with nearby Rush Center for the title of the county seat, which it ultimately won in 1888. Following this designation, a courthouse was erected, and the railroad's presence assisted in bringing about

multiple hotels, churches, banks, newspapers, grain elevators, a post office, an opera house, and a foundry and machine shop. In 1970, the Kansas Barbed Wire Museum was founded at a local storefront. After a series of expansions, the Antique Barbed Wire Society and barbed-wire enthusiasts claim that the museum now showcases over 2,000 unique forms of barbed wire. Other historical points of interest around the city are the Rush County Historical Museum, the Nekoma Bank Museum, the Post Rock Museum, and a schoolhouse.

 **Restaurant Recommendation:**
**Jct 4 Diner**
**1601 Main St**
**La Crosse, KS 67548**

# LIEBENTHAL, KS
## POPULATION: 92 – TOWN 411 OF 627 (8-13-23)
Liebenthal was brought up chiefly by a colony of Volga Germans from Liebenthal, Russia. They sought refuge from Russia after the Czar decreed that German colonists must complete mandatory military duties and other obligations to the Motherland. The townsite had its beginnings in 1876 but did not achieve incorporation status until 1935. Many of the early settlers left to settle in nearby Schoenchen because of that community's closer proximity to a water source. As a result, the population of Liebenthal always remained relatively small, as it had only about 30 people living within its boundaries in 1910 and as many as 265 inhabitants as of the 1940 Census. St. Joseph's Catholic Church is a community focal point, having been built by early parishioners and formally dedicated on May 28, 1905.

# MCCRACKEN, KS
## POPULATION: 152 – TOWN 430 OF 627 (8-15-23)
McCracken's existence owes itself to the determination by several early men that the area would make an excellent townsite and depot for the Missouri Pacific Railroad. One such man in the party was J. K. McCracken, an early trustee and railroad employee, after whom the town was named. After its founding in 1886, it only took a year for the townspeople to erect a theater, bank, grocery and general stores, a newspaper, and the Evangelical United Brethren Church of McCracken. Other religious denominations would follow suit and build their churches, and capitalists would start a creamery, flour mills, and grain elevators. Shale quarries were established in 1939 outside of

town that would sell "wonder mud" to drilling enterprises throughout the country. Drilling fluid or "mud" is still used today in the drilling of oil and gas to help lubricate the drill bit and carry rock remnants to the surface. In the seventies, McCracken was one of several filming locations for the film *Paper Moon*, although the movie sites (the hotel and the cafe) have since been razed. The town started the McCracken Historical & Paper Moon Museum in 2001 to pay homage to the town's history.

# OTIS, KS
## POPULATION: 296 – TOWN 409 OF 627 (8-13-23)
Major E. C. Moderwell, originally of Salina, was the benefactor of this small Rush County community that he named for his son, Otis. Mr. Moderwell was responsible for donating the land for the first public school, and because of his works, the Missouri Pacific Railroad opted to build their line through his townsite. Between the typical early establishments of a bank and post office were two industry gems: a cigar factory, amongst the best in Kansas in the 1910s, and the Otis Helium Plant, primarily in operation circa 1943 and thereon. Although that plant has since closed, The Linde Group of Munich, Germany maintains and operates the second largest helium production facility in the world outside of Otis. They are responsible for supplying the helium for the Macy's Thanksgiving Day Parade.

# RUSH CENTER, KS
## POPULATION: 141 – TOWN 414 OF 627 (8-14-23)
Walnut City was first settled in 1871 and appropriately named by settlers after the nearby Walnut Creek. They soon changed the name (in 1874) to Rush Centre because of the settlement's geographical location at the center of Rush County. For years, it would serve as the judicial seat until a new town named La Crosse sprung up in 1876 and overtook the honor the following year. The county records would continue to be moved between the two communities over the next decade before they finally settled in La Crosse for good. Rush Center pays homage to this "shared county seat" designation by carrying "The Courthouse" by wagon back to Rush Center during the annual St. Patrick's Day Parade. Around the time that a spelling change corrected the suffix of the community's name to "Center" from "Centre" in 1895, the infrastructure of Rush Center truly began to blossom thanks to the presence of the Atchison, Topeka & Santa Fe Railroad. Amongst the typical early-town establishments, The Pennsylvania House (a large hotel with 46 rooms) and The Harvey

House (a 50-room hotel chain famous throughout Kansas) were the most prestigious. Noted Judge of the United States Court of Appeals for the District of Columbia Circuit from 1937 to 1970, Henry White Edgerton, is the most notable former Rush Center resident.

# TIMKEN, KS
## POPULATION: 38 – TOWN 415 OF 627 (8-14-23)

Henry Timken, of German descent, bought up the land that he speculated would later need to be purchased by the Atchison, Topeka & Santa Fe Railroad so they could continue to expand their line westward. His assumptions were correct, and when the railroad came to him with an offer to buy the land, he asserted that he would only sell if the townsite and railroad depot were named in his honor. The railroad obliged, and a little community sprung up in the 1880s that would eventually be home to a grain mill and elevator, a lumber yard, a grocery store, general merchandise establishments, a post office (opened in 1888 to 1996), and exceptionally unusual for that time, a bowling alley. Because the town has such a small population (38 inhabitants), its total area is only 0.15 square miles.

**Adjacent Counties:** Ellis (N), Russell (NE), Baton (E), Pawnee (S), Ness (W)

**Unincorporated/Ghost Towns:** Belfield, Brookdale, Fenton, Flavius, Hampton, Hargrave, Hutton, Lippard, Loretta, Nekoma, Olney, Pioneer, Ryan, Saunders, Schaffer, West Point

**National Register of Historic Places:**
**Bison:** Lone Star School, District 64
**La Crosse:** Miller Farmstead, Rush County Courthouse, Sand Creek Tributary Stone Arch Bridge
**Nekoma:** Walnut Creek Tributary Bridge

**Golf Courses:**
La Crosse Country Club, Semi-Private (La Crosse, KS)

**Town Celebrations:**
Barbed Wire Festival, La Crosse, KS (1st Weekend of May)

# RUSSELL COUNTY
## EST. 1867 - POPULATION: 6,691

Organized in 1867 from the Kansas wilderness, Russell County's namesake is the Union Captain Avra P. Russell.

# BUNKER HILL, KS
**POPULATION: 103 – TOWN 146 OF 627 (4-10-23)**
Bunker Hill's early history starts with Butterfield Overland Despatch mail service that founded a station in 1865. The Kansas Pacific Railway would build its line through the area in 1871, and colonists from Ohio led by J. B. Corbett and Valentine Harbaugh founded a town there. For two brief years, Bunker Hill served as the county seat before nearby Russell overtook the honor in 1874. The Bunker Hill Museum documents the county's history, including a more recent tidbit about the 2008 western drama film *Bunker Hill*, of which the town is the movie's setting and namesake. A restored 1930s Mobil Gas Station helps welcome visitors to the hamlet. Its most notable resident was Mary Ann Bickerdyke, a Union hospital administrator during the Civil War who created an impressive 300 field hospitals throughout the war to treat wounded soldiers.

# DORRANCE, KS
**POPULATION: 146 – TOWN 147 OF 627 (4-10-23)**
Dorrance was founded with the arrival of the Kansas Pacific Railway to the area, a railroad line that would eventually consolidate with the Union Pacific in 1880. The community started in 1870 when a mixture of English, German, Irish, and Pennsylvania settlers decided to lay out a town site and name it in honor of railroad official Oliver Dorrance. The first post office arrived in 1883, and in the Spring of 1910, its residents elected to incorporate the town with the legislature. In popular culture, Dorrance was designated as the equivalent of Smallville, Kansas, the childhood home of Superman (Action Comics #822, Repo Man, part one), and it was one of several small-town filming locations for the 1973 movie *Paper Moon*. Another interesting anecdote is that inventor Ken Mahoney, the inventor of the first "Toss Back" rim used to prevent glass backboards from shattering, was headquartered in Dorrance. The World's Largest Wooden Wheat Threshing Machine, as well as other community artifacts, are on display at the Dorrance Bankery. The Dorrance Historical Society Museum is another local point of interest.

# GORHAM, KS

**POPULATION: 376 – TOWN 149 OF 627 (4-11-23)**

Much of Gorham's early history and growth can be attributed to the discovery of oil buried deep below the surface of Russell County. The community flourished throughout the 1920s to the 1980s because of the discovery, and even to this day, the population has remained relatively steady since the first Census taken of its townspeople. Its first settlers arrived in April 1872 from Lancaster, Pennsylvania, and Elijah Dodge Gorham of Illinois formally platted the townsite in 1879. Gorham, similar to several other area communities, played a role in the making of the 1973 film *Paper Moon*. The plot of the movie begins in Gorham in the 1930s.

# LUCAS, KS

**POPULATION: 332 – TOWN 140 OF 627 (4-10-23)**

Lucas has primarily become known throughout Kansas as the "Grassroots Art Capital of Kansas" (a title given by Governor Bill Graves in 1996) for its numerous folk-art sites and unusual attractions. However, its early history was much more straightforward. The community was established in 1877 under the name Blue Stem, before it was later changed in 1887 after Lucas Place in St. Louis, Missouri. The Union Pacific Railroad would later be constructed through the area. Samuel P. Dinsmoor created the town's first and most notable piece of folk art between 1905 and 1927, which is now known as the Garden of Eden. The outdoor exhibit, consisting of over 200 concrete sculptures depicting world history and scenes from the Bible, was added to the National Register of Historic Places in April of 1977 and now attracts thousands of tourists every year. A now-deceased Dinsmoor and his first wife, Frances A. Barlow Journey, are a part of the exhibit and can be seen in a mausoleum through a glass wall. Other local points of interest include Florence Deeble's rock garden, the Grassroots Art Center, the World's Largest Travel Plate, America's Largest Art Toilet at Bowl Plaza, and the World's Largest Collection of the World's Smallest Version of the World's Largest Things Museum. Bill Volok, an NFL lineman for six seasons in the 1930s, and artist Erika Nelson have ties to Lucas.

# LURAY, KS

**POPULATION: 166 – TOWN 141 OF 627 (4-10-23)**

Lura was the original spelling of this city's name when it was started in the 1870s. Later, a "-y" was added to the name (presumably by the

Union Pacific Railroad), and the addition stuck. In 1904, Luray was incorporated as a city of the third class, with a population in the 300s and a peak of 475 individuals in 1920. However, the population has been steadily declining with each subsequent Census. The first log cabin built in Russell County (circa 1871 by Jonathan Van Scoyoc) can be viewed at Luray City Park. The Luray welcome sign claims Luray is "halfway between Paradise and the Garden of Eden," as its location is literally between the City of Paradise and the Dinsmoor's Garden of Eden in Lucas on Highway 18.

# PARADISE, KS
## POPULATION: 35 – TOWN 143 OF 627 (4-10-23)
Paradise got its namesake from the nearby Paradise Creek, which got its name in 1859. As the story goes, James R. Mead (an early founder of Wichita, Kansas) and other members of a hunting party were following bison along a tributary of the Saline River when they came across a "paradise" setting of water, timber, and wild game. The post office arrived in the area in 1875, and by 1887, the Union Townsite Company formed a townsite and named it Ivamar. The name was a tribute to Iva Marr, the daughter of an early area rancher. The Union Pacific Railroad addressed the town as both Paradise and Ivamar until the city was finally incorporated in 1924 and elected to keep the name Paradise. The Paradise water tower, built from Post Rock Limestone, towers over the city and was added to the National Register of Historic Places in January 2007.

# RUSSELL, KS ★☆
## POPULATION: 4,401 – TOWN 145 OF 627 (4-10-23)
The Butterfield Overland Despatch, an early Great Plains mail service in the 1860s, established Fossil Creek Station in this part of Kansas in 1865 near the area that would ultimately become the city of Russell. Two years later, in 1867, the Kansas Pacific Railroad built a station here, and in 1871, early settlers from Ripon, Wisconsin, moved here and founded a town called "Russell" after the county. Russell and the neighboring city of Bunker Hill fought for the county seat from 1872 to 1874 before Russell gained the permanent honor. There are four museums located in town: the Fossil Station Museum (located in the former sheriff's office and county jail and featuring exhibits on early county history), the Oil Patch Museum (containing exhibits of local petroleum extraction), and two early limestone homes, the Heym-Oliver House and the Gernon House. Deines Cultural Center is another point of interest with an emphasis on art. The town rose to

the attention of the entire country when politicians Bob Dole and Arlen Specter, two natives of the city, campaigned for the United States Presidency in 1996. Other noted Russell citizens are Marj Dusay (actress known for her roles in the 1977 film *MacArthur* and television show *Guiding Light*, Paul Eggert (designer and manager of the time zone database vital for computer programs and operating systems), C.J. Mahoney (a Deputy United States Trade Representative from 2018 to 2020), Wendall Anschutz (KCTV journalist from 1966 to 2001), Philip Anschutz (billionaire businessman known for his sports ventures as the owner of the NHL's Los Angeles Kings, minority owner of the NBA's Los Angeles Lakers, and a co-founder of Major League Soccer), Steven Bender (founder of Altamira Group and iMagic Software), Jim Line (2x NCAA men's basketball champion in 1948 and 1949 with the Kentucky Wildcats, and Walter Sutton (known for helping the Boveri-Sutton chromosome theory), amongst others.

 **Restaurant Recommendation:**
**Meridy's Restaurant & Lounge**
**1220 S Fossil St**
**Russell, KS 67665**

# WALDO, KS
**POPULATION: 30 – TOWN 142 OF 627 (4-10-23)**
This town of thirty residents owes its existence to the Union Pacific Railroad and the Union Town Company, which formed the city on October 1, 1888. Early industries, such as stores and even multiple grain elevators, came to Waldo with the railroad's arrival, leading to the town's formal incorporation in 1911.

**Adjacent Counties:** Osborne (N), Lincoln (E), Ellsworth (SE), Barton (S), Rush (SW), Ellis (W)

**Unincorporated/Ghost Towns:** Bayne, Blue Stem, Dubuque, East Wolf, Fairport, Fay, Forest Hill, Greenvale, Hawley, Jack, Kennebec, Milberger, Success, Winterset, Woodville

**National Register of Historic Places:**
**Dorrance:** Dorrance State Bank, Reiff Building
**Lucas:** Deeble Rock Garden, Garden of Eden, Lucas School Gymnasium
**Luray:** House at 202 West 3rd Street

434

**Paradise:** Kennedy Hotel, Paradise Water Tower
**Russell:** Banks-Waudby Building, Dream Theater, First National Bank-Waudby Building, Nicholas Gernon House, Mann House, Russell County Jail and Sheriff's Residence, U.S. Post Office-Russell, Woelk House

**Golf Courses:**
Russell Memorial Park Golf Course, Public (Russell, KS)

**Town Celebrations:**
Adams Apple Festival, Lucas, KS (Last Saturday of August)
After Harvest Fireworks Display, Waldo, KS (Weekend after July 4th)
April Fools-a-Palooza, Lucas, KS (April 1st)
Friendship Day, Luray, KS (Labor Day Weekend)

# SALINE COUNTY
## EST. 1860 - POPULATION: 54,303

The Saline River, a 397-mile-long river that stretches throughout northwest Kansas, is from where the name of the county was taken.

# ASSARIA, KS
**POPULATION: 428 – TOWN 208 OF 627 (5-2-23)**
Assaria, population 428, began in 1879 under the direction of Highland Fairchild and his town company. The area's post office was founded in February that same year under the name Oban, but by September, it had been renamed Assaria. It was once the site of several small businesses and a line of the Union Pacific Railroad. Incorporation status came in 1886 via an act of the legislature.

# BROOKVILLE, KS
**POPULATION: 247 – TOWN 199 OF 627 (5-1-23)**
Brookville began in 1870 when the Kansas Pacific Railroad (later consolidated with the Union Pacific) was built through the area. It was in the same year that the post office arrived on February 2, 1870. In 1873, the town filed for incorporation, and William Brownhill was elected as the first mayor. The population boomed to 511 residents as of the 1880 Census but has steadily declined and remained between 200 and 300 persons since 1900. A scene of the 1980 comedy film *Up the Academy* was shot at a local gas station. Mushroom Rock State Park, west of Brookville, welcomes visitors to

marvel at its prehistoric mushroom-shaped rocks. It is the smallest of Kansas's state parks at only five acres.

# GYPSUM, KS
**POPULATION: 400 – TOWN 210 OF 627 (5-2-23)**

In 1885, the German Templer Community, a Pietist sect that came about in the mid-1800s, founded the town of Tempelfeld. Residents later elected to rename it Gypsum, after the local creek. The mineral of the same name was abundant in the area, and a local gypsum mill was responsible for sending over 7,000 tons of it to the Chicago World's Fair in 1893. Its central railroad of note was the Missouri Pacific Railroad. The post office underwent a series of name changes before settling on Gypsum in 1886, having formerly been called Pliny from November 1869 to December 11, 1871, Prescott for eight days until December 19, 1871, and then again Pliny until October 21, 1886. Four notable persons have called Gypsum home: a 1936 Olympic gold medalist in basketball, Bill Wheatley, the fourth-place finisher in the 1996 Olympic decathlon event, Steve Fritz, musician JD Andrew of The Boxmasters with Billy Bob Thornton, and explorer and New York Times journalist Frank Wilkeson.

# NEW CAMBRIA, KS
**POPULATION: 106 – TOWN 197 OF 627 (5-1-23)**

New Cambria is an eponym for Cambria County, Pennsylvania, the home area of early town settler S. P. Donmyer. Despite never achieving a Census population higher than 212 citizens (in 1910), the town was once serviced by the Union Pacific, Chicago, Rock Island & Pacific, and the Atchison, Topeka & Santa Fe Railroads. It was in June 1873 that the postal service established an office there, and in 1913, New Cambria was incorporated as a city of the third class.

# SALINA, KS ★☆
**POPULATION: 46,889 – TOWN 198 OF 627 (5-1-23)**

The founding of the county seat of Saline County and the regional trade center for most of North Central Kansas and beyond truly began with the Battle of Indian Rock in 1857. Throughout the 1850s, settlement of the area was deterred by the significant presence of the High Plains tribes of Native Americans, who had used the area as hunting grounds for centuries. After Big Chief of the Cheyenne attacked one of the Eastern tribes of Native Americans-equipped with rifles given to them by the Kaw and early settlers-another battle ensued, leaving behind thousands of arrows and dozens of bodies. Following this show of force, the Cheyenne retreated from the area for good, enabling Colonel William A. Phillips, A.C. Spillman, Robert Crawford, A. M. Campbell, and James Muir to form the Salina Town Company in 1858. Once the Kansas Pacific Railroad was completed about a decade later, incorporation came in 1870, and the town grew to house factories for body braces, sunbonnets, gloves, brooms, mattresses, razor strops, cigars, and other lines of industry from alfalfa, flour, and planing mills to an oil refinery, creamery, carriage and wagon works, machine shops, and more. Three more railroads, the Atchison, Topeka & Santa Fe, the Chicago, Rock Island & Pacific, and the Missouri Pacific, would assist in bringing more industry to the community throughout its early history. The Lee Brand of denim jeans opened its first factory in Salina in 1889, and today, major employers include Tony's Pizza of Schwan's Company (once a sole restaurant called Tony and Dick's Pizzeria), Salina Regional Health Center, USD 305, and Exide Battery. Numerous higher education institutions have called or still do call Salina home today: Kansas Wesleyan University (a private Christian university founded in 1886), Salina Area Technical College (est. 1965), and a branch of the University of Kansas School of Medicine. Salina Normal University remained in operation from 1884 until a fire destroyed it in 1904, and Marymount College operated from 1922 to 1989. Salina was the primary filming site for the 1980 comedy movie *Up the Academy*, and it is featured in the 1955 film *Picnic* and the 1958 psychological thriller *Vertigo*. Songs by Shawn Colvin ("A Few Small Repairs") and The Avett Brothers ("Salina") are mentioned by name. Significant points of interest include The Rolling Hills Zoo, Indian Rock Park, the Smoky Hill Museum, the Salina Art Center, the Yesteryear Museum, and Tony's Pizza Events Center. Schilling Air Force Base, now the Salina Regional Airport, formerly had the longest noncommercially owned runway in the world. It was designated as an emergency landing site for U.S. Space Shuttles because of its length. Dozens of notable persons have connections to the city, a small handful which includes war correspondent Betty Knox, ABC News Radio broadcaster Paull Harvey, U.S. women's national soccer team goalie Adrianna Franch, member of the Women's Basketball Hall of Fame and former head coach Kurt Budke, astronaut Steve Hawley, the 40th and 43rd Governors of Kansas, John W. Carlin and Bill Graves, the inventor of Lee Jeans, Harry Lee, 2x NFL-Pro Bowler and cornerback Terence Newman, actors George Murdock, Dwight Frye, Otto Hulett and Tyrees Allen, and the former CEO of Burlington Northern Santa Fe (Railroad) Corporation, Matthew K. Rose. Steve Fossett made Salina

437

the beginning and ending terminus of his solo, nonstop, unrefueled, fixed-wing, globe-circumnavigated flight around the world in 2005.

**Restaurant Recommendation:**
**The Cozy Inn**
**108 N 7th St**
**Salina, KS 67401**

**Restaurant Recommendation:**
**Martinelli's Little Italy**
**158 S Santa Fe Ave**
**Salina, KS 67401**

# SMOLAN, KS
**POPULATION: 162 – TOWN 209 OF 627 (5-2-23)**
Named after the Swedish province of Småland by a group of early settlers from Sweden, this small town was once served by the Missouri Pacific Railroad. The town post office served two rural routes from its inception on June 15, 1887, and eventually closed on July 5, 1997. The city was not incorporated until 1962. The 40th Governor of Kansas and the 8th Archivist of the United States, John W. Carlin, spent much of his childhood growing up here.

Solomon is only partially located in Saline County (see Dickinson County).

**Adjacent Counties:** Ottawa (N), Dickinson (E), Marion (SE), McPherson (S), Ellsworth (W), Lincoln (NW)

**Unincorporated/Ghost Towns:** Bavaria, Bridgeport, Falun, Glendale, Hedville, Kipp, Mentor, Salemsborg, Shipton, Trenton

**National Register of Historic Places:**
**Brookville:** Brookville Grade School
**Gypsum:** Hobbs Creek Truss Leg Bedstead Bridge
**Lindsborg:** Coronado Heights
**Salina:** Christ Cathedral, Flanders-Lee House and Carriage House, Fox-Watson Theater Building, Lakewood Park Bridge, H. D. Lee Company Complex, Lowell School, Masonic Temple, Mount Barbara, National Bank of America, The Norton Apartments, Pioneer Hall,

Kansas Wesleyan University, John H. Prescott House, Roosevelt-Lincoln Junior High School, A. J. Schwartz House, U.S. Post Office and Federal Building-Salina, Whiteford (Price) Archeological Site

**Breweries/Wineries/Distilleries:**
Blue Skye Brewery & Eats (Salina, KS)
Smoky Hills Vineyards & Winery (Salina, KS)
**Golf Courses:**
Elks Country Club, Private (Salina, KS)
Salina Country Club, Private (Salina, KS)
Salina Municipal Golf Course, Public (Salina, KS)

**Town Celebrations:**
Leadsled Spectacular Car Show, Salina, KS (Last Weekend of July)
Smoky Hill River Festival, Salina, KS (2nd Weekend of June)

Riley County Photos: Leonardville, Manhattan, Manhattan, Manhattan, Manhattan, Manhattan, Manhattan, Riley

440

Rooks County Photos: Damar, Palco, Palco, Plainville, Stockton, Stockton, Stockton, Stockton

Rush County Photos: Alexander, Bison, La Crosse, La Crosse, La Crosse, Liebenthal, McCracken, McCracken

Russell County Photos: Bunker Hill, Dorrance, Lucas, Lucas, Lucas, Paradise, Russell, Waldo

443

Saline County Photos: Brookville, New Cambria, Salina, Salina, Salina, Salina, Salina, Salina

444

# SCOTT COUNTY
## EST. 1873 - POPULATION: 5,151

"Old Fuss and Feathers," perhaps better known as Winfield Scott, the Commanding General of the U.S. Army from 1841 to 1861, is celebrated by the name of Scott County.

# SCOTT CITY, KS ★☆
## POPULATION: 4,113 – TOWN 435 OF 627 (8-16-23)

General Winfield Scott, the Commanding General of the United States Army from 1841 to 1861, had this western Kansas municipality named in his honor. It was in 1884 that the first settlers pegged the land that would later become the townsite, and in the coming months, several other pioneers arrived to claim unsettled lands. The establishment of Scott City by a town company would aid in developing three railroads, the Missouri Pacific, the Atchison, Topeka & Santa Fe, and the Garden City, Gulf, and Northern Railroad (formerly known as the Colorado, Kansas & Oklahoma). The same company donated land so churches of the four largest congregations, a park, a school, and a courthouse (to fulfill its duties as the judicial seat of Scott County) could be erected. Knowing that such infrastructure was already in place, residents quickly established several lines of business, including drug and general stores, banks, grain elevators, and flour mills. The El Quartelejo Museum and the Jerry Thomas Gallery and Collection focus their curations on the Apache and Pueblo tribes of Native Americans, as well as the unique geology of the area. Some pueblo ruins can be seen at Lake Scott State Park, a frequent destination spot for campers, bikers, boaters, and other nature lovers. Former NBA player Ron Baker attended Scott Community High before his professional basketball career.

**Adjacent Counties:** Gove (NE), Lane (E), Finney (S), Kearny (SW), Wichita (W), Logan (NW)

**Unincorporated/Ghost Towns:** Chevron, Grigston, Hutchins, Manning, Modoc, Pence, Shallow Water

**National Register of Historic Places:**
**Beaver Township:** Battle of Punished Woman's Fork, El Cuartelejo, Herbert and Eliza Steele House
**Valley Township:** Shallow Water School

**Golf Courses:**
Scott City Country Club, Public (Scott City, KS)

# SEDGWICK COUNTY
## EST. 1867 - POPULATION: 523,824

The most populous city in the state honors the legacy of John Sedgwick, one of the highest-ranking Union officers to be killed in action in the American Civil War.

# ANDALE, KS
## POPULATION: 941 – TOWN 618 OF 627 (10-12-23)
The surnames of two early families, the Andersons, and the Dales, were honored by having this town named for them when it was founded in the 1880s. The town's early industry and people came with the Missouri Pacific Railroad, which accomplished the construction of the greatest feat of architecture in Andale at that time, the Catholic church and school. Since being incorporated in 1901, Andale's population has grown with every Census except for the 1930 count, which had a net loss of four residents. Colton Haynes, known for his roles in *Teen Wolf* and *Arrow*, and B. J. Finney, an offensive guard in the NFL from 2015 to 2021, have ties to Andale.

# BEL AIRE, KS
## POPULATION: 8,262 – TOWN 575 OF 627 (10-8-23)
Bel Aire was formally incorporated on November 26, 1980, after the State of Kansas legally recognized it following a court battle with the City of Wichita. It began in 1955 as an improvement district for water. As nearby Wichita continued to grow, the residents of Bel Aire found it appropriate to uniquely identify themselves as their own city. The Kansas Supreme Court agreed with them, and thus one of the newest cities in Kansas was formulated. Population growth has been steady over the years. In 1990, it was home to just 3,695 people, but now 8,262 live there in 2020.

# BENTLEY, KS
## POPULATION: 560 – TOWN 616 OF 627 (10-12-23)
Orsemus Hills Bentley was instrumental in bringing the Kansas Midland Railroad to this part of Kansas in 1887, intending to connect Wichita with Ellsworth. His efforts were rewarded by having the town

named in his honor. The Kansas Midland would be annexed by the St. Louis & San Francisco Railroad in 1900, and by 1980, the Frisco became a part of the Burlington Northern. The postal service took an interest in establishing an office there on March 6, 1888, and in 1959, it was finally incorporated as a municipality.

# CHENEY, KS ☆
**POPULATION: 2,181 – TOWN 611 OF 627 (10-12-23)**
Founded in the summer of 1883, Cheney came about as the Atchison, Topeka & Santa Fe Railway was expanding across this portion of Kansas. It was named in honor of Benjamin P. Cheney, the director affiliated with the railroad company. A post office was established only a month after the townsite was laid out, and what followed was the construction of various businesses and an influx of settlers. The population of Cheney surpassed a thousand individuals for the first time in the late 1950s (1,101 people lived there as of the 1960 Census) and two thousand people in the late 2000s (2,094 residents as of the 2010 Census). The Souders Historical Museum is an impressive complex with train depots, a church and a school, and early genuine and fabricated storefronts. Cheney State Park consists of 1,913 acres and allows for ample opportunities to boat, hunt, fish, and camp for area residents and visitors.

# CLEARWATER, KS
**POPULATION: 2,653 – TOWN 591 OF 627 (10-9-23)**
This Missouri Pacific and Atchison, Topeka & Santa Fe Railroad town welcomed its first settlers in 1870 and was formally laid out as a town site in 1872. Its name was given for the exceptionally clear water found on the Ninnescah River. For years, the local post office spelled the name "Clear Water" until they matched the railroad-given spelling for good on February 17, 1894. The Chisholm Trail, used to drive cattle from Texas to northern lands, passed through here and enticed people to set up storefronts. Commerce led to the establishment of banks, and economic activity spurred the founding of several churches and a public school system. Its population has multiplied because of its proximity to Wichita: it had a historical population of 647 people in 1950, less than a quarter of what it has today. The country singer Logan Mize heeds from Clearwater, as does Raymond Goertz, the roboticist who patented the telefactor (a hand-and-arm device that can be controlled from afar by a person). One unique aspect of Clearwater is that many of the town's street signs have been placed on miniature windmills. Exhibits on the town's military, school,

and business history can be viewed at the Clearwater Historical Society Museum.

# COLWICH, KS
**POPULATION: 1,455 – TOWN 617 OF 627 (10-12-23)**
Colwich, another example of a rural Sedgwick County town turned city suburb because of its proximity to Wichita, had its simple beginnings in 1887 when the Colorado & Wichita Railroad (alternatively the Missouri Pacific) created it as one of the many communities along its route. The name "Colwich" is a combination of the terminals of the railroad line, "Col[orado]" and "Wich[ita]." Amongst the earliest noted buildings circa 1912 were an alfalfa mill, a hotel, a post office, and a Catholic and Methodist church. The population has grown with each Census since 1890, except for the 1930 Census, in which it lost two residents from the previous count.

# DERBY, KS
**POPULATION: 25,625 – TOWN 572 OF 627 (10-7-23)**
Derby was first called El Paso from 1871 and 1880 after El Paso, Illinois. When the Atchison, Topeka & Santa Fe Railroad extended one of its lines through the area, the officials considered it wise to adjust the name to "Derby" to avoid confusion with the Texas city of the same name. While some insist that the name was derived from horse derbies, a popular pastime in England at that time, it is a nod to C. F. Derby, who was one of the railroad officials at that time. When applying for incorporation at the turn of the century, it was granted the status with the name "El Paso," although it was still referred to as Derby by the railroad. At this point, Derby was still a small community with a handful of churches, general stores, and other lines of business. As the aviation industry took off in nearby Wichita, hordes of airmen began to move to the area. In 1956, the El Paso nomenclature was formally retired, and Derby has since grown into one of the larger cities of south-central Kansas, with a 2020 population of over 25,000 citizens. Despite its growth, the Derby Historical Society has saved much of the town's early history in its exhibits and archives at the Derby Historical Museum. Robot dinosaurs soar over the Derby sky at Field Station: Dinosaurs and encourage visitors with a mighty roar to explore the 14-acre family attraction. Numerous sports figures have ties to Derby, amongst the most notable being William Campfield (former NFL running back), George Teague (former NFL safety), Nick Reid (former NFL linebacker), Jason Gamble (former NFL lineman), Woody Austin

(golfer and 1995 PGA Tour Rookie of the Year), and David Rickels (mixed martial artist). Voice actress Caitlynn French and cartoonist Grant Snider also heed from Derby.

# EASTBOROUGH, KS
**POPULATION: 756 – TOWN 574 OF 627 (10-8-23)**
Eastborough is an incredibly unique municipality in that Wichita surrounds it on all sides. Founded on April 10, 1929, and named for its location in the "east borough of Wichita," Burdon Hunter is the British architect credited with bringing life to this little community. The subdivision rivaled next door Woodlawn for several years, but the two ultimately decided to work together and become their own independent municipality on June 1, 1937. The city's population has been as high as 1,141 residents (based on 1970 Census data), although today it is home to 756 residents. Olive Ann Beech, the "First Lady of Aviation" and the co-founder of Beech Aircraft Corporation, resided here in the later stages of her life. Eastborough is famous amongst residents of Wichita for being a "speed trap."

# GARDEN PLAIN, KS
**POPULATION: 948 – TOWN 612 OF 627 (10-12-23)**
Established in 1884 and incorporated in 1902, Garden Plain (formally called Southwick Glen) began as a railroad town on the Wichita and Western Railroad that connected Wichita with Kingman, the Kingman county seat. This was eventually known as the Wichita & Pratt division along the Atchison, Topeka & Santa Fe Railway. Garden Plain's early establishment of implement and other general merchandising stores fared well for local farmers, who cultivated fruitful harvests and named the area after its suitableness for agricultural activities. The 1932 Olympic gold medalist in the Decathlon and a member of the College Football Hall of Fame, Jim Bausch, grew up here.

# GODDARD, KS
**POPULATION: 5,084 – TOWN 613 OF 627 (10-12-23)**
The land on which Goddard was built was laid out by Ezekiel Wilder in 1883, who bought it as an investment with the knowledge that the Atchison, Topeka & Santa Fe Railroad would soon be built there. He strategically named it in honor of J. F. Goddard, then vice-president of the railroad company, and the following year, they laid the tracks through the townsite. Blendon was an alternative early name for the

area before the advent of the railroad and was itself its own town until many of the buildings were ultimately moved to Goddard. After the town's Methodist and Baptist churches were built, schools were put into session, and businesses were founded, Goddard applied for incorporation as a city of the third class circa 1910. It has grown from a small community of 533 people in the 1960s to having 5,084 residents as of the 2020 Census. Goddard's Tanganyika Wildlife Park has been named the most interactive zoo in the Midwest because of its opportunities for people to feed and touch exotic animals like giraffes, lemurs, and rhinos. Three former MLB players, pitcher Ed Siever (1902 AL ERA leader), catcher Derek Norris (2014 All-Star), and infielder Logan Watkins heed from Goddard.

## HAYSVILLE, KS
**POPULATION: 11,262 – TOWN 592 OF 627 (10-10-23)**
The sweet town of Haysville, the "Peach Capital of Kansas," was platted in 1891 on the land of W. W. Hays. Its founding date is notably later than most Kansas communities of the twentieth century. It grew slowly as a village on the Chicago, Rock Island & Pacific Railroad and, for many years, had not much more than a hotel, bank, grist mill, post office, and merchandising stores. As Wichita grew due to its manufacturing interests, so did Haysville as its neighbor to the south. When it was incorporated in 1951, its population had already grown into the thousands, and nowadays, those people celebrate all kinds of events to keep their individuality as a city intact. The most historical portion of Haysville was wiped out by a May 3, 1999 tornado that left behind nothing in the district but its destruction and a bank vault. Remarkably, in another section of town, the tornado spared the 1954 Vickers Petroleum Service Station, which is now remembered as the World's First Batwing Gas Station.

 **Restaurant Recommendation: Bionic Burger 243 S Seneca St Haysville, KS 67060**

## KECHI, KS
**POPULATION: 2,217 – TOWN 576 OF 627 (10-8-23)**
The name Kechi honors the tribe of Native Americans of the same name, alternatively known as the K'itaish, Keechi, Kichai, or Kitsai. Like several other Sedgwick County cities that once started as small

rural towns, so too did Kechi begin as a station on the Chicago, Nebraska & Kansas Railway in the 1880s. Growth was steady as the railroad attracted the postal service on May 29, 1888, and other structures were established. It was incorporated in 1957, and since the 1990 Census, its historical population has jumped from 517 residents in 1990 to 2,217 as of the latest federal count. Kechi once claimed to be the "Antique Capital of Kansas" because of its many antique stores.

# MAIZE, KS
**POPULATION: 5,735 – TOWN 614 OF 627 (10-12-23)**
N. F. Neiderlander and the Maize Town Company established this community in 1886 and named it from a derivation of a Native American word meaning "corn." Growth was steady in its primal years as a church, bank, newspaper, and post office were amongst the first institutions to be founded, and in 1915, it was awarded the title of being an incorporated city of the third class. The Missouri Pacific Railway was the principal railroad of interest. The town's population exploded with a 134.2% increase in residents between the 1950 (266 people) and the 1960 Census (623 persons), and from thereon, it continued to grow exponentially alongside Wichita and its other Sedgwick County neighbors. Nancy Kassebaum (the only woman in the U.S. Senate in 1978), Richard Kassebaum (a filmmaker), and Miles Ukaoma (an Olympic hurdler) have connections to the city.

 **Restaurant Recommendation: Barn'rds Soups Sandwiches 3860 N Maize Maize, KS 67101**

# MOUNT HOPE, KS
**POPULATION: 806 – TOWN 619 OF 627 (10-12-23)**
Mount Hope, the former home of the Pirates, was located in 1874 on the Arkansas River and would later be served by the Missouri Pacific Railroad. Its name is an eponym for Mount Hope, Michigan. The Mount Hope Clarion was the community's noted newspaper at the turn of the century, and amongst the other prominent early establishments were the grain elevator and a post office. Its highest number of residents came at the 2000 Census when it was reported that 830 people lived there.

# MULVANE, KS

Railroad official Joab A. Mulvane was honored to have this primarily Sedgwick County community named for him because of his efforts to bring the Atchison, Topeka & Santa Fe Railroad to the area circa 1879. Mulvane was located at the junction of five A, T & SF lines, which resulted in an easy pathway of growth for the city. J. S. Brown and J. N. Trickey operated the first stores of Mulvane, and A. C. Crawford erected the Mulvane House as a hotel for weary travelers. The post office got in on the action in October 1879 and selected J. B. Brown as postmaster. In due time, there was a creamery, flour and feed mills, and an ice and cold storage plant, all of which traded with the other nearby suburbs of Wichita. Mulvane Old Settlers Day is a proud community tradition dating back to 1873, the longest-continuously operating event in the state. The Kansas Star Casino (opened in 2011), the Mulvane Historical Museum in the Santa Fe depot, and the Doc Sunback Film Festival attract droves of tourists. Longtime college football head coach Dennis Franchione partially launched his four-decade coaching career at Mulvane High School as an assistant. Laura M. Cobb, a noted World War II United States Navy Nurse, attended the same school in the early 1900s. Terry and Carol Houck of Mulvane were the founders of the Patriot Guard in 2005, an organization that sends its members to shelter and protect the loved ones of deceased military veterans and first responders at their funerals.

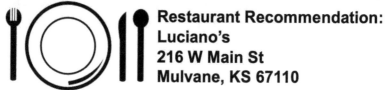

**Restaurant Recommendation:
Luciano's
216 W Main St
Mulvane, KS 67110**

# PARK CITY, KS

The modern-day Park City began in 1953 as the "Park City Improvement District," although its origins date long before then. The first incarnation of the community was in 1870 when it vied for control of the county seat against Wichita. It lost, and the town disappeared into ghost town status after town promoters failed to attract the attention of the railroad. The name resurfaced in the 1950s when the district was being planned. After about two-and-a-half decades of development, it was incorporated in a city of the third class on

November 26, 1980 (the same day that neighboring Bel Aire became a municipality). The town's proudest building is Hartman Arena, completed in 2009 and is the present home of the Wichita Wings team of the Major Arena Soccer League 2 (developmental) league.

# VALLEY CENTER, KS
**POPULATION: 7,340 – TOWN 578 OF 627 (10-8-23)**
Valley Center has been around since 1871 when it was founded and descriptively named for its location in the Arkansas River valley. The Atchison, Topeka & Santa Fe and the St. Louis & San Francisco Railroad primarily served it. Both lines significantly bolstered the local economy, and soon Valley Center had a broom factory, a feed and alfalfa mill, and extensive stock breeding and raising operations alongside other enterprises. In 1885, it would be incorporated under Kansas state law as a municipality. Valley Center made national headlines in July of 2007 when an explosion at Barton Solvents rocked the community and forced residents to evacuate. At the Valley Center Historical Museum, visitors can learn more about the town's role in Sedgwick County history. Former pop and country artist Cady Groves and her family resided here for a short time.

# VIOLA, KS
**POPULATION: 115 – TOWN 590 OF 627 (10-10-23)**
Another commonly used name for this town was Peotone until May 27, 1899, when it was changed to match the railroad name Viola. For some time, it boasted the activity of two rail lines, the Atchison, Topeka & Santa Fe, and the Kansas City, Mexico & Orient. Both enabled a spur of population growth to 537 people in the 1890s, during which all the town's lines of business came to fruition. Viola was incorporated in 1909 and was once home to the Bulldogs of Viola High School.

# WICHITA, KS ★
**POPULATION: 397,532 – TOWN 573 OF 627 (10-8-23)**
"The Air Capital of the World," Wichita, is the largest city in Kansas and the county seat of Sedgwick County. As of the 2020 Census, the city's population sat at 397,532 individuals or about 13.53% of the entire population of the state. Such a high figure places it at the 50th spot of the most populated cities in the United States. Its modern history begins circa 1863 when the city's namesake tribe of Native Americans returned to the area from Indian Territory due to the

ongoing American Civil War. They opted to settle along the banks of the confluence of the Little Arkansas and the Arkansas Rivers. Seeing an investment opportunity, James R. Mead started a trading post there to conduct business with the tribe and other pioneers–and later, those driving cattle along the Chisholm Trail–traveling through the area. In 1868, he created the Wichita Town Company with Governor S. J. Crawford, W. H. Lawrence, I. S. Munger, E. P. Bancroft, and A. F. Horner, and a hotel and a military post office were established. As plats were filed and the town was laid out, the cattle drive was in full effect, marking a rapid time of expansion for the young city. At this point, the cattle drive was so instrumental to the success of the town's economy that it became regionally referred to as "Cowtown." It reached incorporation status on July 21, 1870, and the Atchison, Topeka & Santa Fe Railway was quick to realize the earning potential of the city. As was typical with important economic centers of Kansas at that time, other railroads joined in the pursuit to earn and keep their own slice of Wichita's booming economy: the Missouri Pacific, St. Louis & San Francisco, the Chicago, Kansas, and Nebraska (later the Rock Island), and the Kansas City, Mexico & Orient (later acquired by Santa Fe). By this point, Wichita's early manufacturing interests were in full force, and the city had six foundries, six planing mills, five flour mills, four alfalfa mills, three overall factories, two packing plants, cement works and brick plants, and numerous other factories. Two of these were The Mentholatum Company, then a popular manufacturer of healthcare products, and The Coleman Company, known mainly for their camping gear products. Its infrastructure fared just as well, as in 1912, it was reported as having twenty public schools, sixteen publishers, ten theaters, six specialized hospitals, and two colleges: Fairmount College and Friends University (initially Garfield University). The ten-story Beason building, built in 1910, was then the tallest in the state. The feats of Wichita became all the more impressive when considering that all of the structures mentioned above were in place before the discovery of oil in Butler County and the subsequent boom in the airplane manufacturing industry. What resulted was the formation of Koch Industries by Charles and David Koch, the second-largest privately held company in the United States, as well as Swallow Airplane Company, Stearman Aircraft (later Spirit Aerosystems), Beechcraft, and Cessna Aircraft Company. During World War II, roughly 74,000 new workers and residents came to Wichita to help construct the Boeing B-29 bomber, the only aircraft ever used to carry and utilize nuclear warheads in battle. Regarding warheads, Wichita was one of three locations in the United States where 18 Titan II missiles were on continuous alert at McConnell Air

Force Base from 1963 to 1987. The first of many thousands of the Pizza Hut restaurant chain was started here on May 31, 1958, by Wichita State students Dan and Frank Carney, a few decades after White Castle, the first fast-food hamburger chain in the world, was founded on September 13, 1921. Freddy's Frozen Custard & Steakburgers, yet another fast-food franchise, went into operation in Wichita as recently as 2002 after Scott Redler and Bill and Randy Simon came up with the idea. In the Civil Rights space, Wichita was the site of the Dockum Drug Store sit-in, one of the first organized protests amid the Civil Rights Movement. In the modern age, Wichita's focal points center primarily around manufacturing and healthcare, although it has plentiful sites of interest to historians, locals, and tourists: Wichita-Sedgwick County Historical Museum, Wichita Art Museum, the Kansas African American Museum, the Kansas Sports Hall of Fame, Botanica, The Wichita Gardens, the Allen-Lambe House designed by Frank Lloyd Wright, the Sedgwick County Zoo, the Kansas Aviation Museum, the Museum of World Treasures, Stonehenge Jr. and Central Riverside Park, Old Cowtown, Exploration Place, Riverfront Stadium, Great Plains Nature Center, the Kansas Firefighters Museum, the Great Plains Transportation Museum, Intrust Bank Arena, Old Town, the Mid-America All-Indian Center, and The Keeper of the Plains, a 44-foot tall sculpture and symbol of the city. Sports fans can enjoy watching the Wichita Thunder of minor league hockey (an ECHL affiliate of the NHL's San Jose Sharks) and the Wichita Wind Surge (a Double-A affiliate of the MLB's Minnesota Twins). Wichita State University, the grown-up version of the previously mentioned Fairmount College, has 17,500 students as of the fall semester and has athletic teams that compete at the Division I level. The original Pizza Hut Museum, the Ulrich Museum of Art, and the Lowell D. Holmes Museum of Anthropology are on campus. Friends University, a private Christian institution, and Newman University, a private Roman Catholic university, are the other two institutions of higher learning with their main campuses in Wichita. Hundreds of persons of note have associations to Wichita, some of the more recognizable being: Jimmy Donaldson (YouTuber personality known as MrBeast, the most-subscribed individual on the platform), Mike Pompeo (the 70th United States Secretary of State), Don Johnson (lead actor in the 1980s crime show *Miami Vice* and a Primetime Emmy Award winner), Barry Sanders (member of the Pro Football Hall of Fame and the 1997 NFL's Most Valuable Player), Lynette Woodard (the first female Harlem Globetrotter basketball player), Phil Ruffin (businessman and billionaire), Jim Lehrer (former news anchor of the *PBS Newshour* and a presidential debate moderator), Robert Gates (22nd United

455

States Secretary of Defense), Kirstie Alley (Emmy Award and Golden Globe winning actress in *Veronica's Closet* and *Cheers*), Wyatt Earp (famous early lawman), David L. Payne (the "Father of Oklahoma"), Gale Sayers (NFL Hall of Fame and 4x Pro-Bowler), and the fictional college football head coach Ted Lasso of the sports comedy series.

**Restaurant Recommendation:**
**Bocatto Eatery & Pasta**
**321 N Mead St**
**Wichita, KS 67202**

**Restaurant Recommendation:**
**Doo Dah Diner**
**206 E Kellogg St**
**Wichita, KS 67202**

**Restaurant Recommendation:**
**Georges French Bistro**
**4618 E Central Ave #50**
**Wichita, KS 67208**

**Lodging Recommendation:**
**Hotel at Old Town**
**830 E First St**
**Wichita, KS 67202**

Sedgwick is only partially located in Sedgwick County (see Harvey County).

**Adjacent Counties:** Harvey (N), Butler (E), Cowley (SE), Sumner (S), Kingman (W), Reno (NW)

**Unincorporated/Ghost Towns:** Anness, Bayneville, Berwet, Clonmel, Davidson, Furley, Greenwich, Greenwick Heights, Hatfield, Juckle, Jamesburg, Marshall, McConnell AFB, Murray Gill, Oaklawn-Sunview, Oatville, Peck, Prospect, Schulte, St. Marks, St. Mary Aleppo, St. Paul, Sunnydale, Trails View, Waco, Wego, Wichita Heights

## National Register of Historic Places:

**Derby:** Derby Public School-District 6
**Haysville:** Vickers Petroleum Service Station
**St. Marks:** St. Mark Church
**Wichita:** Frank J. and Harvey J. Ablah House, Adeline Apartment Building, Administration Building, Allen's Market, Henry J. Allen House, Arkansas Valley Lodge No. 21, Prince Hall Masons, Ash-Grove Historic District on East Douglas Avenue, Oscar D. and Ida Barnes House, Battin Apartments Historic District, Belmont Arches, Bitting Building, Bitting Historic District, Frank E. Blaser House, Bond-Sullivan House, Bowers House, Broadview Hotel, Broom Corn Warehouse, Brow Building, Buildings at 800 West Douglas Block, J. Arch Butts Packard Building, Calvary Baptist Church, B. H. Campbell House, Carey House, Century II Performing Arts and Convention Center, Chapman-Noble House, L. W. Clapp House, R. D. W. Clapp House, College Hill Park Bathhouse, Comley House, Commodore Apartment Hotel, E. S. Cowie Electric Company Buildings, Cudahy Packing Plant, Dunbar Theatre, Eagle's Lodge #132, East Douglas Avenue Historic District, Eastwood Plaza Apartments, Ellis-Singleton Building, Engine House No. 6, Fairmount Apartments, Fairmount Congregational Church, Fairmount Cottage, Fairview Apartments, J. E. Farmer House, Farmer's and Banker's Historic District, Fourth National Bank Building, Fresh Air Baby Camp, Garvey Center, Gelbach House, Grace Methodist Episcopal Church, Grandview Terrace Apartments, Guldner House, Hayford Buildings, Henry's Department Store, Hillside Cottage, Holyoke Cottage, Hypatia House, Innes Department Store, International Harvester Building, C. M. Jackman House, Johnson Drug Store Building, Kansas Gas & Electric Company Building, Keep Klean Building, Kellogg Elementary School, Edward M. Kelly House, Knightley's Parking Garage, S. H. Kress Company Building, Lassen Hotel, Governor L. D. Lewelling House, Linwood Park Greenhouse and Maintenance Building, Linwood Place Historic District, Chester I. Long House, Luling's City Laundry, John Mack Bridge, Market Street Cottage, McCormick School, McCormick-Armstrong Press Building, Elizabeth McLean House, Mentholatum Company Building, Mohr Barn, Monroe-Mahan House, Mullen Court Apartments, Darius Sales Munger House, Newbern-Gore House, Nokomis and Navarre Apartment Buildings, North Market Street Apartments Historic District, North Riverside Comfort Station, North Topeka Avenue-10th Street Historic District, North Topeka Avenue Apartments Historic District, Occidental Hotel, Old Mission Mausoleum, Old Sedgwick County Courthouse, Old Wheeler-Kelly-Hagny Building, Orpheum Theater and Office Building, Park Place-Fairview Historic District, Penley House, Powell

457

House, Pryor House, Riverside Cottage, Riverview Apartments, Roberts House, Rock Island Depot, St. James Episcopal Church, Scottish Rite Temple, Sedgwick County Memorial Hall and Soldiers and Sailors Monument, Sim Park Golf Course Tee Shelters, Smyser House, South Kansas Avenue Historic District, Stackman Court Apartments, William Sternberg House, Stoner Apartment Building, Sunnyside School, Sutton Place, Topeka-Emporia Historic District, Union National Bank Building, University Hall, Friends University, U.S. Post Office and Federal Building-Wichita, W. O. Van Arsdale House, Victor Court Apartments, Virginia Apartment Building, Judge T. B. Wall House, Western Union Building, Westside I.O.O.F. Lodge, Wichita City Carnegie Library Building, Wichita City Hall, Wichita High School, Wichita Historic Warehouse and Jobbers District, Wichita Public Library-Main Branch, Wichita Veterans Administration Hospital, Wichita Wholesale Grocery Company, Grace Wilkie House, Wilson-Boyle House, Fred D. Wilson House, Winders Historic District, Woodburn House, Woolf Brothers Clothing Company

## Breweries/Wineries/Distilleries:
Alzavino Wine Tavern (Wichita, KS)
Brew Wagon Tours (Wichita, KS)
Bricktown Brewery – East (Wichita, KS)
Bricktown Brewery – West (Wichita, KS)
Central Standard Brewing (Wichita, KS)
Hank is Wiser Brewery (Cheney, KS)
Hopping Gnome Brewing Company (Wichita, KS)
Nortons Brewing Company (Wichita, KS)
Old School Taphouse & Social (Kechi, KS)
PourHouse by Walnut River Brewing Company (Wichita, KS)
Prairie Hill Vineyard (Colwich, KS)
River City Brewing Company (Wichita, KS)
Sweet Allie B's Limestone Beer Company (Wichita, KS)
Third Place Brewing (Wichita, KS)
Tor Brewing (Wichita, KS)
Wheat State Distilling (Wichita, KS)
White Crow Cider Company (Wichita, KS)
Wichita Brewing Company and Pizzeria – East (Wichita, KS)
Wichita Brewing Company and Pizzeria – West (Wichita, KS)
Wyldewood Cellars Winery (Peck, KS)

## Golf Courses:
Auburn Hills Golf Course, Public (Wichita, KS)
Braeburn Golf Club at WSU, Semi-Private (Wichita, KS)
Cherry Oaks Golf Club, Public (Cheney, KS)

Clearwater Greens Golf Course, Public (Clearwater, KS)
Crestview Country Club, Private (Wichita, KS)
Echo Hills Golf Club, Public (Wichita, KS)
Hidden Lakes Golf Course, Public (Derby, KS)
L W Clapp Golf Club, Public (Wichita, KS)
MacDonald Golf Course, Public (Wichita, KS)
Pine Bay Golf Course, Public (Wichita, KS)
Reflection Ridge Golf Club, Private (Wichita, KS)
Rolling Hills Country Club, Private (Wichita, KS)
Sim Park Golf Course, Public (Wichita, KS)
Tallgrass Country Club, Private (Wichita, KS)
Tex Consolver Golf Course, Public (Wichita, KS)
Valley Point Golf Course, Public (Valley Center, KS)
Wichita Country Club, Private (Wichita, KS)
Willowbend Golf Club, Private (Wichita, KS)

**Town Celebrations:**
4th of July Celebration, Garden Plain, KS (Independence Day)
Colwich Heritage Festival, Colwich, KS (Late September)
Maize Fall Festival, Maize, KS (September or October)
Old Settlers Celebration, Mulvane, KS (3rd Weekend of August)
Vintage Market, Garden Plain, KS (1st Saturday in June)
Wichita Jazz Festival, Wichita, KS (March)
Wichita Riverfest, Wichita, KS (Late May or Early June)

# SEWARD COUNTY
## EST. 1873 - POPULATION: 21,964

William H. Seward, the 12th Governor of New York and later the 24th United States Secretary of State, was honored in 1873 with the naming of Seward County, Kansas.

# KISMET, KS
### POPULATION: 340 – TOWN 489 OF 627 (9-20-23)
Kismet, formerly the home of the Pirates until its school was consolidated, was founded in the 1880s. The local post office entered service in November 1888 before being discontinued in September 1890. It would be a little over seventeen years later that the postal service would re-establish another office there in February of 1908, which remains in operation to this day. The Chicago, Rock Island & Pacific Railroad was the most significant railroad in the town's history, and its largest population of people (484) came in the 2000s.

# LIBERAL, KS ★☆

Liberal's population has grown wildly over the century. It was initially founded in 1888, although Seymour S. Rogers built his home on a section of land some years before then that would ultimately become an impressive city in southwestern Kansas. Rogers was also responsible for building Liberal's first general store and post office. His idea to name it "Liberal" came from a common saying that travelers would give him when he offered them free water: "That's very liberal of you." The name stuck, and by the time the Chicago, Rock Island & Pacific Railroad was built through the townsite later that year, the population expanded to 800 persons. The Oklahoma land runs near the turn of the century caused Liberal to lose about fifty percent of its settlers, but the community rebounded quickly. The first big industry was its broom-corn market, which shipped out over 800 cars of sorghum (used to make brooms and whisk brooms) every year in the 1910s: the largest such market in the country then. The average population of the county seat of Seward County has stayed close to 20,000 citizens since the dawn of the 21st century, thanks mainly in part to the discovery of natural gas in the area in 1920 (the Panhandle-Hugoton Gas Field), oil in the 1950s, the founding of the world's largest helium plant, National Helium in 1963, and the presence of the National Beef Packing Company, which bought a location in Liberal in 1993. The plant employs 3,500 people, or hypothetically about one-sixth of the entire population of the city. Some of its most prominent attractions are the Coronado Museum (featuring Native American exhibits and a handful of artifacts from Coronado's 1541 expedition), the Mid-America Air Museum (home to over one hundred aircraft, it is the fifth largest collection of civilian and military aircraft in the U.S.A.), Adventure Bay water park, the International Pancake Day Hall of Fame, and Seward County Community College (a public community college started in December of 1967). The "Land of Oz" exhibit features a recreation of the Yellow Brick Road and Dorothy Gale's house from *The Wizard of Oz* movie; it was moved to Liberal from Topeka in 1992. The previously mentioned "Pancake Day" museum highlights the storied history of Liberal's Pancake Day race, in which runners from Liberal square off against international contestants in Olney, Buckinghamshire, England, to see who is the pancake-flipping runner. In the 1983 film *National Lampoon's Vacation*, Mr. Griswold suggests that the family detours to Liberal to visit the "world's largest house of mud," an attraction that does not exist in the real world. An episode of *Fargo* from season four is also set here. Jerrod Niemann (country music singer and songwriter), Wayne Angell (economist and former member of the Federal Reserve Board of Governors), Martin Lewis and Melvin Sanders (former NBA players), William Stafford (the 20th Consultant in Poetry to the Library of Congress), Kristin Key (comedian), Wantha Davis (jockey), Chris Brown (the head coach of Fort Hays State football since 2011), Jerame Tuman, Lamar Chapman, and Doug Terry (all former NFL players), Kelli McCarty (Miss USA 1991), Kelly Overton (author and activist noted for his work on the mistreatment of animals), and Kasey Hayes (professional bull rider) are just a few famous individuals with ties to Liberal.

 **Restaurant Recommendation:
BrickHouse BBQ & Brew
24 E 2nd St
Liberal, KS 67901**

**Adjacent Counties:** Haskell (N), Meade (E), Stevens (W)

**Unincorporated/Ghost Towns:** Arkalon, Fargo Springs, Hayne, Springfield

**Golf Courses:**
Liberal Country Club, Private (Liberal, KS)
Willow Tree Golf Course, Public (Liberal, KS)

**Town Celebrations:**
Little World's Fair, Kismet, KS (Labor Day Weekend)
OzFest, Liberal, KS (3rd Saturday October Biannually)
Pancake Day, Liberal, KS (Shrove Tuesday)

# SHAWNEE COUNTY
## EST. 1855 - POPULATION: 178,909

Shawnee County, home to the state capitol in Topeka, was one of the original 33 counties named for the Shawnee Native Americans.

# AUBURN, KS
## POPULATION: 1,273 – TOWN 265 OF 627 (6-10-23)
The beginnings of this Shawnee County town began in the summer of 1854 when John W. Brown acquired 800 acres of land for his

homestead and brought his friends and family to the area. By 1856, he, Henry Fox, M. C. Dickey, and Loring Farnsworth had founded a town company. They sought to call the place "Brownville" until it was discovered that another town of that name already existed in Kansas. They settled on Auburn a year later, and as it quickly attracted settlers and began to furnish storefronts and other industries, it became a serious contender for the title of state capital. But alas, the railroad chose to bypass Auburn, and the population stagnated for several years until incorporation was awarded in 1963. From 1970 to 1980, the number of people living there grew by 241.0% (261 to 890 citizens) as people began to commute between Topeka and Auburn. It is the fictional hometown of Cameron Mitchell from the *Stargate SG-1* sci-fi television series and the legitimate hometown of Nina Evans Allender, a cartoonist known for her work done for the National Woman's Party to advocate for women's suffrage rights.

# ROSSVILLE, KS
**POPULATION: 1,105 – TOWN 262 OF 627 (6-9-23)**
Rossville takes its name from Rossville Township of Shawnee County, which got its name from early Kansas journalist William W. Ross. Located on the Union Pacific Railway, it was founded in 1871 and was the site of an opera house, retail outlets, schools, churches, and a postal office. The first store was founded by J. C. McIlvane in 1873, and H. H. Miller was elected as the first mayor when the town was incorporated in 1881. Following the 1980 Census, the population broke 1,000 persons and has remained relatively steady.

# SILVER LAKE, KS
**POPULATION: 1,345 – TOWN 263 OF 627 (6-9-23)**
Mr. Huntoon of Topeka platted the town of Silver Lake in February 1868, a couple of years after the Union Pacific Railroad had laid tracks in the area. There are two tales as to how it arrived at its present nomenclature. The common story is that the name was derived from the pristine, silvery water of the local oxbow lake, and the other is that it was named after Chief Joseph LaFramboise's dog, "Silver." Settlers C. S. Palmer and M. B. Beaubien were responsible for opening the first store in Silver Lake and, in the following years, a hotel, flour mills, churches, and schools. Incorporation as a city of the third class came in the early months of 1871. Born here in 1952 was Lonnie Duane Kruger, who would go on to be the head coach of the Kansas State (1986-1990), Florida (1990-1996), Illinois (1996-2000), UNLV (2004-2011), and Oklahoma (2011-2021) men's collegiate

basketball programs throughout his career. He was inducted into the College Basketball Hall of Fame in 2022, and for a brief stint, he served as the head coach of the NBA's Atlanta Hawks (2000-2003).

# TOPEKA, KS ★☆

**POPULATION: 126,587 – TOWN 264 OF 627 (6-10-23)**

Topeka had its beginnings in 1854 when a group of nine men of the New England Emigrant Society led by Cyrus K. Holliday (later the mayor of Topeka and the founder of the Atchison, Topeka & Santa Fe Railroad) and C. Robinson sought to establish the Topeka Town Association company. They selected the site because of its proximity to the Kansas River, the strong trade route that had been established in the prior two decades by the Oregon Trail and the military road between Fort Leavenworth and Fort Riley, and the availability of land that would be necessary to constitute a formidable bid for the title of the state capital. The name was chosen by the suggestion of either Joseph James or Mr. Webb for the Kansa-Osage word *Topeka-okie*, which translates to "a good place to dig potatoes." The town multiplied in the following years as significant buildings, including Constitution Hall (where the first free-state legislature opened in March 1856) and The Topeka House were constructed, as well as a sawmill, multiple hotels and stores, factories, brickyards, and other places of industry. It was during this same time that Bleeding Kansas, a series of violent confrontations between abolitionists and pro-slavery settlers who fought for the admission of Kansas into the Union as a free state or a slavery state, resulted in 56 political killings. The City of Topeka headquartered the free-state movement in Kansas, and the townspeople organized a militia and fortifications and underwent a siege from nearby proslavery rivals (primarily out of Lecompton) for a portion of 1856. The following year, Topeka would be incorporated as a city, and in 1861, it was named the permanent state capital, the same year that Kansas was admitted to the Union as the 34th State. Exodusters settled the east side of Topeka's Lincoln Street throughout the 1870s, and in 1893, the first African-American kindergarten west of the Mississippi River was established by Dr. Charles Sheldon. Its progressive stance on African-American equality started early in 1871 when Topeka High School was fully integrated upon its inception, and it was there that the famous Brown v. Board of Education case brought about the requirement of racial integration in the country's public schools. The Monroe Elementary School site is now a part of the Brown v. Board of Education National Historical Park. Some of Topeka's other claims to fame include the origin of the popular Christian phrase, "What would Jesus do?" at

Charles Sheldon's Central Congregational Church and its distinction as the "home of Pentecostalism." Additionally, it was only the second Baha'i community in the Western Hemisphere. In March of 2010, Topeka Mayor Bill Bunten temporarily called for the city to be renamed to "Google, Kansas, the capital city of fiber optics" in a bid to help bring Google's fiber experiments to the area. On April 1 of that year, Google reciprocated the joke and changed their search engine home page to say "Topeka" for the day. Points of interest throughout the city include the Evel Knievel Museum, the Combat Air Museum at Forbes Field, the Kansas Museum of History, the Topeka Computing Museum, Burnett's Mound, the Equality House, the World's Largest Wren Statue, the Topeka Zoo, Great Overland Station, Heartland Park Topeka, Old Prairie Town at Ward-Meade Historic Site, Kansas Expocentre and Landon Arena, the Kansas Children's Discovery Center, Truckhenge, Mulvane Art Museum, Museum of the Kansas National Guard, Kaw River State Park (the only urban state park), and the Kansas State Capitol. Washburn University (formerly known as Lincoln College, Washburn College, and Washburn Municipal University) is the last city-ran university in the country. It had an enrollment of 5,460 students in the Fall of 2022 and has been in operation since February 6, 1865. Several other post-secondary institutions throughout the city are branches of Friends University, Rasmussen College, Baker University, the University of Kansas, and the Washburn Institute of Technology. Hundreds of noteworthy individuals heed from or have connections to the city: Phil Ehart and Kerry Livgren (founders of the progressive rock band Kansas), John F. Kilmartin (former CEO of Mervyn's Department Stores), Annette Bening (four-time Academy Award, two-time Tony and Golden Globe Award-winning actress), Karl Targownik (Holocaust survivor and psychiatrist), Joan Finney (42nd Governor of Kansas), Donald C. Thompson (World War I photographer), John States Seybold (Governor of Panama Canal Zone from 1952 to 1956), John H. Outland (namesake of College Football's Outland Trophy award), Warren Faidley (world's first full-time professional stormchaser), Margaret Murdock (first woman Olympic medalist in Shooting at the Summer Olympics), Ruth Patrick (botanist known for work on developing ways to measure the health of freshwater ecosystems), Aaron Douglas (artist of the Harlem Renaissance period), Charles Curtis (31st Vice President of the United States), Alf Landon (26th Governor of Kansas and 1936 Republican Party Presidential nominee), and Brandon Adams (actor known for his roles as Jesse in The Mighty Ducks and Kenny in The Sandlot), and many others.

**Restaurant Recommendation:**
**Bobo's Drive In**
**2300 SW 10$^{th}$ Ave**
**Topeka, KS 66604**

**Restaurant Recommendation:**
**The Burger Stand**
**2833 SW 29$^{th}$ St**
**Topeka, KS 66614**

**Restaurant Recommendation:**
**The Wheel Barrel**
**925 N Kansas Ave**
**Topeka, KS 66608**

**Lodging Recommendation:**
**PlainsCraft Covered Wagons**
**435 NW Independence Ave**
**Topeka, KS 66608**

# WILLARD, KS
## POPULATION: 74 – TOWN 261 OF 627 (6-9-23)

Once a bustling town complete with a hotel, general store, and other furnishings that came about from the construction of the Chicago, Kansas, and Nebraska Railroad through the city in the late 1880s, Willard has since lost the majority of its population and is now home to only 74 residents. Some estimates place the town's population at over 300 individuals because of their role as a shipping point for cattle. Following the Great Depression and the Great Flood of 1951 (which decimated the community's infrastructure and cut it off from nearby Rossville until 1955), population figures plummeted.

**Adjacent Counties:** Jackson (N), Jefferson (NE), Douglas (SE), Osage (S), Wabaunsee (W), Pottawatomie (NW)

**Unincorporated/Ghost Towns:** Berryton, Calhoun, Dover, Elmont, Indianola, Kiro, Montara, Pauline, Richland, Sumner City, Tecumseh, Uniontown, Wakarusa, Watson

## National Register of Historic Places:
**Auburn:** McCauley Bridge, Thomas Arch Bridge, Union Church Building
**Berryton:** Horace G. Lyons House
**Dover:** Sage Inn
**Silver Lake:** Hard Chief's Village
**Tecumseh:** Hopkins House
**Topeka:** Morton Albaugh House, Solomon A. Alt House, Anton-Woodring House, ATSF Motive Power Building, Blacksmith Creek Bridge, Bowker House, Brown v. Board of Education National Historic Site, Shannon Brown House, Casson Building, Cedar Crest, Central Motor and Finance Corporation Building, Central National Bank, Church of the Assumption and Rectory, Church of the Assumption Historic District, Church of the Holy Name, College Avenue Historic District, Columbian Building, Constitution Hall-Topeka, Country Club Residential Historic District, Crawford Building, Nelson Antrim Crawford House, William T. and Delora Crosby House, Curtis Junior High School, Charles Curtis House, Davies Building, Devon Apartments, Dillon House, East Topeka Junior High School, England Farm, Evergreen Court Apartments, Fire Station No. 1, Fire Station No. 2, Fire Station No. 4, Fire Station No. 6, Fire Station No. 7, Gem Building, Giles-Nellis House, Gordon Building, HTK Architects Office Building, John C. Harmon House, Hicks Block, Holliday Park Historic District I, Holliday Park Historic District II, House at 116 Southwest The Drive, Hughes Conoco Service Station, Jayhawk Hotel, Theater and Walk, Kansas State Capitol, Hazen L. Kirkpatrick House, Charles and Dorothy Kouns House, James and Freda Lippitt House, Fred and Cira Luttjohann House, Masonic Grand Lodge Building, Memorial Building, Menninger Clinic Building, Dr. Karl & Jeanetta Lyle Menninger Education Center, Mill Block Historic District, Morgan House, North Topeka Baptist Church, Old German-American State Bank, Park Plaza Apartments, Pottawatomie Baptist Mission Building, Potwin Place Historic District, Ritchie Cemetery, John and Mary Ritchie House, Ross Row Houses, St. John African Methodist Episcopal Church, St. John's Lutheran School, St. Joseph's Catholic Church, St. Joseph's School-St. Joseph's Convent, St. Mark's African Methodist Episcopal Church, Santa Fe Hospital, John Sargent House, Security Benefit Association Hospital Building, Senate and Curtis Court Apartments Historic District, Shiloh Baptist Church, J. A. Shoemaker House, South Kansas Avenue Commercial Historic

District, Sumner Elementary School and Monroe Elementary School, Thacher Building, Topeka Cemetery Historic District, Topeka Council of Colored Women's Clubs Building, Topeka High School, Topeka Veterans Administration Hospital, Union Pacific Railroad Passenger Depot, United States Post Office and Court House, Tinkham Veale Building, Ward-Meade House, Washburn University Carnegie Library Building, Wea Creek Bowstring Arch Truss Bridge, Westminster Presbyterian Church, Willits Church, Woman's Club Building, Chester B. Woodward House, Wakarusa Hotel, Uniontown Cemetery

## Breweries/Wineries/Distilleries:
785 Beer Company (Topeka, KS)
Blind Tiger Brewery & Restaurant (Topeka, KS)
Glaciers Edge Winery (Wakarusa, KS)
Happy Basset Barrel House (Topeka, KS)
Happy Basset Brewing Company (Topeka, KS)
Iron Rail Brewing (Topeka, KS)
Matrot Castle Winery (Topeka, KS)
Norsemen Brewing Company (Topeka, KS)
Norsemen Lakeheim (Topeka, KS)
Wakarusa Valley Vineyard (Wakarusa, KS)

## Golf Courses:
Berkshire Country Club, Private (Topeka, KS)
Lake Perry Country Club, Private (Topeka, KS)
Lake Shawnee Golf Course, Public (Topeka, KS)
Prairie View Country Club, Private (Topeka, KS)
Shawanee County Parks, Public (Topeka, KS)
Shawnee Country Club, Private (Topeka, KS)
Sports Center Golf Complex, Public (Topeka, KS)
Topeka Country Club, Private (Topeka, KS)
Topeka Public Golf Course, Public (Topeka, KS)
Western Hills Golf Club, Semi-Private (Topeka, KS)

## Town Celebrations:
Country Stampede Music Festival, Topeka, KS (Mid-July)
Dover Heritage Day, Dover, KS (3rd Saturday in June)
Fiesta Topeka, Topeka, KS (Mid-July)
Huff 'n Puff Hot Air Balloon Rally, Topeka, KS (Weekend after Labor Day)
Tall Corn Festival, Rossville, KS (2nd Weekend of August)

# SHERIDAN COUNTY
## EST. 1873 - POPULATION: 2,447

Fightin' Phil Sheridan, a five-star general in the United States Army in his prime, had Sheridan County named for him when it was established in 1873.

# HOXIE, KS ★☆
**POPULATION: 1,211 – TOWN 183 OF 627 (4-13-23)**

This town had its true beginnings in 1886 after a group of nine early town promoters of the Hoxie Town Company convinced residents of the city of Kenneth (the county seat at that time) to move their buildings and residents three miles southward to be located on the forthcoming Union Pacific Railroad. The two towns would consolidate and become Hoxie, the county seat of Sheridan County. It was named in honor of railroad official H. M. Hoxie, general manager of the Missouri Pacific Railroad. A prominent feature of Hoxie is the Sheridan County Historical Society and Mickey's Museum, dedicated to telling the early stories of Sheridan County. Numerous persons of note have connections with the city, including Nick Hague (astronaut formerly onboard the International Space Station), Jacie Hoyt (head coach of the Oklahoma State women's basketball team), Brad Lambert (football head coach), Urbane Pickering and Les Barnhart (MLB players), and Dirk Johnson (former NFL punter).

 **Restaurant Recommendation:
The Elephant Bistro & Bar
732 Main St.
Hoxie, KS 67740**

# SELDEN, KS
**POPULATION: 184 – TOWN 178 OF 627 (4-13-23)**

Sheridan County's city of Selden was laid out in 1888 on the Chicago, Rock Island, and Pacific Railroad and named after its founder, Selden G. Hopkins. The United States Postal Service established a post office here on July 21, 1888. The current President of the NBA's Atlanta Hawks, Travis Schlenk, was born in Selden, as was Norman Malcolm, noted for his work on common sense philosophy. In a bizarre natural event on June 3, 1959, a thunderstorm dropped eighteen inches of hail on the community for an incredible eighty-five minutes straight.

**Adjacent Counties:** Decatur (N), Norton (NE), Graham (E), Gove (S), Thomas (W)

**Unincorporated/Ghost Towns:** Adell, Alcyone, Angelus, Chicago, Lucerne, Museum, Mystic, Phelps, Seguin, Sheridan, Studley, Tasco, Ute, Violenta

**National Register of Historic Places:**
**Valley Township:** John Fenton Pratt Ranch
**West Saline Township:** Shafer Barn

Scott County Photos: Scott City (all)

Sedgwick County Photos: Andale, Cheney, Cheney, Colwich, Haysville, Valley Center, Wichita, Wichita

Seward County Photos: Kismet, Kismet, Liberal, Liberal, Liberal, Liberal, Liberal, Liberal

Shawnee County Photos: Silver Lake, Topeka, Topeka, Topeka, Topeka, Topeka, Topeka, Topeka

Sheridan County Photos: Hoxie, Hoxie, Hoxie, Hoxie, Selden, Selden, Selden, Selden

# SHERMAN COUNTY
## EST. 1873 - POPULATION: 5,927

The etymology of Sherman County comes from William Tecumseh Sherman, the Commanding General of the U.S. Army between March 1869 and November 1883.

# GOODLAND, KS ★☆
## POPULATION: 4,465 – TOWN 165 OF 627 (4-12-23)

When Sherman County was organized, early settlers immediately questioned which town should be awarded the title of county seat: Eustis, Itasca, Sherman Center, or Voltaire. A gentleman named Clark arrived the following year to resolve the issue by founding a brand-new city, Goodland (named after Goodland, Indiana). Citizens of the county ultimately voted on the matter, with 872 votes going to Goodland, 611 to Eustis, and only 12 to Voltaire. Eustis refused to concede the election and involved the Supreme Court of Kansas in the matter, but because the vote had concluded, Goodland was formally awarded the title. The county's records had to be seized in January 1888 because Eustis refused to hand them over. Eustis, Itasca, Sherman Center, and Voltaire have faded away, with the only other incorporated community in the county being Kanorado. The Chicago, Rock Island & Pacific Railroad helped to bring shops, large stockyards, flour mills, grain elevators, and more to the newly founded community. Some of its present attractions are the High Plains Museum (home to a replica of the gyrocopter, the first rotary-winged aircraft to receive a United States patent), the Carnegie Arts Center, the Ennis-Handy Victorian period house, and the World's Largest Easel, an eighty-foot-tall structure that holds a 32-by-34-foot painting of Vincent van Gogh's "3 Sunflowers in a Vase." It was painted by artist Cameron Cross in 2001. Goodland is mentioned in numerous media works, including *Goodland*, a 2014 film by Josh Doke, two of T.D. Shields's novels, *Into Shadow* and *Into Light*, and L.E. Howel's novel *Planetfall*. Notable residents from the community include Brook Berringer (former quarterback for the University of Nebraska), furniture architect Milo Baughman, two former NFL wide receivers, Dave Jones and Mike Friede, and Hollywood actor and NFL defensive back Tinker Keck, alongside others. William J. Purvis and Charles A. Wilson of Goodland are credited with creating "America's First Patented Helicopter," although their design was sadly never successful.

**Restaurant Recommendation:
The Bricks by Maria
1530 Main St
Goodland, KS 67735**

# KANORADO, KS
**POPULATION: 153 – TOWN 166 OF 627 (4-12-23)**

Kanorado's fun name is an amalgamation of the state names "Kansas" and "Colorado" because of its location right along the state line of Colorado. The local post office was called Lamborn from January 1889 to September 1903. Kanorado was given the honorary title of "Top City of Kansas" in 2016 because of its distinction of being the highest-elevated city in the state at approximately 3,907 feet. The highest point in Kansas at 4,039 feet, Mount Sunflower, is located in a remote area about twenty-five miles south of Kanorado.

**Adjacent Counties:** Cheyenne (N), Rawlins (NE), Thomas (E), Logan (SE), Wallace (S)

**Unincorporated/Ghost Towns:** Caruso, Edson, Ruleton, Voltaire

**National Register of Historic Places:**
**Edson:** Kuhrt Ranch
**Goodland:** Mary Seaman Ennis House, Goodland City Library, Grant School, Ruleton School, U.S. Post Office-Goodland, United Telephone Building

**Golf Courses:**
Sugar Hills Golf Club, Semi-Private (Goodland, KS)

**Town Celebrations:**
Flatlander Festival, Goodland, KS (Last Full Weekend of September)

# SMITH COUNTY
## EST. 1867 - POPULATION: 3,570

Smith County, the site of the geographic center of the contiguous 48 states, was named for J. Nelson Smith. He was a Major for the Union in the American Civil War.

# ATHOL, KS
## POPULATION: 41 – TOWN 120 OF 627 (3-29-23)
Athol was founded in 1888 and served as a station and shipping point on the Chicago, Rock Island, and Pacific Railroad in its early days. In February of that same year, a post office was moved to town with the name Corvallis. The official Kansas state song and one of the Top 100 Western songs of all time, "Home on the Range," was written by Dr. Brewster M. Higley at his cabin about eight miles north of town in the early 1870s.

# CEDAR, KS
## POPULATION: 11 – TOWN 117 OF 627 (3-29-23)
"Cedarville" was the original name for this townsite before it was later shortened to Cedar. Although its population today is only 11 people, at its peak in 1910, it was home to 400 residents. It served as an essential trading center for the county and a shipping point on the Missouri Pacific Railroad. It had been home to a hotel, grade school, Christian and Methodist churches, grain elevator, bank, and telegraph, telephone, and postal services.

# GAYLORD, KS
## POPULATION: 87 – TOWN 118 OF 627 (3-29-23)
Gaylord, located on the Missouri Pacific Railway, took its name from one of its founders, C. E. Gaylord, originally of Marshall County, Kansas. It was organized in 1870, welcomed its post office in June 1871, and was formally incorporated in 1886.

# KENSINGTON, KS
## POPULATION: 399 – TOWN 121 OF 627 (3-29-23)
Kensington's founding can be traced to 1887, when it was created along the Chicago, Rock Island, and Pacific Railroad. On January 7,

1888, its post office was established, and in 1900 the town was incorporated.

# LEBANON, KS
**POPULATION: 178 – TOWN 123 OF 627 (3-29-23)**
The original Lebanon was platted in 1876, but from September 1887 to February 1888, its buildings were moved to the present townsite (likely to be located along the newly established Rock Island Railroad) four miles to the northeast. Lebanon is a town of national fame because of its proximity to the geographic center of the 48 contiguous US states located 2.6 miles to the northwest. The location was determined at the coordinates 39°50'N 98°35'W in a 1918 survey. In popular culture, the town has been featured numerous times in the TV series *House of Cards* (Season 6, Episode 7), *American Gods*, *Salvation*, and *Supernatural* (the home base of main characters Sam and Dean Winchester from season 8 onwards). It was also featured in a Super Bowl LV commercial for Jeep in the 1969 film *The Computer Wore Tennis Shoes*, the 2008 documentary *The Return of the Buffalo: Restoring the Great American Prairie*, and Neil Gaiman's 2001 book *American Gods*.

# SMITH CENTER, KS ★☆
**POPULATION: 1,571 – TOWN 119 OF 627 (3-29-23)**
Smith Center was created in 1871 and named for Major J. Nelson Smith of the 2nd Colorado Cavalry. Smith County, of which it is the county seat, was named after the same veteran. On January 8, 1873, the town's post office was formed, and in 1886 it gained incorporation status. Several famous individuals have ties to Smith Center: Mitch Holthus (an ESPN college basketball announcer and the play-by-play announcer for the Kansas City Chiefs), Roscoe "Fatty" Arbuckle (a silent film actor known for mentoring other stars such as Charlie Chaplin), Albert Wagner (the last surviving American Marine veteran to serve in World War I), Steve Tasker (7x NFL Pro Bowl wide receiver), former NFL linebacker Mark Simoneau, and Nolan Cromwell (4x NFL Pro Bowl safety and Super Bowl XXXI champion).

 **Restaurant Recommendation:**
**Jiffy Burger**
**815 US-36**
**Smith Center, KS 66967**

**Adjacent Counties:** Jewell (E), Osborne (S), Rooks (SW), Phillips (W)

**Unincorporated/Ghost Towns:** Anderson, Bellaire, Claudell, Clifford, Cora, Corvallis, Covington, Crystal Plains, Custer, Dispatch, Germantown, Hardilee, Harlan, Jacksonburg, Judson, Ohio, Troublesome, Twelve Mile, Tyner, Uhl

**National Register of Historic Places:**
**Smith Center:** First National Bank Building, Grimes House, Home on the Range Cabin, Martyn House

**Golf Courses:**
Smith Center Country Club, Semi-Private (Smith Center, KS)

**Town Celebrations:**
Old Fashioned Saturday Night, Kensington, KS (3rd Saturday in August)
Veterans Day Parade and Fall Craft Fair, Kensington, KS (Veteran's Day Weekend)

# STAFFORD COUNTY
## EST. 1867 - POPULATION: 4,072

The creators of Stafford County thought it appropriate to name it in honor of Lewis Stafford, a Kansan Union captain who passed away during the Battle of Young's Point.

# HUDSON, KS
## POPULATION: 95 – TOWN 456 OF 627 (8-18-23)

Rattlesnake was the first name for this western Kansas town because of the presence of the reptile found throughout this part of the state. In 1887, the townspeople elected to change the name to Hudson after the town in Wisconsin of the same nomenclature. It was located on the Missouri Pacific Railroad, which brought with its arrival the people and capabilities to begin cement stone works, grain elevators, a creamery, general and drug stores, a post office, and most notable of all, Stafford County Flour Mills. The mill remains Hudson's most significant driver of economic activity and the city's highest employer, as it makes Hudson Cream Flour and Kroger, King Arthur, and Kemach flour brands as well. The mill's name-brand variety of flour is known nationwide and is used explicitly in Marlinton, West Virginia's annual biscuit bake-off contest.

**Restaurant Recommendation:**
**Wheatland Cafe**
**112 N Main St**
**Hudson, KS 67545**

# MACKSVILLE, KS
### POPULATION: 471 – TOWN 453 OF 627 (8-18-23)

The name Macksville was derived from the surname of George Mack, the first postmaster of Stafford County. It was established in 1885 as a station on the Atchison, Topeka & Santa Fe Railroad and boasted several businesses, a couple of banks, and a newspaper and post office in its early days. It was incorporated by an act of the legislature in 1886.

# RADIUM, KS
### POPULATION: 26 – TOWN 454 OF 627 (8-18-23)

Radium has maintained incorporation status since 1934 despite its historical population being at most 85 people (as was recorded in the 1940 Census). It has always served as a small agricultural community, and for eighty years, it boasted a post office that remained in operation from October 17, 1910, to April 28, 1990. It was likely founded in the 1900s.

# SEWARD, KS
### POPULATION: 41 – TOWN 455 OF 627 (8-18-23)

Seward's history dates to the 1870s, not long before the Missouri Pacific Railroad wove its way through Stafford County. Before its incorporation in 1927, it was estimated that the population rose to as many as 300 people in the 1910s. During that time, it was home to a creamery, post office, bank, hotel, and several lines of business like general and drug stores. Its namesake is William H. Seward, the 24th United States Secretary of State and the 12th Governor of New York. The area post office operated from 1878 to 1995.

# STAFFORD, KS ☆

Once a candidate for the title of the Stafford County seat, Stafford began as a prosperous community thanks to its location at the junction of the Missouri Pacific and the Atchison, Topeka & Santa Fe Railroad. It was established in 1878 and named after the county in which it was located, which was, in turn, named for Lewis Stafford, a deceased soldier from the American Civil War. An early 1882 tornado decimated the early sod houses and structures of Stafford, which were later rebuilt of stone and frame to avoid future catastrophe. A planing mill, disc harrow, steam plow and sled factories, a creamery, grain elevators, and a public library were amongst the town's first achievements. Three noted Staffordians are pianist Norma Wendelburg, Neva Egan, the original First Lady of Alaska from 1959 to 1966, and Tony Fields, a dancer known for his roles in Michael Jackson music videos and the 1980s television series *Solid Gold.* The Jones Store, once a chain of department stores of which the first was founded in 1887 by J. Logan Jones in Stafford, would ultimately end up as a part of Dillard's, and now Macy's. Quivira National Wildlife Refuge is a large 22,135-acre protected area that started in 1955 to protect area salt marshes and a range of birds that follow the Central Flyway migration route. The Stafford County Museum exhibits the stories of town residents of the past and present.

 **Restaurant Recommendation: Joan's**
**454 Martin Ave**
**Stafford, KS 67578**

# ST. JOHN, KS ★

William Bickerton of the Church of Jesus Christ (the Mormons) founded a religious settlement in 1875 named Zion Valley. As its infrastructure grew and the Atchison, Topeka & Santa Fe Railroad looked to extend their line, the townsite attracted the attention of some town promoters, who purchased the townsite in 1879 to make it the county seat of Stafford County. They strategically named it St. John in honor of the man who was then the 8th Governor of Kansas, John Pierce St. John, to entice him to award the judicial seat title to the city. The promoters' plan worked. St. John's population grew to as many as 1,785 people by 1910, at which point it had two grain elevators, flour and roller mills, banks, a hotel, a high school, and a post office as its primary businesses of note. It was in 1880 that the postal service changed the name from Zion Valley to St. John to match the town's etymology, although, in the 1970s, they again changed it to Saint John. Some forty-five years later, several citizens banded together to reverse the post office's change and keep the town's name as "St. John" once and for all. William Gray, a noted area photographer, had his studio in the city and was famous for using glass negatives instead of film to document day-to-day life in St. John and nearby Stafford. Despite its location within Tornado Alley, the city has never been struck by a tornado. Locals attest that the reasoning lies within the 1981 book *No Cyclone Shall Destroy: The Story of St. John, Kansas.*

**Adjacent Counties:** Barton (N), Rice (NE), Reno (E), Pratt (S), Edwards (W), Pawnee (W)

**Unincorporated/Ghost Towns:** Dillwyn, Neola, Zenith

**National Register of Historic Places:**
**St. John:** William R. Gray Photography Studio and Residence, Martin Cemetery
**Stafford:** Comanche Archeological Site, Covenanter Church, Farmers National Bank, First Methodist Episcopal Church, Sarah L. Henderson House, Nora E. Larabee Memorial Library, Joseph L. Spickard House

**Golf Courses:**
Stafford County Country Club, Semi-Private (Stafford, KS)

**Town Celebrations:**
Country Christmas, Macksville, KS (1st Weekend of December)
Hudson Chicken Ride, Hudson, KS (1st Saturday in August)
MackFest, Macksville, KS (2nd Saturday in August)
Oktoberfest, Stafford, KS (1st Weekend of October)
St. John Jubilee, St. John, KS (Memorial Day Weekend)

# STANTON COUNTY
## EST. 1887 - POPULATION: 2,084

Stanton County's name remembers Edwin Stanton, the 27th United States Secretary of War responsible for organizing the search for John Wilkes Booth, Lincoln's killer.

# JOHNSON CITY, KS ★☆
**POPULATION: 1,464 – TOWN 482 OF 627 (9-19-23)**
Many American Civil War veterans settled in this far-western corner of Kansas in 1885, so the townsite and respective town company were named Veteran. A year later, they changed the name to Johnson for Colonel A. S. Johnson. There was no railroad connecting Johnson City to the rest of the outside world for many decades, and they relied on a daily stagecoach to Syracuse–located 30 miles north–to have access to a railroad and trade with nearby communities. Their main point of pride was that they were the judicial seat of Stanton County due to their geographical location in the center of the county. While a handful of retail stores, a newspaper, and even a post office flourished for some-odd years, the lack of a railroad proved too detrimental to the community's survival, and settlers began to leave in search of bluer skies. By the early 1890s, not even a decade after the first veterans had arrived, the population had dwindled to a mere ten people. In 1906, it was said to have had only a single resident, making it the smallest county seat in the world. What saved the town was the introduction of a branch of the Atchison, Topeka & Santa Fe Railroad, which wanted to utilize Johnson City as a shipping point between the coal mines of Colorado and the rest of Kansas. The town's fortunes turned heavily, and by the 1930s, it had 514 persons living there. The Stanton County Museum complex pays tribute to the county's unique history in its six structures.

# MANTER, KS
**POPULATION: 132 – TOWN 483 OF 627 (9-19-23)**
Manter's history dates to the arrival of a line of the Atchison, Topeka & Santa Fe Railroad to the area, when the railroad needed to found a station every seven to ten miles for refueling, watering, or changing personnel. Its founding coincides with the establishment of the area post office on February 10, 1923. Since its 1924 incorporation date, there have been as many as 224 residents (1930 Census) and as few as 132 (2020 Census).

**Adjacent Counties:** Hamilton (N), Grant (E), Stevens (SE), Morton (S)

**Unincorporated/Ghost Towns:** Big Bow, Julian, Saunders

**Golf Courses:**
Stanton County Prairie Pines, Public (Johnson City, KS)

**Town Celebrations:**
Pioneer Days, Johnson, KS (4th Saturday of July)

# STEVENS COUNTY
## EST. 1886 - POPULATION: 5,250

Congressman Thaddeus Stevens is the individual honored by this county's name because of his leadership during the Reconstruction period of the country following the Civil War.

# HUGOTON, KS ★☆
**POPULATION: 3,747 – TOWN 487 OF 627 (9-20-23)**
Early settlers from McPherson, Kansas, founded the City of Hugo in 1885 and named it after the French Romantic writer Victor Hugo. Once it was discovered that there was a Hugo, Colorado, not very far away, the suffix '-ton' was added to the name to differentiate the cities from one another. The following year, Hugoton would get its post office, its first church, Hugoton United Methodist (the longest continuous church congregation in Stevens County), and a blessing from then-Governor John Martin to be the county seat of the newly founded Stevens County. A nearby town called Woodsdale, which has faded away entirely, was angry with the decision because they had platted their townsite at the center of the county, intending to become the judicial seat. When ensued was a county seat war between the two towns, which ended with the Hay Meadow massacre on July 25, 1888, when a party of Hugoton supporters (led by town marshal Sam Robinson) and another of Woodsdale supporters (under town marshal Ed Short) clashed with one another, leaving four of five members of the Woodsdale party dead. A court of law handed out no punishment, as nobody had jurisdiction over "No Man's Land" in Oklahoma, where the massacre had taken place. Shortly before the tragic event, town promoters vied to attract the Denver, Memphis & Atlantic Railroad or the Meade Center, Cimarron Valley & Trinidad

Railroad. Both lines failed to reach Hugoton. It wouldn't be until 1913 that the Atchison, Topeka & Santa Fe Railroad reached town, which helped replenish the settlers that had given up hope and moved to Oklahoma during the land runs. The Hugoton Gas Field was first discovered here in 1927 at the Crawford No. 1 well owned by the Independent Oil and Gas Company, and as of 2021, it has produced nearly 19 trillion cubic feet of natural gas. The same field contains the largest helium reserves in the United States, making Hugoton the "Natural Gas Capital of the World." According to local lore, notorious criminals Bonnie and Clyde lived here under the pseudonyms Jewell and Blackie Underwood. Blackie was a local farm hand, and Jewell was the owner of Jewell's Cafe. It is said that the couple hid under the radar operations to evade local law enforcement and keep their true identities hidden. The stories of locals may be factual, as when Bonnie and Clyde perished in a 1934 shootout in Louisiana, receipts from Jewell's Cafe were found in their vehicle. In addition to these historical anecdotes, many more are featured at the Stevens County Gas & Historical Museum, a complex made up of artifacts from the former local grocery store, churches, school, train depot, and numerous other past businesses. The president of the Kansas Senate from 2005 to 2013, Stephen Morris, and actor William Burrows (stage name Billy Drago), known for his roles in Clint Eastwood westerns, come from a Hugoton background.

**Restaurant Recommendation:**
**Bonnie & Clyde Grill**
**615 S Monroe St**
**Hugoton, KS 67951**

# MOSCOW, KS
### POPULATION: 272 – TOWN 480 OF 627 (9-19-23)
The intended name for this Stevens County community was Mosco. However, when the petition was received by the postal service to found an office there, the postal clerk added a "w" to the name, thinking that they desired it to be named after the Russian capital. In reality, town residents had wanted to call it Mosco, a shortened form of "Moscoso," in honor of Spanish conquistador Luis de Moscoso Alvarado, a member of Hernando De Soto's expedition. The first settlers arrived at the townsite in 1887, and a year later, the post office was moved there from the now-defunct town of Valparaiso. After the Cimarron Valley Railroad (a branch of the Atchison, Topeka & Santa Fe) was constructed through this part of Kansas in 1912, Moscow's

residents elected to move 8 miles north in 1913 so they could take advantage of the economic benefits of the railway. They were formally incorporated in 1929, and the population currently sits at 272.

**Adjacent Counties:** Grant (N), Haskell (NE), Seward (E), Morton (W), Stanton (NW)

**Unincorporated/Ghost Towns:** Woodsdale

**Golf Courses:**
Hugoton Country Club, Public (Hugoton, KS)

Sherman County Photos: Goodland, Goodland, Goodland, Goodland, Goodland, Goodland, Kanorado, Kanorado

487

Smith County Photos: Athol, Cedar, Gaylord, Kensington, Lebanon, Lebanon, Smith Center, Smith Center

Stafford County Photos: Hudson, Macksville, Seward, Stafford, Stafford, St. John, St. John, St. John

Stanton County Photos: Johnson City, Johnson City, Johnson City, Johnson City, Johnson City, Johnson City, Manter, Manter

490

Stevens County Photos: Hugoton, Hugoton, Hugoton, Hugoton, Hugoton, Manter, Manter, Manter

491

# SUMNER COUNTY
## EST. 1867 - POPULATION: 22,382

Charles Sumner, a United States Senator from Massachusetts and the Dean of the Senate from March 1869 to March 1874, is the namesake of Sumner County.

# ARGONIA, KS
**POPULATION: 456 – TOWN 586 OF 627 (10-9-23)**

The first woman ever elected to serve as a town's mayor in United States history was Susanna M. Salter of Argonia, Kansas, who took over the honor on April 4, 1887, after taking a surprise victory with the support of the Women's Christian Temperance Union and the Republican Party. She was elected early in the town's history, as Argonia had only recently been established in 1881. It was given its name for the ship Argo, of great importance in Greek mythology, a boat that Jason and the Argonauts used to retrieve the Golden Fleece. The Missouri Pacific and the Atchison, Topeka & Santa Fe Railroads provided the means to expand the community to include numerous places of worship, grain elevators, and a milling industry, amongst other accomplishments. Salter's home is now on display as an 1880s-period house.

# BELLE PLAINE, KS
**POPULATION: 1,467 – TOWN 580 OF 627 (10-9-23)**

In French, "Belle Plaine" literally translates to "beautiful plain," a descriptive term for how the first settlers of this town felt about the land that encompassed it. Located on the Ninnescah River in 1871, the real growth came with the arrival of the Southern Central & Fort Scott Railway, which whisked away the products and materials created by the local flour and planing mills. A few decades later, the Missouri Pacific and the Atchison, Topeka & Santa Fe Railways opted to build through Belle Plaine, increasing the economy to the point where they could upkeep an opera house, public schools, and several churches of different denominations. Residents are exceptionally proud of Bartlett Arboretum, created by Dr. Walter Bartlett, who in 1910 wished to have his arboretum. It has since been developed into a beautiful 15.2-acre area, complete with a stage for events, the former Santa Fe Railroad Depot, and plants from across the globe. Its director, Robin Lynn Macy, co-founded The Chicks country music band (formerly the Dixie Chicks). Jesse Beams, a physicist who worked on the Manhattan Project and was an early patent-holder for air conditioning, was born here on Christmas Day in 1898.

# CALDWELL, KS ☆
**POPULATION: 1,025 – TOWN 584 OF 627 (10-9-23)**

Alexander Caldwell served as a United States Senator for Kansas from March 1871 to March 1873, and because of his status, had a newly-founded community in Sumner County named in his honor. The Chisholm Trail predates the townsite, as it operated from about 1867 to 1871 before the townsite and the area post office (May 1871) were established. C. H. Stone opened the first store in Caldwell to trade with the cattlemen traveling through this part of Kansas. Because of its notoriety amongst the men, it became known as the "Queen of the Cowtowns—The Border Queen." The Chisholm Trail, Chicago, Rock Island, and Pacific Railroad (originally the Chicago, Kansas and Nebraska Railway), the Kansas Southwestern, and the Atchison, Topeka & Santa Fe lines played a crucial role in the development of Caldwell. The arrival of the railroads spurred the townspeople's desire to build flour mills and grain elevators, hotels, schools, churches, and marble works. Caldwell earned a unique designation in the mid-1980s after Larry Miller and his sixth-grade class began a project to designate the ornate box turtle as the official state reptile of Kansas. They succeeded with tremendous support, and on April 14, 1986, Governor John W. Carlin made the designation in a ceremony at the school. Residents of Caldwell hold this accomplishment very highly and refer to themselves as the "Ornate Box Turtle Capital of the World." Max Showalter (pseudonym Casey Adams), a famous television actor, Gladys A. Emerson, the first person to isolate Vitamin E in a pure form, noted fiddle player Byron Berline, and The Dinning Sisters, Lou, Jean, and Ginger, known for the 1940s hits, headline Caldwell's famous past residents.

 **Restaurant Recommendation:
Red Barn Family Restaurant
624 S Main St
Caldwell, KS 67022**

# CONWAY SPRINGS, KS
**POPULATION: 1,086 – TOWN 589 OF 627 (10-9-23)**

The name Conway Springs comes as a combination of its location in Conway Township of Sumner County and the presence of nearby mineral springs that provided a valuable source of water for pioneer settlers. The town's location on the Missouri Pacific and the Atchison, Topeka & Santa Fe Railroad enabled it to establish itself as a viable settlement upon its founding in 1884. The first man to settle the area was Captain Cranmer, and nowadays, there are 1,086 "settled" folks living in the city. The founder of the American Meteorite Museum in Arizona, Harvey H. Nininger, was born here in 1887, as was Lloyd Bishop, who played nine days in the MLB with the Cleveland Naps.

# GEUDA SPRINGS, KS
## POPULATION: 158 – TOWN 564 OF 627 (10-6-23)
Originally a small siding of the Kansas Southwestern Railroad, this town splits the Cowley-Sumner County line. The name was descriptively given when settlers discovered a large mineral spring, and they found that natives called it *Ge-u-da*, meaning healing. The abundance of water enabled easy settlement of the area, first by George B. Green and then by others, including G. A. Cutler (the proprietor of the first drug store), J. R. Musgrave (a general merchandising store owner), and James Stiner (constructor of the Geuda Springs House). A series of newspapers existed between 1882 and 1914, none of which have survived to the present day. Geuda Springs was formally incorporated by an act of the legislature in 1884. Because of its "healing springs," Geuda became a vacation hotspot for those wanting to experience the healing properties of its seven springs. Notorious gunfighter and Old West figure Luke Short, known for his gunfighting skills (and luck), passed away in Geuda Springs in September 1893.

# HUNNEWELL, KS
## POPULATION: 44 – TOWN 583 OF 627 (10-9-23)
H. H. Hunnewell, a noted Kansas railroad financier and director responsible for the Kansas City, Fort Scott, and Gulf Railroad and the Kansas City, Lawrence, and Southern Railroad, had this community named in his honor for his contributions to the railroading industry. The townsite's notable railways were the Leavenworth, Lawrence, and Galveston lines and the Kansas and Southwestern. It was initially a cowtown, and most of its residents were cowboys and railroad employees. They frequented the eight saloons and two dance halls, and due to the lack of any real police force or marshals, violence occurred on the daily. On August 21, 1884, the historical "Hunnewell gunfight" event made headlines after a couple of men perished at Hanley's Saloon. As the cattle trade was pushed westward by

lawmakers, Hunnewell was given the time to grow as an upright community. Frank Shiffdaner was the first manager of the post office upon its establishment in August 1880 (it closed in 1960), and Ford & Leonard built the first home that year. The first mayor was J. A. Hughes when Hunnewell was incorporated in 1881. Hunnewell again made headlines approximately three decades later when a city council of all men attempted to overthrow then-woman mayor Ella Wilson. Hunnewell has since quieted down into a small rural agricultural community and had a population of just 44 people as of the 2020 Census.

# MAYFIELD, KS
**POPULATION: 75 – TOWN 588 OF 627 (10-9-23)**
A post office called Bellevue was established near the future Mayfield townsite in 1877. It was renamed Marengo in 1878 and then moved on September 8, 1880, to Mayfield when the Atchison, Topeka & Santa Fe Railroad developed a railroad siding. Mayfield remained unincorporated for the next forty-seven years until 1927 the population began to subside. It was once the proud home of the *Mayfield Voice* newspaper (March 1894 to 1895), vocational and educational institutions, and two flour mills.

# MILAN, KS
**POPULATION: 56 – TOWN 587 OF 627 (10-9-23)**
Named after its northern Italy counterpart, Milan was founded in 1880 when the Atchison, Topeka & Santa Fe Railroad sought to extend their line through Sumner County. The post office, staffed by the town's primary postmaster and storekeeper, I. D. Moffitt, arrived around the same time and remained open until November 29, 2011. As was typical for the town then, as it is today in rural areas, the locals thrived on its early mills and elevators. It was incorporated in 1890 and today has an all-time low historical population of 56 people.

# OXFORD, KS
**POPULATION: 1,048 – TOWN 565 OF 627 (10-6-23)**
"Nep-tah-wal-lah" (also spelled Napawalla) was the name of an Osage chief who called these lands home before the arrival of European settlers. The town retained the title for a short while before it was changed to Oxford by the Oxford Town and Immigration Company when they purchased the townsite in 1871. The new name was coined after Oxford University in England. Lafe Binkley served

as the postmaster of the original Napawalla post office, and following its closure, T. E. Clark took over the duties for the Oxford, Kansas branch of the postal service. Like most Midwestern communities, Oxford owes its prosperity to the advent of the railroads, namely the Atchison, Topeka & Santa Fe Railway, and the Missouri Pacific and the Midland Valley Railroad. Early officials failed to win the county seat designation as they had hoped, but the city was still incorporated in 1879 and was home to as many as 1,173 people in the 2000s. Keitha Adams, the head women's basketball coach at the University of Texas at El Paso, and author Vingie E. Roe claim Oxford as home.

# SOUTH HAVEN, KS
## POPULATION: 324 – TOWN 582 OF 627 (10-9-23)
This place was called "South Haven" after the City of South Haven, Michigan, when it was laid out in 1872. Aside from a lone store that doubled as the area post office owned by F. F. Meister, the town's activities did not begin until 1879 with the advent of the Atchison, Topeka & Santa Fe Railroad and the Kansas Southwestern Railroad. From thereon, it grew to encompass all of the lines of business found in a typical Kansas farm town of that day, the most noted of which was a milling company. It has no relation to the Haven in Reno County, Kansas, which wasn't founded until 1886. The former General Superintendent of the Church of the Nazarene (the highest possible position within the organization) from 1989 to 1997, Donald Owens, and Forest "Spot" Geyer of the 1973 College Football Hall of Fame class are affiliated with the city.

# WELLINGTON, KS ★
## POPULATION: 7,715 – TOWN 581 OF 627 (10-9-23)
The self-proclaimed "Wheat Capital of the World" came to be in 1871, when the Wellington Town Company, composed of R. A. Davis, A. A. Jordan, P. A. Wood, and five others, banded together to found Wellington. The name honors Arthur Wellesley, the 1st Duke of Wellington and a two-time prime minister of the United Kingdom. By the end of the year, there was already a hotel, drug store, general merchandising store, and a post office managed by postmaster C. R. Godfrey. The following year, county residents voted it in as the county seat over the nearby Sumner City, and it was incorporated that November. The race to extend railroads westward reached the Wellington vicinity in 1880 when the Atchison, Topeka & Santa Fe Railroad made it a division point. In 1887, the Chicago, Kansas, and Nebraska Railway (in modern days now a part of the Union Pacific)

laid its tracks here. The designation of Wellington as a division point for what was one of the most important railroads in Kansas brought enormous fortunes (both financially and in terms of luck) to the area. By 1912, there were hundreds of stores, three flour mills and feed mills, factories for cheese, cigars, plows, salt, marble, and granite, and an ice and cold storage plant. The Sumner County high school building had the largest enrollment of any high school in the state in 1908, even over many Topeka, Kansas City, and Wichita learning institutions. The Chisholm Trail Museum, located in the old Hatcher Hospital, has an impressive forty rooms full of artifacts, many pertaining to its namesake that brought the earliest trade to the area. The National Glass Museum down the street is noted for its emphasis on American-made glass during the era of the Great Depression. Wellington Lake is another area favorite for its angling, camping, boating, and waterfowl hunting opportunities. Many famed individuals are linked to Wellington in one way or another: Ernie Barrett (early NBA player known as "Mr. K-State"), Walter Chrysler (the founder of Chrysler Corporation), Chuck Miller (pianist known for his 1955 hit "The House of Blue Lights"), Kent Whealy (the co-founder of Seed Savers Exchange), David Carradine (actor primarily known for his role as Kwai Chang Caine in the 1970s television series *Kung Fu*), Francis Heydt (four-time NCAA swimming champion in the 1940s), Joseph E. Maddy (conductor and founder of the Interlochen Arts Camp), Loren Hibbs (the longtime head coach of the Charlotte NCAA baseball team from 1993 to 2019), Neil Frank (once a director of the National Hurricane Center), Ryleigh Buck (a member of the United States women's national baseball team), and Arthur S. Champeny (the only American to be honored with the Distinguished Service Cross in three different wars (WWI and WWII, and the Korean War).

 **Restaurant Recommendation:**
**Travelin' Smoke BBQ**
**217 N Washington Ave**
**Wellington, KS 67152**

Mulvane is only partially in Sumner County (see Sedgwick County).

**Adjacent Counties:** Sedgwick (N), Butler (NE), Cowley (E), Harper (W), Kingman (NW)

**Unincorporated/Ghost Towns:** Adamsville, Anson, Ashton, Bushnell, Cicero, Cleardale, Corbin, Dalton, Doster, Drury, Ewell,

Metcalf, Millerton, Milton, Peck, Perth, Portland, Riverdale, Roland, Rome, Sumner City, Suppesville, Zyba

**National Register of Historic Places:**
**Argonia:** Salter House
**Belle Plaine:** Bartlett Arboretum
**Caldwell:** Caldwell Carnegie Library, U.S. Post Office-Caldwell
**Oxford:** Old Oxford Mill
**Wellington:** Downtown Wellington Historic District, Edwin Smith House, H. F. Smith House, Wellington Carnegie Library

**Breweries/Wineries/Distilleries:**
Bluff Creek Distillery & 18 Acres Lounge (Caldwell, KS)

**Golf Courses:**
Caldwell Golf Course, Private (Caldwell, KS)
Suppesville Golf Course, Public (Milton, KS)
Wellington Golf Club, Public (Wellington, KS)

**Town Celebrations:**
Chisolm Trail Festival, Caldwell, KS (1st Weekend of May)
Kansas Wheat Festival, Wellington, KS (2nd Week of July)
Tulip Time Festival, Belle Plaine, KS (2nd Weekend of April)
Watermelon Feed, Oxford, KS (2nd Weekend of September)

# THOMAS COUNTY
## EST. 1873 - POPULATION: 7,930

The designation of this county of "Thomas" seeks to honor George Henry Thomas, a Union Army general.

# BREWSTER, KS
## POPULATION: 291 – TOWN 167 OF 627 (4-12-23)
Robert Brewster, a railroad foreman of the Chicago, Kansas & Nebraska Railway when the town of Brewster was founded, is the namesake of this community. Brewster served as a shipping point along the railroad in its early days, and in September 1888, the postal service arrived. A former name for the area post office was Hastings.

# COLBY, KS ★☆

A post office was established near the center of Thomas County in 1882, and a few years later, land was purchased from the railroad to begin a town to serve the local settlers. It was at this time when J. R. Colby started to work on platting the city in 1885 through the Colby Town Company. In 1886, it was awarded the title of the County Seat of Thomas County, and the Union Pacific and Chicago, Rock Island & Pacific Railroads would build their lines through the area shortly after. The town's population has grown steadily from an initial 1890 Census count of 516 citizens to 5,570 people as of the 2020 Census. Colby Community College, home to the Trojans, was founded as a Kansas Public Community College in 1964. Other local points of interest are the Wheat Jesus Billboard off of Interstate-70, Villa High Lake, Fike Park, and the Prairie Museum of Art and History, known for being the home of the Cooper Barn: "The Largest Barn in Kansas." Outside of the Thomas County Courthouse is a statue of a pioneer woman and her young son, a testament to the spirit of the earliest frontierswomen who braved the wilderness of the open prairie and worked diligently to raise the first children of the area. Some notable figures associated with Colby include the 41st Governor of Kansas, Mike Hayden, the director of the United States Mint from 1969 to 1977, Mary Brooks, opera singer Samuel Ramey, the 44th Lieutenant Governor of Kansas, Sheila Frahm, Zelma Henderson, desegregation activist & a plaintiff in the famous Brown v Board of Education court case, World Heavyweight Champion Wayne Munn, and Christian singer and songwriter Mark Schultz.

**Restaurant Recommendation:**
**B-Hive**
**170 W 4th St**
**Colby, KS 67701**

# GEM, KS

This jewel of a community began as a railroad station on the Chicago, Rock Island & Pacific Railroad in the 1880s. It was named for the Gem Ranch and incorporated as a city of the third class in 1926. The town's post office remained in operation from December 14, 1885, to the spring of 2014.

# MENLO, KS
Menlo, a small rural community of 33 residents located on the eastern border of Thomas County, was once located on the Union Pacific Railroad. It was once home to general stores, two elevators, a bank and post office, and other businesses. The post office arrived on December 20, 1888, and closed its doors on June 27, 1992.

# REXFORD, KS
Rexford, established in 1887 and incorporated in 1917, took its name from the Rexford family of early settlers after one of the family members tragically passed away in a house fire. Rexford's population was 375 individuals as of the 1930 Census, and its present population is 197 residents.

Oakley is only partially located in Thomas County (see Logan County).

**Adjacent Counties:** Rawlins (N), Decatur (NE), Sheridan (E), Gove (SE), Logan (S), Sherman (W)

**Unincorporated/Ghost Towns:** Copeland, Cumberland, Halford, Kuka, Levant, Mingo, Otterbourne, Quickville

**National Register of Historic Places:**
**Colby:** Colby City Hall, Colby Community High School, St. Thomas Hospital, Thomas County Courthouse

**Golf Courses:**
Colby Country Club, Semi-Private (Colby, KS)

**Town Celebrations:**
Pickin' on the Plains Bluegrass Festival, Colby, KS (June)
Sunflower Festival, Colby, KS (4th Weekend in August)

# TREGO COUNTY
## EST. 1867 - POPULATION: 2,808

After it was organized in 1867, it was decided that Trego County would be named in honor of the Union Army captain Edgar P. Trego.

# COLLYER, KS
**POPULATION: 97 – TOWN 154 OF 627 (4-11-23)**
Collyer was founded as a station on the Union Pacific Railroad line in 1879; many of its earliest settlers were from a colony of soldiers and sailors. The name seeks to honor Reverend Robert Collyer, who assisted early settlers in adapting to life in the area. It once was home to Baptist, Catholic, and Congregational churches and multiple schools and general stores.

# WAKEENEY, KS ★☆
**POPULATION: 1,799 – TOWN 153 OF 627 (4-11-23)**
Early settlers of WaKeeney worked to market it as "The Queen City of the High Plains" in a bid to attract immigrants from around the nation. It was principally founded by James Keeney of Chicago, who purchased the townsite from the Kansas Pacific Railroad and worked with Albert Warren to survey and plat a town by 1879 (the same year that it became the county seat of Trego County). The name WaKeeney is a combination of their surnames. Since 1950, the town has created a large Christmas lighting display in the wintertime in which they display a 35-foot Christmas tree and well over 6,000 lights throughout downtown. Because of the display's popularity, the town adopted the name "Christmas City of the High Plains" and even converted an empty lot in its downtown into the "North Pole." Another local point of interest is the Trego County Museum. Cedar Bluff State Park, twenty-one miles southeast of WaKeeney, is separated into two areas: the Bluffton and Page Creek Area. Threshing Machine Canyon is the most historically noted park site because of its mid-19th-century wall carvings. A handful of famous individuals have ties to the city: the leader of the Green Party of Ontario, Canada, Mike Schreiner, PGA Tour golfer Steve Gotsche, painter Frank Mechau, journalist Charles Garrigues, and 1904 Olympic silver medalist in tug of war Orrin Upshaw. Gloria Folkers and her backyard made international news in 1999 when an escaped elephant from a traveling circus wandered into her backyard after the town's tornado sirens went off.

**Adjacent Counties:** Graham (N), Rooks (NE), Ellis (E), Ness (S), Gove (W)

**Unincorporated/Ghost Towns:** Banner, Blufton, Bosna, Cyrus, Ogallah, Riga, Threshing Machine Canyon, Voda, Wilcox

**National Register of Historic Places:**
**Collyer:** Collyer Downtown Historic District, Lipp Barn, St. Michael School & Convent
**Ransom:** Wilcox School-District 29
**WaKeeney:** Keraus Hardware Store, Stradal House, Trego County Fairgrounds Exhibit Building

**Breweries/Wineries/Distilleries:**
Shiloh Vineyard & Winery (WaKeeney, KS)

**Golf Courses:**
Big Creek Golf Course, Semi-Private (WaKeeney, KS)

**Town Celebrations:**
Christmas Tree Lighting, WaKeeney, KS (Saturday after Thanksgiving)

# WABAUNSEE COUNTY
## EST. 1855 - POPULATION: 6,877

Wabaunsee County was named for the leader of the Potawatomi Native American tribe, also spelled Waubonsie.

# ALMA, KS ★☆
**POPULATION: 802 – TOWN 257 OF 627 (6-9-23)**
The county seat of Wabaunsee County, Alma, has a disputed etymology. It is assumed to have been named after Alma, Germany, for a small river in Crimea. Residents have called it the "City of Native Stone" because many of its buildings were constructed with stone from the Flint Hills. The first home was built in 1867, the year the community was founded, and in the following decades, the Chicago, Rock Island & Pacific Railroad and the Atchison, Topeka & Santa Fe Railroads would construct their lines through Alma. Notable early landmarks included three schools, one public and two private (Catholic and Lutheran), a bank, a flour mill, two newspaper offices,

and a post office. The historical population was once as high as 1,125 persons, according to the 1890 Census. Highway 99, which leads into Alma from the south, is part of the Native Stone Scenic Byway. Several miles of stone fences were constructed by early pioneers under government incentives beginnings in the 1860s, many of which can still be seen today. The Wabaunsee County Historical Society operates a local museum that allows a look into the county's past.

# ALTA VISTA, KS
**POPULATION: 409 – TOWN 246 OF 627 (5-4-23)**
Alta Vista's first settlers arrived circa 1887 and decided to name it for its lofty elevation. "Alta Vista" is a Spanish term meaning "high view." The Chicago, Kansas, and Nebraska Railroad, which would eventually be annexed by the Chicago, Rock Island & Pacific Railroad, helped to bring wealthy merchants, bankers, and other commerce and institutions to the surrounding area. It was in the same year that the railroad was built in which the post office, moved from "Pike, Kansas," was established. Another earlier name for the area was Albion. Alta Vista was incorporated in 1905 and reported a high population of 499 residents in the 1910 Census. Ag Heritage Park consists of exhibits ranging from threshing machines to combines that pertain to the agricultural history of the area.

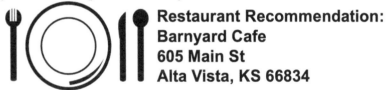 **Restaurant Recommendation:
Barnyard Cafe
605 Main St
Alta Vista, KS 66834**

# ESKRIDGE, KS
**POPULATION: 439 – TOWN 271 OF 627 (6-10-23)**
Named in honor of Charles. V. Eskridge, a noted Emporia-area politician who became the first person to buy a town lot in the newly-founded town, Eskridge was laid out in 1868. E. H. Sanford was its founder and helped to convince the Atchison, Topeka & Santa Fe Railroad to extend their Burlingame & Alma line through this townsite in 1880. The town grew considerably throughout its early decades to a high of 797 citizens in 1910, thanks mainly partly to its importance on the railroad and the town's development. It was once the site of five churches of differing denominations, one of which was affiliated with the Kansas Wesleyan Bible School.

# HARVEYVILLE, KS
**POPULATION: 178 – TOWN 270 OF 627 (6-10-23)**

The original townsite of Harveyville was laid out circa 1880. However, it would later be moved closer to the station on the Burlington & Alma line of the Atchison, Topeka & Santa Fe Railroad. Its name honors Henry Harvey, an early pioneer and missionary to the Shawnee tribe of Native Americans. The town post office arrived in 1869, and amongst its proudest early engineering feats included a public school and a Christian and Methodist church. Incorporation came about in 1905. In modern times, Harveyville was featured as the setting of Sandra Dallas's 1995 novel *The Persian Pickle Club*, and the public school has since been turned into "The Harveyville Project–A Rural Schoolhouse Creative Workshop & Retreat."

# MAPLE HILL, KS
**POPULATION: 631 – TOWN 260 OF 627 (6-9-23)**

The name Maple Hill comes from a large grove of maple trees that sat atop a hill near the original townsite at its founding circa 1882 by George Fowler. It was suggested by early postmistress Mrs. Higgenbotham, whose office was in close proximity to the growth. The Chicago, Kansas, and Nebraska Railway (later annexed by the Chicago, Rock Island, and Pacific in 1891 and ultimately the Union Pacific Railroad in 1997) constructed a railroad line through Maple Hill in 1887, spurring the town's growth. Joseph Norman Dolley, known for being the first promoter of "blue-sky laws," was instrumental in the city's development. A blue-sky law is a state law that regulates the sales or offerings associated with securities to protect the public from being frauded. His idea to implement them came about because many early salesmen would sell stakes in "gold mines" hidden along the back roads of Kansas to early settlers despite the mines not even existing. One of a handful of unusual gravestones found around Kansas, the backward cast of Sarah Oliver, is at the Old Stone Church cemetery.

# MCFARLAND, KS
**POPULATION: 272 – TOWN 258 OF 627 (6-9-23)**

S. H. Fairfield brought this town to life in 1887 and named it in honor of Judge J. N. McFarland, a member of the town company. The two men brought the first homes, hotel, store, and church to the newly founded town with the help of James Sury, George Bates, and C. W. Jewel. Having been established at the junction of two lines of the

Chicago, Rock Island, and Pacific Railroad, other lines of business began to expand, and a post office would eventually be established. It was incorporated as a city of the third class in 1903.

# PAXICO, KS
## POPULATION: 210 – TOWN 259 OF 627 (6-9-23)
This town was founded in 1879 and was once known as "Strong Mill." The post office later changed the name to Paxico in honor of Pashqua, an early Potawatomi medicine man. In 1886, the Chicago, Rock Island & Pacific Railroad was being built through the area, so the entire town, as well as another little community by the name of Newbury, moved to be next to it. The railroad's arrival brought a hotel, flour mill, telegraph offices, and a bank.

St. Marys is only partially in Wabaunsee County (see Pottawatomie County), and Willard is only partially in Wabaunsee County (see Shawnee County).

**Adjacent Counties:** Pottawatomie (N), Shawnee (E), Osage (SE), Lyon (S), Morris (SW), Geary (W), Riley (NW)

**Unincorporated/Ghost Towns:** Bradford, Keene, Newbury, Vera, Volland, Wabaunsee, Wilmington

**National Register of Historic Places:**
**Alma:** Alma Downtown Historic District, Brandt Hotel, Fix Farmstead, Grimm-Schultz Farmstead, Stuewe House, Sump Barn, Peter Thoes Barn, Wabaunsee County Courthouse
**Eskridge:** East Stone Arch Bridge-Lake Wabaunsee, Eskridge Bandstand, Security State Bank, Southeast Stone Arch Bridge-Lake Wabaunsee
**Manhattan:** Pratt-Mertz Barn
**Paxico:** Paxico Historic District, Paxico Rural High School, Snokomo School
**Wabaunsee:** Beecher Bible and Rifle Church, Wabaunsee District No. 1 Grammar School
**Wamego:** Mount Mitchell Heritage Prairie Historic District

**Breweries/Wineries/Distilleries:**
Prairie Fire Winery, Candles & Lavender (Paxico, KS)

**Town Celebrations:**
Eskridge Fall Festival, Eskridge, KS (Last Saturday in October)
Hot Alma Nights, Alma, KS (3rd Saturday of August)
Paxico Blues Festival, Paxico, KS (3rd Saturday of September)

# WALLACE COUNTY
## EST. 1868 - POPULATION: 1,512

Known as the second least-populous county in Kansas and the home
of Mount Sunflower, Wallace County was named after the legendary
Union general W. H. L. Wallace.

# SHARON SPRINGS, KS ★☆
### POPULATION: 751 – TOWN 164 OF 627 (4-12-23)

Eagle Tail station was established in 1868 but was later renamed
Sharon Springs in 1886 once the Western Town Site Company
created a formal townsite. Sharon Springs is an eponym for a town of
the same name in New York. It was assigned the title of the Wallace
County seat in 1887 and, for a long time, served as the largest trading
center in a one-thousand-square-mile radius. In 1903, then-President
Theodore Roosevelt was touring the Midwest and the rapidly
expanding railroad scene. One of his stops was in Sharon Springs,
where he spoke to residents and attended a service at the Methodist
Church. Before departing, Pearl Gorsuch offered Roosevelt a two-
week-old badger as a pet to take back to the White House with him.
He happily obliged and exclaimed that "Wallace County was a corking
good time," and the badger was named Josiah. It lived with Roosevelt
and his family for some time before being relocated to the Bronx Zoo
in New York City when it grew up. The town briefly cracked the 1000-
resident mark in the 1970s when the Census reported its population
as 1,012 individuals. It is the closest city to Mt. Sunflower, the highest
point in Kansas at approximately 4,039 feet above sea level.

# Lodging Recommendation:
## Mt. Sunflower B&B
## 229 N Gardner St
## Sharon Springs, KS 67758

# WALLACE, KS

In 1865, the United States Army constructed Fort Wallace, a significant early US Cavalry Fort utilized until 1882 and occupied by famous military names such as George Custer and George Forsyth. The town of Wallace would come about in the 1870s and would be formally incorporated by an act of the legislature in 1887. The post office preceded the town's founding, as it was opened on August 15, 1872. Fort Wallace Museum invites visitors to see a stage station riddled with bullet holes and a large, barbed wire buffalo.

**Adjacent Counties:** Sherman (N), Logan (E), Wichita (SE), Greeley (S)

**Unincorporated/Ghost Towns:** Weskan

**National Register of Historic Places:**
**Wallace:** Clark-Robidoux House, Pond Creek Station

**Golf Courses:**
Sharon Springs Golf Course, Public (Sharon Springs, KS)

Sumner County Photos: Argonia, Caldwell, Caldwell, Caldwell, Conway Springs, Conway Springs, Oxford, Wellington

Thomas County Photos: Brewster, Brewster, Colby, Colby, Colby, Colby, Gem, Rexford

509

Trego County Photos: Collyer, Collyer, WaKeeney, WaKeeney, WaKeeney, WaKeeney, WaKeeney, WaKeeney

Wabaunsee County Photos: Alma, Alma, Alta Vista, Eskridge, Maple Hill, McFarland, Paxico, Paxico

Wallace County Photos: Sharon Springs, Sharon Springs, Sharon Springs, Wallace, Wallace, Wallace, Wallace, Wallace

# WASHINGTON COUNTY
## EST. 1857 - POPULATION: 5,530

Washington County is officially named after the first President of the United States, George Washington.

# BARNES, KS
## POPULATION: 165 – TOWN 8 OF 627 (2-19-23)
Once known as Elm Grove, the town of Barnes was founded in 1870 as a shipping station on the Missouri Pacific Railroad. It was named for A. S. Barnes, a stockholder of the Central Branch Union Pacific Railroad, the other railroad that went through town. The inventor of the ICEE drink, Omar Knedlik, was born and raised here before he invented the now-famous beverage (also called Slurpees by 7-Eleven) in Coffeyville, Kansas. The founder of the Alaskan Independence Party (an Alaskan nationalist political party that advocated for Alaska to become an independent country), Joe Vogler, was born on a farm outside town.

# GREENLEAF, KS
## POPULATION: 350 – TOWN 9 OF 627 (2-19-23)
Founded in 1876 and incorporated four years later in 1880, Greenleaf was started as a station on the Missouri Pacific Railway. A. W. Greenleaf, once treasurer of the Central Branch Pacific Railroad, is its namesake. Former names for the town's post office included Round Grove, Prospect Hill, and Hopper.

# HADDAM, KS
## POPULATION: 110 – TOWN 20 OF 627 (2-20-23)
Haddam, Kansas, borrowed its name from a town in Connecticut of the same name. It began in 1869 when J. W. Taylor opened his store there, and a post office was established. It was once situated on the Chicago, Burlington & Quincy Railway. For a short while, there was a neighboring town called "West Haddam," founded by a gentleman named Whitney, and the post office would move between the two towns. They consolidated in 1874.

# HANOVER, KS

**POPULATION: 690 – TOWN 24 OF 627 (2-20-23)**

The predominantly German settlement of Hanover began around 1869, and by 1872, it was incorporated as a city of Kansas. Town founders Geret Hollenberg and his wife Sophia Brockmeyer opted to name it after Hanover, Germany. "Hollenberg Station" served as essentially a rest stop for Pony Express riders in 1869, where they could enjoy a warm meal for 27 cents or a night of safety and sleep. It is the final surviving building along the original route, today operated as the Hollenberg Pony Express Station State Historic Site.

 **Restaurant Recommendation:
Ricky's Cafe
323 W North St
Hanover, KS 66945**

# HOLLENBERG, KS

**POPULATION: 10 – TOWN 23 OF 627 (2-20-23)**

Hollenberg's population has dwindled to just ten residents as of the last Census, although its highest recorded population was as many as 250 individuals in 1910. The town was founded in the spring of 1872 by the town's first store owner, G. H. Hollenberg, and it was later that the St. Joseph & Grand Island Railroad would be constructed in the area. In April of the year it was founded, the post office arrived.

# LINN, KS

**POPULATION: 387 – TOWN 10 OF 627 (2-19-23)**

The original name for this community was Summit before it was later changed to honor Lewis F. Linn, a United States Senator for Missouri from 1833 to 1843. Founded along the Missouri Pacific Railroad, the town was established in 1877, and the first post office came to town on January 25, 1878.

# MAHASKA, KS

**POPULATION: 46 – TOWN 19 OF 627 (2-20-23)**

Mahaska was named after "Mah-hos-kah," the Chief of the Kiowa tribe of Native Americans, after it was founded in 1887 by L. Noham. That same year, it received its first post office. The central railroad in its early days was the Chicago, Rock Island & Pacific Railroad. The

40th Parallel, also known as the Sixth Principal Meridian, was marked here in 1856. The marker is significant because it was the origin point for the original land surveys for Kansas and Nebraska, large portions of Colorado and Wyoming, and even part of South Dakota. It wasn't until 1976 that the monument was rediscovered, and a new marker was dedicated in 1987. Charles D. McAtee, a former FBI agent, director of the Kansas prison system, and Marine Corps officer, was from Mahaska.

# MORROWVILLE, KS
**POPULATION: 114 – TOWN 21 OF 627 (2-20-23)**
This small town in the northwestern portion of Washington County was platted in 1884 following the confirmation of the Missouri and Burlington Railroad through the area. For years, the post office was called Morrow Station until, in 1894, it was changed to Morrowville because it was confused with the town of Morrill (located in Brown County). In 1923, Jim Cummings was watching a ditch near his farm being filled with mules and slip scrapers, and he thought that there must be a better way to do the task. With the help of other locals, John Earl McLeod (draftsman) and J. D. Lewis (blacksmith), this idea eventually became the world's first bulldozer. A replica of his invention is still on display at Morrowville city park.

# PALMER, KS
**POPULATION: 125 – TOWN 11 OF 627 (2-19-23)**
Palmer, pop. 125, began as another stopping point for rail traffic along the Missouri Pacific Railroad. It was founded in 1878, the same year it got its first post office, and named in honor of J. Palmer.

# VINING, KS
**POPULATION: 43 – TOWN 13 OF 627 (2-19-23)**
Vining, located adjacent to the larger town of Clifton (population 454), was first called West Clifton when it was platted in 1877. It was ultimately renamed Vining in 1881 for E. P. Vining, a railroad agent. Like its larger counterpart, Vining was noted in its early days for its location at a junction of the Missouri Pacific and Union Pacific Railroads.

# WASHINGTON, KS ★☆

Washington has served as the county seat of Washington County since it was founded in 1860 by George G. Pierce's town company. It was strategically placed where the Missouri Pacific and Chicago, Burlington & Quincy Railroads would meet at a junction. When the American Civil War broke out in 1861, the community's growth reached a standstill until its conclusion half a decade later. During that time, the community was protected primarily by two stockade buildings: the Washington Company House and Woolbert's Stockade Hotel (both built in 1860 and used until 1865). The Washington County Museum invites people to explore more of the stories and the people from previous eras of Washington. The actor who played the mayor of Munchkinland in the 1939 *Wizard of Oz* film, Charlie Becker, lived here for a short while.

Clifton is only partially located in Washington County (see Clay County).

**Adjacent Counties:** Marshall (E), Riley (SE), Clay (S), Cloud (SW), Republic (W)

**Unincorporated/Ghost Towns:** Hopewell, Lanham, Strawberry

**National Register of Historic Places:**
**Barnes:** Washington County Kingpost
**Hanover:** Hollenberg Pony Express Station
**Mahaska:** Mahaska Rural High School #3, Site No. JF00-072
**Morrowville:** Lowe Center School-District 115
**Washington:** Washington County Courthouse, Washington County Jail and Sheriff's Residence, John F. Wayland House

**Breweries/Wineries/Distilleries:**
Kansas Territory Brewing Company (Washington, KS)

**Golf Courses:**
Cedar Hills Golf Course, Public (Washington, KS)

**Town Celebrations:**
Frontier Days, Haddam, KS (2nd Weekend of August)
Hanover Days of 49, Hanover, KS (Weekend before 4th of July)
Labor Day Celebration, Palmer, KS (Labor Day Weekend)

# WICHITA COUNTY
## EST. 1873 - POPULATION: 2,152

Wichita County is one of eleven counties in Kansas that derives its name from a Native American tribe (the Wichita people) that once called Kansas home.

# LEOTI, KS ★☆
## POPULATION: 1,475 – TOWN 436 OF 627 (8-16-23)

Leoti is a town of 1,475 inhabitants that serves as the only municipality and the county seat of Wichita County, Kansas. The etymology of the town's name is widely disputed amongst the locals, as it was potentially named for three varying reasons: after Leoti Gray, the daughter of a member of the town company, in honor of Leoti Kibbee, one of the earliest residents, or for a Native American word that roughly translates to "prairie flower." For a very brief stint between January 1886 and January 1887, the name was changed to Bonasa. The month following the restoration of the name would turn out to be the darkest moment in the community's history, when several men went into the neighboring (presently unincorporated) town of Coronado and injured or killed several people to ensure that Leoti would be awarded the county seat in perpetuity. Another village called Farmer City was equally as eager to win the title, although Leoti came away with the honor as the two other communities faded out of existence. The Missouri Pacific Railroad served the needs of Leoti and allowed it to retain much of its population despite significant drought and famine in the area for years. 7x Pro Bowler Steve Tasker, the only special teams player in NFL history to win the Pro Bowl MVP, has ties to Leoti, as does Ben Diggins, who had a brief stint with the Milwaukee Brewers in 2002. Paleontologist Marion Charles Bonner spent much of his time in Leoti, although he was responsible for significant fossil discoveries throughout Gove, Logan, and Scott County. The Wichita County Historical Society is responsible for two museums in Leoti, the Washington-Ames House and the Museum of the Great Plains.

**Adjacent Counties:** Logan (N), Scott (E), Kearny (S), Hamilton (SW), Greeley (W), Wallace (NW)
**Unincorporated/Ghost Towns:** Coronado, Farmer City, Lydia, Marienthal, Selkirk

**Leoti:** Municipal Auditorium and City Hall, William B. and Julia Washington House

**Golf Courses:**
Leoti Country Club, Semi-Private (Leoti, KS)

# WILSON COUNTY
## EST. 1855 - POPULATION: 8,624

Wilson County was named after Hiero Wilson, a colonel in the Union Army.

# ALTOONA, KS
### POPULATION: 354 – TOWN 352 OF 627 (7-16-23)
The original name of Altoona was Geddesburg when it was organized in 1869 by Dr. T. F. C. Todd, but a year later, it was renamed after the Pennsylvanian city. It was also then that the post office elected to formulate an office there on April 11, 1870. The rise of Altoona came with the Missouri Pacific Railroad when saw and flour mills, a zinc smelter, and cement and brick plants were erected to stimulate the local economy. Four particular persons of note heed from Altoona, them being Benjamin N. Woodson, "Mr. Life Insurance," Oren E. Long, the tenth Territorial Governor of Hawaii, actress Ida Moore, and Tom Hamilton, who had a brief stint in the MLB with the Athletics.

**Restaurant Recommendation:**
**Prairie Nut Hut**
**1306 Quincy St**
**Altoona, KS 66710**

# BENEDICT, KS
### POPULATION: 69 – TOWN 351 OF 627 (7-16-23)
Established at the junction of the Atchison, Topeka & Santa Fe and the Missouri Pacific Railroads in 1866, Benedict takes its name from Honorary S. S. Benedict. Its existence came to be due to the railroads being constructed through the territory, and the town would grow to include a bank, post office, and several iron bridges that crossed the Verdigris River. After being incorporated as a city of the third class in

1905, Benedict would reach its highest number of residents in its recorded history leading up to the 1920 Census at 275 persons.

# BUFFALO, KS
**POPULATION: 217 – TOWN 350 OF 627 (7-16-23)**
Buffalo, once a town with a population of 807 people according to the 1910 Census, was founded in 1867 when the postal service established an office there with Chester Gould at its helm. Buffalo was selected after the nearby tributary of the same name, taking its name from the American bison that once ruled the Great Plains. A store and a hotel were amongst the first buildings to be erected, and in 1886, the Missouri Pacific Railroad arrived to further the town's lines of business and aid in constructing a brief plant and mill. Incorporation as a city of the third class came in 1898, and E. B. Johnson was elected mayor. Buffalo native MLB pitcher Claude Willoughby pitched 219 games for the Phillies and the Pirates throughout the late 1920s, and Milburn G. Apt, a U.S. Air Force test pilot, became the first man to exceed Mach 3 (three times the speed of sound) in an aircraft in 1956. Wilson State Fishing Lake is a favorite amongst locals for hiking and fishing.

# COYVILLE, KS
**POPULATION: 60 – TOWN 403 OF 627 (7-20-23)**
The namesake of this Wilson County hamlet is Oscar Coy, who assumed the duties of postmaster in May 1866. The first store had been opened seven years prior by Albert Hagen, who traded frequently with the local Osage tribe of Native Americans. As the town grew, a sawmill and flour mill were erected, and soon banks, general stores, and other enterprises would come about. The townspeople opted to incorporate as a city in 1906. The city has steadily lost population throughout the years, although it increased from 46 persons to 60 between the 2010 and 2020 Censuses.

# FREDONIA, KS ★☆
**POPULATION: 2,151 – TOWN 402 OF 627 (7-20-23)**
The first settlers of what would shortly become Fredonia were Dr. J. Barrett and Albert Troxel, who worked together to create the town's first store. Justus Fellows arrived around the same time and became president of the town company that worked to plat the townsite in 1868. The city was laid out along the St. Louis & San Francisco Railway and acquired a post office shortly after that, in contrast to a

small town half a mile north, Twin Mounds, which has since been vacated entirely. Soon, a courthouse was erected. Fredonia was formally named the county seat of Wilson County, which attracted the attention of the Missouri Pacific Railroad and the Atchison, Topeka & Santa Fe line. After being incorporated in 1871, the town's population nearly doubled between the 1900 and 1910 Census from 1,650 to 3,040 individuals, and thereafter, a large vein of coal was discovered in the area, furthering its growth. The discovery brought significant industry to the town, such as cement works (in operation from 1907 to 2012), two brick plants and gas plants, oil, flour, and electric mills, a canning factory, and even the most prominent window glass plant in the Western United States at that time. The Archers-Daniel-Midland corporation, now a multinational food processing and trading company, operated a soybean processing facility in Fredonia from 1928 to 2003. Fredonia's Wilson County Historical Museum operates under the direction of the Wilson County Historical Society. Amongst the town's most notable residents are Benjamin S. Paulen, the 23rd Governor of Kansas, Kendall Trainor (the 1988 leader in field goals per game in college football for the University of Arkansas), Brigadier General Marcus B. Bell, and Washington and Nevada Congressmen Charles Stokes and George W. Malone.

**Restaurant Recommendation:
The Kitchen Table
114 S 3rd St
Fredonia, KS 66736**

**Restaurant Recommendation:
Tri-Mee Drive-In
1017 Washington St
Fredonia, KS 66736**

# NEODESHA, KS
**POPULATION: 2,275 – TOWN 353 OF 627 (7-16-23)**
"Neodesha" is derived from an Osage Native American word meaning "meeting of the waters," a name given by the local tribe because of the substantial number of little villages that were located in the area of the confluence of the Fall and Verdigris Rivers. A trading post was established in 1867 by A. McCartney and A. K. Phelon with the blessing of the Osage tribe, and in 1868, two town promoters (John B. Keyes and R S. Futhey) arrived to purchase the site for $500.

Growth within the first few years was rapid as a sawmill and hundreds of other buildings were erected. After the signing of the Drum Creek Treaty, which sent the Osage off to "Indian Territory," the growth expanded exponentially, and incorporation came as soon as 1871. The St. Louis & San Francisco Railroad and the Missouri Pacific Railroad brought with them the capacities to start industries such as a bottle glass factory, a broom factory, a zinc smelter, a cement and brick and tile plant, mills, and oil wells and a refinery. One such well was the Norman No. 1 Oil Well, dug in 1892, that would become the first of many commercially successful wells dug throughout the Mid-Continent oil field that stretches north from Kansas to down south throughout most of Oklahoma, Texas, and Louisiana. The Norman 1. Museum pays tribute to the designation and early community history. Neodesha is one of only about a dozen places in the country that offers their high school district (Kansas USD 461) to attend any U.S. Pell Grant-approved college, community college, or technical school of their choice for a free or discounted rate. Students who attend KS-USD 461 from 6th to 12th grade qualify for 100% paid tuition. Noted Neodeshians are Lyle D. Goodhue, the inventor of the "bug bomb" and aerosol containers, Grimes Poznikov, a decorated street performer from San Francisco, violin instructor Dorothy DeLay, and Clay T. Whitehead, director of the White House Office of Telecommunications Policy under the Richard Nixon administration.

# NEW ALBANY, KS
**POPULATION: 57 – TOWN 401 OF 627 (7-20-23)**
The establishment of New Albany as a townsite came in the same year, 1866 when the postal service placed a post office there. William Hall was named the first postmaster. Its name was given as an eponym for New Albany, Indiana. Men by the names of Hall & Mooney and Jackson & Hickson founded the first store and sawmill and gristmill (respectively), and subsequently, more mills, churches, a brick plant, stone quarries, and banks came to town, as well as the St. Louis & San Francisco Railroad. New Albany's highest population came at the 1920 Census; there were 223 residents then.

**Adjacent Counties:** Woodson (N), Allen (NE), Neosho (E), Montgomery (S), Elk (W), Greenwood (NW)

**Unincorporated/Ghost Towns:** Buxton, Guilford, Lafontaine, Rest, Roper, Vilas

**National Register of Historic Places:**
**Coyville:** Brush Creek Bridge
**Fredonia:** Dr. A. C. Flack House, Gold Dust Hotel, U.S. Post Office-Fredonia
**Neodesha:** Brown Hotel, Dorothy DeLay House, Neodesha City Hall Building, Norman No. 1 Oil Well Site, U.S. Post Office-Neodesha

**Golf Courses:**
Fredonia Country Club, Semi-Private (Fredonia, KS)

**Town Celebrations:**
Fredonia Sausage Fest, Fredonia, KS (Last Saturday in August)
Old Iron Days Show, Fredonia, KS. (Last Weekend in September)

# WOODSON COUNTY
## EST. 1855 - POPULATION: 3,115

Woodson County honors Kansas legend Daniel Woodson, who served as a five-time acting governor of Kansas Territory between 1855 and 1857.

# NEOSHO FALLS, KS
## POPULATION: 134 – TOWN 317 OF 627 (6-28-23)

Neosho Falls was founded in 1857 by brothers Benjamin F. and N. S. Goss, who were the leaders of the town company and the town's first postmaster, respectively. They opted to name the city after the Neosho River, which would ironically be the town's demise when the Great Flood of 1951 decimated its infrastructure and forced large numbers of its population to move elsewhere. Neosho Falls was the first town in Woodson County and the first judicial seat. When it welcomed the Missouri, Kansas & Texas, and the Atchison, Topeka & Santa Fe Railroads to the area, many industries sprouted, ranging from oil wells and flour mills to sorghum mills, sawmills, and a grain elevator. President Rutherford B. Hayes and his wife visited the area in 1879 as attendees of the Neosho Valley fair, and the townspeople gifted him a buckhorn chair to remember the town by. The rock band Kansas immortalized the town's flooding incident in their 1988 album *In the Spirit of Things*.

522

# TORONTO, KS
**POPULATION: 206 – TOWN 404 OF 627 (7-20-23)**

Toronto, one of only three incorporated communities in Woodson County, was founded in 1869 by a town company. The officers named it after Canada's most populous city, Toronto. The arrival of the Missouri Pacific and the Atchison, Topeka & Santa Fe Railroads, firstly in 1882, aided in the construction of over 80 new buildings and ultimately led to the town's incorporation as a municipality three years later. The post office began in 1870, and S. R. Kellogg was named postmaster. Buried in the Toronto Township Cemetery is John C. Woods, a master sergeant of the United States Army who was one of two men to carry out the Nuremberg executions of former leaders of Germany's Third Reich. Cross Timbers State Park is a favorite amongst locals for fishing and birdwatching. *Do Lizards Have Lips?* is a book by Iris Craver that covers tall tales and true stories as told by many of the town's residents, such as a remedy of cow manure and molasses that can allegedly be used to cure headaches.

# YATES CENTER, KS ★☆
**POPULATION: 1,352 – TOWN 349 OF 627 (7-16-23)**

The selection of Yates Center as the judicial seat of Woodson County predates the existence of the town itself, the only instance of such a phenomenon to have occurred in Kansas. In 1867, Neosho Falls in the northeastern portion of the county had already served as the seat for nearly a decade. County residents disliked its location and petitioned for a new town to be founded at the geographical center. Proprietors of the towns of Kalida and Defiance, both of which had aspirations to become the county seat, convinced Abner Yates to plat a townsite on his land so that the two communities could move their buildings there and start a new community. Yates Center would be named the county seat in 1876 after Abner Yates donated land for a courthouse, churches, and parks to be constructed. Another proposed name for the townsite at the time was Butler. Following the arrival of the Atchison, Topeka & Santa Fe, and the Missouri Pacific Railroads, the townspeople erected an opera house and auditorium, stone quarries and bottling works, schools and churches, a furniture factory, and all the other typical lines of enterprise. Yates Center pays tribute to its hay-centric heritage with an annual event called HayFest, a nod to the city's former designation as the "Prairie Hay Capital of the World." This history and more are further explored by the work done at the Woodson County Historical Museum.

**Adjacent Counties:** Coffey (N), Anderson (NE), Allen (E), Neosho (SE), Wilson (S), Greenwood (W)

**Unincorporated/Ghost Towns:** Belmont, Cookville, Defiance, Durand, Kalida, Piqua, Vernon

**National Register of Historic Places:**
**Yates Center:** Stockbrands and Kemmerer Department Store, Woodson County Courthouse, Yates Center Carnegie Library, Yates Center Courthouse Square Historic District

**Golf Courses:**
Lake Side Golf Course, Public (Yates Center, KS)

**Town Celebrations:**
HayFest, Yates Center, KS (2nd Weekend of October)
Toronto Days, Toronto, KS (Independence Day Weekend)
Yates Center Days, Yates Center, KS (Memorial Day Weekend)

# WYANDOTTE COUNTY
## EST. 1859 - POPULATION: 169,245

Wyandotte County, the fourth-most populous in Kansas because of Kansas City, took its name from the Wyandot people who lived in Kansas for some time.

# BONNER SPRINGS, KS
## POPULATION: 7,837 – TOWN 282 OF 627 (6-12-23)
The first settlers arrived at Bonner Springs in 1812, when the Chouteau brothers, a couple of fur traders from France, founded the "Four Houses" trading post along the Kansas River and a local spring. Their post is widely considered the first center of business in the state. Town founder John McDaniel platted the townsite in 1855 and named it for Henry Tiblow, a member of the Delaware tribe of Native Americans who ran a local ferry across the river. It would later be renamed by Philo Clark (who purchased the land from McDaniel in 1885) for Robert E. Bonner, the founder of the former newspaper The New York Ledger. The springs were said to have medicinal and healing properties, which attracted visitors from far and wide. A large cement factory, retail establishments, schools, churches, and lumber yards came about following the arrival of the Union Pacific and the

Atchison, Topeka & Santa Fe Railroads. Its four main tourism draws are the Kansas City Renaissance Festival (held every year since 1977), which brings in upwards of 200,000 visitors on an annual basis, Azura Amphitheater, an outdoor venue with a capacity for 18,000 concert or event-goers, the National Agricultural Center and Hall of Fame, and the Wyandotte County Historical Museum. Locals also heavily recommend the Moon Marble Company, where visitors can watch owner Bruce Breslow hand-blow marbles and tour the business. Musicians Myra Taylor (jazz singer), Bobby Watson (saxophonist), and Gene Clark (founding member of the folk-rock band The Byrds) have Bonner Springs ties, as do athletes Ed Nealy (1993 NBA champion) and David Jaynes (quarterback and finalist for the 1973 Heisman Trophy award).

# EDWARDSVILLE, KS
## POPULATION: 4,717 – TOWN 549 OF 627 (9-29-23)
Edwardsville was named in remembrance of John H. Edwards, who, at the time of the city's establishment, was the general passenger agent of the Union Pacific Railroad. Formerly platted in 1869, the land was once owned by Delaware Chief Half Moon, who elected to sell it to General Smith, who then sold it onward to William Knous, who is credited with being its founder. The post office predates the formation of the town (1867), but the other early town organizations and storefronts came in the late 1860s and the following decade. Since being incorporated in 1915, Edwardsville has enjoyed constant growth in its population, from 243 inhabitants in 1940 to 619 in 1970, 4,146 in 2000, and 4,717 today. Its most famous past resident was Junius George Groves, widely known as the "Potato King of the World" for his incredible potato-producing tactics and notoriety for being one of the wealthiest African Americans of the early portion of the twentieth century.

# KANSAS CITY, KS ★☆
## POPULATION: 156,607 – TOWN 540 OF 627 (9-27-23)
Kansas City was once the principal metropolis of Kansas, having been the largest city in the state for a number of years before neighboring Overland Park and the City of Wichita overtook it in population. Primarily considered a precursor to Kansas City, the town of Wyandotte was laid out in 1857 by John H. Miller, and half of its town board was composed of members of the Wyandot tribe of Native Americans. Sawmills, stores, and congregations were erected, and workers of all professions flocked to start their new lives here. Kansas

City's Missouri counterpart was incorporated in 1850 as the City of Kansas, but because settlements proliferated on the lands both eastern and western of the Missouri River, the City of Kansas (in Kansas) took on incorporation status of its own in October of 1872. The first mayor was James Boyle. Its location at the confluence of the Kansas and the Missouri Rivers made trade and travel convenient for early settlers, and the area was incredibly prosperous. Rails for streetcars were laid out between Armourdale, Kansas City, Missouri and Kansas, and Wyandotte, and the manufacturing industry began to expand at an unbelievable pace. Factories produced everything from brick, furniture, tinware, wheelbarrows, hay presses, gasoline engines, and soap, and cotton and flour mills, meat-packing plants, and stockyards added to the local economy. This vital trade resulted in the formation of numerous other communities in this part of Kansas, including Armstrong, Argentine, Armourdale, Quindaro, Riverview, and Rosedale, all of which were ultimately consolidated into the larger Kansas City between March 1886 and 1922. Numerous railroads, namely the Atchison, Topeka & Santa Fe, the Chicago, Rock Island & Pacific, the St. Louis & San Francisco, the Missouri Pacific, the Union Pacific, the Chicago & Great Western, the Kansas City Northwestern, and the Kansas City Southern Railways, took advantage of the industries. Prominent points of interest throughout the city include Village West, home to Kansas Speedway, a racetrack host to NASCAR Cup Series races, Great Wolf Lodge, and Monarchs Stadium, once the site of the well-established Kansas City Monarchs Negro League baseball team (in operation from 1920 to 1965). The Rosedale Arch, Memorial Hall, Granada Theater, Grinter Place State Historic Site, Strawberry Hill Museum and Cultural Center (known for their display of Pope John Paul II's toothpaste, pillows, and other objects used on his visits to the United States, the Mule Deer Country Museum at Cabela's (the most extensive collection of mule deer on Earth), and the Wyandotte County Courthouse (as Kansas City is the county seat of Wyandotte County) are other noteworthy sites of cultural significance. Sporting Kansas City of Major League Soccer is the city's sole men's professional sports team. It plays its games at Children's Mercy Park, which additionally hosts the soccer matches for the National Women's Soccer League's Kansas City Current. Three institutions aid in bringing higher learning to the area Donnelly College, a private Catholic college founded in 1949, Kansas City Kansas Community College, a public-two year college established in 1923, and the University of Kansas Medical Center, whose primary campus is located in Kansas City as of June 21, 1920. As is to be expected with metropolitan areas, hundreds of figures of note once called Kansas

City their home: Ed Asner (seven-time Primetime Emmy Award winner), Jason Aaron (comic book writer known for his work on *Thor*, *The Avengers*, and other series), Scott Foley (actor in television shows such as *The Unit* and *Scrubs*), Janelle Monáe (eight-time Grammy Award nominated singer and songwriter), Paul Revere Braniff (co-founder of Braniff International Airways), Maurice Greene (once the record holder or the fastest 100m dash in history at 9.79 seconds and a multi-year gold medalist in the 2000 Olympics), Ben Fernandez (the first major presidential candidate of Hispanic origin), Paul Harrington (the inventor of the Harrington Rod, a revolutionary device or straightening the human spine), Earl Cole (the victor of season fourteen of *Survivor: Fiji*), Matt Vogel (the current puppeteer of Kermit the Frog of *The Muppets* and Big Bird of *Sesame Street*), Edward F. Arn (the 32nd Governor of Kansas), Charlie "Yardbird" Parker (saxophonist and pioneer of bebop jazz), Al Christy (noted television and radio broadcaster), William N. Alsbrook (the inventor of the Tuskegee Airmen), and dozens of others.

**Restaurant Recommendation:**
**Chixen Kansas City**
**1407 Southwest Blvd**
**Kansas City, KS 66103**

**Restaurant Recommendation:**
**Fritz's**
**250 N 18th St**
**Kansas City, KS 66102**

**Restaurant Recommendation:**
**Mason Jar Brews & Burgers**
**941 N 74 Dr**
**Kansas City, KS 66112**

Lake Quivira is only partially located in Wyandotte County (see Johnson County).

**Adjacent Counties:** Johnson (S), Leavenworth (W)
**Unincorporated/Ghost Towns:** Argentine, Armourdale, Armstrong, Four Houses, Loring, Morris, Piper, Rosedale, Turner, Welborn, Wyandotte

## National Register of Historic Places:
**Bonner Springs:** Bonner Springs High School, Lake of the Forest Historic District
**Edwardsville:** Roy Williamson House
**Kansas City:** Argentine Carnegie Library, Brotherhood Block, Castle Rock, Fairfax Hills Historic District, Fire Station No. 9, Franklin Elementary School, Judge Louis Gates House, Granada Theater, Grinter Place, H. W. Gates Funeral Home, Hanover Heights Neighborhood Historic District, Huron Cemetery, Kansas City, Kansas City Hall and Fire Headquarters, Kansas City, Kansas High School Gymnasium and Laboratory, Kansas City, Kansas YMCA Building, Lowell Elementary School, Horace Mann Elementary School, Cordell D. Meeks Sr. House, Northeast Junior High School, Quindaro Townsite, Rosedale World War I Memorial Arch, St. Augustine Hall, Saint Margaret's Hospital, Sauer Castle, Schleifer-McAlpine House, Scottish Rite Temple, Theodore Shafer House, Shawnee Street Overpass, Simmons Funeral Home, Soldiers and Sailors Memorial Building, Sumner High School and Athletic Field, Town House Hotel, Trowbridge Archeological Site, Vernon School, Welborn Community Congregational Church, Westheight Apartments Historic District, Westheight Manor District, Whitefeather Spring, Whittier School, Wyandotte County Courthouse, Wyandotte High School

## Breweries/Wineries/Distilleries:
Outfield Beer Company (Bonner Springs, KS)
Range 23 Brewing (Kansas City, KS)
Rowe Ridge Vineyard & Winery (Kansas City, KS)

## Golf Courses:
Dubs Dread Golf Club, Public (Kansas City, KS)
Lake Of The Forest Golf Course, Private (Bonner Springs, KS)
Painted Hills Golf Course, Public (Kansas City, KS)
Sunflower Hills Golf Course, Public (Bonner Springs, KS)

## Town Celebrations:
Edwardsville Days, Edwardsville, KS (April)
Kansas City Renaissance Festival, Bonner Springs, KS (Weekends from Labor Day to Mid-October)
Plaza Art Fair, Kansas City, KS (Third Weekend after Labor Day)
Tacos and Tequila Festival, Kansas City, KS (Varies)
Tiblow Days, Bonner Springs, KS (Last Weekend in August)

Washington County Photos: Barnes, Greenleaf, Haddam, Hanover, Mahaska, Morrowville, Washington, Washington

Wichita County Photos: Leoti (all)

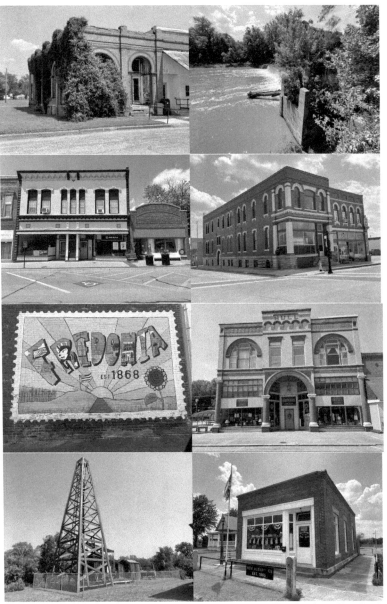

Wilson County Photos: Altoona, Altoona, Fredonia, Fredonia, Fredonia, Neodesha, Neodesha, New Albany

531

Woodson County Photos: Neosho Falls, Toronto, Toronto, Yates Center, Yates Center, Yates Center, Yates Center

Wyandotte County Photos: Bonner Springs, Kansas City, Kansas City, Kansas City, Kansas City, Kansas City, Kansas City, Kansas City

533

# QR Code Tutorial

During a Wandermore project, we snap tens of thousands of photos of businesses, churches, parks, and other points of interest in each community. Since one book cannot possibly have all the photos in print, Wandermore has created a unique QR code system that enables readers to take a virtual tour of every incorporated community in the state. An online photo album of each town can be accessed by scanning a "QR Code." They're quite simple to use, and the instructions below will teach you how to use them with ease!

To scan a QR code, follow these instructions:

1) **Open the "Camera" app on any mobile device.**
2) **Position your camera over the pixelated box (as seen above). Make sure your camera can see the entire box, or it won't work!**
3) **Tap the link or notification bubble that appears at the top of your screen.**
4) **Voila! You now have access to our pictures and videos from the specified town.**
5) **Note: Some users may have to download a "QR code reader" app on their smartphone or device to scan the codes. Several varieties of these apps can be found for free in your device's App Store.**

If the QR codes become defunct in the distant future, please contact wandermorepublishing@gmail.com. We will create new ways to access the photo albums through our website or social media outlets.

# QR Code Photo Albums

Abbyville

Abilene

Admire

Agenda

Agra

Albert

Alden

Alexander

Allen

Alma

Almena

Altamont

Alta Vista

Alton

Altoona

Americus

Andale

Andover

Anthony

Arcadia

Argonia

Arkansas City

Arlington

Arma

| Ashland | Assaria | Atchison |
| Athol | Atlanta | Attica |
| Atwood | Auburn | Augusta |
| Aurora | Axtell | Baldwin City |

| | | |
|---|---|---|
| Barnard | Barnes | Bartlett |
| Basehor | Bassett | Baxter Springs |
| Bazine | Beattie | Bel Aire |
| Belle Plaine | Belleville | Beloit |

Belpre

Belvue

Benedict

Bennington

Bentley

Benton

Bern

Beverly

Bird City

Bison

Blue Mound

Blue Rapids

| Bluff City | Bogue | Bonner Springs |
| Brewster | Bronson | Brookville |
| Brownell | Bucklin | Buffalo |
| Buhler | Bunker Hill | Burden |

Burdett     Burlingame     Burlington

Burns     Burr Oak     Burrton

Bushong     Bushton     Byers

Caldwell     Cambridge     Caney

| Canton | Carbondale | Carlton |
| Cassoday | Cawker City | Cedar |
| Cedar Point | Cedar Vale | Centralia |
| Chanute | Chapman | Chase |

Chautauqua

Cheney

Cherokee

Cherryvale

Chetopa

Cimarron

Circleville

Claflin

Clay Center

Clayton

Clearwater

Clifton

Climax     Clyde     Coats

Coffeyville     Colby     Coldwater

Collyer     Colony     Columbus

Colwich     Concordia     Conway Springs

| Coolidge | Copeland | Corning |
| Cottonwood Falls | Council Grove | Courtland |
| Coyville | Cuba | Cullison |
| Culver | Cunningham | Damar |

Danville   Dearing   Deerfield

Delia   Delphos   Denison

Denton   Derby   De Soto

Dexter   Dighton   Dodge City

Dorrance  Douglass  Downs

Dresden  Dunlap  Durham

Dwight  Earlton  Eastborough

Easton  Edgerton  Edmond

| Edna | Edwardsville | Effingham |
| Elbing | El Dorado | Elgin |
| Elk City | Elk Falls | Elkhart |
| Ellinwood | Ellis | Ellsworth |

Elmdale  Elsmore  Elwood

Emmett  Emporia  Englewood

Ensign  Enterprise  Erie

Esbon  Eskridge  Eudora

Eureka Everest Fairview

Fairway Fall River Florence

Fontana Ford Formoso

Fort Scott Fowler Frankfort

Frederick      Fredonia      Freeport

Frontenac      Fulton      Galatia

Galena      Galesburg      Galva

Garden City      Garden Plain      Gardner

Garfield          Garnett          Gas

Gaylord          Gem          Geneseo

Geuda Springs          Girard          Glade

Glasco          Glen Elder          Goddard

| Goessel | Goff | Goodland |
| Gorham | Gove City | Grainfield |
| Grandview Plaza | Great Bend | Greeley |
| Green | Greenleaf | Greensburg |

Grenola

Gridley

Grinnell

Gypsum

Haddam

Halstead

Hamilton

Hamlin

Hanover

Hanston

Hardtner

Harper

| Hartford | Harveyville | Havana |
| Haven | Havensville | Haviland |
| Hays | Haysville | Hazelton |
| Hepler | Herington | Herndon |

Hesston

Hiawatha

Highland

Hill City

Hillsboro

Hoisington

Holcomb

Hollenberg

Holton

Holyrood

Hope

Horace

| Horton | Howard | Hoxie |
| Hoyt | Hudson | Hugoton |
| Humboldt | Hunnewell | Hunter |
| Huron | Hutchinson | Independence |

Ingalls     Inman     Iola

Isabel     Iuka     Jamestown

Jennings     Jetmore     Jewell

Johnson City     Junction City     Kanopolis

| Kanorado | Kansas City | Kechi |
| Kensington | Kincaid | Kingman |
| Kinsley | Kiowa | Kirwin |
| Kismet | Labette | La Crosse |

La Cygne

La Harpe

Lake Quivira

Lakin

Lancaster

Lane

Langdon

Lansing

Larned

Latham

Latimer

Lawrence

Leavenworth        Leawood        Lebanon

Lebo        Lecompton        Lehigh

Lenexa        Lenora        Leon

Leona        Leonardville        Leoti

Le Roy

Lewis

Liberal

Liberty

Liebenthal

Lincoln

Lincolnville

Lindsborg

Linn

Linn Valley

Linwood

Little River

Logan Lone Elm Longford

Long Island Longton Lorraine

Lost Springs Louisburg Louisville

Lucas Luray Lyndon

Lyons          Macksville          Madison

Mahaska          Maize          Manchester

Manhattan          Mankato          Manter

Maple Hill          Mapleton          Marion

Marquette Marysville Matfield Green

Mayetta Mayfield McCracken

McCune McDonald McFarland

McLouth McPherson Meade

Medicine Lodge     Melvern     Menlo

Meriden     Merriam     Milan

Milford     Miltonvale     Minneapolis

Minneola     Mission     Mission Hills

Mission Woods     Moline     Montezuma

Moran     Morganville     Morland

Morrill     Morrowville     Moscow

Mound City     Moundridge     Mound Valley

Mount Hope    Mulberry    Mullinville

Mulvane    Munden    Muscotah

Narka    Nashville    Natoma

Neodesha    Neosho Falls    Neosho Rapids

Ness City

Netawaka

New Albany

New Cambria

New Strawn

Newton

Nickerson

Niotaze

Norcatur

North Newton

Norton

Nortonville

| Norwich | Oak Hill | Oakley |
| Oberlin | Offerle | Ogden |
| Oketo | Olathe | Olivet |
| Olmitz | Olpe | Olsburg |

Onaga      Oneida      Osage City

Osawatomie      Osborne      Oskaloosa

Oswego      Otis      Ottawa

Overbrook      Overland Park      Oxford

Ozawkie     Palco     Palmer

Paola     Paradise     Park

Park City     Parker     Parkerfield

Parkerville     Parsons     Partridge

Pawnee Rock   Paxico   Peabody

Penalosa   Perry   Peru

Phillipsburg   Pittsburg   Plains

Plainville   Pleasanton   Plevna

| Pomona | Portis | Potwin |
| Powhattan | Prairie View | Prairie Village |
| Pratt | Prescott | Preston |
| Pretty Prairie | Princeton | Protection |

Quenemo

Quinter

Radium

Ramona

Randall

Randolph

Ransom

Rantoul

Raymond

Reading

Redfield

Republic

Reserve  Rexford  Richfield

Richmond  Riley  Robinson

Roeland Park  Rolla  Rose Hill

Roseland  Rossville  Rozel

Rush Center     Russell     Russell Springs

Sabetha     Salina     Satanta

Savonburg     Sawyer     Scammon

Scandia     Schoenchen     Scott City

Scottsville

Scranton

Sedan

Sedgwick

Selden

Seneca

Severance

Severy

Seward

Sharon

Sharon Springs

Shawnee

Silver Lake     Simpson     Smith Center

Smolan     Soldier     Solomon

South Haven     South Hutchinson     Spearville

Speed     Spivey     Spring Hill

St. Francis     St. George     St. John

St. Marys     St. Paul     Stafford

Stark     Sterling     Stockton

Strong City     Sublette     Summerfield

Sun City      Susank      Sylvan Grove

Sylvia      Syracuse      Tampa

Tescott      Thayer      The Highlands

Timken      Tipton      Tonganoxie

Topeka      Toronto      Towanda

Tribune      Troy      Turon

Tyro      Udall      Ulysses

Uniontown      Utica      Valley Center

Valley Falls

Varner

Vermillion

Victoria

Vining

Viola

Virgil

WaKeeney

Wakefield

Waldo

Waldron

Wallace

Walnut

Walton

Wamego

Washington

Waterville

Wathena

Waverly

Webber

Weir

Wellington

Wellsville

West Mineral

Westmoreland    Westphalia    Westwood

Westwood Hills    Wetmore    Wheaton

White City    White Cloud    Whitewater

Whiting    Wichita    Willard

Williamsburg · Willis · Willowbrook

Wilmore · Wilsey · Wilson

Winchester · Windom · Winfield

Winona · Woodbine · Woodston

Yates Center       Yoder       Zenda

Zurich

# Kansas Campgrounds

Looking to enjoy the great outdoors of Kansas? Campgrounds are available to use all throughout the Sunflower State. Check with online sources to check availability prior to traveling and to find contact information.

Abilene – Central Kansas Free Fair (619 N. Rogers)
Abilene – Covered Wagon RV Resort (803 S Buckeye Ave)
Abilene – Walt's Four Seasons Campground (2500 Mink Rd)
Allen – Basecamp Flint Hills (204 W. 2nd St.)
Alma – Lake Wabaunsee (657 E Flint Hills Dr)
Altamont – Altamont City Lake (10500 Ness Rd)
Argonia – River Park (210 S Main)
Arkansas City – Cherokee Strip Campground (6916 306th Lane)
Arkansas City – Lou Ann's Campground (9423 292nd Rd)
Atchison – Warnock Lake Campground (17860 274th Rd)
Atwood – Atwood Lions RV Park (503 N 3rd)
Atwood – Cottonwood Lane RV Campsites at Lake Atwood (N Hwy 25)
Augusta – Santa Fe Lake & Campground (11367 SW Shore Dr)
Baldwin City – Douglas State Fishing Lake (Douglas County Rd 12)
Baxter Springs – Baxter Springs City Campground (Riverside West)
Belleville – Rocky Pond Park (East 12th St)
Beloit – Chautauqua Park & Water Park (301 Chautauqua Drive)
Blue Rapids – Riverside Park Campsite (West 5th St)
Blue Valley – Tuttle Creek – Randolph Park (Randolph Park Rd)
Burlington – Burlington RV Park (1420 Hudson St)
Burlington – John Redmond Lake (1565 Embankment Rd SW)
Burrton – Harvey County West Park Campground (15835 NW 24th St)
Burrton – Pete's Puddle (4801 N. Willow Lake Rd)
Canton – McPherson State Fishing Lake (2565 Pueblo Rd)
Cawker City – West Place RV Park (515 Cawker Lane)
Centerville – Big Sugar Ranch (12156 Ellis Rd)
Chanute – Safari RV Campground (3499 S Santa Fe Ave)
Chapman – Chapman Creek RV Park (2701 N. Marshall St)
Cheney – Cheney State Park (16000 N.E. 50th St.)
Cherryvale – Big Hill Lake (19000 Rd)
Chetopa – Elmore Park Campground (3109 N 3rd St)
Clifton – Berner Memorial Park (West Parallel)
Colby – Colby RV Park (155 E Willow)
Coldwater – Lake Coldwater (RR 1)
Columbus – T & S RV Park (1308 E Hwy 160)
Columbus – VFW Park Campground (660 E. Country Rd)
Concordia – Airport Park RV Park (3015 Blosser Drive)
Cottonwood Falls – Chase State Fishing Lake (1130 Lake Road)
Cottonwood Falls – Swope City Park & Campground (1715 210th Rd)
Council Grove – Canning Creek Cove Park & Campground (945 Lake Rd)
Deerfield – Deerfield Beach Campground (2385 Road 170)
Dexter – 4M Heritage Center (26798 212th Rd)

Dighton – Lane Co. Fairgrounds Campground (N 7th St)
Dodge City – Blue RV Park (2114 E. Wyatt Earp Blvd)
Dodge City – Dodge City KOA (701 Park St.)
Dodge City – Gunsmoke RV Park (11070 108 Rd)
Dodge City – Nendels Inn & Suites RV Sites (2523 E Wyatt Earp Blvd)
Dodge City – Riverside RV Park (500 E Cherry St)
Dorrance – Cedar Ridge Cabins (4420 205th Blvd)
Easton – Tranquility RV Park (201 S 1st Street)
Edna – City of Edna Campground (209 N Delaware)
El Dorado – Deer Grove RV Park (2873 SE US Hwy 54)
El Dorado – Walnut River Campground (618 NE Bluestem Rd)
Elk Falls – Elk Falls RV Park (819 7th St)
Elkhart – Cimarron National Grassland (242 E Hwy 56)
Elkhart – Prairie RV Park (48 East Highway 56)
Ellis – Cedar Bluff State Park (32001 147 Hwy)
Ellis – Ellis Lakeside Campground (815 Jefferson)
Elmdale – Camp Wood YMCA Retreat Center (1101 Camp Wood Rd)
Emporia – Emporia RV Park & Campground (4601 W Hwy 50)
Ensign – Hamilton Acres (10198 Wilburn Road)
Eureka – Bechtel Ranch Field Trial Grounds (957 G Rd)
Fall River – Fall River State Park (2381 Casner Creek Rd)
Fall River – Flint Oak (2639 Quail Rd)
Farlington – Crawford State Park (1 Lake Rd)
Fort Scott – Gunn Park & Campground (1010 Park Avenue)
Fredonia – West Park (199 Jefferson St.)
Garden City – Finney Co. Fair Campgrounds (209 Lake Avenue)
Garden City – R.J.'s RV Park (4100 E Hwy 50)
Garland – Black Dogs Farm (351 230th St.)
Garnett – Cedar Valley Reservoir (Kentucky & 1500 Rd)
Garnett – Garnett Campground (409 W. South Lake Drive)
Garnett – Garnett Hotel & RV Park (109 Prairie Plaza Parkway)
Garnett – Lazy Z RV Park (23211 NW 1700 Rd)
Garnett – North Lake Park Campground (North Lake Rd)
Garnett – Southside RV Park (1312 S. Maple St.)
Glen Elder – Glen Elder State Park (2131 180 Rd)
Glen Elder – Norman's North Shore (2100A 190 Rd)
Glen Elder – The Lazy H Lakeview Campground (2174 Hwy 128)
Goddard – All Seasons RV Park (15520 W. Maple St.)
Goodland – Goodland KOA Journey (1114 E Hwy 24)
Goodland – Mid-America Camp Inn (2802 Commerce)
Goodland – Soldiers Memorial Park at Smoky Gardens (1735 Rd 54)
Great Bend – Cottonwood Grove RV Park (2800 North Main)
Great Bend – Finer Mobile Park (5501 9th Street)
Greensburg – Happy Camper Cabins (504 N. Bay)
Gridley – Gridley City Lake (Emmer Rd)
Halstead – Spring Lake RV Resort (1308 S. Spring Lake Road)
Hays – Creek Side Resort (3301 US Highway 183 Alt)
Herington – Herington Lake & Reservoir (500 Avenue & Sage Rd)
Herington – Railer RV Park (101 S 3rd St)
Hesston – Cottonwood Grove RV Campground (1001 E Lincoln Blvd)
Hiawatha – Mulberry Pond (2252 Mulberry Rd.)
Hillsboro – Memorial Park Campground (West D St)

Hoisington – Hoisington RV Park (1200 Susank Rd)
Holton – Banner Creek Reservoir & Campground (10975 Hwy 16)
Holton – Prairie Lake Campground (14824 246th Rd)
Horton – Mission Lake (120th Rd & Wilson Dr)
Hoxie – Buffalo Bill Park (273 Main St.)
Hugoton – Eagle RV Park (1471 Rd 13)
Hugoton – Hugoton RV Campground (1039 W City Limits)
Humboldt – Camp Hunter – Campground (806 S 1st St)
Hutchinson – Kansas State Fairgrounds RV Park (2000 N Poplar)
Hutchinson – Melody Acres Mobile RV Park (1009 E Blanchard Ave)
Hutchinson – Sand Hills State Park (4207 E 56th)
Independence – Elk City State Park (4825 Squaw Creek Rd)
Iola – Storage and RV of Iola Inc. (1327 US 54 Hwy)
Jetmore – HorseThief Reservoir (19005 SSW Highway 156)
Jetmore – Jetmore City Lake (19997 SW 215 Rd)
Junction City – Curtis Creek Park (4020 W Hwy 57)
Junction City – Farnum Creek Park (4020 W Hwy 57)
Junction City – Geary State Fishing Lake (US-77)
Junction City – Milford Lake-USACE (5203 N. K57 Hwy)
Junction City – Owl's Nest RV Campground (1912 Old Hwy 40)
Junction City – School Creek Park (4020 W Hwy 57)
Junction City – Thunderbird RV Resort (4725 W Rolling Hills Rd)
Junction City – Timber Creek Park (4020 W Hwy 57)
Junction City – West Rolling Hills Park (4020 W Hwy 57)
Kansas City – Suite Tea (3605 N. 59th St)
Kingman – Byron Walker Wildlife Area (8685 W Hwy 54)
Kingman – Kingman Riverside Park RV (100 W 1st Ave)
Kingman – Kingman RV Park (810 East E Avenue)
Kingman – Kingman State Fishing Lake (8685 W Hwy 54)
Kingsdown – Clark State Fishing Lake (HCO 1 Box 58)
Kinsley – 4 Aces RV Campground (Highway 50 & Massachusetts)
Kirwin – Little Bits RV Park (263 E. Main)
La Crosse – Grass Park (1st & Main)
La Cygne – Linn County Park & La Cygne Lake (23095 Valley Rd)
La Harpe – Jayhawker RV Park (403 US Highway 54)
Larned – Camp Pawnee Campground (Jct 264)
Larned – Santa Fe Trail RV Park (125 State St.)
Larned – West Wind Villas & RV Park (1601 Sycamore St)
Lawrence – 500 Road Farms (1867 E 500 Rd)
Lawrence – Clinton State Park (798 N. 1415 Rd)
Lawrence – Kansas City West/Lawrence KOA (1473 Highway 40)
Leavenworth – Riverfront Park (1201 Riverfront Park Rd.)
Leavenworth – Suncatcher Lake RV Park (24836 Tonganoxie Rd)
Lewis – Lewis RV Park (601 S. Edwards St.)
Liberal – Arkalon Park Campground (11123 Arkalon Park Road)
Liberal – Seven Winds RV Park (5924 Old Highway 54)
Liberal – Western Star RV Ranch (13916 Road 7)
Liberty – Junction West Coffeyville RV Park (2649 N Highway 169)
Lindsborg – Coronado Motel & RV Park (305 N Harrison St)
Lindsborg – Dan's RV Park (236 S Cole St.)
Lindsborg – Old Mill Campground (600 Old Mill Rd)
Linn – City Park Campground (Park View Dr)

Louisburg – Foxfire Farm (7195 W 327th Street)
Louisburg – Rutlader Outpost & RV Park (33565 Metcalf Rd.)
Lucas – Lucas RV Park (119 N Wolf Ave)
Lucas – Set in Stone Cabins & RV Park (649 E 1st St)
Lyndon – Crossroads RV Park & Campground (23313 S Hwy 75)
Lyons – Wagon Wheel Inn & Trailer Park (819 US 56)
Manhattan – Pillsbury Crossing Wildlife Area (2464 Pillsbury Crossing Ln)
Manhattan – Tuttle Creek Lake Campground (5020 Tuttle Crk Blvd)
Manhattan – Tuttle Creek State Park (5800 River Pond Rd)
Mapleton – KanRocks Recreation Association, Inc. (2051 130th St)
Marion – Marion County Park & Campground (1 Office Dr)
Marion – Marion Reservoir Campground (2105 N Pawnee)
Marquette – Kanopolis State Park (200 Horsethief Rd)
Marysville – Marysville City Park Campground (10th & Spring St)
Marysville – Oak Springs Campground (1374 U.S. Hwy 77)
Marysville – Thunderbird Motel & RV Park (819 Pony Express Hwy)
Mayetta – Prairie Band RV Park (12305 150 Rd.)
McPherson – McPherson RV Ranch (2201 E. Northview)
McPherson – Mustang Mobile RV Park (1909 Millers Ln)
McPherson – Sunflower RV Patch (1050 W Kansas Ave)
Meade – Lake Meade State Park (13051 V Rd)
Medicine Lodge – Barber State Fishing Lake (Well Rd)
Medicine Lodge – Gyp Hills Guest Ranch (3393 SW Woodward Rd)
Medicine Lodge – Gypsum Hills Trl Rides (1801 N.W. Forest City Rd)
Medicine Lodge – Memorial Peace Park (3091 SE US Hwy 160)
Melvern – Melvern Lake (31051 Melvern Lake Pkwy)
Merriam – Walnut Grove RV Park (10218 Johnson Drive)
Milford – Acorns Resort (3710 Farnum Creek Rd)
Milford – Flagstop Resort & RV Park (302 Whiting St)
Milford – Milford Lake, State Park (3612 State Park Rd)
Miltonvale – The Barn at Bear Bottoms Lodge (505 Meridian Rd)
Minneapolis – Markley Grove Park (161 S Mill)
Montezuma – Prairie Wind RV Park (508 W Cortez)
Neodesha – Norman No. 1 Oil Well RV Park (103 South First St)
Neosho Falls – Riverside Park (N Hwy 54, Willow Rd)
Newton – Harvey County East Park (314 N East Lake Rd)
Newton – Payne Oil Company RV Park (3610 N Hwy 15)
Norton – Prairie Dog State Park (13037 State Highway 261)
Oakley – Hill Plains Camping & RV (462 Hwy 83)
Oakley – Kansas Country Inn & Campground (3538 Hwy 40)
Olathe – Lone Elm Park (167th & Lone Elm Rd)
Osage City – Eisenhower State Park (29810 S. Fairlawn Rd)
Osawatomie – City Lake & RV Campground (327th Bethel Church Rd)
Osawatomie – City of Osawatomie Campground (1000 Main St)
Osawatomie – Mills House RV Park (212 1st St)
Osborne – North 40 Alpacas (460 S Hwy 24)
Osborne – Pine Parks RV (314 E. New Hampshire)
Oskaloosa – Happy Joy Acres (6040 Ferguson Rd)
Oswego – Danny Elliott Park Campground (502 Waterplant Rd)
Ottawa – Camp Chippewa (2577 Idaho Rd Box 134)
Oxford – Napawalla Park (Main & Colorado St)
Ozawkie – Longview Park (10419 Perry Lake Rd)

591

Ozawkie – Perry State Park (5441 W Lake Rd)
Paola – Hillsdale State Park (26001 W. 255th Street)
Paola – Lake Miola (2470 W. 299th St.)
Parsons – Lake Parsons (10355 30th Rd)
Parsons – Marvel RV Park (800 E. Main)
Paxico – Mill Creek Campground & RV Park (22470 Campground Rd)
Perry – Perry Lake Corps of Engineers (10419 Perry Lake Rd)
Phillipsburg – Phillipsburg City Park & Campgrounds (Ft. Bissel Ave.)
Pittsburg – Four Oaks RV & Tent Park (800 W 20th St)
Pittsburg – Parkview RV Park (520 W 20th St)
Plainville – C2T Ranch & Campground (1202 Saline River Road)
Powhattan – Sac & Fox Casino, The Lodge (1322 US Highway 75)
Pratt – Pratt Co. Veterans Memorial Lake Campground (Hwy K64)
Pratt – The Evergreen Inn (20001 W Hwy 54)
Reading – Lyon State Fishing Lake (2272 Road 250)
Rexford – Rexford Hotel (385 Main St)
Rexford – Shepherd's Staff RV Park (240 Main St.)
Robinson – F^3 Fun Family Farm (2127 205th Street)
Russell – Fossil Creek RV Park (833 S. Front St.)
Russell – Triple-J Camper Park (187 E. Edward Ave)
Russell Springs – Butterfield Trail Campground (515 Hilts)
Sabetha – Sycamore Springs Whitetail Ranch (3126 Bittersweet Rd)
Salina – K.O.A. of Salina Kansas (1109 W Diamond Dr)
Salina – Saline County Livestock & Expo Center (900 Greeley)
Salina – Webster Conference Center (2601 N. Ohio Street)
Scott City – Historic Lake Scott State Park (101 West Scott Lake Dr)
Scott City – Pine Tree RV Park (402 N Main)
Seneca – Bailey's RV Resort (1701 North St.)
Sharon Springs – Dinkel RV Sites (525 S. Main St.)
Sharon Springs – Wallace County Fairgrounds (214 W Park)
South Haven – Kansas Badlands Off-Road Park (886 E 160th St. S)
South Hutchinson – Lighthouse Landing RV Park (9 Heartland Dr)
St. Francis – Homesteader Motel (410 W. Business Hwy 36)
St. John – Pine Haven Retreat (217 E Highway 50)
Sterling – Sterling Lake (400 E Van Buren)
Stockton – Stockton City Park (102 Highway 24)
Stockton – Stockton RV Park (115 S. Walnut)
Stockton – Webster State Park (1140 10 Rd.)
Sublette – Golden Prairie Hunting Service (607 W Gwinn Ct)
Sylvan Grove – Wilson State Park (3 State Park Road)
Syracuse – Hamilton County Fairgrounds (806 S Main)
Syracuse – Syracuse Sand Dunes Park (250 W. River Road)
Tipton – Ringneck Ranch, Inc. (655 Solomon Lane)
Topeka – Capital City KOA (1949 SW 49th St)
Topeka – Deer Creek Valley RV Park (3140 SE 21st Street)
Topeka – Forbes Landing RV Park (5932 SW Topeka Blvd)
Topeka – From The Top Glamping (Delivered to your home!)
Topeka – Lake Shawnee Campground (3535 SE East Edge Rd)
Topeka – Lake Shawnee Campgrounds (3137 SE 29th)
Toronto – Cross Timbers State Park (144 Hwy 105)
Toronto – Woodson State Fishing Lake (738 Fegan Rd)
Tribune – Mike's Mountain View Trailer Park (W. Kansas Ave)

Ulysses – Frazier Park Campground (1380 Frazier Park Road)
Vassar – Lamont Hill RV Park (22975 Highway 368)
Vassar – Pomona State Park & Reservoir (22900 S Hwy 368)
WaKeeney – WaKeeney KOA (25027 S Interstate)
Wakefield – Clay County Campground & Park (201 2nd St)
Wallace – Fort Wallace RV Sites (102 Front Street)
Wamego – Riverside Estates & RV Park 105 E Valley St)
Washington – Rose Garden RV Camp (127 E 9th)
Washington – Washington City Park Campgrounds (South D St)
Waterville – Waterville City Campground (400 E Walnut)
Wathena – Riverbend Hide-Out (926 Sheridan Road)
Webber – Lovewell State Park (2446 250 Rd)
Wellington – Wellington KOA (100 S. Koa Drive)
West Mineral – Big Brutus RV Park (6509 NW 60th St)
Westmoreland – Oregon Trail RV Park (202 Main St)
Wichita – Air Capital RV Park (609 E. 47th St. South)
Wichita – Camp The Range RV Park (2920 E. 33rd St. N.)
Wichita – K and R RV Park (3200 S. Southeast Blvd)
Williamsburg – Homewood RV Park (2161 Idaho Rd)
Wilson – Missile Silo Adventure Campground (354 4th Rd)
Wilson – Wilson RV Park (821 27th St)
Winfield – Winfield City Lake (10348 141st Rd)
Winfield – Winfield Fairgrounds (1105 W 9th Ave)
Winona – JL Bar Ranch (1720 Seneca)
Yates Center – South Owl Lake & Campground (Llama Rd)
Yoder – Hitchin' Post RV Park (3415 Switzer Rd)

# Kansas Fast Facts

Kansas was the 34th State admitted to the Union on January 29, 1861. It was named after the Kansas River, which in took its name from the Kansa tribe of Native Americans.

Population: 2,940,865 (36th as of the 2020 Census)
Area: 82,278 square miles (15th)
Highest Elevation: 4,041 feet (Mount Sunflower near Weskan)
Lowest Elevation: 679 feet (Verdigris River near Oklahoma border)

Amphibian: Barred tiger salamander – *Ambystoma mavortium* (2005)
Animal: American bison – *Bison bison bison* (1955)
Bird: Western meadowlark – *Sturnella neglecta* (1933)
Fish: Channel catfish – *Ictalurus punctatus* (2018)
Flower: Sunflower – *Helianthus annuus* (1903)
Flying Fossil: *Pteranodon* (2014)
Fossil: *Tylosaurus* (2014)
Fruit: Sandhill plum – *Prunus angustifolia* (2022)
Gemstone: Jelinite/Amber (2018)
Grass: Little bluestem – *Schizachyrium scoparium* (2010)
Insect: European honey bee – *Apis mellifera* (1976)
March: "The Kansas March" (1935), "Here's Kansas" (1992)
Mineral: Galena (2018)
Motto: *Ad astra per aspera*
Nickname: "The Sunflower State"
Reptile: Ornate box turtle – *Terrapene ornate* (1986)
Rock: Greenhorn Limestone (2018)
Soil: Harney silt loam (1990)
Song: "Home on the Range" (1947)
Tree: Eastern cottonwood – *Populus deltoides* (1937)

# Kansas Governors

1) Charles L. Robinson, Republican (2/9/1861-1/12/1863)
2) Thomas Carney, Republican (1/12/1863-1/9/1865)
3) Samuel J. Crawford, Republican (1/9/1865-11/4/1868)
4) Nehemiah Green, Republican (11/4/1868-1/11/1869)
5) James M. Harvey, Republican (1/11/1869-1/13/1873)
6) Thomas A. Osborn, Republican (1/13/1873-1/8/1877)
7) George T. Anthony, Republican (1/8/1877-1/13/1879)
8) John St. John, Republican (1/13/1879-1/8/1883)
9) George W. Glick, Democratic (1/8/1883-1/12/1885)
10) John A. Martin, Republican (1/12/1885-1/14/1889)
11) Lyman U. Humphrey, Republican (1/14/1889-1/9/1893)
12) Lorenzo D. Lewelling, Populist (1/9/1893-1/14/1895)
13) Edmund N. Morrill, Republican (1/14/1895-1/11/1897)
14) John W. Leedy, Populist (1/11/1897-1/9/1899)
15) William E. Stanley, Republican (1/9/1899-1/12/1903)
16) Willis J. Bailey, Republican (1/12/1903-1/9/1905)
17) Edward H. Hoch, Republican (1/9/1905-1/11/1909)
18) Walter R. Stubbs, Republican (1/11/1909-1/13/1913)
19) George H. Hodges, Democratic (1/13/1913-1/11/1915)
20) Arthur Capper, Republican (1/11/1915-1/13/1919)
21) Henry J. Allen, Republican (1/13/1919-1/8/1923)
22) Jonathan M. Davis, Democratic (1/8/1923-1/12/1925)
23) Benjamin S. Paulen, Republican (1/12/1925-1/14/1929)
24) Clyde M. Reed, Republican (1/14/1929-1/12/1931)
25) Harry H. Woodring, Democratic (1/12/1931-1/9/1933)
26) Alf M. Landon, Republican (1/9/1933-1/11/1937)
27) Walter A. Huxman, Democratic (1/11/1937-1/9/1939)
28) Payne H. Ratner, Republican (1/9/1939-1/11/1943)
29) Andrew F. Schoeppel, Republican (1/11/1943-1/13/1947)
30) Frank Carlson, Republican (1/13/1947-11/28/1950)
31) Frank L. Hagaman, Republican (11/28/1950-1/8/1951)
32) Edward F. Arn, Republican (1/8/1951-1/10/1955)
33) Frederick L. Hall, Republican (1/10/1955-1/3/1957)
34) John B. McCuish, Republican (1/3/1957-1/14/1957)
35) George Docking, Democratic (1/14/1957-1/9/1961)
36) John Anderson Jr., Republican (1/9/1961-1/11/1965)
37) William H. Avery, Republican (1/11/1965-1/9/1967)
38) Robert B. Docking, Democratic (1/9/1967-1/13/1975)
39) Robert F. Bennett, Republican (1/13/1975-1/8/1979)
40) John W. Carlin, Democratic (1/8/1979-1/12/1987)
41) John M Hayden, Republican (1/12/1987-1/14/1991)
42) Joan M. Finney, Democratic (1/14/1991-1/9/1995)
43) Bill P. Graves, Republican (1/9/1995-1/13/2003)
44) Kathleen Sebelius, Democratic (1/13/2003-4/28/2009)
45) Mark V. Parkinson, Democratic (1/28/2009-1/10/2011)
46) Sam D. Brownback, Republican (1/10/2011-1/31/2018)
47) Jeff W. Colyer, Republican (1/31/2018-1/14/2019)
48) Laura J. Kelly, Democratic (1/14/2019-incumbent)

# Kansas Scenic & Historic Byways

Kansas's Byways are a great way to traverse large portions of the state and take in beautiful scenery or strings of historic sites. There are 12 Byways in Kansas, two of which are also categorized as a National Scenic Byway (in **bold**).

**Flint Hills National Scenic Byway (47 miles)**
- Passes through Council Grove, Strong City, Cottonwood Falls, Bazaar, Matfield Green, Cassoday

Frontier Military Historic Byway (168 miles)
- Passes through Leavenworth, Lansing, Maltby, Kansas City, Edwardsville, Lake Quivira, Lenexa, Olathe, Overland Park, Aubry, Louisburg, Linn Valley, Pleasanton, Prescott, Fulton, Fort Scott, Dry Wood, Arma, Franklin, Frontenac, Pittsburg, Crestline, Riverton, Baxter Springs

Glacial Hills Scenic Byway (63 miles)
- Passes through White Cloud, Iowa Point, Sparks, Atchison, Leavenworth

Gypsum Hills Scenic Byway (42 miles)
- Passes through Coldwater, Medicine Lodge

Kansas Route 66 Historic Byway (13 miles)
- Passes through Galena, Riverton, Baxter Springs

Land & Sky Scenic Byway (88 miles)
- Passes through St. Francis, Wheeler, Goodland, Sharon Springs

Native Stone Scenic Byway (75 miles)
- Passes through Dover, Keene, Eskridge, Alma, Wabaunsee, Zeandale, Fairmont, Manhattan

Post Rock Scenic Byway (18 miles)
- Passes through Lucas, Wilson

Prairie Trail Scenic Byway (80 miles)
- Passes through Ellsworth, Kanopolis, Carneiro, Langley, Marquette, Lindsborg, Roxbury, Canton

Smoky Valley Scenic Byway (60 miles)
- Passes through Ogallah, Brownell, Ransom, WaKeeney

Western Vistas Historic Byway (102 miles)
- Passes through Scott City, Elkader, Oakley, Monument, Page City, Winona, McAllaster, Wallace, Sharon Springs

**Wetlands & Wildlife National Scenic Byway (77 miles)**
- Passes through St. John, Claflin, Redwing, Hoisington

For more information, visit https://www.travelks.com/things-to-do/byways-and-highways/byways/

# Sources

With the help of historical sources and town historical societies, Wandermore researched the etymology of each town's name and compiled interesting historical information, fun facts, and stories to include in this book. Many towns have differing accounts as to how they arrived at their present name, and so the most frequently cross-referenced story was utilized.

Parts of the following works were used to help compile figures and historical and travel-related information. Please consider visiting the links below to learn more about Kansas and its communities, history, and people.

Department of Wildlife & Parks Kansas – https://ksoutdoors.com/State-Parks/Locations

History of the State of Kansas by A. T. Andreas (1883) - https://archive.org/details/historyofstateof00andr/page/n3/mode/2up

Kansas: A Cyclopedia of State History, Embracing Events, Institutions, Industries, Counties, Cities, Towns, Prominent Persons, Etc. by Frank W. Blackmar (1912) - https://web.archive.org/web/20060923013205/http://skyways.lib.ks.us/genweb/archives/1912/index.html

Kansas Golf - Golf Course Directory - https://kansasgolf.com/

Kansas Post Offices, May 29, 1828-August 3, 1961 by Robert W. Baughman the Kansas Postal History Society (1961) - https://www.kshs.org/p/post-offices/11307#KSPostOffices

Roadside America Kansas Map - https://www.roadsideamerica.com/map/ks

Twentieth Biennial Report of the Board of Directors of Kansas State Historical Society by Kansas State Historical Society (1916) - https://archive.org/details/bub_gb_5zdAAQAAMAAJ/page/n4/mode/1up

The Origin of Certain Place Names in the United States by Henry Gannett (1905) - https://books.google.com/books?id=9V1IAAAAMAAJ

Travel Kansas – Official State Tourism Site https://www.travelks.com

United States Census Bureau https://www.census.gov/

# Acknowledgements

This book is dedicated to State of Kansas, and the following individuals who helped make the Wandermore journey across Kansas possible. Thank you for your generosity and for allowing us to help others see all that the Sunflower State has to offer!

{The Squirrel Inn}
1JKC Construction Services
A. F. Freund
A.J. Boeckman
Aaleahyah Goering
Aaron & Linda Valentine
Aaron Luthi
Aaron Oestreicher
Aaron Pulliam
Aaron, Stephani, Jade, Brooke & Hope Senst
Abbey Rubottom
Abby McDonald
Abigail A. August
Abigail Oestmann
Adam & Ashley Nelson
Adam J. Chriss
Adam J. Gerber
Addie Osterman
Addison Abitz
Addison Willhite
Addy Trimborn
Adelaide Bowman
Adelina Wright
Adeline Runer
Adlar Detrixhe
Adrian Dwight Marcum II
Adriana Brown
Adriana Laura Davis
Adriana Stavropoulos
Adrianna Cuezze
Adrianne Guillory-Luthi
Adrienne Oestmann
Aileen E. Carr
AJ Boeckman
Al Robke
Alan & Shannon Barus
Alan Brown

Alan Bruster
Alan Charley
Alan Detrixhe
Alan Jacka
Alana Ayers
Albert, Mercedes, Jack, Larry & Susann Depew
Albinus Allen Hooker
Alene Ilene Peterson
Alex & Madisyn Schmitz
Alex & Shelby Otis
Alex J. Buck
Alex James Buck
Alex Muninger
Alex Nasseri
Alex Weller
Alex Zachgo
Alexandria Gumfory
Alexis Hamilton
Alfred & Anita Braun
Ali Maria Davis
Alice (McMillan) Lockridge
Alice Boren (Ashland, KS)
Alice Buckland
Alice E. Lunsford
Alice Franklin
Alice Wiruth
Alicia Bruster
Alieta Meyer
Alisa Sooter
Alissa Horton (Wichita, KS)
Alivia Quillen
Allen Johnson
Allie Miller
Allie Osterman
Allison Luthi
Alma Bakery & Sweet Shoppe
Alma Wick
Alver J. Gillmore

Alvin Urban
Alyson Spradling
Alyssa Carpino
Alyssa Hajny
Alyssa Pollman & Margaret Carlson
Alyvia Moser
Amanda Baumgartner
Amanda J. Geniuk
Amanda Logsdon
Amanda Wood
Amber Brown
Amber D. Farha
Amber Grossardt
Amber M. Farha
Amber Tedder
Ameilianna Mills
Amelia Brown
Amelia Nørgaard Frandsen-Rinck
Amy Barlovic Sanders
Amy L. Robinson
Amy Nichol
Amy Towery-Cole
Amy VanDorn
Anastacia Drake
Andrea Angel
Andrea Hickel
Andrea Kaufman
Andrea White Clark
Andrew & Eden Davis
Andrew Holup
Andrew Kanning Family
Andrew Lloyd
Andrew Ohman
Andrew Smith
Andrews Keith Morgan
Andy & Jeanette Thompson

Andy & Kristen
Britton
Andy & Rebecca
Nickels
Andy Runer
Angela Hollman
Angela Howard &
Zack Edwards
Angela Lamb
Angela Sharma
Angelia Morgan
(Oklahoma City, OK)
Angie Allton
Angie Coomes
Angie Funk
Angie Hammack
Angie Logan
Angie Shimek
Reeves
Anita Felzke
Anita Kay (Colgrove)
Bott
Anita Kultgen White
& Troy Kultgen
Anita Losey Kirkman
Anita Pawlush
Anja & Kira Tabatha
Ossowski
Ann Bicknell Bennett
Ann Jackson
Ann M. Robinson
Vannasdall
Ann Zachgo
Anna Bokern
Anna Murphy
Anna Orcutt
Anna Wick
Annabel Vande Riet
Anne Shearer-
Shineman
Annel Scates
Annelise Scates
Annette Denk Jacka
Annie Mous
Anonymous (x5)
Anthony & Hayden
Munn (Rolla, KS)
April Henderson
April Shankles
Aralen Dabney
Ardan Harp
Ardene Wilkens
(McDonald Schools)
Arhianna Pulliam
Ariadne Snyder

Arianna McMillin-
Osburn
Arizona Spicer
Arlen Goering
Arlene Jean
Peterson
Wheelbarger
Arlene Peterson
Wheelbarger
Arletta Dickman
Arlynn Scadden
Arlyss Vathauer
Armand Gingles &
Lorene Gingles
Armella Schneider
Arnaldo Rodriguez-
Ortiz
Art & Barbara McGee
Arya Thompson
Ashley Boland
Ashley Gilmore Reid
Ashley
Wojciechowski
Ashlie Womack-
Wendt
Ashton Kadel
Asteria Kelley
Atlas LePard
Aubree Ray
Cornelius
Aubrey Hickel
Aubrey Hughes
Audrey Hajek
Mclinden
August & Ann Martin
(Herndon, KS)
August Robke
AuLaura N. Delgado
Austin Hughes
Austyn Hickel
Ava R. Buck
Ava Rae Buck
Ava Wright
Average Joes' Bar &
Grill
Averie Oestreicher
Ayden Kadel
Ayden Muniz
Azela Morales
Azuara Family
Bailey Hajny
Bailey Steckline
Ballers Sports Bar &
Grill
Bane Bunch Children

Banks Farha
Bar K Bar Arena
Barb Depew
Barb Knoll
Barb Oltjen
Barb Rathbun
Barb Young Innes
Barbara Ann Pipkin-
Covey
Barbara
Brueggemann Gitt
Barbara Mosier
Barbara Nordling
Barbara Purdy
Barbara Reser
Barbara Rice
Knowles
Barbara Thomas
Baron Farha
Barry & Cindy Curry
Barry M. Shalinsky
Barry Smith
Bat BD Machine &
Equipment Co.
Be Courageous
Becki Libhart
Becky (Nevitt)
McManus
Becky Greenlee
Becky Meili
Becky Penry
Becky Pivonka
Becky Reedy
Becky Rourk & John
Seidel
Belinda Wessels
Bella Hickel
Ben Boland
Ben Perrin
Benjamin Buckland
Benjamin Curtis
Benn Maddox
Bennett Vann
Bernadette (Noll)
Linss
Bernadette Murphy
Bernard E. "Bernie"
Nordling
Bernie & Dorrene
Peterson
Bernie & Ronny Jo
Hennis
Bernie Zillner
Bertha Mehl
Beryl & Jason Dinges

Beth Brandenburg McIntosh
Beth Gardner
Beth Oltjen Viadales
Beth Scheve
Bethany Cater
Bethany Swafford
Bette Douglas
Betty Fakes
Betty R. Teter & Dorman G. Teter
Betty Wood
Bev Rucker
Beverly & Ed Chapman
Beverly (Bomhoff) Hoffman
Beverly Brueggemann Clark
Beverly Carol (Thompson) Evans
Beverly Meyer Darling
Beverly Osbourn Carlson
Big Chuck (Sr.) & Linda Taylor (Dodge City, KS)
Big Cs Café LLC (Elkhart, KS)
Bill & Brenda Britton
Bill & Brenda Toby
Bill & Carol Gusenius (Fellow KS Travelers)
Bill & Mary Andrews
Bill & Nacy Trauer
Bill & Terri McCauley
Bill Bergmeier Family
Bill Bunyan
Bill Dinkel Family
Bill Estes
Bill Ginder
Bill Johnson
Bill Johnson Jr.
Bill Lawrence
Bill Longbine
Bill Murphy
Bill Nungesser
Bill Reed
Bill Rickenbrode (Hope, KS)
Bill Shute
Bill Thomas
Bill Thompson

Bill Vering
Billie Scott
Billie, Nancy, Sherry, Mike, Susan & Laura Trauer
Billy & Tami Britton
Billy J. Fager
Billy Lawrence
Billy, Chet & Jessie Jordon
Birkley Barnes
Blake & Jene' Bolen
Blake Grams
Blakely Day
Blanche Campbell Massey
Blane Lamb
Blasi Service Station
Blaze Wegele
Bob & Betsy Glunt
Bob & Betty Shubkagel
Bob & Carol Ebert
Bob & Deb Garcia
Bob & Debbi Eickbush
Bob & Edna Grant
Bob "Pa Pa" Palmer
Bob Critser
Bob Koch
Bob Laubengayer
Bob Moser
Bob Ross
Bob Schneider
Bob Settles
Bob Stranathan
Bobbi Halinski
Bobbie Cree Myers
Boston & Parker Woodrum
Bowman Family (McLouth, KS)
Boyd G. Hutchinson
Brad & Jeanie Shearer
Brad & Jill Deutscher
Brad & Myra Howard

Brad Maddox
Brad Wells
Bradley Oestmann
Brady Grams
Brady J. Hendrickson
Bradyn Ebersole
Brandon Depew
Brandon Grossardt
Brandon Hickel
Brandon Mitchell
Brandon Young
Brandy & Tommy Stone & Family
Breanna Bezona Rodriguez
Brenda & Mike Hinkle
Brenda Anderson
Brenda Brueggemann
Brenda Bruster
Brenda Dreyer Edminston
Brenda Karstensen
Brenda Lee Rowley Gray
Brenda Runnebaum
Brenda S. Mattson
Brenda Seger
Brenden & Pamela Wirth
Brendon Boone
Brent & Anne Proksch
Brent Bayliff
Bret & MaryKay Ulrich
Brett Blyholder
Brett Johnson
Brevin Farha
Brian & Amanda Lervold
Brian & Rhonda Newell
Brian A. Ross
Brian Angel
Brian D. Ross
Brian Dohe
Brian E. McDannald
Brian Gregory Davis
Brian J. Ross
Brian Kelly
Brian Miller
Brian R. Stenger
Brian Shaw

Brian Smith
Brian Vasquez
Brian Wahlstrom
Brianna Ault
BrickHouse BBQ &
Brew
Brinleigh Hickel
Britney Nasseri
Brittany Wheatcroft
Brooke Parise
Bruce E. Napier
(2014)
Bruce Franklin
Bryan & Connie
Brown (Iola, KS)
Bryan Cheever
Bryan Wright
Bryan, Kiley & Lena
Van Horn
Bryce Casida
Bryce Cornelius
Bryce Woelk
Buck Beaver &
Woody Harper
Budd Zillner
Burnie Lamb
Burt Sheets
Burton Studt
Butch Rives
Butler County
Historical Society
Butterfly Funhouse
Childcare
Byron Schroder
C. Frank Morgan
C. J. Jack & Etta
Ward
C.J., Becca, Eleanor
& Patrick Mahoney
CA Hayes
Cadey Carney-
Goforth
Caitlin Johnson
Caleb Quillen
Cali Claar
Callan Abitz
Calvin, Oliver, Violet
& Evelyn Dwyer
Camber Boland
Cameron & Lexi
Twombly
Cameron Farha
Cameron Hajny
Cameron Murphy
Camille Bervert

Camille Kay
Vossman
Camille Y. Ellard
Candy Westhoff
Carl Nevitt
Carl Vanderhofe
Carla Hayes Becker
Carla Mann &
Andrew Goodman
Carmen Azuara
Albart
Carmen Gonzales
Carmen Nelson
Carol Gerlits
Carol Gradner
Carol Graney
Carol Harris
Carol James
Carol Jean Miner
Middendorf Stumbo
Hanrahan
Carol Lingo
Carol Madron
Carol Rickenbrode
(Hope, KS)
Carol Shobe
Carol Whittey
Caroline Burnett
Caroline J. Flax
Carolyn Elizabeth
Steele
Carolyn Granger
Austin
Carolyn Johnson
Carrell Family
Carrie Alt
Carrie Benjamin
Carroll Burger
Carson Farha
Carter L. Stevens
Carter T. Olson
Cary Grant Utz
Casey & Aurore
Maxon
Casey Allen Kemp
Catherine Hillis
Catherine Plummer
Cathy (Boyce)
Mendenhall
Cathy A. Huitt
Cathy Baughn
Cathy Maxon
Cathy McVey
Cecelia Nicolet
Cecil Carender

Celebration Centre
Celestine J.
Schneider
Chad Thompson
Chance & Anna Fulls
Chandler B. Birkholz
Chandra Thomas
Charlene Chellew
Charles & Janet
Nichol
Charles A. May
Charles Collins
Charles G. Bright
Charles Jarrell III
Caleb Jarrell
Charles Moser
Charles Reese
Family
Charles Van Megen
(AFS 1976/77
Netherlands Foreign
Exchange Student)
Charles Vest
Charles W. Bright
Charles W. Kauffman
Charles W. Nimz
Charles W. Nimz Jr.
Charlie & Geraldine
Darnall
Charlie & Iva (Chiles)
Moser
Charlie & Teres
Moore
Charlotte Buckland
Charlotte Ruth
(Shaw) Morrell
Charlotte Strubbe
Charmarose Craven
Chase King
Chase T., Dylan W.
& Mateo G.
Chelsea Hughes
Cashier
Chelsie Green
Cheri Kindt-Gonzales
Cheri Williams
Cherie & Marty
Sauers
Cherie Sanders
Cheryl & Lanny
Pauley
Cheryl Cox
Cheryl Flear
Cheryl Hickel

602

Cheryl L., Daniel B.,
Tobias B., Tristan B.
Cheryl Rooker Briggs
Cheryl Wendt
Mussatto
Chief R. Shane &
Sheri Smith
Chip Carl
Chloe E. Pfrimmer
Chloe Vaupel
Chris & Amy Cassell
Chris & Sheri
Thompson
Chris & Tammy
Corum (Allen, KS)
Chris Arpad
Chris Berk (Kressley)
Chris Blockburger
Chris Hiebert
Chris Holderman
Chris Johnson
Chris Palmer
Chris, Brooke, Tess,
Kase & Zoller Mann
Christie Holm
Christie Louthan
Christina Carlson
Reed
Christina King
Christina Lee
Harrison
Christina McDonald
Christine Anderson
Christopher
Blankenship
Christopher J. Drazic
Christopher P.
Shoults
Christopher Reay
Christy Reed
Christy Vogel
Chuck & Jan Kress
Chuck & Kim Stroda
Chuck Denk
Cierra Clark-Knight
Cindy (Baker) Adams
Cindy Bucher
Cindy Hardy
Cindy Knouf-Sipe
Cindy Palmer-Berry
Cindy Rogers
Cindy Stout
Cindy Trimmell
Cindy Walton

Cissy, Milton, Diane,
Phil
City of Fowler, KS
Vickie (Oberle)
Hoffman
Clara Gabelmann
Clarabel's Dance
Citadel (Junction
City, KS)
Clarence Caldwell Jr.
Clarence Caldwell
Sr.
Clarence Roeder
Claude & Pauline
Brill
Claudine Echer
Clay Murphy
Clay Thomas
Clayton & Teddy
Williamson
Cleomarie &
Chancedavid
Cliff & Pauline Mann
Clufford James
Colby, Jaxon & Ella
Durham
Coleton Jennings
Colleen K. Alexander
Collyns Spradling
Colton, Landri &
Quade Estes (Love,
Mom & Dad)
Connie Beals
Connie Driscoll
Griffin
Connie R. McMahan
Cordelia Shirley
Coronado Motel &
RV Park (Lindsborg,
KS)
Cory Hargett
Cory Johnson
County Divide Café
(Clifton, KS)
Courtney E. Coder
Courtney Kaufman
Courtney Pringle
Cozy White Smith
Craig Jaggard
Craig Neubecker
Craig Scherling
Craig Turrentine
Craig Zachgo
Crawfords (Solomon,
KS)

Crimson Concepts
(Centralia, KS)
Crooked Creek
Ranch
Crosby, Jill, Erin,
John, Summer &
Matthew Gernon
Crystal Dana
Crystal Miller
Curly & Barbara
Decker
Curry's Body Shop
Curry's Golf Cars
Curt & Valerie
Hazlett
Curt Strubbe
Curtis & Shelley
Weilert
Curtis Rush
Curtiss Family
(Lawrence, KS)
Cynthia Smith
D. K. Freund
D'Ete Payne
Meacham Family
Dakota Bennett
Dakota Buchanan
Dakota Oestmann
Dale & April Droste
Dale & Valda Haug
Dale Fakes
Dale Kolterman
Dale McBride
Dallas Brady
Dallas Coker
Dalles Lincoln Carr
Dalton Gang Hideout
Dalton Murphy
Damian Murphy
Dan & Eleanor
Seemann
Dan A. Nixon
Dan Biehler
Dan Farha
Dan Pearce
Dana K. McDaniel
Dane M. Rodriguez
Daniel & Ashley
Landis
Daniel & Misty
O'Brien
Daniel D Harrell (Hill
City, KS)
Daniel Day
Daniel Meyer

603

Daniel Ming
Daniel W. Jones
Daniel Wilkens
(McDonald Schools)
Danielle Davis
Danielle Detrixhe
Danielle Dunlap &
Brett Dunlap
Danielle Jameson
Danielle Terrill
Danny & Dana
Young
Danny Brewer
Danny Fabrizius
Danny Julian
Danny Lee Powell
Darcey Evans
Darcie Holthaus
Darcie Moske
Darius Bussen
Darla Fuller-Brock
Darlene Rosetta
Darold & Geneva
Wedel
Darral VanGoethem
Darrell Bowersox
Darrin Simmons
Daryl & Dee
Thornburg
Daryl & Marjorie
Hartzog
Daryl Dickman
Daugherty Family
Davault Family
Dave & Diane Scott
Dave & Georgiea
Slyter
Dave & Leigh
(Petersen) Varner
Dave Davis
Dave Little
Dave McKane
Dave Vance
DaVern & Pamela
Spreier
David & Deniece
Detjen
David & Donna Brill
David & Gerianne
Harrington
David & Karen Hinz
David & Lynett
Becker
David Charles Gray
David Charley

David Hickel
David Lawrence
David Leroy
Thompson
David M. August
David Massey
David Reed
David Sanders
David Schneider
David Simmons
David Utermoehlen
David Whorrall
Dawkins Farha
Dawn & Marc
Toomey
Dawn Burgardt
Dawn Chulsky
Dawn Harper
Daytan Moore
Dayton,
Pennsylvania
Dé Oehm (Oketo,
KS)
Deacon Terrill
Dean & Stacey
Ellington
Dean Cauble
Dean Dohe
Dean Jerome
Dean Reese Family
Dean Taton
Deanna Ebert
Pierson
Deanna Lanter
Deb Hanes-Nelson
Deb Perrin (Heston)
Deb Rice & Cathy
Lake
Debbie (Smith)
LeBleu
Debbie Berges
Debbie Fuller-
Bennett
Debbie Johnson
Debbie Pearce
Debbie Smiley
Debbie Thomas
Allton
Debbie Thornton
Schultz
Debby Benjamin
Haley
Deborah Ann Sapp
Deborah Duncan

Deborah Miller
Bolling
Debra Miller
Deceased Members
of the Stephen &
Chacon Families
Dedicated to the
Brave Pioneer
Women of Kansas
Dedicated to the
Mathews Family
(Lyons, KS)
Dedicated to the
Sidebottom Family
(Ransom, KS)
Dee Daugherty
Dee Nunnink
Dee Perez
Dee, Candy, Ricardo,
Sara, Dominick,
Ricky, Terry & Toni
Deedee Little
DeeDee Wells
Deidra Casida
Deidra Hendricks
Delaney Hastings
Delanie Moske
Delilah Benjamin
Pate
Delker & Addie Shaw
(Waldron, KS)
Della Tomanek
Deloras Baker
(Ashland, KS)
Deloris J. Vollmar
Delwin H. Locke
Dena (Saenger)
Bronson
Deneen Urbanek
Denise & Joni White
Denise Hastings
Denise Hollrah
Denise M. Thomason
Denise Montague
Denise Palmer
Dennis & Iva Krien
Dennis & Jennifer
Runyan
Dennis & Susan
Barnes
Dennis & Tammy
Grabmiller
Dennis Davis
Dennis Hughes
Dennis Schneider

604

Denton & Christine Roetter
Denton Rohrer
Deona Joy
Derek & Franscine Whitehouse
Derek Brady
Derek Wright
Derrek, Krystal, Aiden, Jalynn & Dylan Duerksen
Destiny & Killian Mason
Destiny Love
Devin M. August
Devin Strecker
Devon Grossardt
DeVore, Suiter, Hager & Crotts Families
DeVoss & Davault Families
DeVoss Family
Dewey Breese
Dewi Rusli
Diana Bright Ramsey
Diana Linn Ennis
Diana Sauder Miller George
Diane & Barry Walton
Diane (Hachmeister) Hill
Diane Foster-Parrett
Diane VanGoethem
Diane Wilkens Moro (McDonald Schools)
Dick Stoffer
Dillon Trimmell
Dimitri Beauregard
Dixie Nicholson
Dohe Peterson
Dolan K, McDaniel
Dominic Rockford
Dominic Slotto
Dominique Holliday
Don & Carol Stephen
Don & Cathy Hanken
Don & Gerry Bain
Don & Grace Cole
Don & Leslie Brown
Don & Sandy Francis
Don Kindt
Don Nelson
Don R. Danenberg

Don Reese Family
Don Schneider
Donald & Marie Hrabe
Donald Boos
Donald Eugene Hazen
Donald VanWey
Donald, Ramona, LaDonna, Shelley & Beverly Gordonauer
Donals Virginis
Donita Hayes
Donna Casteel
Donna Cochran Boyles
Donna Hamel
Donna Longbine
Donna Medek
Donna Oehm (Oketo, KS)
Donna Schneider Moranville
Donna Sue Davis
Donnie V. Bugbee
Donnie, Donna & Heather Wilkinson
Dorian Tanuis
Doris Nordyke Betsworth
Dorothy & Darren Becker
Dorothy (Colgrove) Brandt
Dorothy Bird
Dorothy Denk
Dorothy King Ketterer
Dorsett Markham
Doug Daugherty
Doug Nelson
Doug Sivils
Doug Strubbe
Douglas & Martha Schamle
Dr. Bob & Betty Moore (Caney, KS)
Dr. Curtis McElroy
Dr. Dave George
Dr. Elizabeth Tew
Dr. James and Gloria Croy (1972-1998)
Dr. John & Patricia Atkin

Dr. Lewis S. Henderson III DDS
Frances A. Henderson
Dr. Robert R. Snook
Dr. Shashi Sharma
Duane Lanter
Duane M. Stoskopf
Duane Ogren (Memorial)
Duane Wilkens (McDonald Schools)
Durham, Quinter & Lawrence
Durrenberger Family
Dustin & Courtney Hecht
Dustin & Monica McCown
Dustin Froelich
Dustin Kleekamp Family
Dustin Locke
Dustin Mathes & Kelby Mathes (Oberlin, KS)
Dustin Taylor
Dustin Wallman
Dwight Charles Colgrove
Dwight Hartman
Dwight Vallin
Dylan Boone
Dylan Murphy
E.H. & Marie Reese
Earl & Charla Seger Family
Earl E. Harrell (Hill City, KS)
Easton Dabney
Easton Murphy
Ed & Ann Riedel
Ed & Leba Shubkagel
Eddie Vering
Eden LePard
Edie Bastin Adamson
Edna Dean Harrell (Hill City, KS)
Edward Burnett
Edward Robert Ten Eyck
Edwin & Juanita Carswell

Elaine Bell (Danville & Louisburg, KS)
Elaine Ketterer Beckwith
Elaine Lortscher
Elaine Ragan
Elbert & Bessie Copple
Elbert Joe Charley
Elby R. Adamson
Eldon & Arlyss (Roepke) Wendland
Eldon & Karla Reif
Eldon Cress
Eldon Pate
Eleanor Hickel
Eliese Ueding
Elijah Vap
Elisabeth Oestmann
Elise McLeod
Elise Suarez
Elizabeth E. Nimz
Elizabeth E. Schulz
Elizabeth Eileen (Dye) Bailey
Elizabeth Losey
Elizabeth S. Treger
Elizabeth Shove
Elizabeth Sith
Elizabeth Thompson
Ella Cater
Ella Oehm (Oketo, KS)
Ella Schreiber
Ella Vap
Ellamae Watts
Ellie Abitz
Ellie Sharp
Elmir Family
Elsie P. Napier (2006)
Elspeth Rose Huerter
Elton & Marcella Smith
Elvin (JC) Betts
Elvin J. Reedy
Elwin E. McDannald
Elwood Olson
Elysa Griffiths
Em's Repair
Emberlyn LePard
Emil Gabelmann
Emilina Mills
Emilio LJ Lopez
Emily Boyd

Emily Jackson
Emily Lynn
Emily Miller
Emily Vallin
Emma Ohman
Emma Schreiber
Emmy Parks
Emory J. McKenzie
Ensley Vaupel
Eric Hadley
Eric Harper
Eric Ohman
Eric Simmons
Erica Barnes
Erica Locke
Erica Terrell
Erie Library
Erin Meierhoff
Erin Thompson
Erin Vaupel
Erma Bokern Robke
Ernest Wolff
Ernie & Karen Augustein
Ervin Miller & Jeanne Miller
Eryn Cox
Esther (Wendlandt) Obermeyer
Ethan Knoll
Eva Hazen
Eva Strecker
Evan Carter
Evan Lamb
Evelyn Aumiller
Evelyn Evans
Evelyn Miller
Everett Moddie
Evie Schreiber
Ewan Shortess
Fairbanks
Fairlene Swanson
Family of H.H. & Myrtle Stewart
Family of Wade Woodring
Fannie Persell
Fay F. Cochran
Fay Warders
Faye Ann Breese Hunziker
Faye Bausch
Fee & Cindy Monshizadeh

Florence "Dolly" Thomas
Florence McCarthy
Floyd Dean & Mary E. Fix
Floyd H. Beck
Floyd Hardy Jr.
Forgey Family
Fort Scott Museum of Creativity
Fr. Jim Hoerter
Frances Ashlock
Frances Biehler
Frances J. Morgan
Francis J. Ross Family
Frank & Margret Ball
Frank & Nan Vyzourek
Frank & Tammy Guilfoyle
Frank Kaiser
Frank Toman
Fred Hammack
Fred Holman
Frederick L. Peterson
Friends of the Ornate Box Turtle
G. Arnold Brooks
G. Marcene (Smith) Locke
Gabe, Toby & Henry Roetter
Gabriel Clark
Gabriella Quillen
Gage Guiot (Kansas Muralist, Instagram @jargon_ks)
Gail Barnard
Galan Family
Gale Binder
Galen & Shari Monaghan
Galloway Family (Allen, KS)
Garnett Fire Department
Garret & McLaren Armstrong
Garret E. McDannald
Garrett Family
Garrett Farha
Garrett Forshee
Garrett Roskam
Garrett Thompson

Gary & Jaccie
Gary & Lynnette
Curtis
Gary & Rose Pearce
Gary & Susan
Wescoat
Gary & Wendy
Walker
Gary Aumiller
Gary Gilchrist &
Grace Gilchrist
Gary Gonzales
Gary Grigsby
Gary Knoll
Gary Kussman
Gary Marshall
Gary Stafford
Gavin Robert
Gavynn Maddox
Gayle Avery & Mike
Avery
Gearold Wright
Gene & Lynn Angel
Gene Laverty
Gene Scott
Gene Whittey
Genia Deets
Genny Dixon
Gentry Upton
Whitaker
Geoffrey L.
Christensen
George & Annette
Ravens
George & Elizabeth
Lewis
George & Marjorie
Withroder
George Benjamin
George Galliart
George Stavropoulos
George W. Rogers
George, Elmer &
Marie Henderson
Georgia Stumpff
Rose
Gerald & Elsie
Haines (Butler
County, KS)
Gerald & Lynda
Harris
Gerald H. (Jerry)
Miner
Geraldine B.

Geraldine Reboul
Garrett
Gerard Holup
Geri "Ra Ra' Palmer
Gerry Jackson
Gertrude Grady
Elson
Gilbert Rodriguez
Gillin Newell
Gillis & Ernestin
Partin
Gina Farra
McClintick
Gina McBride
Ginger Howell
Gladys & Andy
Leinmiller – George,
Carol, Lloyd & Ginny
Gladys
(Lunkenheimer)
Beeson
Gladys Louise Swart
Rowley
Gladys Stinson
Glen & Louise
Stevenson
Glen & Pat Boren
Glen E. Napier
(2018)
Glen Sheets
Glen Smith
Glen, Vickie, Genay,
Grant & Greg Gibson
Glenda Harvey
Glenn & Ruth M.
Cunningham
Glenn B. Schulz
Gloria Stafford
Golda Blair
Golda Goforth
Goodland Games
Gordon R. Schulz
Gordon, Alma, Cody
& Christopher Trauer
Grace & Joey
Brandenburg
Grace & Kathleen
Carpenter
Grace Toman
Gracie Defore
Graham, Tasha,
Keagin & Maci
Grant Tew
Graysen DeJarnett
Grayson Farha

Greeley County
Library
Greg & Carla
Morrical
Greg & Carol Howard
Greg & Irene Burtin
Greg & Mallory Metz
Greg Herzog
Greg, Tracey, Katy &
Hannah
Gregg & Diane Barr
Gregg & Shelly
Hadley
Gregg Swanson &
Keli Reid
Greylen Heersche
Gudrun Tyler
Guy Justis
Gwen B.
Harshbarger
H. Lynn Smith
Hailee Gehlen
Hailey Smith-Knoll
Hal Brandenburg
Haly Hendricks
Handy LLC
Hannah K. Franklin
Hannah Karlin
(Grose)
Hannah Louise Gray
Hannah Zimbal
Hap (Henry) & Rose
Meier
Hard At Play (Garden
City, KS)
Harma P. McKenzie
Harold & Barbara
Muiller
Harold & Ina Jeanne
Dody
Harold & Lourine
Baker
Harold Atkins Garrett
Harold Joseph Davis
Jr.
Harold P.
Brandenburg Jr.
Harriet Bowman
Harry & Anna May
McKenzie
Harvey Wood
Haskell &
Shawnettee Williams
Haskell Cultural
Center & Museum

607

Hatt Hickey Family
Hattie (Ferris)
McMillan
Hayden Middleton
Hayes Breeding
Hayes Ross
Hazel Bright
Hazel L. Robb
Hazel Loraine
Heather Grossardt
Family
Heather Hansen &
James Wright
Heather Jennings
Heather Murphy
Helen K. Treger
Helen King & Family
Hellers
Henry Arthur Harrouff
Henry F. McMillan
Henry Moczygemba
Herald L. Willey
Herb Keck
Herbert C. Hoover Jr.
(Pleasanton, KS)
Herbert Treger
Herschel Eck
Historic Wolf Hotel
Staff
Hobie & Mary Ahrens
Holly Bane
Holly Schneider
Hotel Leatherock
Howard Raymond
Hoyt Wilhite
Hubert Heasty
Hudson Swagerty
Hugh Heasty
Hunter Asher Talon
Blocker
Hunter Hastings
Hunter L. Ullum
Hyla Wiles Winters
Ida Cheever
Ida May (Hooker)
Harrouff
Ida Studt
Iishshaa (Roberson)
Snoe
Ike Sheets
Ilamae James
Immanuel Jacob
Christian Betts

In Honor & Memory
of Harvey & Patricia
(Pat) Wood
In Honor of Alfred &
Bonita Heim Lager
In Honor of Beverly
O'Neal
In Honor of Bo Dillon
In Honor of Dianna
Dillon
In Honor of Dina
Dillon
In Honor of Lisa
Dillon
In Honor of Rhett
Kemp
In Honor of Slade
Dillon
In Honor of Tara
Kemp
In Honor of Tayvia
Kemp
In Honor of the
Tarlton &
McAlexander
Families (Hamilton,
KS)
In Honor of Tom
Dillon
In Honor of Travis
Dillon
In Honor of Trevor
Kemp
In Honor of Ty Kemp
In Loving Memory of
Don W. Wilkinson
In Loving Memory of
Donalee Sue Smith
In Loving Memory of
Esther Neubecker
In Loving Memory of
Jerry Caldwell
In Loving Memory of
Joseph Allen Wible
III
In Loving Memory of
Lela & Stanley Morey
In Loving Memory of
Norm Hosterman
In Loving Memory of
Sarah Elizabeth
Colling
In Memory of Alan,
Janey & Alana
Osborn

In Memory of Albert
& Velma
Schwerdtfeger
In Memory of Allen
D. Johnson
In Memory of B.
Brustowicz
In Memory of Benny
Miller
In Memory of Betty
Loy & Le Roy Loy
In Memory of Bill
Beals
In Memory of
Brandon T.
Cartwright
In Memory of Bud &
Mary Dodge
In Memory of Candis
Jerome
In Memory of Carolyn
Turvey
In Memory of Carrie
Kubin Buryanek
In Memory of Cassy
Linder
In Memory of Cecil &
Florence Thompson
In Memory of
Clarence & Ruth
Buryanek
In Memory of Clifford
& Val Wallace
In Memory of Cody
Gettler (Garnett, KS)
In Memory of Connie
Grossardt
In Memory of Craig
Moritz
In Memory of Dan &
Ellen Murphy
In Memory of
Darlene Horn
In Memory of Dean &
Genevieve Townley
In Memory of Delores
Koss
In Memory of
Demaree Hammond
In Memory of Dennie
Reed
In Memory of Donald
Lykins
In Memory of Donna
Studley

In Memory of Dr. Dallas E. Dillon

In Memory of Duane & Donita Goyen

In Memory of Duane Horn

In Memory of Earl & Willetta McBride

In Memory of Elbert & Wilma Frey

In Memory of Elden (Tubby) & Frauenfelder (Hanover, KS)

In Memory of Ernest Collard

In Memory of Florance Bottger Denk

In Memory of Frances Hagel (McLouth, KS)

In Memory of Fred Knoche

In Memory of Garold & Eleanor Mayfield

In Memory of Gene & Fawna Barrett

In Memory of George Hachmeister

In Memory of George Williams

In Memory of Gerald (Dean) Taylor

In Memory of Harold & Myrland Tonn

In Memory of Harold & Virginia Wenzel

In Memory of Ilah (Metz) Taylor

In Memory of Jack Vandeveer

In Memory of James (Jim) Taylor

In Memory of Jean Kunze Peterson

In Memory of Jeff Little

In Memory of Jeremiah M. O'Gara

In Memory of Jim & Lola Goff

In Memory of Jim Miller

In Memory of Jim Moore

In Memory of Joe Buryanek

In Memory of Joe Walker

In Memory of John Joseph Cannaley

In Memory of Jon Kreifels

In Memory of Justin Riley

In Memory of Katrina Fox

In Memory of Kelly Franklin

In Memory of Kenneth M. Stanley

In Memory of Lance Reichenberger

In Memory of Lauree Young

In Memory of Lawrence D. Biehler

In Memory of Leon Reeves

In Memory of Loy O. Carlson (Wichita, KS)

In Memory of Makinna Ann Krebaum

In Memory of Margaret Schulz

In Memory of Marvin Salber

In Memory of Mary F. Biehler

In Memory of Mary Ruth Spiegel Woerner

In Memory of Maxine Zuercher

In Memory of Meriden Locke

In Memory of Milton Bryan

In Memory of Norb & Joanne Bussen

In Memory of Pete Bottger & Florence Bottger Denk

In Memory of Pierre Carpentier

In Memory of Richard E. "Dick" Johnson

In Memory of Robert & Carol Brubaker

In Memory of Roberta Craig

In Memory of Roger & Judy Bales (Sawyer, KS)

In Memory of Roy Kreger

In Memory of Roy. M Johnson & Goldie May Frost Johnson

In Memory of Ruth Holle Collard

In Memory of Sally Hays Reed

In Memory of Sandra Schiff Vandeveer

In Memory of Sharon Shroyer-Johnson

In Memory of Sherri McBride

In Memory of Stanley & Edna Lee Withiam

In Memory of Stephanie Horn

In Memory of Teddy & Phyllis Zimmerman

In Memory of the Fred Farm (Herndon, KS)

In Memory of Tom Ramseier

In Memory of Wayne & Alice Dick (Zenda, KS)

Indiana County, Pennsylvania

Indie Workman

Ingrid Webster

Inman Harvest Cafe

Irene Hendershott

Irv & Marietta (Ward) Miller

Isaac Joaquin Christian Betts

Isaac McCoy

Isaac Trimmell

Isabel Lloyd

Isabella Murphy

Ivy Carrey

J. Bradley Lowell

J. D. Baughn

J. T. Blair

Jace & Samantha Beavers
Jace Collins
Jacinta Jarrell
Jack & Connie Percival
Jack & Victoria Haag
Jack Kelley
Jack McGonigal
Jack, Jerry, Barbara & Gary Monasmith
Jacki Clinton
Jackie Burns
Jackie Farra
Jackie Tedder
Jacob Barnes
Jacob Bowman
Jacob Heersche
Jacob Lindenman
Jacob P. Flax
Jacob Reichard
Jacqueline Thompson
Jadeane Laflen
Jaden Boone
Jaden Farha
Jake Dreyer
Jake Geisinger (Selden, KS)
Jake Jones
Jake Vasquez
Jake Worthington
James & Melva Barlow
James "JD" Biehler
James A. Evans
James Boddiger
James Dinkel & Michelle Dinkel
James E. Eliasen
James E. Harrell (Hill City, KS)
James E. Ross
James Flax
James H. Gordon
James Harold Nichols (Bronson, KS)
James Herken Jr.
James M. Ross
James Michael Gustafson
James Nelson
James Noble
James R. Flax

James Rohan
James Smiley
Jami Burger
Jami, Adam & Anna North
Jamie Balman Wallace
Jamie Penry
Jan Kindt
Jana Kahle
Jana Voitenko
Jane Cauble
Jane Henry-Johnson
Jane Hoerter
Janelle Domoney
Janelle Fowler
Janese Little
Janet Avery Wright
Janet Bair
Janet Fakes
Janet Hopson
Janet L. Kohls
Janet Lawrence
Janet M. Reynolds
Janet McDonald
Janet Schreiber
Janet Tygart Davis
Janice Brenner
Janice James
Janice Parks
Janice Turrentine
Janice Wentworth
Janie Brandenburg Jacobs
Jared D. Morey
Jared Davis
Jarek Baughn
Jaretta Ward
Jarrod Helms
Jason & Cheyenne Chrisanthon
Jason Abitz
Jason K. Davis
Jason McGahey
Jason Moske
Jason Rule
Jason Wesoloski
Jaxon Rice
Jay & Tami Mars
Jay & Vonda Copeland
Jay Dee Buchanan
Jay Perez
Jay Templin
Jayme Tillitson

Jayne Ceballos
Jayse Baughn
Jean Cashman Pearson
Jeanette M. Weiser
Jeanie Rose
Jeanine Brannan
Jeanine Reser
Jeanne (Meyer) Quinn
Jeff & Carla Hickey
Jeff & Dawn Unruh
Jeff & Eddie Chaney
Jeff Boyce
Jeff Hagerman
Jeff Hall
Jeff Hoyt
Jeff Kahle
Jeff Laha
Jeff Osterman
Jeff Roskam
Jeff Shufelt
Jeff Souter
Jeff, Robin, Darby & Sam Lampe
Jeffrey & Caryl Fank
Jeffrey & Jettie Zoller
Jeffrey Boddiger
Jen Tarter
Jen Taylor
Jene & Robin Allen
Jenna Morris
Jenna R. Rodriguez
Jennetta Scego
Jenni Hamman
Jennifer (Walker) Braun
Jennifer Brammer Curtis
Jennifer Dalton
Jennifer Duncan
Jennifer Harp
Jennifer McAlexander
Jennifer Schneider
Jennifer Weir
Jennifer Widmer Sullivan
Jennifer Zamora
Jenny Buckley
Jenny Cheatham
Jeremy "Scooter" Brown
Jeremy Hunt
Jeri Biehler

Jeri Davis Shute
Jeri Wright
Jerome Trimmell
Jerrald Colstrom
Jerry & Stacy
Wagoner
Jerry Benjamin
Jerry Caldwell
Jerry Ediger
Jerry Simmons
Jerry Sisler Family
(Kipp, KS)
Jerry Wade
JerryAnn Goding
Jesse Fern Charley
Jesse W. Flax
Jessica & Keith
Hannah
Jessica (Bernal Flora
Wright)
Jessica Farra
Hanson
Jessica Horn-
Carpino
Jessica Murphy
Jessica Reichard
Jessica Robinson
Jewel Farra Owen
Jewell Ceballos
Jill Danielle Koch
Jill, Matt & Jake Lee
Jim & Colleen Mann
Jim & Diana Schmidt
Jim & Donna Rourk
Jim & Karma Michael
Jim & Nancy Furney
Jim & Nancy Gruber
Jim Clopton
Jim Herbic & Lynn
Herbic
Jim McDonald
Jim Nusz
Jim Pritchard
Jim Pulliam
Jim Rhodes
Jim Springston
Jim Swan
Jim, Helen & Yvonne
Cook
Jo Buryanek Schmidt
Jo Herian
Joan Beamer
Joan Debord
Joan Dingwerth
Joan Holup

JoAnn Crow
JoAnn LeRoy
Stoskopf
Jocelyn Colby
Jock Farra
Jodi & Joel Mumma
Jodi Rosenberry
Jody Harbaugh
Jody K. Morey
Jody Robison
Stoskopf
Joe & Debbie Burns
Joe & Debra Banks
Joe & Jessica
Hoffman
Joe & Kay Religa
Joe & Linda Heinen
Joe Baughn
Joe Bodine
Joe Echer
Joe Perez
Joe Perry
Joe Watts
Joe, Shelby, Finlee &
Charlie Succi
John & Carol
Fletcher
John & Kris Ball
John & Mary
Harrington
John & Ruth Walker
John "Duke" Duncan
John "Jack" Hoffman
John Balman
John Baumgartner
John Blair
John Boone
John Brandenburg
John C. & Mary Marr
Kinter
John C. Hudson
John D. Augustus
John D. Scott
John Dandurand
John Edie
John Griffin
John Griffith
John H. Locke
John Hamernick-
Ramseier
John Hendricks
John Hoerter
John Holderness
Tom
John Just

John K. Ball
John K. Bestor
John Koepke
John L. Blair
John Lawrence
John R. Massey
John Rogers
John Sanz
John Shankles
John Sommers
John Stavropoulos
John T. Bird
John T. Meitner
John Urban & Ronna
Urban
John W. Ullum
John Yonke Family
Johnathan Bowman
Johnathen Freeman
Johnette Massey
Hodgin
Johnny Sanz
Johnsie Just
Joleen D. Dibben
Joleen Scheck
Meusburger
Jolene Evans
Joli Ridpath Root
Jon Farra
Jon Steuart
Jon, Alexis, Sam &
Jase Bailey
(Waverly, KS)
Jonah Hoerter
Jonathan & Kasey
Ulrich
Jone Minnie Williams
Jordan & Kori
Hartwell
Jordan M. Stevens
Jordan Parks
Jordan Rinck-Taylor
Joseph (Joe Mac)
Roy
Joseph Barbeau
Joseph Cuezze
Joseph Fuerch
Joseph Guillory
Joseph L. Whitaker
Joseph Quincy Ten
Eyck Sr.
Joseph Rockford
Joseph Vap II
Lissy Wines

Josephine Farra Wilson
Josephine Rockford
Josh & Amanda Guilfoyle
Josh & Jessica Bennett
Josh & Jordyn Britton
Josh Perez
Josh Strathman
Joshua Butler
Josie M. McDannald
Josie Mardis
Joy McDonald
Joyce Clennan Snodgrass
Joyce Ediger
Joyce Heilman
Joyce Keck
Joyce Koehn
Joyce Marrs
JT Construction Company
Juanita C. Gordon
Juanita Gonzales
Juanita Kuntz Carr
Judith Ann Ten Eyck
Judith Bright Russell
Judy Bond
Judy Corley
Judy Edie
Judy Ginder
Judy Graney Bond
Judy Lee Bean
Judy Marshall
Judy Montgomery
Judy Potter
Judy Siemsen
Judy Toman
Judy Wade Siragusa
Julia Bauer
Julia Lamb
Julia Wright Simens
Juliana Bernardo
Julie & Jerry Tynon
Julie & John Geisinger (Selden, KS)
Julie (Nordling) Andrews
Julie Clement
Julie Jelks
Junction City High Class of 1985
June I. Nimz

Junior "Cotton" Hunziker
Just For You Jewelry & Gifts (Hiawatha, KS)
Justin A. Wilton
Justin Bruster
Justin Lamb
Justin M. Geniuk
Justin Wesoloski
K. E. Freund
K. Voth
Kaci Y. Bayless
Kaden O'Mara
Kaden Vering
Kady M. Stevens (Smith)
Kaiden Tanuis
Kaleb Johnson
Kaleb O'Keeffe
Kaleigh Oestreicher
Kaley Froelich
Kallee Tucker
Kalyn Baughn
Kameron O'Keeffe
Kamilla Jones
Kannon Taylor
Kansas Oil Museum
Kara Guillory Stierman
Karen & Ernie Augustein
Karen & Keith Simmons
Karen (Lunsford) Compton
Karen Castillo
Karen Cochran Hanks
Karen Gates
Karen Guillory Bridges
Karen J. McKenzie-McAdoo
Karen Napier
Karen Whorrall
Karen Wolford
Karl O'Brien Smith
Karl Rohlich
Karla Shute Essmiller
Karla Sullivan
Karla, Brecken, Latham & Nola Kramer
Karol Hastings

Karsyn Ross
Kate Bachman (Neilson)
Kate Berney Werring
Kate Duncan
Katha Allison
Kathel L. Snook
Katherine H. White
Kathleen Kilian-Smith
Kathleen Schmidt
Kathryn Pauley Heslep
Kathy Basinger
Kathy Hartman
Kathy P. Thomas
Kathy Woelk
Kathy Wohlgemuth
Katie Claar
Katie Nollette
Katy Ast
Katy Hendricks Cater
Katy M. Wheeler
Kautzer Family
Kay Dalton
Kay Lawrence
Kay Lykins
Kay Nocktonick
Kay Reeder
Kay Steckman
Kayden Tappendick
Kayla Brown
Kayla Hall
Kaylie J. Ullum
Kaylin Detrixhe
KC R. Willey
Keaton Metcalf
Keegan T. August
Keela Riedel
Keenan Meierhoff
Keith & Jerri White
Keith & Mary Ann Drummet
Keith Just
Keith Wohlgemuth
Keith, Lei, Madison, Kyle, Kolton & Karter Eklund
Kelli Penner
Kelly Calton
Kelsen Day
Kelsey Abitz
Kelsey Darnall
Ken C. Jones
Ken Collins, Kansas State Representative

Ken Underwood
Kendall M. Hopp
Kendelle Runer
Kendi Hickel
Kennedy Trimble
Kenneth & Connie
Schaben
Kenneth & Taylor
Patterson
Kenneth A. Russell
Kenneth Cheever
Kenneth Eugene
Peterson
Kenneth H. Estes
(Class of 1956)
Kenneth M. Harrell
(Hill City, KS)
Kenneth Morrow Jr.
Kenneth Paul Jocius
Kenny & Mariah Jay
Kenny & Patsy Miller
Kenny Hamman
Kenny Walburn
Family
Kent Fuller
Kent Studt
Kenzy Tillitson
Keri Jenkins &
Darrell Jenkins
Kerry J. Locke
Kerry O'Connor &
Rick Banning
Kevin & Debbie
Witthuhn
Kevin & Glenda Little
Kevin & Lori Burk
Kevin & Marsha
Reynolds
Kevin Howton
Kevin J. Barnes
Kevin McDonald
Kevin Parks
Kevin Simens
Kevin The Burt
Kevin White
Kiddie Garden Day
Care
Kiefer Lucas Davis
Kim & Guy Price
Kim & Wendy Brotton
Kim Mick
Kim Olivar
Kim Vanderhofe
Kimberley (Rediker)
Stewart

Kimberly Bright
Kimi Zeman
Kinley Swagerty
Kinsel "Bob" Kincaid
Kirby & Brenda
Thowe
Kirby Shineman
Kirk & Krystal Potter
Kirk & Maddy Camac
Kirk Coomes
Kirk R. Chandler
Kirsten Elson
K-Motel
Knox Taylor
Koal Gibson
Kohart Family
Kora Lynn Louthan
Kortney Khan
Krista Johnson
Kristeena Thompson
Kristen F. Ball
Kristen Murphy
Kristi & William
(Jody) Herrman
Kristie O'Keeffe
Kristin Metcalf
Kristina Gann-
Albright
Kristina Hartman
Kristy Ebersole
Kristy Lee
Krysta Baughn
Kurt Pfannenstiel
Kyla Scherling
Kyle Johnson
Kyle Rodriguez
Kyle, Kaitlin,
Danielle, Dawson &
Dalaini Munstermann
Kyleb Collins
Kynli Baughn
Kyrsten Ross
LaCygne Historical
Society Museum
LaDeen White Allen
LaDonna Urban
Laikyn Rice
Lainey Scherling
Lakeside Auction &
Consignment
Lakeside Auction &
Consignments
Lamoine Nelson
Lana Kincheloe Stark
Landis Fischer

Landry Mastellar
Lane Heersche
Lane Moczygemba
Lanetta Wheatcroft
Lanny Hess
Larisa Watts
Larry & Ann Wassom
Larry & Eydie Green
Larry & Lori Senne
Larry & Martha Slack
Larry & Tammy
Roetter
Larry D. Mater
Larry Jerome
Larry L. Miller
Larry Nichols
Larry Rippe
Larry Rohrer
Larry Walton
Larry Wheatcroft
Larue Lennen
Lateef & Carrie
Dowdell
Lathan Mastellar
Laura A. Miller-Beck
Laura A. Pivonka
Laura Benjamin
Laura Evans
Laura Heide
Norwicke
Laura M. Roy
Laura Newsom
Laura Riley
Laura Swoyer
Laura Walker
Laura West
Lauranell Westberry
Laurel (Dandurand)
Ford
Lauren & Deanna
Rundle
Laurence Brammer
Laurie Simmons
Laurie Wilson
Laurine Brown
LaVelle Wheatcroft
LaVetta Stephens
Lawrence Bennett
Lawrence Bowman
Lawrence Burhenn
Layne Riot Martin
Leah Lindenman
Leann Lamb
Leatha A. Russell
Leatrice Ivy White

613

LeDena Laha
Lee & Pam Vyzourek
Lee Eslick-Huff
Lee Hastings
Lee Jones
Lee Jones & Monica
Jones
Lee McVey
Lee Wilson
Leland G. Gerber
Leland Schreiber
Leon & Margaret
Plante (Plainville,
KS)
Leon Marrs
Leon T. Glover
Leonard & Halen
Vyzourek
Leonard Anderson
Leonia Jean Bullock
(Weege)
Leroy Hickman
Family
Lesley D. Eliasen
Leslie Myers
Leslie Struckhoff
Levi Oehm (Oketo,
KS)
Levi Schreiber
Liam Gomel Thornhill
Library District #2
(LaCygne, KS)
Lilia Holup
Lillian Haden
Lillianna Jennings
Lily & Jackson Ryan
Lincoln Schreiber
Linda & Glenda
Rocco
Linda & Ken
Rousselle
Linda Bestest
Goodman
Linda Bird Brown
Linda Bullock
Linda Cutshaw
Linda Gieser
Linda Jerome
Linda Linderman
Benjamin
Linda O'Keeffe
Linda Oestmann
Linda Penner
Linda Pulliam
Linda Tessendorf

Linda Tillitson
Linda Wrench (Love,
Mom)
Lindsay B. Chriss
Lindsay C. Vaughn
Lindsey Oehm
(Oketo, KS)
Lindsey Rubottom
Lisa (Frerking) Carter
Lisa Dettmer
Lisa Diederich
Lisa Haverkamp
Murry
Lisa Jo Schmidt
Lisa K. Judd
Lisa K. Lugar
Lisa Seirer
Lisa Smith
(Gilmartin)
Lisa Thomas
Sorenson
Lisa Vasquez
Lisa Worthington
Little Blue River
Rentals
Little Creek Farms
(Benton, KS)
Liz Boltz
Lizabeth A. Hoffman
Lloyd & Pearl Ann
Shubkagel
Lloyd Haile (Rusty)
Smith
Lloyd Pearson
Lloyd R. Beeson
Loen & Janet Morris
Logan Terrill
Lois Jane Roberts
Lois Settles
Lonnie & Janice
Adamson
Lonnie Olivar
Lora Flock
Loren & Marge
Hemphill
Loren & Peggy
Metcalf
Loren Charles
Blecha
Lorena Wilton
Loretta Bussen
Loretta D. Pinick
Lori Ann White
Lori Baumgartner
Lori Boyce

Lori Lamb
Lori Royal
Lori Sulzen
Lori Worthington
Lorin & Jennifer
Corbett
Lorina Bowman
Lorraine & Wm.
Muckenthaler
Lorraine C. (Krampe)
Belford
Lou Boeckman
Louise Copeland
Louise Cumming-
Simmons
Lowell "Buck"
McDaniel
Loyal & Mackenzi
Jacob
Loyal Peevyhouse
Lucille Spencer
Lucy Lou Labranese
Lucy Marion
Brammer
Luella (Harrouff)
Durham
Luis Wells
Luke & Carolyn
Cochren
Luke Hoerter
Luke Kaufman
Luke Orcutt
Luke Schreiber
Lydia Evans
Lydia G. Flax
Lydia Gomel West
Lydia Hickel
Lyle Ratliff
Lynda Borth
Lynda Johnson
Lyndsi Oestmann
Lynell Kinish
Lynette Schmidt
Lynn & George
Drake
Lynn & Susan
Applegate
Lynn Tomanek
M.D. Marrs
M-A Garage
Mac Sanborn
Mack Newell
Mackenzie Carroll
Mackenzie
VanGoethem

Macon Farha
Madeleine A. Bock
Madeleine F. (Durham) McMillan
Madeline Owen
Madelynne Hawkinson
Madison Scherling
Madiynn Heersche
Maela Brown
Magen Hawkinson
Maggie Moser
Maggie Schneider
Mai Nnerd
Makayla Carroll
Malinda Wright
Mallory Brown
Mandy Trimmell
Marcena S. Gerber
Marcene L. Carstensen
Marcia Cook
Marcia Lecklider Newlin
Marcie Smith
Marcus Baumgartner
Marcy Sanz
Mardell (Randall) Wilhite
Marearl
Margaret Moore
Margaret Odegard
Margaret Weilert
Maria Luthi
Marianne McCorkill
Marie Grant
Marie Henry
Marie Miller Dutton
Marilee Williams
Marilyn Coxwell (Ashland, KS)
Marilyn Harbaugh
Marilyn Morrissey Lampman
Marilyn Walton
Marion Lesovsky
Marissa Ostrander
Marjorie Anderson
Marjorie Heasty
Marjorie Roeder
Marjorie Zillner
Mark & Charity Horinek (Sublette, KS)

Mark & Debbie Lehman
Mark & Kay Moore
Mark Coomes
Mark Julian
Mark Moulden
Mark Pawlush
Mark Rogers
Mark Scheve
Mark Wann
Marla D. (Locke) Ford
Marlene Johnson
Marlene Pfeifer Family
Marliegh Wright
Marlin Leon Sherfick
Marner Family
Marsh D. Rucas
Marsha Wells
Marshall & Jan Jernigan Stewart
Marshall Bowman
Marshall Elson
Marshall Hastings
Martha Dandurand
Martha Gene Burhenn Linville
Martha Hugo
Martha Sommers
Martha T. Burress
Martha Young Dreyer
Marty L. Hoffman
Marty Wells
Marva Blubaugh
Marvin Coker
Marvin Obermeyer Jr.
Marvin Obermeyer Sr.
Marvin, Cheryl, Marvin II & Drichelle
Mary (Dodd) Colgrove
Mary Adkins
Mary Ann Miner
Mary Ann Steward
Mary Anne Bernal
Mary Barbara Boddiger
Mary Bernard
Mary Boos
Mary Calderwood
Mary E. Gillmore
Mary Gale

Mary Jane Baker Miner
Mary Jane Ullum
Mary Jo Julian
Mary Kate Blankenship
Mary Kathryn Fuerch
Mary Kincaid
Mary Lou Holman
Mary Lou Peterson Heller
Mary Miller
Mary Sanz
Mary Westbrook
Mary Whitaker
Masie Sheets
Mason Angel
Mason Claar
Mason Hickel
Mathilde Strubbe
Mathis Lueker Real Est. & Property Mgmt
Matilda Mae (Tucker)
Matt & Kate Danders
Matt & Kate Dixon
Matt & Lacey Grogan
Matt Jordan – KGGF
Matt McDonald
Matt W. Smith
Matt, Joni, Idalynn & Dorothea Porter
Matthew Curtis
Matthew E. Ross
Matthew Hawkinson
Matthew Jones
Matthew Vaupel
Matthew William Smith
Mattison Love
Maureen (Hancock) Obermeyer
Mavon & Naomi Copeland
Max & Dixie Hudson
Max & Kelly Albin
Max Besinger
Max Empson
Max Mountford
Maxine Balderston
Maxine Swickard
McCaela Nelson
McFerrin
McKinsey Thompson
McLouth, McPherson & Oskaloosa

Meade County
Historical Society
Megan Holliday
Megan Jones
Melanie Kauffman
Melanie
Stavropoulos
Melchizedek
Hawkinson
Meleah Schrepel
Melissa Blocker
Melissa Boland
Melissa L. Rogers
Melissa Lindenman
Mellenbruch Family
(Fairview, KS)
Melody Colby
Melvin D. Epp
Melvin Kenworthy
Memory of Hazel
Perkins
Memory of Orval
Henry
Meredith Kate Pickert
Merit Carter
Merle Norman
Cosmetics
Merrilee Betts
Micah Hawkinson
Micah Kaufman
Michael & Mimi
Carpenter
Michael & Shelly
Essary
Michael Baumgartner
Michael Blankenship
Michael Burger
Michael Cater
Michael Dandurand
Michael E. Ullum
Michael Elson
Michael Haley
Michael J. Pivonka
Michael Raymond
Peebles
Michael Ryan Lee
Michael S. Gerber
Michael T. Ullum
Michael W. Shove
Michael Wayne
Michael Williams
Michele R. August
Michelle & Michael
Chilcott
Michelle Bradford

Michelle Cooper
Michelle Douglas
Gressel
Michelle Feltner
Michelle Ohman
Michelle Robert
Michelle Tyler
Michelle White
Micki (Beeson)
Marion
Mickie Gillette
Mikaelynn Scates
Mike & Becky Seeber
Mike & Cindi Vlach
Mike & Debbie
Snyder (Smith)
Mike & Denice
McCarty
Mike & Jill Carroll
Mike & Lachel Dreyer
Mike & Louann
Hatfield
Mike & Marjie Lewis
Mike & Phyllis
Farney
Mike & Steph
Phetteplace
Mike "Brainzooming"
Brown
Mike Benjamin
Mike E. Miner
Mike Getto SR &
Ginna Getto
Mike Louthan
Mike Oswald
Mike Rickenbrode
(Wichita, KS)
Mike Schneider
Mike Smith
Mike Stephens
Mike Thomas
Mike Woelk
Mike Worthington
Mila Scherling
Milani Quillen
Mildred Caldwell
Miles & Kim Pepperd
Millicent Craig Tygart
Mindy & Rick
Danberry
Miranda Read
MisFit Cattle Co.
Mit S. Winter
Mitch & Shelly Hewitt
Mitch Staatz

Mitch, Nancy, Aaron
& Scooter
Mona Broomfield
Monica Jones
Monte & Terri Hayes
Moore Family Library
MoPac Railroad
Depot Museum
Morgan Blockburger
Moriah Carpenter
Moses J. Dabney
Mound Valley
Housing
Mr. & Mrs. Patrick
Laham
Mr. and Mrs. Kerry
Scott
MSC Boutique
Mullen Family
Muller Family
Munn Family &
Wagner Family
Murphys Seamless
Roofing Inc.
Mylee Maddox
Myra L. Hutchinson
Myrick Hawkinson
Nada Belle McCool
Nancy (Mosher)
Clopton
Nancy Ann Drovetta
Hughes
Nancy Brandenburg
Nancy Cruce
Nancy Davis
Nancy Hartke
Housewright
Nancy Holsinger
Nancy Howerter
Nancy Marengo
Wyatt
Nancy Reese-Dillon
& Pat Dillon
Nash Farha
Natalie Boone
Natasha Rowley-
Phipps
Nathan Schmidt
Nathan Smalley
National Tax Colby
Neal & Joan Lehew
Neal & Manda
Graham
Neal Julian
Neal Sharma

Neil Crow
Nels, Karen, Nash &
Mac Lindberg
Newman V. Treger
Nicholas Brim
Nicholas Cerre
Nicholas Hargett
Nicholas Rickford
Grant
Nick McMillin
Nick, Katy, Coleman
& Nathan Reinecker
Nicki, Larry, Kadyn,
Marek & Janicka
Williams
Nicole Brewer
Nicole Noble
Nik Stavropoulos
Noah Erichsen &
Logan Erichsen
Noah Wallace
Nora Jo Thomas
Cavanaugh
Nora Lloyd
Noreen Markham
Norma Allison
Norman Walton
Nuthin' Fancy Bakery
O.P. Miller
Obe William
Morrissey
Ola Miller Anderson
Olive Graham
Olivia Cheatham
Olivia Lara
Olivia Murphy
Olivia Sharma
Olivia, Kyle, Luther &
Clara Peterson
Olivia's LLC
(Gardner, KS)
Ollen W. Linss
Omer E. Roy
Opal Rhodes
Orlis Allison
Orpha L. Carlson
(Wichita, KS)
Osawatomie History
Museum
Oscar M. Burrows &
Alvin Dwaine
Burrows
Othelia S. Funk
Owen Campbell
Oz Brewing

Ozzie Bakes LLC
P. H. Roy
Paige Hamman
Paisley Locke
Pam Koehn
Pam Scott-Rippe
Pam Spencer
Pamela Nordhus
Pamela Steinmeyer
Pamela Toman
Pamela Wills Burnett
Parker Feris
Parker Zachgo
Pat C. McDaniel
Pat Haremza
Pat Nichols
Pat Stranathan
Patricia Sheets
Patrick Eslick-Huff
Patrick Kelly
Patrick VanGoethem
Patsy Giangrosso
Patsy Vann
Patti Jorgensen
Patty & Dan Foss
Patty Roskam
Patty St. Clair
Patty Wheelbarger
Loy
Paul & Cheryl Jones
Paul & JoElla Phares
Paul & Nancy Roth
Paul & Vee
Carrington
Paul (Blade)
Schauner
Paul Anderson
Paul Bird
Paul Boeckman
Paul Boone
Paul Craig
Paul D. Freeman
Paul G. Schulz Sr.
Paul Hansen
Paul Kitzke
Paul Pawlush
Paul R. Oltjen
Paul West
Paul Whitaker
Paula Oltjen Willman
Paula Robke
Pauline Gerstner
Elson
Pauline Kaiser
Paxtyn Birdsong

Payton Stevenson
Pearl Just
Pearl Rice
(Lancaster, KS)
Peggy D. Chandler
Peggy Henderson-
Widenor
Penny Boyce
Penny Dorado
Penny Garrett
Nemechek
Pete Bogerd
Peyton & Jacob
Kocur
Phelps-Mendenhall
Phil Cook
Phil Klinkhardt
Phil Oestmann
Phil Pfister & Bev
Pfister
Philip A. Niblock
Phove T. Hopp
Phylis L. Dozier
Phyllis K. (Bugbee)
Hunter
Phyllis Rogers
(VanOverschelde)
Phyllis Smith
Phyllis Springston
Piper Murphy
Pizza Time
Pizza Village
Portia (Wools)
Murphy
Prairie Family Dental
(Junction City, KS)
Prairie Museum of
Art & History
Prairie Psychiatric
Care (Jennifer Kubin,
MSN, APRN,
PMHNP-BC)
Prairie View
Education
Foundation (PVEF)
Preston Bodine
Priscilla "Pat"
Sumearll
Quintin Robert
R. Brustowicz (KSU
'14)
R. Janet Walraven
R. Marl Ford
R. R. Freund

Raceile (Lichtenhan)
Owen
Rachael Wohletz
Rachel Hink
Rachel Kelly
Rachel Louise Gray
Rachel R. Rodriguez
Raelei Thornton &
Rylan Thornton
Raeli Orr
Raichelle Freeman
Raina Heinrich
Ralph & Lorette
Rogers
Ralph Kleekamp
Family
Ralph Massey
Ramon & Lyla
Ramirez
Ramon Alvarez
Ramona Garvey
Ramona June
(Bugbee) Tinsley
Ramona West
Randall Rogers
Randall Winter
Randy & Karen
Young
Randy & Mariann
Affolter
Randy Barnes &
Tara Barnes
(Knudsen)
Randy Benjamin
Randy Heilman
Randy Herzog
Randy Laflen
Randy Linderman
Randy, Elisa, Rex &
Alex Lundgren
Ray & Verena Wetter
(Hanover, KS)
Ray Oehm (Oketo,
KS)
Ray Rosetta
Ray Shobe
Raymond E.
Lunsford
Raymond Thomas
Reagan Gehlen
Reba Erickson
Rebecca & Jim
Meairs
Rebecca Kelly
Rebekah Hink

Reese B. Birkholz
Regina Mayer
Reighney Boone
Reka (Turley)
Beeson
Remington
Stevenson
Remmi Knoll
Renn Allsman
Rev. Sam Leonard
Rex Cheever
Rex Gene
Wheelbarger
Rheva Boswell
Rhonda & Steve
Lorenz
Rhonda
Siebenmorgen
Rian Zimbal
Rice County Tourism
Rich & Terri Powers
Rich Holderman
Richard & Cindy
Williams
Richard & Debra
Stafford Shearer
Richard & Jana
Angel-Ross
Richard & Kathy
Buessing
Richard & Linda
Inman (Hanover, KS)
Richard & Mary Jo
Carswell
Richard & Maureen
Richard Brown
Family
Richard Evans
Richard J. & Mary
Elizabeth Fischli
Richard Lee
McMillan
Richard VanWey
Rick & Juana Uht
Rick & Stephanie
Guilfoyle
Rick & Susan
Fitzgerald
Rick Allison
Rick Hays
Rick Mick
Rickee Maddox
Rik Vanessa
Rileigh Brewer
Riley ReQua

Riley Tillitson
Rina N.
Ripp Freeman
Rita Cochran Davis
Rita Marie (Schmidt)
Koehn
Rj Maldonado &
GoodFinds
(Burlington, KS)
Rob Rowe & Rika
Rowe
Robby McCurdy
Robert & Jeanie
Shearer
Robert & Sheila Weis
Robert & Shirley
Petrey
Robert "Bob" Goltra
III
Robert C. Beeson
Robert Craven
Robert Detwiler
Robert Dreyer
Robert E. "Bob"
Thomas Jr.
Robert E. "Bobby"
Thomas Jr.
Robert F. (Bob)
Wilhite
Robert Hahn
Robert J. Thomas
Robert Jr. & Jennifer
Kempin
Robert O'Gara
Robert R. Beeson
Robert S. Heller
Robert Siemsen
Robert Tygart
Robert VanWey Sr.
Robert Wayne
McCool
Robert, Deanna,
Emma, Isaac & Aden
Morris
Roberta (Wilhite)
Mardis
Robin Eshelman
Robin Froese
Robin Roberts
Robin Roberts
Racing
Rocky Seirer
Rod & Barbara
Dryden
Rod & Ginny Tolle

618

Rod Bussen
Rodger & Jane Linn
Rodney Casida
(1956-2022)
Rodney Cooper
Rodney Evans
Rodney R. Napier
(2018)
Rogena Grigsby
Roger & Janet
Henderson
Roger Boland
Roger Borth
Roger Grossardt
Roger Loder
Roger Nelson
Roger Tanuis
Romney Runyan
Ron & Cherie Jantz
Ron & Kay Kelly
Ron & Mary Lou
Bowen
Ron & Susan
Hughes
Ron Balderston
Craig Balderston
Ron Beggs
Ron Calvaruso
Ron Chellew
Ron Ediger
Ron Jennings
Ron Luhring
Ronald & Jeanne
Sturgeon
Ronald & Karen
Deutscher
Ronald Carlson
Ronald G. Lunsford
Ronald Spencer
Roni Rogers
Rosalie M. Banks
Rose & Faye Siegle
Rose Morgan
Sanders
Rosella Jacka
Roselynn Boone
Rosemary Ann
Beaman
Rosemary Kennedy
Rosetta "Babe"
Breese
Rosie Hastings
Ross Tygart Jr.
Rossman Family

Roxanne (Nevitt)
England
Roy & Dorothy Ruhl
Roy Currie
Roy Goding
Royal Valley Middle
School 7th Grade
History – Mrs.
DelToro
Ruby Gomel Osthoff
Russ McDonald
Russell & Leah
Redding
Russell Smith
Russell, Leann,
Alyvia & Amara
Johnson
Ruth Critser
Ruth Heasty
Ruth Shepherd Wolff
Ruth Thompson
Ruthie LePard
Ruthie Vance
Ruxton Workman
Rvey Rosson
Ryan & Kirsten Zoller
Ryan Claar
Ryan Cook
Ryan D. August
Ryan Lara
Rydge Oestreicher
Ryker J. Bennett
Rylan Thompson
Rylynn Wilper
S. Baylee (Ford)
Engle
Sabrina Anderson
Richards
Sadie Ann Russell
Sadie Hayden
Sadina Marie
Wagner-Walraven
Sally J. (Livingston)
Boyce
Salvador Del Real
Corona
Sam McMillin
Samantha Brox
Samantha Castoldi-
Ennis
Samantha Kempher
Samantha Tremblay
Family
Samantha Wilper
Sammy Spears

Samuel & Pennie
Nicholson
Samuel M. Brown II
Sandra Sherraden
Jaggard
Sandy Pagacz
Sandy Reed Mitchell
Sara Lewis
Sara McFarland
Sara McGinnis
Sara Osterman
Sara Ross
Sarah Dehn
Sarah Opal Cochran
Satchel Creek Ranch
Sawyer Robinson
Scooters Lawn &
Leisure Repair
(Rossville, KS)
Scott & Donna
Anderson
Scott & Julie Gregory
Scott & Kris
Lundgren
Scott Heilman
Scott Holder
Scott J. Ricke
Scott Landreth
Family
Scott Neubecker
Scott Walker
Scott, Carrie, Zellie &
Lorynn Goodheart
Scott, Regina, Erika
& Sydney Erickson
Sean & Stephanie
Schraeder
Sean Olivar
Seeker Bruce Bodine
Serena McCurdy
Serenity Violet
Blocker
Sereta R. Fager
Service Systems
Seth Harp
ShananiGanns
Shane Jarvis
Shane Love
Shane Ross
Shanna Maddox
Shannon & Kimberly
Bowie
Shannon Purdy &
Heather Purdy

Sharon & Bobby
Scroggins
Sharon (Balderston)
Saulnier
Sharon Henning
Sharon Koepke
Sharon Saulnier
Sharon Schwemmer
Shaun O'Keeffe
Shawn & Christina
Carpentier
Shawn & Lorelei
McFarland
Shawn Davis
Shawn Lindenman
Shawn Staatz Bruner
Shawn Wick
Shawn, Cammy,
Sarah, Reilly, Quincy
& Parker Jensen
Shawna Tunnell
Shawnn Adams
Shay Ledbetter
Shayne Allen
(Jackie) & Brailynn
Johnson
Shed & June
Degenhardt
Sheila Baumgartner
Sheila Maas
Sheila Meyer
Shelby & Christopher
Grissom
Shelby Liang
Shelley Culver &
Wallace Culver
Shelley Robertson
Shelly Farha
Shelly Murphy
Sheri Gray
Sheri Lynn Cavin
Sheri Yager
Sherri & Max Grogan
Sherrill A. Hoover
(Chanute, KS)
Sherry Carlson Hess
Sherry Watts
Sherry, Mike & Laura
Sheryl Hansford
Shirley & Dennis
Dobbs
Shirley Devanney
Shirley Vasquez
Shirley Wolff Ackley
Shurelle Wegele

Sierra Ravin Blocker
Sims Family
Snake Blocker
Sneary Family
Soeken
Sonia Derusseau
Sonja Griffith
Sonny Singhisen
Sophia Sharma
Spencer Farha
Spencer Zachgo
Spike's Café (Ingalls,
KS)
St. Mary's Real
Estate, Inc.
Stacey Moddie
Staci Hunt
Stacy Taylor
Stacy Waters
Stan & Kathy Utting
Stan Ewy
Stella McElroy
Stephanie & Jay
Scott
Stephanie Grams
Stephanie McDonald
Stephen A. Baldwin
Steve & Katie Pope
Steve & Mary
Skubkagel
Steve & Sherry
Bullock
Steve & Sue
Stutterheim
Steve Blubaugh
Steve Buchanan
Steve D. McDannald
Steve D. McDannald
Jr.
Steve Fuller
Steve Logan
Steve M. Stoskopf
Steve McCorkill
Steve Sherrow
Steve Walton
Steve, Carla, William
& Audra Rush
Steven & Donna
Johnson
Steven O'Keeffe
Steven Wessels
Store Gypsum
Stormie Brown
Strauss Family
Stringer Family

Stuhn Family
Sue Herman
Sula Thomas
Summer Root
Summers Brown
Susan A. Winter
Susan Brewer
Susan Bunyan
Susan G. Hammond
Susan Goering
Susan Runyan
Susie Reed Henry
Suzanne Franz
Swaffer Family
Sweet Dreams B&B
Sylvester Byrd
Sylvia K. Epp
T. J. Stout
Taevian Dabney
Tagan Evans
Talynn Franks
Tamara Ann Green
Tamera Wood
Tammi Knight
Tammy Gerlits
Tammy J. Phillips
Overton
Tammy Meyer Moore
Tammy Nichols
Tammy Strawn
Moulden
Tammy Wentz
Tanner Beach
Tanner Cheatham
Tara Ferguson
Tara Richardson
Tasha Krebaum
Family
Tatum D. Stevens
Tatum, Kendal &
Maggie Doebele
Taylor Weishaar
Taylour Tedder
Teagen Tanuis
Teckla J. Wattman
Ted & Carol Murphy
Ted & Diora,
Josephine, Brenda
Teda Princ-Huskey
Teddi Sue Osborn
(Ashland, KS)
Teresa Gorman
Teresa Meitl
Teresa Wesoloski
Terrance Thompson

Terri Hughes Kruetzer
Terry & Karen Frederick
Terry & Rita LeDuc
Terry & Robyn Siegle
Terry Bright
Terry Bussen
Terry Lee Hargett
Terry Lynn Bunnell Hargett
Terry Mann
Terry V. Boyce
Terry Wade
Thatcher Moddie
The Boston Meyer Family
The Bradbury Family
The Brustowicz Family (NJ & KS)
The Cherryvale Bed & Breakfast
The Class of 79
The Cuzzo Family (NJ)
The DeWitt Family
The DuBois Family
The Dunning Family
The Fiene Family
The Galen Bennett Family
The Grabill Family
The Hageman Family
The Henke Family of Kansas
The Herrman Family
The Hrabe Family
The Humpert Family
The Hurt Family
The Ireland Family
The James & Carol Smith Family
The Kansas Gastronomist (TKG)
The Lafferty Family
The Leidig's (Lenora, KS)
The Loerger Family
The McNitt Family
The Pearlsnaps (Garden Plain, KS)
The Raymond Parks Family
The Rick Wiley Family

The Robert Family (Englewood, KS)
The Rumbaugh Family
The Sister's Boutique
The Stanley Harding Family
The Sutton Family
The Torn Edge (Wellsville, KS)
The Turnbull Family
The Ward Siblings (5)
The Wymer Family (Protection, KS)
Theo Stavropoulos
Theodore Bowman
Theodore Meyer Family
Theodore Plummer
Theresa & David Whatley
Theresa Rohrer
Thomas Wesoloski
Tiiu Haamer
Tilly Newell
Tim & Emma Brownell
Tim & Kim Nollette
Tim Cheatham
Tim Miller
Tim O'Mara
Tina Estes
Tina Peevyhouse
Tina Schenherr-Peery
Tina Tomanek Hoerter
Tinsley Runer
Tisha Ross-Miller
Tiya Tonn
TNT Auto
Tod Stafford
Todd Calderwood
Todd Quillen
Todd Schneider
Tom & Anita Harvey McDaniel
Tom & Pearl Sullivan
Tom & Roberta Harkness
Tom & Toni Scimeca
Tom Ayers
Tom Gerlits
Tom Thurston

Tomi Carpenter
Tommy, Holly, Moses, Olympas, Jewel & Styles Peterson
Tonalea Dody
Toni (Nevitt) Scallion
Toni Nusz
Toni Stafford (Erwin)
Tonja & Craig Davis
Tonja Vallin
Tony Vlach
Tony, Gerilynn, Shannon & Annalise Martinez
Tony, Jennifer, Kendall, Brandt, Berklee & Locklyn Clark
Tonya (Grosfield) Jones
Tracie Morgan
Tracy M. Byrd-Hudson
Tracy Myrick
Tracy Senne
Travis & Loriett Puryear
Travis Angel
Travis Hageman
Travis Scates
Travis Vallin
Trent & Kendra Witthuhn
Trevor Goforth
Trevor K. Alexander
Trevor Vsetecka
Trey Ediger
Tricia Rex Carnes
Trina Rush
Triple K Farm
Trish Poage
Trista Rosenberger
Tristan W. Jones
Troy Ochsner
Troy Toman
Truitt & Hadley Witthuhn
Trystan Pringle
Twila (Colgrove) Brandt
Two Boys & A Tee
Ty & Abbie Mosier
Ty, Janna, Maya & Reese Pattison

Tyson Rosenberger
Una O'Gara
Valeria Marrs Edwards
Valerie Rito-Mastellar
Valley View Ranch
Vella Mae (Kraft) Jantz
Vera Dreyer Watts
Verl & Betty Stevens
Vern "Tuffy" Rhodes
Vern Rhodes
Vernon Sommers
Veronica (Aitken) Olivar
Veronica Nimz
Vicki Larson
Vickie (Belford Smith)
Vickie Deines
Victor & Deanna Hagy
Victoria & Douglas Hochstetler
Victoria Rush
Victoria Stephen
Virgel Fakes
Virgie Ratliff
Virgil E. Belford Jr.
Virgil Palmer "A Walking Legend"
Virginia Marshall
Vivian Bowman
Vula Mae Roy
W. F. Freund
Walker Trimble
Wallace J. Bugbee
Wallace M. Carter Jr.

Walter "Doc" & Irene Nichols (Builder of 30+ Grain Elevators in KS)
Walter Brown
Warren D. Chriss
Warren Schoming
Wayne & Linda Jones
Wayne & Louise Cressler
Wayne A. & Martha Jo Clark
Wayne Bird
Wayne Jacka
Wayne K. Funk
Waynetta (Kitsl) Shove Maynor
Webster L. Elson Sr.
Wendell Anderson
Wendy Skinner
Wes & Susie Fisk
Wes Tillitson
Wesley Skillman
Wesley T. Ford
Weston A. Bohrer
Wheeler Family
Whiskey Bin Grainery
Whitey Neubecker
Whitney Wilson
Wilbur Colgrove
Will Toman
William & Alice Trauer
William A. (Trey) Jones III
William A. Dozier
William Blaine Ennis

William C. Nimz
William E. Durham
William E. May
William Henry
William L. Audrey Louise Fix
William Rosson
William, Stephanie & Matthew Bryan
Williams Family
Willie Christman
Wilma VanWey
Wilmer (Baldy) Balderston
Wilmer Dean Cossaart
Winston Wayne Shove
Wood Wiles
Wretha L. (White) Locke
Wright & Johnson Families
Xander Sharma
Xavier Rodriguez
Yoder Thrift Shop (9815 S. Main, Yoder, KS 67585)
Yvette Ediger
Zac Engle
Zachary Love
Zachary R. Allen
Zander Colt Saber Blocker
Zayn Orr
Zayne Godbout
Zeke Fira & Mikaela Fira
Zowie Fraser

…and to everybody else who helped me along the way. Thank you!

VISIT627*Kansas*

# Town Index

Deerfield 248
Delia 217
Delphos 371
Denison 217
Denton 131
Derby 448
Dexter 107
Dighton 267
Dodge City 163
Dorrance 431
Douglass 59
Downs 368
Dresden 118
Dunlap 334
Durham 293
Dwight 335
Earlton 350
Eastborough 449
Easton 268
Edgerton 234
Edmond 356
Edna 257
Edwardsville 525
Effingham 30
El Dorado 60
Elbing 60
Elgin 69
Elk City 330
Elk Falls 143
Elkhart 338
Ellinwood 37
Ellis 152
Ellsworth 156
Elmdale 66
Elsmore 21
Elwood 131
Emmett 379
Emporia 288
Englewood 85
Ensign 186
Enterprise 127
Erie 350
Esbon 225
Eskridge 503
Eudora 135
Eureka 194
Everest 52
Fairview 52
Fairway 234

Fall River 195
Florence 293
Fontana 318
Ford 165
Formoso 225
Fort Scott 48
Fowler 311
Frankfort 301
Frederick 409
Fredonia 519
Frontenac 112
Fulton 50
Galatia 38
Galena 80
Galesburg 351
Galva 304
Garden City 160
Garden Plain 449
Gardner 235
Garfield 373
Garnett 26
Gas 21
Gaylord 477
Gem 499
Geneseo 409
Geuda Springs 494
Girard 113
Glade 376
Glasco 92
Glen Elder 323
Goddard 449
Goessel 294
Goff 346
Goodland 475
Gorham 432
Gove City 179
Grainfield 179
Grandview Plaza 177
Great Bend 38
Greeley 26
Green 88
Greenleaf 513
Greensburg 253
Grenola 144
Gridley 100
Grinnell 180
Gypsum 436

Haddam 513
Halstead 203
Hamilton 195
Hamlin 52
Hanover 514
Hanston 215
Hardtner 32
Harper 201
Hartford 290
Harveyville 504
Havana 330
Haven 396
Havensville 379
Haviland 255
Hays 152
Haysville 450
Hazelton 33
Hepler 113
Herington 127
Herndon 394
Hesston 204
Hiawatha 53
Highland 131
Hill City 182
Hillsboro 294
Hoisington 40
Holcomb 162
Hollenberg 514
Holton 218
Holyrood 157
Hope 128
Horace 193
Horton 54
Howard 144
Hoxie 468
Hoyt 219
Hudson 479
Hugoton 484
Humboldt 22
Hunnewell 494
Hunter 324
Huron 30
Hutchinson 397
Independence 330
Ingalls 186
Inman 305
Iola 23
Isabel 33
Iuka 391

Jamestown 93
Jennings 118
Jetmore 216
Jewell 226
Johnson City 483
Junction City 177
Kanopolis 157
Kanorado 476
Kansas City 525
Kechi 450
Kensington 477
Kincaid 27
Kingman 250
Kinsley 142
Kiowa 33
Kirwin 376
Kismet 459
La Crosse 427
La Cygne 276
La Harpe 24
Labette 257
Lake Quivira 235
Lakin 249
Lancaster 30
Lane 167
Langdon 400
Lansing 268
Larned 374
Latham 61
Latimer 335
Lawrence 136
Le Roy 101
Leavenworth 269
Leawood 237
Lebanon 478
Lebo 101
Lecompton 138
Lehigh 295
Lenexa 236
Lenora 356
Leon 62
Leona 132
Leonardville 419
Leoti 517
Lewis 142
Liberal 460
Liberty 332
Liebenthal 428
Lincoln Center 274

Lincolnville 295
Lindsborg 305
Linn 514
Linn Valley 276
Linwood 271
Little River 410
Logan 376
Lone Elm 27
Long Island 377
Longford 88
Longton 145
Lorraine 158
Lost Springs 296
Louisburg 318
Louisville 380
Lucas 432
Luray 432
Lyndon 359
Lyons 410
Macksville 480
Madison 196
Mahaska 514
Maize 451
Manchester 128
Manhattan 419
Mankato 226
Manter 483
Maple Hill 504
Mapleton 50
Marion 296
Marquette 307
Marysville 301
Matfield Green 67
Mayetta 219
Mayfield 495
McCracken 428
McCune 114
McDonald 394
McFarland 504
McLouth 221
McPherson 307
Meade 311
Medicine Lodge 34
Melvern 359
Menlo 500
Meriden 221
Merriam 237
Milan 495
Milford 178

Miltonvale 93
Minneapolis 372
Minneola 86
Mission 238
Mission Hills 238
Mission Woods 239
Moline 145
Montezuma 186
Moran 24
Morganville 89
Morland 182
Morrill 54
Morrowville 515
Moscow 485
Mound City 277
Mound Valley 258
Moundridge 308
Mount Hope 451
Mulberry 114
Mullinville 255
Mulvane 452
Munden 406
Muscotah 31
Narka 406
Nashville 251
Natoma 368
Neodesha 520
Neosho Falls 522
Neosho Rapids 290
Ness City 353
Netawaka 219
New Albany 521
New Cambria 436
New Strawn 101
Newton 204
Nickerson 400
Niotaze 70
Norcatur 118
North Newton 206
Norton 356
Nortonville 221
Norwich 251
Oak Hill 89
Oakley 279
Oberlin 119
Offerle 143
Ogden 421

Oketo 302
Olathe 240
Olivet 359
Olmitz 41
Olpe 291
Olsburg 380
Onaga 380
Oneida 346
Osage City 360
Osawatomie 319
Osborne 369
Oskaloosa 222
Oswego 258
Otis 429
Ottawa 167
Overbrook 360
Overland Park 241
Oxford 495
Ozawkie 222
Palco 424
Palmer 515
Paola 320
Paradise 433
Park 180
Park City 452
Parker 277
Parkerfield 108
Parkerville 335
Parsons 259
Partridge 401
Pawnee Rock 41
Paxico 505
Peabody 297
Penalosa 252
Perry 223
Peru 70
Phillipsburg 377
Pittsburg 114
Plains 312
Plainville 424
Pleasanton 278
Plevna 401
Pomona 168
Portis 370
Potwin 62
Powhattan 55
Prairie View 378
Prairie Village 243
Pratt 391

Prescott 278
Preston 392
Pretty Prairie 401
Princeton 169
Protection 104
Quenemo 361
Quinter 180
Radium 480
Ramona 298
Randall 226
Randolph 421
Ransom 354
Rantoul 169
Raymond 411
Reading 291
Redfield 50
Republic 406
Reserve 55
Rexford 500
Richfield 338
Richmond 169
Riley 422
Robinson 55
Roeland Park 244
Rolla 339
Rose Hill 63
Roseland 81
Rossville 462
Rozel 375
Rush Center 429
Russell 433
Russell Springs 280
Sabetha 346
Salina 436
Satanta 214
Savonburg 24
Sawyer 392
Scammon 81
Scandia 407
Schoenchen 154
Scott City 445
Scottsville 324
Scranton 361
Sedan 70
Sedgwick 206
Selden 468
Seneca 347
Severance 132

Severy 196
Seward 480
Sharon 35
Sharon Springs 506
Shawnee 244
Silver Lake 462
Simpson 324
Smith Center 478
Smolan 438
Soldier 219
Solomon 129
South Haven 496
South Hutchinson 402
Spearville 165
Speed 378
Spivey 252
Spring Hill 245
St. Francis 84
St. George 381
St. John 481
St. Marys 381
St. Paul 351
Stafford 481
Stark 351
Sterling 411
Stockton 425
Strong City 67
Sublette 214
Summerfield 302
Sun City 35
Susank 41
Sylvan Grove 274
Sylvia 402
Syracuse 198
Tampa 298
Tescott 372
Thayer 352
The Highlands 403
Timken 430
Tipton 325
Tonganoxie 271
Topeka 463
Toronto 523
Towanda 63
Tribune 193
Troy 132
Turon 403

Tyro 332
Udall 108
Ulysses 183
Uniontown 51
Utica 354
Valley Center 453
Valley Falls 223
Vermillion 302
Victoria 154
Vining 515
Viola 453
Virgil 197
WaKeeney 501
Wakefield 89
Waldo 434
Waldron 202
Wallace 507
Walnut 116
Walton 207

Wamego 382
Washington 516
Waterville 303
Wathena 133
Waverly 102
Webber 227
Weir 81
Wellington 496
Wellsville 170
West Mineral 82
Westmoreland 382
Westphalia 27
Westwood 245
Westwood Hills 246
Wetmore 348
Wheaton 383
White City 336
White Cloud 133

Whitewater 64
Whiting 220
Wichita 453
Willard 465
Williamsburg 170
Willis 55
Willowbrook 403
Wilmore 104
Wilsey 336
Wilson 158
Winchester 224
Windom 309
Winfield 108
Winona 280
Woodbine 129
Woodston 425
Yates Center 523
Zenda 252
Zurich 426

627

# About the Author: Seth Varner

Hey! I'm Seth Varner, the CEO of Wandermore Publishing, and the author of this book. I was raised in a small town called Wahoo, Nebraska, home to about five-thousand residents. I spent my early days living on an acreage between a couple of communities with double-digit populations before moving to Wahoo at ten years old. It was there where I attended Bishop Neumann High School and participated in journalism, FBLA, Spanish, and helped with the basketball program. I went on to obtain my bachelor's degree in business administration from the University of Nebraska at Omaha in the subsequent years. While in college, I conceived the idea for Wandermore Publishing and visited every incorporated community in Nebraska, Iowa, South Dakota, and Kansas. Travel has always been my passion. I've been fortunate to have had the opportunities to visit thirty-one states and nine foreign countries as of November 2023, and I hope that someday I can make the claim that I've visited every municipality in at least ten states. When I'm not working away on the Wandermore social media pages or learning more about Midwest history and tourism, I look for any excuse to hit the road with my friends and family to attend concerts and sporting events, tour museums and parks, and eat at small-town eateries. Otherwise, I don't mind sticking around the Omaha-Wahoo area to hang out with loved ones, listen to the hottest new country songs, or spend a night out on the town. It's a pleasure to call a state like Nebraska home, and I love waking up every morning with the joy of knowing that my work at Wandermore is helping to preserve Midwest history and expand tourism opportunities for its communities. Keep an eye on my Facebook pages to see if I'm in your area for book talks or presentations, or if I'm back in town for a local event!

You can get in touch with me about all things travel on my Facebook pages, or at sethvarner@wandermorepublishing.com

# More by Wandermore Publishing

Enjoying your copy of "Wandermore in Kansas"?

Learn more about town history, travel vicariously through each state via thousands of photos, and explore what Nebraska, Iowa, and South Dakota have to offer with the help of our other three books!

*Visit531Nebraska: A Guide to Nebraska's 531 Incorporated Communities*

*Wandermore in Iowa: Your ultimate guide to the Hawkeye State!*

*Wandermore in South Dakota: Your ultimate guide to the Mount Rushmore State!*

Available for purchase at wandermorepublishing.com/shop!